VOCANIO

NEW 보카니오

VOCA

기출편 논리와 어휘 해결사 보카니오
무한반복! 합격의 지름길이다

김앤북
KIM&BOOK

PREFACE

이 책의 머리말

어휘를 잘정리한 책은 차고 넘치지만 편입어휘라는 방대한 분량을

어떻게 제대로 공부해야 하는지 방법을 가르쳐주는 책은 찾아보기 어렵습니다.

최근 편입시험에서는 어근,접두어를 통해

동의어를 맞추는 문제도 상당히 중요하지만

단순암기된 단어들을 해석과 추론능력을 통해

빈칸을 완성하는 형태로 트렌드가 바뀌고 있는것입니다

결국 단순어휘암기에 만족하지 말고

외운어휘들을 문장으로 규정하는 작업을 반복적으로 연습하지 않게 되면

중상위권대학 해석형어휘문제와 논리형어휘문제 그리고 독해에서 고득점을 맞을수가 없습니다.

보카니오 기출편은 는 기존의 어휘책들과 달리

가장많이 출제되는 편입 단어들을 최신경향에 맞추어

논리완성과 독해의 완성도까지 도움이 될수있는

예문과 동의어, 반의어까지 정리할수 있는 내용으로 구성되었습니다.

가장 단시간내 편입공부에 가장 중요한 내용을 군더더기 없이 정리한 책입니다.

결국 보카니오는 편입어휘의 핵심예문을 바탕으로 연결고리를 파악해

독해와 논리완성의 빈칸을 정확히 적중시킬 수 있는

편입만을 위한 단시간 가장 효과가 좋은 학습법을 명확히 제시합니다.

CONTENTS

이 책의 목차

PART 01 NEW 보카니오 기출편 총정리(A-Z) · 7

1강	8
2강	14
3강	20
4강	26
5강	31
6강	36
7강	41
8강	46
9강	51
10강	56
11강	61
12강	66
13강	71
14강	77
15강	82
16강	87
17강	92
18강	97
19강	103
20강	108
21강	113
22강	118
23강	123
24강	128
25강	133
26강	139
27강	144
28강	149
29강	155
30강	160
31강	165
32강	170
33강	175
34강	180
35강	185
36강	190
37강	195
38강	200
39강	205
40강	210

PART 02 독논주보(독해, 논리, 주제별 보카니오) · 215

PART 03 숙토니오 · 247

PART 01

NEW 보카니오 기출편 총정리(A-Z)

LESSON 01

0001
autograph [ɔ́ːtəgræ̀f]

서명, 자서, 자필
IN BRIEF A person's own signature or handwriting
(특히 작가나, 예능인 등 유명인이 자기 저서나 사진에 하는 서명)

> Janet is interested in autographs of famous jazz performers.
> (자넷은 유명한 재즈 연주가들의 자필 사인에 관심이 있다.)

0002
adversity [ædvə́ːrsəti]

역경 → 불행 → 불운 (misfortune)
IN BRIEF Adverse fortune or fate; a condition marked by misfortune
[+] catastrophe, disaster, trouble

> She overcame many adversities.
> (그녀는 많은 역경들을 이겨냈다.)

0003
ambivalent [æmˈbɪvələnt]

서로 용납하지 않는 → 상극인 → 양면 가치의
IN BRIEF Uncertain or unable to decide about what course to follow
[+] undecided, mixed, conflicting, opposed, uncertain, doubtful, unsure, contradictory, wavering, unresolved, fluctuating, hesitant, inconclusive, debatable, equivocal, vacillating, warring, irresolute

> She is ambivalent about her future career.
> (그녀는 자기 미래 직업에 대해 서로 상반되는 감정을 지니고 있다.)

0004
anti-monarchist [æ̀ntimάnərkist]

군주정치 반대자
(왕이나 여왕의 통치를 반대 → An enemy to monarchial government)

> Brought up "vehemently anti-monarchist," the actress says her parents, now deceased, would be horrified that she is playing Queen Elizabeth.
> (열렬하게 군주정치 반대자로 길러졌기 때문에 그 여배우는 지금은 돌아가신 부모님이 그녀가 엘리자베스 여왕 역을 연기한다는 것에 충격을 받을지 모른다고 말한다.)

0005
affiliation [əfìliéiʃən]

n. 친밀 → 협력관계 → 제휴 → 가입 → 가맹 → 양자결연
IN BRIEF Associate or be associated with a larger organization
[+] incorporate, annex, confederate, amalgamate → unite, join, link, ally, combine

> Having ended his affiliation with the university, Dr. Smith went to work for the government.
> (대학과의 결연이 종료된 후, 스미스 박사는 정부에서 일하기 시작했다.)

0006
asceticism [əsétisìzəm]

금욕주의 → 고행[수도] 생활
IN BRIEF The practice of self-denial for spiritual improvement
[+] self-denial, self-discipline, monasticism

> He is living in a mountain, practicing asceticism.
> (그는 산에서 수도 생활을 하고 있다.)

0007
artifice [άːrtəfis]

기교, 책략 → 구실 → 핑계 → 속임수
IN BRIEF Deception or trickery
[+] deception, device, dodge, feint, gimmick, imposture, jig, maneuver, ploy, ruse, sleight, stratagem, subterfuge, trick, wile

> The Trojan War proved to the Greeks that cunning and artifice were often more effective than military might.
> (트로이전쟁(The Trojan War)은 그리스인들에게 교활함과 책략이 종종 군사력보다 더 효과적이라는 것을 증명했다.)

0008
adapt [ədǽpt]

IN BRIEF To change or get in line with new circumstances
적응 → 조화 → 순응시키다 → 개조하다 → (소설·극)개작[번안, 각색]하다(modify)

> Mel Brooks's newest musical, *Young Frankenstein*, opens on Broadway this week, adapted from his 1974 movie comedy starring Gene Wilder.
> (멜 브룩스(Mel Brooks)의 최신 뮤지컬인 『영 프랑켄슈타인(Young Frankenstein)』은 1974년 진 와일더(Gene Wilder)가 주연한 코미디 영화를 각색한 것으로 이번 주 브로드웨이에서 개봉한다.)

0009
adopt [ədάpt]

채용[채택]하다(employ → take up)
입양하다 (To take into one's family → adoption)

IN BRIEF Choose and follow

[+] choose or take something as one's own
[−] disown, leave alone, reject, repudiate, repulse

> we adopted the resolution over the opposition of the other party.
> (우리는 다른 당의 반대에도 불구하고 그 결의안을 채택했다.)
> they adopted the child as their heir.
> (그들은 그 아이를 상속자로 입양했다.)

0010
acceptable [ækséptəbəl]

받아들일만한 → 수용할만한 → 조건이나 기준에 맞는

IN BRIEF Adequate to satisfy a need, requirement, or standard; satisfactory

[+] satisfactory, agreeable
[−] disagreeable, disturbing, unacceptable, unsatisfactory, unwelcome

> Politicians no longer think that what is good for individuals is necessarily acceptable for the nation.
> (정치인들은 개인들에게 좋은 것이 꼭 전체나라에 바람직하다고는 더 이상 생각하지 않는다.)

0011
act out

(정신분석)행동화하다 → 실연(實演)하다 → 연출하다 → 실행에 옮기다

IN BRIEF The process of doing or performing something: the act of thinking

[+] act, play, represent

> We are taught not to act out our repressed desires.
> (우리는 억압된 욕구를 행동으로 옮기지 않도록 교육을 받았다.)

0012
annoy [ənɔ́i]

성가시게 하다 → 괴롭히다

IN BRIEF To bother or disturb

[+] aggravate, bother, bug, chafe, disturb, exasperate, fret, gall, get, irk, irritate, nettle, peeve, provoke, put out, rile, ruffle, vex

> She was annoyed at his rude manner.
> (그녀는 그의 무례한 태도에 화가 났다.)

0013
autonomy [ɔːtánəmi]

자치(자치권)

IN BRIEF The condition of being politically free

[+] freedom, independence, independency, liberty, self-government, sovereignty
[−] dependence

> The angry factory workers were demanding autonomy.
> (화가 난 공장 근로자들은 자치권을 요구하고 있었다.)

0014
abortion [əbɔ́ːrʃən]

낙태, 임신중절 → 《구어》(계획) 실패

IN BRIEF Induced termination of a pregnancy with destruction of the embryo or fetus

[+] termination, miscarriage, failure, terminate

> Abortion is forbidden by law.
> (낙태는 법률로 금지되어 있다.)

0015
addictive [ədíkt]

habit-forming (Antonym: nonaddictive)
(약)중독[습관]성의 → 중독이 되기 쉬운 → 탐닉하기 쉬운.

[+] habit, compulsive, obsessive, attached, uncontrollable, driving

> Heroin is highly addictive.
> (헤로인은 중독성이 대단히 높다.)

0016
adjacent to [ədʒéisənt]

~에 인접한 (공간적인 개념)

IN BRIEF Being near or bordering upon

[+] next to, touching, contiguous, nearby, neighboring, proximate, abutting, bordering, juxtaposed, tangent

> Our farm land was adjacent to the river.
> (우리 농지는 강에 인접해 있었다.)

0017
ajar [ədʒάːr]

조금 열린
[+] open, agape, unclosed, Partially opened

ajar1 [ədʒάːr]
ad, a. 「형용사로는 서술적」(문이) 조금 열리어
leave the door ~ 문을 조금 열어 두다.

ajar2
ad, a. 「형용사로는 서술적」 조화되지 않아; 티격이 나서(with)

> The door was ajar.
> (문이 약간 열려 있었다.)

0018
appalled [əpɔ́:l]
a. 놀라게 된, 소름끼치게 된(shock)

IN BRIEF To fill with horror and amazement; dismay greatly

+ consternate, daunt, dismay, horrify, shake, shock

> She was appalled when she learned that the teacher did not care about his students.
> (선생님이 학생들에게 신경 쓰지 않는다는 것을 알았을 때 그녀는 소스라치게 놀랐다.)

0019
ample [ǽmpl]
a. 광대한, 넓은, 충분한, 넉넉한, 풍부한

IN BRIEF Of large or great size, amount, extent, or capacity

+ extensive, sufficient → plenty of, abundant, plentiful

> There is ample evidence to support this view.
> (이 견해를 뒷받침하는 충분한 증거가 있다.)

0020
absolute [ǽbsəlù:t]
① 절대적인(opp. relative), 완전한, 전면적인
② 무제한의, 무조건의(opp. limited)
③ (왕권·정부) 절대적인, 독재적인

IN BRIEF Unqualified in extent or degree; total

+ complete, perfect, unlimited, undoubted, certain

> A(n) absolute ruler is one who is ruled by no one else.
> (절대 군주는 어느 누구에 의해서도 지배를 받지 않는 사람이다.)
> A(n) absolute mess is a total mess.
> (전적인 혼란은 온통 뒤죽박죽임을 의미한다.)
> A(n) absolute rule is one that has no exceptions and that you must follow.
> (절대적인 규칙은 예외가 없고 당신이 반드시 따라야하는 규칙이다.)

0021
adamant [ǽdəmənt]
a. 견고한; 단호한, 확고한

IN BRIEF Unyielding; unbreakable

+ obdurate, relentless, implacable, incompliant, inexorable, inflexible, intransigent, iron

> Adamant students were given detention as a matter of course after school.
> (고집불통인 학생들은 당연하게도 방과 후에 학교에 남게 되었다.)

0022
appliance [əpláiəns]
n. 기계, 기구, 용구; 장치, 설비, 보조 기구

+ device, tool, instrument, apparatus, machine

> They sell all sorts of domestic appliances – washing – machines, dishwashers, and so on.
> (그들은 세탁기, 식기세척기 등, 모든 종류의 가정용 기구를 판다.)

0023
arbitrary [á:rbitrèri]
제멋대로인, 변덕스러운, 전제적인, 독단적인, 횡포한

IN BRIEF Determined by chance, whim, or impulse, and not by necessity, reason, or principle

+ random, whimsical, willful, capricious, dictatorial, dogmatic

> She does not make an arbitrary decision.
> (그녀는 멋대로 결정을 내리지 않는다.)

0024
arid [ǽrid]
마른; 습기가 없는, 불모(不毛)의, 메마른

+ dry, desert, sterile, barren ; dry and barren: uninteresting

> Nothing grows in these arid conditions.
> (이렇게 건조한 환경에서는 아무것도 자라지 않는다.)

0025
assertive [əsə́:rtiv]
단정적인(positive), 독단적인(dogmatic), 자기 주장이 강한

IN BRIEF Given to making assertions or bold demands; dogmatic or aggressive

+ confident, firm, decided, forceful, aggressive

> If you really want the promotion, you'll have to be more assertive.
> (정말로 승진하기를 원한다면 좀 더 확고한 태도를 취해야 할 것이다.)

0026
auspicious [ɔːspíʃəs]
길조의, 전조가 좋은, 상서로운; 순조로운

IN BRIEF Attended by favorable circumstances; propitious

+ favorable, timely, prosperous, opportune, propitious, fortunate

> Our first meeting was no auspicious.
> (우리의 첫 모임은 순조롭지 못했다.)

0027
across-the-board
① 전면적인, 전체에 미치는
   an across-the-board pay raise (일괄 임금 인상)
② (경마에서 한 장으로 1등·2등·3등을 거는) 복합식의
③ 【라디오·TV】 월요일부터 금요일 주 5일에 걸친 〈프로〉
   an across-the-board program (연속 프로)

IN BRIEF Applying to or impacting every part or individual in a group or spectrum of things

> The company increased the salaries by 10% across the board.
> (회사는 임금을 일괄적으로10% 인상했습니다.)

0028
be at odds with
~와 사이가 나쁘다, ~와 불화(갈등)하다

IN BRIEF Not match or correspond to each other

[+] in disagreement → conflicting, contradictory, self-contradictory

> The U. S. and North Korea have been at odds with Pyongyang's nuclear ambitions for years.
> (미국과 북한은 평양의 핵에 대한 야심 때문에 오랫동안 갈등을 겪어 왔습니다.)

0029
acceleration [æksèləréiʃən]
가속; 촉진, (물리)가속도

IN BRIEF Increase of speed or velocity

positive[negative] acceleration (가[감]속도)
the acceleration of gravity (중력 가속도)

[+] increasing speed, timing
[−] deceleration, deferral, hindrance, retardation, slowing down

0030
aversion [əvə́ːrʒən]
n. 혐오감; 싫음

IN BRIEF Strong dislike or opposition

[+] antipathy, distaste, avoidance, shunning, turning away, dodging

> The female aversion to mice is often considered absurd by boys.
> (쥐에 대한 여성의 혐오감은 종종 남자 애들에 의해 어리석은 것으로 생각된다.)

0031
account for [əkáunt fɔːr]
설명하다; 책임이 있다; 원인이다; (비율) 차지하다

IN BRIEF Give reasons for (an event, act, etc)

[+] explain, explicate

> The supect could not account for the time leading up to the murder.
> (그 피의자는 살인이 일어나기까지의 시간에 대해 해명하지 못했다.)

0032
antithesis [æntíθəsis]
n. 대조, 대립, 반정립

IN BRIEF Contrast or opposition

[+] contrast, opposition, contradiction, reversal, inversion

> Death is the antithesis of time, since death means infinite stopping, while time means infinite motion.
> (죽음은 시간과 대조된다. 왜냐하면 죽음은 영원한 정지를 뜻하고, 반면 시간은 영원한 운동을 뜻하기 때문이다.)

0033
at random
무작위로, 임의적으로(aimlessly)

IN BRIEF With no discernable pattern or reasoning

[+] by chance, haphazard

> He asked a lot of questions at random.
> (그는 무작위로 많은 질문을 했다.)

0034
amorphous [əmɔ́ːrfəs]
a. 형태가 없는, 조직이 없는

IN BRIEF Without definite shape, character

[+] shapeless, vague, irregular, nondescript, indeterminate, unstructured, nebulous

> The sculptor will convert this amorphous piece of clay into a beautiful bust.
> (그 조각가는 무형의 찰흙을 아름다운 흉상으로 변화시킬 것이다.)

0035
ambidextrous [æ̀mbidékstrəs]
a. 양손잡이의, 두 마음을 품은

IN BRIEF Able to use both hands equally well, double-dealing; deceitful

[+] double-dealing, duplicitous, two-faced, deceitful, double-faced

> By dint of much practice, he became ambidextrous and was able to sign his name with either hand.
> (많은 연습으로, 그는 양손잡이가 되었고, 어느 쪽 손으로도 이름을 서명할 수 있었다.)

0036
aggrieved [əgríːvd]
고민하는 → 고통받는 → 화가 난 → 기분이 상한(mistreated)

IN BRIEF Feeling burdened ; very distressed

[+] hurt, wronged, injured, harmed, disturbed, distressed
[−] Antonyms: happy, pleased

> Mary Lou was aggrieved by the salesman's attitude.
> (Mary Lou는 판매원의 태도에 화가 났다.)

0037
allegation [æ̀ligéiʃən]
n. 근거 없는 주장

IN BRIEF An assertion made with little or no proof

[+] affirmation, assertion, asseveration, averment, claim, declaration, statement

> Even though the public allegation proved untrue, the mayor lost the public's confidence.
> (대중들의 근거 없는 비난의 말은 허위로 밝혀졌지만, 시장은 대중들의 신망을 잃었다.)

0038
augment [ɔːgmént]
v. 증가시키다, 증대시키다(increase)

IN BRIEF To enlarge or make bigger, make greater; improve

+ aggrandize, amplify, boost, build, build up, burgeon, enlarge, escalate, expand, extend, grow, increase, magnify, mount, multiply, proliferate, rise, run up, snowball, soar, swell, upsurge, wax
− Antonyms: decrease, degrade

> If we augment the article, we may have to edit it later.
> (기사를 늘리면, 나중에 수정해야 할 수도 있다.)

0039
ad hoc [æd-hák]
a. 특별한; 임시의(provisional) → 임시변통의

IN BRIEF Formed for or concerned with one specific purpose. Improvised and often impromptu

+ makeshift, emergency, improvised, impromptu, expedient, stopgap

> The office manager called security, and with an adhoc posse, pursued me through the labyrinthine halls, nearly to my editor's door.
> (그 사무실 관리자는 경비를 불렀고, 임시 수색대와 함께, 미로 같은 집회장들을 지나, 거의 편집장 사무실까지 나를 추격하였다.)

0040
awash [əwɔ́ːʃ]
ad. a. 물에 덮여, 침수하여; 가득한, 넘쳐[with, in]

IN BRIEF Filled with, covered with water

+ afloat, flooded, inundated, overflowing

> With society awash in personal data that is bought and sold daily, those who would use it as a weapon have few barriers.
> (매일 사고파는 개인적인 데이터로 가득 차있는 사회에서는 그 자료를 무기로 사용하려는 사람들에게 방해물은 거의 없다.)

0041
accomplished [əkɑ́mplɪʃt]
뛰어난, 완성된

IN BRIEF Successfully completed or brought to an end

+ Skilled; expert → skilled in activity
 → finished, practiced
− inept, inexpert, unable

> He is considered one of the most accomplished writers of his generation.
> (그는 그 세대의 가장 뛰어난 작가 중의 하나로 여겨진다.)

0042
adversity [ædvə́ːrsəti]
n. 역경, 불행(misfortune)

IN BRIEF State of hardship or affliction; misfortune

+ hardship, distress, suffering, trial, disaster, reverse, misery, catastrophe, sorrow, woe, deep water, calamity, mishap, affliction, wretchedness

> He has shown himself to be a really strong character, and he will surely continue to fight in the face of adversity.
> (그는 자신이 정말로 강한 사람이라는 것을 보여주었고, 확실히 역경에 맞서서 싸우는 것을 계속할 것이다.)

0043
ambivalent [æmbívələnt]
a. 양면 가치의; 상반되는 감정[태도·의미]을 가진

> The latest review for the restaurant was ambivalent, suggesting that the sublime cuisine came close to compensating for the insipid decor.
> (그 레스토랑에 대한 최근의 평가는 양면 가치적인 것이어서, 훌륭한 요리가 멋없는 실내장식을 거의 상쇄할 정도임을 말해주었다.)

0044
abstemious [æbstíːmiəs]
a. 절제하는, 검소한

IN BRIEF Pertaining to self-denial

(Exercising moderation and self-restraint in appetites and behavior)

+ continent, sober, temperate, austere, frugal, ascetic

> Some research suggests that people with an abstemious lifestyle tend to live longer than people who indulge their appetites.
> (어떤 조사는 절제하는 생활방식을 가진 사람들이 자기들의 욕구들을 탐닉하는 사람들보다 더 오래 사는 경향이 있음을 시사한다.)

0045
amenity [əménəti]
n. 쾌적함, 즐거움

IN BRIEF Something that makes life more pleasant

+ affability, agreeability, amiability
+ amiableness, congeniality

> No longer satisfied with a minor amenity like a mint on the pillow, frequent guests at five-star hotels demand much more.
> (베개 위에 올려놓는 박하사탕과 같은 작은 즐거움에 더 이상 만족하지 않는 오성급 호텔의 단골손님들은 훨씬 더 많은 것을 요구한다.)

0046
atheist [éiθiist]
n. 무신론자

IN BRIEF One who believes there is no God

+ nonbeliever, pagan, sceptic, disbeliever, heathen, infidel, unbeliever

> Dan says he is an atheist.
> (댄(Dan)은 자기는 무신론자라고 말한다.)

0047
acumen [əkjúːmən]
n. 총명; 날카로운 통찰력

IN BRIEF Skill in perceiving, discriminating, or judging

+ astuteness, clear-sightedness, discernment, discrimination

> Ruth Bader Ginsburg's legal acumen led to her appointment to a position on the Supreme Court.
> (루스 베이더 긴즈버그(Ruth Bader Ginsburg)는 법률업무에서 날카롭고 깊이 있는 통찰력을 갖고 있었기 때문에 대법원 판사에 임명되었다.)

0048
adulation [ædʒəlèit]
n. 지나친 찬사, 과찬

IN BRIEF Excessive flattery or admiration

+ extravagant flattery, worship, fawning, sycophancy, fulsome praise, blandishment

> The director was overjoyed after she won the adulation from the public for her latest film.
> (자신이 만든 최근의 영화에 대해 대중들로부터 엄청난 찬사를 들은 후, 그 감독은 기뻐서 어쩔 줄을 몰랐다.)

0049
attack [ətǽk]
v. 공격하다

IN BRIEF To set upon with force or violence

+ aggress, assail, assault, beset

> In his controversial bestseller The God Delusion, evolutionary biologist and atheist Richard Dawkins attacked religious beliefs.
> (논란을 일으킨 자신의 베스트셀러 『신의 미혹(The God Delusion)』에서, 진화생물학자이자 무신론자인 리처드 도킨스(Richard Dawkins)는 종교적 신앙을 공격했다.)

LESSON 02

0050
abandon [əbǽndən]

v. (사람, 지위, 장소를) 버리다; (계획, 습관을) 단념하다, 포기하다(give up)

IN BRIEF To forsake completely; desert; leave behind

➕ give up, abdicate, cede, relinquish, surrender, withdraw, yield, renounce

> I hope you are not going to **abandon** your project.
> (나는 당신이 계획을 포기하지 않을 거라고 생각한다.)

0051
antidote [ǽntidòut]

n. 해독제; 교정수단; 해결방법

IN BRIEF Counteracting the effects of a poison

➕ corrective, countermeasure, curative, cure, remedy

> Literary awards are inherently subjective and potentially corrupting, but they are also perhaps the most powerful **antidote** (we have regarding the decline of serious fiction) and the best way (of bringing good narrative to a wider world) that desperately needs it.
> (문학상은 본질적으로는 주관적이고 그리고 잠재적으로는 타락성이 있지만, 또한 아마도 순수(본격) 소설의 쇠퇴에 대해 우리가 갖고 있는 가장 강력한 해독제일 것이며, 좋은 이야기를 몹시 필요로 하는 보다 넓은 (독자들의)세계에 그것을 소개하는 최선의 방법일 것이다.)

0052
abbreviate [əbríːvièit]

v. (이야기를) 단축하다; (어구를) 생략하여 쓰다, 간략하게 하다 (shorten, curtail)

IN BRIEF To make shorter → See increase/decrease, long/short. shorten, abridge, condense, curtail, reduce, shorten

➕ curtail → summarize, curtail, abridge, reduce, shorten

> It's not easy to read Prof. Kim's writing, because he often **abbreviates** words where other professors normally wouldn't.
> (김 교수의 글을 읽는 것은 쉽지 않다. 왜냐하면 그는 다른 교수들이 보통 줄여 쓰지 않는 단어를 종종 줄여 쓰기 때문이다.)

0053
abhor [æbhɔ́ːr]

몹시 싫어하다 → 혐오하다

IN BRIEF To regard with horror or loathing; detest

➕ hate, loathe, scorn, detest, abominate, despise, execrate

> They **abhor** all forms of racism.
> (그들은 모든 형태의 인종차별을 혐오한다.)

0054
aberrant [əbérənt]

a. 정도(正道)를 벗어난, 정상에서 벗어난

IN BRIEF Deviation from the normal; mental disorder

➕ deviant, errant, abnormal, anomalous, odd, bizarre

> It can provoke **aberrant** behavior on the part of both parents and children when emotional resources to deal with aberrance are completely drained.
> (탈선에 대처하기 위한 정서적인 해결 수단마저 다 없어져 버리면 부모와 아이들 양쪽 편 모두 정상을 벗어난 행동을 야기할 수 있다.)

0055
abbreviation [əˌbriːviéiʃn]

n. 생략; 생략형, 약어(contraction → a shortened form of a word or phrase)

IN BRIEF The act or product of shortening

➕ abridgment, compression, reduction

> IAEA is the **abbreviation** for International Atomic Energy Agency.
> (IAEA는 국제 원자력 에너지 기구(International Atomic Energy Agency.)의 약어이다.)

0056
abhorrence [æbhɔ́ːrəns]

n. 혐오(loathing); 딱 질색인 것

IN BRIEF The act of detesting extremely

➕ abomination, antipathy, aversion, detestation, hate, hatred, horror, loathing, repellence, repellency, repugnance, repugnancy, repulsion, revulsion

> For Koreans, losing face is a very serious matter, so negotiations involve a great deal of high-context behavior, including an **abhorrence** of saying no directly.
> (한국인들에게 있어 체면을 잃는다는 것은 매우 심각한 문제이다. 그래서 협상은 직접적으로 '아니요(no)'라고 말하는 것과 같이 싫어하는 것을 포함하여 상황에 맞는 상당한 처신을 필요로 한다.)

0057
abiding [əbáidiŋ]

영원한 → 변함없는 → 오래 지속되는

IN BRIEF Existing or remaining in the same state for an indefinitely long time

➕ unceasing, imperishable, continuing, durable, enduring, long-lasting, perdurable, perennial, permanent, persistent

> He has a genuine and **abiding** love of the craft.
> (그는 동업자에게 진실 되고 변함없는 사랑을 가지고 있다.)

0058
abolish [əbάlɪʃ]
v. (관례, 제도를) 폐지하다, 철폐하다(abrogate); 아주 없애다

IN BRIEF To do away with; put an end to; annul

⊕ do away with → to get rid of completely → put an end to, abrogate, annihilate, annul, cancel, invalidate, negate, nullify, void, eliminate

> After years of civil protest, the discriminatory law was finally abolished.
> (수 년 동안 시민들의 저항을 받은 후에, 그 차별적인 법은 마침내 폐지되었다.)

0059
abortion [əbɔ́ːrʃən]
낙태, 임신중절 → 《구어》(계획) 실패

IN BRIEF Induced termination of a pregnancy with destruction of the embryo or fetus

⊕ termination, miscarriage, failure, terminate

> Abortion is forbidden by law.
> (낙태는 법률로 금지되어 있다.)

0060
abound [əbáund]
v. (사물이 ~에) 많다(be plentiful); 그득하다, 풍부하다, 충만하다

IN BRIEF To be great in number or amount

⊕ plentiful, overflow, swarm, teem, flourish, proliferate

> Rumors abound as to the reasons for his resignation.
> (그가 사임한 까닭에 대해 근거 없는 소문들이 무성하다.)

0061
abruptly [əbrʌ́pt]
ad. 뜻밖에, 갑자기(suddenly), 급격히; 무뚝뚝하게, 퉁명스럽게

IN BRIEF Unexpectedly sudden

⊕ suddenly, short, unexpectedly, all of a sudden, hastily, precipitately, all at once, hurriedly

> He ended his speech abruptly.
> (그는 연설을 갑자기 끝냈다.)

0062
abscond [æbskάnd]
v. 도망하다, 달아나다(run off)[from, with]

IN BRIEF To leave quickly and secretly and hide oneself, often to avoid arrest or prosecution

⊕ vanish, flee, disappear, escape, get away, run off

> Big-business crooks enter poor countries in order to abscond with their natural resources.
> (악덕 기업들이 후진국의 천연 자원을 가지고 달아나기 위해 들어온다.)

0063
abstain [æbstéin]
v. 그만두다, 끊다, 삼가다(refrain from); 금주하다

IN BRIEF To withhold something from oneself

⊕ forbear, hold off, keep, refrain, withhold

> My dentist said I would have fewer decayed teeth if I abstained from eating candy.
> (내가 사탕 먹는 것을 자제했더라면 충치가 덜 생겼을 거라고 치과의사가 말했다.)

0064
abstract [æbstrǽkt]
n. 개요, 요약, 발췌, 추출
v. 떼어내다, 분리·추출(抽出)하다[from]
a. 추상적인, 관념적인(intangible), 공상적인(opp. practical)
(Difficult to understand; abstruse: recondite)

IN BRIEF Considered apart from concrete existence

⊕ theoretical, general, complex, academic, intellectual, subtle, profound

> This philosophy paper is extremely confusing. Its key concepts are so abstract.
> (이 철학 논문은 매우 혼란스럽다. 그 논문의 주요 개념들이 너무나 추상적이다.)

0065
abstruse [æbstrúːs]
a. 심원한, 난해한(abstract)

IN BRIEF Hard to understand; esoteric

⊕ obscure, complex, confusing, puzzling, subtle, mysterious

> Baffled by the abstruse philosophical texts assigned in class, Jane asked Mark to explain Kant's "Critique of Pure Reason."
> (Jane은 학급에 할당된 난해한 철학 주제에 어리둥절하여 Mark에게 칸트의 '순수 이성 비판'을 설명해달라고 했다.)

0066
absurd [æbsə́ːrd]
a. 불합리한, 부조리한; 엉터리없는, 터무니없는; 우스꽝스런, 어리석은(foolish)

IN BRIEF Extremely unreasonable, incongruous, or inappropriate

⊕ ridiculous, unbelievable, ludicrous, unreasonable, inane, foolish, preposterous → zany → imbecile

> Even reasonable men sometimes do absurd thing.
> (분별 있는 사람도 때때로 어리석은 일을 저지른다.)

0067
abundance [əbʌ́ndəns]

n. 풍부, 많음(plenty); 부유

IN BRIEF More than enough; in great supply

+ plenty, exuberance, plethora, excess, affluence

> There is such an *abundance* of apples this year that many of them are not picked.
> (금년에는 사과가 너무 많이 달려서 따지 못한 것들이 많이 있다.)

0068
abundant [əbʌ́ndənt]

a. 풍부한, 많은(plentiful)

IN BRIEF Occurring in abundance

+ ample, bounteous, bountiful, copious, generous

> Calcium, the body's most *abundant* mineral, works with phosphorus in maintaining the skeletal system.
> (인체에 가장 풍부한 무기물인 칼슘은 인(燐)과 함께 골격체제를 유지하는 일을 한다.)

0069
abuse [əbjúːz]

남용하다 → 악용하다 → 욕하다(욕설)

IN BRIEF Mishandle; misapply; pervert; revile, malign; mistreat

+ maltreatment, wrong, misapplication, misappropriation, misuse

> The country must extirpate the evils of drug *abuse*.
> (그 나라는 마약 남용이라는 악을 뿌리 뽑아야 한다.)

0070
abysmal [əbízməl]

a. 심연(深淵)의, 나락의, 끝없이 깊은; 지독히 나쁜, 형편없는(awful)

IN BRIEF Immeasurably deep or extreme, fathomless

+ endless, immeasurable, immense, infinite, unfathomable

> The Internet probably deserves its *abysmal* reputation among business executives. They're barraged daily with hype about the World Wide Web and the Net's flashy multimedia strip with its glitzy movie clips and virtual shopping malls.
> (인터넷이 기업의 중역들 사이에서 악명을 얻을만한 이유가 충분하다. 그들에게 월드 와이드 웹에 관한 과대광고와 현란한 영화 장면들과 가상 쇼핑몰이 들어 있는 멀티미디어 플래시 영상이 매일 매일 쏟아지기 때문이다.)

0071
accede [æksíːd]

v. (요구에) 동의하다(agree); (높은 지위에) 오르다, 취임하다; 계승하다; 참가하다, 가맹하다

IN BRIEF Assent or yield; give consent; agree

+ agree to, accept, yield to, acquiesce, concede, submit

> My wife didn't *accede with* what you suggested to us.
> (제 아내는 당신이 우리에게 제안했던 것에 동의하지 않았습니다.)

0072
accentuate [ækséntʃuèit]

v. 강조하다(emphasize), 두드러지게 하다

IN BRIEF To stress or emphasize; intensify

+ emphasize, highlight, punctuate, stress, underscore

> Laws such as these simply serve to *accentuate* inequality.
> (이와 같은 법들은 단지 불평등을 강조하는데 도움이 될 뿐이다.)

0073
accept [æksépt]

v. 받아들이다; (초대, 제안을) 수락하다; (설명, 학설을) 인정하다, 용인하다(permit, allow)

IN BRIEF To answer affirmatively

+ embrace, admit, allow, assume, accede to, acquiesce to, agree to

> Slang is not generally *accepted* in published scientific papers.
> (속어(俗語)는 간행된 과학 논문에서는 일반적으로 용인되지 않는다.)

0074
accessible [æksésəbəl]

a. 접근하기 쉬운, 입수하기 쉬운, 이용할 수 있는(available)

IN BRIEF Easy to approach, reach, enter, or use: an accessible road

+ handy, near, nearby, at hand, within reach

> The students' records were not readily *accessible* for their perusal.
> (학생들의 성적은 열람용으로 쉽게 이용할 수 없다.)

0075
accidental [æ̀ksidéntl]

a. 우연한, 고의가 아닌(not deliberately intended); 비본질적인, 부수적인

IN BRIEF Occurring by chance, unexpectedly, or unintentionally

+ unintentional, unexpected, incidental, unintended, unplanned, unpremeditated

> In contrast to the conventional symbol, the *accidental* symbol cannot be shared by anyone else except as we relate the events connected with the symbol.
> (전통적인 상징과는 달리, 우연한 상징은 우리가 관계된 사건들을 그 상징과 연관시킬 때를 제외하고는 누구와도 공유될 수 없다.)

0076
accomplice [əkɑ́mplis]

n. 공범자(helper), 동료, 협력자

IN BRIEF A person who helps another in committing a crime

+ partner in crime, ally, associate, assistant, companion, accessory, comrade

> The criminal and his *accomplice* were captured by the alert detectives.
> (범인과 그의 공범은 민완 형사들에 의해 붙잡혔다.)

0077
accomplishment [əkάmpliʃmənt]

n. 성취, 달성; 이행, 수행; 공로, 업적(achievement)

IN BRIEF The act of accomplishing or the state of being accomplished; completion

➕ achievement, feat, attainment, act, stroke, triumph, coup, exploit, deed

> When he was an executive of the company, his first accomplishment was to bring about better working conditions.
> (그가 회사의 중역이 되었을 때 최초의 업적은 더 나은 작업 조건을 만드는 것이었다.)

0078
accountable [əkáuntəbl]

a. 책임 있는(responsible), 해명할 의무가 있는; 설명할 수 있는

IN BRIEF Expected or required to account for one's actions; answerable

➕ answerable, subject, responsible, obliged, liable, amenable, obligated, chargeable

> The woman won an $800,000 judgment against the company that employed the drunken driver who killed her son in an accident. She said she wanted corporate America to get the message that they had to be accountable.
> (그 여자는 사고를 내어 자신의 아들을 죽인 술 취한 운전사를 고용했던 회사를 상대로 한 재판에서 승소하여 80만 달러를 받았다. 그녀는 아메리카 회사로부터 그들에게 책임이 있다는 메시지를 받기 원했다고 말했다.)

0079
accumulate [əkjúːmjəlèit]

v. 조금씩 모으다, 축적하다(hoard)

IN BRIEF To gather or cause to increase; amass

➕ build up, increase, grow, be stored, collect, gather, pile up, amass, stockpile, hoard, accrue, cumulate

> Primitive peoples do devote certain types of goods to facilitating production, and from time to time accumulate them in advance for this specific purpose.
> (원시인들은 정말로 생산을 촉진하는데 특정 종류의 물건들을 바치며 때로는 이러한 특별한 목적을 위해 미리 이 물건들을 모아둔다.)

0080
acme [ǽkmi]

정점, 최고조, 절정; 극도, 극치 → (인생의) 전성기

IN BRIEF The peak of perfection

➕ zenith, pinnacle, peak, climax, apogee, culmination, apex

> He reached the acme of success.
> (그는 성공의 최정상에 도달했다.)

0081
acquaint [əkwéint]

알려주다, 전하다(inform) [with] → 잘 알게[정통하게] 하다 (familiarize)

IN BRIEF To make (a person) familiar or conversant (with); inform (of)

➕ tell, reveal, inform, familiarize, apprise, accustom, introduce

> Please acquaint me with the facts of the case.
> (그 사건의 사실들을 내게 알려주시오.)

0082
acquire [əkwáiər]

v. 손에 넣다, 획득하다(obtain); 몸에 익히다, 습득하다

IN BRIEF To get or gain (something, such as an object, trait, or ability)

➕ get, win, buy, receive, land, score (slang), gain, achieve

> The company has just acquired a further 5% of the shares.
> (그 회사는 막 추가 5%의 배당금을 받았다.)

0083
acquiesce [æ̀kwiés]

v. 묵묵히 따르다, 잠자코 받아들이다, 묵인하다, (마지못해) 동의하다(consent)

IN BRIEF To assent tacitly; submit or comply silently or without protest

➕ submit, agree, accept, approve, yield, bend, surrender, consent, tolerate, comply, give in

> After she acquiesced on her employer's suggestions, things went much more smoothly.
> (그녀가 고용주의 제안에 동의하고 난 후에 일이 훨씬 더 순조롭게 진행되었다.)

0084
acquit [əkwít]

v. 석방하다, 무죄로 하다(formally declare not to have committed the crime); 면제해주다

IN BRIEF To free or release (from a charge of crime)

➕ absolve, clear, exculpate, exonerate, vindicate

> Two years after charging the leader of the militia with treason, the government had no choice but to acquit him. But he still faces a possible death sentence if convicted of a separate charge of having organized a protest against the government.
> (그 국민군 지도자를 반역 혐의로 고발하고 2년이 지난 뒤에 그 정부는 그를 석방할 수밖에 없었다. 그러나 정부에 저항하는 단체를 조직했다는 개별 혐의에 대해 유죄가 선고되는 경우, 그는 여전히 사형 선고에 직면할 가능성이 크다.)

0085
acrimonious [æ̀krəmóuniəs]

a. 매서운, 신랄한(bitter), cf) bitter a. 쓴; 모진, 살을 에는 (듯한); 호된, 가차[용서] 없는, 신랄한; 견디기 어려운, 쓰라린

IN BRIEF Bitter and sharp in language or tone; rancorous

+ bitter, cutting, biting, sharp, severe, hostile, crabbed, sarcastic

> There was an acrimonious dispute about the new labor law between the two parties.
> (두 정당 간에 새로 개정된 노동법을 둘러싸고 신랄한 토론이 있었다.)

0086
activate [ǽktəvèit]

v. 활발하게 하다; 켜다, 작동시키다(turn on)

IN BRIEF To make active or capable of action

+ start, move, trigger (off), stimulate, turn on, set off, initiate

> activate the alarm
> (경보기를 작동시켜라.)

0087
acutely [əkjúːt]

ad. 예리하게, 날카롭게; 격심하게 (strongly); 예민하게

IN BRIEF Reacting readily to stimuli or impressions; sensitive

+ painfully, clearly, markedly, excessively, alarmingly, dreadfully, distressingly

> I am acutely aware that my beliefs have never been tested by personal experience.
> (나는 내 신념이 개인적인 경험에 의해 결코 평가받은 적이 없다는 것을 강하게 인식하고 있다.)

0088
adamant [ǽdəmənt]

a. 더없이 단단한; 강직한, 완강한(inflexible); 강경히 주장하는; 불굴의

IN BRIEF Not willing to change one's opinion, purpose, or principles; unyielding

+ determined, firm, fixed, stiff, rigid, set, relentless, stubborn

> The mayor is adamant that he will not purchase more computers.
> (시장은 더 이상 컴퓨터를 구입하지 않겠다는 완강한 입장이다.)

0089
address [ədrés]

n. 주소; 인사말, 연설(speech)

IN BRIEF To make a formal speech to

+ speech, talk, lecture, discourse, sermon, dissertation, harangue

> The president's address lasted three hours.
> (그 회장의 연설은 3시간 동안 계속되었다.)

0090
adduce [ədjúːs]

v. (이유, 증거를) 제시하다(present), 예증하다

IN BRIEF To cite as an example or means of proof in an argument

+ mention, offer, name, present, advance, quote, allege, cite, designate

> He adduced several facts to support his theory.
> (그는 자신의 이론을 뒷받침하기 위해 여러 가지 사실들을 제시했다.)

0091
adept [ədépt]

a. 숙련된(skillful); 정통한, 환한

IN BRIEF Thoroughly proficient; an expert

+ skilful, able, skilled, expert, masterly, practised, accomplished, versed

> They showed themselves adept at many stratagems for obtaining them.
> (그 사람들은 그것들을 구하기 위한 많은 계략에 능숙함을 보여주었다.)

0092
ad-hoc [ˈhɑːk]

임시의 → 특별한 → 임시변통으로(temporary)

IN BRIEF For a particular purpose only; lacking generality or justification

+ makeshift, emergency, improvised, impromptu

0093
adjacent [ədʒéisənt]

a. 접근한, 인접한(touching), 이웃의, 인근의, 부근의

IN BRIEF Being near or close, esp having a common boundary; adjoining; contiguous

+ adjoining, neighbouring, nearby, abutting

> There are eighteen adjacent metropolitan areas.
> (대도시에 인접한 18개 지역이 있다.)

0094
adequate [ǽdikwət]

a. 어울리는, 적당한, 적절한, 적임의; 충분한(sufficient)

IN BRIEF Sufficient to satisfy a requirement or meet a need

+ passable, acceptable, middling, average, fair, ordinary

> One of the big city's greatest problems is providing adequate water to meet the needs of its expanding population.
> (그 대도시의 가장 큰 문제 중 하나는 날로 늘어나는 도시 인구의 필요에 응할 충분한 물을 공급하는 것이다.)

0095
adjust [ədʒʌ́st]

v. 조절하다, 맞추다, 순응시키다(accustom)

IN BRIEF To alter slightly, esp to achieve accuracy; regulate

[+] acclimate, acclimatize, accommodate, adapt, conform, fashion, fit

> You should adjust yourself to a new environment. Accepting the customs of the place you are living in helps you get along well with the local people.
> (당신은 새로운 환경에 순응해야 한다. 당신이 지금 살고 있는 곳의 관습을 받아들이는 것은 당신으로 하여금 그 지역 사람들과 사이좋게 잘 지낼 수 있도록 도와준다.)

0096
admit [ædmít]

허가하다, 인정하다[to, into]

IN BRIEF To give access to, To accept as being true; to confess

[+] concede, allow, grant, permit, let in, receive

> George would never admit to being wrong.
> (George는 잘못을 결코 인정하지 않을 것이다.)

0097
adorn [ədɔ́ːrn]

꾸미다, 장식하다[with]

IN BRIEF To decorate or add a beautiful accent

[+] decorate, enhance, embellish, ornament, garnish, beautify

> Her hair was adorned with flowers.
> (그녀의 머리는 꽃으로 장식되었다.)

0098
adornment [ədɔ́ːrnmənt]

n. 장식(decoration, ornamentation)

IN BRIEF Something that adds attractiveness; an ornament; accessory

[+] decoration, trimming, supplement, accessory, ornament, frill, festoon, embellishment

> In many cultures, costumes are worn largely as adornment on social or religious occasions.
> (많은 문화권에서, 대체로 사회적, 종교적 행사에 장식으로서, 특유한 복장들이 착용된다.)

0099
adroit [ədrɔ́it]

a. 교묘한, 솜씨 좋은(skillful); 기민한, 빈틈없는

IN BRIEF Quick and skillful in body or mind; deft

[+] skilful, able, skilled, expert, bright (informal), clever

> I think my brother is very adroit as a negotiator.
> (내 생각에 우리 형은 협상가로서 아주 능숙한 사람이다.)

LESSON 03

0100
adulterate [ədʌ́ltərèit]

(식품·약) 섞다 (debase, spoil → doctor) → 품질을 떨어뜨리다 [with]

IN BRIEF To make impure

- weaken, deteriorate, mix with, devalue, defile, pollute, taint

> As early as 1800, the poor in Britain were subsisting on a vastly less nutritions meal of often adulterated white bread with cheese, tea and sugar.
> (1800년대 초 영국에서 가난한 사람들은 종종 질 낮은 흰 빵에 치즈, 차, 설탕을 곁들인 매우 영양이 낮은 식사로 연명하고 있었다.)

0101
advance [ædvǽns]

발전하다 → 진보하다 → 나아가다(progress, proceed)

IN BRIEF To move forward

- go forward, encourage, foster, further, promote, elevate, exalt

> The U. S. economy advanced briskly.
> (미국 경제는 활발하게 신장했다.)

0102
advent [ǽdvent]

n. 도래, 출현(appearance, arrival, coming)

IN BRIEF An important arrival of an event or change

- coming, approach, appearance, arrival, entrance, onset, occurrence, visitation

> The traditional craft of hand loom weaving was eradicated by the advent of mechanized factory looms.
> (전통적인 수동 직조 기술은 기계화된 공장 직조기의 출현으로 인해 완전히 사라졌다.)

0103
abdicate [ǽbdikèit]

(권리) 버리다, 포기하다, 양위하다(renounce)

IN BRIEF To give up power

- abandon, cede, demit, forswear, hand over
- quitclaim, relinquish
- render, renounce, resign, surrender, waive, yield

> There's no handbook for how to abdicate, but Oprah Winfrey offered up a pretty good model for monarchs who don't want to go quietly.
> (권리포기에 관한 지침서는 없다. 그러나 오프라 윈프리는 조용히 물러나고 싶지 않은 많은 군주들(거물급 인사들.)에게 아주 훌륭한 모델을 제시했다.)

0104
advocate [ǽdvəkit]

옹호하다 → 지지하다

IN BRIEF To speak or write in support of something or someone

- recommend, support, promote, uphold

> I advocate a policy of gradual reform.
> (나는 점진적인 개혁 정책을 주장한다.)

0105
affability [æ̀fəbíləti]

상냥함, 붙임성 있음 → 사근사근함(pleasantness)

IN BRIEF A disposition to be friendly and approachable

- affableness, amiableness, congeniality, cordialness, sociableness

> Mr. White plays a character of enormous affability.
> (Mr. White는 엄청나게 상냥한 인물을 연기한다.)

0106
anticlerical [ˌænti'klerɪkl]

a. 교권(敎權) 개입에 반대하는

IN BRIEF Opposed to the influence of the church or the clergy in political affairs

> Unlike Continental anticlerical literature about monks and nuns, the saga was not directly pornographic.
> (수도사와 수녀에 관한 유럽의 반교권적인 문학작품과 달리, 북유럽 전설은 노골적으로 외설적이지는 않았다.)

0107
anemic [əníːmik]

빈혈의; 무기력한, 허약한(feeble)

IN BRIEF Lacking vitality; listless and weak

> World leaders suddenly seem more concerned with the irrational excitement of tomorrow than the anemic economy of today.
> (세계 지도자들은 오늘의 무기력한 경제보다는 내일의 비합리적인 흥분에 갑자기 더 관심이 있는 것 같다.)

0108
adverse [ædvə́ːrs]

적대적인 → 불리한 → 반대하는

IN BRIEF Acting or serving to oppose; antagonistic

- unfavorable, antagonistic

> This drug is known to have adverse side effects.
> (이 약물은 좋지 않은 부작용이 있는 것으로 알려져 있다.)

0109
affirm [əfə́:rm]

단언하다, 주장하다

IN BRIEF Declare the truth of something

➕ assert, allege, attest, avow, maintain, profess, confirm, establish, validate, declare

> He affirm that he was telling the truth.
> (그는 자신이 진실을 말하고 있다고 단언했다.)

0110
afflict [əflíkt]

심하게 괴롭히다, 성가시게 굴다

IN BRIEF To distress with mental or bodily pain; trouble grievously

➕ hurt, torment, pain, distress, harass

> Severe drought has afflicted the countryside.
> (심한 가뭄이 시골 지역을 괴롭혀 왔다.)

0111
affliction [əflíkʃən]

(마음, 몸)고통 → 질병 → 괴로움(misery)

IN BRIEF A condition of pain, suffering, or distress

➕ misfortune, suffering, trouble, trial, disease, pain, distress

> The affliction is snoring.
> (그 병은 코를 고는 것이다.)

0112
affluence [ǽflu(:)əns]

(물질적인) 풍부함, 풍요, 유복

IN BRIEF A plentiful supply of material goods; wealth

➕ wealth, plenty, abundance, fortune, opulence, prosperity

> Their affluence is more apparent than real.
> (그들의 부유함은 사실보다는 겉보기이다.)

0113
agitate [ǽdʒətèit]

vt. 선동하다 → 동요시키다(disturb) → 혼란시키다

IN BRIEF To excite or activate

➕ protest, campaign, push, demonstrate, drive, crusade, cry out

> Carl and Martin may inherit their grandmother's possessions when she dies. The thought agitates her.
> (할머니가 돌아가시면 칼(Carl.)과 마틴(Martin.)이 재산을 상속받을 것이다. 이 생각은 그녀를 심란하게 한다.)

0114
afford [əfɔ́:rd]

(시간적·경제적) 여유가 있다 → 제공하다, 주다

IN BRIEF To have enough money to pay for, To be able to spare

➕ manage, offer, provide, support, sustain, furnish, grant, supply

> They walked because they couldn't afford to take a taxi.
> (그들은 택시를 탈만한 여유가 없었기 때문에 걸었다.)

0115
aftermath [ǽftəmæθ]

n. (전쟁·재해) 결과, 여파, 영향 (consequence)

IN BRIEF Consequence; outcome

➕ effects, end, results, wake, consequences, outcome, sequel

> Poverty and sickness are often the aftermaths of war.
> (가난과 병은 대개 전쟁의 여파이다.)

0116
agenda [ədʒéndə]

n. 의제, 의사일정, 협의 사항 (program, list, plan, schedule)

IN BRIEF A list or program of things to be done or considered

➕ programme, list, plan, schedule, diary, calendar, timetable

> The environment is high on the political agenda at the moment.
> (환경 문제가 요즘 정치권에서 중요한 의제이다.)

0117
aggravate [ǽgrəvèit]

v. (병)를 악화시키다, (부담·죄) 무겁게 하다
(구어) 화나게 하다, 괴롭히다

IN BRIEF To make worse or more bothersome

➕ make worse, exaggerate, worsen, intensify
➕ annoy, bother, provoke, irritate

> He aggravated his condition by leaving hospital too soon.
> (그는 너무 일찍 퇴원함으로써 자신의 상태를 악화시켰다.)

0118
agile [ǽdʒəl]

민첩한, 경쾌한; 생기가 도는, 활기 찬; 머리의 회전이 빠른

IN BRIEF Ability to move or think easily and quickly

➕ nimble, active, quick, swift, brisk, supple, facile

> My grandmother isn't as agile as she used to be.
> (우리 할머니는 예전처럼 민첩하지 못하시다.)

0119
affluent [ǽflu(ː)ənt]

풍부한; 유복한; 거침 없이 흐르는(rich)

IN BRIEF Generously supplied with money, property, or possessions; prosperous or rich

[+] wealth, riches, plenty, fortune, prosperity, abundance, big money, exuberance

> Only affluent families were invited to the gala event.
> (단지 부유한 가족들만이 화려한 행사에 초청을 받았다.)

0120
agitation [æ̀dʒətéiʃən]

선동, (선동적) 운동, 부르짖음, 외침 (in agitation: 흥분상태)

IN BRIEF The act of agitating or the state of being agitated.

[+] tumult, turmoil, upset, uproar, anxiety ↔ calmness, relaxation

> She was in a state of great agitation.
> (그녀는 대단히 흥분한 상태에 있었다.)

0121
agnostic [ægnάstik]

(철학) 불가지론(자)의

IN BRIEF One who believes that it is impossible to know whether there is a God

[+] disbeliever, sceptic, doubter

> Although he was born a Catholic, he was an agnostic for most of his adult life.
> (그는 카톨릭 교도로 태어났지만, 성인이 된 후엔 대부분 불가지론자로 지냈다.)

0122
agreeable [əgríːəbəl]

기분 좋은, 쾌적한, 느낌이 좋은, 마음에 드는

IN BRIEF Pleasant; pleasing

[+] pleasant, delightful, enjoyable, congenial, likeable, friendly

> The boy had a charming and agreeable manner.
> (그 소년은 매력 있고 기분 좋은 매너를 가지고 있었다.)

0123
amenable [əmíːnəbəl]

(의견)잘 받아들이는(agreeable) → 유순한, 고분고분한

IN BRIEF Willing to change or submit

[+] compliant, conformable, docile
[+] obedient, submissive, supple, tractable

> Gallup polling (in India) reveals Indians are more amenable than hostile to closer ties with China, and see the country's growing influence as beneficial to India.
> (인도에서 갤럽 조사에 따르면, 인도인들은 중국과의 관계 개선에 반대하기보다는 흔쾌히 받아들이고 있으며, 중국의 영향력 증대가 인도에 이익이 되는 것이라고 간주한다.)

0124
alienate [éiljənèit]

(친구) 멀리하다, 소원하게 하다; 이간하다

IN BRIEF To cause one to leave or turn away

[+] antagonize, anger, annoy, irritate, cause unfriendliness, hostility

> The prime minister's policy has alienated many of his supporters.
> (수상의 정책은 그의 많은 지지자들을 떨어져 나가게 했다.)

0125
alleged [əlédʒid]

(근거없이) 주장된 → 단정된 → 의심스러운 → 가정(假定)의

IN BRIEF Supposed; unproven

[+] doubtful, claimed, supposed, assumed, described, asserted, presumed

> It is alleged that a number of unauthorized payments were made.
> (인가 받지 않은 지불이 많이 행해졌다는 주장이 제기되고 있다.)

0126
allegedly [ə'ledʒıdli]

ad. 소문에 의하면, 주장하는 바에 따르면

IN BRIEF Reportedly; supposedly

[+] supposedly, apparently, reportedly, by all accounts, reputedly, purportedly

> Every few minutes, someone introduces a new antiaging cream that allegedly supersedes all the existing ones on the market.
> (몇 분마다, 시장에 나와 있는 기존의 모든 제품을 대신한다고 하는 새로운 노화방지 크림이 출시되어 나오고 있다.)

0127
alleviate [əlíːvièit]

완화시키다 → 경감시키다 → 덜어주다(relieve)

IN BRIEF To make (pain, for example) less intense or more bearable

[+] relieve; lessen allay, assuage, mitigate, palliate

> As a nurse, she was able to alleviate anxiety as well as pain.
> (간호사로서 그녀는 (환자의) 고통뿐 아니라 걱정까지도 덜어줄 수 있었다.)

0128
allocate [ǽləkèit]

(일·임무) 할당하다; (이익) 배분하다(assign)

IN BRIEF To share in portions; to distribute

[+] assign, grant, distribute, earmark, set aside

> He allocated each of us our tasks.
> (그가 우리들 각자에게 할 일을 할당해 주었다.)

0129
all-out
총력을 기울인, 전면적인 → 전체적인

IN BRIEF With every possible effort → overall

+ total, full, complete, determined, supreme, maximum, outright, thorough

> The team is going all-out to win the championship.
> (그 팀은 우승하기 위해 전력을 다하고 있다.)

0130
allowance [əláuəns]
n. (일정한) 할당액[량], 용돈

IN BRIEF A certain amount of money given to a child

+ portion, share, lot, pension, allocation, pocket money

> My monthly allowance is 200,000won.
> (나의 한 달 용돈은 20만원이다.)

0131
aloof [əlúːf]
떨어져서, 멀어져서[from]; 냉담한, 무관심한

IN BRIEF Showing little or no concern

+ distant, cold, remote, detached, reserved, indifferent, apart, separate

> She kept herself aloof from her fellow students.
> (그녀는 동료 학생들과 어울리지 않았다.)

0132
alter [ɔ́ːltər]
v. 바꾸다, 변경하다, 고치다(transmute; adjust, adapt)

IN BRIEF Change: alter a will; adjust

+ modify, change, reform, shift, vary, transform, adjust, adapt, revise, amend
diversify, remodel, tweak (informal), recast, reshape, metamorphose

> Today's parents seem to believe they can alter their child's destiny by picking the perfect — preferably idiosyncratic — name.
> (오늘날의 부모들은 완벽한, 되도록 개성적인, 이름을 선택함으로써 아이들의 운명을 바꿀 수 있다고 믿고 있는 듯 보인다.)

0133
alteration [ɔ̀ːltəréiʃən]
변경 → 개조 → 수정(renovation)

IN BRIEF The process or result of making or becoming different

+ change, convert, modify, revise, shift, transformation

> The house needed extensive alteration when we moved in.
> (우리가 이사 갔을 때 그 집은 대대적인 개조가 필요했다.)

0134
agree on
동의하다 → 찬성하다 → 승인하다

IN BRIEF To have the same opinion or feeling

+ accede, accept, acquiesce
+ assent, consent, nod, subscribe, yes

> Despite the fact (that the two council members belonged to different political parties), they agreed on the issue of how to finance the town debt.
> (두 의원은 다른 정당 소속이라는 사실에도 불구하고, 도시채무의 재정을 어떻게 충당할 것인지에 대한 문제에는 의견을 같이하고 있다.)

0135
alternative [ɔːltə́ːrnətiv]
(보통 the alternative) 둘 중에서의 선택, 양자택일(대안)

IN BRIEF A choice between two or more things

+ substitute, choice, other (of two), option, preference, recourse

> New ways to treat arthritis may provide an alternative to painkillers.
> (관절염을 치료하는 새로운 방법이 진통제 대체물로 공급될 것 같다.)

0136
altruism [ǽltruːìzəm]
이타주의 (opp. egoism)

IN BRIEF Service to others without thinking of one's self

+ selflessness, charity, consideration, goodwill, generosity, self-sacrifice, philanthropy

> The philanthropist was noted for his altruism.
> (그 자선가는 자신의 애타주의[박애주의]로 널리 알려졌다.)

0137
assess [əsés]
(사람, 사물) 성질[가치]을 평가하다(evaluate)

IN BRIEF Capable of being considered carefully

> The process (of assessing the small actions you can take in the immediate future) can take a lot of pressure off and help you achieve larger goals.
> (가까운 장래에 당신이 취할 수 있는 작은 조치들을 평가하는 과정은 많은 부담감을 덜어줄 수 있으며 더 큰 목표를 달성하는 데 도움을 줄 수 있다.)

0138
amalgam [əmǽlgəm]
아말감(수은과 다른 금속과의 합금) → 혼합물

IN BRIEF Something produced by mixing

+ a mixture or blend, combination, mixture, fusion, alloy

> A subtle amalgam of spices
> (향신료의 미묘한 혼합물)

0139
amalgamate [əmǽlgəmèit]
v. (회사) 통합[합병]하다(combine)
IN BRIEF To combine into a unified or integrated whole; unite
➕ combine, unite, ally, compound, blend, incorporate, integrate, merge

> The firm was amalgamated into another.
> (그 회사는 다른 회사에 합병되었다.)

0140
amass [əmǽs]
v. 쌓다, 모으다, 축적하다(accumulate)
IN BRIEF To gather together or accumulate a large quantity of (something)
➕ collect, gather, assemble, compile, accumulate, aggregate, pile up, garner

> Karen's aptitude for business enabled her to amass a small fortune before she was thirty.
> (카렌(Karen)의 사업 수완은 그녀가 30세가 되기 전에 약간의 재산을 모을 수 있게 해주었다.)

0141
amazing [əméiziŋ]
놀랄 만한, 놀라운(astonishing, surprising)
IN BRIEF To impress strongly by what is unexpected or unusual
➕ impressive, astounding, marvelous, remarkable

> I find it amazing that you can't swim.
> (네가 수영을 못한다니 놀랍다.)

0142
ambience [ǽmbiəns]
n. 주변의 상황, 분위기, 주위, 환경(ambiance)
IN BRIEF Atmosphere, feel, setting, air, quality, character, spirit, surroundings
➕ atmosphere, air, surrounding, impression, mood, aura, feel

> We've tried to create the ambience of a French bistro.
> (우리는 프랑스식 소규모 식당의 분위기를 창출하려고 애써 왔다.)

0143
ambiguous [æmbígjuəs]
두 가지 이상의 뜻이 있는, (의미) 애매모호한
IN BRIEF Difficult to understand or classify; obscure
➕ unclear, uncertain, obscure, doubtful, dubious, equivocal

> His closing words were deliberately ambiguous.
> (그의 마무리 말들은 의도적으로 애매하게 표현되었다.)

0144
ambition [æmbíʃən]
대망, 갈망, 포부; 야심의 목적, 야망의 대상
IN BRIEF A strong drive for success; A cherished desire
➕ goal, end, desire, aspiration, enthusiasm; desire to succeed

> Her ambition knows no limits.
> (그녀의 야망은 끝이 없다.)

0145
ambivalence [æmbívələns]
동요함 → 양면가치 → 모호함 → 주저함
IN BRIEF The coexistence of opposing attitudes or feelings, such as love and hate, toward a person, object, or idea
➕ wavering, fluctuation, hesitancy, equivocation, vacillation, irresolution

> Many people feel some ambivalence towards television and its effect on our lives.
> (많은 사람들이 텔레비전과 그것이 우리 삶에 미치는 영향에 대해 어느 정도 상반된 감정을 동시에 갖는다.)

0146
ambush [ǽmbuʃ]
n. 매복, 잠복; 매복 기습(매복하다, 기습하다)
IN BRIEF To attack suddenly and without warning
➕ trap, attack, surprise, ensnare, waylay: attack by surprise

> The thieves were lying in ambush for their victims.
> (그 도둑들은 숨어서 범행 대상을 기다리고 있었다.)

0147
ameliorate [əmíːljərèit]
v. 개량[개선]하다, 좋아지다, 향상되다
IN BRIEF To make or become better; improve
➕ improve, reform, promote, advance, make better, upgrade

> Steps have been taken to ameliorate the situation.
> (상황을 개선하기 위한 조치들이 취해져 왔다.)

0148
amenities [əménəti]
편의시설, 문화적 설비(facility, service)
IN BRIEF Things that make you comfortable and at ease
➕ convenience, comfort, accommodations, conveniences facilities

> People who retire to the country often miss the amenities of a town.
> (시골로 은둔해 들어간 사람들은 흔히 도시의 문화적 설비들을 그리워한다.)

0149
amiable [éimiəbəl]

a. 붙임성 있는; 상냥한(agreeable)

IN BRIEF To perform a task pleasantly or in a friendly manner

+ affable, agreeable, congenial, cordial, genial, good-natured, good-tempered, pleasant, sociable, warm

> I could submit and live the life of an amiable slave, but that was impossible.
> (나는 굴복하고 상냥한 노예의 삶을 살 수도 있었으나 그것은 불가능하였다.)

LESSON 04

0150
amicable [ǽmikəbəl]

(행위·태도·관계)우호적인, 사이좋은, 원만한; 온화한
IN BRIEF Characterized by friendship and good will
+ kindly, friendly, amiable, cordial, sociable

> His manner was perfectly amicable but I felt uncomfortable.
> (그의 태도는 아주 우호적이었지만 나는 불편했다.)

0151
amity [ǽməti]

n. 친선, 친교, 우호 관계
IN BRIEF Friendship
+ friendship, accord, peace, harmony

> She lived in amity with neighbors for many years.
> (그녀는 이웃과 몇 년 동안 사이좋게 지냈다.)

0152
anachronism [ənǽkrənizəm]

시대착오, 시대착오의 것, 시대에 맞지 않는 것[사람]
IN BRIEF The placement of an event or person out of its proper chronological relationship
+ misdating, mistiming

> The monarchy is seen by some as an anachronism in present-day society.
> (현대사회에서는 군주제가 일부 사람들에게는 시대착오로 여겨진다.)

0153
analogy [ənǽlədʒi]

n. 유사, 비슷함, 닮음(between; to; with), 유사(성), 유추
IN BRIEF A similarity between like features of two things, on which a comparison may be based
+ similarity, relation, parallel, likeness

> There is no analogy with any previous case.
> (어떤 이전의 경우와도 유사점이 없다.)

0154
anchor [ǽŋkər]

정박하다 → 닻을 내리다 → 고정시키다
IN BRIEF To secure (a vessel with an anchor)
+ secure, tie, fix, bind, attach → To make secure

> They brought the boat into the harbour and dropped the anchor.
> (그들은 배를 항구로 끌고 들어와 닻을 내렸다.)

0155
annual [ǽnjuəl]

1년의, 1년간의; 1년을 단위로 하는, 해마다의
IN BRIEF Once a year or every year; yearly
+ yearly, once a year, anniversary

> You will receive annual salary increments every September.
> (당신은 매년 9월에 연중 봉급 인상을 받게 될 것입니다.)

0156
anonymous [ənάnəməs]

작자[저자] 불명의 → 익명[가명]의
IN BRIEF Having an unknown name or author
+ unnamed, unknown, incognito, unauthenticated, unsigned

> An anonymous benefactor donated 2 million dollars.
> (한 익명의 은인이 2백만 달러를 기증했다.)

0157
anorexia [æ̀nəréksiə]

[의학] 식욕 부진, 식욕 감퇴
IN BRIEF A loss of appetite or lack of desire to eat

> Anorexia has been dubbed 'the slimming disease'.
> (거식증은 '살 빠지는 병'으로 일컬어져 왔다.)

0158
antagonistic [æntæ̀gənístik]

적대의, 반대하는
IN BRIEF One who opposes and contends against another; an adversary
+ hostile, opposed, resistant, incompatible

> Cats and dogs are antagonistic.
> (고양이와 개는 사이가 나쁘다.)

0159
antecedent [æ̀ntɪ'siːdnt]

선행자 → 선례 → 원형 → 전신 → 조상(prior)
IN BRIEF One that precedes another
+ preceding, earlier, former, previous, prior, preliminary, foregoing, anterior, precursory

> The horse-drawn wagons are antecedent of the modern automobiles.
> (말이 끄는 마차는 현대 자동차의 전신이다.)

0160
anticipate [æntísəpèit]
v. 예상하다, 예감하다; 고대하다

IN BRIEF To look forward to; to expect

⊕ expect, predict, forecast, foresee, hope for

> We anticipate that demand is likely to increase.
> (우리는 수요가 증가할 것으로 예상한다.)

0161
antiquated [ǽntikwèitid]
낡은 → 구식의 → 시대에 뒤진

IN BRIEF Of a style or method formerly in vogue

⊕ obsolete, ancient, out-of-date, outmoded, passe, behind the times

> Most businessmen ardently hope that the lash of competition willtransform that antiquated banking system.
> (대부분의 사업가들은 경쟁이라는 자극이 그런 낡은 금융 제도를 변화시킬 것을 열렬히 희망하고 있다.)

0162
anxiety [æŋzáiəti]
걱정, 근심; 불안, 염려 (worry)

IN BRIEF A troubled or anxious state of mind

⊕ uneasiness, concern, doubt, tension, alarm, distress, suspicion, angst, unease, apprehension

> We waited for news with a growing sense of anxiety.
> (우리는 점점 더 커지는 우려 속에서 소식을 기다렸다.)

0163
apathetic [æpəθétik]
무감각한 → 감정이 없는 → 냉담한 → 무관심한

IN BRIEF The condition of having no interest

⊕ indifferent, uninvolved, uninterested, dispassionate, impassive, languid, lethargic, listless, torpid

> You are totally apathetic about world affairs
> (당신은 세계 문제들에 대해 완전히 무관심하다.)

0164
aperture [ǽpərtʃər]
구멍, (째진) 틈, 간격; 틈이 생긴 것; 〈광학〉(렌즈의) 구경(口徑)

IN BRIEF A hole, gap, crack, slit, or other opening

⊕ opening, crack, orifice, fissure

> The camera adjusts the lens aperture and shutter speed automatically.
> (이 사진기는 자동으로 렌즈 구경과 셔터 속도를 조절한다.)

0165
api(bee)
☑ apiarist [éipiərist] 양봉가
☑ apiary [éipièri] 양봉장(場)
☑ apian [éipiən] 꿀벌의
☑ apiculture [éipəkÀltʃər] 양봉

0166
apologetic [əpàlədʒétik]
변명의, 해명의; 사과의, 사죄의 (full of excuses)

IN BRIEF Expressing or anxious to make apology; contrite

⊕ regretful, contrite, penitent, remorseful, repentant sorry

> He was very apologetic about arriving late.
> (그는 늦게 도착한 데 대해 매우 미안해했다.)

0167
appalling [əpɔ́:liŋ]
소름끼치는, 무서운(dreadful)

IN BRIEF Causing consternation or dismay; frightful

⊕ horrifying, shocking, terrible, awful, fearful

> The food was just about tolerable, but the service was appalling.
> (음식은 그냥 참고 먹을 만했지만, 서비스는 정말 끔찍했다.)

0168
apparel [əpǽrəl]
《집합적》옷, (여성·아동) 의류; 겉옷; 기성복

IN BRIEF Clothing, especially outer garments; attire

⊕ clothing, dress, garment, costume, clothes

> Does this store sell women's apparel?
> (이 상점에서 여성복을 팝니까?)

0169
apparent [əpǽrənt]
a. 눈에 보이는; 분명한, 명백한, 뚜렷한

IN BRIEF Obvious; clearly seen

⊕ obvious, clear, patent, manifest, conspicuous

> This fact is apparent to everybody.
> (이 사실은 모두에게 명백하다.)

0170
apparently [əpǽrəntli]
ad. 겉보기에는, 외관상으로는, 명백히; 분명히

IN BRIEF It appears that; as far as one knows; seemingly

⊕ seemingly, outwardly, ostensibly, speciously

> The two crimes are apparently unconnected.
> (그 두 범죄는 분명히 연관이 없다.)

0171
appease [əpíːz]

달래다; 〔슬픔 따위〕를 가라앉히다; 진정시키다

IN BRIEF To bring to a state of calm; pacify

+ pacify, soothe, placate, mollify, conciliate, calm, alleviate, assuage

> He tried to appease the crying child by giving him candy.
> (그는 우는 아이에게 캔디를 주어 달래려 했다.)

0172
appliance [əpláiəns]

n. 기계, 기구, 용구; 장치, 설비, 보조 기구

IN BRIEF A device or instrument designed to perform a specific function, especially an electrical device

+ device, tool, instrument, apparatus, machine

> They sell all sorts of domestic appliances – washing – machines, dishwashers, and so on.
> (그들은 세탁기, 식기세척기 등, 모든 종류의 가정용 기구를 판다.)

0173
appraise [əpréiz]

(물건·재산) 값 매기다 → 견적[감정]하다 → (사람·능력) 평가하다

IN BRIEF To make an estimate of a thing's value

+ assay, assess, calculate, estimate, evaluate, gauge, judge, rate, size up, valuate, value

> I had an expert appraise the house beforehand.
> (미리 전문가에게 그 집을 평가하게 했다.)

0174
appreciate [əpríːʃièit]

v. 평가, 감상, 감사, 존중(인정), 이해(하다), 상승하다

IN BRIEF To recognize the quality, significance, or magnitude of

+ value, esteem, be aware of, understand, realize, be obliged, be thankful

> My boss doesn't appreciate me.
> (우리 사장은 내 진가를 알지 못한다.)

0175
apprehend [æprɪ'hend]

v. 염려하다; 체포하다; 이해하다

IN BRIEF 1. to take into custody
2. to grasp the meaning of; understand
3. to expect with anxiety, suspicion, or fear; anticipate

+ arrest, seize/compass, comprehend, fathom, grasp

> Tess was apprehended by the local police and subsequently accused for her misdemeanor.
> (테스는 지역 경찰에 체포되었으며, 그 후에 경범죄로 기소되었다.)

0176
apprehension [æprihénʃən]

n. 걱정, 염려, 이해, 체포(dread)

> He could see the mixture of suspicion and apprehension on their faces.
> (그는 그들의 얼굴에서 의심과 우려가 뒤섞인 표정을 읽을 수 있었다.)

0177
apprehensive [æprihénsiv]

a. 우려(염려)하는[about, for], 이해가 빠른

IN BRIEF Anxious or fearful about the future; uneasy/quick to learn or understand

+ fearful, anxious, worry, concerned/discerning

> I feel apprehensive about the results of the exams.
> (나는 시험결과에 대해 우려한다.)

0178
apprise [əpráiz]

알리다, 통고[통지]하다(inform)

IN BRIEF Give notice of; acquaint; inform

+ tell, warn, inform, acquaint, make aware
  apprise(inform) A of B : A에게 B를 알리다, 통고하다

> The magazine has apprised its readers of an increase in rates beginning January 1.
> (그 잡지는 독자들에게 1월 1일부터 요금이 인상된다고 통지했다.)

0179
approbation [æproubéiʃən]

① 허가, (공식) 인가, ② 찬양, 칭찬

IN BRIEF An expression of warm approval; praise

+ approval, support, sanction, assent

> I receive official approbation.
> (나는 공적인 인가를 받았다.)

0180
appropriate [əpróuprièit]

① 적당한, 적절한, 알맞은, 어울리는(suitable, relevant)
② 사적인 용도로 쓰다 (사용(私用): (공금) 착복(횡령)하다
③ (특수목적) 〈돈〉 충당하다; (지출을) 승인하다

IN BRIEF Suitable for a particular person, condition, occasion, or place; fitting

+ proper, pertinent, seize, confiscate, commandeer

> You will be informed of the details at the appropriate time.
> (적절한 시기에 상세한 내용을 알려 드리겠습니다.)

0181
approximate [əpráksəmèit]
대략의, 거의 정확한; 비슷한, 근사한(nearly correct)

IN BRIEF Almost exact or correct

[+] rough, close, near, estimated

> What is the approximate size of this room?
> (이 방의 대략적인 크기가 얼마입니까?)

0182
apt [æpt]
a. 적절한, 적당한(appropriate)

IN BRIEF Exactly suitable; appropriate

[+] suitable, proper, relevant, pertinent

> His choice of music was most apt.
> (그의 선곡은 대단히 적절했다.)

0183
aqueduct [ǽkwədʌ̀kt]
n. (토목) 수로(水路)

IN BRIEF A channel designed to carry water from one site to another

[+] conduit, channel, passage, canal, waterway, duct

> During the drought, the aqueduct was dry.
> (가뭄이 있는 동안, 수도관은 건조한 상태였다.)

0184
arable [ǽrəbəl]
경작할 수 있는, 경작에 알맞은(농토, 토지)

IN BRIEF The quality of land that is appropriate for cultivation

[+] productive, fertile, fecund, cultivable, plowable

> A lot of the arable land was under-used and poorly tended.
> (경작 가능한 토지상당 부분이 이용이 안 되고 있으며 형편없이 관리되고 있다.)

0185
astound [əstáund]
크게 놀라게 하다
(amaze, astonish, startle, surprise → consternate)

> evening, they were astounded to hear a man's voice coming from the living room. The husband gripped his umbrella and tiptoed towards the door, flung the door open, switched on the light, and charged in to find that the radio set had been left on.
> (젊은 부부가 어느날 저녁 극장에서 귀가했을 때. 그들은 한 남자의 목소리가 거실에서 들려오는 것을 듣고 깜짝 놀랐다. 남편은 우산을 움켜쥐고 문을 향해 발끝으로 걸으며 문을 거칠게 열어 불을킨 다음 안으로 뛰어 들어 갔더니 라디오를 켜두고 갔었음을 알아챘다.)

0186
archaic [ɑːrkéiik]
고풍의, 형태가 오래된

IN BRIEF Old-fashioned, ancient

[+] Definition: very old

[+] Antonyms: current, modern, new, present, young

1) A(n) meaning of a word is one that isn't used anymore
   (고어(古語)란 더 이상 사용되지 않는 단어이다)
2) civilizations are ones that appeared a long time ago
   (고대 문명이란 오래전에 나타났던 문명들이다)

0187
abrogate [ǽbrəgèit]
[법령·협정·관습] (공식으로) 폐지하다 → 폐기[철폐]하다

IN BRIEF Revoke formally; To abolish, do away with, or annul (especially by authority)

[+] abolish, annihilate, annul, cancel, invalidate, negate, nullify, void.

[−] approve, establish, fix, institute, legalize, ratify, sanction, support

> Guidelines for bone health maintenance have been recently developed. Practical strategies designed to monitor bone health offer the potential to abrogate increased fracture risk.
> (뼈 건강유지를 위한 지침이 최근에 개발되었다. 뼈의 건강을 살펴보기 위해 고안된 실용적인 전략들을 골절의 위험이 증가되지 않도록 할 가능성을 제시한다.)

0188
armchair [άːrmtʃɛ̀ər]
① 안락의자
② 탁상공론의; 관념적인; 실제로 겪지 않은(간접)

IN BRIEF Remote from active involvement: impractical

[+] worthless, abstract, hypothetical, theoretical, ineffective, useless

> They are armchair critics
> (그들은 관념적 비평가들이다.)

0189
austerity measures
긴축정책

> Markets responded positively to Friday's actions after weeks of turmoil after the Spanish government approved new austerity measures and a limited economic stimulus package to ease investor fears about its debt — and insisted again it was taking strong steps to right its ailing economy.
> (스페인 정부가 채무에 관한 투자자의 우려를 불식시키기 위해 새로운 긴축 정책들과 제한된 경기 부양책을 승인하고, 침체된 경제를 바로잡기 위해 강력한 조치들을 취하고 있다고 거듭 강조한 후, 시장은 수 주간에 걸친 동요를 끝내고 금요일의 조치들에 대해 긍정적인 반응을 보였다.)

0190
argument [ά:rgjəmənt]

논쟁, 언쟁(controversy)

IN BRIEF A quarrel; altercation

➕ reason, dialectic, debate, discussion, claim

> His argument seems logical.
> (그의 주장은 논리 정연한 것처럼 보인다.)

0191
arid [ǽrid]

마른; 습기가 없는, 불모(不毛)의, 메마른

IN BRIEF Having little or no rain; dry; parched with heat

➕ dry, desert, sterile, barren ; dry and barren: uninteresting

> Nothing grows in these arid conditions.
> (이렇게 건조한 환경에서는 아무것도 자라지 않는다.)

0192
acclaim [əkleɪm]

칭찬하다 → 환호하다 → 인정하다

IN BRIEF To praise enthusiastically and often publicly

➕ praise, celebrate, honour, cheer, admire, hail, applaud, compliment, salute, approve, congratulate, clap, pay tribute to, commend, exalt, laud, extol, crack up, big up, give it up for, eulogize

> Writer of outstanding books on ancient civilizations, Thomas Wright is internationally acclaimed for his work as researcher.
> (고대 문명에 대한 뛰어난 책들의 저자인 토마스 라이트는 학자로서의 연구로 국제적으로 인정받은 분이다.)

0193
armistice [ά:rməstis]

n. 휴전, 정전; 휴전 조약

IN BRIEF A temporary suspension of hostilities by agreement of the warring parties; truce

➕ cease-fire, agreement, pact, treaty

> The Armistice was signed in late 1918 and the Great War came to an end.
> (휴전 조약이 1918년 말에 체결되고 대전이 끝났다.)

0194
arrange [əreɪndʒ]

정리(정돈)하다(put in order);배열하다, 준비(계획)하다

IN BRIEF Place in a certain order; adjust properly; array, group, sort, classify

➕ plan, prepare, schedule, organize, order, set up

> Let's arrange a time and place for our next meeting.
> (우리의 다음 회의를 위한 시간과 장소를 정합시다.)

0195
arduous [ά:rdʒuəs]

a. (일)고된, 힘드는, 끈기 있는

IN BRIEF Very difficult; hard

➕ difficult, hard, tough, painful, severe

> The work is extremely arduous.
> (그 일은 지극히 힘이 들었다.)

0196
arrogant [ǽrəgənt]

a. 건방진, 거만한, 교만한, 젠체하는; 무례한

IN BRIEF Having or showing an exaggerated opinion of one's own importance, merit, ability, etc; conceited

➕ conceited, haughty, insolent, self-important

> She felt belittled by her husband's arrogant behaviour.
> (그녀는 남편의 거만한 행동 때문에 부끄러웠다.)

0197
articulate [ɑ:rtíkjəlit]

a. (말, 생각) 명확한, 조리 있는, 분명한, v. (음절·단어, 생각, 감정) 똑똑히 발음하다, 분명하게 표현하다 (clear, vocalize, definite, distinct, lucid)

IN BRIEF Composed of distinct, meaningful syllables or words

➕ expressive, clear, effective, vocal, meaningful, understandable

> She's a little deaf, so articulate your words carefully.
> (그녀는 귀가 약간 먹었으니 조심스럽게 또렷이 발음하십시오.)

0198
artificial [ὰ:rtəfíʃəl]

a. 인공의; 인조의; 모조의

IN BRIEF Made by human beings instead of nature

➕ unnatural, phoney, spurious, manufactured, synthetic, fake, imitation, counterfeit, feigned

> This yoghurt contains no artificial flavoring or coloring.
> (이 요구르트에는 인공향료나 착색제가 함유되어 있지 않다.)

0199
ardent [ά:rdənt]

a. 열렬한, 열심인, 정열적인, 심한, 격렬한

IN BRIEF Passionate; enthusiastic

➕ enthusiastic, eager, avid, zealous, passionate

> He is an ardent student of Greek history.
> (그는 그리스 역사를 열심히 연구하는 학생이다.)

LESSON 05

0200
aspiration [æ̀spəréiʃən]

n. 열망(desire), 대망, 큰 뜻, 염원

IN BRIEF A wish or hope

+ aim, longing, end, plan, hope, goal, design, dream

A new civilization is always being made: the state of affairs that we enjoy today illustrates what happens to the aspirations of each age for a better one.
(새로운 문명은 항상 만들어지고 있다. 오늘날 우리가 향유하고 있는 상황은 더 나은 문명을 위한 각 세대의 열망에 어떤 일이 일어나는 지를 설명해 준다.)

0201
assailant [əséilənt]

n. 공격자, 습격자; 가해자; 논적

IN BRIEF A murderer or attacker

+ attacker, invader, assaulter, aggressor

He was unable to see his assailant clearly in the dark.
(그는 어두워서 자기를 공격한 사람을 분명히 볼 수 없었다.)

0202
admonish [ədmάniʃ]

꾸짖다 → 책망하다 → (강력히)충고하다(reprimand)

The witness was admonished by the judge for failing to answer the question.
(그 증인은 질문에 대답하지 못해 판사에 의해 경고를 받았다.)

0203
astonish [əstάniʃ]

깜짝 놀라게 하다, 경악케하다(greatly surprise)

IN BRIEF Affect with wonder

+ amaze, surprise, stagger, bewilder, astound, confound

The news astonished everyone.
(그 뉴스는 모든 사람들을 깜짝 놀라게 했다.)

0204
astronomy [əstrάnəmi]

n. 천문학

IN BRIEF A system of knowledge or beliefs about celestial phenomena

+ planets, stars, constellations

The professor is devoted to astronomy.
(그 교수는 천문학에 전념하고 있다.)

0205
ambivalent [æmbívələnt]

① 상반하는 감정을 품은
② 상반된 감정이 공존하는
③ 불확실한(uncertain)

+ conflicting → undecided, mixed, contradictory, debatable, vacillating
− certain, definite, resolved, settled, sure, unequivocal

Often the characters of great novels are ambivalent and hard to figure out.
(위대한 소설의 등장인물들은 종종 성격이 애매하고 (양면적이고) 이해하기 힘들다.)

0206
astute [əstjú:t]

기민한, 통찰력이 있는, 날카로운, 뛰어난

IN BRIEF Performing in a clever manner
(cagey, canny, knowing, perspicacious)
(shrewd, slick, smart, wise)

Having learned it in youth, Thomas is astute in the art of archery.
(젊어서 배웠기 때문에 토마스는 궁술 솜씨가 뛰어나다.)

0207
attenuate [əténjuèit]

v. 가늘게 하다, 작게 하다, 묽게 하다, 줄이다

IN BRIEF To weaken or become weak; reduce in size, strength, density, or value

+ weaken, reduce, lower, diminish

The years will attenuate his desire for revenge.
(세월이 그의 복수의 욕망을 약하게 했다.)

0208
attest [ətést]

v. 증명하다, 입증하다(confirm), 진실성을 나타내다

IN BRIEF To affirm to be correct, true, or genuine

+ testify, prove, show, declare, exhibit, manifest

This attests to his honesty.
(이 일로 그가 정직하다는 것을 알 수 있다.)

0209
altercation [ɔːltərˈkeɪʃn]
언쟁 → 논쟁 → 격론

IN BRIEF An angry or heated discussion or quarrel; argument

+ argument, row, clash, disagreement, dispute, controversy, contention, quarrel, squabble, wrangle, bickering, discord, dissension

> The angry altercation started with a seemingly innocent remark by the taxi driver.
> (그 격론은 택시 운전사의 별 악의 없는 말에 의해 시작되었다.)

0210
attribute [əˈtrɪbjuːt]
(원인) 돌리다 → 탓으로 하다 / n. 속성, 특징

IN BRIEF A quality proper to a particular person or thing

+ ascribe, impute, apply, charge, assign

> She attributes her success to hard work and a bit of luck.
> (그녀는 자신의 성공을 근면과 약간의 행운의 덕분으로 여긴다.)

0211
audacious [ɔːˈdeɪʃəs]
a. 대담한(unrestrained); 넉살좋은, 철면피의; 무례한

IN BRIEF Invulnerable to fear or intimidation; unrestrained by existing ideas, conventions

+ daring, enterprising, brave, bold, risky, rash, adventurous, reckless
courageous, fearless, intrepid, valiant, daredevil, death-defying, dauntless

> This sort of audacious prediction used to be commonplace in the bio fuel industry.
> (이런 종류의 대담한 예측은 바이오 연료 업계에서는 흔해 빠진 것이었다.)

0212
audacity [ɔːˈdæsəti]
n. 대담(성), 담대함; 무모함, 뻔뻔스러움

IN BRIEF Fearless daring; intrepidity

+ daring, courage, rudeness, boldness, shamelessness

> He had the audacity to tell me I was too fat.
> (그는 내가 너무 뚱뚱하다고 뻔뻔하게 말했다.)

0213
audible [ˈɔːdəbl]
들리는, 청취할 수 있는

IN BRIEF To make noise loudly enough to be heard

+ clear, discernible, hearable, detectable

> Her voice was scarcely audible because of the noise of the wind.
> (그녀의 목소리는 바람 소리 때문에 거의 들리지 않았다.)

0214
auspicious [ɔːˈspɪʃəs]
a. 전조가 좋은, 길조의, 상서로운 (favorable)

IN BRIEF Presenting favorable circumstances or showing signs of a favorable outcome; propitious

+ favourable, timely, happy, promising, encouraging

> With a hundred people promising donations of $100 each, the fund-raising drive got off to a most auspicious start.
> (100명의 사람들이 각각 100달러를 기부할 것을 약속하면서 모금 운동은 매우 기분 좋은 출발을 했다.)

0215
austere [ɔːˈstɪər]
a. (태도·용모) 엄격한; 금욕적인, 검소한, 평이한

IN BRIEF Stern or severe in attitude or manner

+ stern, severe, strict, grim, rigorous, ascetic, rigid, plain

> My father was always a rather distant, austere figure.
> (나의 아버지는 항상 다소 엄격하고 쌀쌀한 분이셨다.)

0216
authorization [ˌɔːθərɪˈzeɪʃən]
n. 권한 부여, 허가, 면허, 공인

IN BRIEF The approving of an action, especially when done by one in authority

+ sanction, permission, licence, warrant

> May I see your authorization for this?
> (허가서 좀 보여주시겠습니까?)

0217
autocratic [ˌɔːtəˈkrætɪk]
전제의, 독재의; 독재적인

IN BRIEF Having and exercising complete political power and control

+ tyranny, dictatorial, despotic, tyrannical, authoritarian

> The president resigned after 30 years of autocratic rule.
> (그 대통령은 30년간의 독재 통치 끝에 사임했다.)

0218
autonomous [ɔːˈtɒnəməs]
자치의, 자치적인; 독립된, 독자적인

IN BRIEF Self-governing

+ independence, self-ruling, sovereign, self-governing

> The local groups are autonomous of the national organization.
> (그 지역 단체들은 국가 조직으로부터 독립해 있다.)

0219
available [əvéiləbə]

이용할 수 있는, 입수[이용] 가능한(obtainable)

IN BRIEF Possible to get, use, or reach

➕ acquirable, attainable, gettable, obtainable, procurable

> Erik Peterson of the Center for Strategic and International Studies in Washington points out that as small an amount as three percent is available to us for daily use.
> (워싱턴에 소재한 국제 전략문제 연구소의 에릭 피터슨은 3%만큼 적은 양만을 우리가 입수하여 매일 이용할 수 있다고 지적한다.)

0220
avaricious [ævəríʃəs]

a. 욕심 많은, 탐욕스러운

IN BRIEF Characterized by greed

➕ grasping, greedy, covetous, ravenous, voracious

> He is avaricious of power.
> (그는 권력에 굶주려 있다.)

0221
avert [əvə́ːrt]

돌리다, 비키다 [from], (사고·위험) 피하다, 막다, (시선, 얼굴 등을 다른 데로) 돌리다

IN BRIEF To turn away; to keep something from happening

➕ deflect, deviate, divert, pivot, shift, swing, turn, veer

> I tried to avert my thoughts from the subject.
> (나는 그 주제로부터 생각을 돌이키려고 애를 썼다.)

0222
augur [ɔ́ːgə(r)]

전조[조짐]가 되다 → 점치다 → 예언하다 (herald)

IN BRIEF To make predictions from signs or omens

➕ auspicate, bode, omen, portend, foreshadow, presage, prognosticate, predict, prefigure, betoken, forecast, foretell

> For boys, impulsivity in the early years may augur a heightened risk of delinquency.
> (남자 아이들의 경우, 유년기의 충동이 청소년 비행이나 폭력의 높은 위험성을 예고하는 것일지도 모른다.)

0223
awkward [ɔ́ːkwərd]

a. 서투른, 미숙한[at, in]

IN BRIEF Not having grace or skill; clumsy. Uncomfortable

➕ unskilled, uncomfortable, clumsy, inept, maladroit

> He is awkward in his gestures. (그는 몸짓이 어색하다.)

0224
avid [ǽvid]

a. 탐욕스런, 열렬한

IN BRIEF Excessively eager or greedy

➕ enthusiastic, devoted, fervent, zealous, greedy

> The dictator had an avid desire for power.
> (그 독재자는 권력에 대한 불타는 욕망을 가지고 있었다.)

0225
awry [ərái]

ad., a. 구부러져, 비뚤어져, (사람의 행동이나 사물이) 잘못되어

IN BRIEF Askew, twisted to one side

➕ distorted, wrong, amiss, askew, crooked, twisted

> His analysis is wildly awry.
> (그의 분석이 턱없이 잘못됐다.)

0226
bachelor [bǽtʃələr]

n. 독신(미혼)남성↔학사

IN BRIEF A man who is not married

➕ single man, unmarried man, celibate ↔ spinster

> The young bachelor will soon be taking a wife.
> (그 젊은 독신 남자는 머지않아 아내를 맞을 것이다.)

0227
backlash [bǽklæʃ]

n. 반동, 반발, 반격 (negative reaction), (개혁에 대한 격렬한)반발, 반동

IN BRIEF A sudden or violent backward whipping motion

➕ reaction, response, resistance, resentment

> It has not yet risen to an organized consumer movement, but there are unmistakable signs of a backlash against the 75 million handheld communications devices now on the American scene.
> (아직 조직적인 소비자 운동으로까지 발전하지는 않았지만 오늘날 미국에는 7,500만대나 되어 휴대용 통신장에 대한 반발의 기미가 있다는 데에는 의심의 여지가 없다.)

0228
backwater [bǽkwɔ̀ːtər]

(nonentity) 역수(逆水: 둑에 부딪쳐 되밀리는 물), (문화) 침체상태[지역] → 벽지 → 오지

IN BRIEF Water held or pushed back by or as if by a dam or current

➕ A place, situation regarded as isolated, stagnant, or backward

> The city remained a backwater until now.
> (그 도시는 지금까지 낙후지역이었다.)

0229
barter [báːrtər]
v. 물물 교환, 교역, 물물 교환하다, 교역하다

IN BRIEF To trade goods or services without the exchange of money

+ trade, exchange, swap, sell

> The prisoners tried to barter with the guards for their freedom.
> (죄수들은 간수들과 그들의 자유를 위해 물물교환 하려고 했다.)

0230
balm [baːm]
n. 향유, 진통제, 마음을 진정시켜 주는 것

IN BRIEF To make or become calm

+ allay, becalm, calm (down), lull, quiet, settle, still, tranquilize, comfort

> The gentle music was (a) balm to his ears.
> (부드러운 음악은 그의 귀에 위안이 되었다.)

0231
ban [bæn]
n. 금지(령), 반대, 압력, 비난

IN BRIEF To prohibit (an action) or forbid the use of (something), especially by official decree

+ prohibit, forbid, proscribe, bar

> The United States and China are holding talks about a ban against nuclear testing programs.
> (미국과 중국은 핵실험 금지에 관한 회담을 개최하고 있습니다.)

0232
bankruptcy [bǽŋkrʌptsi]
n. 파산, 도산

IN BRIEF Inability to pay debts: insolvency

+ insolvency, failure, crash, disaster, ruin, liquidation, indebtedness

> His incompetence has brought the company to the brink of bankruptcy.
> (그의 무능 때문에 회사가 부도 일보직전까지 갔다.)

0233
a banner year for the team
우수한, 주요한, 일류의(first-rate), 대성공의;(정당지지) 두드러진(Unusually good; outstanding)

IN BRIEF Unusually good; outstanding

+ excellent, extremely successful, very good

0234
barren [bǽrən]
불모의, 메마른, 불임의, 시시한, 무력한, 어리석은, 빈약한

IN BRIEF Infertile, sterile, bare, desolate, dry, Unable to produce anything

+ sparse, unable to support growth

> A sandy desert is barren.
> (모래사막은 불모지다.)

0235
bedrock [bédrɑ̀k]
근본(기초적인 사실), 근본 원리

IN BRIEF The very basis; the foundation

+ first principle, rule, basis, foundation, roots, nuts and bolts

> Ownership of land is the bedrock of democracy.
> (토지소유는 민주주의의 근본 원리이다.)

0236
beatific [biːətífik]
축복받은; 행복에 넘친

IN BRIEF Having a blissful appearance

+ happy, blissful, giving-bliss, rapturous, euphoric

> The angels in the painting have beatific smiles.
> (그 그림 속의 천사는 사람들을 행복하게 하는 웃음을 지녔다.)

0237
beat-up
(물건이) 써서 낡은, 모양이 망가진 (rundown)

IN BRIEF Damaged or worn because of neglect or heavy use

+ dilapidated, shabby, debilitated, exhausted, fatigued, weary

> It's a beat-up old car.
> (이것은 완전 낡아빠진 차이다.)

0238
bed
하천 바닥, 호수 바닥

IN BRIEF A depression forming the ground under a body of water

+ bottom, ground, floor

> He searched for treasure on the ocean bed.
> (그는 해저에서 보물을 찾았다.)

0239
benign [bináin]
a. 자비로운, 인자한, 친절한/ (종양 등이) 양성(良性)의(benign/malignant tumors)

IN BRIEF Kind and gentle; mild (climate)

+ benevolent, generous, kind, gentle, obliging)

> On a warm sunny day the river seems placid and benign.
> (따뜻하고 햇볕 나는 날에는 그 강은 평온하고 온화해 보인다.)

0240
beneficial [bènəfíʃəl]
a. 유익한, 이로운

IN BRIEF Being of help or use

+ useful, helpful, profitable, benign, advantageous

> Using computers has a beneficial effect on children's learning.
> (컴퓨터 이용이 어린이들의 학습에 유익한 영향을 미친다.)

0241
belated [biléitid]
a. 늦어진; 뒤늦은; 시대에 뒤진

IN BRIEF Having been delayed; done or sent too late

+ late, delayed, overdue, tardy

> Two days after he had crashed my car he made a belated apology.
> (그는 내 차를 들이받은 지 이틀이 지나서 뒤늦게 사과했다.)

0242
bellicose [belɪkoʊs]
호전적인, 투쟁[싸움]을 좋아하는(warlike)

IN BRIEF Warlike or hostile in manner or temperament

+ aggressive, offensive, hostile, belligerent combative, antagonistic

> The general made some bellicose statements about his country's military strength.
> (장군은 자국의 군사력에 대해 호전적인 발언을 했다.)

0243
belligerent [bəlídʒərənt]
교전 중인; 교전국의; 호전적인

IN BRIEF Inclined or eager to fight; hostile or aggressive

+ aggressive, hostile, combative, warlike, bellicose

> I don't know why she always seems so belligerent toward me.
> (왜 그녀가 늘 나에게 그렇게 호전적인지 모르겠다.)

0244
bemused [bimjúːzd]
a. 멍한, 넋이 나간; 마음을 빼앗긴

IN BRIEF To cause to be bewildered; confuse

+ puzzled, bewildered, baffled, confused, perplexed

> He was totally bemused by all the activity around him.
> (그는 주변의 엄청난 활기에 완전히 어리벙벙했다.)

0245
benediction [bènədíkʃən]
n. 축복; 감사기도; 축도 ↔ anathema, execration

IN BRIEF An invocation of divine blessing

+ blessing, grace, prayer, thankfulness

> Jack and Jill were married without their parents' benediction.
> (Jack 과 Jill은 그들 부모의 축복 없이 결혼했다.)

0246
benefactor [bénəfæktər]
은혜를 베푸는 사람, 은인; 후원자

IN BRIEF One that gives aid, especially financial aid

+ supporter, defender, patron, sponsor, helper

> The money was donated by an anonymous benefactor.
> (익명의 후원자가 그 돈을 기증하였다.)

0247
beforehand [bifɔ́ːrhænd]
ad., a. 미리, 사전에, 전부터, 이전에

IN BRIEF Early; in advance; in anticipation

+ in advance, already, previously, before, ahead

> We were aware of the problem beforehand.
> (우리는 미리 그 문제를 알고 있었다.)

0248
benevolent [bənévələnt]
a. 자비로운, 인자한, 자선을(위한), 호의적인

IN BRIEF Having a desire to do good

+ kind, good, generous, benign, amicable, amiable

> She believed in the existence of a benevolent God.
> (그녀는 자비로운 신의 존재를 믿었다.)

0249
balk [bɔːk]
n. 망설이다; 갑자기 멈추다; 방해하다

IN BRIEF To stop short and refuse to go on

+ block, recoil, resist, hesitate

> His parents balked at the cost of the guitar he wanted.
> (부모님은 그가 원하는 기타의 가격을 알고서 망설였다.)

0250
bent [bent]
경향, 소질, 재능, 좋아함, 기호
IN BRIEF Turned in a specific direction
[+] disposition, partiality, penchant, predilection, predisposition, tendency, trend, bias, propensity

He has a strong bent for painting.
(그는 그림을 매우 좋아한다.)

0251
bereave [birí:v]
(희망·기쁨·이성, 가족) 앗아가다, 잃게하다(deprive of)
IN BRIEF Deprive through death
[+] death; loss, dispossess, rob, strip ↔ birth

His death bereaved her of all her hope.
(그의 죽음은 그녀의 모든 희망을 앗아갔다.)

0252
besiege [bisí:dʒ]
vt. 포위하다, 둘러싸다, 공격하다, 괴롭히다
IN BRIEF To crowd around; beset, pester, harass, hound
[+] besiege, beleaguer, blockade, invest, siege, bother; assault

The fans excitedly besieged the escaping musicians in an attempt to get their autographs.
(그 팬들은 도망가려는 음악가들의 사인을 받아내려고 흥분하며 둘러쌌다.)

0253
bibliophile [bíbliəfàil]
애서가, 서적 수집가
IN BRIEF Lover of books, collector of books
[+] book lover, booklover

He is a great bibliophile.
(그는 대단한 애서가이다.)

0254
better off
(경제적으로) 부유한(richer) (well-off의 비교급)
IN BRIEF In a more fortunate or prosperous condition
[+] fortunate

They were better off than most of their neighbors.
(그들은 대부분의 이웃들보다 더 잘살았다.)

0255
beverage [bévəridʒ]
n. 음료(drinks)

Soon after the colonists arrived in the New World, they learned to produce beverages from fruit and grain.
(개척자들은 미대륙에 도착하고 얼마 지나지 않아 과일과 곡식에서 음료수를 얻는 법을 알았다.)

0256
blandishment [blǽndiʃ]
아첨(Excessive, ingratiating praise, flatter)
감언이설로 속임

He refused to be moved by either threats or blandishments.
(그는 협박에도 감언이설에도 마음을 움직이려 하지 않았다.)

0257
biased [báiəsd]
치우친, 편견을 지닌, 편향된(prejudiced)
IN BRIEF Marked by or exhibiting bias; prejudiced
[+] predisposed, weighted, prejudiced, one-sided, partial

The newspapers gave a very biased report of the meeting.
(신문들은 그 회동에 대해 매우 편향된 보도를 했다.)

0258
besmirch [bismə́:rtʃ]
(인격·명예·평판) 더럽히다, 손상시키다
IN BRIEF To make dirty; soil
[+] smear, smudge, smut, soil, spatter, stain, sully, impair, taint, tarnish, blemish

The scandalous remarks in the newspaper besmirch the reputations of every member of the society.
(신문의 수치스러운 발언들이 협회 구성원 모두의 평판을 욕되게 했다.)

0259
bicker [bíkər]
말다툼하다(quarrel, argue)
IN BRIEF To argue over something unimportant
[+] argue, contend, dispute, fight, quarrel, quibble, spat, squabble, wrangle, conflict

I wish you two would stop bickering.
(나는 둘이 그만 다투었으면 좋겠어.)

0260
biennially [baiéniəm]

2년마다, 2년에 한 번씩(every two years)

IN BRIEF Lasting or living for two years

+ biyearly

> The plant bore flowers biennially.
> (그 식물은 2년마다 꽃을 피운다.)

0261
bizarre [bizá:r]

a. 기괴한(grotesque) → 이상야릇한 → 이상한

IN BRIEF Very unusual or strange

+ strange, wild, eccentric, erratic, freakish, idiosyncratic, odd, outlandish, crazy, peculiar, quaint, queer, singular, unnatural, weird, antic, fantastic, far-fetched

> The plot of the novel was too bizarre to be believed.
> (그 소설의 구성은 너무나도 이상해서 믿어지지 않았다.)

0262
blanch [blæntʃ]

v. 희게(표백)되다(whiten, bleach), (과일)데치다, 창백하게 되다 (etiolate, pale, wan)

IN BRIEF To remove colour from, or (of colour) to be removed; whiten; fade

+ turn pale, fade, pale, drain, bleach, wan, whiten

> He blanched with fear at the sight of the snake.
> (뱀을 보자 그는 얼굴이 겁에 질렸다.)

0263
beguiling [bigáil]

a. 속이는; 매력적인(alluring)

IN BRIEF Charming or fascinating

+ charming, interesting, pleasing, attractive, engaging

> Unfortunately the gadgets often have a beguiling way of appearing useful until you look a bit closer.
> (불행히도 그 장치들은 당신이 조금 더 가까이에서 볼 때까지는 쓸모 있어 보이게 하는 매력적인 면이 종종 있다.)

0264
blankly [blǽŋkli]

무표정하게, 멍하니, 멍청하게

IN BRIEF Devoid of writing, images, or marks

+ bare, clear, empty, vacant, vacuous, void

> He stared blankly into space, not knowing what to say next.
> (그는 다음에 무슨 말을 할지 몰라서 멍하니 허공을 바라보았다.)

0265
blatant [bléitənt]

a. 시끄러운, 떠들썩한, 노골적인, 심한, 눈에 거슬리는

IN BRIEF Offensively noisy or loud; brazenly obvious

+ boisterous, clamorous, obstreperous, strident, vociferous; obtrusive, obvious

> It is difficult to think of a more blatant example of unlawful sex discrimination.
> (불법적 성차별의 예로 이보다 더 명백한 것은 생각하기 힘들다.)

0266
bleak [bli:k]

a. 황폐한, 쓸쓸한; 냉혹한; 구슬픈(desolate)

IN BRIEF Gloomy and somber

+ dismal, black, dark, depressing, grim, discouraging, gloomy

> The Pentagon's bleak progress report offers good reasons for a speedier withdrawal of American troops from Afghanistan.
> (미국 국방성의 우울한 경과보고서는 미군이 아프가니스탄에서 보다 신속하게 철수해야 하는 타당한 이유들을 제시하고 있다.)

0267
bemoan [bimóun]

v. 한탄하다, 슬퍼하다, 유감으로 생각하다

IN BRIEF To express grief over; lament

+ regret, complain about, rue, deplore

> There will be those who have looked forward to the initiation of the new policy, whereas others bemoan either its necessity or its effectiveness.
> (새로운 정책의 시행을 고대해온 사람들이 있을 것이고, 반면에 그 정책의 필요성이나 효과에 대해 유감스럽게 생각하는 다른 사람들도 있을 것이다.)

0268
blithe [blaið]

a. 즐거운, 유쾌한, 명랑한, 쾌활한

IN BRIEF Carefree and lighthearted

+ happy, cheerful, merry, jaunty, delighted, glad

> The little girl is very blithe, so everybody like her.
> (그 조그만 소녀는 매우 명랑하다. 그래서 모든 사람들이 그녀를 좋아한다.)

0269
block [blɑk]

방해하다, 막다, 차단하다

IN BRIEF A solid piece of hard material; an obstruction

+ bar, dam, impede, obstruct, close

> A large crowd blocked the corridors and exits.
> (많은 사람이 복도와 출입구를 막았다.)

0270
blue [bluː]

a. 기운이 없는, 풀이 죽은, 낙담한, 우울한

IN BRIEF Depressed in spirits; dejected; melancholy

+ depressed, sad, gloomy, dismal, dejected, despondent

> I felt blue when I failed in the exam.
> (시험에 실패해서 나는 우울했다.)

0271
blunder [blʌ́ndər]

n. 큰 실수, 대실책, 대실패(fiasco)

IN BRIEF Mistake typically caused by ignorance or confusion

+ mistake, bull, bungle, foozle, fumble, muff, stumble

> He was very careful not to commit a blunder.
> (그는 큰 실수를 하지 않도록 무척 조심했다.)

0272
blurred [bləːrd]

(눈·시력·시야·경치가)흐릿한; (사진)핀트가 안맞는

IN BRIEF To make indistinct and hazy in outline or appearance; obscure

+ indistinct, faint, vague, unclear, misty

> His eyes blurred with tears.
> (그의 두 눈은 눈물로 흐릿해졌다.)

0273
board [bɔːrd]

타다(get on), (on board) 배 위[안]에, 차[비행기] 안에

+ get on, enter, mount, embark, get on board

> When a car with a child on board gets into a traffic accident, physical injuries aren't the only thing to be worried about.
> (어린이를 태운 차가 교통사고를 당했을 때, 걱정해야 할 일은 신체적 상해만이 아니다.)

0274
bolster [bóulstər]

지지(지원)하다, 보강(강화)하다

IN BRIEF To support; reinforce

+ propup, sustain, uphold, buttress, sustain, encourage, strengthen

> New camera and film technology will bolster the company's market share.
> (새로운 카메라와 영화 기술은 그 회사의 시장 점유율을 강화할 것이다.)

0275
bombshell [bάmʃèl]

폭탄(bomb);포탄(shell)/ (구어) 깜짝 놀라게 하는 일, 충격적인 소식[뉴스], 돌발사건/ 굉장히 매력적인 미인

IN BRIEF Unexpected and very shocking piece of news

+ complete surprise, shock, revelation, jolt, bolt from the blue

> The news of his death was a bombshell.
> (그의 사망 소식은 날벼락이었다.)

0276
bona fide

진실한[하게] → 성실하게 → 선의를 가지고

IN BRIEF Not counterfeit or copied

+ authentic and genuine; actual, authentic, genuine, indubitable, good, original, real, true, undoubted, unquestionable

> Because she tried continually bona fide, could got on in life.
> (그녀는 계속해서 성실히 노력했기 때문에 출세할 수 있었다.)

0277
bond [bɑnd]

묶는[매는, 잇는]것, 속박, 구속, 유대, 결속, 계약, 동맹, 접착제(본드)

IN BRIEF Something, such as a fetter, cord, or band, that binds, ties, or fastens things together

+ tie, union, coupling, association, relation, connection, alliance

> There should be a bond of affection between the members of a family.
> (가족 구성원 간에는 애정의 결속이 있어야 한다.)

0278
boost [buːst]

v. 밀어올리다, 후원하다, 인상하다, 증가하다, (사기)돋우다

IN BRIEF Make higher or greater

+ aggrandize, amplify, augment, build, build up, burgeon, enlarge, escalate, expand, extend, grow, increase, magnify, mount, multiply, proliferate, rise, run up, snowball, soar, swell, upsurge, wax

> This will be a boost for the president's popularity.
> (이것은 대통령의 인기에 도움이 될 것이다.)

0279
bountiful [báuntifəl]

a. 풍부한

IN BRIEF Marked by or producing abundance

+ plentiful, ample, abundant, copious, exuberant

> We found a bountiful supply of coconuts on the island.
> (우리는 그 섬에 코코넛이 풍부하다는 것을 알았다.)

0280
brag [bræg]
v. 자랑하다, 뽐내다, 호언장담하다, 허풍떨다[of, about]

IN BRIEF To talk or write about oneself in a proud or self-impressed way

+ boast, swagger, blow your own trumpet/horn, vaunt

> He's been bragging about his new car.
> (그는 자기 새 차를 자랑하고 있다.)

0281
brandish [brændiʃ]
vt. (칼·창) 휘두르다; 과시하다

IN BRIEF To wave or flourish (a weapon in a triumphant, threatening, or ostentatious way)

+ wave, flourish, sweep, flaunt, display, exhibit, show

> The demonstrators brandished banners and shouted slogans.
> (시위대들은 깃발을 흔들며 슬로건을 외쳤다.)

0282
brawl [brɔːl]
vi. 말다툼, 싸움(종종 거리에서 주고받는)(fight)

IN BRIEF A noisy quarrel or fight

+ broil, donnybrook, fracas, melee fray, free-for-all, row

> The meeting turned into an undignified brawl.
> (그 회의는 품위 없는 언쟁으로 변해 버렸다.)

0283
break [breik]
v. 밝히다, 알리다 → (구어) 기회(s)

IN BRIEF Make known to the public information that was previously known only to a few people or that was meant to be kept a secret

+ tell, reveal, disclose, divulge

> She held back, not knowing how to break the terrible news.
> (그녀는 끔찍한 소식을 어떻게 알려야 할지 몰라, 말하지 않았다.)

0284
breakthrough [|breɪkθruː]
돌파구 → 큰 발전 (advance)

IN BRIEF An act of overcoming or penetrating an obstacle or restriction

+ development, advance, progress, improvement, discovery, finding, invention

> Doctors believe they've made a breakthrough in the treatment of breast cancer using drugs instead of surgery.
> (의사들은 수술 대신 약물을 이용한 유방암 치료에 큰 발전을 이룩시켰다고 믿고 있다.)

0285
brevity [brévəti]
(시간·기간의) 짧음; 간결

IN BRIEF Brief or short in duration

+ shortness, briefness, succinctness, terseness

> Simon's poems were known for their brevity.
> (사이먼의 시는 간결함으로 유명했다.)

0286
brilliantly [bríljəntli]
ad. 찬란하게, 환하게; 훌륭히, 멋지게

IN BRIEF Full of light; shining

+ intelligently, brightly, sharply, acutely, cleverly, perspicaciously, masterly

> She performed quite brilliantly.
> (그녀는 정말 훌륭히 연기를 했다.)

0287
bristle [brís-əl]
발끈하다(become irritated)

IN BRIEF Short, course, or prickly hair from a hog or boar

+ angry, rage, irritate, wrath

> She was bristling with anger.
> (그녀는 잔뜩 화내고 있었다.)

0288
brittle ['brɪtl]
a. 부서지기[깨지기] 쉬운(fragile); 덧없는

IN BRIEF Easily cracked, snapped, or broken; fragile

+ fragile, delicate, crisp, crumbling, frail, crumbly, breakable

> This may help to undermine the brittle truce that exists between the two countries.
> (이번 사건은 어쩌면 두 나라 사이의 취약한 정전 상태를 손상시킬 수도 있다.)

0289
bulk [bʌlk]
부피, 용적, 크기, 대부분 → 중요하다

IN BRIEF Size, mass, or volume, especially when very large

+ size, volume, dimensions, magnitude, substance

> It is of no great bulk.
> (그것은 그리 크지 않다. (size))
>
> The eldest son inherited the bulk of the estate.
> (장남이 토지의 대부분을 상속받았다. (majority))
>
> The case bulked large in his thoughts.
> (그의 생각에는 그 사건이 중요하게 여겨졌다.)

0290
brochure [brouʃúər]

n. 팸플릿, 소책자, 광고 전단

IN BRIEF A small booklet or pamphlet

➕ booklet, leaflet, pamphlet

> The computer's features are detailed in our brochure.
> (그 컴퓨터의 특징은 저희 책자에 상세히 나와 있습니다.)

0291
bullion [búljən]

금괴, 은괴

IN BRIEF Gold or silver in bars, ingots, or plates

➕ precious metal

> The robbers ran off with a thousand bars of gold bullion, stolen from Fort Knox.
> (강도들은 녹스 요새에서 훔친 금괴 천 개를 가지고 달아났다.)

0292
bulwark [búlwəːrk]

성채, 보루, 방벽, 방패, 방파제(strong) → 보호자(fortification, support)

IN BRIEF Something that provides defense or security

➕ barricade, breastwork, earthwork, rampart, bastion, parapet

> The soldiers built a bulwark to protect the east side of the city.
> (군인들은 도시의 동쪽을 보호하기 위해 성벽을 세웠다.)

0293
burgeon [bə́ːrdʒən]

싹트다 → (급격히)성장하다 → 발전하다(grow rapidly) ↔ shrink

IN BRIEF To put forth new buds, leaves, or greenery; sprout

➕ develope, increase, grow, thrive, flourish; grow and flourish

> Korea's burgeoning auto industry will threaten the foreign carmakers.
> (한국의 급성장하는 자동차산업은 외국 자동차 메이커들에 위협이 될 것이다.)

0294
burglar [bə́ːrgləːr]

n. 빈집털이범, 도둑

IN BRIEF A person who commits burglary; housebreaker

➕ housebreaker, thief, rubber, filcher, bandit

> The burglars got into the house through the bedroom window.
> (도둑들은 침실 창문을 통해 그 집으로 들어왔다.)

0295
burrow [bə́ːrou]

굴을 만들다, 구멍을 파다

IN BRIEF Hole dug in the ground; to dig a hole

➕ hole, tunnel, dig, excavate, exhume, unearth

> I saw a fox burrowing in the field.
> (나는 여우가 들판에서 굴을 파고 있는 것을 보았다.)

0296
bustle [bʌ́sl]

활발하게 움직이다; 분주히 돌아다니다; 법석을 떨며 돌아다니다

IN BRIEF To move very quickly; to hurry

➕ quick and busy activity; haste, hasten, hurry, hustle, rush, stir (move)

> Grandma likes to bustle around the kitchen while the family eats dinner.
> (할머니는 가족들이 저녁을 먹는 동안 부엌에서 바쁘게 움직이는 것을 좋아한다.)

0297
buttress [bʌ́tris]

지지하다, 옹호하다, 보호하다, 버팀벽, 지지물, 버티는 것

IN BRIEF Any support or prop

➕ support, bolster, reinforcement, brace, foundation

> You need more facts to buttress your argument.
> (당신의 주장을 뒷받침하려면 더 많은 사실이 필요하다.)

0298
cacophony (bad) [kækáfəni]

귀에 거슬리는 소리, 불협화음, 잡음, 소음 ↔ euphony 기분좋은 소리(good)

IN BRIEF Harshness or discordancy of sound; the opposite of euphony

➕ discord, racket, din, dissonance, disharmony, stridency

> Some people seemto enjoy the cacophony of an orchestra that is turningup.
> (몇몇 사람은 관현악단이 조율할 때, 나오는 불협화음을 즐기는 것 같다.)

0299
cadaverous [kədǽvərəs]

송장 같은; 새파랗게 질린; 빼빼 마른

IN BRIEF Resembling a corpse

➕ pale, suggestive(시사, 암시하는) of death; corpselike

> The hikers looked cadaverous after they were found a week later.
> (등산객들은 일주일 후에 발견된 후, 매우 흉측해 보였다.)

LESSON 07

0300
cajole [kedʒóul]

구슬리다, 회유하다, 부추기다(coax)

IN BRIEF Use flattery(아첨) or deceit(속임) to persuade

+ coax, flatter, blandish, honey, wheedle,
Informal soft-soap, sweet-talk

The children will try to cajole their mother into giving them more dessert.
(아이들은 엄마를 부추겨 디저트를 더 주도록 할 것이다.)

0301
caliber [kǽlibər]

재능, 도량; 인품, 사람됨

IN BRIEF Degree of excellence, see value

+ worth, quality, ability, talent

The firm needs more people of your caliber.
(그 회사는 당신 같은 재능을 지닌 사람들을 더 많이 필요로 한다.)

0302
callous (hard skin) [kǽləs]

a. 냉담한 → 무관심한 → 무감각한 → (피부)굳은

IN BRIEF Without regard for the feelings or sufferings of others

+ heartless, cold, harsh, hardened, indifferent

The company showed callous disregard for the safety of their employees.
(회사는 직원들의 안전을 냉담하게 무시했다.)

0303
callow [kǽlou]

미숙한, 경험이 없는, (새가) 아직 깃털이 나지 않은

IN BRIEF Lacking adult maturity or experience; immature

+ inexperienced, naive, puerile, immature, unfledged

You are a just callow youth.
(너는 단지 풋내기 청년일 뿐 이다.)

0304
camouflage [kǽmuflὰːʒ]

위장하다, 눈가림하다 (conceal)

IN BRIEF Anything used to disguise or mislead

+ disguise, cover, dissemble, dissimulate, mask, masquerade

Insects are masters of camouflage because of their coloring.
(곤충은 그들의 색깔 덕분에 위장의 달인이 된다.)

0305
campaign [kæmpéin]

(사회적·정치적) 운동, 캠페인 → 선거운동, 유세, 군사행동, 전쟁(war)

IN BRIEF To support or take part in a political contest, An organized effort to accomplish a purpose

+ drive, movement, push

The presidential campaign was long, but exciting.
(대선은 길었지만, 흥미진진했다.)

0306
candor [kǽndər]

n. 솔직함; 정직함

IN BRIEF Frankness or sincerity of expression; openness

+ honesty, fairness sincerity, frankness, outspokenness, forthrightness

His candor at the meeting was praiseworthy.
(회의에서 보여준 그의 솔직함은 칭찬할 만했다.)

0307
candid [kǽndid]

솔직한, 자연스러운, 공평한

IN BRIEF People appearing natural and not posed for a photograph

+ sincere honesty, forthright, frank

They preferred candid shots instead of posed picture from the wedding.
(그들은 결혼식에서 포즈를 취한 사진 대신 솔직하게 찍힌 사진을 선호했다.)

0308
candidate [kǽndidèit]

지원자, 지망자; 수험자, 후보(자)

IN BRIEF A person who seeks or is nominated for an office, prize, or honor

+ contender, applicant, nominee

The candidate emphasized his excellent credentials.
(그 후보는 자신의 뛰어난 능력을 강조했다.)

0309
cancel [kǽnsəl]

지우다 → 무효로 하다 → 취소[철회]하다(call off)

IN BRIEF To annul or invalidate

+ annul, abolish, repeal, abrogate, rescind, countermand

I was ill and had to cancel all my appointments.
(나는 몸이 아파서 모든 약속을 취소해야만 했다.)

0310
capacity [kəpǽsəti]

(See ability/inability) (최대) 수용능력, 지적능력, 재능, (방·건물·탈것)정원(定員)

IN BRIEF Physical, mental, financial, or legal power to perform

+ ability, capability, competence, competency, faculty

> She has an enormous capacity for hard work.
> (그녀는 힘든 일을 해내는 능력을 가지고 있다.)

0311
capital [ˈkæpɪtl]

수도, (산업 따위의) 중심지 /대문자, 두문자(letter) /자본(금); 자산, 원금(interest, money, funds, property, wealth, resources) / 처벌 (capital punishment : 사형제도)

> London, Paris and Washington DC are capital cities.
> (런던, 파리, 워싱턴 DC는 수도인 도시들이다.)
> London is spelt with a capital 'L'.
> (London은 대문자 L로 쓴다.)
> They lacked the capital to develop the business.
> (그들은 사업을 전개할 자본금이 부족했다.)

0312
capitalize [kǽpitəlàiz]

v. 이용하다, 투자하다

IN BRIEF To take advantage (of); profit (by)

+ dispose of, make the most of

> However Forrester's been able to capitalize on the issue.
> (그러나 포레스터는 이 문제를 교묘하게 이용해왔습니다.)

0313
capitulate [kəpítʃəlèit]

항복하다

IN BRIEF Give in, yield, concede, submit, surrender, comply, give up

+ give in, yield to, concede, submit, surrender, succumb

> We had no choice but to capitulate to their demands.
> (우리는 그들의 요구에 항복할 수밖에 없었다.)

0314
capricious [kəpríʃəs]

변덕스러운, 변하기 쉬운, 바람기 있는

IN BRIEF Given to sudden behavior change

+ arbitrary, whimsical, changeable, erratic, unpredictable, variable, fickle, mercurial, unstable

> He was a cruel and capricious tyrant.
> (그는 잔인하고 변덕스러운 폭군이었다.)

0315
capsize [ˈkæpsaɪz]

뒤집히다 → 전복하다(overturn)

IN BRIEF To overturn or cause to overturn

+ overthrow, topple, turn over, upset

> We capsized in heavy seas.
> (거친 파도에 우리가 전복되었다.)

0316
cardinal [káːrdənl]

근본적인 → 아주 중요한 → 주요한(main) → 진홍색의(새빨간)

IN BRIEF Most important, influential, or significant, leading, main, major

+ capital, chief, first, foremost, key, number one, paramount

> Harmony, balance and order are cardinal virtues to the French.
> (프랑스 사람들에게는 조화와 균형과 질서가 주요한 덕목이다.)

0317
careless [kɛ́ərlis]

a. 부주의한, 신중하지 않은

IN BRIEF Without concern

+ slapdash, reckless, cursory, thoughtless, negligent

> Careless drivers cause accidents.
> (부주의한 운전자는 사고를 일으킨다.)

0318
carnage [káːrnidʒ]

대량 학살; (전쟁터) 시체, 주검

IN BRIEF Massacre[mǽsəkə:r]대량학살 or slaughter살인

+ mass murder, massacre, slaughter, butchery

> There was much carnage on the battlefield.
> (전쟁터에서 많은 대학살이 있다.)

0319
categorize [kǽtigəràiz]

vt. 범주에 넣다; 분류하다

IN BRIEF To put into a category or categories; classify

+ assort, class, classify

> The books were categorized by language.
> (그 책들은 언어에 따라 분류되어 있었다.)

0320
catastrophe [kətǽstrəfi]

큰 재해, 대참사, 파국, 비극적 결말

IN BRIEF A great, often sudden calamity

➕ disaster, tragedy, calamity, cataclysm, mishap

> The earthquake was the country's worst catastrophe.
> (그 지진은 그 나라 최악의 재난이었다.)

0321
catchy [kǽtʃi]

(Attractive or appealing) 사람의 마음을 끄는 → 걸려들기 알맞은 → 현혹되기 쉬운

IN BRIEF Attractive or appealing

➕ captivating, addictive, pleasant

> We need a catchy advertising slogan.
> (눈길을 끄는 광고 슬로건이 필요하다.)

0322
categorize [kǽtigəràiz]

vt. 범주에 넣다; 분류하다

IN BRIEF To put into a category or categories; classify

➕ assort, class, classify

> The books were categorized by language.
> (그 책들은 언어에 따라 분류되어 있었다.)

0323
catholic [kǽθəlik]

전반적인, 보편적인, (취미나 감정) 넓은

IN BRIEF Broad in tastes or interests

➕ wide, general, global, universal, ecumenical

> He is a man of catholic tastes.
> (그는 폭넓은 취미를 가진 사람이다.)

0324
cavernous [kǽvərnəs]

동굴의, 동굴 모양의, 움푹 들어간 ↔ filled

IN BRIEF Suggestive of a cavern in vastness, darkness

➕ vast, spacious, commodious, large and hollow

> The hall is cavernous depths
> (그 구멍은 동굴같이 깊은 곳이다.)

0325
celebrity [kǽθəlik]

⟨famous person⟩ 명사, 유명 인사

IN BRIEF Fame or popular renown

➕ publicity, personality, fame, reputation, popularity

> She found herself something of a celebrity.
> (그녀는 자신이 상당한 유명인사가 되어 있음을 알았다.)

0326
celerity [səlérəti]

n. (행동의) 민첩함, 기민함

IN BRIEF Rapidness of movement or activity

➕ swiftness, dispatch, expedition, expeditiousness, fleetness

> They moved with great celerity when they heard about the flood.
> (그들은 홍수에 대해 들었을 때 매우 침착하게 움직였다.)

0327
censorship [sénsərʃip]

n. 검열(제도)

IN BRIEF The act, process, or practice of censoring

➕ expurgation, purgation, supervision

> Once he starts talking about censorship you can't stop him.
> (일단 그가 검열에 대해 이야기를 시작하면 말릴 수가 없다.)

0328
censure [sénʃər]

견책, 징계; 비난, 책망, 혹평

IN BRIEF Expression of blame or disapproval

➕ criticize, blame, condemn, reprimand, reproach, scold, berate

> His dishonest behavior came under severe censure.
> (그의 부정직한 행동은 호된 비난을 받았다.)

0329
census [sénsəs]

n. 통계 조사; 인구 조사

IN BRIEF A periodic count of the population

➕ nose count, nosecount

> According to the U. S. census of 1860, the number of slave-owning blacks in Manchester County, Virginia, would be down to five.
> (1860년 미국 인구 조사에 의하면, 버지니아 주의 맨체스터 카운티에서 노예를 소유하고 있는 흑인의 숫자는 5명이었다.)

0330
centennial [senténiəl]

a. 100주년의, 100년마다의 (one hundredth)

IN BRIEF Of or relating to an age or period of 100 years

➕ centenary

> Sookmyung Women's University is preparing to celebrate its centennial anniversary.
> (숙명여자대학교는 개교 100주년 기념 행사를 준비하고 있다.)

0331
chagrin [ʃəˈgrɪn]

n. 원통함, 분함, 유감(embarrassment)

IN BRIEF A feeling of annoyance or mortification

[+] annoyance, embarrassment, humiliation, dissatisfaction, displeasure, mortification

> There was nothing remarkable about the man save his blazing red head, and the expression of extreme chagrin and discontent upon his features.
> (그 사람에게 주목할 만한 점은 단지 불타는 듯한 붉은 머리카락과 얼굴 이목구비에 나타난 극도의 유감과 불만의 표정이었다.)

0332
charitable [tʃǽrətəbəl]

a. 자비로운, 관대한

IN BRIEF The giving of money or help to those in need

[+] generous, benevolent, altruistic, philanthropic, merciful, kind, magnanimous

> He was a very charitable person.
> (그는 무척 자비로운 사람이었다.)

0333
chasten [tʃéisən]

(벌하여) 바로잡다, 단련시키다

IN BRIEF To correct using punishment or suffering

[+] subdue, discipline, cow, curb, humble, soften

> He was greatly chastened by his failure.
> (그는 실패에 의해 크게 단련되었다.)

0334
chatterbox [tʃǽtərbàks]

수다쟁이

IN BRIEF An extremely talkative person

[+] chatterer, babbler, prater, spouter

> Ahntonio is a chatterbox!
> (안토니오는 수다쟁이야!)

0335
check [tʃek]

v. 조사하다, 확인하다, 점검하다

IN BRIEF The act or an instance of inspecting or testing something, as for accuracy or quality

[+] examine, test, stop, control, restrain

> You must check your work more carefully. it's full of mistakes.
> (네가 하는 일을 좀 더 꼼꼼히 점검해야 해. 실수투성이야.)

0336
chestnut [tʃésnʌt]

n. 밤(나무) → 케케묵은 이야기 (old story)

IN BRIEF An old, frequently repeated joke, story, or song

> The title comes from the hoary sci-fi chestnut that modifying a tiny aspect of the past will create seismic changes in the present.
> (그 제목은 과거의 아주 작은 외형만을 수정하여 현재에 커다란 변화를 일으키는 진부한 공상과학 소설의 케케묵은 이야기에서 유래한다.)

0337
chilly [tʃíli]

a. 으슬으슬한; 차가운, 추운, 한기가 드는

IN BRIEF Very hot and finely tapering pepper of special pungency

[+] cool, hostile, frigid, frighten

> The speech met with a chilly reception.
> (그 연설은 냉랭한 반응을 받았다.)

0338
chronic(time) [kránik]

a. 장기간에 걸친, 만성적인, 오래 계속되는

IN BRIEF Of long duration; continuing

[+] persistent, continuous, Lasting for a long period of time confirmed, habitual, inveterate, incessant, never-ending

> His disease passed into a chronic state.
> (그의 병은 만성이 되었다.)

0339
chronological [ˌkrɑːnəˈlɑːdʒɪkl]

연대순의 (in chronological order : 연대순으로)

IN BRIEF Arranged according to the order of time

[+] sequential, ordered, historical, progressive, consecutive

> The whole report was written in chronological order.
> (천체 보고서는 연대순으로 작성되었다.)

0340
coagulate [kouǽgjəlèit]

응고시키다, 굳히다

IN BRIEF To cause (a fluid, such as blood) to change into a soft semisolid mass or (of such a fluid) to change into such a mass

[+] congeal, clot, curdle → jelly, set

> Blood coagulates in air.
> (혈액은 공기 중에서는 응고한다.)

0341
circumference [sərkʌ́mfərəns]

원주, 주위, 주변, 경계선, 영역, 범위

IN BRIEF The boundary line of a figure, area, or object

+ border, circuit, compass, periphery, edge, perimeter

> This lake is about three miles in circumference.
> (이 호수는 둘레가 약 3마일이다.)

0342
circumvent [sə̀ːrkəmvént]

vt. (곤란·문제점) 교묘하게 회피하다

IN BRIEF To get the better of by using cleverness

+ avoid, get around, outwit, burke, bypass, elude, escape, eschew, evade, frustrate

> He circumvented this serious problem.
> (그는 심각한 문제를 교묘하게 회피했다.)

0343
cite [sait]

vt. (구절·판례) 인용[인증(引證)]하다(quote)

IN BRIEF To quote; refer to as an example; commend

+ instance, mention, specify, adduce, lay, present, summon

> The devil can cite Scripture for his purpose.
> (악마도 자신의 목적을 위하여 성경을 인용할 수 있다.)

0344
clandestine [klændéstin]

a. 비밀의, 남몰래 하는

IN BRIEF Kept or done in secret

+ secret, hidden, closet, furtive, surreptitious, covert

> The group held weekly clandestine meetings in a church.
> (그 그룹은 교회에서 매주 비밀만남을 가졌다.)

0345
clemency [klémənsi]

n. 관용, 아량, 관대함

IN BRIEF Mercy or leniency

+ mercy, pity, compassion, leniency

> He appealed to the judge for clemency.
> (그는 판사에게 관대한 조처를 간청했다.)

0346
client [kláiənt]

n. 소송 의뢰인, (상점) 고객, 단골손님

IN BRIEF A customer or patron

+ customer, consumer, patient, patron

> He is going to meet with an important client.
> (그는 중요한 의뢰인과 만날 예정이다.)

0347
common [kɑ́mən/kɔ́m-]

a. 공통의; 일반적인, 평범한; 품위 없는

IN BRIEF Belonging equally to, or shared alike by, two or more or all in question

+ usual, standard, daily, regular, ordinary, familiar, plain, conventional

> The elegant Princess Ingrid has ling complained about Duchess Sarah Norton's common accent.
> (기품 있는 잉그리드 공주는 사라 노튼 공작부인의 저속한 말투에 관해 오랫동안 불평해 왔다.)

0348
crass [kræs]

a. 우둔한, 아주 어리석은; 형편없는, 지독한(nasty)

IN BRIEF So unrefined as to be lacking in discrimination and sensibility

+ insensitive, stupid, gross, blundering, dense, coarse, witless, boorish, obtuse, unrefined, asinine, indelicate, oafish, lumpish, doltish

> Some people were shocked by a loudmouthed jerk's rude jokes and crass comments.
> 일부 사람들은 시끄러운 얼간이의 무례한 농담과 지독한 말에 경악했다.

0349
converse [kənvə́ːrs]

a. (의견) 반대의; (방향) 정반대의

IN BRIEF Opposite or contrary in direction, action, sequence

+ opposite, counter, reverse, contrary

> The candidate's speech was converse to her usual pattern, and this became the turning point in her political career.
> (그 후보자의 연설은 그녀가 늘 하던 형식과는 정반대였고, 이것이 그녀의 정치이력에 있어 일대 전환점이 되었다.)

LESSON 08

0350
clog [klɑg]

v. 방해하다; 막다, 막히게 하다; (up)[with]

IN BRIEF An obstruction or hindrance

[+] obstruct, block, hamper, hinder, congest

> The pipes are clogging up.
> (배관이 막히고 있다.)

0351
clue [kluː]

n. 단서, 실마리

IN BRIEF Something that helps to solve a problem or unravel a mystery

[+] indication, sign, trace, hint

> There is no clue to the identity of the killer.
> (살해자의 정체에 대한 아무런 단서도 없다.)

0352
coagulate [kouǽgjəlèit]

응고시키다, 굳히다

IN BRIEF To cause transformation of (a liquid or sol, for example into or as if into a soft, semisolid, or solid mass)

[+] congeal, clot, curdle → jelly, set

> Blood coagulates in air.
> (혈액은 공기 중에서는 응고한다.)

0353
coerce [kouə́ːrs]

vt. 강요하다, 강제하다

IN BRIEF To pressure, intimidate, or force (someone into doing something)

[+] force, compel, intimidate, pressurize

> We were coerced into signing the contract.
> (우리는 강제로 그 계약서에 서명해야 했다.)

0354
cognizant [kágnəzənt]

인식하고 있는, 알고 있는, 깨닫고 있는

IN BRIEF Having cognizance; aware

[+] knowledgeable, familiar, aware, conscious

> Regrettably, we were not cognizant of the facts.
> (유감스럽게도 우리는 그 사실을 알고 있지 못했습니다.)

0355
coerce [kouə́ːrs]

vt. 강요하다, 강제하다

IN BRIEF To pressure, intimidate, or force (someone into doing something)

[+] force, compel, intimidate, pressurize

> His arguments lack coherence.
> (그의 주장은 조리가 없다.)

0356
coincide [kòuinsáid]

vi. 일치하다, 동시에 일어나다

IN BRIEF To occur or exist simultaneously

[+] occur simultaneously, synchronize, occur at the same time

> Her arrival coincided with our departure.
> (그녀의 도착은 우리의 출발과 동시에 일어났다.)

0357
collapse [kəlǽps]

v. 붕괴, 파탄, 허물어지다; (계획·제도 등이) 무너지다, 쓰러지다

IN BRIEF To fall down or inward suddenly; cave in

[+] fall down, subside, crumple, founder, breakdown

> The company is on the point of collapse.
> (그 회사는 붕괴 직전이다.)

0358
colleague [káliːg]

n. 동료, 파트너

IN BRIEF A fellow member of a profession, staff, or academic faculty; an associate

[+] partner, ally, associate, assistant, co-worker

> I visited a colleague for a week.
> (나는 1주일 동안 동료의 집에 머물렀다.)

0359
collision [kəlíʒən]

n. 충돌, 마찰

IN BRIEF The act of colliding; a crash

[+] crash, accident, disagreement, conflict

> The ship had to take evasive action in order to avoid a collision.
> (그 배는 충돌을 피하기 위해 도피 조치를 취해야만 했다.)

0360
colony [kάləni]

n. 식민지

IN BRIEF An area subject to rule by an outside power

[+] dependency, possession, province, territory

Once India was a colony of England.
(한때 인도는 영국의 식민지였다.)

0361
colossal [kəlάsəl]

a. 거대한, 엄청난

IN BRIEF Of great size, extent, or amount; immense

[+] huge, massive, enormous, gigantic, immense

In the center of the hall stood a colossal wooden statue, decorated in ivory and gold.
(홀의 중심에 상아와 금으로 장식된, 나무로 만든 거대한 상이 서 있었다.)

0362
coma [kóumə]

n. 혼수상태, 무감각(deep unconsciousness)

IN BRIEF Deep prolonged unconsciousness

[+] unconsciousness, oblivion, stupor, torpor

He has been in a coma for the past six weeks.
(그는 지난 6주 동안 혼수상태에 빠져 있었다.)

0363
combustible [kəmbʌ́stəbəl]

가연성의, 불붙기 쉬운, 흥분하기 쉬운, 잘 달아오르는

IN BRIEF Able to be exploded

[+] flammable, explosive, incendiary, hotheaded

Gasoline is highly combustible.
(가솔린은 연소성이 높다.)

0364
comely [kʌ́mli]

보기 좋은, 잘생긴

IN BRIEF Pleasing and wholesome in appearance; attractive

[+] good looking, attractive, winsome, pretty, handsome

She might be rather called comely than beautiful.
(그녀는 아름답다기보다 잘생겼다고 해야 할 것 같다.)

0365
commence [kəméns]

v. 시작하다, 개시하다

IN BRIEF To begin or start

[+] embark, begin, start, initiate, inaugurate

We will commence with this work.
(우리는 이 일부터 시작합니다.)

0366
commensurate [kə'menʃərət]

같은 정도의, ~에 상응하는, 적당한[to, with]

IN BRIEF Equal; properly proportioned

[+] equivalent, consistent, compatible, proportionate to

Her low salary is not commensurate with her abilities.
(그녀의 낮은 봉급은 그녀의 능력에 상응하지 않는다.)

0367
commodity [kəmάdəti]

n. (경제) 상품, 원자재, 일용품, 생활필수품; 유용[편리]한 것

IN BRIEF Something bought and sold

[+] goods, stock, products, wares

Trading in commodities was brisk.
(일용품의 거래는 활발했다.)

0368
complacent [kəmpléisnt]

(부정적) 자기만족의 → 현실에 안주하는 → 무관심한(unconcerned)

IN BRIEF Self-satisfied; smug; unbothered

[+] smug, self-satisfied, pleased with yourself, resting on your laurels

All his life he had to work hard under extreme conditions and now he has a complacent feeling about what he has done.
(평생을 극한의 조건에서 열심히 일을 해야 했고 이제는 자신이 한 일에 대해 안일한 감정을 가지고 있다.)

0369
compartment [kəmpάːrtmənt]

(객차·객선의) 칸막이된 객실, 칸

IN BRIEF One of the parts or spaces into which an area is subdivided

[+] section, carriage, chamber, category

The first-class compartments are in front.
(1등 칸은 앞쪽에 있습니다.)

0370
compelling [kəmpéliŋ]

a. 강제적인 → 마음끄는 → 주목할만한(noteworthy) → 설득력 있는(unavoidable)

IN BRIEF Urgently requiring attention

[+] convincing, pressing, urgent, unavoidable, fascinating

The most compelling market for voice-recognition software might be Asia.
(음성인식 소프트웨어의 가장 주목할 만한 시장은 아시아일 것이다.)

0371
compel [kəmpél]
v. 억지로 ~시키다, 강제하다
IN BRIEF To make or force someone to act
+ force, urge, coerce, impel

> You can compel obedience, but not affection.
> (복종은 강요할 수 있지만 애정은 그럴 수 없다.)

0372
compatible [kəmpǽtəbəl]
양립(호환)할 수 있는, 모순 없는 → 사이좋게 지낼 수 있는 (harmonious)
IN BRIEF Able to be together and get along
+ consistent, congruent, consonant, congenial, accordant

> IBM-compatible machines
> (IBM과 호환 가능한 기계)

0373
competent [kámpətənt]
a. 유능한; 적당한, 충분한
IN BRIEF Properly or sufficiently qualified; capable
+ able, skilled, fit, capable, proficient

> He is a competent language teacher.
> (그는 유능한 어학 교사이다.)

0374
complacency [kəm-plā′sən-sē]
n. (부정적인)자기만족 → 무관심
IN BRIEF A feeling of satisfaction, esp extreme self-satisfaction; smugness
+ smugness, self-satisfaction, satisfaction, contentment

> There's an air of complacency in his behaviour which I dislike.
> (그의 태도에는 내가 싫어하는 자기만족적인 분위기가 있다.)

0375
compliant [kəmpláiənt]
a. 고분고분한
IN BRIEF Agreeable; willing to yield ↔ recalcitrant
+ conformable, docile, obedient, submissive, supple, tractable

> By then, Henry seemed less compliant with his wife's wishes than he had been six months before.
> (그때는 이미 Henry(헨리)가 6개월 전 보다 부인의 요구에 덜 순종적인 것처럼 보였다.)

0376
complexity [kəmpléksəti]
n. 복잡성
IN BRIEF The quality or condition of being complex
+ complication, intricacy, entanglement

> It's a matter of considerable complexity.
> (그것은 꽤 복잡한 문제다.)

0377
compliance [kəmpláiəns]
(명령·요구) 따르기, 승낙(conformity)
IN BRIEF The act of complying with a wish, request, or demand; acquiescence
+ agreement, assent, acquiescence, consent, submissiveness

> her reluctant compliance
> (그녀의 마지못한 승낙)

0378
commotion [kəmóuʃən]
혼란, (정신적인) 동요, 흥분; 소동, 폭동
IN BRIEF Noisy confusion → A condition of turbulent motion
+ disturbance, riot, disorder, fuss, turmoil, agitation

> The children are making a lot of commotion.
> (아이들이 야단법석을 떨고 있다.)

0379
comply [kəmplái]
vi. 따르다, 응하다 (규칙, 명령)
IN BRIEF Abide by, follow agreement or instructions
+ obey, follow, agree to, submit, yield to

> It is very stupid of you to comply with his request.
> (네가 그의 요구에 응한다는 것은 참으로 어리석은 짓이다.)

0380
component [kəmpóunənt]
구성 요소[성분]를 이루는, 구성하고 있는, 구성 요소, 성분
IN BRIEF One of the individual entities contributing to a whole
+ part, piece, ingredient, element

> Surprise is an essential component of my plan.
> (깜짝 놀라게 하는 것도 내 계획의 필수 구성 성분이다.)

0381
composite [kəmpázit]
a. 각종 요소로 된; 합성의, 복합의, 합성물, 복합물
IN BRIEF Made up of distinct components; compound
+ compound, mosaic, combination, mixture, fusion, synthesis

> The play is a composite of reality and fiction.
> (그 연극은 사실과 허구의 복합물이다.)

0382
compose [kəmpóuz]

구성, 작곡하다 → 마음을 가라앉히다

IN BRIEF Create or put together; constitute; to calm one's mind or body

➕ organize, constitute, make up, comprise, be, represent

> I ran out of the office until I could compose myself enough to face them.
> (사무실 밖으로 뛰쳐나온 뒤에야 나는 그들과 대면할 수 있을 만큼 마음을 진정시킬 수 있었다.)

0383
comprehensive [kàmprihénsive]

포괄적인 → 넓은 → 종합적인(overall)/이해력이 있는 → 이해가 빠른

IN BRIEF Of large scope; inclusive; having an extended mental range or grasp

➕ broad, inclusive, extensive, complete, encyclopedic, thorough, cover

> The book is a comprehensive guide to Korea.
> (그 책은 한국에 대한 포괄적인 안내서이다.)

0384
compromise [kámprəmàiz]

n. 타협(안), 화해

IN BRIEF To settle an argument by giving up something wanted

➕ agreement, concession, accommodation

> They reached a satisfactory compromise.
> (그들은 만족할 만한 타협을 보았다.)

0385
compulsive [kəmpʌ́lsiv]

(compulsion : 강박관념) 강제적인 → 억지의 → 강박관념에 사로잡힌

IN BRIEF Having the capacity to compel

➕ obsessive, chronic, persistent, addictive, incorrigible, irresistible

> Ahntonio is a compulsive worker.
> (안토니오는 강박적인 일꾼이다/ 강박적으로 일을 한다.)

0386
compulsory [kəmpʌ́lsəri]

의무 → 강제 → 필수적인 (required, mandatory)

IN BRIEF Absolutely required or forced

➕ imperative, mandatory, necessary, obligatory, required, requisite

> Attendance at the meeting is compulsory.
> (회의에 참석하는 것은 필수이다.)

0387
conceited [kənsíːtid]

a. 자만심이 강한, 우쭐대는

IN BRIEF Holding or characterized by an unduly high opinion of oneself; vain

➕ self-important, arrogant, proud, vainglorious

> He is conceited with his won talents.
> (그는 자기 재능에 대해 자만에 빠져 있다.)

0388
concentrate [kánsəntrèit]

v. 집중시키다; 전념하다

IN BRIEF To direct or draw toward a common center; focus

➕ focus on, pay attention to

> She couldn't concentrate on her work.
> (그녀는 자신의 일에 집중할 수 없었다.)

0389
concession [kənséʃən]

양보용인; (주로 정부에 의한) 허가 → 면허 → 특허, 권(利權) (compromise)

IN BRIEF The act of conceding

➕ yielding, adjustment, allowance

> The government had hoped that its concession would draw desperately needed foreign aid and investment.
> (정부 측에서는 그 양보 조처로 인하여 절실히 필요했던 외국의 원조와 투자를 끌어들이기를 희망했다.)

0390
conciliatory [kənsíliətɔ̀ːri]

a. 융화적인, 달래는; 회유적인

IN BRIEF Tending to conciliate; pacific; mollifying; propitiating

➕ pacific, diplomatic, appeasing, placid, pacifying, friendly

> His letter was couched in conciliatory terms.
> (그의 편지는 회유적인 말들로 표현되어 있었다.)

0391
concise [kənsáis]

a. (말·문체 따위가) 간결한, 간명한

IN BRIEF Expressing much in few words; clear and succinct

➕ brief, short, compact, terse, laconic, succinct, pithy, summary

> Make your answers clear and concise.
> (대답은 명료하고 간결하게 하시오.)

0392
condense [kəndéns]

v. 압축하다; 요약하다 (abridge, contract)

IN BRIEF To make more dense or compact

⊕ concentrate, shorten, constrict, abbreviate, compact, summarize

> I've tried to condense ten pages of comments into two.
> (나는 10페이지에 달하는 논평을 2페이지로 요약하려고 했다.)

0393
condone [kəndóun]

vt. (죄·과실 등을) 용서하다, 너그럽게 봐주다(overlook)

IN BRIEF To overlook, forgive, or disregard (an offense without protest or censure)

⊕ overlook, excuse, forgive, pardon, disregard, turn a blind eye to, wink at

> Legalization of addictive drugs would not condone use of any addictive substance.
> (중독성 약물을 합법화한다고 해도 어떤 중독성 물질이나 사용하도록 눈감아주지는 않을 것이다.)

0394
conduct [kándʌkt]

n. 행위, 행동

IN BRIEF To act as a director or conductor

⊕ behavior, attitude, manners, demeanor, deportment

> His conduct disappointed us.
> (그의 행동에 우리는 실망했다.)

0395
confederation [kənfèdəréiʃən]

동맹, 연합(국)

IN BRIEF Being united or joined together in an alliance

⊕ association, alliance, colleague, coalition

> Switzerland is a heterogeneous confederation of 26 self-governing cantons.
> (스위스는 26개의 자치 주로 이루어진 이질적인 연방 국가이다.)

0396
confined [kənfáind]

한정된, 좁은

IN BRIEF To keep within bounds; restrict

⊕ restricted, limited, narrow, enclosed

> I don't like a job in which I'm confined to doing only one thing.
> (나는 오직 한 가지 일만 해야 하는 일은 좋아하지 않는다.)

0397
concede [kənsíːd]

v. 인정하다, 시인하다

IN BRIEF Yielding without necessarily agreeing

⊕ admit, allow, accept, acquiesce, acknowledge, confess

> She grudgingly had to concede defeat.
> (그녀는 억지로 패배를 인정해야 했다.)

0398
canvass [kǽnˈvəs]

v. 조사하다, 검토하다; 유세하다; 여론조사

IN BRIEF To examine carefully or discuss thoroughly; scrutinize

⊕ poll, study, examine, investigate, analyse, scan, inspect, sift, scrutinize

> Over 15 Igbo groups of fields had met to work out a position that could be canvassed by the Southeast geopolitical zone.
> (다양한 분야에 걸친 15개 이상의 이그보우 족 단체들이 남동부의 지정학적 지대에 의해 검토 될 수 있는 입장을 내놓기 위해 모임을 가졌다.)

0399
come down with

(병) 걸리다

IN BRIEF To become sick with (an illness)

⊕ catch a cold, fall[get, be taken] ill[sick]

> Aid organizations are also mounting information campaigns to make people know how to prevent cholera and what to do if someone comes down with the disease.
> (구호단체들은 또한 어떻게 콜레라를 예방하고 누군가 (그 병에) 걸리면 무엇을 해야 하는지에 관해 사람들에게 알리기 위한 안내 캠페인을 벌이고 있다.)

LESSON 09

0400
confirm [kənfə́ːrm]

확신시키다; 확인하다, 비준하다, 승인하다(verify)

IN BRIEF To support or establish the certainty or validity of; verify

+ prove, affirm, declare, assert, testify

> The announcement confirmed my suspicions.
> (그 발표는 나의 의심을 확인시켜 주었다.)

0401
conflicting [kənflíktiŋ]

a. 서로 상반되는, 모순되는, 일치하지 않는

IN BRIEF A state of open, often prolonged fighting; a battle or war

+ incompatible, opposed, contrary, discordant, disagree

> She experienced a maelstrom of conflicting emotions.
> (그녀는 상충되는 감정의 대혼란을 겪었다.)

0402
confront [kənfrʌ́nt]

vt. 직면하다; 맞서다, 대처하다(challenge, face)

IN BRIEF To come face to face with

+ accost, encounter, face, front

> We must confront the future of our nation with optimism.
> (우리는 우리나라의 미래에 낙관적으로 대처해야 한다.)

0403
congenial [kənˈdʒiːniəl]

a. 적합한, 쾌적한(favorable)

IN BRIEF Having the same tastes, habits, or temperament; sympathetic. Pleasant and friendly in disposition

+ affable, agreeable, amiable, cordial, genial, good-natured, good-tempered, pleasant, sociable, warm

> This city is a quite congenial place for someone with depression or neurosis to work in.
> (그 도시는 우울증 또는 신경과민증으로 고생하는 사람들이 일하기에 꽤 적합한 곳이다.)

0404
conglomerate [kənglʌ́mərət]

a. 집성(체); 경제(거대) 복합(複合) 기업, 재벌 그룹

IN BRIEF To form or gather into a mass or whole

+ corporation, multinational, aggregate, agglomerate, assortment

> The firm has been taken over by an American conglomerate.
> (그 회사는 미국 복합 기업에 인수되었다.)

0405
congregate [káŋgrigèit]

모이다, 집합하다(gather together)

IN BRIEF To bring or come together in a group, crowd, or assembly

+ come together, mass, collect, convene

> A crowd quickly congregated round the speaker.
> (연설자 주위로 관중이 재빨리 모여들었다.)

0406
congruent [káŋgruənt]

(격식) 일치하는, 어울리는

IN BRIEF To be in harmony and equal

+ compatible, according, corresponding, congruous

> This measures are congruent with the seriousness of the situation.
> (이 조치들은 상황의 심각성에 어울린다.)

0407
conjugal [kándʒəgəl]

a. 부부(간)의, 혼인(상)의

IN BRIEF Having to do with marriage → connubial, hymeneal

+ marital, married, matrimonial, nuptial, spousal, wedded

> Some prisoners are to be permitted conjugal visits.
> (몇몇 죄수들에게는 부부의 방문이 허용된다.)

0408
connoisseur [kànəsə́ːr]

(미술품) 감정가, 감식가, 전문가

IN BRIEF An expert able to appreciate a certain field

+ expert, judge, specialist, appreciator

> I'm no connoisseur but I know a good champagne when I taste one.
> (나는 전문가는 아니지만 좋은 샴페인은 마셔 보면 알 수 있다.)

0409
consanguineous [kànsæŋgwíniəs]

혈족의, 동족의, 혈연의(related by blood, akin)

IN BRIEF Of the same lineage or origin; having a common ancestor

+ agnate, akin, allied, cognate, connate, connatural, consanguine, kindred, related

> They are consanguineous brothers.
> (그들은 혈연관계의 형제이다. → sibling)

0410
consecrate [kánsəkrèit]
신성하게 하다, 성화(聖化)하다, 성직에 임명하다

IN BRIEF To declare or set apart as sacred

+ sanctify, dedicate, hallow, devote, bless

> He was consecrated Archbishop last year.
> (그는 작년에 대주교로 임명되었다.)

0411
consecutive [kənsékjətiv]
연속적인, 계속되는(successive, straight, in turn)

IN BRIEF Coming one after another, in a regular order

+ successive, following, succeeding, in turn, uninterrupted, chronological, sequential

> This is the fifth consecutive weekend that I've spent working, and I'm a bit fed up with it.
> (이것으로 연속 5주째 주말을 일하며 보내고 있는데 이제는 좀 질렸다.)

0412
consequence [kánsikwèns]
결과; 귀추

IN BRIEF Having important effects or influence

+ result, outcome, upshot, effect, aftermath

> The accident was the inevitable consequence of carelessness.
> (그 사고는 부주의에서 발생한 필연적 결과였다.)

0413
contemporary [kəntémpərèri]
동시대의(동시발생) → 같은 시대의 → 현대의 → 최신의 → 같은 나이의

IN BRIEF Modern; of current times; present day

+ modern, latest, recent, current, with it (informal), trendy (Brit. informal), up-to-date

> My studies were devoted almost entirely to contemporary literature.
> (나의 연구들은 거의 전적으로 현대 문학에 바쳐졌다.)

0414
consign [kənsáin]
vt. 넘겨주다, 인도하다; 위임하다, 맡기다

IN BRIEF To give over to the care or custody of another

+ deposit, commit, put away, entrust, remit

> She consigned a child to its uncle's care.
> (그녀는 아이를 그 애의 삼촌이 보살피도록 맡겼다.)

0415
console [kənsóul]
vt. 위로하다, 달래다

IN BRIEF To offer comfort or aid in an attempt to lessen sadness or trouble

+ comfort, solace, soothe, appease, mollify, pacify, placate

> It is a consoling thought that there are others in a much worse position.
> (다른 사람들은 훨씬 더 나쁜 처지에 있다는 생각이 위안이 된다.)

0416
conspicuous [kənspíkjuəs]
a. 눈에 잘 띄는

IN BRIEF Easy to see; remarkable

+ obvious, clear, apparent, visible, prominent

> There was no conspicuous road sign in that highway.
> (그 도로에는 눈에 들어오는 도로 표지가 없었다.)

0417
construe [kənstrú:]
v. 해석하다, 이해하다(interpret)

IN BRIEF To adduce or explain the meaning of; interpret

+ interpret, explain, comprehend

> Her remarks were wrongly construed.
> (그녀의 발언은 잘못 해석되었다.)

0418
contract [kántrækt]
① 계약(하다) (agreement, commission, commitment)
② 수축하다 (constrict, tighten, shorten)
③ 병에 걸리다, 감염되다 (catch, acquire, infected with)

> The contract is void.
> (그 계약은 무효다.)
> Metals contract as they get cooler.
> (금속은 차가워지면 수축한다. ↔expand)
> The computer contracts a virus.
> (컴퓨터가 바이러스에 걸리다.)

0419
considerably [kənsídərəbli]
ad. 상당히, 어지간히, 꽤(greatly, very much)

IN BRIEF Large in amount, extent, or degree

+ seriously, notably, remarkably, significantly, substantially

> Prices have increased considerably.
> (물가가 상당히 올랐다.)

0420
contempt [kəntémpt]

n. 경멸, 멸시, 모욕

IN BRIEF Disregard or despise for something or someone

⊕ scorn, disdain, mockery, disregard

> She showed him contempt.
> (그녀는 그를 경멸했다.)

0421
contentious [kənténʃəs]

a. 논쟁[토론]을 좋아하는, 논쟁을 일으키는, 이론의 여지가 있는

IN BRIEF Given to contention; quarrelsome

⊕ argumentative, pugnacious, quarrelsome, querulous, controversial

> It's currently a very contentious issue.
> (그것은 현재 매우 논쟁적인 안건이다.)

0422
contagious [kəntéidʒəs]

전염성의, 옮기기 쉬운

IN BRIEF A disease that is easily spread

⊕ communicable → infectious, transmittable

> The viruses can spread easily and it is very contagious.
> (바이러스는 쉽게 퍼질 수 있고 매우 잘 전염된다.)

0423
contradict [kàntrədíkt]

v. 반박하다; 모순되다

IN BRIEF To assert to be untrue, often by saying the opposite

⊕ deny, dispute, oppose, counter, negate

> The facts contradict the theory.
> (그 사실은 이론과 상반된다.)

0424
contrary [kántreri]

a. 반대되는, 위배되는, 배치되는

IN BRIEF Opposed, as in character or purpose

⊕ opposite, different, adverse, antithetical

> The results were contrary to all expectation.
> (그 결과는 모든 기대에 반하는 것이었다.)

0425
copious [kóupiəs]

a. (공급량·사용량)풍부한, 막대한 → 내용이 풍부한

IN BRIEF More than enough; plentiful, abundant

⊕ abundant, generous, lavish, full, rich

> She supports her theory with copious evidence.
> (그녀는 자기의 이론을 풍부한 증거로 뒷받침했다.)

0426
controversial [kàntrəvə́ːrʃəl]

논란의 소지가 많은, 물의를 일으키는

IN BRIEF Of, producing, or marked by controversy

⊕ disputed, contentious, issue, debatable, subject to debate

> It is a controversial policy which has attracted international censure.
> (그것은 국제적인 비난을 야기하는 논쟁의 여지가 있는 정책이다.)

0427
convalescence [kànvəlésns]

n. (병의) 차도 → 회복기

IN BRIEF The stage of recovery from an illness, operation or injury

⊕ recovery, rehabilitation, recuperation

> It is an operation that requires a long convalescence.
> (그것은 장기 요양을 필요로 하는 수술이다.)

0428
conventional [kənvénʃənəl]

전통적인, 관습적인, 인습적인, 틀에 박힌(진부한)

IN BRIEF Conforming to established practice or accepted standards; traditional

⊕ proper, conservative, formal, usual, ordinary, traditional

> 31 He took a stand opposed to conventional wisdom.
> (그는 전통적인 생각(통념.)과 정반대의 입장을 취했다.)

0429
convert [kənvə́ːrt]

v. 바꾸다, 개종하다

IN BRIEF To change into a different form, substance, or state

⊕ change, turn, transform, alter

> Japan has converted manufacturing muscle into financial might.
> (일본은 막강한 제조력을 금융력으로 전환시켰다.)

0430
contrite [kəntráit]

(죄를) 깊이 뉘우치고 있는

IN BRIEF To be repentant or sorry for wrong-doing

⊕ humble, sorrowful, remorseful, regretful, penitent, repentant

> Ahntonio looked contrite, even distressed.
> (Ahntonio는 회개하는 듯, 심지어 비통해 하는 듯 보였다.)

0431
corollary [kɔ́:rəlèri]
(당연한)결과 → 부수적인 것(consequence, result, outcome)

IN BRIEF Something that follows directly from something that has been proven

➕ consequence, result, effect, outcome, sequel, end result, upshot

> Good health is a corollary of having good habits.
> (건강은 좋은 습관을 가진 데서 오는 당연한 결과이다.)

0432
correspond [kɔ̀:rəspánd]
vi. 일치(조화)하다 → 상응(상당, 해당)하다 → 서신왕래하다

IN BRIEF To be in agreement, harmony, or conformity

➕ consistent, match, accord, coincide, harmonize, equivalent

> I think it to correspond to facts.
> (그것은 사실과 일치한다고 생각한다.)

0433
corroborate [kərábərèit]
(증거 따위로) 확증하다, 입증하다; 뒷받침하다

IN BRIEF To prove with evidence

➕ support, establish, confirm, sustain, validate

> Recent research in this field seems to corroborate he theory.
> (이 분야의 최근 조사는 그 이론을 입증하는 것처럼 보인다.)

0434
council [káunsəl]
n. (지방)의회, 위원회

IN BRIEF A gathering of people for consultation

➕ committee, parliament, congress, ministry, diet, assembly

> You must first obtain permission from your council.
> (당신은 먼저 위원회의 허가를 받아야 한다.)

0435
count [kaunt]
v. 세다; 간주하다, 중요하다

IN BRIEF To have importance

➕ matter, be important, weigh

> First impressions of people count.
> (사람들의 첫인상이 중요하다.)

0436
counterfeit [káuntərfit]
a. 가짜, 모조품, 위조품

IN BRIEF To make an imitation or copy of (something, usually with the intent to defraud)

➕ fake, false, forged, spurious, phony

> This ten-dollar bill is counterfeit.
> (이 10 달러 짜리 지폐는 가짜다.)

0437
courier [kúriər]
특사, 급사, 스파이

IN BRIEF A messenger

➕ messenger, carrier, envoy, herald

> We sent the documents by courier.
> (우리는 특사를 통해 서류를 보냈다.)

0438
crafty [kræfti]
간교한, 교활한 (Deceitfully clever)

IN BRIEF Skilled in or marked by underhandedness, deviousness, or deception

➕ cunning, sly, devious, tricky

> He's a crafty old fox.
> (그는 교활한 여우다.)

0439
crash [kræʃ]
충돌하다, 추락하다, 충돌, 추락

IN BRIEF To break violently or noisily; smash

➕ collision, accident, smash, clash, bang

> There were no survivors from the plane crash.
> (비행기 추락 사고의 생존자는 없었다.)

0440
crave [kreiv]
v. 갈망하다, 열망하다

IN BRIEF To want or desire very much

➕ long for, yearn for, want, need, desire, aspire to

> I crave that she come.
> (그녀가 꼭 와 주었으면 한다.)

0441
craven [kréivən]
겁많은, 소심한; 비열한, 비겁한

IN BRIEF Cowardly → Characterized by abject fear

- cowardly, scared, fearful, dastardly, timorous

> Ahntonio admitted to a craven fear of spiders.
> (안토니오는 소심하게 거미를 두려워함을 인정했다.)

0442
criterion [kraitíəriən]
n. 기준, 척도

IN BRIEF A standard used to decide the correctness of a judgment or decision

- standard, measure, principle, norm, yardstick, touchstone

> Success in making money is not always a good criterion of success in life.
> (돈벌이에 있어서의 성공이 항상 성공한 삶의 좋은 기준이 되는 것은 아니다.)

0443
critical [krítikəl]
① 비평[평론]의
② 중대한; 결정적인

IN BRIEF Being unfavorably judgmental, very important

- crucial, momentous, serious, pivotal, important

> The depth of the foundations is critical.
> (기초의 깊이가 중요하다.)

0444
criticize [krítisàiz]
비판하다, 비평하다; 비난하다

IN BRIEF To find fault with

- censure, blame, carp, disparage, find fault with

> It is easy to criticize.
> (비판하기는 쉽다.)

0445
contemptible [kəntémptəbəl]
a. 경멸할 만한, 비열한(low-down)

IN BRIEF Deserving of contempt or scorn

- nefarious, obnoxious, odious, repugnant

> Over the past few years, the Indian government has established a contemptible pattern of defending consular officials accused of labor exploitation and human trafficking in the United States.
> (지난 몇 년 동안, 인도 정부는 미국에서 노동착취와 인신매매로 고발당한 영사관 직원을 비호하는 비열한 관행을 밝혀냈다.)

0446
corporeal [kɔːrpɔ́ːriəl]
a. 육체상의, 형체를 가진, 손으로 만져지는; 물질적인

IN BRIEF Of the nature of the physical body; bodily, material; tangible

- substantial, tangible; physical, somatic

> Venus is the rare film that suggests that the aged are neither magical saints nor tragic cases, but corporeal creatures like the rest of us.
> (영화 [비너스]는 노인들이 마술과 같은 능력을 지닌 성자도 아니요, 비극의 주인공도 아닌, 다만 우리와 같은 몸을 지닌 존재라는 것을 보여주는 드문 영화이다.)

0447
clout [klaut]
n. 영향력

IN BRIEF Power or influence, esp in politics

- influence, power; prestige

> Mary has enormous clout in the company because her father is its president.
> (메리는 아버지가 사장이기 때문에 그 회사에서 영향력이 엄청나다.)

0448
collateral [kəlǽtərəl]
a. 부수적인, 이차적인

IN BRIEF Coinciding in tendency or effect; concomitant or accompanying

- ancillary, assistant, auxiliary

> A collateral aim of the government's industrial strategy is to increase employment.
> (정부의 산업 전략의 부수적인 목표는 고용을 늘리는 것이다.)

0449
corporal [kɔ́ːrpərəl]
a. 육체의, 신체의(physical); 개인적인

> What constitutes corporal punishment is also wide-ranging: everything from a light slap on the hand to an all-out whipping with a belt or a paddle.
> (체벌을 구성하는 것은 또한 광범위하다. 손을 가볍게 찰싹 때리는 것에서부터 벨트나 회초리로 온힘을 다해 때리는 것에 이르기까지 온갖 것들이 있다.)

LESSON 10

0450
cross-current
주류(主流)와 교차하는 흐름 → 대립되는 의견 (counter-current)
IN BRIEF A current flowing across another current

It is a cross-current of opinion against the prevailing view.
(그것은 주도적인 견해에 대립되는 의견(역류)이다.)

0451
crowd [kraud]
밀어넣다
IN BRIEF To force by or as if by pressing or shoving
➕ throng, company, press, army, host, pack, mob, flock, herd

Police crowded the spectators back to the viewing stand.
(경찰들이 관람석으로 관중들을 연이어 몰아넣었다.)

0452
crucial [krúːʃəl]
a. 매우 중대한, 결정적인
IN BRIEF Being very important → Extremely significant or important
➕ vital, important, essential, urgent, critical, significant

That was a crucial experiment.
(그것은 결정적인 실험이었다.)

0453
crude [kruːd]
천연 그대로의; 저속한 → 조잡한 → 초기의 → 야한
IN BRIEF Being in an unrefined or natural state
➕ rough, undeveloped, primitive, coarse

That country exports crude oil.
(그 나라는 원유를 수출한다.)

0454
crumble [krʌ́mbl]
산산조각으로 부서지다, 힘없이 무너지다(reduce to tiny bits)
IN BRIEF To break into small fragments or pieces
➕ disintegrate, collapse, deteriorate, decompose

His power was crumbling away.
(그의 권력은 허무하게 사라졌다.)

0455
cryptic [kríptik]
숨은, 비밀의; 불가해한, 수수께끼 같은
IN BRIEF Mysterious, concealing → Difficult to explain or understand
➕ mysterious, puzzling, obscure, vague, enigmatic, abstruse

I found a scrap of paper with a cryptic message saying.
(나는 수수께끼 같은 메시지를 담은 종이 쪽지를 발견했다.)

0456
culmination [kʌ̀lmənéiʃən]
n. 절정, 정점, 최고점
IN BRIEF The highest point or state: acme, apex, apogee
➕ climax, crest, height, meridian, peak, pinnacle, summit, top, zenith

the successful culmination of a long campaign
(오랜 캠페인의 성공적인 정점)

0457
culpable [kʌ́lpəbl]
a. 비난할 만한, 유죄의(blameworthy, wrong, guilty)
IN BRIEF Guilty → Deserving blame
➕ blamable[blameable], blameful, blameworthy, censurable

He was held culpable for all that had happened.
(그는 일어난 모든 일에 대해 과실이 있다는 판결을 받았다.)

0458
culprit [kʌ́lprit]
n. 범인, 죄인
IN BRIEF One charged with an offense or crime
➕ offender, criminal, villain, sinner, felon, cause

Police are searching for the culprits.
(경찰이 범인들을 쫓고 있다.)

0459
cultivate [kʌ́ltəvèit]
vt. 경작하다, 재배하다, 양성하다
IN BRIEF To improve and prepare (land, as by plowing or fertilizing, for raising crops; till)
➕ farm, till, develop, foster

The farmer cultivates flowers.
(그 농부는 꽃을 재배한다.)

0460
cumbersome [kʌ́mbərsəm]
방해가 되는, 번거로운; 성가신(inconvenient)

IN BRIEF Awkward to carry due to weight or size

- bulky, burdensome, unmanageable, unwieldy, inefficient

> He's got a cumbersome old computer.
> (그는 번거로운 오래된 컴퓨터를 가지고 있다.)

0461
curb [kə:rb]
구속하다, 억제하다

IN BRIEF Something that restrains or holds back

- restrain, check, restrict, hinder, impede

> We tried to keep a curb on their activities.
> (우리는 그들의 활동을 억제하려고 노력했다.)

0462
cure [kjuər]
(환자·병을) 고치다, 치유하다

IN BRIEF A drug or course of medical treatment used to restore health

- make better, heal, restore to health, remedy

> Aspirin will cure your pain.
> (아스피린이 네 고통을 없애 줄 것이다.)

0463
currency [kə́:rənsi]
n. 통화, 화폐(money)

IN BRIEF The paper money in common use in any country

- money, coinage, legal tender, medium of exchange, bills, notes, coins

> The currency of Korea is won.
> (한국의 통화는 원화이다.)

0464
currently [kə́:rəntli]
ad. 현재, 지금 (now)

IN BRIEF At the present time

- presently, actually, now

> It's currently a very contentious issue.
> (그것은 현재 굉장히 논쟁을 일으키는 안건이다.)

0465
curse [kə:rs]
욕설; 저주, 저주하다

IN BRIEF To utter curses; swear

- blaspheme, abuse, scold, bane

> Ahntonio cursed his bad luck.
> (안토니오는 그의 나쁜 운수를 저주했다.)

0466
cursory [kə́:rsəri]
a. 서두르는, 되는 대로의, 대강의

IN BRIEF Quick and superficial

- casual, brief, rapid, careless, superficial, hasty, perfunctory

> The book is cursory in its treatment of his early life.
> (그 책은 그의 유년시절을 대충 다루고 있다.)

0467
curtail [kə:rtéil]
vt. 줄이다, 단축하다

IN BRIEF To cut short or reduce

- reduce, cut, diminish, shorten, lessen

> We must try to curtail our spending.
> (우리는 지출을 줄이도록 해야 한다.)

0468
customary [kʌ́stəmèri]
a. 습관적인 → 관습상의 → 전통상의(traditionally)

IN BRIEF By custom → according to common practice

- usual, general, common, accepted, established, traditional, normal, ordinary

> American children customarily go trick-or-treating on Halloween.
> (미국 아이들은 할로윈에 관습적으로 '사탕을 안주면 장난칠테야' 라는 놀이를 한다.)

0469
cutting edge
신랄함, 날카로움 → (기술) 최첨단

IN BRIEF In accord with the most fashionable ideas or style

- most advanced, up to date, state of the art, high-tech

> He is working at the cutting edge of computer technology.
> (그는 컴퓨터 기술의 최첨단에서 일하고 있다.)

0470
convincingly [kənvínsiŋli]

ad. 납득이 가도록(persuasively), (경기) 압도적으로

IN BRIEF Showing clearly the excellence

> She won Wimbledon convincingly, solidifying her No. 1 ranking.
> (그녀는 윔블던 대회에서 압도적으로 우승하여 랭킹 1위 자리를 굳혔다.)

0471
dabble [ˈdæbl]

물을 튀기다, 물장난을 하다, 취미삼아해보다

IN BRIEF To do something lightly or playfully

+ splash, spatter

> She dabbled her fingers in the fountain.
> (그녀는 분수에 손가락을 넣고 물을 튀겼다.)

0472
dally [dǽli]

v. 꾸물거리다, 꾸물대다 → 가지고 놀다(toy)

IN BRIEF Delay; waste time

+ waste time, delay, linger, dawdle, drag, loiter, procrastinate

> Stop dilly-dallying and make up your mind!
> (꾸물거리지 말고 마음을 정해요!)

0473
dank [dæŋk]

a. 축축한, 구중중한

IN BRIEF Disagreeably damp or humid

+ damp, moist, soggy, dripping, damp and cold

> Wow! Ahntonio's house is a dark dank cave!!
> (와우! 안토니오의 집은 어둡고 축축한 동굴이구만!!)

0474
dart [dɑːrt]

휙 던지다; 돌진하다

IN BRIEF A slender, pointed missile, often having tail fins, thrown by hand, shot from a blowgun, or expelled by an exploding bomb

+ dash, run, shoot

> Swallows are darting through the air.
> (제비들이 하늘을 휙휙 날아다니고 있다.)

0475
deadlock [ˈdedlɑːk]

막다른 골목, 교착 상태 → (경기)동점 → 이중 자물쇠

IN BRIEF A standstill resulting from the opposition of two unrelenting forces or factions

+ impasse, stalemate, cessation, standstill

> The negotiations have reached deadlock.
> (협상이 교착상태에 빠졌다.)

0476
deadly [dédli]

생명에 관계되는, 치명적인, 극도로, 몹시, 지독히(lethal, fatal)

IN BRIEF Causing or tending to cause death

+ mortal, murderous, poisonous, virulent, noxious, extremely

> It was a deadly wound.
> (그것은 치명적인 상처였다.)

0477
dearth [dəːrθ]

n. 결핍, 부족, 식량 부족, 기근

IN BRIEF A scarce supply; a lack

+ lack, absence, poverty, shortage, deficiency

> There seems to be a dearth of good young players at the moment.
> (지금은 훌륭한 젊은 선수가 부족한 것 같다.)

0478
debase [dibéis]

vt. (인격·품성 가치)를 떨어뜨리다, 천하게 하다

IN BRIEF To lower in character, quality, or value; degrade

+ corrupt, devalue, pollute, impair, lower, degrade

> You debase yourself by telling such lies.
> (그런 거짓말이 너의 격을 떨어뜨리고 있어.)

0479
debatable [dibéitəbəl]

a. 문제되는, 논쟁의 여지가 있는

IN BRIEF Being such that formal argument or discussion is possible

+ doubtful, uncertain, dubious, controversial, undecided, unsettled

> It's debatable whether or not the reforms have improved conditions.
> (개혁으로 사정이 나아졌는지 아닌지는 논쟁의 여지가 있다.)

0480
debris [dəbríː]

파편(더미), 잔해, 부스러기 (leftover)

IN BRIEF The remains of something destroyed, disintegrated, or decayed

[+] rubble, ruin, wrack, wreck, wreckage

> Rescue workers have found *debris* floating on the surface of the water.
> (구조 요원들은 바다 위에 떠있는 잔해를 발견했습니다.)

0481
decade [dékeid]

n. 10년간 (ten years)

IN BRIEF A period of ten years

[+] decennary, decennium

> They lived there for a *decade*.
> (그들은 십 년간 그 곳에 살았다.)

0482
deceased [disíːst]

a. 죽은; 작고한, 고(故)

IN BRIEF No longer alive, late

[+] asleep, dead, defunct, departed, extinct, gone, lifeless, expired

> Did you know the *deceased*?
> (고인과 아시는 사이였나요?)

0483
decent [díːsənt]

a. 점잖은 → 예절 바른 → (수입) 꽤 좋은, 근사한, (사회기준) 남 부럽지 않은, 관대한

IN BRIEF In accordance with the standards of proper behavior, speech, manners or dress; respectable

[+] good, kind, friendly, neighbourly (neighborly), generous, helpful

> He's a thoroughly *decent* man.
> (그는 정말 점잖은 사람이다.)

0484
deception [disépʃən]

n. 속임수, 기만

IN BRIEF The use of deceit

[+] trickery, fraud, deceit, guile

> His wife was a victim of *deception*.
> (그의 아내는 사기의 희생자였다.)

0485
decimate [désəmèit]

vt. (전쟁·질병) 많은 사람 죽이다

IN BRIEF To kill savagely and indiscriminately

[+] annihilate, butcher, massacre, slaughter

> Disease has *decimate*d the population.
> (질병이 수많은 생명을 앗아갔다.)

0486
decipher [disáifər]

vt. (암호문 따위)해독하다, 번역하다

IN BRIEF Figure out, understand

[+] decode, solve, reveal, interpret, make out

> Can you *decipher* Ahntonio's handwriting?
> (넌 안토니오의 필체를 알아보겠니?)

0487
decline [dikláin]

v. 감소, 쇠퇴, 하강; 내리막, 거절하다; 감소하다

IN BRIEF To grow smaller; diminish

[+] fall, lower, diminish, decrease → refuse

> Manufacturing output is in *decline*.
> (제조업 생산고가 감소하고 있다.)

0488
decriminalize [diːkrímənəlàiz]

(사람·행위) 기소[처벌] 대상에서 제외하다 → (범죄자) 정신 치료 하다

IN BRIEF To reduce or abolish criminal penalties for

[+] decriminalise, legalise, legalize, legitimate

> The question of whether prostitution should be *decriminalized*
> (성매매를 비범죄화 해야하느냐에 대한 문제)

0489
decry [dikrái]

vt. 비난하다, 헐뜯다(criticize, blame)/【경제】(통화) 가치를 떨어 뜨리다

IN BRIEF To express disrespect and scorn for; to disapprove of or condemn

[+] disparage, depreciate, derogate, belittle, minimize, downgrade

> He *decried* her efforts as a waste of time.
> (그는 그녀의 노력을 시간 낭비라고 폄하했다.)

0490
deduce [didjúːs]

vt. 추론하다

IN BRIEF Infer; draw a logical conclusion

+ conclude, gather, infer, presume, reason, suppose

> If a=b and b=c, we can deduce that a=c.
> (만약에 a=b이고 b=c이면, 우리는 a=c라고 추론할 수 있다.)

0491
deem [diːm]

v. 생각 → 간주하다

IN BRIEF To regard as; consider

+ consider, think, believe, suppose, judge, infer

> We deem that he is honest.
> (우리는 그가 정직하다고 생각한다.)

0492
defective [difěktiv]

결함이 있는, 불완전한

IN BRIEF Having or showing a defect; faulty

+ faulty, broken, imperfect, deficient

> Ahntonio is mentally defective.
> (안토니오는 정신적으로 결함이 있다.)

0493
deference [défərəns]

n. 경의, 존경 (respect, honor, courtesy)

IN BRIEF Courteous respect for another's opinion, wishes, or judgment

+ respect, regard, consideration, attention, honour, esteem

> He treats his mother with as much deference as if she were the Queen.
> (그는 자기 어머니를 마치 여왕인 것처럼 최대의 존경을 다해 대했다.)

0494
defiant [difáiənt]

a. 도전적인, 반항적인, 거만한

IN BRIEF Marked by defiance

+ contumacious, recalcitrant, disobedient, disregardful, boldly

> She is not cowed but defiant.
> (그녀는 겁을 먹는게 아니라 반항적이다.)

0495
deflect [diflékt]

v. (광선·탄알 한쪽으로) 빗나가다, (생각) 편향되다, 치우치다 (deviate)

IN BRIEF To cause to turn aside or downward

+ avert, deviate, divert, pivot, shift, swing, turn, veer

> The bullet deflected from the wall.
> (총알이 벽에 빗맞았다.)

0496
de-forestation [fɔ(ː)ristéiʃ-ən]

산림벌채, 산림개간(root out the trees)

IN BRIEF The act or process of removing trees from or clearing a forest

+ disforestation

> The pace of deforestation is so great that many scientists predict it will soon have an effect on the world weather.
> (산림이 너무나 빠르게 벌채되고 있어서 조만간 세계 기후에 영향을 미칠 것이라고 많은 과학자들이 예측하고 있다.)

0497
deftly [déftli]

교묘하게, 능숙하게

IN BRIEF Quick and neat in action; skillful

+ skillfully, adroitly, aptly, adeptly, dexterously

> He deftly removed his glasses before she sat on them.
> (그는 그녀가 그의 안경 위에 앉기 전에 교묘하게 그 안경을 치웠다.)

0498
diversity [divə́ːrsəti]

n. 차이; 변화, 다양성

IN BRIEF State or quality of being different or varied

+ difference, variety, divergence, multiplicity, heterogeneity

> The intellectual flexibility distinctive in a multicultural nation has been restrained in classrooms where the cultural diversity of our country has not been reflected.
> (다문화 국가의 특징인 지적 융통성은 우리나라의 문화적 다양성이 반영되지 않은 교실에서는 제한되어왔다.)

0499
derivative [dirívətiv]

a. 파생적인

IN BRIEF Not original; secondary

+ by-product, spin-off, offshoot, descendant, derivation, outgrowth

> English is a derivative language. It is made up of words that originated in many other languages.
> (영어는 파생 언어이다. 영어는 다른 많은 언어에서 기원한 단어들로 이루어져 있다.)

LESSON 11

0500
defuse [di(ː)fjúːz]

vt. 위기를 해제하다 → (긴장) 완화시키다, (폭탄·지뢰) 신관을 제거하다

IN BRIEF To make less dangerous, tense, or hostile

+ calm, smooth, stabilize, alleviate

The two groups will meet next week to try to defuse the crisis.
(그 두 그룹은 다음 주에 만나 위기를 해소하기로 했다.)

0501
degrade [digréid]

v. 지위(품위)를 떨어뜨리다

IN BRIEF To lower in quality or value; make inferior or less valuable

+ demean, disgrace, humiliate, lower in esteem

Pollution is degrading the environment.
(공해가 환경의 질을 떨어뜨리고 있다.)

0502
deign [dein]

(See over/under, rise/fall)
① (윗사람이) 황송하게도 ~해주다
② (부정문) (자존심을 버리고) ~하다
③ (격식·유머) 젠체하다

IN BRIEF To descend to a level considered inappropriate to one's dignity

+ submit, condescend, stoop, vouchsafe, lower oneself

If she deigns to reply to my letter, I'll be extremely surprised.
(만약 그녀가 황송하게도 내 편지에 답장을 한다면, 나는 몹시 놀랄 것이다.)

0503
delegate [déligit]

대표로 파견하다; (권한·임무 등을) 위임하다(assign)

IN BRIEF A person authorized to act as representative for another; a deputy or agent

+ representative, agent, deputy, ambassador, proxy

A boss must know how to delegate work.
(상사는 일을 위임할 줄 알아야 한다.)

0504
delete [dilíːt]

vt. 삭제하다, 지우다

IN BRIEF To strike out or cancel, as from a text

+ remove, cancel, erase, dfface

Delete his name from the list.
(그의 이름을 명단에서 삭제하시오.)

0505
deleterious [dèlətíəriəs]

a. (심신)해로운 → 유독한

IN BRIEF Harmful, hurtful, morally or physically

+ bad, detrimental, evil, harmful, hurtful, ill, injurious, mischievous

Using steroids can be deleterious to your health.
(스테로이드를 사용하면 건강에 해로울 수 있다.)

0506
deliberately [dilíbəritli]

ad. 일부러, 고의로, 신중히

IN BRIEF Done with or marked by full consciousness of the nature and effects; intentional

+ intentionally, planned, consciously, purposefully

I'm sure he says these things deliberately to annoy me.
(나를 성가시게 하기 위해 그가 일부러 이런 말을 하는 게 틀림없다.)

0507
delicate [délikət]

a. 민감한, 섬세한, 깨지기 쉬운(fragile, feeble)

IN BRIEF Pleasing to the senses, especially in a subtle way

+ decrepit, flimsy, frail, insubstantial, puny)

That's a delicate problem.
(그것은 민감한 문제이다.)

0508
delineate [dilínièit]

윤곽을 그리다, 묘사[서술]하다

IN BRIEF To draw or depict

+ depict, describe, express, image, limn, picture, portray, render, represent, show

you must delineate your plans.
(너는 반드시 너의 계획들을 상술해야 한다.)

0509
delivery [dilívəri]
배달, 연설, 발표

IN BRIEF The act of conveying or delivering

⊕ pronunciation, diction, presentation/transfer, distribution, transmission, speech, expression

> We demand cash on delivery.
> (배달과 동시에 대금을 지불해 주십시오.)
> Her poor delivery spoilt an otherwise excellent speech.
> (그녀의 서투른 연설 태도가 훌륭했을 연설을 망쳐 놓았다.)

0510
demise [dimáiz]
서거, 사망

IN BRIEF The end of existence or activity; termination

⊕ death, dying, passing, decease, expiration, disappearance

> On the demise of my father, the family house will go to me and my brother.
> (아버지가 돌아가실 경우, 가족이 살던 집은 나와 내 동생에게 넘겨질 것이다.)

0511
demolish [dimáliʃ]
v. 〔건물 따위〕를 파괴하다, 〔계획·제도 따위〕를 폐지[폐기]하다

IN BRIEF To tear down or break apart the structure of; raze

⊕ destroy, ruin, wreck, undo, overturn, smash, tear down, raze

> They've demolished the slum district.
> (그들은 빈민굴 지역을 철거했다.)

0512
denizen [dénəzən]
서식하는 생물 → (어떤 장소) 주민, 거주자

IN BRIEF An inhabitant; a resident

⊕ inhabitant, resident, citizen, dweller

> Deer, foxes and squirrels are among the denizens of the forest.
> (사슴, 여우, 다람쥐는 모두 그 숲의 주민이다.)

0513
denote [dinóut]
vt. 표시이다, 이름[명칭]이다, 뜻하다, 나타내다, 의미하다

IN BRIEF Be a sign of; convey; stand as a name for; indicate

⊕ indicate, express, mean, represent, imply, designate

> This map symbol denotes historic places.
> (이 지도 기호는 사적지(역사적 의미가 있는 곳)를 표시한다.)

0514
denounce [dináuns]
vt. 비난(고발)하다 (condemn)

IN BRIEF Be a sign of; convey; stand as a name for; indicate

⊕ censure, decry, proscribe, vilify, stigmatize, accuse

> She denounced the government's handling of the crisis.
> (그녀는 정부의 위기 상황 대처를 비난했다.)

0515
privation [praivéiʃən]
n. 결핍, 궁핍(destitution) → 박탈, 몰수

IN BRIEF The condition of being extremely poor

⊕ deprivation, dispossession

> Poverty had by no means been eliminated, but the extreme privation that had earlier characterized large sections of the country had disappeared.
> (가난이 결코 없어지진 않았지만, 예전에 그 나라 대부분 지역의 특징이었던 극단적인 궁핍은 사라졌다.)

0516
derelict [dérəlikt]
a. 임무[직무] 태만의; 유기된, 버려진, 방치된

IN BRIEF Deserted by an owner or keeper; abandoned

⊕ abandoned, deserted, ruined, neglected, discarded, forsaken

> There are plans to redevelop an area of derelict land near the station.
> (기차역 근처에 버려진 땅이 있는 지역을 재개발할 계획이 있다.)

0517
deplorable [diplɔ́:rəbl]
a. 슬픈, 슬퍼할 만한; 유감스러운; 처참한, 비참한

IN BRIEF Worthy of severe condemnation or reproach

⊕ terrible, distressing, dreadful, disastrous, melancholy, dire

> The acting was deplorable.
> (그 연기는 한심스러웠다.)

0518
deport [dipɔ́:rt]
vt. (국외로) 추방하다; 퇴거시키다

IN BRIEF Expel from a country; banish

⊕ banish, exile, expatriate, expel, ostracize, transport

> He was convicted of drug offences and was deported.
> (그는 마약 범죄로 기소되어 국외로 추방되었다.)

0519
deprecate [déprikèit]
옳지 않다고 역설하다 → 비난하다 → 경시하다

IN BRIEF To express disapproval of; deplore

+ condemn, disapprove of, object to, disparage, criticize, scorn

> The article deprecates their negative attitude.
> (그 기사는 그들의 부정적인 태도를 비난한다.)

0520
densely [dénsli]
빽빽하게, 조밀하게

IN BRIEF Crowded closely together; compact

+ thickly, compactly, closely, heavily

> South Korea is densely populated.
> (남한은 인구 밀도가 높다.)

0521
deprivation [dèprəvéiʃən]
n. 박탈, 상실

IN BRIEF The state of being without; dispossession

+ deprival, dispossession, divestiture, loss, privation, poor

> Loss of hearing is a great deprivation.
> (청각 상실은 엄청난 상실이다.)

0522
dependable [dipéndəbl]
a. 신뢰할 수 있는, 의지할 수 있는

IN BRIEF Able to be depended on; reliable; trustworthy

+ reliable, responsible, steady, faithful, trusty

> He is a dependable person for you.
> (그는 네가 의존할 수 있는 인물이다.)

0523
deride [diráid]
vt. 비웃다, 조롱하다, 바보 취급하다[as]

IN BRIEF To laugh at, speak of, or write about dismissively or contemptuously

+ mock, ridicule, scorn, sneer, disdain, insult

> They derided his efforts as childish.
> (그들은 그의 노력을 유치하다고 비웃었다.)

0524
derision [diríʒən]
n. 조소, 비웃음, 조롱

IN BRIEF The act of ridiculing or laughing at someone or something

+ mockery, laughter, contempt, bleak, ridicule, scorn, disrespect

> They treated his suggestion with derision.
> (그들은 그의 제안을 조롱했다.)

0525
descent [disént]
n. 가계(家系), 혈통

IN BRIEF Downward incline or passage

+ origin, ancestry, lineage, parenage, herediy, extraction

> The American is proud that he is of Korean descent.
> (그 미국인은 한국계임을 자랑으로 여기고 있다.)

0526
desert [dézərt]
사막의, 불모의/ (신념) 버리다; 포기하다

IN BRIEF Often deserts something that is deserved or merited, especially a punishment

+ arid, wilderness, waste, wilds, dust bowl/ abandon, leave, relinquish, renounce, give up, forsake

> It was an endless desert.
> (그것은 끝이 없는 사막이었다.)
>
> He isn't the man to desert me.
> (그는 나를 버릴 남자가 아니다.)

0527
designate [dézignèit]
vt. 가리키다, 지명하다, 선정하다, 임명하다

IN BRIEF To give a name or title to; characterize

+ appoint, name, choose, delegate, select, assign, depute

> The chairman is allowed to designate his own successor.
> (의장이 자기 후임자를 지명하는 것이 허용된다.)

0528
desolate [désəlit]
a. (토지 따위가) 황량한, 삭막한; 사람이 살지 않는

IN BRIEF Devoid of inhabitants; deserted

+ uninhabited, deserted, bare, waste, barren

> I have never been anywhere so desolate.
> (그렇게 삭막한 곳은 가본 적이 없다.)

0529
despicable [déspikəbəl]
경멸할 만한, 비열한

IN BRIEF Hateful; beyond contempt; bad

+ contemptible, awful, worthless, disgraceful, sordid, detestable

> It was despicable of him to desert his family.
> (그는 비열하게도 가족을 버렸다.)

0530
despise [dispáiz]

vt. 경멸하다, 얕보다(look down upon; scorn)

IN BRIEF To regard with contempt or scorn

➕ despise, contemn, disdain, scorn, scout

> Ahntonio despises liars.
> (안토니오는 거짓말쟁이를 경멸한다.)

0531
despotic [dispátik]

절대 군주의, 전제 정치의; 독재적인, 전제적인

IN BRIEF A ruler with absolute power

➕ tyrannical, authoritarian, autocratic, dictatorial

> The nation is a despotic monarchy.
> (그 나라는 전제 군주국이다.)

0532
destitute [déstətjùːt]

a. 빈곤한, 극빈의, 궁핍한, 결핍한[없는][of]

IN BRIEF Lacking resources or the means of subsistence; completely impoverished

➕ penniless, poor, impoverished, needy, distressed

> When he died, his family was left completely destitute.
> (그가 죽자, 그의 가족은 완전히 빈곤에 처하게 되었다.)

0533
desultory [désəltɔ̀ːri]

a. 일관성 없는 → 산만한 → 주제를 벗어난 → 탈선적인

IN BRIEF Moving or jumping from one thing to another; disconnected

➕ random, vague, irregular, inconsistent, cursory, unmethodical

> I wandered around in a desultory.
> (나는 종잡을 수 없이 이리저리 돌아다녔다.)

0534
detached [ditǽtʃt]

a. 분리(파견)된, 고립된(isolated), (의견) 사심 없는, 공평한

IN BRIEF Separated; disconnected

➕ loose, objective, neutral, impartial, aloof, impersonal, disconnected, separated

> The parcel could not be delivered because the label became detached from it in the post.
> (우체국에 주소가 적힌 라벨이 떨어져 나갔기 때문에 그 소포는 배달 될 수 없었다.)

0535
detain [ditéin]

vt. (사람) 가지 못하게 붙들다, 유치[구류, 감금]하다

IN BRIEF To keep from proceeding; delay or retard: To keep in custody or confinement

➕ confine, arrest, delay, hamper, restrain, impede

> Since you are busy, I won't detain you.
> (바쁘신 분이니 못 가게 붙들지는 않겠습니다.)

0536
deter [ditə́ːr]

vt. 단념하게 하다 → 방해하다

IN BRIEF To prevent or discourage from acting, as by means of fear or doubt

➕ discourage, inhibit, prevent, restrain, prohibit, dissuade, keep

> Nothing can deter me from my determination.
> (어떤 일이 있어도 내 결심은 불변이다.)

0537
deteriorate [ditíəriərèit]

(질·건강·날씨) 나빠지다, 악화[저하]하다, 타락하다

IN BRIEF To become lower in quality, character, or condition

➕ decline, descend, retrograde, worsen, fade, fail, flag, anguish, sink, wane

> The flight has been cancelled due to deteriorating weather conditions.
> (기상조건 악화로 비행이 취소되었다.)

0538
determine [ditə́ːrmin]

v. 결정하다, 결심하다; 판단하다

IN BRIEF To establish or ascertain definitely, as after consideration, investigation, or calculation

➕ decide, purpose, conclude, resolve, choose, fix

> The exam results could determine your career.
> (그 시험 결과가 너의 직업을 결정할 수도 있다.)

0539
deterrent [ditə́ːrənt]

억제물, 방해물; 저지력

IN BRIEF Tending to deter

➕ preventive measures, dissuasion, discouragement, obstacle, curb, restrain, disincentive, determent

> His punishment will be a deterrent to others.
> (그의 처벌이 다른 사람들에 대한 억제책이 될 것이다.)

0540
detest [ditést]
vt. 혐오하다, 몹시 싫어하다

IN BRIEF To dislike or hate with intensity

+ hate, loathe, despise, abhor, abominate

> Ahntonio detests having to get up early.
> (안토니오는 일찍 일어나는 것을 몹시 싫어한다.)

0541
detriment [détrəmənt]
n. 손상, 손실

IN BRIEF Damage, harm, or loss

+ damage, injury, prejudice, impairment, harm

> Ahntonio works long hours, to the detriment of his health.
> (안토니오는 장시간 일을 하여 건강을 손상시킨다.)

0542
detrimental [dètrəméntl]
a. 유해한 → 해로운

IN BRIEF Causing damage or harm; injurious

+ damaging, destructive, harmful, adverse, baleful, deleterious, injury

> These chemicals have a detrimental effect on the environment.
> (이 화학제품들은 환경에 해로운 영향을 끼친다.)

0543
devastate [dévəstèit]
vt. 황폐시키다, 철저하게 파괴하다; (사람) 압도하다, 망연자실케 하다

IN BRIEF To destroy completely as or as if by conquering

+ disastrous, destroy, waste, ruin, wreck, spoil, demolish, ravage

> Bombs had devastated the town.
> (폭탄이 그 도시를 초토화했다.)

0544
devour [diváuər]
vt. 게걸스럽게 먹다

IN BRIEF To eat up greedily or to destroy as if by eating

+ consume, swallow, bolt, dispatch, gorge, gulp, gobble

> In no time at all they had devoured the entire loaf.
> (그들은 즉시에 빵 한 덩이를 다 먹어 치웠다.)

0545
devout [diváut]
a. 믿음이 깊은, 독실한; 헌신적인 → 독실한, 성실한

IN BRIEF Devoted to a religion or to the fulfillment of religious obligations

+ religious, godly, pious, orthodox, saintly, reverent, sincere

> He was a devout Roman Catholic.
> (그는 독실한 가톨릭 교도였다.)

0546
dexterity [dekstérəti]
n. 손재주, 솜씨, 수완; 기민함 (adroitness)

IN BRIEF Skill and grace in physical movement, especially in the use of the hands

+ skill, expertise, mastery, facility, craft, proficiency, adroitness

> A juggler needs great dexterity.
> (저글러는 굉장한 손재주를 필요로 한다.)

0547
dominant [dámənənt]
a. 지배적인; 유력한, 우세한

> A subculture is a system of perceptions, values beliefs, and customs that are significantly different from those of the dominant culture.
> (하위문화는 주류문화의 그것과 현저하게 다른 인식, 가치관, 믿음, 관습의 체계이다.)

0548
destitution [dèstətjù:t]
n. 빈곤, 궁핍

> With improved access to education and health, people see new opportunities for making a living and no longer consider children a needed insurance against destitution in old age.
> (교육과 건강 서비스를 보다 쉽게 이용할 수 있게 됨에 따라, 사람들은 생계유지를 위한 새로운 기회를 맞이하고 있으며, 더 이상 아이들을 노년의 궁핍함에 대비하기 위해 필요한 보험으로 간주하지 않는다.)

0549
disposal [dispóuzəl]
n. 처리, 처분; 처분권, 자유 재량권

> Professor Singh argues that the major aid institutions could make better use of the funds that they have at their disposal.
> (싱 교수는 주요 원조 기관들은 그들이 자유롭게 사용할 수 있는 기금을 더 잘 활용할 수 있을 것이라고 주장한다.)

LESSON 12

0550
dichotomy [daikátəmi: 다이카토미]
(논리, 철학)이분법(둘로 갈림) → 양단법; 이분, 양분《between》
IN BRIEF A division into two especially mutually exclusive or contradictory groups
+ division, split, separation, polarity, gulf, disjunction

> There is often a dichotomy between what politicians say and what they do.
> (정치인들이 하는 말과 행동은 양분되어 있는 경우가 많다.)

0551
differentiate [dìfərénʃièit]
v. 구별하다
IN BRIEF To recognize as being different
+ distinguish, separate, discriminate, contrast, discern

> Can you differentiate one variety from the other?
> (한 가지 종류를 다른 것과 구별할 수 있겠습니까?)

0552
digress [daigrés]
vi. (이야기·의제 따위가) 빗나가다 → 주제에서 벗어나다
IN BRIEF To turn aside from the main subject
+ wander, drift, ramble, meander, expatiate, stray, deviate

> Let me digress for a moment and explain what had happened previously.
> (잠깐 본론을 벗어나서 전에 무슨 일이 일어났었는지 설명하겠다.)

0553
dilapidated [diláepədèitid]
a. 황폐한, 파손된, 헐어빠진, 낡아빠진(disintegrated)
IN BRIEF Falling to pieces from lack of care
+ ruined, battered, decayed, shabby, crumbling, run-down

> The hotel we stayed in was really dilapidated.
> (우리가 묵은 호텔은 정말로 허름한 곳이었다.)

0554
dilate [dailéit]
v. 확장하다[확장되다]; 팽창하다(become wider)
IN BRIEF To make wider or larger; cause to expand
+ enlarge, extend, stretch, expand, broaden

> The pupils of your eyes dilate when you enter a dark room.
> (어두운 방에 들어가면 눈동자가 팽창한다.)

0555
dilute [dilú:t]
v. 희석하다, 묽게 하다
IN BRIEF To thin out or weaken by adding some other substance
+ water down, weaken, adulterate, thin

> Dilute the juice with water before you drink it.
> (마시기 전에 주스를 물로 희석하시오.)

0556
diminish [dəmíniʃ]
v. 줄이다, 감소하다(fade)
IN BRIEF To make smaller or less; reduce or lessen
+ decrease, decline, lessen, contract, dwindle, recede, wane

> China has diminishing leverage over North Korea.
> (북한에 대한 중국의 영향력이 점차 줄고 있다.)

0557
diminutive [dimínjətiv]
a. 소형의 → 조그마한 → 아주 작은
IN BRIEF Very small
+ small, tiny, minute, pocket, miniature

> She has diminutive hands for an adult.
> (그녀는 어른치고는 아주 작은 손을 가졌다.)

0558
din [din]
소음
IN BRIEF A jumble of loud, usually discordant sounds
+ loud noise, row, racket, crash, shout, outcry, uproar

> What a terrible din that machine makes!
> (저 기계 소음이 정말 심하구나!)

0559
dire [daiər: 다이얼]
무서운, 무시무시한; 비참한, 끔찍한, 긴박한(위험, 필요)
IN BRIEF Warning of or having dreadful or terrible consequences
+ terrible, awful, appalling, dreadful, frightful, disastrous

> The country is in dire need of food.
> (그 나라는 식량을 시급히 필요로 한다.)

0560
discard [diskáːrd]
v. (불필요한 것·습관·신념) 버리다; 포기하다

IN BRIEF To throw away; reject

+ remove, reject, abandon, relinquish, repudiate, throw away

> Remove the skins from the tomatoes and discard them.
> (토마토에서 껍질을 벗겨내고 그것을 버리시오.)

0561
discern [disə́ːrn]
v. 깨닫다; 분별하다, 인식하다(know)

IN BRIEF To perceive with the eyes; detect or distinguish

+ distinguish, perceive, notice, recognize, behold

> She cannot discern good from evil.
> (그녀는 선악을 구별하지 못한다.)

0562
discernible [dĭ-sûrʹnə-bəl]
a. 인식[식별]할 수 있는

IN BRIEF Perceptible, as by vision or the intellect

+ recognizable; distinct → perceptible, seeable

> Divergence in response to evolution is commonly expressed by altering the form and function of some part of the organism, the original identity of which is clearly discernible.
> (진화에 따른 분지(分枝)는 일반적으로 유기체의 특정 신체부위의 형태와 기능이 변하는 것으로 표현되는데, 그 특정 부위의 원래의 동일성은 분명히 식별할 수 있다.)

0563
discharge [distʃáːrdʒ]
v. 해방하다; 내보내다; 배출하다(release), 해고하다(fire, dismiss, lay-off)

IN BRIEF To release, as from confinement, care, or duty

+ release, free, liberate, pardon, acquit, exonerate

> The government decided to discharge the rice in stock.
> (정부는 보유미를 방출하기로 결정했다.)

0564
discipline [dísəplin]
훈련하다, 징계하다

IN BRIEF Control obtained by enforcing compliance or order

+ control, rule, regulation, orderliness

> They are in need of discipline.
> (그들은 단련할 필요가 있다.)

0565
disclaimer [dɪsˈkleɪmə(r)]
기권, 부인 → 권리포기각서

IN BRIEF A repudiation or denial of responsibility or connection

+ contradiction, denial, disaffirmance, disaffirmation, negation, rejection

> To avoid these problems, some infomercial producers and television stations voluntarily include a disclaimer to avoid lawsuits claiming deception.
> (이런 문제를 방지하기 위해서, 일부 정보 광고 제작사들과 TV방송국들은 사기 고소사건을 방지하기 위해 광고의 내용에 대해 자신들은 책임이 없다는 문구를 자발적으로 포함시켜 놓는다.)

0566
discomfit [diskʌ́mfit]
vt. 타파하다, 좌절시키다, 당황하게 하다

IN BRIEF To make uneasy or perplexed; disconcert

+ embarrass, confuse, confound, perplex, unnerve, thwart, upset

> She was not in the least discomfited by the large number of press photographers.
> (그녀는 많은 신문기자들 앞에서도 전혀 당황하지 않았다.)

0567
disconcert [diskənsə́ːrt]
vt. 당황하게 하다 → 좌절시키다

IN BRIEF Disturb the self-control of

+ disturb, embarrass, confuse, baffle, bewilder

> Ahntonio was disconcerted to find the other guests formally dressed.
> (안토니오는 다른 손님들이 정장을 입은 것을 알고 당황했다.)

0568
discreet [diskríːt]
a. 신중한, 삼가는

IN BRIEF Judicious in one's conduct or speech; careful; circumspect; prudent; modest

+ careful, cautious, discerning, prudent, considerate, judicious

> A discreet person does not spread rumor.
> (분별 있는 사람은 풍문을 퍼뜨리지 않는다.)

0569
discrepancy [diskrépənsi]
n. 불일치, 차이

IN BRIEF Divergence or disagreement, as between facts or claims; difference

+ disagreement, difference, variation, conflict, disparity

> There is some discrepancy between the two accounts.
> (두 설명에 서로 어긋나는 점이 있다.)

0570
discrete [diskríːt]
a. 분리된, 별개의; 따로따로의

IN BRIEF Constituting a separate thing; distinct; different; individual; unconnected

[+] separate, individual, distinct, detached, disconnect, unattached

> These small companies now have their own discrete identity.
> (이 작은 회사들은 이제 그들 별개의 정체성을 지니고 있다.)

0571
discretion [diskréʃən]
n. 신중, 분별, 사려 → 판단[선택·행동]의 자유, 결정권

IN BRIEF The quality of being discreet; circumspection

[+] judgment, prudence, caution
[−] throw caution (discretion) to the winds

> Instructing an actor how to play the part, Hamlet advises, "Let your own discretion be your tutor."
> (어떤 배우에게 그 역할을 어떻게 연기할 것인지를 가르치면서 햄릿(Hamlet)은 "자신의 판단을 자신의 가정교사가 되게 하라(자신이 내린 판단력을 근거로 연기하라"고 조언했다.)

0572
discriminating [diskrímənèitiŋ]
a. 식별력 있는 → 구별할 수 있는(discerning)

IN BRIEF Able to recognize or draw fine distinctions; perceptive

[+] discerning, particular, keen, critical, acute, sensitive, refined, cultivated

> The delicate aroma and subtle flavor of this wine need a sensitive nose and discriminating palate to be appreciated.
> (이 포도주의 은은한 냄새와 섬세한 맛을 제대로 감상하려면 민감한 후각과 식별력 있는 미각을 가져야 한다.)

0573
discrimination [diskrìmənéiʃən]
구별 (식별 → 판별 → 차별 대우(differentiation))

IN BRIEF The act of discriminating

[+] differentiation, distinction, separation

> The movement is necessary to combat genuine discrimination.
> (진정한 차별대우에 맞서 싸우려면 운동이 필요하다.)

0574
disinclination [dìsinklinéiʃən]
싫증 → 마음이 안 내킴

IN BRIEF Unwillingness to do: An attitude or feeling of aversion

[+] reluctance, aversion, unwillingness, opposition, dislike

> A disinclination to travel at night
> (밤에 여행하는 것이 내키지 않음)

0575
disembark [dìsembáːrk]
(화물·승객 등을) 내리다, 하선하다

IN BRIEF To land or cause to land from a ship, aircraft, etc

[+] land, alight, arrive, get off

> Passengers may disembark from the plane by the front or rear doors.
> (승객들은 비행기의 앞문이나 뒷문을 통해서 내릴 수 있다.)

0576
disgrace [disgréis]
n. 불명예, 체면 손상; 치욕

IN BRIEF Loss of honor, respect, or reputation; shame

[+] shame, contempt, discredit, degradation, disrepute

> He got drunk and disgraced himself at the wedding.
> (그는 술이 취해서 결혼식에서 망신을 당했다.)

0577
disparate [díspərit]
a. (본질적으로) 다른 → 이종의 → 유사점[공통점]이 없는

IN BRIEF Utterly different or distinct in kind

[+] different, contrary, distinct, diverse, dissimilar, discordant

> He is trying to bring together the disparate elements of three cultural viewpoints.
> (그는 세 가지 문화적 견해의 이질적인 요소들을 규합하기 위해 애쓰고 있다.)

0578
disguise [disgáiz]
변장[위장]시키다 → (의도·감정)속이다, 감추다(hide)

IN BRIEF To modify the manner or appearance of (a person, for example in order to prevent recognition)

[+] hide, conceal, screen, withhold

> There's no disguising the fact that he's a liar.
> (그가 거짓말쟁이라는 사실은 숨길 수가 없다.)

0579
disdain [disdéin]
경멸하다, 멸시하다

IN BRIEF To regard or treat with haughty contempt

[+] scorn, reject, despise, slight, disregard, deride

> Students treated Ahntonio's attempts to please them with cool disdain.
> (학생들은 자기들을 즐겁게 해주려는 안토니오의 시도들을 싸늘한 경멸로 대했다.)

0580
disintegrate [disíntigrèit]
v. 분해하다, 붕괴[분열]시키다, 해체하다

IN BRIEF To fall apart

[+] fall apart; reduce to pieces, collapse

> The family is starting to disintegrate.
> (가족이 해체되고 있다.)

0581
dismal [dízməl]
a. 음울한, 음침한, 어두운; 울적한, 우울한

IN BRIEF Tending to cause sadness or low spirits; terrible, sad, awful

[+] gloomy, melancholy, depressing, bleak, dreary

> The news was as dismal as ever.
> (뉴스는 예나 다름없이 우울했다.)

0582
dismiss [dismís]
해고하다; 물리치다, (생각) 떨치다 (버리다, 배제하다); 해산하다

IN BRIEF To end the employment or service of; discharge

[+] reject, repudiate, banish, dispel, sack, discharge, lay-off

> He tried to dismiss the suspicions from his mind.
> (그는 마음속에서 의혹을 지워 버리려고 애썼다.)

0583
dismount [dismáunt]
v. (말·자전거·오토바이)내리다

IN BRIEF To get down from a horse or other steed

[+] get off something higher, get off, descend, alight, get down

> He helped me dismount from my pony.
> (그는 내가 말에서 내리는 것을 도와주었다.)

0584
disparage [dispǽridʒ]
vt. 비난하다 → 얕보다

IN BRIEF To degrade, to speak slightingly about

[+] belittle, decry, negative, underestimate, ridicule, disdain

> He disparaged her achievements.
> (그는 그녀의 업적들을 비하했다.)

0585
disguise [disgáiz]
변장[위장]시키다 → (의도·감정)속이다, 감추다(hide)

[+] hide, conceal, screen, withhold

> There's no disguising the fact that he's a liar.
> (그가 거짓말쟁이라는 사실은 숨길 수가 없다.)

0586
disparity [dispǽrəti]
n. 격차, 불균형, 불일치, 차이

IN BRIEF The condition or fact of being unequal, as in age, rank, or degree; difference

[+] gap, inequality, distinction, imbalance, discrepancy, difference

> There is a big disparity in their ages.
> (그들은 나이 차가 크다.)

0587
dispatch [dispǽtʃ]
v. (군대, 특사) 파견하다/(일, 식사) 신속히 처리하다/ (사람, 사형수) 죽이다, 처형하다

IN BRIEF The act of sending off something; Killing a person or animal; The property of being prompt and efficient; An official report usually sent in haste

[+] send, transmit, kill, murder, destroy, haste, promptness, alacrity, rapidity

> The government welcomed the dispatch of the peace-keeping force.
> (정부는 평화유지군의 파견을 환영했다.)

0588
dispose of [dispóuz]
처리하다, 결말을 짓다/ 처분하다, 양도[매각]하다/ 제거하다, 버리다; 죽이다

IN BRIEF To put into a willing or receptive frame of mind; incline

[+] arrange, settle, sell/distribute/move, remove

> We will take away your old cooker and dispose of it for you.
> (당신의 낡은 요리 기구는 우리가 가져가서 처리해 드리겠습니다.)

0589
disposition [dispəzíʃən]
n. 경향, 소질, 재능

IN BRIEF A person's usual nature

[+] tendency, propensity, habit, inclination, character, temperament

> The compliment failed to sweeten her disposition.
> (그 칭찬이 그녀의 성질을 누그러뜨리지 못했다.)

0590
dissect [disékt]
v. 해부하다 → (주장·학설)분석하다, 세밀히 조사하다

IN BRIEF To separate into parts for study

[+] analyze, anatomize, break down, resolve, investigate, scrutinize

> The film has been minutely dissected by the critics.
> (그 영화는 비평가들에 의해 세세히 분석되었다.)

0591
disseminate [disémənèit]
흩뿌리다 → (정보·지식, 사상) 퍼뜨리다, 보급[유포]시키다

IN BRIEF To scatter widely, as in sowing seed

+ spread, publish, scatter, proclaim, disperse, diffuse, distribute

The mass media are used to disseminate information.
(대중 전달 매체가 정보를 유포시키는데 이용된다.)

0592
dissenting [diséntiŋ]
a. 의견을 달리하는, 이의를 제기하는, 반대하는

IN BRIEF Disagreeing, especially with a majority

+ disagreeing, opposing, conflicting, differing, dissident

There were many dissenting voices among the students.
(학생들 사이에 많은 반대의 목소리가 있었다.)

0593
dissipate [dísəpèit]
(구름·안개, 바람) 흩뜨리다/(슬픔·공포) 가시게 하다, 없애다/(시간·재산) 낭비하다, 탕진하다(waste)

IN BRIEF To break apart or attenuate to the point of disappearing

+ scatter, disapper, fade, vanish, dissolve, disperse, diffuse

The mist quickly dissipated as the sun rose.
(해가 떠오르자 안개는 빠르게 걷혔다.)

0594
dissuade [diswéid]
단념시키다

IN BRIEF To persuade (a person not to do something)

+ deter, put off, discourage, disincline, urge not to, prevent

I'm trying to dissuade her from buying a TV.
(나는 지금 그녀를 설득하여 TV 사는 것을 단념케 하려고 노력 중이다.)

0595
distraction [distrǽkʃən]
정신을 산란하게 하는 것, 주의산만; 기분전환[오락]거리

IN BRIEF The act of distracting, or the condition of being distracted

+ entertainment, recreation, diversion, pastime, divertissement

TV can be a welcome distraction after a hard day's work.
(하루 종일 힘들게 일한 뒤에는 TV가 반가운 기분전환 거리가 될 수 있다.)

0596
diurnal [daiə́:rnəl]
a. 낮동안의, 주간의, 주행성의↔nocturnal (야행성의)

IN BRIEF Everyday. Relating to daylight

+ daily, daytime, daily, non-nocturnal, quotidian

Unlike most other bats, this specilikis diurnal.
(대부분의 다른 박쥐들과는 달리, 이 종류는 주행성이다.)

0597
dormant [dɔ́:rmənt]
a. 잠자는, 활동이 없는; 잠복한

Indeed, after a couple of centuries of lying dormant, China may once again dictate the narrative of our age.
(참으로, 이삼백년 동안 잠복해 있은 후에, 중국은 다시 한 번 우리 시대의 이야기를 받아쓰게 할 수도 있다.)

0598
deluge [délju:dʒ]
n. 대홍수; 쇄도

The deluge of information generated in recent years placed a burden on the government.
(최근 발생한 정부의 홍수는 정부에게 부담을 안겨 주었다.)

0599
distant [dístənt]
a. 거리가 먼; 감정이 서먹서먹한(aloof)

After a severe quarrel, the old bosom friends remained bitter and distant even while they were sitting in the same classroom.
(절친했던 친구들은 크게 싸우고 난 뒤, 계속 감정이 상해서 같은 교실에 앉아있을 때조차도 서먹서먹하게 있었다.)

LESSON 13

0600
diverse [divə́ːrs]
가지가지의, 다양한
IN BRIEF Not all the same
+ various, different, diversified, assorted, several, sundry

Her interests are very diverse.
(그녀의 관심사는 매우 다양하다.)

0601
divine [diváin]
a. 신의; 거룩한
IN BRIEF Term referring to the Judeo-Christian God; heavenly sacred; holy
+ heavenly, spiritual, holy, immortal, celestial, sacred

To err is human, to forgive divine.
(죄는 인간이 짓고, 용서는 신이 한다.)

0602
divulge [divʌ́ldʒ]
누설하다 → 파헤치다 → 폭로하다
IN BRIEF To disclose or reveal (something private, secret, or previously unknown)
+ expose, give away, let out, reveal, tell, uncover, unveil

The accused would not divulge his connection with the crime.
(그 피고인은 자신의 범죄 연관성을 밝히려 하지 않았다.)

0603
docile [dóusail]
a. 유순한, 고분고분한(obedient)
IN BRIEF Easy to handle
+ obedient, manageable, compliant, amenable, submissive, pliant, tractable, biddable, ductile, teachable

We need creative alternatives to the onslaught of talking heads, all saying much the same thing to docile audiences.
(우리는 고분고분한 청중들에게 모두가 정말 똑같은 말만 하는 사람들의 공격에 대해 창의적인 대안들이필요하다.)

0604
doleful [dóulfəl]
슬픈, 슬픔에 잠긴; 울적한, 음울한(melancholy)
IN BRIEF Filled with or expressing grief; mournful
+ mournful, gloomy, forlorn, woeful, sorrowful, lugubrious

The dog looked at me with a doleful expression.
(그 개는 슬픔에 잠긴 표정으로 나를 바라보았다.)

0605
domesticate [douméstəkèit]
길들이다, 가정적으로 되게 하다 ↔ wild
IN BRIEF To train to live with and be of use to people
+ tame, train, house-train, break, gentle

Most wives try to domesticate their husbands.
(아내들은 대부분 남편을 길들이려고 한다.)

0606
dominion [dəmínjən]
n. 지배권, 통치권, (개인·국가의) 영지 (power)
IN BRIEF Control or the exercise of control; sovereignty
+ control, government, sway, domination, jurisdiction, authority

The king's dominion was devastated by the invading army.
(왕의 영지는 침략군에게 짓밟혔다.)

0607
dormant [dɔ́ːrmənt]
a. 잠자는것 같은 → 수면 상태의 → 잠복의(resting)
IN BRIEF Not awake; asleep
+ resting, motionless, latent, inert, quiescent, suspended, asleep

Scientists discovered recently that the virus is dormant in most brain tissue.
(과학자들은 최근 그 바이러스가 대부분의 뇌 조직에 잠복해 있다는 사실을 발견했다.)

0608
dose [dous]
n. (약의) 1회 복용량, 한 첩, (쓴) 약; 약간의 경험
IN BRIEF Pharmacology med a specific quantity of a therapeutic drug or agent taken at any one time or at specified intervals
+ measure, amount, allowance, ration, dosage

Take one dose of the medicine at bedtime.
(취침시에 1회분의 약을 드세요.)

0609
dote [dout]
맹목적으로 사랑하다

IN BRIEF To show excessive fondness or love

+ adore, prize, admire, treasure, idolize

> She dotes on her grandchildren.
> (그녀는 손자들을 애지중지한다.)

0610
dour [dauər]
뚱한, 음침한 우울한, 뚱한, 시무룩한(sullen) → 엄한; 완고한 (stubborn)

IN BRIEF Unfriendly and sullen

+ gloomy, grim

> A powerful orator, Jim is, in fact, less dour than he's made out to be.
> (영향력 있는 연설자인 짐(Jim)은 사람들의 말에 비해 실제로는 덜 시무룩하다.)

0611
dowdy [dáudi]
(옷)단정치 못한 → 시대에 뒤떨어진 → 맵시 없는 → 촌스러운(누추한)

IN BRIEF Not stylishly or well dressed

+ frumpy, old-fashioned, shabby, drab, tacky unfashionable, dingy

> Her dowdy overcoat alarmed her teenage children.
> (그녀의 단정치 못한 외투는 그녀의 십 대 아이들을 놀라게 했습니다.)

0612
downpour [-pɔ́:r]
호우(downpouring) 엄청나게 비가오는(showering)

IN BRIEF A heavy continuous fall of rain

+ rainstorm, flood, deluge, cloudburst, inundation, showering

> I was caught in a torrential downpour.
> (나는 억수 같은 호우를 만났다.)

0613
down-to-earth
실제적인(realistic) → 철저한

IN BRIEF Having or indicating an awareness of things as they really are

+ matter-of-fact, objective, practical, pragmatic, pragmatical, prosaic, realistic

> Both speakers reached their audience by talking in a down-to-earth manner, strongly expressing their opinions.
> (두 연사 모두 현실적인 방식으로 말함으로써 청중에 접근해서 자기들의 의견을 강력하게 표현했다.)

0614
doze [douz]
v. 졸다, 선잠[풋잠] 자다(sleep lightly)

IN BRIEF To sleep lightly and intermittently

+ nap, slumber, nod, catnap, drowse

> I dozed off during the film.
> (나는 영화를 보는 중에 졸았다.)

0615
draft [dræft]
n. 밑그림(초고), (단숨에) 마시기, 징병, 수표(어음) (스포츠)드래프트제(신인 선수 선발 제도), 기안하다, 선발하다, 잡아당기다

IN BRIEF A plan, sketch, or drawing of something

+ outline, plan, sketch, abstract, delineation, manuscript

> He made a draft for the poster.
> (그는 그 포스터의 도안을 했다.)

0616
drop [drɑp]
(말·한숨) 무심결에 불쑥 나오다 (mentioning)

IN BRIEF Utter with seeming casualness

+ give tongue to, utter, express, verbalise, verbalize

> In response, funeral directors act more like event planners, keeping prop rooms, offering video services and dropping words like "choreography" and "production quality" into their spiels.
> (장의사들은 소품실을 관리하고, 비디오 서비스를 제공하고, 그들의 말에서 '안무'나 '작품의질'과 같은 어들을 언급하며 마치 공연 기획자에 더 가까운 듯 행동한다.)

0617
drawback [drɔ́:bæk]
n. 단점, 결점, 문제점

IN BRIEF A disadvantage or inconvenience

+ disadvantage, trouble, handicap, defect, flaw

> Everyone has his own drawbacks.
> (누구나 결점은 있다.)

0618
dread [dred]
v. 매우 두려워하다 → 겁내다(intimidate)

IN BRIEF To be very afraid

+ fear, shrink from, be anxious about, flinch from, quail from

> Cats dread water.
> (고양이는 물을 두려워한다.)

0619
drench [drentʃ]
vt. 흠뻑 적시다

IN BRIEF To wet through and through; soak

+ soak, flood, wet, drown, saturate, inundate

> She drenched her sleeves with tears.
> (그녀는 눈물로 옷소매를 흠뻑 적셨다.)

0620
drone [droun]
v. 단조로운 소리를 계속 내다/ n. 게으름뱅이(idler, lazy person)
→ 농땡이(sluggard)

IN BRIEF To make a continuous low dull humming sound

+ hum, buzz, vibrate, purr, thrum

> The chairman droned on for hours about the company's performance.
> (의장은 회사의 성과에 대해 몇 시간동안 계속해서 말을 질질 끌었다.)

0621
drastic [drǽstik]
a. 강렬(맹렬)한/ 대담한, 철저한

IN BRIEF Extreme in effect; severe or radical

+ extreme, radical, harsh, severe, huge

> Their policies are currently undergoing drastic revision.
> (그들이 제시한 정책은 지금 대대적으로 수정되고 있다.)

0622
drudgery [drʌ́dʒəri]
단조롭고 고된 일

IN BRIEF Tedious, menial, or unpleasant work

+ labour, hard work, slavery, chore, fag, toil

> Automation has done away with much of the drudgery of work.
> (자동화는 고된 작업을 많이 제거해주었다.)

0623
duplicity [djuːplísiti]
일구이언(이중성), 표리부동; 불성실, 사기

IN BRIEF Deliberate deceptiveness in behavior or speech; The act or practice of deceiving

+ cunning, deceit, deceitfulness, deception, double-dealing, guile, shiftiness.

> Liars engage in duplicity all the time; they say one thing and do another.
> (거짓말쟁이들은 언제나 표리부동한 언행을 한다: 그들은 말과 행동이 다른 사람들이다.)

0624
dubious [djúːbiəs]
a. 의심하는, 의심스러운

IN BRIEF Fraught with uncertainty or doubt; undecided

+ doubtful, suspicious, suspect, doubtful, questionable, unreliable, untrustworthy

> Ahntonio is a dubious character.
> (안토니오는 의심스러운 인물이다.)

0625
dumb [dʌm]
a. 벙어리의, 말 못하는, 말문이 막힌(구어) 둔감한, 우둔한

IN BRIEF Lacking the power of speech

+ silent, mute, stupid, dull, inarticulate, obtuse

> She's been dumb from birth.
> (그녀는 태어날 때부터 말을 하지 못한다.)

0626
duplicate [djúːpləkit]
복사하다; 되풀이하다. 사본

IN BRIEF A thing exactly like another. to make an exact copy

+ repeat, reproduce, copy, clone, replicate, replica

> The thieves were equipped with duplicate keys to the safe.
> (도둑들은 복제한 금고 열쇠를 가지고 있었다.)

0627
dub [dʌb]
별명을 붙이다(~라고 부르다), 재녹음하다, 더빙하다, 번역녹음하다

IN BRIEF To give a name to facetiously or playfully; nickname

+ name, label, designate, denominate, entitle, nick name

> The papers dubbed the Beatles 'The Fab Four'.
> (신문들은 비틀스를 '굉장한 4인조'라고 별칭 했다.)

0628
eccentric [ikséntrik]
a. 별난, 괴짜 같은, 괴상한

IN BRIEF Not ordinary or usual in behavior or appearance; odd or peculiar

+ strange, bizarre, abnormal, odd, peculiar, quaint, queer, quirky, strange, unusual, weird

> There is something eccentric in his composition.
> (그의 성질에는 좀 별난 데가 있다.)

0629
earmark [íərmà:rk]
지정, 할당, 결정하다 → 귀표 → 특징

IN BRIEF To set aside or apart for a specified purpose

➕ designate, allocate, set aside, decide

> Peter has already been earmarked for the job.
> (피터가 그 일에 벌써 책정되었다.)

0630
ebullient [ibúljənt]
(정열 따위가) 용솟음치는 → 열광적인[with], 끓어오르는

IN BRIEF Overflowing with enthusiasm or excitement; exuberant

➕ exuberant, enthusiastic, vivacious, buoyant, elated, zestful

> His CEO was the ebullient cheerleader.
> (그의 CEO는 사기를 높이는 원기 왕성한 리더였다.)

0631
drop the ball
일을 망치다, 중대한 실수를 하다

> Matthew really dropped the ball on this project by letting Susan to be a part of the project team.
> (매튜는 수잔을 그 사업팀의 일원이 되도록 함으로써 이 사업에 있어서 중대한 실수를 했다.)

0632
eccentricity [èksentrísəti]
n. 남다름, 기행, 이상함

IN BRIEF The quality of being eccentric

➕ oddity, peculiarity, bizarreness, singularity, irregularity

> One of his eccentricities is sleeping under the bed instead of on it.
> (그의 희한한 점 중 한 가지는 침대 위에서 자는 것이 아니라 그 아래서 잠을 자는 것이다.)

0633
ecological [ì:kəlɒdʒɪkl]
생태학[계]의 → 생태상의(environmental, green)

IN BRIEF The science of the relationships between organisms and their environments

➕ environmental, green

> The oil spill was an ecological disaster for thousands of birds.
> (그 기름 유출사고는 수천 마리의 새들에게 생태계 재앙이었다.)

0634
edible [édəbəl]
식용이 되는, 먹을 수 있는

IN BRIEF Fit to be eaten, especially by humans

➕ eatable, harmless, wholesome, palatable, digestible, comestible

> This food is scarcely edible.
> (이 음식은 거의 먹을 수가 없다.)

0635
edify [édəfài]
vt. (도덕적·정신적으로) 교화하다, 계발하다

IN BRIEF To improve the morality, intellect, etc, of, esp by instruction

➕ instruct, inform, enlighten, improve, guide

> The President's appearance on a TV talk show was not an edifying spectacle.
> (대통령의 TV 대담 출연은 교훈적인 볼거리가 아니었다.)

0636
eerie [íəri]
a. 무시무시한, 섬뜩한, 오싹하는, 기분 나쁜(weird)

IN BRIEF Inspiring inexplicable fear, dread, or uneasiness; strange and frightening

➕ uncanny, strange, frightening, scary, awesome

> When dolls are too well-made, there is something eerie about them.
> (인형이 너무 잘 만들어지면 뭔가 섬뜩한 느낌이 든다.)

0637
efface [iféis]
(글자·자국) 지우다, 삭제하다 → (기억) 지워 없애다

IN BRIEF To rub or wipe out; erase

➕ obliterate, remove, destroy, erase, eradicate, excise, delete, annihilate

> Time alone will efface those unpleasant memories.
> (오직 시간만이 그 불쾌한 기억들을 지워 줄 것이다.)

0638
egregious [igríːdʒəs]
지독한, 소문난, 터무니없는(terrible)

IN BRIEF Conspicuously bad or offensive

➕ grievous, notorious, infamous, outrageous, intolerable

> It was an egregious error for a statesman to show such ignorance.
> (정치인으로써 그런 무지를 보여주었다는 것은 엄청난 실수이다.)

0639
eject [idʒékt]
v. 탈출하다; 추방하다

IN BRIEF To throw out forcefully; expel

+ expel, exile, oust, banish, deport, evict

> Press 'Eject' to release the cassette from the recorder.
> (레코드에서 카세트를 뽑으려면 '이젝트'를 누르세요.)

0640
elapse [ilǽps]
vi. (시간) 경과하다

IN BRIEF The passage or termination of a period of time

+ pass, lapse, go by, slip away, glide by

> Three years elapsed before they met again.
> (3년이 지나서야 그들은 다시 만났다.)

0641
elastic [ilǽstik]
a. 탄성 있는, 탄력 있는, 신축성 있는

IN BRIEF Easily resuming original size or shape after being stretched or otherwise deformed; flexible

+ flexible, pliable, plastic, ductile, tensile, rubbery

> Our plans are fairly elastic.
> (우리의 계획은 꽤 융통성이 있다.)

0642
elective [iléktiv]
a. 선택의, 필수가 아닌

IN BRIEF Of or relating to a selection by vote

+ selected, chosen, elite, optional

> She is taking French as an elective next year.
> (그녀는 내년에 선택과목으로 프랑스어를 들을 것이다.)

0643
elevate [éləvèit]
vt. 올리다, 높이다, 격상시키다

IN BRIEF To move (something) to a higher place or position from a lower one; lift

+ promote, raise, advance, increase, exalt, upgrade, boost

> She's been elevated to the post of trade minister.
> (그녀는 통상장관 자리로 승진했다.)

0644
elicit [ilísit]
vt. 이끌어내다

IN BRIEF To draw or bring out; educe; evoke

+ derive, bring out, evoke, cause, draw out, draw forth

> At last we've elicited the truth from him.
> (마침내 우리는 그에게서 진실을 이끌어 내었다.)

0645
eligible [élidʒəbəl]
적격의 → 피선거 자격이 있는 → 적임의 → 바람직한 → (특히 결혼상대로서) 적당한

IN BRIEF Having the qualities or conditions required

+ entitled, fit, qualified, suited, suitable

> Here is a decisively eligible young man.
> (여기에 단연 적격인 청년이 있습니다.)

0646
excrete [ıkˈskriːt]
v. 배설하다, 분비하다

IN BRIEF To separate and discharge (waste matter) from the blood, tissues, or organs

+ purge, eliminate, evacuate

> The most medically interesting amphibians found to date are the dart-poison frogs of Central and South America, whose skins excrete a variety of valuable compounds.
> (지금까지 발견된 의학적으로 가장 흥미로운 양서류는 중미와 남미에 사는 독화살 개구리인데, 그것의 피부는 여러 가지 유용한 화합물을 분비한다.)

0647
emaciated [iméiʃièit]
a. 쇠약한, 수척한

IN BRIEF Physically haggard

+ cadaverous, gaunt, haggard

> Mozambique's hospitals are overflowing with famine victims. Most are skeletal and silent. At a hospital in the coastal town of Vilanculos, two brothers lie side by side in a ward filled with emaciated children. They are the only survivors of a family of eleven who walked 65 miles from their village in search of food.
> (모잠비크의 병원들은 기근 희생자들로 넘쳐나고 있다. 대부분은 수척하며 말수가 적다. 빌란쿨로스라는 연안 도시의 한 병원에서는 두 형제가 수척한 아이들로 넘쳐나는 병실에 나란히 누워있다. 그들은 음식을 찾아 고향에서 65마일을 걸어온 11명의 가족 중 유일하게 살아남은 생존자들이다.)

0648
eliminate [ilímənèit]

vt. 제거하다

IN BRIEF To get rid of; remove

⊕ remove, withdraw, terminate, banish, eradicate, abolish, get rid of

> Eliminate all errors from the manuscript.
> (원고에서 틀린 것을 모두 제거해라.)

0649
effulgence [efʌ́ldʒəns]

n. 광휘; 광채

IN BRIEF The quality of being bright and sending out rays of light

⊕ radiancy, refulgence, refulgency, shine, radiance

> To capture on canvas the effulgence of the eastern sky at sunrise is a challenge to any painter.
> (동쪽 하늘에 떠오르는 태양의 광채를 화폭 위에 잡아두는 것은 어떤 화가에게나 쉽지 않은 과제이다.)

LESSON 14

0650
eloquent [éləkwənt]

a. 웅변의, 말 잘하는, (연설 따위가) 감동적인, 청중을 사로잡는

IN BRIEF Capable of or characterized by eloquence

+ effective, stirring, articulate, persuasive, fluent, expressive

> He was an eloquent preacher.
> (그는 말 잘하는 설교사–목사였다.)

0651
elucidate [ilú:sədèit]

(사실·기술) 밝히다, 해명하다, 설명하다

IN BRIEF To make clear or plain, especially by explanation; clarify

+ explain, illustrate, interpret, annotate, explicate, clarify

> You have not understood; allow me to elucidate.
> (당신이 이해를 못하셨군요. 설명을 해 드릴게요.)

0652
emancipate [imǽnsəpèit]

vt. 해방하다

IN BRIEF To free from bondage, oppression, or restraint; liberate

+ release, liberate, discharge, untie, enfranchise

> In many countries women are still struggling to be fully emancipated.
> (많은 국가들에서 여자들은 아직도 완전한 해방을 위해 투쟁하고 있다.)

0653
embark [embá:rk]

v. 승선하다, 탑승하다(begin)

IN BRIEF To cause to board a vessel or aircraft

+ climb aboard, go aboard, board ship, take ship

> Passengers should embark early.
> (승객들은 일찍 배를 타야 합니다.)

0654
embargo [imbá:rgou]

(출입항·통상) 금지

IN BRIEF Legal prohibition or restriction of foreign commerce or trade

+ ban, bar, restriction, boycott, prohibition, interdiction

> EU OKays Total Arms Embargo on Nigeria.
> (EU(유럽공동체)는 나이지리아에 대한 전면적인 무기거래금지 조치에 합의했다.)

0655
embellish [imbéliʃ]

vt. 꾸미다, 장식하다

IN BRIEF To make beautiful, as by ornamentation; decorate

+ decorate, adorn, ornament, enrich, garnish

> She embellished her story with a few lurid details.
> (그녀는 몇 가지 선정적인 세부내용들로 자기 소설을 장식했다.)

0656
emblem [émbləm]

n. 상징, 표상(表象)(symbol)

IN BRIEF An object associated with and serving to identify something else

+ crest, mark, design, image, figure, seal, shield, badge, insignia

> The dove is an emblem of peace.
> (비둘기는 평화의 상징이다.)

0657
embolden [embóuldən]

vt. 용기를 주다; 대담하게 하다

IN BRIEF To foster boldness or courage in

+ encourage, cheer, strengthen, nerve, stimulate, animate

> His success emboldened him to expand the business.
> (그는 성공으로 대담해져서 사업을 확장했다.)

0658
embodiment [imbá:rgou]

(사상·특질을 보여주는) 전형[화신] (epitome)

IN BRIEF The act of embodying or the state of being embodied

+ personification, example, model, type, ideal, expression, symbol, representation, manifestation, realization, incarnation

> He is the embodiment of the young successful businessman.
> (그는 성공한 젊은 사업가의 전형이다.)

0659
embryo [émbriòu]

(발달의) 초기의 것, 싹 → (보통 임신 8주일까지의) 태아

IN BRIEF A source of further growth and development

+ foetus, unborn child, fertilized egg

> My plans are still very much in embryo at this stage.
> (내 계획은 현 단계에서는 아직도 지극히 초기 단계이다.)

0660
emerge [imə́ːrdʒ]

나오다, 나타나다(appear) → 알려지다, 판명되다

IN BRIEF To appear, To rise from

[+] appear, surface, proceed, emanate, issue

> The moon emerged from behind the clouds.
> (달이 구름 뒤에서 모습을 드러냈다.)

0661
emergence [imə́ːrdʒəns]

n. 출현; (문제 등의) 발생

IN BRIEF The act or process of emerging

[+] arrival, surfacing, rise, appearance, advent, emanation

> They saw the emergence of a superstar.
> (그들은 한 슈퍼스타의 출현을 보았다.)

0662
emigrant [éməgrənt]

(자국에서 국외로의) 이민, 이주자(settler, migrant)

IN BRIEF A person who moves from one place to settle in another

[+] immigrant, migrant, transmigrant.

> The number of emigrants is increasing.
> (이민의 수가 증가하고 있다.)

0663
eminent [émənənt]

a. 신분이 높은, 유명한, 저명한(famous and admired)

IN BRIEF High in station, merit, or esteem

[+] prominent, noted, celebrated, outstanding, notable, renowned

> He is an eminent philosopher and mathematician.
> (그는 저명한 철학자이자 수학자이다.)

0664
emissary [éməsèri]

사절, 밀사(messenger)

IN BRIEF A person sent to represent another

[+] envoy, agent, deputy, ambassador, delegate, consul

> The government appointed him President's special emissary to China.
> (정부는 그를 대중국 대통령 특사로 임명했다.)

0665
emit [imít]

vt. (빛·열·향기) 발하다, 내뿜다

IN BRIEF To send or give out

[+] release, shed, radiate, eject, exhale, diffuse

> The garbage dump will emit a foul smell.
> (쓰레기장에서 악취가 날 것이다.)

0666
emission [imíʃən]

n. (빛·열·가스 등의) 방출 → 방사

IN BRIEF An act of sending something out → issuance, diffusion

[+] giving off or out, release, shedding, leak, radiation, discharge, transmission, venting

> Methane is made by decaying plants or found in the burps, belches and other emissions of animals from termites to cattle and people.
> (메탄은 썩어가는 식물에 의해 생기거나, 흰개미로부터 소와 사람들에 이르는 동물들의 트림과 여타 가스방출에서도 발견된다.)

0667
empower [empáuər]

vt. 권한을 부여하다, 권력을 위임하다 [to do]

IN BRIEF To give certain rights or authority to

[+] authorize, allow, commission, qualify, permit, entitle

> Science empowers men to control natural forces.
> (과학은 인간에게 자연의 힘을 제어할 능력을 준다.)

0668
emulate [émjəlèit]

vt. 본뜨다, 흉내내다; 경쟁하다, 겨루다; 필적하다

IN BRIEF To imitate with intent to learn

[+] imitate, copy, compete, match

> She is keen to emulate her sister's sporting achievements.
> (그녀는 언니의 스포츠 업적에 필적하려고 열심이다.)

0669
encompass [inkʌ́mpəs]

vt. 에워싸다, 둘러싸다, 포위하다[with, by]/ 싸다; 내포[포함]하다, 망라하다

IN BRIEF To surround. To contain or include

[+] include, involve, admit, deal with, contain, take in, embrace, incorporate, comprise, embody

> Her knowledge encompasses all aspects of the business.
> (그녀의 지식은 그 사업의 모든 측면을 마무른다.)

0670
encounter [enkáuntər]

(우연)만나다, 마주치다 → (위험)부닥치다 → (meet with) → (적) 교전(충돌)하다

IN BRIEF A chance meeting. A meeting in battle

[+] confront, face, meet, run into

> When did you first encounter Buddhism?
> (당신은 언제 처음으로 불교를 접했습니까?)

0671
encroach [enkróutʃ]
vi. (남의 재산·권리) 침해하다, 위반하다 (trespass (upon))

IN BRIEF Invade another's property, business

[+] breach, break, contravene, transgress, violate, infringe(on), encroach, impinge

> The sea is gradually encroaching.
> (바다가 서서히 침식해 들어오고 있다.)

0672
endemic [endémik]
a. (질병 따위가) 어떤 지방 특유한, 풍토성의(local, native)

IN BRIEF Found especially or only in a certain region

[+] widespread, common, extensive, prevalent, pervasive

> This is an endemic problem.
> (이건 이 지역의 문제예요.)

0673
endorse [endɔ́ːrs]
시인[승인]하다 → 보증하다 → (수표, 어음) 이서하다 → 뒷받침하다

IN BRIEF To sign one's name on the back of a check in order to cash it

[+] support, authorize, approve, warrant, sign, sustain

> I endorse everything that the speaker has said.
> (그 연사가 한 말은 내가 전부 보증한다.)

0674
enforce [enfɔ́ːrs]
vt. 시행하다; 강요하다(put a rule, plan in force)

IN BRIEF To make people obey, To bring about by being strict

[+] impose, require, urge, insist on, compel, exact, oblige, carry out

> The General Assembly has no power to enforce them.
> (총회로서는 이 법안들이 실제 효력을 갖도록 강제할 권한이 없습니다.)

0675
engender [endʒéndər]
[감정·상태] 일으키다, 낳다, 유발하다(beget, create)

IN BRIEF To bring into existence; give rise to

[+] produce, cause, breed, generate, induce, incite

> Some people believe that poverty engenders crime.
> (어떤 사람들은 가난이 범죄를 불러온다고 믿는다.)

0676
engross [engróus]
vt. (주의·시간)집중시키다 → 몰두[열중]시키다(absorb), (시장)독점하다 → (상품) 매점(買占)하다 → (권력)독점하다(monopolize)

IN BRIEF To occupy completely

[+] absorb, consume, immerse, monopolize, preoccupy

> The subject continues to engross her.
> (그 주제가 계속해서 그녀의 마음을 빼앗았다.)

0677
enhance [enhǽns]
(질·능력)높이다 → 강화하다;(가격) 올리다

IN BRIEF To intensify

[+] improve, increase, raise, boost, reinforce, augment

> Those clothes do nothing to enhance her appearance.
> (그 옷들은 그의 외모를 향상시키는 데 아무런 도움이 못된다.)

0678
enigma [inígmə]
n. 수수께끼, 불가사의한 일[사람]

IN BRIEF Something that is puzzling

[+] conundrum, mystery, perplexity, puzzle, puzzler, riddle

> Albert Schweitzer remains something of an enigma.
> (앨버트 슈바이처는 불가사의한 위인으로 남아있다.)

0679
enkindle [enkíndl]
vt. (불을) 타오르게 하다; (정열, 정욕) 불러일으키다, 자극하다; (전쟁) 일으키다

IN BRIEF To set afire; light

[+] fire, ignite, kindle, light

> The surest way to an enlightened society is through the hope enkindled in child- ren's eyes.
> (개화된 사회로 가는 가장 확실한 방법은 어린이들의 눈망울 속에 타오르는 희망을 통하는 것이다.)

0680
enmesh [enméʃ]
그물로 잡다 → 그물에 걸리게 하다 → (곤란)빠뜨리다 → 말려들게 하다

IN BRIEF Involve in situation, entangle

[+] catch, ensnare, ensnarl, entrap, snare, tangle, trammel, trap, web

> He soon became enmeshed in a world of crime.
> (그는 곧 범죄의 세계로 빠져들었다.)

0681
enormous [inɔ́ːrməs]
a. 거대한, 막대한, 심한, 엄청난

IN BRIEF Very large

+ large, huge, vast, extensive, tremendous, titanic, immense

> My dog is enormous.
> (내 개는 매우 크다.)

0682
en route
도중에(on the way to destination)

IN BRIEF On or along the way; on the road

+ along the way, on the road, journey, on the way

> They passed through Paris en route for Rome.
> (그들은 로마로 가는 도중에 파리를 경유했다.)

0683
ensue [ensúː]
v. 뒤따르다, 뒤이어 일어나다

IN BRIEF To follow

+ follow, result, proceed, derive, befall, stem, supervene

> What will ensue on this?
> (이 결과로 무슨 일이 생길까?)

0684
ensuing [inˈsjuːiŋ]
a. 결과로서 계속되는(resulting)

IN BRIEF To take place afterward or as a result

+ following, resulting, succeeding, subsequent, later, consequent

> With the rapid spread of industry and the ensuing transformation of the urban landscape, city dwellers have found themselves living in increasingly bleak surroundings.
> (빠르게 퍼져나간 산업화와 그에 따른 도시경관의 변화에 함께, 도시 거주자들은 그들이 갈수록 더 암울한 환경에 살고 있음을 알게 되었다.)

0685
entail [entéil]
vt. (필연적 결과를) 초래하다, 수반하다, 필요로 하다

IN BRIEF To have, impose, or require as a necessary accompaniment or consequence

+ involve, require, cause, produce

> This job entails a lot of hard work.
> (이 직업은 수많은 힘든 일을 수반한다.)

0686
enthrall [enθrɔ́ːl]
vt. 마음을 사로잡다, 매료하다(captivate)

IN BRIEF To captivate or charm; spellbind

+ engross, charm, grip, fascinate, absorb, entrance, intrigue, enchant

> His thrillers make enthralling reading.
> (그의 스릴러 소설은 읽기에 매혹적이다.)

0687
entrepreneur [à:ntrəprənɔ́ːr]
n. 기업가, 창업가, 사업가

IN BRIEF One who organizes and manages an enterprise

+ tycoon, director, executive, contractor, speculator, enterpriser

> There's an interview with Mr. Pitman in this week's edition of Entrepreneur magazine.
> (이번 호 '기업가'잡지에 피트먼씨와의 인터뷰 기사가 실렸어요.)

0688
evasion [ivéiʒən]
n. (법률, 책임, 의무 등의) 회피, 빠져나감, 탈세, 얼버무림, 핑계

IN BRIEF The act or an instance of evading, an act or instance of escaping, avoiding, or shirking something

+ avoidance, escape, dodging, shirking, cop-out (slang), circumvention, elusion

> The point of the chapter is that the unconscious mind often opposes what the conscious mind wants to do or say, and frequently trips it up with all kinds of evasions, deceits, gags, and kicks in the pants.
> (그 장의 요지는 의식이 행동하거나 말하고자 하는 것을 무의식이 종종 반대하며, 온갖 종류의 회피, 속임수, 억압, 그리고 노골적인 비난을 통해 자주 그것을 좌절시킨다는 것이다.)

0689
enumerate [injúːmərèit]
vt. (일일이) 열거하다(give a list of)

IN BRIEF To count off or name one by one; list

+ list, detail, relate, mention, specify, incite

> She enumerated her objections to the proposals.
> (그녀는 그 제안들에 대한 자신의 반대 이유를 열거했다.)

0690
epitome [ipítəmi]
전형, 표본, 완벽한 보기(example → abbreviation)

IN BRIEF A representative or perfect example of a class or type

+ abridgment, abstract, brief, condensation, synopsis

> He was a model student and the epitome of a hard worker.
> (그는 모범이 되는 학생이었고, 부지런한 사람의 완벽한 본보기였다.)

0691
epitomize [ipítəmàiz]
요약하다; 완벽한 보기이다, 전형적으로 보여주다(embody)

IN BRIEF To make an epitome of; sum up

+ typify, represent, illustrate, embody, exemplify, symbolize, personify, incarnate

> This building epitomizes the spirit of the 19th century.
> (이 건물은 19세기적인 기풍을 잘 보여주고 있다.)

0692
epoch [épək]
n. (획기적인) 시대; 신기원 (long period of time)

IN BRIEF A point in time beginning a new or distinctive period

+ era, period, age, aeon, date

> The emancipation of slaves marks an epoch in American history.
> (노예 해방은 미국사에서 한 시대의 획을 긋는다.)

0693
equanimity [i:kwənímət i]
n. 마음의 평정, 침착(calmness)

IN BRIEF Evenness of mind or temper

+ composure, calm, serenity, tranquillity, aplomb

> He received the news of his mother's death with remarkable equanimity.
> (그는 어머니의 사망 소식을 놀랄만한 담담함으로 받아들였다.)

0694
equilibrium [ì:kwɪ|líbriəm]
n. 평형상태, 균형; 평정

IN BRIEF A condition in which all acting influences are canceled by others, resulting in a stable, balanced, or unchanging system

+ stability, balance, symmetry, steadiness, evenness, equipoise, counterpoise

> Any shift by China concerning North Korea has the potential to significantly alter the political equilibrium in Asia.
> (북한에 대한 중국과 그 어떤 입장변화도 아시아의 정치적인 균형을 크게 바꿀 수 있는 잠재력을 갖고 있다.)

0695
equivalent [ikwívələnt]
a. 동등한 → 상당하는

IN BRIEF The same in amount, value, or meaning

+ equal, counterpart, correspondent, parallel, match, peer

> These two diamonds are equivalent in value.
> (이 두 개의 다이아몬드는 동등한 값어치를 지니고 있다.)

0696
empirical [empírikəl]
a. 경험의, 실험에 의한(Relying on experiment)

> Where science provides explanations that are open to new data and explicitly acknowledges a possibility of various alternatives, religious systems tend not to be open to empirical testing.
> (과학이 새로운 정보를 받아들이는 설명을 제공하고 다양한 대안이 존재할 가능성을 분명하게 인정하는 데 반해, 종교 체계는 경험에 의거한 실험을 받아들이지 않는 경향이 있다.)

0697
erratic [irǽtik]
a. 불규칙한, 일정치 않은, 변덕스러운

IN BRIEF Having no fixed or regular course, irregular in performance, behavior, or attitude; inconsistent and unpredictable

+ changeable, variable, unpredictable, unstable, irregular, erratic, uneven, fickle, capricious, unsteady, inconstant

> The erratic dance moves and catchy electronic sounds from the title song have captivated every listener.
> (주제곡의 일정치 않은 춤동작과 사람의 마음을 끄는 전자음은 모든 청자들의 마음을 사로잡았다.)

0698
ephemeral [ifémərəl]
a. 일시적인, 덧없는

IN BRIEF Lasting a very short time

+ transient, temporary, fugitive, momentary, evanescent, transitory

> Journalism is important but ephemeral.
> (저널리즘은 중요하긴 하지만 덧없다.)

0699
ethereal [iθíːriəl]
a. 가뿐한; 공기 같은; 하늘의; 무형의, 에테르의

IN BRIEF Extremely delicate or refined; exquisite, almost as light as air; impalpable; airy, celestial or spiritual

+ delicate, light, fine, subtle, refined, exquisite, insubstantial, light, fairy, aerial, airy, intangible, spiritual, heavenly, unearthly, sublime, celestial, unworldly

> In his recent study of the ethereal aspects of sound, David Toop defines sound as formlessness, a medium that haunts places and people.
> (소리의 무형적 측면에 대한 그의 최근 연구에서, 데이비드 톱은 소리를 모양이 없는 것으로서, 여러 장소와 사람들을 따라다니는 매개물로 정의하고 있다.)

LESSON 15

0700
eradicate [irǽdəkèit]
vt. 근절하다 → 박멸하다 → 절멸시키다 → 뿌리뽑다
IN BRIEF To destroy thoroughly
+ eliminate, remove, obliterate, uproot, efface, exterminate

Smallpox has now been eradicated.
(천연두는 이제 근절되었다.)

0701
erode [iróud]
v. 부식(침식)되다 (gradually wash away)
IN BRIEF To wear away
+ disintegrate, crumble, spoil, abrade, deteriorate, corrode

Metals are eroded by acids. (금속은 산에 부식한다.)

0702
erroneous [iróuniəs]
a. 잘못된 → 그릇된 → 틀린
IN BRIEF Wrong; illusion
+ incorrect, false, fallacious, invalid, inaccurate, spurious

He had the erroneous impression that the more it cost the better it must be.
(그는 값이 비쌀수록 더 좋을 것이라는 잘못된 생각을 가지고 있었다.)

0703
erudite [érjudàit]
a. 학식이 있는, 박식한; 학자적인(specialized)
IN BRIEF Having or showing great knowledge or learning
+ learned, scholarly, educated, literate, cultivated

Dr. Ahn is a witty and immensely erudite man.
(안 박사는 기지가 있고 엄청나게 박식한 사람이다.)

0704
eschew [ɪs'tʃuː]
v. 피하다, 삼가다
IN BRIEF To avoid using, accepting, participating in, or partaking of
+ avoid, burke, bypass, circumvent, dodge, duck

A young doctor with psychiatric training eschewed the science that had so enamored earlier child-rearing professionals.
(정신의학 교육을 받은 젊은 의사는 초창기 육아 전문가들을 그렇게도 매료시켰던 학문을 회피했다.)

0705
essential [isénʃəl]
a. 필수의
IN BRIEF Most important or absolutely necessary
+ vital, important, necessary, crucial, key

Good health is essential to success in life.
(건강은 인생의 성공에 필수 불가결하다.)

0706
establish [istǽbliʃ]
vt. 설립하다; 확립하다; 증명하다
IN BRIEF To set up or to settle, to show to be true or to prove
+ found, institute, prove, confirm, verify, ratify

They plan to establish an art institute.
(그들은 미술 협회를 설립할 계획이다.)

0707
estate [istéit]
n. 재산, 소유지; 단지
IN BRIEF One's interest in land or other property
+ assets, domain, property, manor

He succeeded to his father's estate.
(그는 아버지 재산을 상속했다.)

0708
esteem [istíːm]
vt. 존경[존중]하다 → (물건) 소중하게 여기다
IN BRIEF To have a good opinion of or regard as valuable
+ respect, regard, honour, admiration, reverence, veneration

She is held in high esteem by those who know her well.
(그녀는 그녀를 잘 아는 사람들로부터 높은 존경을 받고 있다.)

0709
evaporate [ivǽpərèit]
v. (물) 증발시키다 → (희망·열의) 사라지다(disappear)
IN BRIEF To change from a liquid or solid into a gas, to fade away or disappear
+ dry up, dissolve, dehydrate, vaporize, desiccate

The water soon evaporated in the sunshine.
(그 물은 햇빛에 곧 증발해 버렸다.)

0710
eulogy [júːlədʒi]

n. 찬미(praise), 칭송, 찬양, 찬사

IN BRIEF A formal speech praising a person who has just died

➕ praise, acclamation, applause, celebration, commendation, compliment, encomium, kudos, laudation, panegyric, plaudit

> The song was a eulogy to the joys of travelling.
> (그 노래는 여행의 기쁨에 대한 찬미였다.)

0711
evacuate [ivǽkjuèit]

v. 철수시키다, 피난시키다; 소개하다

IN BRIEF To withdraw or depart from; vacate

➕ withdraw, expel, clear, remove, vacate

> Families in the area were urged to evacuate their homes immediately.
> (그 지역에 사는 가족들은 집에서 즉시 대피하도록 재촉 받았다.)

0712
etymologist [ètəmálədʒist]

어원학자, 어원 연구가(A specialist in etymology)

IN BRIEF A lexicographer who specializes in etymology

➕ lexicographer, lexicologist

0713
evince [ivíns]

vt. (감정) 분명히 나타내다, 명시하다(show clearly)

IN BRIEF To show clearly or to indicate

➕ evidence, reveal, demonstrate, manifest, express, attest

> He evinced a strong desire to be reconciled with his family. (그는 가족과 화해할 강한 바람을 나타냈다.)

0714
evoke [ivóuk]

vt. (기억) 되살려내다, 일으키다, 자아내다, 불러일으키다

IN BRIEF To call or summon forth; stimulate

➕ arouse, cause, stimulate, induce, awaken, provoke, elicit

> The music evoked memories of her youth.
> (그 음악은 그녀에게 젊은 시절의 기억을 불러일으켰다.)

0715
evolve [ivάlv]

서서히 발전[전개]하다 → 점진적으로 변화하다 → (생물)진화하다

IN BRIEF To develop or achieve gradually

➕ develop, adapt, progress, elaborate, enlarge, expand

> There are lots of factors that evolve living things.
> (생물을 진화시키는 많은 인자(요소)가 있다.)

0716
exacerbate [igzǽsərbèit]

(병) 악화시키다, (감정) 격화시키다

IN BRIEF To make more sharp, severe, or virulent

➕ irritate, worsen, intensify, infuriate, aggravate

> Scratching exacerbates a skin rash.
> (피부발진은 긁으면 악화된다.)

0717
exaggerate [igzǽdʒərèit]

v. 과장하다↔understate

IN BRIEF To make seem larger or greater than it really is

➕ emphasize, enlarge, embroider, overstate

> Ahntonio always exaggerates to make his stories more amusing.
> (안토니오는 자신의 이야기를 더 재미있게 만들기 위해 항상 과장을 한다.)

0718
exasperate [igzǽspərèit]

성나게 하다 → 격분시키다(야마돌게 하다)

IN BRIEF To trouble the nerves or peace of mind of, especially by repeated vexations

➕ upset, provoke, aggravate, annoy, bother, irritate, frustrate

> The constant noise exasperated him.
> (그 끊임없는 소음이 그를 노하게 했다.)

0719
exceed [iksíːd]

v. (수량·정도·한도)넘다, 초과하다(more than)

IN BRIEF Be or do something to a greater degree

➕ surpass, transcend, surmount, excel, outstrip

> The price will not exceed $100.
> (가격이 100달러를 넘지는 않을 것이다.)

0720
exclusively [iksklúːsivli]

ad. 배타적으로; 전적으로

IN BRIEF Excluding or tending to exclude

➕ solely, totally, fully, entirely, wholly, uniquely

> With the terrorist attacks of 2001, a new era began and the "war on terror" was launched. Before 2001, the government focused its efforts almost exclusively on a handful of immigrants and activists and especially on immigrant activists.
> (2001년의 테러 공격으로, 새로운 시대가 시작되었고 '테러와의 전쟁'이 개시되었다. 2001년 이전에는 정부가 그 노력을 거의 전적으로 그 수가 얼마 안 되는 이민자들과 운동가들 그리고 특히 이민자 운동가들에게만 집중했다.)

0721
exonerate [ɪɡ|zɑːnəreɪt]

v. 결백을[무죄를] 증명하다; ~의 혐의를 벗겨 주다; 면제하다, 해방하다

IN BRIEF To free from blame

+ absolve, clear, exculpate, vindicate

> A thorough investigation exonerated the school from any blame and recommended only a few minor changes.
> (철저한 조사를 통해 학교는 모든 비난으로부터 벗어났고, 몇 가지 사소한 변화를 권고 받았을 뿐이다.)

0722
exhaustive [ɪɡzɔ́ːstɪv]

a. 철저한 → 속속들이 규명해 내는 → 남김 없는(thoroughgoing) / 고갈시키는(소모적인)

IN BRIEF Complete or thorough

+ all-inclusive, complete, thorough

> These are findings we should not dismiss without exhaustive testing.
> (이것들은 철저한 검증 없이는 종결시킬 수 없는 조사 결과들이다.)

0723
exhilarating [ɪɡzíləreɪtɪŋ]

a. 신나는, 유쾌한, 상쾌한(cheerful)

IN BRIEF Causing exhilaration; invigorating

+ exciting, thrilling, stimulating, breathtaking, cheering, exalting

> My first parachute jump was an exhilarating experience.
> (나의 첫 낙하산 점프는 유쾌한 경험이었다.)

0724
exhort [ɪɡzɔ́ːrt]

간곡히 타이르다, 권하다(urge) → 훈계[권고]하다 (admonish)

IN BRIEF To try to influence by words or advice

+ to impel to action(press, urge, advise)

> The teacher kept exhorting us to work harder.
> (선생님은 우리들에게 더 열심히 공부하라고 계속 타일렀다.)

0725
exhortation [èɡzɔːrtéɪʃən]

간곡한 권유, 충고, 훈계(advice, urging)

IN BRIEF A speech or discourse that encourages, incites, or earnestly advises

+ urging, warning, advice, counsel, lecture, caution

> In spite of my exhortation, they went ahead with the plan.
> (내 충고에도 불구하고, 그들은 그 계획을 계속 추진했다.)

0726
excel [ɪksél]

v. 뛰어나다 → 탁월하다 → 빼어나다 → 탁월하다(very good)

IN BRIEF To be superior or distinguished

+ be superior; surpass, exceed, transcend, outdo

> She excels me in English. (그녀는 영어에서 나보다 뛰어나다.)

0727
exorbitant [ɪɡ|zɔːrbɪtənt]

a. 과도한, 지나친

IN BRIEF Going beyond what is reasonable or customary, especially in cost or price

+ extortionate, usurious, outrageous, steep, unconscionable

> Three telecommunications companies have threatened to sue the government over the cancellation of the original arrangement, claiming that the recent increases in operation costs are too exorbitant for them to absorb.
> (3개의 통신회사는 정부가 당초의 합의를 취소한 것에 대해 정부를 고소할 조짐을 보여 왔는데, 그들은 최근에 운영경비의 증가가 감당할 수 없을 정도로 너무 과도하다고 주장하고 있다.)

0728
exotic [ɪɡzátɪk]

a. 외래의, 외국산의; 이국풍의; 별난, 색다른

IN BRIEF Alien, foreign, strange

+ unusual, extraordinary, bizarre, curious, glamorous, peculiar

> She was attracted by his exotic features.
> (그녀는 그의 이국적인 용모에 끌렸다.)

0729
exploit [éksplɔɪt]

n. 영웅적 행위, 공훈, 위업(feat, achievement) / v. (이용)개발하다(use) → 착취하다 → 과대선전하다

IN BRIEF An act or deed, especially a brilliant or heroic one/To employ to the greatest possible advantage

+ feat, effort/take advantage of, abuse, use, manipulate, milk

> His exploits as an explorer brought him fame and wealth.
> (그의 탐험가로서의 공적은 그에게 영예와 부를 가져다주었다.)

0730
exponent [ɪkspóʊnənt]

n. 주창자, 옹호자, 대표자; 설명자

IN BRIEF One that expounds or interprets

+ advocate, supporter, defender, promoter, proponent

> Huxley was an exponent of Darwin's theory of evolution.
> (헉슬리는 다윈의 진화론 옹호자였다.)

0731
expostulation [ikspɑ̀stʃuléiʃən]

훈계, 충고, 권고(exhortation)

IN BRIEF The act of expressing strong or reasoned opposition

+ challenge, demur, exception, objection, protest

> Despite the teacher's scoldings and expostulations, the class remained unruly.
> (교사의 꾸지람과 훈계에도 불구하고, 학생들은 제멋대로 굴었다.)

0732
exposure [ikspóuʒər]

n. 드러남 → 노출(experience of) → 탄로, 폭로

IN BRIEF Position in relation to the sun, elements, or points of the compass

+ uncovering, exhibition, baring, revelation, display

> The color faded from long exposure to the sun.
> (장시간 태양에 노출되어 빛깔이 바랬다.)

0733
expound [ikspáund]

vt. 자세히 설명하다 → 해석[해설]하다

IN BRIEF To explain clearly

+ construe, decipher, explain, explicate, interpret

> He expounded his views on education to me at great length.
> (그는 교육에 대한 자신의 견해를 내게 장황하게 설명했다.)

0734
expurgate [ékspərgèit]

(영화, 책에서 불온한 대목을) 삭제하다; 정화하다(censored)

IN BRIEF To amend by removing words deemed objectionable

+ censor, cut, clean up, purge, purify, blue-pencil, sanitize, bowdlerize

> Perhaps an expurgated edition of the novel would be more appropriate for the less sophisticated students.
> (아마도 그 소설의 검열 삭제판이 덜 세속적인 학생들에게는 더 적절할 것이다.)

0735
entitlement [intáitlmənt]

n. 권리, 자격

IN BRIEF The act or process of entitling, The state of being entitled

+ right, claim, due, licence, permission, privilege, prerogative, allowance, grant, quota, ration, allocation, allotment, apportionment

> Being the favorite may boost self-esteem and confidence. But studies show it can also leave kids with a sense of arrogance and entitlement.
> (부모의 편애를 받는 것은 자존감과 자신감을 높여줄지 모른다. 그러나 연구조사가 보여주는 바로는 그것은 또한 아이들에게 오만감과 당연시하는 권리의식을 갖게 한다.)

0736
extemporize [ikstémpəràiz]

즉석에서 만들다 → 즉석에서 연설[작곡, 연주, 노래]하다 → 임시변통 하다

IN BRIEF To improvise a speech

+ improvise, ad-lib, fake, improvise: without preparation

> He forgot his words and had to extemporize.
> (그는 연설 내용을 잊어 버려서 즉흥 연설을 해야 했다.)

0737
extensive [iksténsiv]

a. 광범위한, 광대한, 넓은 (affluent, broad)

IN BRIEF Having a wide scope, effect or influence

+ large, considerable, substantial, spacious, wide, sweeping

> The school has extensive grounds.
> (그 학교에는 아주 넓은 운동장이 있다.)

0738
extinct [ikstíŋkt]

(불)꺼진(extinguished) → (희망)끊어진, 사라진 → (생명·생물)멸종된

IN BRIEF No longer in use; no longer existing

+ asleep, dead, deceased, defunct, departed, gone, late, lifeless

> These animals are virtually extinct.
> (이들 동물은 사실상 멸종된 상태다.)

0739
extirpate [ékstərpèit]

v. (해충) 근절[절멸]하다(root out)

IN BRIEF To destroy, to pull up by the roots

+ destroy; uproot, eradicate, annihilate, obliterate

> The country must extirpate the evils of drug abuse.
> (그 나라는 마약 남용이라는 악을 뿌리 뽑아야 한다.)

0740
embrace [embréis]

v. 포옹하다, 기꺼이 받아들이다, 수용하다

IN BRIEF To clasp or hold close with the arms, usually as an expression of affection

+ hug, hold, cuddle, seize, squeeze, grasp, clasp, accept, support, receive, welcome, adopt, grab, take up, seize, make use of, espouse, include, involve, cover, deal with, contain, take in, incorporate, comprise

> Nancy and Heather discovered how to embrace each other's differences and a strong bond grew between the two women.
> (낸시와 헤더는 서로의 차이를 수용하는 방법을 깨달았고 그 두 여성 사이에 강한 유대감이 생겨났다.)

0741
extraneous [ikstréiniəs]
a. 이질적인, (주제와) 관계없는

IN BRIEF Not forming an essential part

+ irrelevant, inappropriate, unrelated, impertinent, inapt, inapposite

> Your comment is actually extraneous to the topic.
> (너의 말은 사실 이 주제와 관련이 없다.)

0742
envisage [invízidʒ]
v. 마음속에 그리다, 상상하다

IN BRIEF To form a mental image of; visualize; contemplate

+ conceive of, ideate, imagine

> How can you get ahead of competition? First, you need to develop a business plan and clearly envisage how you will make money, what your expenses will be and what will make your business unique and superior.
> (어떻게 하면 경쟁에서 앞설 수 있을까? 우선, 사업계획을 세우고, 어떻게 돈을 벌 것인지, 비용은 얼마가 될 지, 무엇이 사업을 독특하고 뛰어나게 해줄지를 명확하게 구상해야 한다.)

0743
endowment [indáumənt]
n. 기부금

IN BRIEF Funds or property donated to an institution, individual, or group as a source of income

+ provision, fund, funding, award, income, grant, gift, contribution, revenue, subsidy, presentation, donation, legacy, hand-out, boon, bequest, stipend, bestowal, benefaction

> Officials at private institutions of higher learning do not have to worry about budget issues since they have huge endowments.
> (사립 고등교육기관의 직원들은 예산문제에 관해 걱정할 필요가 없는데, 왜냐하면 이들은 막대한 기부금을 받고 있기 때문이다.)

0744
exalt [igzɔ́:lt]
v. (지위, 명예 등을) 높이다(promote)

IN BRIEF To raise or elevate in rank, position, dignity, etc. to praise highly; glorify; extol

+ praise, acclaim, applaud, pay tribute to, bless, worship, magnify (archaic), glorify, reverence, laud, extol, crack up

> In recent manifestations, Western civilization has tended to exalt science and its technological applications at the expense of the arts.
> (최근 징후를 보면, 서구 문명은 인문과학을 희생시킨 채 과학과 기술의 응용을 숭상하는 경향이 있어 왔다.)

0745
extract [ikstrǽkt]
vt. (이빨)뽑다 → 발췌(인용)하다 → 추출하다

IN BRIEF To draw or pull out, often with great force or effort

+ take out, draw, remove, withdraw, bring out

> I can extract it very slowly if you like.
> (원하시면 천천히 뽑아 드릴수도 있어요.)

0746
equality [i(:)kwáləti]
n. 같음; 평등

IN BRIEF The state or quality of being equal

+ equation, equivalence, equivalency, par, parity, sameness

> Forget what you may have heard about a digital divide or worries that the world is splintering into "info haves" and "info have nots." The fact is, technology fosters equality, and it's often the relatively cheap and mundane devices that do the most good.
> (정보격차에 대해 들어보았을지 모르는 말 혹은 세상은 '정보유산자'와 '정보무산자'로 나눠지고 있다는 걱정의 말들은 잊어버려라. 사실, 기술은 평등을 촉진하며, 가장 도움이 되는 것이 상대적으로 저렴하고 일상적인 장치인 경우가 종종 있다.)

0747
expatriate [ekspéitrièit]
n. 국외에 거주하는 사람, 해외 주재[근무]하는 사람

IN BRIEF Resident in a foreign country, exiled or banished from one's native country

+ banish, deport, exile, expel, ostracize, transport

> He's been working in Barcelona for a year, but his friends are all expatriates, not local people.
> (그는 1년 동안 바르셀로나에서 일하고 있지만, 그의 친구들은 모두 현지인들이 아닌 국외 거주자들이다.)

0748
extravagance [ikstrǽvəgəns]
사치(품), 낭비(wastefulness)

IN BRIEF The quality of being extravagant

+ overspending, squandering, profusion, lavishness, improvidence

> He can not afford such extravagances.
> (그는 그러한 사치를 즐길 여유가 없다.)

0749
exquisite [ikskwízit]
아주 아름다운(very beautiful) → 정교한(delicate); 우아한 → 섬세한(nice)

IN BRIEF Very beautiful, done with great care and skill

+ beautiful, excellent, dainty, delicate, elegant

> The jewellery showed exquisite craftsmanship.
> (그 보석은 장인의 정교한 솜씨를 보여주었다.)

LESSON 16

0750
extol [ɪk|stoʊl]
칭찬하다, 극찬하다
IN BRIEF To pay tribute or homage to
[+] exalt, hail, laud, praise

Where reason finds regularity in nature, faith extols miracles that overturn that regularity.
(이성이 자연 속에서 질서를 찾아내는 반면, 믿음은 그러한 질서를 뒤집는 기적들을 찬양한다.)

0751
fable [féibəl]
n. 우화
IN BRIEF A very short story, usually dealing with animals, that teaches a lesson
[+] legend, myth, parable, apologue, tale

Aesop wrote many fables.
(이솝은 많은 우화를 썼다.)

0752
fabrication [fæ̀brikéiʃən]
n. 조작, 날조; 제작
IN BRIEF Manufacture; something fabricated; an untruthful statement
[+] forgery, fiction, invention, figment, fable

The newspaper story turned out to be a complete fabrication.
(그 신문기사는 순전히 날조된 것으로 밝혀졌다.)

0753
face [feis]
n. 정면으로 맞서다, 향하다
IN BRIEF To have the face or front turned in a specific direction
[+] encounter, cope with, confront, defy, oppose

We are powerless in the face of such a threat.
(그러한 위협에 직면하면 우리는 무력해진다.)

0754
facility [fəsíləti]
n. 쉬움, 유창함, 재주, 솜씨, 설비(시설)
IN BRIEF Something that serves a specific function
[+] amenity, means, aid, convenience, appliance, fluency

They afforded every facility for the students.
(그들은 학생들에게 온갖 편의를 제공했다.)

0755
facet [fǽsit]
n. (다각형 기둥의) 면, 일면, 국면, 양상
IN BRIEF A small polished surface of a cut gem; aspect; phase; side
[+] aspect, part, phase, angle, side

Now let's look at another facet of the problem.
(자 이제 그 문제의 또 다른 일면을 살펴보기로 합시다.)

0756
faint [feint]
a. (빛·소리·색깔·기억·생각·기회) 희미한, 어렴풋한, 엷은; 흐릿한
IN BRIEF Done with little strength or vigor; feeble
[+] indistinct, slight, feeble, remote, vague, slender, unenthusiastic

I heard a faint voice. (나는 어렴풋한 목소리를 들었다.)

0757
fair [fɛər]
a. 전적으로 공정한 [공평한] / n. 품평회, 전시회, 박람회, 시장 (market)
IN BRIEF In a proper or legal manner
[+] impartial, unprejudiced, equal, equitable, trustworthy

She deserves a fair trial.
(그녀는 공정한 재판을 받을 권리가 있다.)
I have an exhibit at the science fair.
(나는 과학 박람회에 출품했다.)

0758
fallacious [fəléiʃəs]
불합리한, 틀린(faulty)
IN BRIEF Containing or based on a fallacy
[+] incorrect, misleading, deceptive, fictitious, delusive

His argument is based on fallacious reasoning.
(그의 주장은 잘못된 추론에 근거를 두고 있다.)

0759
fallout [fɔ́ːlàut]
n. 방사성 낙진; 부산물, (예상치 못한) 무수석인 결과, 여파, 영향
IN BRIEF The slow descent of minute particles of debris in the atmosphere following an explosion, especially the descent of radioactive debris after a nuclear explosion.
[+] consequences, results, outcome, repercussions, effects

Nuclear-fallout pollutes Antarctic snow.
(핵폐기물이 남극의 눈을 오염시킨다.)

0760
falter [fɔ́ːltər]

v. 움찔하다(비틀거리다), 망설이다, 말을 더듬다, 우물거리다

IN BRIEF To be unsteady in purpose or action, as from loss of courage or confidence; waver

+ hesitate, pause, stutter, stumble, stammer

> Never falter in doing good.
> (선행을 하는 데 망설이지 마라.)

0761
fancy [fǽnsi]

n. 기호; 상상, 환상

IN BRIEF Imagination or fantasy, esp. as exercised in a capricious manner

+ imagine, delusion, fantasy, daydream, vision, phantasm

> Fancy never having seen the sea!
> (바다를 한번도 못 봤다고 상상해 봐!)

0762
far-fetched [faːr fetʃ]

빙 둘러서 말하는; 무리한(forced); 부자연한, 억지의

IN BRIEF Not readily believable because of improbable elements therein

+ unconvincing, dubious, doubtful, implausible, improbable

> The film's plot is interesting but rather far-fetched.
> (그 영화의 플롯은 재미있지만 좀 억지스럽다.)

0763
far-reaching

멀리까지 미치는(광범위한), (계획 따위가) 원대한(extensive)

IN BRIEF Having a wide range, influence, or effect

+ all-around, all-inclusive, all-round, broad, broad-spectrum, comprehensive

> Cuts in educational spending will have far-reaching implications for the future.
> (교육비 삭감은 미래에 대해 원대한 영향을 미치게 될 것이다.)

0764
fascinate [fǽsənèit]

v. 황홀하게 하다, 매혹하다 (attract)

IN BRIEF To capture and hold the interest and attention of

+ entrance, absorb, intrigue, allure, bewitch, beguile, captivate

> She was a fascinating young lady.
> (그녀는 매혹적인 젊은 숙녀였다.)

0765
fashionable [fǽʃənəbəl]

a. 유행하는

IN BRIEF Conforming to the current styles or trends; stylish

+ popular, trendy, stylish, customary, prevailing

> It is becoming fashionable to have short hair again.
> (다시 짧은 머리를 하는 것이 유행이 되고 있다.)

0766
fatal [féitl]

a. 치명적인 (mortal), 결정적인, 피할 수 없는 (숙명적인, 불가피한)

IN BRIEF Causing death. disastrous or very unfortunate

+ disastrous, lethal, calamitous, baleful, baneful, catastrophic

> The drunk driver caused a fatal accident.
> (그 음주 운전자는 치명적인 사고를 일으켰다.)

0767
fathom [fǽðəm]

(수심)을 재다; (마음)을 헤아리다, 추측하다

IN BRIEF To penetrate to the meaning or nature of; comprehend

+ understand, grasp, comprehend, interpret

> I'm trying to fathom out the motives behind his proposal.
> (나는 그의 제안 이면에 있는 동기를 헤아리려고 노력하는 중이다.)

0768
fatigue [fətíːg]

n. 피로

IN BRIEF Physical or mental weariness resulting from effort or activity

+ tiredness, lethargy, weariness, ennui, debility

> He was suffering from fatigue.
> (그는 피로에 괴로워하고 있었다.)

0769
fatuous [fǽtʃuəs]

a. 어리석은, 얼빠진

IN BRIEF Foolish or silly, especially in a smug or self-satisfied way

+ Foolish or stupid. insensate, mindless, senseless, silly

> Insisting on a luxury car you cannot afford is fatuous.
> (당신이 살 여유도 없는데 고급 차를 고집하는 것은 어리석은 일이다.)

0770
feasible [ˈfiːzəbl]

a. 실행할 수 있는, 실행 가능한

IN BRIEF Capable of being accomplished or brought about; possible

[+] executable, viable, workable, practicable

> While it is feasible to build a balloon and sent it up into space, no amateur-made spacecraft has reached the limits of the Earth's atmosphere.
> (기구를 만들어 우주로 보내는 것은 실행 가능하지만, 비전문가가 만든 어떠한 우주 비행선도 지구 대기권의 경계선에 도달하지 못했다.)

0771
feast [fiːst]

n. 축제, 연회

IN BRIEF To give a feast for; entertain or feed sumptuously

[+] festival, celebration, holiday, banquet

> The feast is toward.
> (잔치가 막 시작되려 하고 있다.)

0772
feeble [ˈfiːbəl]

약한, 가냘픈, 연약한

IN BRIEF Weak, infirm, insubstantial

[+] not strong; ineffective, decrepit, delicate, flimsy, fragile, frail, puny

> Superstition is the religion of feeble minds.
> (미신은 연약한 마음들이 믿는 종교이다.)

0773
felicity [fəˈlɪsəti]

n. 더할 나위 없는 행복; 절묘하게 어울림

IN BRIEF Great happiness; bliss; a skillful faculty

[+] happiness, joy, ecstasy, bliss, delectation, blessedness, blissfulness

> Human felicity is produced not so much by great pieces of good fortune that seldom happen, as by little advantages that occur every day.
> (인간의 행복은 좀처럼 일어나지 않는 큰 행운에 의해서보다는 매일매일 일어나는 작은 좋은 일들에 의해서 발생된다.)

0774
ferocious [fəˈroʊʃəs]

a. 흉포한, 사나운, 잔인한

IN BRIEF Extremely aggressive or violent

[+] violent, barbaric, fierce, savage, predatory, cruel, ruthless, relentless

> He is no better than a ferocious beast.
> (그는 사나운 짐승이나 다름없다.)

0775
fertile [ˈfɜːrtl]

a. (땅이) 기름진, 비옥한; 다산의

IN BRIEF Biology capable of producing offspring

[+] productive, prolific, plentiful, fruitful, fecund, abundant

> The soil here is fertile.
> (이곳은 땅이 비옥하다.)

0776
fickle [ˈfɪkəl]

a. 변하기 쉬운, 변덕스러운

IN BRIEF Vacillating, blowing hot and cold

[+] capricious, volatile, mercurial, mutable, temperamental, variable

> The weather here is notoriously fickle.
> (이곳의 날씨는 변덕스럽기로 악명 높다.)

0777
fictitious [fɪkˈtɪʃəs]

a. 거짓의, 허구의, 진짜가 아닌, 가공의

IN BRIEF Spurious, fake; fictional; created or assumed with the intention to conceal

[+] false, bogus, counterfeit, artificial, spurious, apocryphal

> All the places and characters in my novel are entirely fictitious.
> (내 소설 속의 모든 장소와 인물은 전적으로 허구이다.)

0778
filthy [ˈfɪlθi]

불결한, 더러운

IN BRIEF Covered or smeared with filth; disgustingly dirty

[+] dirty, nasty, slimy, squalid, feculent

> The whole Ahntonio's house is absolutely filthy.
> (안토니오의 온 집안은 너무도 불결하다.)

0779
fix [fɪks]

n. 고정적으로 공급되는 일정량의 소식; 일정량의 마약 v / 고정, 수리, 마련(준비), 집중하다

IN BRIEF Cause to be firmly attached

[+] place, join, stick, attach, set, position, couple, plant, link

> Click here to get your daily fix of showbiz and celebrity news.
> (매일 연예계와 유명 인사들의 소식을 전달받기 위해서는 여기를 클릭하시오.)

0780
firsthand [-hǽnd]
a. 직접, 바로; 직접 체험에 의해

IN BRIEF From the first or original source; directly

➕ direct, immediate, personal

> He always experience everything firsthand.
> (그는 항상 모든 것을 직접 경험한다.)

0781
fit [fit]
a. 체력이 튼튼한, 건강한; 적합한(healthy, in good health)

IN BRIEF To be appropriate or suitable for

➕ appropriate, suitable, robust, athletic, competent

> "What do you do to keep fit?" "I swim and play tennis."
> ("건강을 지키기 위해 뭘 하세요?" "수영과 테니스를 합니다.")

0782
finite [fáinait]
a. 제한[한정]된, 유한의

IN BRIEF Having bounds; limited

➕ limited, restricted, conditioned, circumscribed, terminable

> Human understanding is finite.
> (인간의 이해력은 한정되어 있다.)

0783
flank [flæŋk]
n. 옆구리; (건물·산 따위의) 측면

IN BRIEF The side of a man or animal between the ribs and the hip

➕ side, quarter, aspect, sector

> The rider dug his spurs into the horse's flank.
> (그 기수는 말의 옆구리에 박차를 가했다.)

0784
flat [flæt]
a. 평평한, 기복이 없는, 평탄한; 밋밋한; 수평의(inactive)

IN BRIEF Having a smooth, even surface

➕ level, plane, uniform, horizontal, planar

> People used to believe that the world was flat.
> (사람들은 예전에 지구가 평평하다고 믿었다.)

0785
flatter [flǽtər]
vt. 아첨하다, 알랑거리다, 비위 맞추다

IN BRIEF Praise too much

➕ compliment, fawn, cajole, soap, blandish

> He flatters her outrageously, and she swallows it whole.
> (그는 그녀에게 터무니없는 아부를 하고 그녀는 그것을 그대로 믿는다.)

0786
flaw [flɔː]
n. 결점, 흠

IN BRIEF An imperfection, often concealed, that impairs soundness

➕ error, fault, blunder, spot, defect, scar

> The vase is perfect except for a few small flaws in its base.
> (그 꽃병은 바닥에 작은 흠이 몇 개 있는 것 외에는 완벽하다.)

0787
flee [fliː]
도망치다, 달아나다

IN BRIEF Vanish; evade, escape, avoid, shun, elude; to run away from

➕ leave, escape, vanish, depart, abscond, avoid

> The customers fled from the bank when the alarm sounded.
> (경보가 울리자 손님들이 은행에서 도피했다.)

0788
flimsy [flímzi]
a. 부서지기 쉬운, 약한, (근거·이론) 설득력이 없는, 불충분한

IN BRIEF Light, thin, and insubstantial

➕ weak, not strong; light, thin, decrepit, delicate, feeble, fragile, frail, infirm, insubstantial, puny, unsound, unsubstantial, weak

> The evidence against him is pretty flimsy.
> (그에 반대되는 증거는 상당히 박약하다.)

0789
flip [flip]
튀기다; 홱 던지다

IN BRIEF To throw or toss with a light brisk motion

➕ flick, throw, cast, snap, pitch

> He gave a coin a flip.
> (그는 동전을 홱 던졌다.)

0790
farrago [fəréigou]
n. 잡동사니; 뒤죽박죽

IN BRIEF An assortment or a medley; a conglomeration

➕ hotchpotch, mixture, jumble, medley, hash, mixed bag, miscellany, mishmash, hodgepodge, salmagundi, gallimaufry

> This research paper contains proactive and affirmative insights but they were buried in a farrago of half-truth and groundless speculation.
> (이 연구논문은 사전대책을 강구하는 긍정적인 통찰력을 포함하고 있지만, 절반의 진실과 근거 없는 추측의 뒤죽박죽 속에 그 통찰력들은 묻혀버렸다.)

0791
float [flout]
v. 띄우다; 뜨다; 떠돌아다니다

IN BRIEF To remain suspended within or on the surface of a fluid without sinking

+ glide, coast, drift, waft, hover

> A balloon floated across the sky.
> (풍선이 하늘을 둥둥 떠갔다.)

0792
figure [fígjər]
n. 숫자; 합계, 값; 모양; 인물

IN BRIEF A written or printed symbol representing something other than a letter, especially a number, Mathematical calculations, An amount represented in numbers, One of the digits specified as making up a larger number

+ price, cost, value, amount, total, sum

> The sculpture has been purchased for an undisclosed figure with assistance from the art fund.
> (그 조각상은 미술품 펀드의 도움을 받아 밝혀지지 않은 액수에 구입되었다.)

0793
fluorescent [flù-ərésnt]
형광성의, 형광을 발하는(luminous)

IN BRIEF Brilliantly colored and apparently giving off light

+ fluorescent fixture

> Change the a fluorescent lamp!
> (형광등을 갈아라!)

0794
flush [flʌʃ]
v. (볼의) 홍조, 얼굴 붉힘

IN BRIEF To turn red, as from fever, embarrassment, or strong emotion; blush

+ red, blush, flame, crimson, redden, glow

> A pink flush spread over his cheeks.
> (그의 두 뺨에 홍조가 번졌다.)

0795
foliage [fóuliidʒ]
n. 잎

IN BRIEF Plant leaves, especially tree leaves

+ leaf, needle, leaves

> My flower arrangement needs more foliage.
> (나의 꽃꽂이에는 잎이 좀 더 많아야겠다.)

0796
flippant [flípənt]
a. 경솔한, 경박한; 건방진, 뻔뻔스러운

IN BRIEF Marked by inappropriate levity; frivolous or offhand

+ frivolous, rude, irreverent, impertinent, impudent

> Don't be so flippant this is an important matter.
> (그렇게 까불지 마. 이건 중요한 문제야.)

0797
fluctuate [flʌ́ktʃuèit]
v. 변동하다, 오르락내리락 하다, 동요하다

IN BRIEF To vary irregularly, especially in amount

+ vary, alter, hesitate, alternate, oscillate, vacillate

> Vegetable prices fluctuate according to the season.
> (채소 가격은 계절에 따라 변동한다.)

0798
facetious [fəsí:ʃəs]
a. 익살맞은, 우스운

IN BRIEF Cleverly amusing in tone; cleverly amusing in tone

+ flippant, funny, amusing, witty, merry, humorous, playful, pleasant, frivolous, tongue in cheek, comical, jesting, droll, jocular, waggish, unserious, jocose

> Our proposal about shipping our town's garbage to the moon was facetious, but the first selectman took it seriously.
> (우리 도시의 쓰레기를 달로 보내는 것에 관한 우리의 제안은 우스운 것이었지만, 행정위원장은 그 제안을 진지하게 받아들였다.)

0799
fertility [fəːrtíləti]
n. 다산; 풍부, 기름짐, 비옥, 독창성, 생식력

IN BRIEF The condition, quality, or degree of being fertile, The birthrate of a population

+ fecundity, fruitfulness, productiveness, productivity, prolificacy, prolificness, richness

> Ball games were connected to fertility in primitive societies. People believed that success in ball games would help their crops to grow and help the players to produce children as well.
> (원시 사회에서 구기경기는 다산과 관련되어 있었다. 사람들은 구기경기에서의 승리가 곡식이 잘 자라도록 도와주고 또한 선수들이 자녀를 얻도록 도와준다고 믿었다.)

LESSON 17

0800
folly [fáli]

n. 어리석음, 우둔

IN BRIEF Lack of good sense, understanding, or foresight

➕ stupidity, absurdity, silliness, imprudence, idiocy

> It's utter folly to go swimming in this weather.
> (이런 날씨에 수영을 하러 가는 것은 완전히 바보 같은 행위다.)

0801
foolproof [fú:lprù:f]

잘못될 수가 없는, 바보라도 할 수 있는, 아주 간단한 (fully reliable)

IN BRIEF Designed so as to be impervious to human incompetence, error, or misuse

➕ infallible, certain, guaranteed, unassailable, unbreakable, safe

> It is a foolproof security system.
> (그것은 절대 안전한 보안 시스템이다.)

0802
forage [fɔ́:ridʒ]

n. 마구 뒤지며 찾다(search for, rummage), 침입하다

IN BRIEF The act of looking or searching for food or provisions

➕ search, scavenge, seek, explore, plunder, rummage

> She foraged about in her handbag, but couldn't find her keys.
> (그녀는 핸드백을 뒤졌지만 열쇠를 찾을 수가 없었다.)

0803
forbidden [fərbídn]

금지된; 금단의(not allowed to do)

IN BRIEF Not permitted by order or law

➕ prohibited, banned, taboo, proscribed, outlawed

> Forbidden fruit is sweetest.
> ((속담) 금단의 열매는 달다.)

0804
foreboding [fɔ:rbóudiŋ]

n. (불길한) 예감, 전조; 예언(presentiment)

IN BRIEF A prediction; a portent of future misfortune; presentiment

➕ omen, prediction, portent, presage, foreshadowing, token

> The letter filled him with foreboding.
> (그 편지를 읽고 그는 불길한 예감에 가득 찼다.)

0805
forsake [fər|seɪk]

그만두다, 버리다

IN BRIEF To give up (something formerly held dear); renounce

➕ desert, abandon, give up

> Due to financial reasons, some scientists are often compelled to forsake their ongoing research projects.
> (재정상의 이유 때문에, 일부 과학자들은 종종 그들이 진행 중인 연구 프로젝트를 그만둘 수밖에 없다.)

0806
forge [fɔ:rdʒ]

이끌어내다(form, establish, shape, frame, create), 위조하다(counterfeit)

IN BRIEF To fashion or reproduce for fraudulent purposes; counterfeit

➕ create, establish, set up, fashion, shape, frame, construct, invent, devise

> The government intends to forge ahead with the job of deregulating the economy.
> (정부는 경제에 대한 규제 철폐 작업을 서서히 추진할 의향이다.)

0807
formerly [fɔ́:rmərli]

ad. 이전에(는), 옛날에는

IN BRIEF Happening earlier in time

➕ previously, earlier, already, in the past, before, lately

> The program will employ devices formerly used only for defense purposes.
> (이 프로젝트를 위해 예전에는 국방 프로그램에만 썼던 장비들이 활용될 예정입니다.)

0808
formidable [fɔ́:rmɪdəbl]

가공할만한, 어마어마한

IN BRIEF Arousing fear, dread, or alarm

➕ challenging

> While dealing with formidable economic and diplomatic tasks, President Mubarak embarked on plans for sweeping health care reform.
> (무바라크 대통령은 어려운 경제문제와 외교문제를 처리하면서 전면적인 의료개혁 계획을 시작했다.)

0809
formal [fɔ́ːrm-əl]

a. 형식적인; 의례적인; 정식의

IN BRIEF Relating to or involving outward form or structure, often in contrast to content or meaning

+ official, conventional, traditional, ceremonial, ritualistic

> His politeness is merely formal.
> (그의 정중함은 단지 형식적일 뿐이다.)

0810
forerunner [fɔ́ːrrʌ̀nəːr]

n. 전조; 선구자; 선인(ancestor)

IN BRIEF One that precedes, as in time; a predecessor

+ sign, token, portent, precursory, predecessor, harbinger

> Snowdrops are the forerunner of spring.
> (아네모네는 봄의 전조이다.)

0811
fortify [fɔ́ːrtəfài]

v. 강화하다; 기운을 북돋우다; 요새화하다

IN BRIEF To make strong

+ strengthen, encourage, confirm, cheer, invigorate, supply

> They went into battle fortified by prayer.
> (그들은 기도로 힘을 얻고 전장으로 나갔다.)

0812
fortitude [fɔ́ːrtətjùːd]

n. 인내, 꿋꿋함, 불굴의 정신, 용기

IN BRIEF Strength of mind that allows one to endure pain or adversity with courage

+ courage, strength, guts, patience, endurance, bravery

> He bore the pain with great fortitude.
> (그는 엄청난 인내심으로 그 통증을 감내했다.)

0813
fortuitous [fɔːrtjúːətəs]

a. 우발적인, 우연의, 뜻밖의

IN BRIEF Happening by accident or chance

+ chance, casual, accidental, arbitrary, incidental

> The collapse of its rivals brought fortuitous gains to the company.
> (경쟁 회사의 몰락이 그 회사에 뜻밖의 이득을 가져다주었다.)

0814
foster [fɔ́(ː)stəːr]

(성장·발달) 촉진하다, 육성[조장]하다

IN BRIEF To bring up; nurture

+ raise, nurse, look after, care for, nurture, promote

> They've fostered over 60 children in the last ten years.
> (그들은 지난 10년 동안 60명의 아이들을 양육했다.)

0815
founder [fáundəːr]

(배) 침몰하다, (건물·토지) 붕괴하다, (계획) 실패하다, 설립자

IN BRIEF To fall or sink down; to become wrecked; to stumble; collapse; succumb

+ fail, collapse, sink, submerge, capsize

> The project foundered as a result of lack of finance.
> (그 기획은 재정부족으로 무산되었다.)

0816
fowl [faul]

n. 닭, (집오리·꿩·칠면조 따위의) 가금

IN BRIEF A bird used for food or hunted as game; chicken, turkey, duck, pheasant

+ poultry, bird

> It has led to the culling of millions of fowl.
> (수백만 마리의 가금류가 폐사됐습니다.)

0817
fragile [frǽdʒail]

a. 깨지기 쉬운, 망가지기 쉬운, 부서지기 쉬운

IN BRIEF Easily broken, damaged, or destroyed

+ unstable, weak, vulnerable, delicate, flimsy, insecure, breakable

> Human happiness is so fragile.
> (인간의 행복은 너무도 깨어지기 쉽다.)

0818
fragmentary [frǽgməntèri]

단편으로 이루어진, 단편적인; 부서진; 미완의

IN BRIEF Consisting of small, disconnected parts

+ incomplete, scattered, partial, discrete, sketch

> Early memories of childhood are mostly fragmentary.
> (유년 시절에 대한 어릴 때 기억은 대체로 단편적이다.)

0819
frail [freil]

a. (체질이) 허약한, 약한, 연약한

IN BRIEF Weak; Not physically strong

[+] decrepit, delicate, feeble, flimsy, fragile, infirm, insubstantial, puny, unsound, unsubstantial, weak, weakly

> He is old and rather frail.
> (그는 나이 들고 다소 허약하다.)

0820
frank [fræŋk]

솔직한

IN BRIEF Open and sincere in expression; straightforward

[+] candid, plain, outright, sincere, ingenuous, blunt, honest

> Your answer is not frank.
> (너의 대답은 솔직하지 못하다.)

0821
fraternal [frətə́:rnəl]

형제의, 우애의

IN BRIEF Of or like brothers

[+] brotherlike, brotherly

> There's always been a lot of fraternal rivalry between my sons.
> (나의 아들들 사이에는 항상 형제간의 경쟁의식이 많았다.)

0822
fratricide [frǽtrəsàid]

형제[자매] 살해(죄) (brother kill)

IN BRIEF The killing of one's brother or sister

[+] liquidator, manslayer, murderer

> The life-long rivalry between the brothers ended tragically in fratricide.
> (형제들 간의 일생에 걸친 경쟁은 형제살해라는 비극으로 막을 내렸다.)

0823
freaked [frí:kt]

《美속어》화난, 흥분한(충격을 받은), (upset)화나게 하다, 흥분하다

IN BRIEF Lose one's nerve

[+] go crazy, irritate, annoy, aggravate, bother

> My parents really freaked when they saw my purple hair.
> (내 자주색 머리를 보시자 우리 부모님은 그야말로 길길이 뛰었다.)

0824
frenzy [frénzi]

열광, 광란

IN BRIEF A state of violent mental agitation or wild excitement

[+] fit, burst, outburst, spasm, convulsion

> The news threw him into a frenzy.
> (그 소식을 듣자 그는 광분했다.)

0825
frequent [frí:kwənt]

a. 자주 일어나는, 빈번한, 흔히 있는(visit)

IN BRIEF Occurring or appearing quite often or at close intervals

[+] common, constant, persistent, recurrent, incessant, habitual

> Ahntonio suffers from frequent bouts of depression.
> (안토니오는 잦은 우울증에 시달린다.)

0826
fret [fret]

v. 애타다, 안달하다, 고민하다

IN BRIEF To become worried or annoyed

[+] worry, anguish, agonize, obsess, brood, annoy

> Don't fret yourself, we'll get there on time.
> (안달하지 마. 우리가 제시간에 거기 도착할거야.)

0827
friction [fríkʃ-ən]

n. 마찰

IN BRIEF The rubbing of one object or surface against another

[+] rubbing, scraping, grating, fretting, rasping

> Heat is produced by friction.
> (열은 마찰에 의해 생긴다.)

0828
frigid [frídʒid]

a. 몹시 추운, 무관심한

IN BRIEF Freezing cold, extremely cold

[+] freezing, cold, frozen, icy, chill, arctic

> There's a very frigid atmosphere in the school.
> (학교에는 몹시 냉담한 분위기가 퍼져 있다.)

0829
frivolous [frívələs]

a. 경박한, 천박한

IN BRIEF Given to lighthearted silliness

[+] careless, trivial, silly, flippant, superficial, shallow, juvenile, idle

> When we were young, we were so frivolous and carefree.
> (젊었을 때, 우리는 너무도 경솔하고 태평했다.)

0830
frolic [frálik-]
장난, (신명이 나서) 까불기
IN BRIEF Playful behavior or merriment
+ merriment, amusement, fun, drollery, skylarking, play

> It was just a harmless frolic.
> (그것은 그냥 악의 없는 장난이었다.)

0831
frown [fraun]
눈살(얼굴)을 찌푸리다(wrinkle one's blow)
IN BRIEF To wrinkle the brow, as in thought or displeasure
+ glare, scowl, glower, make a face, look daggers, lower

> "Stop doing that," she said with a frown.
> ("그 짓 좀 그만 해"하고 그녀는 찡그린 얼굴로 말했다.)

0832
frugality [fruːgǽləti]
n. 검약, 절약, 검소(spending little)
IN BRIEF Practicing or marked by economy, as in the expenditure of money or the use of material resources
+ thrift, economy, conservation, providence, husbandry, moderation

> He believes in a life of simplicity and frugality.
> (그는 간소하고 검소한 삶의 가치를 믿는다.)

0833
fruition [fruːíʃ-ən]
n. (계획·목표 따위의) 달성, 실현, 성취
IN BRIEF Realization of something desired or worked for; accomplishment
+ fulfilment, maturity

> After months of hard work, our plans finally came to fruition.
> (몇 달 동안의 힘든 작업 끝에 우리의 계획이 마침내 결실을 맺게 되었다.)

0834
frustration [frʌstréiʃ-ən]
n. 좌절, 낙담, 욕구불만, 좌절감, 장애물, 방해물
IN BRIEF Feeling of being unable to get anything done
+ annoyance, disappointment, resentment, irritation, exasperation, dissatisfaction

> Every job has its frustrations.
> (모든 직업에는 실망스러운 구석이 있는 법이다.)

0835
fugitive [fjúːdʒətiv]
a. 도망자, 탈주자, 일시적인, 덧없는(temporary)
IN BRIEF Running away or fleeing, as from the law
+ runaway, refugee, deserter, escapee, runagate

> After three weeks, the police finally caught the fugitives.
> (3주 후에 경찰은 마침내 도망자들을 체포했다.)

0836
furious [fjúː-əriəs]
a. 격노한, 격렬한
IN BRIEF Full of or characterized by extreme anger; raging
+ anger, frantic, infuriated, incensed, frenzied, enraged

> I was furious and told him to get out of my house.
> (나는 몹시 화가 나서 그에게 내 집에서 나가라고 말했다.)

0837
furor [fjúərɔːr]
격렬한 감격;(일시적인) 열중, 열광, 분노
IN BRIEF Rage or uproar
+ disturbance, excitement, fad, craze, furore, cult, rage, outburst, frenzy, outcry

> The news touched off a furor across the nation.
> (그 소식은 전국을 열광의 도가니로 만들었다.)

0838
furtive [fɔ́ːrtiv]
a. 은밀한, 내밀한, 남몰래 하는(elusive)
IN BRIEF Characterized by, acting with, or suggesting stealth or a desire to avoid discovery
+ secretive, clandestine, sneaky, under-the-table

> My movements feel unwittingly furtive. I turn into something of a ghost.
> (나의 움직임은 나도 모르는 사이에 은밀하게 느껴진다. 나는 다소 귀신같은 것으로 변한다.)

0839
fusion [fjúːʒ-ən]
n. 용해, 융해; 융합
IN BRIEF The act or process of fusing or melting together; union
+ merging, union, federation, mixture, integration, synthesis

> How long will it be before nuclear fusion becomes practical?
> (핵융합이 실용화되려면 얼마나 시간이 더 걸릴까?)

0840
fussy [fʌ́si]

까다로운, 성가신

IN BRIEF Very difficult to please; Excessively filled with detail

⊕ fastidious, finical, finicky, meticulous, nice, articular, persnickety, squeamish, picky

> Don't be so fussy about your food.
> (음식에 대해 그렇게 야단스럽게 굴지 마라.)

0841
futile [fjúːtl]

a. 쓸데없는, 무익한, 시시한 (inefficient)

IN BRIEF Ineffectual; useless; incapable of producing any result; not successful

⊕ useless, empty, sterile, fruitless, forlorn, barren, abortive

> All my attempts to unlock the door were futile.
> (문을 열기 위한 나의 모든 시도는 수포로 돌아갔다.)

0842
gallant [gǽlənt]

a. 용감한, 씩씩한, 늠름한

IN BRIEF Brave, daring, bold, heroic, courageous, dashing

⊕ audacious, bold, brave, courageous, dauntless, doughty, fearless

> King Arthur was a gallant knight.
> (아서 왕은 용감한 기사였다.)

0843
galvanize [gǽlvənàiz]

vt. 활기를 띠게 하다

IN BRIEF To stimulate or shock with an electric current

⊕ egg on, excite, foment, goad, impel, incite, inflame

> She has galvanized into activity an industry notoriously bad at working together.
> (함께 일하기 힘들다고 악명 높던 산업체에 그녀가 활기를 불어넣었다.)

0844
forbearance [fɔːrbérəns]

n. 참음; 삼감, 자제; 인내(patience)

IN BRIEF Tolerance and restraint in the face of provocation

⊕ patience, resignation, restraint, tolerance, indulgence, long-suffering, moderation, self-control, leniency, temperance, mildness, lenity

> You must use forbearance in dealing with him because he is still weak from his illness.
> (그가 여전히 병으로 쇠약하기 때문에 당신은 그를 대할 때 인내심을 발휘해야 한다.)

0845
garrulous [gǽrjələs]

a. 잘 지껄이는, 수다스러운, 다변의

IN BRIEF Given to constant and frivolous chatter; loquacious; talkative

⊕ chatty, conversational, loquacious, talkative, talky, voluble

> I had expected her to be fat and garrulous.
> (나는 그녀가 뚱뚱하고 수다스러울 거라고 예상했었다.)

0846
fraudulently [frɔ́ːdʒulənt]

ad. 속여서, 부정하게, 사기를 쳐서(deceitfully)

IN BRIEF Engaging in fraud; deceitful, in a dishonest and fraudulent manner

> The report concluded that he acted neither fraudulently nor improperly.
> (보고서는 그가 부정직하거나 부적절한 행동을 하지 않았다고 결론을 내렸다.)

0847
feud [fjuːd]

n. 싸움, 반목, 불화, 다툼

IN BRIEF A bitter, often prolonged quarrel or state of enmity, especially such a state of hostilities

⊕ altercation, conflict, fight, fracas, vendetta

> His bitter feud with club managing director Karren Brady coupled with a faltering bid towards the Premiership has not made St. Andrew's the happiest of places.
> (프리미어리그에 진입하려는 시도가 좌절되고 있는데다 클럽 관리 이사 캐런 브래디(Karren Brady.)와의 극심한 불화까지 겹쳐 그에게는 세인트 앤드류 경기장이 가장 행복한 곳이 되지 못했다.)

0848
garner [gáːrnər]

(곡물 창고 따위에) 축적하다, 모으다(amass)

IN BRIEF To gather and save or to store up

⊕ collect, accumulate, cull, extract, gather, glean

> They garnered information about the accident.
> (그들은 그 사건에 대한 정보를 모았다.)

0849
facilitate [fəsílətèit]

v. 용이하게 하다; 촉진하다(promote)

IN BRIEF To make easy or easier; assist the progress of

⊕ speed up, pave the way for, fast-track

> The moral treatment philosophy had an optimistic view that the provision of an appropriate environment can facilitate cure, especially to those with acute ailments.
> (도덕적 치료 철학은 적절한 환경의 제공이 특히 급성질환을 앓고 있는 환자들의 치유를 촉진할 것이라는 낙관적인 견해를 가지고 있었다.)

LESSON 18

0850
gastronomy [gæstrάnəmi]

n. 미식법; 요리학

IN BRIEF The art or science of good eating

+ gourmet, bon vivant, connoisseur, epicure

> The food writer Elizabeth David introduced gastronomy to many Britons.
> (음식 기고가인 엘리자베스 데이빗은 많은 영국인에게 미식법을 소개했다.)

0851
gateway ['geɪtweɪ]

n. (벽·담·울타리) 대문, 출입구, 통로(어떤 장소로 들어가는) 관문, 현관;
(성공 등에)이르는 길/ (통신)게이트웨이《서로 다른 컴퓨터 네트워크 등을 상호 접속시키기 위한 장치》

IN BRIEF An entrance that may be closed by or as by a gate

+ entrance, entranceway, entryway, entree, entry

> A good education can be the gateway to success.
> (좋은 교육은 성공으로 가는 길이다.)

0852
gelid [dʒélid]

a. 얼음 같은, 얼어붙는 듯한, 매우 차가운(icy) → 냉담한(frigid)

IN BRIEF Extremely cold or frozen

+ arctic, boreal, freezing, frigid, frosty, glacial, icy, polar, wintry

> They wanted to skate, but they were worried that the gelid pond was not quite ready.
> (그들은 스케이트를 타고 싶었지만, 유리로 된 연못이 아직 완전히 얼지 않은 것을 걱정했다.)

0853
generous [dʒénərəs]

a. 인심 좋은, 후한, 관대한 (not severe)

IN BRIEF Liberal in giving or sharing; unselfish

+ freehanded, lavish, liberal, munificent, openhanded

> Aspirin was originally a brand name used by the Bayer Company, but as use of the product spread rapidly, the name became so common that it was accepted as a generic term.
> (아스피린은 원래 바이어 제약회사(Bayer Company.)에 의해 사용된 상표명이었으나 제품의 사용이 급속히 퍼지면 그 이름이 일반화되어 일반적인 용어로 받아들여졌다.)
> Our principal is very generous.
> (우리 교장 선생님은 매우 인자하시다.)

0854
gauge [geɪdʒ]

n. 측정 기준, 규격; 척도, 측정하다, 판단하다

IN BRIEF A measuring device; to test; a size

+ benchmark, criterion, mark, norm, measure, standard

> It was difficult to gauge how people would respond.
> (사람들이 어떤 반응을 보일지는 판단하기가 어려웠다.)

0855
gem [dʒem]

n. 보석, 귀중품, 매우 도움이 되는 사람

IN BRIEF A person or thing held to be a perfect example; treasure

+ bijou, jewel, marvel, prize

> My secretary is a real gem.
> (내 비서는 진짜 주옥같은 인물이다.)

0856
gelatinous [dʒəlǽtənəs]

a. 젤라틴[아교]모양의 → 아교질의(semiliquid)

IN BRIEF Having a dense or viscous consistency

+ coagulated, heavy, stodgy, thick

> Between the two cell layers of jellyfish there is a firm, gelatinous middle layer.
> (해파리의 두 세포층 사이에는 단단하고 젤라틴 같은 중간층이 있다.)

0857
genial [dʒíːnjəl]

따뜻한, 온난한, 쾌적한; 상냥한, 다정한(friendly)

IN BRIEF Having a pleasant or friendly disposition or manner

+ affable, agreeable, amiable, congenial, cordial, good-natured

> Our neighbor has a genial personality.
> (우리 이웃은 다정한 인품을 지녔다.)

0858
genocide [dʒénəsàid]

n. 대량 학살, 집단 학살

IN BRIEF The systematic and widespread extermination or attempted extermination of a national, racial, religious, or ethnic group

+ decimate, massacre, carnage, holocaust, kill

> You know it's more than 100 weeks of genocide.
> (당신도 알다시피 100주 이상의 대량학살이 있었다.)

0859
genuine [dʒénjuin]

a. 진짜의(real) → 참된, 진실된(sincere)

IN BRIEF Actually possessing the alleged or apparent attribute or character

+ actual, authentic, bona fide, indubitable, original, real

> He guaranteed the jewel genuine.
> (그는 그 보석이 진짜임을 보증했다.)

0860
germane [dʒəːrméin]

밀접한 관련이 있는, 적절한(applicable, appropriate)

IN BRIEF Related to a matter at hand, especially to a subject under discussion

+ apropos, fitting, pertinent, apposite, relevant

> I don't think that question is really germane.
> (내 생각에 그 질문은 그다지 밀접한 관계가 없다.)

0861
germinate [dʒə́ːrmənèit]

성장[발달]하기 시작하다 → (종자) 발아하다(grow, cultivate)

IN BRIEF To cause to sprout or grow

+ plant, produce, raise, sprout, flourish, increase, thrive, progress

> The seeds germinated within a week
> (그 씨앗들은 1주일 이내에 싹이 텄다.)

0862
gingerly [dʒíndʒərli]

ad. 주의깊게, 신중하게

IN BRIEF Very cautious or careful

+ careful, cautiously, chary, circumspect, prudent

> She gingerly tested the water with her toe.
> (그녀는 조심스럽게 발가락 끝으로 물을 살펴보았다.)

0863
glimmer [glímər]

n. 깜박이는 빛; 희미한 빛, 미광

IN BRIEF Faint unsteady lights

+ blink, flash, flicker, glance, gleam, glint

> There is still a glimmer of hope.
> (아직 실낱같은 희망은 있다.)

0864
glamorize [glǽməràiz]

vt. 매력 있게 하다, 미화[이상화]하다

IN BRIEF To cause to be or seem glamorous; romanticize or beautify

+ idealize, exemplary, romanticize

> Television tends to glamorize acts of violence.
> (텔레비전은 폭력적인 행동을 미화하는 경향이 있다.)

0865
gloomy [glúːmi]

a. 어두운, 암흑의; 우울한, 마음을 답답하게 하는

IN BRIEF Dimly lit or sadly

+ blue, dark, desolate, dismal, dreary, dejected, sorrowful, bleak, dingy, cloudy

> She was in a gloomy mood.
> (그녀는 우울한 기분이었다.)

0866
gluttony [glʌ́təni]

n. 대식, 폭음 폭식; 탐닉

IN BRIEF Excess in eating or drinking

+ edacity, gourmandism, voracity, excess, greed

> Gluttony is just as much a vice as drunkenness.
> (과식은 만취 못지않은 악습이다.)

0867
goad [goud]

vt. 자극하다, 선동하다, 부추기다(urge)

IN BRIEF Urging a person to action

+ egg on, excite, foment, galvanize, impel, incite, inflame, inspire

> I keep trying to goad these lazy fellows into action.
> (나는 계속 이 게으른 녀석들을 움직이도록 자극을 주고 있다.)

0868
gorge [gɔːrdʒ]

게걸스럽게 먹다 (fill oneself with)

IN BRIEF To satisfy to the full or to excess

+ cloy, engorge, glut, sate, satiate, surfeit

> She gorged herself on cream-cakes.
> (그녀는 크림 케이크를 실컷 먹었다.)

0869
grapple [ɡrǽpəl]

v. 맞붙어 싸우다; 붙들고 씨름하다

IN BRIEF To fight or struggle. To grip or seize

fight, scuffle, struggle, wrestle, grip, seize

> She grappled with her assailant but he got away.
> (그녀가 자신을 공격한 자를 움켜잡았지만, 그가 달아나 버렸다.)

0870
grasp [ɡræsp]

붙잡다 → 이해(파악)하다

IN BRIEF To take hold of intellectually; comprehend

understanding, appreciation, awareness, insight, grapple, grip, seize

> It's important to grasp the meaning from the context.
> (문맥으로 뜻을 파악하는 것이 중요하다.)

0871
gratify [ɡrǽtəfài]

만족시키다, 기쁘게 하다 → 만족하다, 즐거워하다

IN BRIEF To please or satisfy

please, satisfy, appease, cheer, delight, overjoy, pleasure, tickle

> I was most gratified by the outcome of the meeting.
> (나는 그 회의의 결과에 대단히 만족했다.)

0872
gratis [ɡréitis]

무료로 → 공짜로(for nothing)

IN BRIEF Without payment or charge

complimentary, free, gratuitous, on the house

> The sample is sent gratis on application.
> (견본은 신청하시는 대로 무료로 보내드립니다.)

0873
green light [ɡriːn lait]

파란불 → 청신호 → (구어) 정식 허가, 승인(permission)

IN BRIEF To give permission to proceed or authorization to (a project or person)

authorization, sanction, approval, go-ahead, permission, confirmation

> The government has given the green light to the scheme.
> (정부가 그 기획에 공식허가를 해주었다.)

0874
greet [ɡriːt]

v. 인사하다, 경의를 표하다

IN BRIEF To meet or receive with expressions of gladness or welcome

hail, salute, welcome

> The little girl was too bashful to greet us.
> (그 어린 소녀는 너무 부끄러워 우리에게 인사를 하지 못했다.)

0875
gregarious [ɡriɡɛ́əriəs]

(동물) 군거(群居)하는, (동물) 떼 지어 사는, 사교적인(friendly)

IN BRIEF Liking to be with other people; sociable

outgoing, friendly, social, cordial, sociable, affable, convivial, companionable

> She's very outgoing and gregarious.
> (그녀는 대단히 외향적이고 사교적이다.)

0876
grievance [ɡríːvəns]

n. 불만, 고충

IN BRIEF An actual or supposed circumstance regarded as just cause for complaint

complaint, gripe, objection, protest

> He has many grievances against the management.
> (그는 경영자에 대해 많은 불만을 가지고 있다.)

0877
grim [ɡrim]

a. (구어) 불쾌한, 싫은 (unpleasant), 잔인한, 엄격한

IN BRIEF Stern, harsh or unpleasant

hopeless, horrible in manner, appearance

> He looked as grim as if he were made of stone.
> (그는 마치 돌로 만들어 놓은 듯 엄하게 보였다.)

0878
grotesque [ɡroutésk]

a. 기괴한, 괴상한, 기묘한

IN BRIEF Unnaturally odd or ugly

freakish, dreadful, oddity, freaky, monstrous

> That politician's speech was one of the most grotesque, I've ever heard.
> (그 정치인의 연설은 여태껏 내가 들어본 적 없는 가장 괴상한 연설 중에 하나였다.)

0879
ground [graund]

이륙시키지 않다(이륙[비행]시키지 않다) → n. 땅, 입지

IN BRIEF To prevent (an aircraft or a pilot from flying)

+ land, country, field, turf, terrain, area, tract

> The hydrogen leak forced NASA to ground the space shuttle.
> (수소 누출 때문에 NASA는 우주왕복선을 이륙시키지 못했다.)

0880
grown-up [groun ʌp]

a. (구어)어른(adult), 성인 → 성숙한 → 어른이 된(adult)

IN BRIEF Having reached full growth and development

+ adult, developed, full-fledged, full-grown, grown, mature, ripe

> If you're good, you can eat with the grown-ups.
> (네가 얌전히 굴면 어른들하고 식사할 수 있어.)

0881
grudge [grʌdʒ]

원한, 유감, 인색하게 굴다, 불만을 품다

IN BRIEF A persistent feeling of resentment, esp one due to some cause, such as an insult or injury

+ resentment, bitterness, grievance, malice, hate, spite

> He has a grudge against her.
> (그는 그녀에게 원한을 품고 있다.)

0882
grudgingly [grʌ́dʒiŋli]

마지못해, 억지로

IN BRIEF Reluctant, unwilling

+ Reluctantly; unwillingly

> She grudgingly conceded that I was right.
> (그녀는 마지못해 내가 옳음을 인정했다.)

0883
grueling [grúːəliŋ]

녹초(기진맥진)로 만드는; 엄한, 아주 힘든 (arduous, laborious)

IN BRIEF Requiring extreme effort ↔ easy, facile

+ backbreaking, gruelling, hard, heavy, punishing, toilsome

> I've had a gruelling day.
> (오늘은 녹초가 될 만큼 힘든 날이었다.)

0884
gruesome [grúːsəm]

무시무시한 → 소름 끼치는

IN BRIEF Horrible(무서운) or disgusting(메스꺼운)

+ ghastly, grim, grisly, hideous, horrible, horrid, lurid, macabre, horrible, awful

> The gruesome sight sent a shiver down my spine.
> (그 소름끼치는 장면을 보자 나는 등골이 오싹했다.)

0885
gullible [gʌ́ləbəl]

a. 잘 속는 (easily-deceived; naive, trusting)

IN BRIEF Easily cheated or tricked, credulous, dupable

+ easy, exploitable, naive, susceptible

> Fame is proof that the people are gullible.
> (명성은 사람들이 속기 쉽다는 증거이다.)

0886
guts [gʌt]

내장 → 용기(끈기) → 내용(contents) → 본능

IN BRIEF The quality of mind enabling one to face danger or hardship resolutely

+ bravery, courage, dauntlessness, doughtiness, fearlessness, fortitude

> He disagrees with her but doesn't have the guts to say so.
> (그는 그녀에게 동의하지 않았지만 그렇게 말할 배짱이 없었다.)

0887
habitat [hǽbətæt]

n. (생물을 둘러싼) 환경, 거주 환경; 서식지

IN BRIEF The natural environment in which a species or group of species lives

+ home, environment, milieu, surroundings

> Today the plant is rare in its natural habitat.
> (오늘날 그 식물은 자연 서식지에서 찾아보기 힘들다.)

0888
haggard [hǽgərd]

a. 여윈, 초췌한

IN BRIEF Exhausted or distraught and often gaunt in appearance

+ careworn, gaunt, hollow-eyed, skeletal

> He looks haggard.
> (그는 초췌해 보인다.)

0889
hail [heil]

v. 환호하여 맞이하다

IN BRIEF To salute or greet

+ salute, call, greet, address, welcome, speak to

The book was immediately hailed as a masterpiece.
(그 책은 즉각 걸작으로 찬양을 받았다.)

0890
hallmark [hɔ́:lmà:rk]

n. (사람, 사물)특성, 특징

IN BRIEF Distinguishing characteristic

+ trait, earmark, feature, point, idiosyncrasy, individuality, peculiarity

Attention to detail is the hallmark of a fine craftsman.
(세부적인 데 신경을 쓰는 것이 훌륭한 장인의 특질이다.)

0891
hallow [hǽlou]

신성하게[정하게] 하다(make holy)

IN BRIEF Render holy by means of religious rites

+ sanctify, bless, consecrate

One of the theatre's most hallowed traditions
(연극계의 가장 성스러운 전통 중 하나)

0892
hamlet [hǽmlit]

n. 작은 마을 (small village)

IN BRIEF A small village

+ village

He was born in a hamlet, many miles from the nearest city.
(그는 가까운 도시로부터 수마일 떨어진 작은 마을에서 태어났다.)

0893
gluttonous [glʌ́tənəs]

a. 게걸 들린; 탐욕스러운, 욕심 많은; 열중하는

IN BRIEF A person who eats or consumes immoderate amounts of food and drink. A person with an inordinate capacity to receive or withstand something

+ edacious, greedy, hoggish, piggish, ravenous, voracious

Gluttonous when it comes to Italian food especially, Grace ate a pound of rigatoni, seven meatballs, and two servings of tricolor salad at her midday meal.
(특히 이탈리아 음식에 관해서라면 게걸스러워서, 그레이스는 1파운드의 리가토니, 7개의 고기 완자, 3색 샐러드 2인분을 그녀의 점심으로 먹었다.)

0894
handout [hǽnd'out']

광고전단, (교실)인쇄물, (가난사람)동냥, 공식성명(정부발표)

IN BRIEF Something given to a charity or cause; charity

+ assistance, charity, beneficence, contribution, donation, gift

Okay, but we'll need your handouts.
(알겠어요. 하지만 회의 때 당신이 준비한 자료가 있어야 합니다.)

0895
handy [hǽndi]

a. 솜씨 좋은; 유용한; 편리한; 가까이에 있는(convenient)

IN BRIEF Easily or effectively used; convenient or useful

+ adroit, clever, deft, dexterous, facile, nimble

Korean-English dictionaries come in handy.
(한영사전은 도움이 된다.)

0896
hamper [hǽmpər]

vt. 저지하다, 방해하다

IN BRIEF To prevent the free movement, action, or progress of

+ obstruct, impede, inhibit, thwart, stymie, hinder, handicap, hold up, prevent, restrict, frustrate, curb

Our progress was hampered by the bad weather.
(우리의 진행은 나쁜 날씨로 방해를 받았다.)

0897
gibberish [dʒíbəriʃ]

n. 횡설수설 (nonsense talk)

IN BRIEF Unintelligible or nonsensical talk or writing

+ babble, blather, blatherskite, double talk, gabble, jabber, jabberwocky, jargon, nonsense, prate, prattle, twaddle

The first two comments on his article were off-topic and unintelligible nonsense, just complete gibberish.
(그의 글에 대한 첫 두 논평은 주제와 무관하며 이해도 되지 않는 허튼소리들로서, 완전히 횡설수설이었다.)

0898
gratification [græ̀təfikéiʃən]

n. 만족, 희열 (satisfaction); (욕구) 충족

IN BRIEF To please or satisfy. To give in to (a desire); indulge

+ satisfaction, delight, pleasure, joy, thrill, relish, enjoyment, glee

The ability to voluntarily delay immediate gratification, to tolerate self-imposed delays of reward, is at the core of most conceptsof willpower, ego strength, and ego resilience.
(즉각적인 만족을 자발적으로 지연시키는 능력(즉 보상을 자진해서 미루는 것을 견뎌내는 능력)은 의지력, 자아 강도 그리고 자아 회복력에 대한 대부분의 개념에서 핵심적이다.)

generosity [dʒènərásəti]

n. 관대함, 너그러움

IN BRIEF Willingness and liberality in giving away one's money, time, etc; magnanimity

+ kindness, benevolence, selflessness, charity

> A desire (to be applauded by those in attendance), not his sensitivity to the plight of the underprivileged, was the reason for generosity at the charity affair.
> (혜택을 받지 못한 사람들이 처한 곤궁에 대한 헤아림이 아니라 참석한 사람들에게 박수갈채를 받으려는 바람이 그가 자선행사에서 너그러움을 보인 이유였다.)

0900
hangar [hǽŋɡər]

vt. (비행기) 격납고에 넣다

IN BRIEF A shelter especially for housing or repairing aircraft

+ airdock, repair shed

> The airplane is entering the hangar.
> (비행기가 격납고로 들어가고 있다.)

0901
hangover [|hæŋoʊvər]

n. 잔존물, 유물《美속어》숙취; (약의) 부작용

IN BRIEF Trace, relic, remains, vestige, result of heavy drinking

+ aftereffects, morning after, head, crapulence

> This procedure is a hangover from the old system.
> (이 절차는 구체제의 유물이다.)

0902
haphazard [hæphǽzərd]

우연의; 무계획의, 되는 대로의

IN BRIEF Dependent upon or characterized by mere chance

+ chance, desultory, hit-or-miss, indiscriminate, random, unplanned

> The government's approach to the problem was haphazard.
> (그 사안에 대한 정부의 접근법은 막무가내였다.)

0903
hapless [hǽplis]

a. 불행한, 불운한

IN BRIEF Luckless; unfortunate

+ ill-fated, ill-starred, luckless, unfortunate, unhappy, unlucky

> Many children are hapless victims of this war.
> (많은 어린이들이 이 전쟁의 불행한 희생자이다.)

0904
harass [hǽrəs]

괴롭히다; 시달리게 하다; 애먹이다(badger, bother)

IN BRIEF To disturb persistently; torment; pester; persecute

+ annoy, disturb, tease, aggravate, exasperate, irk, vex

> He complained of being harassed by the police.
> (그는 경찰에게 괴롭힘을 당하고 있노라고 불평했다.)

0905
hardship [hάːrdʃip]

n. 고난, 곤경

IN BRIEF Conditions of life difficult to endure

+ tribulation, burden, difficulty, travail, trial, difficulty

> There is so much financial hardship.
> (재정적 어려움이 대단히 크다.)

0906
harass [hǽrəs]

괴롭히다; 시달리게 하다; 애먹이다 (badger, bother)

IN BRIEF Annoy, disturb, tease, aggravate, exasperate, irk, vex

+ harry, hound, importune, pester, plague, solicit

> He complained of being harassed by the police.
> (그는 경찰에게 괴롭힘을 당하고 있노라고 불평했다.)

0907
harry [hǽri]

v. 고민하게 하다, 괴롭히다

IN BRIEF To disturb, distress, or exhaust by repeated demands or criticism; harass

+ annoy, harass, pester, plague, plunder

> He was harried by press reporters wanting a story
> (그는 기사감을 원하는 신문 기자들에게 시달렸다.)

0908
harsh [hɑːrʃ]

a. 가혹한 난폭한; 거친 (cruel, brutal, heartless)

IN BRIEF Rough or grating to the senses

+ coarse, cragged, craggy, jagged, ragged, rough, rugged

> She was harsh to her servants.
> (그녀는 하인들에게 엄했다.)

0909
harvest [hάːrvist]

v. 거두어들이다, 수확하다(pick)

IN BRIEF The act or process of gathering a crop

+ crop, produce, outcome, product, result, autumn, yield

> Farmers are very busy during the harvest.
> (농부들은 수확기에는 아주 바쁘다.)

0910
havoc [hǽvək]

n. 대 파괴, 참혹한 피해, 황폐(disorder)

IN BRIEF Widespread destruction; devastation

+ bane, destruction, devastation, ruin, ruination, wreckage

> The floods created havoc throughout the area.
> (홍수로 그 지역 전역이 엉망이 되었다.)

0911
hazard [hǽzərd]

n. 위험 (danger)

IN BRIEF A chance of being injured or harmed

+ accident, jeopardy, menace, peril, threat, hap, happenstance

> Wet roads are a hazard to drivers.
> (젖은 도로는 운전자들에게는 위험요소이다.)

0912
hazardous [|hǽzərdəs]

모험적인, 위험한

IN BRIEF Marked by danger; perilous

+ dangerous, perilous

> With hazardous road conditions expected tomorrow after the snow tapers off overnight, Governor Lee has ordered only essential personnel to report to work on Monday under the Inclement Weather Policy.
> (눈이 밤새 그치면서 내일은 위험한 도로상태가 예상되는 가운데 Lee주지사는 악천후 일기 방침에 따라 필수 직원들에게만 월요일에 출근하라는 지시를 내렸다.)

0913
headstrong [|hedstrɔːŋ]

완고한, 고집 센

IN BRIEF Tenaciously unwilling to yield

+ bullheaded, dogged, hardheaded, mulish, obstinate, willful, pertinacious, perverse, pigheaded, stiff-necked, tenacious.

> The members of Mary Wilcher's family were notorious for their headstrong temperaments.
> (Mary Wilcher의 가족들은 고집 쎈 성격으로 악명이 높았다.)

0914
heinous [héinəs]

극악[흉악]한, 가증스러운(shocking and immoral)

IN BRIEF Utterly reprehensible or evil; odious; abominable

+ hateful, atrocious, monstrous, outrageous, scandalous, shocking

> It is a heinous crime!!
> (그것은 극악한 범죄다!!)

0915
helm [helm]

키(자루), 주도권, 실권

IN BRIEF A position of leadership or control

+ in charge, in control, in command, directing, at the wheel

> The helm of state
> (국가의 정권)

0916
henceforth [hènsfɔ́ːrθ]

ad. 지금부터는, 이제부터는

IN BRIEF From this time forth, from now on, henceforward

+ from now on, in the future, hereafter, hence

> Henceforth I expect you to be punctual for meetings.
> (이후로는 당신이 회의 시간을 엄수하기를 기대한다.)

0917
hereditary [hirédətèri]

a. 유전(성)의, 유전하는(genetically passed)

IN BRIEF Genetically passed from parent to offspring

+ inherited; transmitted at birth, ancestral, patrimonial

> The disease is hereditary.
> (그 질병은 유전적이다.)

0918
heredity [hirédəti]

n. 유전; 유전 형질(genetics)

IN BRIEF The genetic transmission of characteristics from parent to offspring

+ genetics, inheritance, genetic make-up, congenital traits

> Diet and exercise can influence a person's weight, but heredity is also factor.
> (식사와 운동은 사람의 체중에 영향을 주지만 유전도 한 요인이다.)

0919
heresy [hérəsi]

n. 이교, 이단

IN BRIEF An opinion or doctrine contrary to the orthodox tenets of a religious body or church

+ apostasy, dissent, pagan, iconoclasm, infidelity

> He was burned at the stake in the fifteenth century for heresy.
> (그는 15세기에 이단으로 몰려 말뚝에서 화형당했다.)

0920
hermitage [hə́ːrmitidʒ]

수도원; 은둔 생활, 은신처, 외딴 집

IN BRIEF The habitation of a hermit or group of hermits

⊕ retreat, refuge, sanctuary, haven, shelter, asylum

> A hermitage is a place where a religious person lives on their own apart from the rest of society.
> (은신처는 종교인이 사회의 다른 사람들로부터 떨어져 혼자 살아가는 곳을 말한다.)

0921
hesitant [hézətənt]

머뭇거리는, 주저하는, 내키지 않아 하는(reluctant)

IN BRIEF Wavering, hesitating, or irresolute

⊕ indecisive, irresolute, pendulous, shilly-shally, tentative, timid

> She gave me a hesitant smile.
> (그녀는 나에게 내키지 않은 웃음을 지었다.)

0922
hesitate [hézətèit]

v. 주저하다, 머뭇거리다, 망설이다

IN BRIEF To pause or wait in uncertainty

⊕ dither, falter, shilly-shally, stagger, vacillate, waver

> She hesitated before replying.
> (그녀는 대답하기 전에 머뭇거렸다.)

0923
heterogeneous [hètərədʒíːniəs]

a. 이종의, 이질의, 잡다한

IN BRIEF Composed of unrelated or differing parts or elements

⊕ assorted, divers, diverse, diversified, miscellaneous, mixed

> There was a heterogeneous gathering of people at the party.
> (그 파티에는 이질적인 사람들이 모였다.)

0924
heyday [héidèi]

전성기

IN BRIEF Most successful period; golden years

⊕ peak, climax, apogee, culmination, apex, prim, leading, paramount

> She was a great singer in her heyday.
> (그녀는 전성기 때 위대한 가수였다.)

0925
hiatus [haiéitəs]

(일·활동) 중단, 단절 / 갈라진 틈

IN BRIEF A gap or interruption in space, time, or continuity; a break

⊕ break, gap, interim, lacuna, void, open

> There will be a two-week hiatus before the talks can be resumed.
> (그 회담들이 재개되기 전에 2주간의 휴지가 있을 것이다.)

0926
hideous [hídiəs]

a. 끔찍한, 무시무시한(horrible), (도덕) 극악무도한, 불쾌한, (예상외로)엄청난

IN BRIEF Horrible, disgusting or very ugly

⊕ dreadful, repulsive, ugly, ghastly, grim, grisly, gruesome, horrible, horrid, lurid

> It was hideous to watch.
> (그것은 보기에 소름끼쳤다.)

0927
hierarchy [háiərɑ̀ːrki]

계급제도 (graded orders)

IN BRIEF Any group in which there are higher and lower positions of power

⊕ grading, ranking, social order, pecking order, class system, social stratum

> There's a very rigid social hierarchy in their society.
> (그들의 사회에는 매우 엄격한 사회 계급 제도가 있다.)

0928
hilarious [hiléəriəs]

유쾌한, 즐거운(comical)

IN BRIEF Very funny and loud

⊕ riotous, side-splitting, exuberant, high-spirited, jubilant

> I found the whole situation hilarious.
> (나는 그 전체적인 상황이 재미있다는 걸 알았다.)

0929
hind [haind]

a. 뒤쪽의, 후부의, 후방의

IN BRIEF Located at or forming the back or rear; posterior

⊕ rear, back, hindmost, posterior, postern

> The horse reared up on its hind legs.
> (그 말이 뒷다리로 몸을 받치고 고개를 쳐들었다.)

0930
hinder [híndər]

v. 방해하다 (impede)

IN BRIEF To obstruct or delay the progress of

+ encumber, block, inhibit, thwart, hold back, obstruct

> Don't hinder her work.
> (그녀의 일을 방해하지 마라.)

0931
hoarse [hɔːrs]

a. 목쉰, 목쉰 소리의

IN BRIEF Rough or grating in sound

+ rough, croaking, croaky, gruff

> His voice sounded hoarse.
> (그의 목소리가 쉰 것처럼 들렸다.)

0932
hole [houl]

n. 구멍; 누추한 집, 소굴; 함정 (hellhole)

IN BRIEF A hollowed place in something solid; a cavity or pit

+ cavity, hollow, pocket, vacuity, void

> I am not going to bring up my child in this hole.
> (나는 이런 소굴[불결한 곳]에서 내 아이를 키우지는 않을 것이다.)

0933
homogeneous [hòumədʒíːniəs]

동질적인, 동종의(↔heterogeneous), 동질화된(homogenized), 동종의(identical)

IN BRIEF Of the same kind or nature; unvarying; unmixed

+ alike, consistent, identical, similar, uniform, unvarying, same kind

> It's a dull city of homogeneous buildings.
> (그곳은 같은 모양의 건물들로 이루어진 따분한 도시이다.)

0934
horrid [hɔ́ːrid]

무시무시한(frightful), 지독한, 매우 불쾌한, 지겨운(nasty)

IN BRIEF Causing horror; dreadful; Extremely disagreeable; offensive

+ unpleasant, terrible, awful, offensive, nasty, disgusting

> It was a horrid spectacle.
> (그것은 무서운 광경이었다.)

0935
hospitable [háspitəbəl]

a. 다정한, 친절한

IN BRIEF Receiving or treating guests or strangers warmly and generously

+ accommodating, amiable, cordial, courteous, pleasant

> She is always hospitable to visitors from abroad.
> (그녀는 해외에서 온 방문객을 항상 환대한다.)

0936
hostile [hástil]

a. 적대적인

IN BRIEF Of, relating to, or characteristic of an enemy

+ unfriendly, belligerent, combatant, militant

> He seems to have some hostile feeling toward me.
> (그는 내게 다소 적의를 품고 있는 것 같다.)

0937
howl [haul]

v. 짖다, 소리를 길게 뽑으며 울다

IN BRIEF To utter or emit a long, mournful, plaintive sound

+ moan, groan, wail, yowl, yell

> We heard the wolf's howl.
> (우리는 늑대가 울부짖는 소리를 들었다.)

0938
hub [hʌb]

n. 중심, 중추(center)

IN BRIEF The center part of a wheel, fan, or propeller

+ core, focus, heart, middle, nucleus, crux, essence, gist, heart

> They operate in the hub of the business world.
> (그들은 실업계의 심장부에서 활동한다.)

0939
hubris [hjúːbris]

n. 오만, 자만

IN BRIEF Overbearing pride or presumption; arrogance

+ self-respect, conceit, egotism, immodesty, vanity, haughtiness

> Hubris is one of the vices.
> (오만함은 죄악중의 하나이다.)

0940
humdrum [hʌ́mdrʌ̀m]
평범한, 단조로운, 지루한

IN BRIEF A monotonous routine, task, or person

+ dreary, dry, dull, irksome, monotonous, stuffy, tedious

It is a humdrum business of making money.
(돈을 벌기 위한 평범한 생업이다.)

0941
humid [hjúːmid]
a. 습기 찬, 습한, (고온) 다습한(damp)

IN BRIEF Containing or characterized by a high amount of water or water vapor

+ clammy, dank, stuffy, sultry, sweltering muggy, soggy

The humid climate didn't agree with him.
(습한 기후는 그에게 맞지 않았다.)

0942
humiliate [hjuːmílièit]
vt. 굴욕감을 느끼게 하다, 창피를 주다

IN BRIEF To cause (someone to feel a loss of pride, dignity, or self-respect)

+ abase, degrade, demean, humble, mortify, disgrace, embarrass

She had been disappointed, hurt, even humiliated.
(그녀는 실망하고 상처받았으며 심지어 굴욕감을 느꼈다.)

0943
hush [hʌʃ]
v. 조용히 하다, 조용해지다, 입 다물게 하다

IN BRIEF To make silent or quiet

+ quiet, quieten, calm, sooth, shush, silence, still

Hush! The baby is sleeping.
(쉬! 아기가 자고 있다.)

0944
hyperbole [haipə́ːrbəliː]
n. 과장(법); 과장 표현

IN BRIEF An exaggeration used as a figure of speech

+ exaggeration, hyperbolism, overstatement, tall talk

The blurb on the back of the book was full of the usual hyperbole - enthralling, fascinating and so on.
(책 뒷면의 추천문은 '마음을 사로잡는'이나 '매혹적인' 등의 흔한 과장 어구로 넘쳐 났다.)

0945
hypocrite [hípəkrìt]
a. 위선(자)의

IN BRIEF A person given to hypocrisy

+ liar, pharisee, phony, tartuffe, fraud

You're just a bunch of hypocrites!
(당신들은 그냥 한 떼의 위선자들일 뿐이다!)

0946
hypodermic [hàipədə́ːrmik]
a. 피하에 주입되는, 피하 주사의

IN BRIEF Under the skin; for use under the skin

+ syringe, needle, works

Give him a hypodermic.
(그에게 피하주사를 놓으세요.)

0947
hidebound [ˈhaɪdbaʊnd]
a. 편협한, 완고한

IN BRIEF Stubbornly prejudiced, narrow-minded, or inflexible

+ conventional, set, rigid, narrow, puritan, narrow-minded, strait-laced, brassbound, ultraconservative, set in your ways

Brian is a(n) hidebound Boston Red Sox fan; he has rooted for the team all his life.
(브라이언은 보스턴 레드삭스의 골수팬이다. 그는 평생 동안 그 팀을 응원해왔다.)

0948
homage [hάmidʒ]
n. 존경, 충성

IN BRIEF A public show of respect or honour towards someone or something

+ honor, respect, veneration, adulation, praise, tribute

We have to pay homage to her because she is an amazing artist.
(그녀는 매우 놀라운 예술가이기 때문에 우리는 그녀에게 경의를 표해야 한다.)

0949
harrowing [hǽroʊɪŋ]
a. 고뇌를 주는, 비참한, 괴로운

IN BRIEF Extremely distressing; agonizing

+ agonizing, anguishing, excruciating, tormenting, torturous

We stayed up all night listening to Tom and Bill talk about their harrowing adventures at sea.
(우리는 톰과 빌이 바다에서 겪은 괴로운 모험담을 듣느라 밤을 새웠다.)

LESSON 20

0950
identical [aidéntikəl]
a. 동일한, 똑같은
IN BRIEF Being the same
⊕ identic, same, selfsame, twin, analogous, duplicate

> This is the identical room we stayed in last year.
> (이 방은 우리가 작년에 묵었던 방과 동일한 방이다.)

0951
idiosyncrasy [ìdiəsíŋkrəsi]
(개인)특질, 특징, 개성, 기행(奇行), 특이체질
IN BRIEF Personal mannerism: Peculiar behavior
⊕ eccentricity, peculiarity, quirk, quirkiness, singularity, unusual

> One of her little idiosyncrasies is always washing in cold water.
> (그녀의 소소한 특징들 중 한 가지는 언제나 찬물에 씻는다는 것이다.)

0952
idolize [áidəlàiz]
v. 우상화[우상시]하다
IN BRIEF To regard with great or uncritical admiration or devotion
⊕ adore, revere, reverence, venerate, worship

> She was idolized as a movie star.
> (그녀는 영화 스타로서 우상화되었다.)

0953
ignominious [ìgnəmíniəs]
a. 불명예스러운 → 수치스러운 → 경멸할 만한 → 비열한
IN BRIEF Shameful; dishonorable
⊕ discreditable, disgraceful, dishonorable, disreputable, opprobrious

> This is only an ignominious end in his tiny mind.
> (이는 그의 속좁은 쏨쏨이로 인해 도래된 수치스러운 결과일 뿐이다.)

0954
ignore [ignɔ́ːr]
vt. 무시하다, 모르는 체하다
IN BRIEF To pay no attention to: disregard on purpose
⊕ disregard, neglect, slight, overlook, scorn

> The former president just began to ignore mundane affairs.
> (전직 대통령은 세속적인 일을 무시하기 시작했다.)

0955
illegible [ilédʒəbəl]
a. 판독하기[읽기] 어려운; 불명료한
IN BRIEF Hard or impossible to read; unreadable
⊕ indecipherable, unreadable, faint, crabbed, scrawled, hieroglyphic

> The doctor's signature was completely illegible.
> (그 의사의 서명은 전혀 알아볼 수 없었다.)

0956
illicit [illísit]
a. 위법의, 불법의; (사회 일반에) 인정되지 않은; 무면허의
IN BRIEF Not legally permitted; unlicensed; unlawful
⊕ unlawful, illegal, illegitimate, lawless, outlawed, unlawful

> They were all prosecuted for illicit liquor selling.
> (그들은 모두 불법 주류판매 죄목으로 기소됐다.)

0957
illiterate [ilítərit]
a. 문맹의, (언어·문학) 교양 없는; (어떤 분야) 소양이 없는
IN BRIEF Not able to read or write (Without education or knowledge
⊕ ignorant, uneducated, uninstructed, unlearned, unschooled, untaught

> A surprising percentage of the population are illiterate.
> (인구의 놀랄 만큼 많은 비율이 문맹자이다.)

0958
illuminate [ilúːmənèit]
(물건·장소) 밝게 비추다, 조명하다, 밝게 하다
IN BRIEF To provide or brighten with light
⊕ brighten, illumine, irradiate, lighten, clarify, elucidate

> We have several miniature lamps that can illuminate small areas remarkably well.
> (우리는 작지만 좁은 공간을 아주 환하게 해주는 램프가 몇 가지 있다.)

0959
illustration [ìləstréiʃən]
삽화, (설명하기 위한) 실례(example)
IN BRIEF Pictorial matter used to explain or decorate a text
⊕ depiction, painting, picture, portrayal, vignette, diagram

> Illustration can be more useful than definition for showing what words mean.
> (낱말들의 뜻을 보여주는 데는 정의보다 예시가 더 유용할 수 있다.)

0960
imbibe [imbáib]
마시다, (물·빛·열)를 빨아들이다, 흡수[흡입]하다

IN BRIEF To absorb or take in as if by drinking

+ drink, quaff, sip, swallow, drain, gulp, guzzle, swill

> Plants imbibes moisture from the soil.
> (식물은 토양으로부터 수분을 흡수한다.)

0961
imitation [imətéiʃən]
모조품, 위조품, 가짜[from], 모방, 흉내(copy)

IN BRIEF The act, practice, or art of imitating; mimicry

+ reproduction, mimicry, parody, simulation

> This is not an imitation.
> (이것은 모조품이 아니다.)

0962
immaculate [imækjəlit]
(셔츠·시트) 티 하나 없이 깨끗한, 더러워지지 않은, (도덕) 더럽혀지지 않은, 순결한, 오점 없는 [흠 없는]

IN BRIEF Impeccably clean; spotless

+ chaste, pristine, pure, impeccable, innocent, sinless, completely

> She always looks immaculate.
> (그녀는 항상 티 한 점 없이 깨끗해 보인다.)

0963
immaterial [imətíəriəl]
a. 중요하지 않은, 무형의, 실체가 없는

IN BRIEF Of no importance or relevance; inconsequential or irrelevant

+ extraneous, inconsequential, insignificant, irrelevant, unimportant

> The cost is immaterial.
> (비용은 중요하지 않다.)

0964
immune [imjúːn]
a. (전염병·독) 면한, 면역(성)의(to, from), (과세·공격) 면제된(exempt), (…을) 당할 염려가 없는(from, against)

IN BRIEF Safe from undergoing something or from disease.

+ impervious, insusceptible, proof, resistant, resistive, unsusceptible

> AIDS is an acronym for Acquired Immune Deficiency Syndrome.
> (AIDS는 후천성 면역 결핍증의 약어이다.)

0965
immutable [imjúːtəbəl]
a. 불변의

IN BRIEF Incapable of changing or being modified

+ inflexible, invariable, ironclad, rigid, unalterable, unchangeable

> Some people regard grammar as an immutable set of rules that must be obeyed.
> (어떤 사람들은 문법을 반드시 지켜야 할 불변의 규칙으로 여긴다.)

0966
impact [impækt]
n. 충돌(collision), 격돌, 충격; 영향, 효과

IN BRIEF The striking of one body against another; collision

+ effect, blow, force, shock, collision, crash, jolt, smash

> His father's teachings had a great impact on him.
> (아버지의 가르침이 그에게 큰 영향을 주었다.)

0967
impair [impέər]
악화[약화]시키다 → (건강, 명성) 해치다, 손상시키다

IN BRIEF To cause to weaken, be damaged, or diminish, as in quality

+ damage, destroy, handicap, hurt, injure, undermine, worse, taint

> Too much alcohol impairs your ability to drive.
> (지나친 알코올은 운전 능력을 저해한다.)

0968
impartial [impáːrʃəl]
a. 한쪽으로 치우치지 않은, 편견 없는, 공정한; 공평한(fair)

IN BRIEF Not partial or biased; unprejudiced

+ disinterested, dispassionate, neutral, objective, fair, unbiased

> It's an admirably objective and impartial report.
> (그것은 놀라울 만큼 객관적이고 공정한 보도이다.)

0969
impasse [impǽs]
난국, 곤경, 막다름(dilemma)

IN BRIEF A predicament with no possible escape

+ stalemate, mire, quagmire, bog-down, dilemma, bad situation

> The two countries tried to divide the land equally, but reached an impasse.
> (두 나라는 땅을 균등하게 나누려 노력했으나, 교착상태에 이르렀다.)

0970
impassioned [impǽʃənd]
열정적인, 열렬한; 감동적인, 흥분시키는; 힘을 돋우는

IN BRIEF Filled with passion; fervent

+ passionate, ardent, fervent, fervid, vehement

> As his speech became more impassioned, the audience's reception grew chiller.
> (그의 연설이 점점 열정적이 될수록 청중들의 반응은 냉담해 졌다.)

0971
impatient [impéiʃənt]
a. 성급한, 조바심하는, 참을성 없는

IN BRIEF Very eager, exasperated

+ anxious, eager, enthusiastic, restless, hasty, precipitate

> Don't be so impatient!
> (그렇게 조급하게 굴지 마!)

0972
impeccable [impékəbəl]
a. 완벽한 → 결점[흠]이 없는 → 나무랄데 없는

IN BRIEF Supremely excellent in quality or nature: Blameless, faultless

+ absolute, consummate, faultless, flawless, indefectible, perfect, above suspicion

> His written English is impeccable.
> (그가 쓴 영어는 나무랄 데 없다.)

0973
impede [impíːd]
v. 지연시키다, 방해하다(hinder)

IN BRIEF To retard or obstruct the progress of

+ block, check, halt, obstruct, thwart, delay, frustrate, hamper, hinder, inhibit, restrict

> He continues to impede their progress, even after he was cautioned.
> (심지어 그는 경고를 받은 이후에도 계속해서 그들의 진행을 방해하고 있다.)

0974
impediment [impédəmənt]
n. 장애, 방해, 신체장애

IN BRIEF Something that impedes; a hindrance or obstruction

+ barrier, block, hindrance, obstacle, obstruction

> Ahntonio has a speech impediment.
> (안토니오는 언어 장애가 있다.)

0975
impending [impéndiŋ]
a. 임박한, 시급한

IN BRIEF About to occur at any moment

+ forthcoming, imminent, momentary, proximate

> Let's discuss the impending matter first.
> (우선 시급한 문제부터 논의합시다.)

0976
imperative [impérətiv]
n. 명령(command); (정세) 필요(성) 의무, 책무, 요청(demand), 강제적인 원칙
a. 피할 수 없는, 긴급한, 꼭 해야 할; 필수적인, 긴요한, 명령적인, 단호한; 위엄 있는, 엄숙한

IN BRIEF Necessary or urgent

+ urgent, essential, pressing, vital, crucial, compulsory, indispensable, obligatory, exigent

> Reducing air pollution has become an imperative.
> (대기 오염을 줄이는 것이 필수적인 것이 되었다.)

0977
imperceptible [impərséptəbəl]
a. 지각[감지]할 수 없는, (변화·차이)미세한, 경미한(very slight)

IN BRIEF Impossible or difficult to perceive by the mind or senses

+ hard to sense; faint, impalpable, imponderable, inappreciable, indiscernible, indistinguishable, insensible, intangible, invisible, unnoticeable, unobservable

> The light faded almost imperceptibly.
> (그 빛은 거의 알아볼 수 없을 정도로 희미해졌다.)

0978
imperil [impéril]
(endanger) (생명·재산) 위태롭게 하다, 위험하게 하다

IN BRIEF To subject to danger or destruction: endanger, jeopardize

+ menace, peril, risk, threaten

> We must never imperil the safety or lives of ourpassengers.
> (우리는 절대 승객의 생명을 위태롭게 해서는 안 된다.)

0979
impetuous [impétʃuəs]
(바람·속도, 기질, 행동) 맹렬[격렬]한, 열렬한, 성급한, 충동적인

IN BRIEF Characterized by sudden and forceful energy or emotion

+ brash, foolhardy, hasty, headlong, improvident, impulsive, incautious, rash, reckless, temerarious, unconsidered

> Don't be so impetuous!
> (그렇게 성급하게 굴지 마!)

0980
impetus [ímpətəs]

n. 자극, 추진력

IN BRIEF An impelling force; an impulse

+ encouragement, impulse, incentive, force, motivation

His ambition was an impetus to work for success.
(그의 야망이 성공을 위한 노력의 원동력이었다.)

0981
implacable [implǽkəbəl]

a. 누그러뜨릴 수 없는, 화해하기 어려운, 앙심 깊은

IN BRIEF Impossible to placate or appease

+ inexorable, intractable, uncompromising, unrelenting, unyielding

They are an implacable enemy.
(그들은 화해할 수 없는 적이다.)

0982
implausible [implɔ́ːzəbəl]

a. 받아들이기 어려운, 믿기지 않는

IN BRIEF Difficult to believe; not plausible

+ improbable, inconceivable, incredible, preposterous, unbelievable

This book has really an implausible story.
(이 책은 정말 믿기 어려운 이야기를 담고 있다.)

0983
implement [ímpləmənt]

도구, 용구, 기구 → 이행하다, 실행하다

IN BRIEF Carry out, carry off, put in practice

+ carry out, effect, carry through, complete, apply, perform, fulfil, enforce, execute, discharge

I propose that we implement the plan and see if it will work.
(계획을 실행하고 그 계획이 잘 되어 가는지 살펴보기를 나는 제안한다.)

0984
implode [implóud]

v. (진공관) 안쪽으로 파열하다, 내파(內破)하다(opp. explode)

IN BRIEF To collapse inward violently

+ go off, collapse

The windows on both sides of the room had imploded.
(그 방의 양쪽 창문이 내파되었다.)

0985
imply [implái]

vt. 암시하다, 넌지시 비추다, 함축하다

IN BRIEF To express or state indirectly

+ insinuate, intimate, suggest, denote, indicate

His silence seemed to imply agreement.
(그의 침묵은 동의를 암시하는 것 같았다.)

0986
impose [impóuz]

(세금·형벌·의무)지우다, (의견)강요하다[on, upon]

IN BRIEF To establish or apply as compulsory; levy

+ assess, charge, enact, exact, levy

She imposed her ideas on the group.
(그녀는 그 그룹에 자기 생각을 강요했다.)

0987
impromptu [ɪmˈprɑːmptuː]

준비 없는 → 즉석의 → 즉흥적인 → 임시변통의

IN BRIEF Prompted by the occasion rather than being planned in advance

+ ad-lib, extemporaneous, extempary, extempore, improvised, offhand, off the cuff

We were treated to an impromptu dance display by local schoolchildren.
(우리는 지역 어린 학생들의 즉흥 춤 솜씨를 구경했다.)

0988
impoverish [impávəriʃ]

(사람·국가)가난하게 하다, (토지)불모로 만들다, (사람의 질·능력·활기) 저하시키다, 허약하게 하다

IN BRIEF To reduce to poverty; make poor

+ bankrupt, ruin, beggar, break, pauperize

Intensive cultivation has impoverished the soil.
(집약적인 경작으로 토양이 척박해졌다.)

0989
impregnable [imprégnəbəl]

난공불락의, 견고한 → (신념, 생각)흔들리지 않는 → 확고한

IN BRIEF Impossible to capture or enter by force

+ unconquerable, formidable, invincible invulnerable, secure, strong

They have an impregnable fortress.
(그들은 난공불락의 성채를 가지고 있다.)

0990
impotent [ímpətənt]
a. 무력한, 무능력한, …할 수 없는

IN BRIEF Lacking physical strength or vigor; weak

+ helpless, powerless, ineffective, inept

> Without the chairman's support, the committee is impotent.
> (회장의 후원이 없이는, 그 위원회는 무력하다.)

0991
improvise [ímprəvàiz]
(시, 곡, 연설)즉석에서 하다[짓다, 연주하다]

IN BRIEF To compose or recite without preparation

+ ad-lib, extemporize, fake, make up (Idioms: wing it)

> In jazz, the performers often improvise their own melodies.
> (재즈에서, 공연을 하는 사람들은 종종 자신들의 멜로디를 즉흥에서 만든다.)

0992
imprudent [imprúːdənt]
a. 경솔한, 사려가 없는, 무분별한, 신중치 못한

IN BRIEF Unwise or indiscreet; not prudent

+ foolhardy, hasty, indiscreet, rash, reckless, unwise

> She was imprudent to go out at midnight.
> (그녀는 분별없이 한밤중에 외출했다.)

0993
impudent [ímpjədənt]
a. 뻔뻔스러운, 염치없는, 무례한, 건방진(rude)

IN BRIEF Offensively bold or disrespectful; insolent or impertinent

+ arrogant, audacious, brazen, insolent, presumptuous

> He is an impudent visitor.
> (그는 건방진 손님이다.)

0994
impulse [ímpʌls]
n. 충동, 욕구, (물리적인) 충격, 자극(whim)

IN BRIEF An impelling force; an impetus

+ bent, inclination, proclivity, tendency, impetus, stimulus

> Ahntonio bought the car on impulse.
> (안토니오는 충동적으로 그 차를 샀다.)

0995
impulsive [impʌ́lsiv]
감정에 끌린, 충동적인, (힘이) 추진적인, 추진력이 있는

IN BRIEF Inclined to act on impulse rather than thought

+ headlong, hotheaded, impetuous, improvident, incautious

> She made an impulsive decision.
> (그녀는 충동적인 결정을 내렸다.)

0996
ingrained [ingréind]
a. 깊이 스며든, 뿌리 깊은

IN BRIEF Firmly established, as by long conditioning; deep-seated

+ confirmed, deep-rooted, deep-seated, entrenched, hard-shell, ineradicable, inveterate, irradicable, set, settled

> Despite my close familiarity with the wolf family, this was the kind of situation where irrational but deeply ingrained prejudices completely overmaster reason and experience.
> (내가 늑대과에 대해 매우 잘 알고 있음에도 불구하고, 이 상황은 불합리하지만 뿌리 깊은 편견들이 이성과 경험을 완전히 압도하는 상황이었다.)

0997
intervene [ìntərvíːn]
v. 사이에 들다; 방해하다, 개입하다; (방해 되는 일)생기다

IN BRIEF To involve oneself in a situation so as to alter or hinder an action or development

+ interfere, mediate, intrude, intercede, arbitrate, interpose

> Tom had planned to go to the beach, but a typhoon intervened.
> (톰은 해변에 가려고 계획했었으나, 태풍이 방해했다.)

0998
inordinately [inɔ́ːrdənət]
ad. 과도하게, 지나치게; 엄청나게

IN BRIEF Exceeding reasonable limits; immoderate

+ extraordinarily

> In his late years, it is widely known that Picasso was inordinately frustrated about his age, impending death, and his loss of sexuality. It appears throughout his work at this stage of his life.
> (만년에, 피카소는 자신의 나이, 임박한 죽음, 성욕을 잃어버린 것에 대해 지나치게 좌절했던 것으로 널리 알려져 있다. 그의 생애의 이 시기에 만든 작품 전반에 그것은 두루 나타나있다.)

0999
intuition [ìntjuíʃən]
n. 직관; 직관적 통찰

IN BRIEF Knowing without the use of natural processes; acute insight

+ instinct, perception, insight, sixth sense, discernment

> His telling of the discovery of PAS reads more like a spiritual vision based on scientific intuition, rather than a methodical piece of inference.
> (PAS의 발견에 대한 그의 이야기는 체계적인 추론보다 과학적인 직감에 기초한 영적인 비전 더 가깝게 읽혀진다.)

LESSON 21

1000
inadvertent [inədvə́ːrtənt]
a. 우연히, 무심코, 부주의하게

IN BRIEF Unintentional, accidental

➕ inadvertently, accidently, unintentionally, unwittingly, thoughtlessly

> Some professional sports stars serve as inadvertent role models for young people.
> (몇몇 프로 스포츠 스타들은 젊은이들에게 뜻하지 않게 롤모델이 되기도 한다.)

1001
inaccessible [inəksésəbəl]
가까이 하기[도달하기, 얻기] 어려운(장소), 친해지기 어려운(사람); 움직여지지 않는(감정), (작품, 책) 난해한, 이해할 수 없는

IN BRIEF Not accessible; remote or unapproachable

➕ inapproachable, unapproachable, unattainable, unavailable, unreachable

> These mountain villages are completely inaccessible in winter.
> (이 산골 마을들은 겨울에는 완전히 접근할 수 없다.)

1002
inactive [inǽktiv]
a. 활동하지 않는, 활발치 못한; 움직이지 않는

IN BRIEF Not active or tending to be active

➕ dormant, idle, languid, passive, sedentary, immobile, inert

> Some animals are inactive during the daytime
> (일부 동물들은 낮 시간에는 활동을 하지 않는다.)

1003
inadequate [inǽdikwit]
a. 부적당한, 불충분한[for, to, to do]

IN BRIEF Not adequate to fulfill a need or meet a requirement; insufficient

➕ deficient, insufficient, meager, incapable, incompetent, inappropriate

> He is inadequate for the job.
> (그는 그 일에 부적당하다.)

1004
impute [impjúːt]
vt. A를 B의 탓으로 돌리다

IN BRIEF To attribute or ascribe something discreditable

➕ assign, blame, accuse, ascribe, attribute

> Don't impute me with it.
> (그 일로 나를 책망하지 마.)

1005
inadvertently [ìnədvə́ːrtəntli]
ad. 우연히, 무심코, 부주의로(accidentally)

IN BRIEF Not deliberate or considered; unintentional

➕ unintentionally, accidentally, by accident, mistakenly, unwittingly

> In 2000 the U. S. Postal Service inadvertently printed a stamp showing a tree upside down.
> (2000년에 미국의 우편국은 나무 한 그루가 거꾸로 보이는 우표를 실수로 발행했다.)

1006
inappropriate [inəpróupriit]
a. 부적절한, 부적당한

IN BRIEF Unsuitable or improper

➕ improper, indecorous, unbecoming, unseemly, inapplicable, unfit

> It seems inappropriate for us to intervene at this stage.
> (우리가 이 단계에 끼어드는 것은 부적절한 것 같다.)

1007
incalculable [inkǽlkjələbəl]
a. 헤아릴 수 없는, 무수한, 예측할 수 없는(countless)

IN BRIEF Impossible to calculate

➕ immeasurable, incomputable, inestimable, infinite, innumerable

> Ahntonio is a person of incalculable moods.
> (안토니오는 기분을 종잡을 수 없는 사람이다.)

1008
incapacitate [inkəpǽsətèit]
vt. 무능력하게 하다, ~할 수 없게 하다

IN BRIEF To deprive of strength or ability; disable

➕ cripple, disable, handicap, maim, paralyze, damage, impair

> Persistent pain is incapacitating.
> (끊임없는 통증은 (사람을) 무력하게 만든다.)

1009
inchoate [inkóuèit]
방금 시작한, 불완전한, 미완성의, 불분명한 (↔ explicit)

IN BRIEF Not completely formed. undeveloped, beginning

+ amorphous, formless, shapeless, unformed, unshaped

> She had a child's inchoate awareness of language.
> (그녀는 어린이의 초기 언어 인지력을 지니고 있다.)

1010
incidence [ínsədəns]
발생률, 발생정도[영향범위]

IN BRIEF The rate or range of occurrence or influence of something

+ frequency, occurrence, percentage

> The incidence of such crimes is increasing at a steady rate.
> (그런 범죄발생이 꾸준한 속도로 증가하고 있다.)

1011
incompatible [inkəmpǽtəbəl]
a. 양립할 수 없는, 서로 맞지 않는

IN BRIEF Opposed to, not to be harmonized

+ antagonistic, factious, hostile, inharmonious, irreconcilable, contradictory

> I've never seen such an incompatible couple.
> (나는 그렇게 마음이 맞지 않는 연인은 처음 본다.)

1012
incompetent [inkάmpətənt]
a. 무능한, 부적격의

IN BRIEF Lacking qualities necessary for effective conduct or action

+ incapable, ineffectual, inefficient, inept, unfit

> He's incompetent and not worth keeping on.
> (그는 무능력해서 계속 고용될 가치가 없다.)

1013
indecent [indíːsnt]
버릇없는, 점잖지 못한, 추잡한, 음란[외설]한

IN BRIEF Not in keeping with conventional mores

+ obscene, vulgar; offensive, immodest, improper, indecorous, indelicate, naughty, unbecoming, unbefitting, unseemly, untoward (Idioms: out of line)

> She hit the headlines with her indecent book.
> (그녀는 외설적인 책으로 갑자기 유명해졌다.)

1014
inconspicuous [inkənspíkjuːəs]
눈에 띄지 않는, 주의를 끌지 않는

IN BRIEF Not readily noticeable

+ unnoticeable, obscure, unobtrusive, unassuming

> Ahntonio tried to make himself as inconspicuous as possible.
> (안토니오는 가능한 한 눈에 띄지 않으려고 노력했다.)

1015
incontrovertible [inkὰntrəvə́ːrtəbəl]
논쟁의 여지가 없는, 부정할 수 없는; 명백한

IN BRIEF Impossible to dispute; unquestionable

+ incontestable, indisputable, irrefutable, undebatable

> It is incontrovertible that they have made a mistake.
> (그들이 실수를 했다는 것에는 논쟁의 여지가 없다.)

1016
incredible [inkrédəbəl]
믿을 수 없는, 거짓말 같은, 터무니없는, 놀라운

IN BRIEF So implausible as to elicit disbelief; unbelievable

+ absurd, implausible, impossible, improbable, inconceivable, unbelievable

> She's an incredible actress.
> (그녀는 믿을 수 없을 만큼 훌륭한 배우이다.)

1017
incumbent [inkΛ́mbənt]
a. 현직의, 재직 중의, 의무가 있는 [on, upon]

IN BRIEF The holder of an office who runs for reelection

+ obligatory, required, necessary, essential, binding, compulsory, mandatory, imperative

> The present incumbent at the White House.
> (백악관에서 현재 재직하고 있는 사람, 즉 현 미국 대통령)

1018
inconceivable [ìnkənsíːvəbəl]
a. 믿을 수 없는; 상상할 수도 없는

IN BRIEF Not to be believed

+ incredible, unbelievable, unimaginable, unthinkable

> We are surrounded by the inconceivable vastness of space.
> (우리는 상상하기 힘들 정도로 광대한 우주공간에 둘러싸여 있다.)

1019
indefinitely [indéfənətli]
ad. 무(기)한으로; 불명확하게, 막연히

IN BRIEF Without any limit of time or number

[+] ambiguous, general, indeterminate, indistinct, obscure, vague

> A decision has been postponed indefinitely.
> (결정은 무기한 연기되었다.)

1020
indelible [indéləbəl]
a. 지울[제거할] 수 없는; 잊을 수 없는; 지워지지 않는

IN BRIEF Impossible to remove, erase, or wash away; permanent

[+] fast, lasting, memorable, permanent, unforgettable

> She made indelible memories on me.
> (그녀는 나에게 지워지지 않는 기억(추억)을 주었다.)

1021
indict [indáit]
vt. 기소하다

IN BRIEF Charge with an offense; criticize

[+] accuse, arraign, charge, cite, inculpate

> He was indicted for charges of corruption.
> (그는 매수혐의로 기소되었다.)

1022
indifferent [indífərənt]
a. 무관심한, 냉담한; 중립의

IN BRIEF Not interested, uninterested

[+] apathetic, careless, detached, impassive, impervious, nonchalant

> Many people are indifferent to politics.
> (많은 사람들이 정치에 대해 무관심하다.)

1023
indolence [índələns]
n. 나태, 게으름(sloth, idleness)

IN BRIEF Habitual laziness; sloth

[+] idleness, inactivity, laziness, lethargy, procrastination

> His failure was due to indolence and lack of motivation.
> (그의 실패는 게으름과 동기 부족이 원인이었다.)

1024
indigent [índidʒənt]
a. 가난(해서 생필품에도 궁색)한, 빈곤한

IN BRIEF Experiencing want or need; impoverished

[+] destitute, impoverished, needy, penurious, poor

> Ahntonio is very indigent person.
> (안토니오는 매우 가난한 사람이다.)

1025
indignation
화, 분개(심), 분노

IN BRIEF Anger aroused by something perceived as unjust, mean, or unworthy

[+] anger, pique, resentment, fury, rage, wrath

> Much to my indignation, he sat down in my seat.
> (엄청 화나게도, 그가 내 자리에 앉았다.)

1026
indiscriminate [indiskrímənit]
a. 가리지 않는, 무차별의(indiscreet)

IN BRIEF Not making or based on careful distinctions; unselective

[+] haphazard, arbitrary, random, slapdash, unsystematic

> Indiscriminate attacks by terrorists on civilians are still occurring.
> (민간인에 대한 테러리스트들의 무차별적 공격이 여전히 일어나고 있다.)

1027
indispensable [indispénsəbəl]
절대로 빼놓을 수 없는, 없어서는 안 되는, 필수의, 긴요한

IN BRIEF Absolutely necessary

[+] essential, fundamental, necessary, requisite, vital

> A good dictionary is indispensable for learning a foreign language.
> (좋은 사전은 외국어를 배우는데 있어서 필수 불가결하다.)

1028
indigenous [indídʒənəs]
a. 토착의, (동·식물이) 어느 지역 원산의, 토종의(자생종의)

IN BRIEF Originating, growing, or produced in a certain place or region

[+] endemic, local, native, inborn, inherent, innate

> The kangaroo is indigenous to Australia.
> (캥거루는 오스트레일리아가 원산지이다.)

1029
induce [indjúːs]
꾀다, 권유하다; 권유[설득]하여 …하게 하다[to, to do]

IN BRIEF To lead or move, as to a course of action, by influence or persuasion

[+] coax, encourage, influence, convince, persuade, bring on, cause

> We could not induce her to come.
> (우리는 그녀를 오도록 유도할 수 없었다.)

1030
indulge [indʌ́ldʒ]

(욕망·쾌락 따위에) 빠지다, 탐닉하다, (술을) 과음하다, (아이를) 버릇없게 키우다

IN BRIEF To yield to (a desire or whim; gratify)

+ gratify, satisfy, fulfil, feed, give way to, yield to, cater to, pander to

> He indulges too much.
> (그는 술을 과음한다.)

1031
industrious [indʌ́striəs]

열심히 일하는, 부지런한; 열심인(constant, diligent)

IN BRIEF Energetic in application to work or study

+ indefatigable, persistent, tenacious, assiduous, hard working

> She is an industrious student.
> (그녀는 근면한 학생이다.)

1032
inept [inépt]

a. 부적절한, 무능한

IN BRIEF Unskillful; or not fit or suitable

+ awkward, clumsy, gauche, incompetent

> His behavior at the meeting was inept.
> (회의에서의 그의 태도는 부적절했다.)

1033
inevitable [inévitəbəl]

a. 필연적인; → 피할 수 없는(unavoidable)

IN BRIEF Not able to be avoided; bound to happen

+ inescapable, sure, unavoidable, certain

> Death is inevitable.
> (죽음은 피할 수 없다.)

1034
infamous [ínfəməs]

a. 악명 높은, 평판이 나쁜[for]

IN BRIEF Having a bad reputation

+ ignoble, inglorious, nefarious, notorious, abhorrent, despicable

> His manner was infamous.
> (그의 태도는 형편없었다.)

1035
infectious [infékʃəs]

a. 전염성의 → 전염병을 일으키는 → 전염병의

IN BRIEF Spreading rapidly to others

+ communicable, contagious, transmissible, transferable

> Panic is infectious.
> (공포심은 전염성이 높다.)

1036
influx [ínflʌks]

n. 유입

IN BRIEF The arrival or entry of many people or things

+ flood, incursion, inflow, inrush, inundation, invasion

> Tourism has brought a huge influx of wealth into the country.
> (관광 산업으로 그 나라에 많은 부[돈]가 유입되었다.)

1037
infest [infést]

vt. (해충·도둑 등이) 들끓다

IN BRIEF To inhabit or overrun in numbers or quantities large enough to be harmful, threatening, or obnoxious

+ beset, overrun, pervade, plague, crawl, swarm

> Their clothing was infested with lice.
> (그들의 옷에는 이가 들끓었다.)

1038
infidelity [infidéliti]

불신, 배신; 부정(不貞), 불의(不義), 간통; 배신

IN BRIEF Lack of faith or constancy, esp sexual faithfulness

+ disloyalty, duplicity, unfaithfulness, perfidy, treachery, adultery

> Marriage destroyed by infidelity.
> (외도로 결혼생활이 끝났다.)

1039
infraction [infrǽkʃən]

n. 위반, 침해 (violation)

IN BRIEF The act or an instance of infringing, as of a law or rule; a violation

+ breach, encroachment, infringement, offense, transgression

> Speeding is the infraction of the traffic laws.
> (과속은 교통법 위반이다.)

1040
inflexible [infléksəbəl]
구부러지지 않는, 경직된, 융통성 없는, 완고한, 단호한

IN BRIEF Not easily bent; stiff or rigid

➕ firm, rigid, stiff, unbending, intractable, obdurate

> Ahntonio is obstinate and inflexible.
> (안토니오는 고집이 세고 완고하다.)

1041
infer [infə́ːr]
v. 추론하다, 추측하다; 암시하다

IN BRIEF To conclude from evidence or by reasoning

➕ assume, conclude, deduce, gather, judge

> How you infer that she is dishonest!
> (어떻게 네가 그녀가 부정직하다고 추정할 수 있니!)

1042
infinitesimal [ìnfinitésəməl]
a. 지극히 작은, 아주 작은(극소)

IN BRIEF Infinitely or immeasurably small

➕ microscopic, minuscule, minute, teeny, tiny, inappreciable

> The amounts of radioactivity were infinitesimal.
> (방사능 양이 지극히 미미하다.)

1043
infringe [infríndʒ]
v. (권리를) 침해하다; (법 등을) 어기다

IN BRIEF To transgress or exceed the limits of; violate

➕ breach, break, contravene, transgress, trespass, violate

> Good care must be taken not to infringe copyright.
> (저작권을 침해하지 않기 위한 충분한 주의가 필요하다.)

1044
infuriate [infjúərièit]
vt. 격노하게 만들다

IN BRIEF To make furious; enrage

➕ anger, enrage, incense, inflame, madden, outrage

> Their constant criticism infuriated him.
> (그들의 상습적인 비판이 그를 매우 화나게 했다.)

1045
ingenious [indʒíːnjəs]
a. 재주 있는, 재간이 많은; 영리한

IN BRIEF Having great inventive skill and imagination

➕ astute, bright, brilliant, canny, clever, artful, creative, inventive

> She's very ingenious when it comes to finding excuses.
> (변명하는 것에 관해서라면 그녀는 매우 재간이 있다.)

1046
ingratiate [ingréiʃièit]
vt. 알랑거리다, 비위를 맞추다[with]

IN BRIEF Bring oneself into favor

➕ cajole, curry favor, flatter, toady, wheedle

> He's always trying to ingratiate himself with people in authority.
> (그는 언제나 권력자들에게 알랑거리려고 한다.)

1047
introverted [íntrəvə̀ːrtid]
a. 내성적인, 내향적인

IN BRIEF Given to examining own sensory and perceptual experiences

➕ introspective, withdrawn, inward-looking, self-contained, self-centred, indrawn, inner-directed

> The introverted student became outspoken after a life-changing experience.
> (내성적인 그 학생은 삶을 변화시키는 경험을 한 후에 솔직해졌다.)

1048
inscrutable [inˈskruːtəbl]
a. 불가사의의, 예견할 수 없는, 수수께끼 같은

IN BRIEF Difficult to understand or interpret; impenetrable

➕ enigmatic, impenetrable, deadpan, mysterious, incomprehensible, inexplicable, unintelligible, unfathomable, unexplainable, undiscoverable

> Daisy stated that it was a rather inscrutable work of art, but he liked it.
> (데이지는 그것이 다소 이해할 수 없는 예술작품이라고 말했지만, 그는 그것이 마음에 들었다.)

1049
impervious [impə́ːrviəs]
a. 스며들지 않게; 무감각한

IN BRIEF Incapable of being penetrated; Incapable of being affected

➕ immune, insusceptible, proof, resistant, resistive, unsusceptible

> A study suggests that vitamin E supplements may be good for some Alzheimer's patients after all. The benefit was not huge, but for a devastaing disease that has proved almost impervious to treatment, it was notable.
> (한 연구에서는 비타민 E 보충제가 노인성 치매 환자에게 결국에는 효험이 있을 것으로 보고 있다. 효과가 크지는 않았지만, 치료가 거의 듣지 않는 것으로 드러난 파괴적인 질병치고는 효과가 주목할 만했다.)

LESSON 22

1050
ingredient [ingrí:diənt]

(혼합물의) 성분, 요소; (요리의) 재료, 구성 요소

IN BRIEF An edible substance that is used in making a dish or other food

[+] component, constituent, element, factor, part

> Mix all the ingredients in a bowl.
> (사발 안에 있는 모든 재료들을 섞어라.)

1051
inherent [inhíərənt]

a. 고유의, 타고난

IN BRIEF Innate; existing as a permanent, inseparable element or quality

[+] inborn, innate, intrinsic, native, natural, essential, hereditary

> I have an inherent distrust of politician.
> (나는 본래부터 정치인에 대한 불신감을 가지고 있다.)

1052
inherit [inhérit]

v. (재산·권리) 상속하다, 물려받다

IN BRIEF Receive a right as an heir

[+] acquire, be bequeathed, be willed, get, receive

> She inherited a large fortune.
> (그녀는 많은 돈을 물려받았다.)

1053
inhibit [inhíbit]

vt. 금하다, 못하게 막다[from …ing]

IN BRIEF To hold back; restrain

[+] bridle, constrain, curb, obstruct, restrain, restrict, hinder

> Shyness inhibited him from speaking.
> (소심함 때문에 그는 말을 하지 못했다.)

1054
inhibition [inhəbíʃən]

n. 금지, 억제; 방지

IN BRIEF The act of inhibiting or the condition of being inhibited

[+] shyness, restraint, curb, limitation, constraint, constriction, impediment, coercion, compulsion, restraint

> She had no inhibitions about making her opinions known.
> (그녀는 그녀의 생각을 표현하는데 있어서 아무런 거리낌이 없다.)

1055
inimical [inímikəl]

a. 적대하는, 불리한, 해로운

IN BRIEF Injurious or harmful in effect; adverse

[+] antagonistic, contrary, hostile, malevolent, malicious

> Their policies are inimical to national unity.
> (그들의 정책은 국가 통합에 유해하다.)

1056
inimitable [iními təbəl]

a. 흉내낼 수 없는, 비길 데 없는, 독특한

IN BRIEF Incapable of being duplicated or imitated; unique

[+] incomparable, matchless, peerless, unequaled, unique

> He related, in his own inimitable way, the story of his journey through Tibet.
> (그는 티베트를 일주한 그의 여행담을 그의 특유의 방식으로 말했다.)

1057
initial [iníʃəl]

a. 처음의, 발단의, 초기의

IN BRIEF Of, relating to, or occurring at the beginning; first

[+] beginning, first, introductory, opening, original, starting

> My initial reaction was to refuse.
> (나의 최초의 반응은 거절하는 것이었다.)

1058
initiate [iníʃièit]

vt. (사업·계획) 시작하다, 개시[창시]하다, 착수하다

IN BRIEF To set going by taking the first step; begin

[+] begin, inaugurate, introduce, launch, open, start

> He herded hundreds of heads of cattle to North Korea in 1998, to initiate trade with the North.
> (그는 1998년 수백 마리의 소 떼를 이끌고 방북 북한교역의 물꼬트기 시작했다.)

1059
injurious [indʒúəriəs]

a. 해로운, 유해한[to]

IN BRIEF Causing or tending to cause injury; harmful

[+] damaging, deleterious, destructive, detrimental, harmful

> Smoking is injurious to health.
> (흡연은 건강에 해롭다.)

1060
innate [inéit]

a. 타고난, 선천적인

IN BRIEF Existing in a person or animal from birth; congenital; inborn

+ inborn, inherent, native, natural

A good comedian has an innate wit.
(훌륭한 코미디언은 타고난 재치가 있다.)

1061
innocuous [inάkjuːəs]

a. 해가[독이] 없는, 악의가 없는

IN BRIEF Having no adverse effect; harmless

+ harmless, innocent, inoffensive

Some mushrooms look innocuous but are in fact poisonous.
(어떤 버섯들은 해가 없어 보이지만 실제로는 독성이 있다.)

1062
innovation [inouvéiʃən]

n. 혁신, 개혁

IN BRIEF The act of introducing something new

+ alteration, change, modernization, novelty, modify, transform

My sentence is against innovation.
(내 의견은 개혁에 반대이다.)

1063
innumerable [injúːmərəbəl]

a. 무수한, 헤아릴 수 없는; 아주 많은, 엄청난 (countless)

IN BRIEF Too great to be calculated; incalculable

+ immeasurable, incalculable, incomputable, inestimable, infinite

He has invented innumerable excuses.
(그는 무수한 변명들을 만들어냈다.)

1064
inoperable [inάpərəbəl]

a. 실행[실시]할 수 없는, 〈의학〉수술 불가능한

IN BRIEF Not able to perform its normal function

+ unusable, impossible, impractical

The policy was rendered inoperable.
(그 정책은 실행할 수 없게 되었다.)

1065
inquisitive [inkwízətiv]

호기심이 많은, 꼬치꼬치 캐묻는

IN BRIEF Excessively curious, esp about the affairs of others; prying

+ nosy, snoopy, questioning, meddlesome, prying

Ahntonio is very inquisitive.
(안토니오는 캐묻기를 매우 좋아한다.)

1066
insatiable [inséiʃəbəl]

a. 만족할 줄 모르는, 매우 탐욕스러운

IN BRIEF Impossible to satiate or satisfy

+ greedy, ravenous, unquenchable, voracious, avaricious, covetous

He had an insatiable desire for power.
(그는 권력에 대한 만족할 줄 모르는 욕망을 가졌다.)

1067
inscribe [inskráib]

vt. 새기다, 기입하다; 등록하다

IN BRIEF To write, print, carve, or engrave (words or letters on or in a surface)

+ print, record, write, carve, engrave, imprint

The book was inscribed "To Ahntonio, with warmest regards."
(그 책은 "가장 따뜻한 관심과 함께 안토니오에게"라는 헌사가 적혀 있었다.)

1068
insert [insə́ːrt]

vt. 끼워 넣다, 삽입하다

IN BRIEF To put or set into, between, or among

+ inject, interject, interlard, interpolate, interpose, place

Please insert your card.
(카드를 넣으세요.)

1069
insight [ínsàit]

n. 견식, 식견, 안식, 통찰력 (instinct, inspiration)

IN BRIEF The ability to perceive clearly or deeply; penetration

+ intuition, intuitiveness, penetration, sixth sense

Ahntonio has a keen insight into human character.
(안토니오는 사람의 성격을 꿰뚫어 보는 날카로운 통찰력을 지니고 있다.)

1070
insolent [ínsələnt]

a. 건방진, 오만한

IN BRIEF Audaciously rude or disrespectful; impertinent or impudent

+ haughty, high-and-mighty, lofty, lordly, overbearing

He was the sort of child that teachers would describe as insolent.
(그는 교사들이 건방지다고 묘사하는 종류의 아이였다.)

1071
insipid [insípid]
a. 재미없는, 무미건조한, 지루한, 맛이 없는, 김빠진

IN BRIEF Lacking flavor or zest; not tasty

+ banal, dull, flat, savorless, tasteless, flavorless, unsavory

> Why anyone buys music with such insipid lyrics is a mystery.
> (왜 사람들이 그런 지루한 가사가 담긴 음악을 사는지가 수수께끼이다.)

1072
insinuate [insínjuèit]
넌지시 비추다; (사상 등을) 교묘하게 심어주다, 암시하다

IN BRIEF Hint, suggest, imply, introduce artfully

+ hint, imply, intimate, suggest

> He insinuates to me that you are a liar.
> (그는 나에게 네가 거짓말쟁이라고 넌지시 비추고 있다.)

1073
insolvent [insálvənt]
지급 불능의, 채무를 이행할 수 없는; 파산한

IN BRIEF Unable to meet debts or discharge liabilities; bankrupt

+ bankrupt, broke, destitute, impoverished, destituted, in the red

> They were insolvent within weeks.
> (그들은 몇 주 안 되서 파산했다.)

1074
inspire [inspáiər]
v. 고무하다, 불어넣다, 영감을 주다; 들이마시다

IN BRIEF Fill with high emotion; to guide by divine influence; stimulate creativity

+ animate, enkindle, impassion, kindle, stir, encouraging

> His success inspired the rest of us to greater efforts.
> (그의 성공은 우리(그를 제외)로 하여금 더 많은 노력을 하도록 고무시켰다.)

1075
instill [instíl]
vt. (사상·감정) 서서히 불어넣다, 주입하다[into, in]

IN BRIEF Inculcate, introduce; insinuate; infuse slowly into the mind or feelings

+ impart, implant, inculcate, inspire, introduce, teach, pour

> You have to instilling a sense of responsibility into your children.
> (당신은 당신의 아이들에게 책임감을 가르쳐줘야 한다.)

1076
institute [instətjùːt]
vt. 〔규칙·관례·제도〕마련하다, 제정하다

IN BRIEF To establish, organize, or introduce

+ constitute, create, establish, found, organize, originate, start

> Government institutes a ban on the movement of livestock
> (정부는 가축의 이동에 대한 금지령을 제정한다.)

1077
instrument [instrəmənt]
n. (정밀) 기구, 도구

IN BRIEF A tool or implement used to do or facilitate work

+ device, means, tool, device, implement

> The instrument has different uses.
> (그 기구에는 여러 가지 용도가 있다.)

1078
insurmountable [insərmáuntəbəl]
넘을 수 없는; 빠져나올 수 없는, 극복할 수 없는

IN BRIEF Too large and difficult to be deal with

+ impassable, insuperable, hopeless, overwhelming

> The problems are not insurmountable.
> (그 문제는 극복할 수 없는 것이 아니다.)

1079
intact [intǽkt]
a. 손상되지 않은, 완전한

IN BRIEF Remaining sound, entire, or uninjured; not impaired in any way

+ complete, entire, full, integral, perfect, whole

> This vase has been preserved intact.
> (이 꽃병은 본래대로 보존되어 왔다.)

1080
interact [intərǽkt]
vi. 서로에게 영향을 주다, 상호 작용하다

IN BRIEF To act on each other

+ associate, mingle, socialize, alloy, blend, combine

> Perfume interacts with the skin's natural chemicals.
> (향수는 피부의 자연 화학물질과 상호 작용한다.)

1081
intercede [ìntərsíːd]
vi. 사이에 들어 중재[조정]하다 [with, for]

IN BRIEF To plead on another's behalf

+ arbitrate, intervene, mediate, negotiate

> He had tried to intercede with the authorities for me.
> (그는 나를 위해 당국과 중재하려고 애썼다.)

1082
interference [íntərfíərəns]
n. 간섭, 개입; 방해

IN BRIEF Get into someone else's business

+ intervention, intrusion, meddling, obtrusion

> Ahntonio cannot brook interference.
> (안토니오는 간섭 받는걸 못 참는다.)

1083
interim [íntərim]
a. 한동안, 중간기, 잠시

IN BRIEF An interval of time between one event, process, or period and another

+ break, gap, hiatus, lacuna, void, temporary

> What are you doing in the interim?
> (공백기간 동안 너는 뭘 할 거니?)

1084
interject [ìntərdʒékt]
v. 불쑥 끼어들다

IN BRIEF To interpose abruptly or sharply; interrupt with; throw in

+ inject, insert, interfere, interpolate, interpose

> 'Oh, don't worry about the cost', he interjected.
> ('오! 비용은 걱정하지 말아요' 라고 그가 불쑥 끼어들었다.)

1085
intermittent [ìntərmítənt]
a. 때때로 끊기는, 간헐성의, 주지적인; 때때로의

IN BRIEF Not continuous

+ occasional, periodic, periodical, sporadic

> There will be intermittent rain in the north.
> (북부 지방에는 간헐적으로 비가 내리겠습니다.)

1086
interrupt [ìntərʌ́pt]
v. (흐름·진행·교통)훼방 놓다, 방해하다, 차단하다

IN BRIEF To break the continuity or uniformity of

+ cease, discontinue, suspend, terminate

> Please don't interrupt! (방해 좀 하지 마!)

1087
intertwine [ìntərtwáin]
v. ~을 서로 얽히게[꼬이게] 하다

IN BRIEF To join or become joined by twining together

+ braid, coil, entwine, plait, weave

> Their fingers intertwined. (그들은 손깍지를 꼈다.)

1088
intimate [íntəmit]
a. 친밀한, 친한, 사이좋은, 암시하다, 넌지시 말하다

IN BRIEF To indicate or make known indirectly

+ hint, chummy, close, familiar, friendly, trusted, confidential

> We are intimate friends. (우리는 절친한 친구이다.)

1089
intimidate [intímədèit]
vt. 협박하다, 위협하다

IN BRIEF To make timid; fill with fear

+ browbeat, bully, bullyrag, harass, threaten, frighten

> I find a black cat very intimidating.
> (난 검은 고양이가 참 무서워요.)

1090
intractable [intrǽktəbəl]
고분고분 하지 않은, 다루기 어려운, 고집 센

IN BRIEF Not easily controlled; not manageable; stubborn; obstinate

+ disorderly, fractious, indocile, obstinate, inflexible, obdurate, resolute

> When Ahntonio was little boy, he is really intractable child.
> (안토니오가 작은 아이였을 때, 그는 정말 다루기 힘든 아이였다.)

1091
intrepid [intrépəd]
a. 두려움을 모르는, 용기 있는, 대담한

IN BRIEF Resolutely courageous; fearless

+ audacious, bold, brave, courageous, dauntless, doughty, fearless

> Other intrepid entrepreneurs are making counterfeits.
> (또 다른 대담한 기업가들은 모조품을 만들고 있다.)

1092
intricate [íntrəkit]
a. 뒤얽힌, (기계·일·줄거리 따위가) 복잡한, 난해한

IN BRIEF Having many complexly arranged elements; elaborate

+ detailed, complicated, elaborate, difficult, involved

> The watch mechanism is extremely intricate and very difficult to repair.
> (시계구조는 극히 복잡해서 수리하기가 대단히 어렵다.)

1093
intrigue [intríːg]
v. 음모를 꾸미다; 호기심을 돋우다(fascinate, interest)

IN BRIEF To arouse the interest or curiosity of

➕ cabal, collusion, connivance, conspiracy, machination

> What you say intrigues me.
> (너의 이야기가 나의 흥미를 끈다.)

1094
inference [ínfərəns]
n. 추리, 추측, 추론

IN BRIEF The act or process of deriving logical conclusions from premises known or assumed to be true

➕ deduction, conclusion, assumption, reading, consequence, presumption, conjecture, surmise, corollary

> The relation between the two languages in the district settled by the Danes is a matter of inference rather than exact knowledge.
> (데인족이 정착한 지역에서 사용했던 두 언어 사이의 관계는 정확한 지식보다는 추론의 문제이다.)

1095
inculpatory [inkʌ́lpətɔ̀ːri]
a. 죄를 씌우는, 비난하는

IN BRIEF Causing blame to be imputed to

➖ inculpability—a state of innocence, blamelessness, guiltlessness, inculpableness

> The newspaper reported that the man was poisoned to death by an overdose of arsenic, and a bottle of arsenic was found in the purse of his secretary. The district attorney presented that bottle as inculpatory evidence to prosecute his secretary.
> (신문 기사에 의하면, 그 남자는 다량의 비소를 먹고 중독되어 사망한 것이며, 비서의 핸드백에서 비소가 들어 있는 병이 발견됐다. 지방검사는 비서를 기소 할 수 있는 유죄의 증거로 그 병을 제출했다.)

1096
incoherent [ìnkouhíərənt]
a. 일관되지 않는

IN BRIEF Lacking cohesion, connection, or harmony; not coherent. Unable to think or express one's thoughts in a clear or orderly manner

➕ unintelligible, wild, confused, disordered, wandering, muddled, rambling, inconsistent, jumbled, stammering, disconnected, stuttering, unconnected, disjointed, inarticulate, uncoordinated

> His speech last night was incoherent because it lacked unity, organized ideas illogically, and alternated between formal and informal style.
> (어젯밤 그의 연설은 통일성이 부족했고, 생각들을 비논리적으로 전개했으며, 격식을 갖춘 말과 구어체를 번갈아 가며 이야기했기 때문에 일관성이 없었다.)

1097
ignorance [ígnərəns]
n. 무지

IN BRIEF The condition of being uneducated, unaware, or uninformed

➕ lack of education, stupidity, foolishness, blindness, illiteracy, benightedness, unenlightenment, unintelligence

> Socrates insists that his understanding of his own ignorance is the greatest understanding that he has. "I know, " he says in the Apology, "that I have no wisdom, small or great. "
> (소크라테스는 자신의 무지를 아는 것이 그가 가진 가장 큰 깨달음이라고 주장한다. 그는 [변명]이라는 책에서 "나는 나에게 작든 크든 그 어떤 지혜도 없음을 안다."고 말하고 있다.)

1098
implicit [implísit]
a. 은연중의, 함축적인, 암시적인

IN BRIEF Implied or understood though not directly expressed

➕ implied, understood, suggested, hinted at, taken for granted, unspoken, inferred, tacit, undeclared, insinuated, unstated

> Virtue is measured by one's approximation to proper class appearances. Even a simple adventure story like Treasure Island manifests this implicit class perspective.
> (미덕은 계급이 가진 고유한 모습에 얼마나 가까운지 여부로 측정된다. 심지어 [보물섬]같은 간단한 모험 소설조차도 이런 암묵적인 계급적 시각을 분명하게 드러내고 있다.)

1099
initiative [iníʃiətiv]
n. 계획, 주도권, 진취성

IN BRIEF 1. the first step or action of a matter; commencing move: he took the initiative; a peace initiative

IN BRIEF 2. the right or power to begin or initiate something: he has the initiative

IN BRIEF 3. the ability or attitude required to begin or initiate something

➕ plan, deal, proposal, act, action, measure, scheme, strategy, technique, suggestion, procedure, gambit

➕ advantage, start, lead, upper hand

➕ enterprise, drive, push, energy, spirit, resource, leadership, ambition, daring, enthusiasm, pep, vigour, zeal, originality, eagerness

> Local residents are launching a new initiative to promote greater involvement in community affairs.
> (지역주민들은 지역사회의 일에 보다 적극적인 참여를 장려하기 위해 새로운 계획에 착수하고 있다.)

LESSON 23

1100
intrinsic [ɪn|trɪnsɪk]

본질적인, 고유의(inherent, belonging naturally)

IN BRIEF Of or relating to the essential nature of a thing; inherent

➕ congenital, connatural, constitutional, elemental, inborn, inbred

> The concept of liberty is intrinsic to Western civilization.
> (자유의 개념은 서양 문명에 내재되어 있다.)

1101
inundate [ínəndèit]

vt. 범람하다, 넘치게 하다, 밀어닥치다

IN BRIEF To cover with water, especially floodwaters

➕ deluge, drown, engulf, flood, flush, overflow

> The river burst its banks and inundated nearby villages.
> (강물이 강둑을 허물어서 근처의 마을을 침수시켰다.)

1102
inure [injúər]

v. 단련시키다, 익숙하게 만들다

IN BRIEF To habituate to something undesirable, especially by prolonged subjection; accustom

➕ accustom, familiarize, habituate, naturalize

> After living here for years I've become inured to the damp climate.
> (몇 년 동안 이곳에 살고 난 이후로 나는 습한 기후에 익숙해졌다.)

1103
invincible [ɪnvínsəbəl]

무적의, 정복당하지 않는, (정신) 불굴의(unconquerable)

IN BRIEF Incapable of being overcome or defeated; unconquerable

➕ impregnable, indomitable, indefatigable, unconquerable

> She has an invincible will.
> (그녀는 꺾을 수 없는 의지를 가지고 있다.)

1104
invaluable [ɪnvǽljuəbəl]

a. 값을 헤아릴 수 없는, 매우 귀중한

IN BRIEF Of inestimable value; priceless

➕ costly, inestimable, precious, priceless, worthy

> This book will be invaluable to all students of history.
> (이 책은 역사를 공부하는 모든 학생들에게 매우 귀중할 것이다.)

1105
invariable [ɪnvɛ́əriəbəl]

a. 바꿀 수 없는, 불변의, 일정한

IN BRIEF Not changing or subject to change; constant

➕ changeless, constant, equable, even, invariant, regular, same, uniform

> The invariable answer to my questions was 'No!'.
> (나의 질문에 대한 변함없는 대답은 '아니오!'였다.)

1106
invidious [ɪnvídiəs]

비위에 거슬리는, 불쾌한 (arousing dislike)

IN BRIEF Tending to rouse ill will, animosity, or resentment

➕ malicious, malignant, spiteful, vicious, insulting, objectionable

> It is invidious to deprive workers of health insurance.
> (직원들의 의료 보험 혜택을 없애는 것은 불쾌한 일이다.)

1107
invigorating [ɪnvígərèitiŋ]

기운 나게 하는, 활력을 주는, (공기·미풍)상쾌한

IN BRIEF To impart vigor, strength, or vitality to; animate

➕ exhilarant, exhilarating, refreshing, rejuvenated, cheerful, delightful

> It's invigorating to swim in the sea.
> (바다에서 수영하는 것은 상쾌하다.)

1108
invalid [ínvəlid]

병약자, 환자; 병약한, 병든; 환자용의, (법)효력이 없는

IN BRIEF One who is disabled for illness or injury, having no force or weight

➕ convalescent, debilitated, disabled, incapacitated, sick, defective

> Ahntonio have an invalid mother to be taken care of.
> (안토니오에게는 돌봐드려야 할 병약한 어머니가 계시다.)

1109
involve [ɪnvάlv]

vt. 끌어들이다, 관여하게 만들다; 포함하다

IN BRIEF To have as a necessary feature or consequence; entail

➕ comprehend, comprise, contain, embody, embrace, encompass

> Don't involve me in your quarrels.
> (너희들의 싸움에 나를 끌어들이지 마.)

1110
irksome [ə́:rksəm]
a. 짜증스러운, 진력나는

IN BRIEF Causing annoyance, weariness, or vexation

(+) bothersome, galling, irritating, nettlesome, plague, provoking

> It is irksome to listen to his constant complaints.
> (그의 끊임없는 불평을 듣는 것에 진력이 난다.)

1111
irreconcilable [irékənsàiləbəl]
화합할 수 없는, 조화를 이룰 수 없는

IN BRIEF Impossible to reconcile

(+) conflicting, contention, controversy, confrontation, incompatible

> The talks have become irreconcilable.
> (회담은 화해할 수 없는 지경에 이르렀다.)

1112
irrelevant [iréləvənt]
a. 관계없는, 무관한, 부적절한 (extraneous)

IN BRIEF Unrelated to the matter being considered

(+) immaterial, impertinent, inapplicable, inappropriate, unsuited, beside the point

> If you can do the job well, your age is irrelevant.
> (네가 일만 잘할 수 있다면, 나이는 상관없다.)

1113
irritable [irətəbəl]
a. 화를 잘 내는, 성급한, 짜증내는, 흥분하기 쉬운(grouchy)

IN BRIEF Easily irritated or annoyed

(+) bad-tempered, cantankerous, crabbed, cranky, cross, disagreeable

> Ahntonio was nervous and irritable from lack of sleep.
> (안토니오는 수면 부족으로 말미암아 신경질적이 되어 있었다.)

1114
irritant [irətənt]
a. 자극하는, 흥분시키는; (약 따위가) 자극성의

IN BRIEF Causing irritation, especially physical irritation

(+) aggravation, annoyance, bother, irritation, nuisance

> The noise of traffic is a constant irritant.
> (교통 소음은 계속적인 자극을 준다.)

1115
irritate [irətèit]
v. 짜증스럽게[성가시게] 하다; 자극하다

IN BRIEF Exasperate; provoke; inflame or chafe

(+) aggravate, annoy, bother, bug, chafe, disturb

> He irritates me very often.
> (그는 매우 자주 나를 화나게 한다.)

1116
iterate [itərèit]
되풀이하다, 요약하다

IN BRIEF To say or perform again; repeat

(+) repeat, reiterate, ingeminate, restate, recapitulate

> I will iterate the warning I have previously given to you.
> (나는 이전에 당신에게 했던 경고를 되풀이해서 말하고자 한다.)

1117
itinerary [aitínərèri]
n. 여정, 여행 일정

IN BRIEF A description of a journey → route or proposed route of a journey

(+) agenda, outline, route, travel plan

> The professor has not fully outlined the trip's itinerary.
> (교수들이 여행 스케줄을 완벽하게 윤곽을 잡지 않았다.)

1118
in disarray
혼란해져, 어지럽게 뒤섞여

IN BRIEF A state of disorder; confusion, A lack of order or regular arrangement

(+) chaos, clutter, confusedness, confusion, derangement, disarrangement, disorder

> The room was in disarray.
> (그 방은 어지럽혀 있었다.)

1119
jaunt [dʒɔ:nt]
n. 소풍, 짧은 유람 여행

IN BRIEF A short trip or excursion, usually for pleasure; an outing

(+) excursion, outing, expedition, journey, voyage, trip

> She's gone on a jaunt to town.
> (그녀는 마을로 산책 갔다.)

1120
javelin [dʒǽvəlin]

n. 던지는 창; 투창

IN BRIEF A light spear thrown with the hand and used as a weapon

+ spear, lance, the light spear

> She came second in the javelin.
> (그녀는 투창에서 2등을 했다.)

1121
jeopardize [dʒépərdàiz]

v. 위험에 빠뜨리다

IN BRIEF To expose to loss or injury; imperil

+ endanger, imperil, menace, peril, risk, threaten

> She knew that by failing her exams she could jeopardize her whole future.
> (그녀는 시험에 떨어지면 자신의 장래가 위태로울 수 있음을 알고 있었다.)

1122
jeopardy [dʒépərdi]

n. 위험

IN BRIEF Risk of loss or injury; peril or danger

+ danger, endangerment, hazard, imperilment, peril, risk

> Thousands of jobs are now in jeopardy.
> (수천 개의 직장들이 이제 위태롭게 된다.)

1123
jostle [dʒásl]

v. 떠밀다

IN BRIEF To come in rough contact while moving; push and shove

+ jostling, push, bump, jiggle, shove

> The youths jostled her.
> (젊은이들이 그녀를 밀쳤다.)

1124
judicious [dʒuːdíʃəs]

a. 현명한, 사려 분별이 있는

IN BRIEF Having or proceeding from good judgment

+ wise, sapient, smart, commonsensible, commonsensical, prudent, rational, careful, cautious, circumspect, discreet

> A little judicious prodding may be necessary at this stage.
> (이 단계에서는 약간의 현명한 자극이 필요할 수 있다.)

1125
juice [dʒuːs]

n. 주스, 즙; 진수; 영감, 기운, 활력(inspiration)

IN BRIEF To give energy, spirit, or interest to

+ liquid, extract, fluid, liquor, sap, nectar

> An increasing number of photography breaks are helping amateur photographers tap their creative juices.
> (점점 늘어나고 있는 많은 사진 촬영 기회는 아마추어 사진사들이 창조적인 영감을 발휘하도록 도와주고 있다.)

1126
junk [dʒʌŋk]

n. 못 쓰는 물건, 쓰레기, 고철

IN BRIEF Discarded material, such as glass, rags, paper, or metal

+ filth, remains, rubbish, trash, waste

> We must get rid of all this junk.
> (우리는 이 모든 쓰레기를 치워야 한다.)

1127
keen [kiːn]

a. 날카로운, 예리한

IN BRIEF Having a fine, sharp cutting edge or point

+ sharp, edged, bright, clever, acute

> Ahntonio's taste is very keen.
> (안토니오의 미각은 매우 예민하다.)

1128
kidnap [kídnæp]

(어린이) 유괴하다, 꾀어내다; (사람)납치하다

IN BRIEF To carry off and hold (a person, usually for ransom)

+ abduct, snatch, carry away, shanghai, hijack

> Two businessmen have been kidnapped by terrorists.
> (두 명의 사업가가 테러리스트들에게 납치당했다.)

1129
kindle [kíndl]

v. (연료·가연물) 불을 붙이다, 태우다, 점화하다

IN BRIEF To set alight or start to burn

+ enkindle, fire, ignite, light, foment, incite, provoke, stir up, inspire

> She had kindled a flame within him.
> (그녀가 그에게 격정을 불러 일으켰다.)

1130
kitschy [kítʃi]

(작품) 저속한, 저질의

IN BRIEF Effusively or insincerely emotional

[+] funny and cheap, shallow, debauched, lascivious, prurient

> Isn't this lamp kitschy?
> (이 램프 질이 안좋은 것 같지 않니?)

1131
kleptomania [klèptəméiniə]

절도광(狂), 병적 도벽

IN BRIEF Compulsion to steal, usually without either economic need or personal desire

[+] cacoethes, mania, passion

> Ahntonio is a kleptomania.
> (안토니오는 절도광이다.)

1132
kernel [kə́ːrnəl]

핵심 → 요점 → 가장 중요한 부분(core)
핵심 (核心) [核 씨 핵] [心 마음 심]
사물의 가장 중심이 되는 부분이나 요점

IN BRIEF A seed essence, core, substance, gist

[+] marrow, germ, nub, pith

> The kernel (of that message) was that peace must not be a source of advantage or disadvantage for anyone.
> (그 메시지의 핵심은 평화가 어느 누구에게도 이익이나 불이익의 근원이 되어서는 안 된다는 것이다.)

1133
labyrinth [lǽbərinθ]

n. 미로, 미궁(maze), 복잡하게 뒤얽힌 것

IN BRIEF An intricate combination of paths or passages in which it is difficult to find one's way or to reach the exit

[+] entanglement, jungle, knot, maze

> She disappeared into the labyrinth.
> (그녀는 미궁 속으로 사라졌다.)

1134
laconic [ləkánik]

a. 간결한; 말수가 적은

IN BRIEF Using or marked by the use of few words; terse or concise

[+] brief, compendious, concise, short, succinct, summary

> She had a laconic sense of humor.
> (그녀는 간결한 유머감각을 지니고 있다.)

1135
lamentable [lǽməntəbəl]

a. 슬픈, 애처로운, 통탄할, 유감스러운

IN BRIEF Inspiring or deserving of lament or regret; deplorable or pitiable

[+] doleful, dolorous, grievous, mournful, regrettable, rueful

> It was a really lamentable accident.
> (그것은 정말 슬픈 사고였다.)

1136
languid [lǽŋgwid]

노곤한, 나른한, 기운 없는

IN BRIEF Lacking energy or disinclined to exert effort; listless

[+] sluggish, torpid, lackadaisical, languorous, listless, indolent, lethargic, apathetic, indifferent, unconcerned

> I feel too languid to work.
> (몸이 나른해서 일할 생각이 안 든다.)

1137
lassitude [lǽsitjùːd]

n. 나른함, 권태, 무기력

IN BRIEF A state or feeling of weariness, diminished energy, or listlessness

[+] apathy, listlessness, passivity, indolence, laziness, sloth, languor, lethargy

> I felt a sudden lassitude descend on me.
> (나는 갑작스러운 피로가 엄습함을 느꼈다.)

1138
latent [léit-ənt]

a. 숨은, 잠재한, 보이지 않는, 잠복해 있는

IN BRIEF Present or potential but not evident or active

[+] hidden, dormant, inert, quiescent, passive, unconscious, potential, undeveloped

> The virus remains latent in the body for many years.
> (그 바이러스는 인체 내에 여러 해 동안 잠복해 있다.)

1139
lateral [lǽtərəl]

a. 측면의, 좌우의, 바깥쪽의; 옆의, 옆에서의

IN BRIEF In a sideways manner

[+] flanking, left, right, sideways, edgewise

> Strong lateral forces are exerted on the driver of a racing car.
> (경주용 차의 운전자에게는 강력한 측면 에너지가 가해진다.)

1140
laudatory [lɔ́:dətɔ̀:ri]

a. 기리는, 찬미하는, 찬양의

IN BRIEF Expressing or containing praise; eulogistic

+ acclamatory, approbatory, commendatory, complimentary

> She was the subject of laudatory articles in several New York magazines.
> (그녀는 몇몇 뉴욕 잡지에 실린 찬양성 기사의 주제였다.)

1141
launch [lɔ:ntʃ]

v. 진수시키다, 시작하다

IN BRIEF To begin a new venture or phase; embark

+ send-off, begin, establish, instigate, introduce, originate

> She wants to be more than just a singer and is launching out into films.
> (그녀는 단순한 가수를 넘어서고 싶어서 영화배우를 시작하고 있다.)

1142
lavish [lǽviʃ]

a. 아끼지 않는, 흥청망청 쓰는, 낭비적인

IN BRIEF Characterized by or produced with extravagance and profusion

+ luxurious, opulent, palatial, plush, rich, sumptuous, prodigal

> He is never lavish with his money.
> (그는 돈을 낭비하는 법이 결코 없다.)

1143
law-abiding [lɔ: əbáidiŋ]

법을 따르는, 준법의

IN BRIEF Obeying legal rules

+ well behaved, non-criminal

> Government promotes law-abiding spirit
> (정부는 준법정신을 장려했다.)

1144
lay off [lei ɔ:f]

구조조정으로 해고하다; 그만두다, 끊다

IN BRIEF The act of dismissing employees, esp. temporarily

+ dismiss, fire, discharge, ditch

> The company will lay off half its workers.
> (그 회사는 직원의 반을 해고할 거야.)

1145
leading [lí:diŋ]

a. 주요한, 중견[중진]의; 일류의, 뛰어난

IN BRIEF Having a position in the lead; foremost

+ primary, capital, cardinal, chief, first, foremost, key, main, major

> He is one of the leading brains in the country.
> (그는 그 나라 최고 두뇌 중 한 명이다.)

1146
legitimate [lidʒítəmit]

a. 합법적인; 도리에 맞는

IN BRIEF Being in compliance with the law; lawful

+ justifiable, innocent, lawful, legal, licit

> I'm not sure that his business is strictly legitimate.
> (나는 그의 사업이 엄격히 합법적인지 확실히 모르겠다.)

1147
lenient [lí:niənt]

a. 너그러운, 관대한

IN BRIEF Being allowing or not strict

+ generous, not serve, charitable, clement, merciful, benevolent, compassionate, humane, sympathetic, mild

> I hope the judge will be lenient with them.
> (판사가 그들에게 관대한 처벌을 내리길 바란다.)

1148
lessen [lésn]

v. 줄다

IN BRIEF To cause to decrease; to belittle; to become less; reduce

+ decrease, diminish, fall

> Many economists believe that the latest figures show that the risk of inflation has lessened slightly over the past six months.
> (최근 수치는 인플레이션 위험이 지난 6개월 동안 약간 줄어들었다는 것을 보여준다고 많은 경제학자들이 믿는다.)

1149
legible [lédʒəbəl]

(필적·인쇄) 읽기 쉬운(easily read); (마음속 따위를) 훤히 알 수 있는, 명료한(clean, clear, neat, plain, readable)

IN BRIEF Clear enough to be read easily

> The poster was written in letters big enough to be legible across the room.
> (그 포스터는 그 방 어디서나 읽을 수 있을 정도로 충분히 큰 글씨로 쓰여 있었다.)

LESSON 24

1150

lethal [líːθ-əl]

a. 죽음을 초래하는, 치사의, 치명적인

IN BRIEF Capable of causing death → Deadly

+ critical, deadly, deathly, fatal, mortal

> The closure of the factory dealt a lethal blow to the town.
> (공장폐쇄는 도시에 치명적인 타격을 주었다.)

1151

lethargic [leθáːrdʒik]

졸리는, 둔감한, 활발치 못한, 감동이 없는, 무기력한

IN BRIEF Deficient in alertness or activity

+ apathetic, inactive, sluggish, stuporous, torpid, languid, phlegmatic, drowsy

> The hot weather made her listless and lethargic.
> (더운 날씨 때문에 그녀는 노곤하고 기력이 없었다.)

1152

level [lév-əl]

평평한, 평탄한, 높낮이가 없는

IN BRIEF Having a flat

+ flat, straight, horizontal, exactly

> The two pictures aren't quite level.
> (그 두 그림이 나란하지가 않다.)

1153

levy [lévi]

부과하다 → 징수하다

IN BRIEF One that imposes or collects a tax

+ assess, exact, impose, put, charge

> They are going to levy some new taxes.
> (그들은 몇 가지 새로운 세금을 징수하려고 한다.)

1154

lewd [luːd]

a. 음탕한, 음란한; 방탕한 (obscene, amative)

IN BRIEF Indecent → Preoccupied with sex and sexual desire; lustful

+ amorous, concupiscent, erotic, lascivious, lecherous, libidinous

> He said lewd jokes.
> (그는 외설적인 농담을 했다.)

1155

lexicon [léksəkən]

n. 사전, 어휘집

IN BRIEF A dictionary

+ dictionary, glossary, vocabulary, wordbook

> She compiles a lexicon.
> (그녀는 사전을 편찬한다.)

1156

liability [làiəbíləti]

n. 책임 있음, 책임; 부담, 의무/ 부채, 채무/불리한 일

IN BRIEF The state of being liable

+ answerability, responsibility ; burden, debt

> His lack of education is his biggest liability.
> (교육을 받지 못한 점이 그의 가장 큰 장애이다.)

1157

libel [láib-əl]

n. 명예 훼손

IN BRIEF Defamation by written or printed words, pictures, or the like, rather than by spoken words

+ slander, aspersion, calumniation, calumny, defamation, denigration

> This picture is a libel on her.
> (이 사진은 그녀에게 모욕이 된다.)

1158

license [láis-əns]

n. 면허(증) (allowance)

IN BRIEF Official or legal permission to engage in a regulated activity

+ approbation, approval, authorization, consent, endorsement

> Please produce your driver's license.
> (운전 면허증을 보여주십시오.)

1160

licentious [laisénʃəs]

부도덕한, (특히) 방탕한, 성적으로 음탕한

IN BRIEF Lacking moral restraint, especially in sexual conduct

+ lewd, profligate, depraved, dissolute, lascivious, salacious, wanton

> The licentious monarch brought about the kingdom's downfall.
> (방탕한 군주는 왕국의 몰락을 야기했다.)

1161
likeness [láiknis]
n. 닮음, 비슷함 (resemblance)

IN BRIEF The state, quality, or fact of being like; resemblance

➕ affinity, alikeness, analogy, comparison, correspondence, parallelism

> I see no likeness between them.
> (그들은 닮은 데가 안 보인다.)

1162
limp [limp]
vi. 발을 절다, 느릿느릿 걷다, 흐느적거리는

IN BRIEF To walk with an uneven step, esp with a weak or injured leg

➕ falter, hobble, stagger, stumble, lifeless and drooping

> The bird was limping, dragging its injured wing along the ground.
> (새는 다친 날개를 끌고 절뚝거리며 땅위를 걸어가고 있었다.)

1163
liquidate [líkwidèit]
지불[청산]하다, 변제하다, 해산[정리]하다, 퇴출시키다, 해치우다, 죽이다

IN BRIEF To pay off (a debt, claim, or obligation; settle)

➕ abolish, annihilate, blot out, clear, eradicate, erase, exterminate

> He retained power by liquidating his opponents.
> (그는 적들을 숙청함으로써 권력을 유지했다.)

1164
livid [lívid]
흙빛의, 납빛의; 격노한, 창백한

IN BRIEF Extremely angry; furious

➕ colorless, lurid, pale; enraged, fuming, furious, incensed, irate

> He'd be livid if he knew you were here.
> (네가 여기 있는 걸 알면 그가 노발대발할 거야.)

1165
load [loud]
n. 짐

IN BRIEF A burden or cargo

➕ place, burden, cargo, freight, baggage, merchandise

> Put down your load and rest.
> (짐을 내려놓고 쉬어라.)

1166
loath [louθ]
a. 지긋지긋하여, 싫어서, 질색으로

IN BRIEF Not willing

➕ dislike, averse, disinclined, indisposed, reluctant, unwilling

> He is loath to go there.
> (그는 그 곳에 가기를 정말 꺼린다.)

1167
loathe [louð]
몹시 싫어하다, 질색이다 (dislike very strongly)

IN BRIEF To hate or despise

➕ abhor, abominate, despise, detest, execrate, hate

> I loathe snakes.
> (나는 뱀이라면 질색이다.)

1168
locomotion [lòukəmóuʃən]
n. 이동(력), 여행

IN BRIEF Movement, act or power to move from one place to another

➕ movement, travel, travelling, moving, action, progress, motion

> A fish uses its fins for locomotion.
> (물고기는 지느러미를 이용해 이동한다.)

1169
loophole [lúːphòul]
n. 빠져나갈 구멍, 허점

IN BRIEF Means of escape, avoid, elude

➕ let-out, escape, excuse, plea, avoidance, evasion

> He found a loophole in the rules.
> (그는 규칙의 허점을 찾았다.)

1170
loquacious [loukwéiʃəs]
a. 수다스러운, 말 많은

IN BRIEF Talkative

➕ chatty, conversational, garrulous, talkative, talky, voluble

> She was very loquacious about her experiences.
> (그녀는 자신의 경험에 대해 너무 떠벌였다.)

1171
lubricant [lúːbrikənt]
n. 매끄럽게 하는 것; 윤활유

IN BRIEF A substance, as oil or grease, for lessening friction, esp. in a mechanism

[+] lubricator, lubricating substance, grease, oil, wax

> Engines won't run without lubricants.
> (엔진은 윤활유가 없으면 작동하지 않는다.)

1172
lucid [lúːsid]
a. 빛나는, 맑은, 투명한, 알기 쉬운, 명백한

IN BRIEF Easily understood. Thinking clearly

[+] understandable, perceptive, rational, translucent, transparent

> His style is very lucid.
> (그의 문체는 매우 명료하다.)

1173
lucrative [lúːkrətiv]
a. 이익이 있는, 유리한, 수지맞는 (well-paying)

IN BRIEF Highly profitable

[+] advantageous, moneymaking, profitable, remunerative, rewarding

> The merger proved to be very lucrative for both companies.
> (그 합병은 양쪽 회사에 매우 득이 되는 것으로 판명되었다.)

1174
ludicrous [lúːdəkrəs]
a. 우스운, 익살맞은, 웃기는, 바보 같은

IN BRIEF So absurd or incongruous as to be laughable

[+] comic, comical, farcical, funny, laughable, laughing, ridiculous

> You look absolutely ludicrous in those clothes.
> (그 옷을 입으니까 정말로 우스꽝스럽다.)

1175
lukewarm [lúːkwɔ̀ːrm]
미적지근한 → 마음 내키지 않는(halfhearted) → 열의 없는 → 냉담한

IN BRIEF Tepid. Not enthusiastic

[+] indifferent, halfhearted, tepid, warm, unenthusiastic

> Heat the milk until it is just lukewarm.
> (우유가 미지근해질 정도까지만 데워.)

1176
luminous [lúːmənəs]
빛을 발하는, 빛나는, 번쩍이는, 명쾌한

IN BRIEF Giving off light

[+] bright, brilliant, effulgent, incandescent, irradiant, lambent, clear

> The sun and stars are luminous bodies.
> (태양과 별들은 빛을 내는 천체이다.)

1177
lunatic [lúːnətik]
a. 정신 이상자, 미친 사람

IN BRIEF A person who is affected by lunacy; a mentally deranged person

[+] disordered, deranged, insane, mad, bizarre, odd, queer

> You're driving on the wrong side of the road, you lunatic!
> (너 도로 엉뚱한 곳으로 달리고 있잖아, 이 미친놈!)

1178
lure [luər]
vt. 유혹하다, 유인하다, 매력 (allure, attract)

IN BRIEF To attract or lead by offering something that seems pleasant

[+] entice, tempt, bewitch, charm, enchant, seduce, attraction

> Don't let money lure you into a job you don't like.
> (돈에 유혹되어 좋아하지도 않는 직업을 갖지 마라.)

1179
lucubrate [lúːkjubrèit]
v. (등불 밑에서)밤늦도록 공부하다, 부지런히 일하다, 열심히 갈고닦다(moil)

IN BRIEF Write in a scholarly way; to work, write, or study laboriously, especially late at night

형설지공 (螢雪之功)(고생을 하면서 꾸준히 공부하여 얻은 보람)

> The government should lucubrate on the shortcomings unveiled by the recent evaluation.
> (정부는 최근의 평가에 의해 밝혀진 문제점들에 대해 부지런히 노력해야 한다.)

1180
leaps and bounds
급속도로, 비약적으로(by far: Very quickly)

> This rule is leaps and bounds better than what we have now.
> (이 규칙은 우리가 현재 가지고 있는 것보다 비약적으로 나아진 것이다.)

1181
lanky [lǽŋki]
a. 호리호리한, 마른(lean)

IN BRIEF Tall and thin

gangling, gangly, rangy, spindling, spindly, angular, bony, fleshless, gaunt, lank, lean, meager, scrawny, skinny, slender, slim, spare, thin,

We climbed to our peanut gallery seats just as Miss Rodeo America, a lanky brunette swaddled in a lavender pantsuit, gloves, and a cowboy hat, loped across the arena.
(라벤더 슈트, 장갑, 카우보이 모자로 온몸을 둘러싼 삐쩍 마른 흑갈색 머리의 백인 여성인 미스 로데오 아메리카(Miss Rodeo America)가 공연장을 가로질러 성큼성큼 달려간 바로 그때 우리는 맨 뒷좌석으로 올라갔다.)

1182
layman [ˈleɪmən]
n. 속인(俗人); 아마추어, 비전문가(non-specialist)

IN BRIEF A man who is a nonprofessional: amateur person

nonprofessional, amateur, outsider, lay person, non-expert, nonspecialist

The surgeon tried to describe the procedure in terms of a layman, but he used so much medical jargon that I had no idea what he was talking about.
(외과의사는 그 절차를 일반인의 말로 설명하려고 했지만, 그가 무슨 말을 하는지 모를 정도로 의학 용어를 많이 사용했다.)

1183
maelstrom [méilstrəm]
n. 큰 소용돌이, 대혼란

IN BRIEF Confused disordered state of affairs, chaos

commotion, confusion, turbulence, turmoil

She experienced a maelstrom of conflicting emotions.
(그녀는 상충되는 감정의 대혼란을 겪었다.)

1184
magnitude [mǽgnətjùːd]
n. (굉장한)크기; 중대함

IN BRIEF Relative importance or significance

importance, amplitude, bulk, mass, size

You don't appreciate the magnitude of her achievement.
(당신은 그녀가 이룬 업적의 중대성을 알지 못한다.)

1185
maintain [meintéin]
vt. 주장하다; 유지하다; 지지하다

IN BRIEF To keep up or carry on; continue

support, keep, retain, preserve, sustain

Food is necessary to maintain life.
(음식은 생명을 유지하는 데 필요하다.)

1186
makeshift [méikʃìft]
임시변통의, 대용품; 미봉책

IN BRIEF Suitable as a temporary or expedient substitute

shift, stopgap, impromptu, provisional, temporary

We'll build a makeshift shelter until help arrives.
(구조가 올 때까지 임시방편으로 거처를 만들자.)

1187
malady [mǽlədi]
n. (만성적인) 병, 질병

IN BRIEF A disease, disorder, or ailment

affliction, ailment, disease, disorder, ill, illness, sickness

We have to take
(자신감이 부족해서 그녀는 사교 생활이 다소 서투르다.)

1189
malediction [mæ̀lədíkʃ-ən]
n. 저주

IN BRIEF The calling down of a curse

curse, anathema, execration, imprecation, condemnation

Princess is trapped in a death-like sleep because of the malediction uttered by an angry witch.
(공주는 화난 마녀가 말한 저주에 걸려서 죽은 듯이 잠들게 된다.)

1190
malevolent [məlévələnt]
a. (…에) 악의[적의]를 가진

IN BRIEF Having or exhibiting ill will; wishing harm to others; malicious

wicked, invidious

They were aware of the landlord's malevolent purpose.
(그들은 집주인의 악의적인 의도를 알고 있었다.)

1191
malicious [məlíʃəs]

a. 악의[적의] 있는, 심술궂은 (wicked, baleful)

IN BRIEF Characterized by malice

⊕ hateful, nasty, spiteful, vicious, malevolent, malign, malignant

> That story is nothing more than malicious gossip.
> (그 얘기는 순전히 악의적인 험담이다.)

1192
malign [məláin]

vt. (남)을 나쁘게 말하다, 헐뜯다, 중상하다, 해로운

IN BRIEF To make evil, harmful, and often untrue statements about (someone)

⊕ slander, asperse, backbite, calumniate, defame, defamation, libel, misrepresentation, evil

> Don't malign an innocent person.
> (무고한 사람을 비방하지 마라.)

1193
malnourished [mælnə́ːriʃt]

a. 영양 불량[실조]의

IN BRIEF Not being provided with adequate nourishment, underfed

> A UNICEF nutrition representative Karen Codling says China hascut its proportion of malnourished children from 19percent to 8 percent.
> (유니세프 영양대표 카렌 코들링씨는 중국이 영양불균형아이들 비율을 19 퍼센트에서 8퍼센트로 줄였다고 밝혔다.)

1194
mandate [mǽndeit]

vt. 명령하다, 요구하다

IN BRIEF An authoritative command or instruction

⊕ decree, direct, legislate, order, command, commandment, dictate

> He was appointed managing director with a mandate to reverse the company's decline.
> (그는 회사의 쇠락 기조를 되돌리라는 명령과 함께 전무이사에 임명되었다.)

1195
mandatory [mǽndətɔ̀ːri]

a. 의무적인, 강제적인

IN BRIEF Required or commanded by authority; obligatory

⊕ prescribed, compulsory, imperative, necessary, obligatory, required, requisite

> Tuition is mandatory for all students.
> (개인지도를 받는 것은 모든 학생들에게 필수다.)

1196
manifest [mǽnəfèst]

a. 명백한, 분명한, 명백하게 하다, 분명히 나타내다

IN BRIEF Clearly apparent to the sight or understanding; obvious

⊕ apparent, evident, obvious, plain, clear, clear-cut, display, show

> His guilt was manifest.
> (그의 유죄는 명백했다.)

1197
manipulate [mənípjəlèit]

v. 조종(조작)하다

IN BRIEF To handle or use, esp with some skill, in a process or action

⊕ maneuver, handle physically, control, exploit, steer, handle, manage, operate

> The wheelchair is designed so that it is easy to manipulate.
> (그 휠체어는 조작하기 쉽게 설계되었다.)

1198
manuscript [mǽnjəskrìpt]

n. 원고

IN BRIEF Literary & Literary Critical Terms a book or other document written by hand

⊕ document, record, register, text

> I read his novel in manuscript.
> (나는 그의 소설을 원고로 읽었다.)

1199
masquerade [mæ̀skəréid]

vi. 가장하다, 변장하다

IN BRIEF The act of hiding who one is or how one feels

⊕ fake, camouflage, disguise, disguisement, facade

> Her sorrow is just a masquerade.
> (그녀의 슬픔은 가장일 뿐이다.)

1200
material [mətíːəriəl]

a. 중대한; 물질적인 / n. 구성 물질; 재료, 원료

IN BRIEF Of, relating to, or composed of matter

⊕ a. crucial, significant /n. matter, stuff, substance

> Is this point material to your argument?
> (이 점이 당신의 주장에 중요한가요?)

LESSON 25

1201
matriarch [méitriɑ̀:rk]
n. 여가장, 여족장
IN BRIEF A woman who rules a family, clan, or tribe
[+] female ruler, a strong mother

> She saw herself as an elderly matriarch.
> (그녀는 자신을 장년의 여가장으로 간주했다.)

1202
maul [mɔ:l]
(나무로 만든) 큰 메, 망치 → 난폭하게[거칠게] 때리다; 혹평하다
IN BRIEF A heavy hammer; to use roughly; to injure
[+] batter, beat, mangle

> Her novel was badly mauled by the critics.
> (그녀의 소설은 비평가들의 호된 혹평을 받았다.)

1203
maxim [mǽksim]
n. 격언, 금언; 좌우명
IN BRIEF A succinct formulation of a fundamental principle, general truth, or rule of conduct
[+] byword, motto, saying, adage, apothegm, aphorism, axiom, precept, proverb, epigram, saw

> It is a valid maxim that competition increases productivity.
> (경쟁이 생산성을 높인다는 것은 타당한 금언이다.)

1204
mean [mi:n]
v. 의미하다; 의도하다(connote, denote) / a. 인색한, 천한, 비열한 (parsimonious, stingy) / n. 평균, 중용(average, median, common, mediocre)

> I mean you no harm.
> (너를 해 할 생각은 없었어.)
> He looks like a mean character.
> (그는 성격이 비열한 것 같다.)
> You must find a mean between frankness and rudeness.
> (솔직함과 무례함 사이의 중용을 찾아야 한다.)

1205
mediocre [mì:dióukər]
a. 보통의, 평범한, 열등한
IN BRIEF Of ordinary or undistinguished quality
[+] common, commonplace, cut-and-dried, formulaic, inferior

> Although the critics enthused, I thought it was a mediocre play.
> (평론가들은 찬탄했지만, 나는 그것이 평범한 연극이라고 생각했다.)

1206
meditate [médətèit]
v. 심사숙고하다, 명상하다
IN BRIEF To think about something deeply
[+] consider, contemplate, deliberate, entertain, excogitate, mull

> I like to meditate before an important exam.
> (나는 중요한 시험 전에 명상하기를 좋아한다.)

1207
medium [mí:diəm]
n. 중간, 중용, 중간 위치[성질]의 것, (…의) 매개물
IN BRIEF A middle state or condition; mean
[+] a means of doing, average, mean, median, norm, par

> A newspaper is a good medium for advertising.
> (신문은 좋은 광고 매체이다.)

1208
meek [mi:k]
a. 얌전한, 유화한, 온순한; 참을성 있는
IN BRIEF Showing patience and humility; gentle
[+] modest, forbearing, gentle, patient, tolerant, acquiescent

> Ahntonio looks meek and mild but you should see him when he's angry.
> (안토니오가 순하고 부드러운 것처럼 보이지만 넌 그가 화났을 때를 봐야 해.)

1209
meet [mi:t]
v. (요구)만족시키다, 응하다
IN BRIEF Fitting; proper
[+] fill, fulfill, satisfy, cater, pander

> I can't possibly meet that deadline.
> (저는 그 기한을 맞출 수 없습니다.)

1210
melt [melt]
v. 녹다; (서서히) 사라지다

IN BRIEF To be changed from a solid to a liquid state especially by the application of heat

+ disappear, deliquesce, liquefy, dissolve, disintegrate, dissipate, blend

> Great heat melts iron.
> (높은 열은 철을 녹인다.)

1211
memento [miméntou]
n. 기억, 추억, 추억거리; 기념(품), 유물

IN BRIEF Something that reminds one of past events; souvenir

+ keepsake, remembrance, reminder, souvenir, token, trophy

> These postcards are mementos of our trip abroad.
> (이 그림엽서들은 우리 해외여행의 기념물이다.)

1212
mendicant [méndikənt]
a. 탁발하는, 구걸하는, 거지의, 거지와 같은

IN BRIEF One who begs habitually or for a living

+ beggar, cadger, indigent, pauper

> A mendicant monk visited the rich man.
> (탁발승이 부잣집 남자를 방문했다.)

1213
menial [míːniəl]
(일)시시한 → 지루한 → 천한(mean) → 비굴한 (노예근성 있는)

IN BRIEF Of or relating to work or a job regarded as servile

+ lowly, obsequious, servile, slavish, subservient

> He was given the menial job of operating the office photocopying machine.
> (그에게는 사무실 복사기를 다루는 허드렛일이 주어졌다.)

1214
merge [məːrdʒ]
v. 어우러지다, 뒤섞이다; 합병하다

IN BRIEF To combine or unite into a single entity

+ blend, commingle, fuse, combine, unify, amalgamate, incorporate

> They decided to merge the two companies into one.
> (그들은 두 회사를 하나로 합병하기로 결정했다.)

1215
merit [mérit]
n. 뛰어남, 빼어남; 장점, 좋은 점

IN BRIEF Superior quality or worth; excellence

+ caliber, quality, stature, value, virtue, worth

> His chief merit is kindness.
> (그의 주된 장점은 친절이다.)

1216
mercurial [məːrkjúəriəl]
〈천문〉수성의;〈로마 신화〉머큐리 → 신의, 변덕스러운

IN BRIEF Following no predictable pattern

+ capricious, changeable, erratic, fickle, whimsical

> Ahntonio has a mercurial temperament.
> (안토니오는 변덕스런 성질을 가지고 있다.)

1217
meticulous [mətíkjələs]
a. 세심한, 꼼꼼한, 정확한 → 성실한

IN BRIEF Giving great attention to details

+ very careful, fastidious, painstaking, punctilious, scrupulous

> Many hours of meticulous preparation have gone into writing this book.
> (이 책을 쓰는 데에는 여러 시간에 걸친 꼼꼼한 준비가 들어갔다.)

1218
middle-of-the-road
(정책·정치가) 중도(中道)의(Not extreme) → 중용의 → 온건한 → 무난한 → 대중적인

IN BRIEF Not extreme, esp in political views; moderate

+ moderate, central, intermediate, mean, medial, mid, middle

> Her political views are very middle-of-the-road.
> (그녀의 정치적 견해는 대단히 온건하다.)

1219
migrate [máigreit]
v. 이주하다, 이동하다

IN BRIEF Move, travel to another place

+ move from one place to another, emigrate, immigrate, transmigrate

> These birds migrate to North Africa in winter.
> (이 새들은 겨울이면 북미로 이동한다.)

1220
milestone [máilstòun]

n. 이정표; 중대한 사건[국면]

IN BRIEF A significant event or point in development

[+] significant, event, landmark, occasion, turning point

His election victory was an important milestone.
(그가 선거에서 승리한 것은 중대 사건이었다.)

1221
milk [milk]

(구어) (돈·정보) 짜내다, 끌어내다, 착취하다

IN BRIEF To obtain money or benefits from, in order to achieve personal gain; exploit

[+] extract money by guile from, extract, wrest, pluck, deduce, derive

Cows must be milked twice a day.
(젖소들은 하루에 두 번 젖을 짜 주어야 한다.)

1222
millennium [miléniəm]

n. 천년(간)

IN BRIEF Span of one thousand years, thousands of years

[+] millenary

Big celebrations are planned for the arrival of the next millennium.
(다음 1,000년의 도래를 맞는 큰 축하 행사가 계획되고 있다.)

1223
minuscule [mínʌskjùːl]

(문자가) 소문자인, 소문자로 쓴, 대단히 작은; 하찮은

IN BRIEF Very small; tiny

[+] diminutive, Lilliputian, midget, miniature, tiny

For his first course all he got was two minuscule pieces of toast.
(첫 코스에서 그가 먹은 것이라곤 아주 작은 토스트 두 조각뿐이었다.)

1224
misdemeanor [mìsdimíːnər]

n. 나쁜 행실, 비행; (중죄가 아닌) 경(범)죄

IN BRIEF Wrong doing, a minor offence

[+] infraction, misdemeanour, violation, infringement

He committed a misdemeanor.
(그는 경범죄를 범했다.)

1225
miser [máizər]

n. 구두쇠, 수전노, 자린고비

IN BRIEF Person who hoards money

[+] niggard, skinflint, cheapskate, money-grubber, tightwad, stinginess

A typical miser, he hid his money in the house in various places.
(전형적인 구두쇠인 그는 집안의 여러 곳에 돈을 숨겼다.)

1226
miserly [máizərli]

인색한, 욕심 많은(stingy)

IN BRIEF Relating to one who stores riches selfishly

[+] mean, stingy, penny-pinching, parsimonious

Time was, national crises stimulated saving. But thrift today has a negative, miserly connotation.
(국가의 위기가 저축을 장려하던 시기가 있었다. 그러나 오늘날 절약은 부정적이고, 인색한 의미를 내포하고 있다.)

1227
miserable [mízərəbəl]

(사람·기분·생활 따위가) 비참한, 불행한, 슬픈

IN BRIEF Very unhappy. Poor in quality

[+] woebegone, woeful, wretched, dejected, mournful, sorrowful

Don't look so miserable!
(그렇게 불쌍하게 굴지 마!)

1228
mishap [míshæp]

n. 사고, 불행한 일

IN BRIEF A misfortune

[+] accident, casualty, contretemps, misadventure, mischance

Our journey ended without mishap.
(우리 여행은 사고 없이 끝났다.)

1229
misgiving [misgíviŋ]

n. 걱정, 의혹, 불안, 불길한 예감

IN BRIEF Doubt, distrust, or apprehension

[+] distrust, apprehension, doubt, foreboding, qualm, suspicion, anxiety

I have serious misgivings about taking the job.
(난 그 직장을 갖는 것에 대해 몹시 불안하다.)

1230
misnomer [misnóumər]

잘못된 명칭 → (인명·지명의) 잘못 부르기 → (법률 문서 중의) 인명[지명] 오기

IN BRIEF Error in naming a person or place

They found a *misnomer* in their will so they had to rewrite it.
(그들은 유언장에서 잘못된 이름을 발견했기 때문에 그것을 다시 써야 했다.)

1231
mite [mait]

n. 소액 화폐, 잔돈

IN BRIEF A very small contribution or amount of money

+ bit, money, crumb, fragment

She offered the beggar a *mite*.
(그녀는 그 거지에게 약간의 잔돈을 주었다.)

1232
mock [mɑk]

v. 조롱하다, 비웃다, 업신여기다

IN BRIEF To make fun of with scorn. Not real

+ deride, gibe, jeer, jest, laugh, ridicule, scoff

They have insulted us and *mocked* our religion.
(그들은 우리를 모욕하고 우리의 종교를 비웃었다.)

1233
modest [mάdist]

a. 겸손한; 정숙한; 적당한

IN BRIEF Having or showing a moderate estimation of one's own abilities, accomplishments, or value

+ unassertive, unassuming, chaste, demure, moral

Really great men are *modest*.
(정말 위대한 사람들은 겸손하다.)

1234
modify [mάdəfài]

v. (부분적으로)변경하다, 수정하다

IN BRIEF To make a small or partial change in

+ alter, change, mutate, turn, vary

The union has been forced to *modify* its position.
(노조는 입장을 수정하라는 압력을 받아오고 있다.)

1235
moist [mɔist]

a. 습한, 축축한, 젖은

IN BRIEF Slightly wet; damp

+ damp, dank, humid, wet

It's cool and *moist* and almost fragrant.
(공기가 시원하고 촉촉하며 향기로울 정도다.)

1236
moisture [mɔ́istʃər]

n. 습기

IN BRIEF Condensed or diffused liquid, esp. water

+ damp, dank, humidity, wet

Plants cannot live without *moisture*.
(식물은 물 없이 살 수 없다.)

1237
mold [mould]

n. 형, 틀 / v. 본뜨다

IN BRIEF To form (something out of a fluid or plastic material)

+ stamp, mould, cast

Melted metal is poured into a *mold* to harden into shape.
(녹은 금속은 굳어 형체를 이루도록 일정한 틀에 붓는다.)

1238
momentous [mouméntəs]

a. 중대한, 중요한, 심상치 않은

IN BRIEF Of great importance

+ important, earnest, grave, heavy, serious, weighty

Choosing between peace and war is a *momentous* decision.
(평화와 전쟁 중 택일하는 것은 중대한 결정이다.)

1239
monumental [mὰnjəméntl]

a. 기념비적인, 기념이 되는

IN BRIEF Like a monument, esp in large size, endurance, or importance

+ outstanding, enormous, immense, massive, vast, classic, historic

It was a *monumental* achievement.
(그것은 지대한 업적이었다.)

1240
moody [mú:di]

a. 시무룩한, 침울한, 변덕스러운; 성미가 까다로운

IN BRIEF Having frequently changeable and often negative emotions

+ depressed, temperamental, dour, gloomy, glum, morose, saturnine

I keep away from him when he's *moody*.
(나는 그가 시무룩할 때에는 가까이 가지 않는다.)

1241
moribund [mɔ́(ː)rəbʌ̀nd]

a. 죽어가는, 소멸해 가는(die)

IN BRIEF Approaching death; about to die

➕ deteriorating, dying, failing, waning

> Linguists have studied moribund languages.
> (언어학자들은 사라져 가는 언어들을 연구해 왔다.)

1242
mortify [mɔ́ːrtəfài]

굴욕감을 주다, (정욕·감정) 억제하다, 극복하다

IN BRIEF To cause to experience shame, humiliation, or wounded pride

➕ abase, degrade, abash, disgrace, humble, humiliate, shame

> He was mortified that he hadn't been invited.
> (그는 초대받지 않은 것에 대해 굴욕감을 느꼈다.)

1243
motivation [mòutəvéiʃən]

n. 자극; 동기 부여; 열의

IN BRIEF Something that encourages

➕ encouragement, inspiration, stimulation, impetus, impulse, incentive

> They lack the motivation to study.
> (그들은 공부하려는 동기가 부족하다.)

1244
mourn [mɔːrn]

v. 애도하다, (죽음을) 슬퍼하다

IN BRIEF To be sad over someone's death or a loss

➕ grieve, lament, sorrow, deplore

> Black is a token of mourning.
> (검은색은 애도의 표시이다.)

1245
meteorologist [mìːtiərɑ́lədʒist]

n. 기상학자, 기상 캐스터

IN BRIEF One who studies meteorology. One who reports and forecasts weather conditions

> Chicago could see as much as 6-8 inches of snow from late Tuesday Through late Thursday, which WGN meteorologist Tom Skilling says will arrive "in waves rather than a single stretch." (WGN: a television station in Chicago, Illinois, USA)
> (시카고에는 화요일 오후에 목요일 오후까지 눈이 6내지 8인치나 올 수 있는데, WGN의 기상캐스터인 톰 스킬링에 따르면, 눈이 '한번에 다 오고 그치는 것이 아니라 연달아' 올 것이라고 한다.)

1246
mitigate [‘mɪtɪgeɪt]

v. 누그러뜨리다, 완화시키다, (형벌)경감시키다

IN BRIEF To make or become less severe or harsh; moderate

➕ allay, blunt, moderate, palliate, temper

> These should be understood if they are to be properly mitigated.
> (이것들은, 만일 적절하게 완화되어야 한다면, 이해되어야 한다.)

1247
monstrous [mɑ́nstrəs]

a. 괴물 같은, 기괴한; 엄청난

IN BRIEF Shockingly hideous or frightful in appearance

➕ outrageous, shocking, evil, horrifying, vicious, foul, cruel, infamous, intolerable, disgraceful, scandalous, atrocious

> The stadium can only hold 10,000 people but a monstrous crowd came for the concert.
> (그 경기장은 불과 10,000명을 수용할 수 있지만, 그 콘서트를 보러 엄청난 관객들이 왔다.)

1248
mollify [mɑ́ləfài]

v. 완화 시키다; 달래다, 진정시키다

IN BRIEF To calm in temper or feeling; soothe, appease, assuage, calm (down)

➕ conciliate, dulcify, gentle, pacify, placate, propitiate, soften, soothe

> I had every intention to raise liberated, nonviolent sons whose aggressive tendencies would be mollified by sensitivity and compassion
> (나는 아들들을 자유롭고 폭력적이지 않게 키울 의사가 분명히 있었으며 아들들의 공격적 성향은 감성과 동정심으로 누그러질 것이었다.)

1249
mawkish [mɔ́ːkiʃ]

a. 몹시 감상적인, 눈물을 잘 흘리는

IN BRIEF Excessively and objectionably sentimental

➕ Definition: sentimental, emotional, maudlin, slushy, schmaltz
➕ Antonyms: calm, serious, unemotional

> The critic's review of the movie seems mawkish and overwrought.
> (그 영화에 대한 비평가의 평은 감상적이고 지나치게 공을 들인 것 같다.)

1250
measured [méʒərd]

a. 신중한, 침착한(prudent); 정확히 잰

IN BRIEF Careful and slow in acting, moving, or deciding

+ deliberate, leisurely, unhurried: restrained

> Let's say that he should have come to me first,' George said in a heavy, measured tone.
> ("그가 먼저 나에게 왔어야 했다고 칩시다"라고 조지(George)가 진지하고 신중한 어조로 말했다.)

LESSON 26

1251
mournful [mɔ́ːrnfəl]
a. 슬픔에 잠긴, 한탄하는
IN BRIEF Full of or expressive of sorrow
+ sad, doleful, dolorous, lugubrious, plaintive, rueful, sorrowful

We saw a mournful expression on her face.
(우리는 그녀의 얼굴에 어린 슬픈 표정을 보았다.)

1252
moving [múːviŋ]
움직이는, 이동하는, 동기가 되는, 감동시키는
IN BRIEF Arousing or touching the emotions
+ heart-rending, touching, inspiring, stirring, motivating

His speech was deeply moving.
(그의 연설은 아주 감동적이었다.)

1253
muggy [mʌ́gi]
a. (기후 따위가) 찌는 듯이 더운, 무더운
IN BRIEF Warm and humid
+ hot and humid, soggy, sultry, damp, tropical

The day was unusually muggy.
(그 날은 유난히 무더웠다.)

1254
multiracial [mʌ̀ltiréiʃ-əl]
a. 다민족의, 여러 민족으로 이루어진
IN BRIEF Made up of various races
+ racial

I live in a multiracial society.
(나는 다민족 사회에서 산다.)

1255
mumble [mʌ́mb-əl]
v. 중얼거리다
IN BRIEF To utter indistinctly, as with the mouth partly closed; mutter
+ murmur, speak indistinctly mutter, whisper, grumble, complain

Ahntonio always mumbles when he's embarrassed.
(안토니오는 당황할 때면 항상 중얼거린다.)

1256
mundane [mʌ́ndein]
a. 현세의; 세속적인(earthly), 평범한, 흔히 있는, 우주의
IN BRIEF Everyday, ordinary, or banal
+ commonplace, routine, uneventful, terrestrial, worldly, everyday

I lead a pretty mundane life.
(나는 상당히 평범한 삶을 살고 있다.)

1257
muse [mjuːz]
v. 깊이 생각하다, 숙고하다
IN BRIEF Think, ruminate on, dream, ponder, contemplate
+ ruminate, meditate, think about, cogitate, mull over

'I wonder if I will ever see them again', he mused.
('내가 그들을 과연 다시 볼 수 있을지 모르겠다.' 그는 생각에 잠겼다.)

1258
muster [mʌ́stəːr]
모으다, 소집하다
IN BRIEF To call (troops together, as for inspection)
+ collect, gather, summon, recruit

Bring all the players you can muster.
(불러 모을 수 있는 선수는 모조리 데려와라.)

1259
mutual [mjúːtʃuəl]
a. 서로의, 상호의; 상호적인
IN BRIEF Directed and received by each toward the other; reciprocal
+ reciprocal, reciprocative, bilateral, common, joint

The agreement was terminated by mutual consent.
(그 협정은 상호 동의에 의해 종결되었다.)

1260
mutiny [mjúːt-əni]
n. 폭동, 반란, 하극상
IN BRIEF Open rebellion against constituted authority
+ insurgence, insurgency, insurrection, rebellion, revolt

The team manager nearly had a mutiny on his hands.
(그 팀장은 그의 고용인들에게 거의 하극상을 당할 뻔했다.)

1261
myth [miθ]

n. 신화; 미신

IN BRIEF A traditional story accepted as history

+ story that isn't true, fable, legend, parable, story, tale

> Greek myths retold for children
> (아이들이 읽기 쉽게 개작된 그리스 신화)

1262
malfeasance [mælfíːzəns]

n. (공무원)부정행위, 위법행위, 부정

IN BRIEF Inappropriate conduct by a public official

> The governor was impeached for gross malfeasance, although embezzlement charges were never filed.
> (그 주지사는 횡령 혐의로 기소되지는 않았지만, 총체적인 부정행위 때문에 탄핵되었다.)

1263
nomadic [nouméedik]

a. 유목민의; 방랑의

IN BRIEF Leading the life of a person without a fixed domicile; moving from place to place

+ peripatetic, vagrant, gypsy, itinerant, roving, traveling, vagabond, wandering — ant. resident

> Chinese states experienced tense relations with the nomadic people in the past.
> (중국의 여러 왕조 국가들은 과거에 유목민들과의 긴장 관계를 경험했다.)

1264
normative [nɔ́ːrmətiv]

a. 표준의, 규범적인, 기준을 세우는

IN BRIEF Dealing with norms: standardizing, controlling, regulating, prescriptive

+ normalizing, regularizing

> The alternative mechanism of normative morphogenesis is the accumulation of innovations.
> (규범적 형태생성의 대안적 기제는 혁신을 축적하는 것이다.)

1265
nadir [néidər]

n. 최하점, 밑바닥; 천저

IN BRIEF The lowest point, bottom

+ bottom, depths, lowest point, rock bottom, all-time low

> Company losses reached their nadir in 1992.
> (회사 손실은 1992년에 최저점에 이르렀다.)

1266
nebulous [nébjələs]

a. 흐린, 불투명한(dim, hazy, amorphous)

IN BRIEF Lacking definite form or limits; vague

+ vague, confused, uncertain, obscure, unclear, ambiguous, indefinite, hazy, indeterminate, imprecise, indistinct

> During the campaign, the candidate promised to fight crime. But when reporters asked for details, his plan was nebulous he could not say whether he would hire more police or support longer jail sentences.
> (선거운동이 진행되는 동안, 그 후보는 범죄와 싸우겠다고 약속했다. 그러나 기자가 자세한 방안을 물었을 때, 그의 계획은 불투명했다. 그는 자신이 더 많은 경찰을 고용한다거나 형기를 더 늘리는 것을 지지할 것인지를 말하지 못했다.)

1267
nagging [nǽgiŋ]

a. 끊임없이 잔소리하는, 성가시게 잔소리를 늘어놓는, 끈질긴

IN BRIEF Continually complaining or faultfinding

+ badger, bother, harass, hassle, pester, plague, torment

> Stop nagging, I'll do it as soon as I can.
> (잔소리 그만해. 할 수 있는 대로 빨리 할 거니까.)

1268
narrative [nǽrətiv]

(사건·경험 따위를) 서술한 것, 이야기, 담화

IN BRIEF A narrated account; a story

+ account, report, story, tale

> The novel contains more narrative than dialogue.
> (그 소설에는 대화보다 서술문이 더 많다.)

1269
nascent [nǽsənt]

a. 태어나려고 하는, 발생기의, 초기의

IN BRIEF Inceptive, incipient (come into being)

+ fledgling, just beginning to exist, budding, embryonic, emerging

> It's just a nascent stage
> (그것은 이제 막 시작한 단계이다.)

1270
nearly [níərli]

ad. 거의, 얼추, 대략

IN BRIEF Almost, about, approximately

+ roughly, essentially, practically, virtually

> We're nearly there now.
> (우린 이제 거의 그곳에 다 왔다.)

1271
needle [níːdl]
n. 바늘, 바느질 바늘 / (pin) v. 갉아대다, 괴롭히다, 자극하여 … 시키다

IN BRIEF Make cutting little remarks, goad, pester, prod, provoke, tease

[+] irritate, anger, provoke, annoy, sting, bait, harass

> I could see that my questions were needling him.
> (나는 내 질문이 그를 자극하고 있음을 알 수 있었다.)

1272
negligence [néglidʒəns]
n. 과실; 태만; 부주의

IN BRIEF The state or quality of being negligent

[+] laxity, laxness, carelessness, inattentive, remissness, slackness

> The accident was the result of negligence.
> (그 사고는 부주의의 결과였다.)

1273
negotiation [nigòuʃiéiʃən]
n. 협상, 교섭

IN BRIEF The act or process of negotiating

[+] arbitrate, intercede mediate

> A treaty is currently under negotiation in Vienna.
> (현재 비엔나에서 조약이 협상 중에 있다.)

1274
nepotism [népətizəm]
n. 연고자[친족] 등용; 족벌주의

IN BRIEF Favouritism shown to relatives or close friends by those with power or influence

[+] favoritism towards relatives, inequity, partisanship, patronage

> So, he says, nepotism was not involved.
> (따라서 그의 말대로 하면 어떤 연줄도 작용하지 않은 것이다.)

1275
nerve [nəːrv]
n. 신경, 용기, 신경과민, (구어)무례, 뻔뻔함

IN BRIEF The quality of mind enabling one to face danger or hardship resolutely

[+] mettle, audacity, effrontery, impudence, insolence, presumption

> Everyone's nerves are on edge after the accident.
> (그 사고 이후 모든 사람들의 신경이 날카로워졌다.)

1276
niggardly [nígərdli]
a. 인색한, 쩨쩨한

IN BRIEF Ungenerously or pettily reluctant to spend money

[+] begrudging, cheap, miserly, stingy

> They pay a niggardly 3% on loans.
> (그들은 대출금에 인색하게 3%를 낸다.)

1277
nimble [nímb-əl]
a. 민첩한, 재빠른, 민활한, 이해가 빠른, 영리한

IN BRIEF Quick, light, or agile in movement or action; deft

[+] agile, lively, quick-moving, sprightly, spry, adroit, deft, dexterous

> She's very nimble on her feet.
> (그녀는 발이 아주 재빠르다.)

1278
nocturnal [nɑktə́ːrnl]
a. 밤의, 야간의(야행성의)

IN BRIEF Of, relating to, or occurring in the night

[+] nightly, night, of the night, night-time

> Most bats and owls are nocturnal.
> (대부분의 박쥐와 부엉이는 야행성이다.)

1279
nominal [nάmənl]
a. 이름뿐인, 명목[명의]상의, 유명무실한, 아주적은

IN BRIEF Very small (titular, ostensible, insignificant)

[+] titular, formal, purported, in name only, supposed, so-called, pretended

> His position as chairman is purely nominal.
> (회장으로서 그의 지위는 순전히 명목뿐이다.)

1280
nominate [nάmənèit]
v. 지명하다; 임명하다(recommend)

IN BRIEF To choose a candidate for election

[+] appoint, choose, designate, name, propose, put forward

> He was nominated as best actor.
> (그는 최고 배우로 지명 추천되었다.)

1281
nonchalant [nÀnʃ-əláːnt]
a. 태연한, 무관심한, 냉담한

IN BRIEF Showing no concern

[+] calm, composed, unconcerned, indifferent, unruffled

> Ahntonio tried to appear nonchalant.
> (안토니오는 태연한 척 보이려고 노력했다.)

1282
nonsense [nánsens]
n. 허튼소리[짓], 시시한 것

IN BRIEF Words or signs having no intelligible meaning

[+] foolishness, idiocy, imbecility, inanity, stupidity

> The plan was all nonsense.
> (그 계획은 모두 엉터리였다.)

1283
nosy [nóuzi]
a. 《구어》 꼬치꼬치 캐기 좋아하는; 참견하기 좋아하는

IN BRIEF Given to or showing an intrusive curiosity about the affairs of others; prying

[+] inquisitive, intrusive, prying, snoopy

> Don't be so nosy, it's none of your business.
> (그렇게 참견하지 마. 그건 당신하고 상관없는 일이야.)

1284
noted [nóutid]
a. 유명한

IN BRIEF Widely known and esteemed

[+] celebrated, eminent, famed, famous, prominent, renowned

> He came to be a noted scientist.
> (그는 유명한 과학자가 되었다.)

1285
notify [nóutəfài]
vt. 통고하다, 통지하다, 알리다

IN BRIEF To give notice to; inform

[+] inform, announce, apprise, communicate, enlighten, inform, warn

> He notified us that he was going to leave.
> (그는 우리에게 떠날 것이라고 통고했다.)

1286
notorious [noutɔ́ːriəs]
a. 악명 높은

IN BRIEF Infamous, nefarious, widely and unfavourably known

[+] infamous, disreputable, opprobrious

> Politicians are notorious egotists, interested only in promoting themselves.
> (정치가들은 오직 자기 승진에만 관심이 있는 악명 높은 이기주의자들이다.)

1287
novelty [nÁv-əlti]
n. 신기함; 새로움

IN BRIEF The quality of being new and fresh and interesting

[+] freshness, newness, originality, uniqueness

> The novelty of her poetry impressed me.
> (그녀 시의 참신함은 내게 깊은 인상을 주었다.)

1288
noxious [nÁkʃəs]
a. (몸에) 해로운, 유독한

IN BRIEF Physically harmful

[+] deleterious, harmful, malignant, nocuous, pernicious, poisonous

> The people in the house had died from inhaling noxious smoke.
> (그 집에 있던 사람들은 유독성 연기를 마시고 죽었다.)

1289
nullify [nÁləfài]
vt. (법적) 무효로 하다, 취소하다, 헛되게 하다

IN BRIEF To remove legitimacy

[+] invalidate, abolish, abrogate, annul, rescind, revoke, void

> An unhealthy diet will nullify the effects of training.
> (건강에 해로운 식이요법은 운동의 효과를 수포로 돌리게 될 것이다.)

1290
nurture [nə́ːrtʃəːr]
vt. 양육하다; (영양을 주어) 키우다, 양성하다

IN BRIEF The action of raising or caring for offspring

[+] nourish, parent, rear, sustain, advance, cultivate, develop

> The Smiths nurture their children in a lovingenvironment.
> (스미스 부부는 자녀들을 사랑의 환경에서 양육한다.)

1291
nutty [nʌ́ti]

a. (속어) 머리가 어떻게 된, 약간 맛이 간, 미친

IN BRIEF Nutsy insane; crazy

+ mad, goofy, loony, silly, crazy, hysterical, insane

> She's got some nutty friends.
> (그녀는 괴짜친구가 몇 명 있다.)

1292
obediently [oubí:diəntli]

복종하여, 고분고분하게, 순순히

IN BRIEF Dutifully complying with the commands, orders, or instructions of one in authority

+ compliant, docile, manageable, submissive, tractable, yielding

> She whistled, and the dog came obediently.
> (그녀가 휘파람을 불자 개가 순순히 왔다.)

1293
obese [oubí:s]

a. 뚱뚱한, 살찐, 비만의

IN BRIEF Having excessive body weight caused by the accumulation of fat

+ corpulent, fat, overweight, portly, rotund

> She is grossly obese.
> (그녀는 끔찍하게 뚱뚱하다.)

1294
obfuscate [ɑbfʌ́skèit]

vt. …을 혼란 시키다, 모호하게 하다, …을 알기 어렵게 만들다

IN BRIEF To make so confused or opaque as to be difficult to perceive or understand

+ complicate, confuse, distort, muddle, obscure

> He accused the government of obfuscating the issue.
> (그는 정부가 그 쟁점을 흐리게 했다고 비난했다.)

1295
object [ɑ́bdʒikt]

n. 물체; 목적; 목적어(aim, end, goal, objective, purpose, receiver, recipient)
v. 반대하다; 싫어하다(demur, dispute, oppose, protest)

IN BRIEF A specific, individual, material entity, especially one that is not living or not sentient

> Weird glass and plastic objects lined the shelves.
> (기이한 유리 및 플라스틱 물건들이 선반들에 늘어서 있었다.)

1296
obligation [ὰbləgéiʃən]

의무, 책임(duty)

IN BRIEF A moral or legal requirement; duty

+ burden, charge, commitment, duty, imperative

> Being himself a second son, he could qualify for a woman who was also looking for a mate free of parental obligations.
> (둘째 아들이어서, 그는 마찬가지로 부모님을 모시지 않아도 되는 배우자를 찾고 있는 여성의 신랑감이 될 수 있었다.)

1297
oblique [əblí:k]

a. 비스듬한, 기울어진(diagonal, inclined)

IN BRIEF Having a slanting or sloping direction, course, or position; inclined

+ sloping, tilted, askew, crooked, lopsided, devious, indirect

> In through the window came the last few oblique rays of evening sunshine.
> (창을 통해서 저녁 햇빛의 마지막 몇 줄기가 비스듬히 들어왔다.)

1298
obliterate [əblítərèit]

vt. (글자 따위를) 지우다, 말소하다; (기억에서) 지우다

IN BRIEF To remove or destroy completely so as to leave no trace

+ eradicate, liquidate, wipe out, efface, erase, expunge, remove

> She tried to obliterate the memory of her childhood.
> (그녀는 어린 시절의 기억을 지워 버리려고 애썼다.)

1299
oblivion [əblíviən]

n. (세상에서)잊혀져 있는 상태, 망각

IN BRIEF The condition of being forgotten or disregarded

+ blackness, obscurity, forgetfulness, lethe, unconsciousness

> His work fell into oblivion after his death.
> (그의 작품은 그가 죽고 나자 세간에서 잊혀졌다.)

1300
omnipresent [ὰmnəprézənt]

a. 편재하는, 동시에 어디든지 있는

IN BRIEF Present everywhere simultaneously

+ ubiquitous, ever-present, pervasive

> Thanks to technological progress, Big Brother can now be almost as omnipresent as God. Nor is it only on the technical front that the hand of the would-be dictator has been strengthened.
> (기술력 진보 덕분에 현재 빅 브라더는 신만큼이나 거의 어디에나 있을 수 있다. 또한 독재자가 되려는 사람의 영향력이 강화된 것은 기술적인 영역에서만도 아니다.)

LESSON 27

1301
obscure [əbskjúər]
a. 분명하지 않은, 애매한, 가리다, (본심을)숨기다, (명성을)가리다
IN BRIEF Deficient in light; dark
[+] cryptic, recondite, veiled, unfamiliar, unknown, vague, block, conceal, hide

> Their real intention is obscure.
> (그들의 진짜 의도가 애매하다.)

1302
obscurity [əbskjúərəti]
n. 세상에 알려지지 않음, 모호함; 불분명
IN BRIEF Deficiency or absence of light; darkness
[+] unknown, anonymity, oblivion, ambiguity, uncertainty, vagueness

> After years of working in obscurity, he at last found recognition.
> (수년 동안 무명으로 일을 한 후, 마침내 그가 인정을 받게 되었다.)

1303
obsolete [àbsəlíːt]
a. 사라진, 폐기된, (사물) 시대에 뒤떨어진, 구식의
IN BRIEF No longer in use
[+] antiquated, outdated, old-fashioned, out-of-date, outmoded, disused

> This new computer rendered my old one obsolete.
> (이 새 컴퓨터를 보니까 내 오래된 컴퓨터는 구식이 돼버렸다.)

1304
obstinacy [ábstənəsi]
n. 고집, 완고, 완강
IN BRIEF The state or quality of being obstinate
[+] obstinateness, pertinacity, tenaciousness, tenacity

> His obstinacy is proverbial.
> (그의 완고함은 소문났다.)

1305
obtain [əbtéin]
v. (노력하여) …을 얻다, 손에 넣다, 획득하다
IN BRIEF To gain possession of; acquire; get
[+] acquire, gain, procure, purchase, capture, grasp, seize

> How did you obtain your data?
> (자료를 어떻게 얻은 거예요?)

1306
obstinate [ábstənit]
a. 완고한, 고집 센
IN BRIEF Stubbornly adhering to an attitude, opinion, or course of action; obdurate
[+] adamant, implacable, inflexible, obdurate, resolute, stubborn, determined

> He has an obstinate belief in his own ability.
> (그는 자신의 능력을 고집스럽게 믿고 있다.)

1307
obtrude [əbtrúːd]
(의견)강요하다, 억지로 내밀다
IN BRIEF To push out or forward
[+] emerge, intrude, horn-in, impose, invade

> Don't obtrude your opinions on others.
> (남에게 자신의 의견을 강요하지 마라.)

1308
occult [əkʌ́lt]
a. 신비로운, 불가사의한, 비밀의
IN BRIEF To conceal or cause to disappear from view
[+] concealed, dark, hidden, mysterious, mystical

> He's interested in the occult.
> (그는 비학에 관심이 있다.)

1309
odds and ends [ɑdz]
여러 가지 잡다한 일, 여분, 찌꺼기, 쓰레기
IN BRIEF Too small or numerous to be specified, miscellaneous task
[+] hodgepodge, hotchpotch, melange, mingle-mangle

> There are just a few odds and ends left.
> (남은 것은 조금의 잡동사니뿐이다.)

1310
odor [óudər]
n. 냄새, 향기(fragrance, perfume)
IN BRIEF A quality of something that is perceived by the sense of smell
[+] redolence, aroma, bouquet, scent, smell, effluvium

> Bad eggs have an offensive odor.
> (상한 달걀은 고약한 냄새가 난다.)

1311
offensive [əfénsiv]

a. 화나게 하는, 불쾌한, 싫은, 비위에 거슬리는

IN BRIEF Causing anger, displeasure, or resentment

⊕ disgusting, distasteful, obnoxious, unpleasant, repugnant, repulsive

> I find that kind of language offensive.
> (그런 말투는 듣기가 거북하군요.)

1312
offhand [ɔ́(:)fhǽnd]

a. 준비 없이, 즉석에서, 그 자리에서

IN BRIEF Without preparation or forethought; extemporaneously

⊕ casual, at once, impromptu, spontaneous, haphazard, nonchalant

> The question is too important to answer offhand.
> (그 문제는 너무 중요해서 즉답을 할 수 없다.)

1313
officious [əfíʃəs]

a. 말참견하는, 주제넘은

IN BRIEF Meddlesome; intrusive in an offensive manner

⊕ intrusive, meddlesome, nosy, obtrusive

> Ahntonio is an officious man and widely disliked in the company.
> (그는 참견하기 좋아하는 남자로 회사에서 널리 미움을 받았다.)

1314
omnipotent [ɑmnípətənt]

a. 전능한, 무엇이든 할 수 있는

IN BRIEF Having very great or unlimited power

⊕ all-powerful, almighty, sovereign, supreme

> Is God the only omnipotent being?
> (신만이 전능한 존재인가?)

1315
onset [ánsèt]

n. 착수, 시작, 개시

IN BRIEF The beginning or start of something

⊕ beginning, commencement, outset, start, appearance, outbreak

> A rise in interest rates could hasten the onset of recession.
> (금리인상이 경기 침체의 시작을 재촉할지도 모른다.)

1316
omniscient [ɑmníʃənt]

a. 전지의; 박식한

IN BRIEF Having total knowledge; knowing everything

⊕ all-knowing, all-seeing, all-wise

> Christians believe that God is omniscient.
> (기독교인들은 하느님이 전지하다고 믿는다.)

1317
ooze [uːz]

v. 스며 나오다, 배어 나오다, 새다

IN BRIEF To flow or leak out slowly, as through small openings

⊕ drip, flow, leak, trickle, exude, radiate

> They oozed confidence.
> (그들은 자신감이 넘쳐흘렀다.)

1318
ophthalmologist [àfθəlmálədʒist]

안과 의사

IN BRIEF Physician specializing in the eye

⊕ eye doctor, oculist

> An ophthalmologist is a doctor who treats eye diseases.
> (안과 의사는 눈병을 치료하는 의사이다.)

1319
opportune [àpərtjúːn]

a. (…에) 적당한, 시기가 좋은, 시기적절한

IN BRIEF Suited or right for a particular purpose

⊕ right, fitting, timely, fortunate, lucky, propitious, providential

> Your arrival was most opportune.
> (당신의 도착은 아주 시의 적절했다.)

1320
optimistic [àptəmístik]

낙천적인, 낙관적인(hopeful)

IN BRIEF One who usually expects a favorable outcome

⊕ cheerful, confident, hopeful, sanguine, idealistic, auspicious, propitious

> I'm very much optimist, and I believe that progress on even the world's toughest problems is possible.
> (나는 매우 낙천주의자라서 세상에서 가장 어려운 문제조차도 발전이 가능하다고 믿는다.)

1321
opt [ɑpt]

vi. (…중에서) 선택하다, 고르다

IN BRIEF To make a choice or decision

+ choose, cull, elect, pick out, select

> He opted to go to Stanford rather than Yale.
> (그는 예일대보다 스탠퍼드대로 가는 쪽을 택했다.)

1322
optimum [ɑ́ptəməm]

최적의, 가장 알맞은; (한정된 조건 아래 얻을 수 있는) 최대

IN BRIEF The point at which the condition, degree, or amount of something is the most favorable

+ finest, choicest, perfect, supreme, peak, outstanding, first-class, foremost

> For efficient fuel consumption a speed of 60 mph is about the optimum.
> (효율적인 연료 소모를 위해서는 시속 60마일이 거의 최적 속도이다.)

1323
opulent [ɑ́pjələnt]

a. 부유한; 호사스러운, 풍부한, 윤택한

IN BRIEF Possessing or exhibiting great wealth; affluent

+ bounteous, copious, plentiful, extravagant, lavish, rich, sumptuous

> Most of the cash went on supporting her opulent lifestyle.
> (돈의 대부분은 그녀의 호사스런 생활을 유지하는데 사용됐다.)

1324
orbit [ɔ́ːrbit]

n. 궤도; (인생의) 궤도

IN BRIEF To revolve around a center of attraction

+ influence, circuit, course, path, revolution, trajectory

> The spacecraft went into orbit around the earth.
> (우주선은 지구 궤도에 진입했다.)

1325
orient [ɔ́ːriənt]

…로 향하게 하다, (새 환경 등에) 적응[순응]시키다

IN BRIEF To place so as to face the east; to become familiar with a situation

+ adjust, settle, adapt, tune, convert, alter, compose, accommodate

> Indeed, print-oriented novelists seem doomed to disappear, as electronic media and computer games are becoming more influential.
> (전자 매체와 컴퓨터 게임들이 점점 영향력을 갖게 됨에 따라 사실상, 인쇄 지향적인 소설가들은 사라져야 하는 운명에 처해 있는 것처럼 보인다.)

1326
originate [ərídʒənèit]

v. 비롯하다, 생기다, 시작하다

IN BRIEF To bring into being; create or start

+ start, generate, derive, emanate, stem, initiate

> Where did that story originate?
> (그 이야기는 어디서 시작되었는가?)

1327
ornamental [ɔ̀ːrnəméntl]

a. 장식용의, 장식적인

IN BRIEF Of value as an ornament; decorative

+ decorative, elaborate, ornate, accessory, adornment, embellishment

> These buttons are only ornamental.
> (이 단추들은 장식용일 뿐이다.)

1328
ornate [ɔːrnéit]

a. 꾸민, 화려하게 장식한; (문체가) 화려한

IN BRIEF Elaborately, heavily, and often excessively ornamented

+ decorated, embellished, fancy, baroque, flamboyant, florid, rococo

> She likes ornate furniture.
> (그녀는 화려한 가구를 좋아한다.)

1329
ostensible [ɑsténsəbəl]

a. 표면상의, 겉으로 만의, 겉치레의

IN BRIEF Represented or appearing as such; ostensive

+ specious, apparent, nominal, outward, seeming, alleged, pretended

> The ostensible reason for his absence was illness.
> (그가 결근한 표면상의 이유는 병이었다.)

1330
ostentatious [ɑ̀stentéiʃəs]

a. 허세 부리는; 과시하는, 자랑해 보이는

IN BRIEF Characterized by or given to ostentation

+ pompous, high-flown, bombastic, showy, snobbish, pretentious

> They criticized the ostentatious lifestyle of their leaders.
> (그들은 자기 지도자들의 허세부리는 삶의 방식을 비난했다.)

1331
ostracize [ástrəsàiz]

국외로 추방하다; 배척하다, 따돌리다, 「왕따」시키다

IN BRIEF To exclude from a group or society

[+] exclude, isolate, shun, shut out, banish, cast out, deport, exile

> He was ostracized by his colleagues.
> (그는 동료들에게 배척을 받았다.)

1332
outcome [áutkʌm]

n. 결과

IN BRIEF An end result; a consequence

[+] aftermath, consequence, effect, end, result

> The outcome is still uncertain.
> (결과는 아직 분명치 않다.)

1333
outdistance [àutdístəns]

vt. …을 훨씬 리드하다[앞서다], 이기다

IN BRIEF To surpass by a wide margin, especially through superior skill or endurance

[+] outstrip, exceed, surpass, outclass, outdo, overtake

> She easily outdistanced the other runners.
> (그녀는 쉽게 다른 주자들을 앞섰다.)

1334
outlet [áutlet]

n. 출구, 통로, 배출구

IN BRIEF A passage for escape or exit; a vent

[+] escape, release, channel, opening, plug

> I play racquet ball as an outlet for stress.
> (나는 스트레스 해소책으로 라켓볼을 친다.)

1335
output [áutpùt]

n. 생산(량)

IN BRIEF The act of production or manufacture

[+] product, production, turnout, result, commodity, outcome, outgrowth

> Manufacturing output is in decline.
> (제조업 생산고가 감소하고 있다.)

1336
outrage [áutrèidʒ]

n. 분개; 격노

IN BRIEF An act of extreme violence or viciousness

[+] anger, shame, fury, wrath, exasperation, indignation, resentment

> She was filled with a sense of outrage.
> (그녀는 격분에 휩싸였다.)

1337
outright [áutràit]

a. 명백한; 솔직한, 노골적인

IN BRIEF Without reservation or qualification; openly

[+] absolute, all-out, direct, perfect, plain, unreserved

> I didn't expect his outright refusal.
> (나는 그의 노골적인 거절을 예상치 못했다.)

1338
outspoken [áutspóukkən]

a. 솔직한, 거침없이 말하는

IN BRIEF Spoken without reserve; candid

[+] candid, direct, forthright, frank, honest

> You'd better tone down the more outspoken passages in your article.
> (당신 글 속의 더 노골적인 구절들의 어조를 누그러뜨리는 게 좋을 것 같다.)

1339
outstanding [àutstǽndiŋ]

a. 뛰어난, 눈에 띄는, 현저한

IN BRIEF Excellent or exceptionally good

[+] excellent, striking, notable, prominent, renowned

> It's an outstanding novel.
> (이것은 뛰어난 소설이다.)

1340
outweigh [àutwéi]

vt. 압도하다; …보다 중요하다, 능가하다

IN BRIEF To exceed in value or importance

[+] exceed, better, excel, predominate, surpass

> The book's virtues far outweigh its faults.
> (그 책은 장점이 결점보다 훨씬 많다.)

1341
ominous [ámənəs]

a. 불길한, 나쁜 징조의

IN BRIEF Threatening or foreshadowing evil or tragic developments

[+] apocalyptic, apocalyptical, baneful, dire, direful, fateful, fire-and-brimstone, grave, hellfire, portentous, unlucky

> Not many groups became universally recognizable during the twentieth century, and those that did often had ominous overtones, such as the Mafia.
> (20세기 동안 일반적으로 알아볼 수 있게 된 집단들은 많지 않았는데, 그렇게 된 집단들은 종종 마피아와 같은 그런 불길한 의미를 갖고 있었다.)

1342
opaque [oupéik]

a. 불투명한; 불명료한, 이해하기 힘든

IN BRIEF Not letting light pass through; neither transparent nor translucent

[+] dark, impenetrable, ambiguous, hazy, nebulous, unclear, vague

> Iraq has been stripped of the politics that have made the country opaque to the world.
> (이라크는 지금까지 그 나라를 세계에서 불투명한 나라로 만들어온 정치에서 이제 벗어났다.)

1343
pace [peis]

n. 페이스, 보조, (생활·일·걸음 등의) 속도

IN BRIEF A step made in walking; a stride

[+] footstep, gait, stride, speed, tread, rate, tempo, velocity

> We stepped up our pace.
> (우리들은 걸음을 빨리했다.)

1344
page [peidʒ]

이름을 불러 (…를) 찾다, 호출하다(call aloud, label)

IN BRIEF To summon or call (a person by name)

[+] name, term, cry, summon, announce, declare, proclaim

> Can you page Dr Berry, please?
> (베리 박사를 호출 해주시겠어요?)

1345
palliate [pǽlièit]

vt. 가볍게 하려고 하다, 누그러지게 하다, 일시적으로 완화하다

IN BRIEF To make less severe or intense; mitigate

[+] extenuate, justify, mitigate, alleviate, ease, reduce, relieve

> Many modern drugs palliate but do not cure illness.
> (많은 현대 약품은 병을 완화시키기는 하지만 치유하지는 못한다.)

1346
palpable [pǽlpəbəl]

a. 명백한; 지각할 수 있는

IN BRIEF Capable of being handled, touched, or felt; tangible

[+] apparent, discernible, noticeable, obvious, perceptible, tangible

> His statement is palpable nonsense.
> (그의 진술은 명백한 넌센스다.)

1347
pamphlet [pǽmflit]

n. 소책자, 팸플릿

IN BRIEF An unbound printed work, usually with a paper cover

[+] booklet, brochure, bulletin

> The pamphlet contains full details of the national park's scenic attractions.
> (그 소책자에는 국립공원의 경치 좋은 곳에 대한 완벽한 세부 정보가 담겨 있다.)

1348
panacea [pæ̀nəsíːə]

n. 만능제, 만병치료제

IN BRIEF Something believed to cure all human disorders

[+] cure-all, elixir, nostrum, heal-all

> These measures will all help, though they cannot be anything like the panacea that the would-be regulators dream of.
> (이러한 조치들은 비록 총기규제 담당자가 될 사람들이 꿈꾸는 만능해결책이 될 수 없다 하더라도, 아주 많은 도움이 될 것이다.)

1349
pandemonium [pæ̀ndəmóuniəm]

n. 아수라장, 대혼란

IN BRIEF A wild uproar, bedlam, chaos, confusion, disorder, disturbance

[+] bedlam, chaos, topsy-turvydom, topsy-turvyness

> Pandemonium broke out when the news was announced.
> (그 소식이 발표되자 아수라장이 벌어졌다.)

1350
pandemic [pændémik]

a. (세계적으로) 전국적으로 유행하는

IN BRIEF Widespread; general; So pervasive and all-inclusive; catholic, cosmic

[+] cosmopolitan, ecumenical, global, planetary, universal, worldwide

> During the eighteenth and nineteenth centuries, there were about eight influenza epidemics; during the winter 1889-90 it is estimated that more than 10 million people died worldwide. The worst flu pandemic on record was that caused by the infamous Spanish flu which killed many people.
> (18세기와 19세기 동안 약 8번의 독감이 유행했다. 1889년에서 1890년 겨울동안 전 세계에서 1천만 명이 넘는 사람들이 사망한 것으로 추정된다. 공식적으로 기록된 전 세계적으로 유행한 가장 끔찍한 독감은 많은 사람들을 사망케 한 악명 높은 스페인 독감으로 인해 발생된 것이었다.)

1351
paralyze [pǽrəlàiz]
vt. …을 마비시키다

IN BRIEF To affect with paralysis

+ disable, stun, stupefy, deaden, freeze, numb, petrify

The effect of the drug is to paralyze the nerves.
(그 약의 효과는 신경을 마비시키는 것이다.)

1352
paramount [pǽrəmàunt]
a. 최고의, 가장 주요한

IN BRIEF Of chief concern or importance

+ capital, chief, dominant, foremost, preeminent, premier

This matter is of paramount importance.
(이 문제는 가장 중요하다.)

1353
paranormal [pæ̀rənɔ́ːrməl]
a. 과학적으로 알[인식할] 수가 없는

IN BRIEF Psychology beyond normal explanation

+ unusual, atypical, peculiar, rare, singular, uncommon, unique

This book is about people who claim to have paranormal abilities.
(이 책은 과학적으로 알 수 없는 능력을 가졌다고 주장하는 사람들에 관한 것이다.)

1354
parsimonious [pàːrsəmóuniəs]
인색한

IN BRIEF Excessively sparing or frugal

+ mean, stingy, penny-pinching, miserly, near, saving

To a great extent, they've been hectored into behaving more like their parsimonious Pilgrim forebears, whose expression of gratitude America has celebrated every year in November.
(상당한 정도로, 그들은 검소한 청교도 조상처럼 행동하도록 괴롭힘을 당해왔는데, 미국은 매년 11월에 청교도들의 감사표시를 기념해왔다.)

1355
parity [pǽrəti]
n. 동등, 동격

IN BRIEF Equality, as in amount, status, or value

+ equality, equation, equivalence, equivalency, par, sameness

Primary school teachers are demanding parity with those in secondary schools.
(초등학교 교사들은 중등학교 교사들과의 동등성을 요구하고 있다.)

1356
pastoral [pǽstərəl]
a. 양치기의; 전원의, 목가적인

IN BRIEF Of or relating to the country or country life; rural

+ rural or rustic, bucolic, country, provincial

The painting showed a pastoral scene.
(그 그림은 목가적인 풍경을 보여 주었다.)

1357
paterfamilias [pèitərfəmíliəs]
n. 가장, 호주, 가부장(家父長)

IN BRIEF Head of a household

+ patriarch

Some man relish the role of paterfamilias.
(몇몇 남자는 가부장 역할을 좋아한다.)

1358
paternity [pətə́ːrnəti]
n. 아버지임, 부권(父權), (생각의) 기원

IN BRIEF The state of being a father; fatherhood

+ fatherhood, fathership

He denied paternity of the boy.
(그는 그 소년의 아버지임을 부인했다.)

1359
patron [péitrən]
n. 단골손님; 후원자

IN BRIEF One that supports, protects, or champions someone or something

+ client, customer, advocate, benefactor, sponsor, supporter

The princess is a well-known patron of several charities.
(공주는 몇몇 자선단체의 잘 알려진 후원자이다.)

1360
pathetic [pəθétik]
n. 불쌍한, 애처로운

IN BRIEF Arousing or deserving of sympathetic sadness and compassion

[+] forlorn, piteous, pitiful, doleful, miserable, rueful, wretched

> He was often cast as a pathetic little man.
> (그는 종종 애처롭고 작은 남자 배역을 맡는 경우가 많았다.)

1361
peculiar [pikjú:ljər]
a. 특별한, 독특한; 기묘한

IN BRIEF Not ordinary or usual; odd or strange

[+] idiosyncratic, eccentric, odd, queer, strange, quaint, unusual

> It looks peculiar.
> (이것은 독특해 보인다.)

1362
pecuniary [pikjú:nièri]
a. 금전(상)의, 재정상의

IN BRIEF Consisting of or relating to money

[+] financial, fiscal, monetary, budgetary, economic

> It is a pecuniary advantage.
> (그것은 금전상의 이득이다.)

1363
pedagogic [pèdəgádʒik]
a. 교육학의, 교수법의

IN BRIEF Of, relating to, or characteristic of pedagogy

[+] pedagogical, lecture, professor

> You have to learn pedagogic skills.
> (당신은 교수법(강의법)들을 배워야 한다.)

1364
peer [piər]
n. 동료, 또래, 한패

IN BRIEF A person who has equal standing with another or others, as in rank, class, or age

[+] contemporary, friends at the same age, counterpart, equal, match

> He doesn't spend enough time with his peers.
> (그는 또래들과 충분한 시간을 보내지 않는다.)

1365
penetrate [pénətrèit]
v. 관통하다; 침입하다

IN BRIEF To enter, pass into, or force a way into

[+] pass through, infiltrate, invade, perforate, pierce

> The bullet could not penetrate the wall.
> (총알은 벽을 관통하지 못했다.)

1366
pensive [pénsiv]
a. 깊은 생각에 잠긴, 명상에 잠긴

IN BRIEF Engaged in deep and serious thought

[+] absorbed, engrossed, immersed, melancholy, morose, somber

> She looked pensive when she heard the news.
> (그 소식을 듣자 그녀는 시름에 잠기는 것 같았다.)

1367
pensively [ˈpensɪvlɪ]
ad. 수심에 잠겨

IN BRIEF Engaged in deep and serious thought

> I knew immediately that Mary's father was very ill by the way she pensively asked us to come over.
> (나는 메리가 수심에 잠겨 우리에게 와줄 것을 부탁해서 메리의 아버지가 매우 편찮으시다는 것을 즉각 알았다.)

1368
penury [pénjəri]
n. 극빈, 빈곤; 부족, 결핍

IN BRIEF Extreme want or poverty; destitution

[+] destitution, indigence, insolvency, poverty, privation, want

> He lives in penury.
> (그는 빈궁하게 산다.)

1369
perennially [pəréniəl]
a. 연중 계속되어; 지속되어, 영속적으로

IN BRIEF Lasting an indefinitely long time; enduring

[+] year-round, ceaseless, constant, continual, perpetual, enduring, fixed, immutable, permanent, undying

> Ahntonio seems to be perennially short of money.
> (안토니오는 일 년 내내 돈이 부족한 것 같다.)

1370
perforate [pə́:rfərèit]

…에 구멍을 뚫다, …을 꿰뚫다, 관통하다

IN BRIEF To pierce, punch, or bore a hole or holes in; penetrate

⊕ bore, cut, drill, pierce, punch, puncture

A metal spike had perforated the fuel tank.
(금속 못이 연료탱크에 구멍을 뚫었다.)

1371
perfunctory [pə:rfʌ́ŋktəri]

a. 형식적인, 마지못한, 되는 대로의

IN BRIEF Done superficially, only as a matter of routine; careless or cursory

⊕ cursory, haphazard, halfhearted, nonchalant, superficial, shallow

She gave him no more than a perfunctory "So glad you could come."
(그녀는 그에게 "그래 당신이 오게 돼서 기뻐요." 하는 형식적인 인사 밖에 건네지 않았다.)

1372
perish [périʃ]

v. 멸망하다; 죽다; 사라지다

IN BRIEF Expire, shrivel, wither, rot, vanish

⊕ expire, pass away, decline, fade, subside, wane

Thousands of people perished in the earthquake.
(그 지진으로 수천 명의 사람들이 비명횡사했다.)

1373
perjury [pə́:rdʒəri]

n. 위증, 거짓 맹세

IN BRIEF The crime of willfully and knowingly making a false statement about a material fact while under oath

⊕ dishonesty, falsehood, forswearing, lying under oath, prevarication

She was sentenced to 2 years in jail for committing perjury.
(그녀는 위증죄로 2년간 복역하라는 선고를 받았다.)

1374
permanent [pə́:rmənənt]

a. 영구(永久)한, 영원의, 불변의

IN BRIEF Lasting or remaining without essential change

⊕ constant, durable, fixed, lasting, immutable, invariable, unalterable, unchanging, continuous, eternal, infinite, undying

I mean permanent.
(영구적으로 말이에요.)

1375
permeate [pə́:rmièit]

v. 스며들다, 침투하다, 가득 차다, 퍼지다

IN BRIEF To spread or flow throughout; pervade

⊕ spread into, infiltrate, ingress, invade, perforate, pervade

The smell of cooking permeated through the house.
(요리 냄새가 집안 전체에 퍼졌다.)

1376
pernicious [pə:rníʃəs]

a. 해로운, 유독한, 파괴적인; 치명적인

IN BRIEF Tending to cause death or serious injury; deadly

⊕ deadly, destructive, fatal, lethal, mortal, noxious, damaging, deleterious, detrimental, harmful

Most doctors agree that smoking is a pernicious habit.
(대부분의 의사는 흡연이 해로운 습관이라는 데 의견을 같이 한다.)

1377
perpetrate [pə́:rpətrèit]

vt. (나쁜 짓)을 하다, (죄·잘못)을 저지르다

IN BRIEF To be responsible for; commit

⊕ carry out, commit, enact, execute, perform

Many computer frauds are perpetrated by authorized users.
(많은 컴퓨터 사기 행위는 권위 있는(인정받은) 사용자들에 의해 저질러진다.)

1378
perpetual [pərpétʃuəl]

a. 영원한, 영속하는, 불후의, 무궁한

IN BRIEF Lasting forever; never-ending

⊕ undying, ceaseless, constant, continuous, incessant, interminable

They heard the perpetual noises of the machines.
(그들은 기계의 끊임없는 소음을 들었다.)

1379
perplex [pərpléks]

vt. 당황하게[황당하게] 하다

IN BRIEF To confuse or trouble with uncertainty or doubt

⊕ bewilder, confuse, mystify, nonplus, puzzle

I was perplexed by Ahntonio's strange behavior.
(나는 안토니오의 이상한 행동에 난감했다.)

1380
persistent [pəːrsístənt]
a. 고집하는[in], 집요한, 끈기 있는; 끊임없는(continuous)

IN BRIEF Showing persistence

+ determined, insistent, resolute, stubborn, tenacious, chronic

> The school expelled him for persistent misbehavior.
> (끊임없는 비행 때문에 학교 측은 그를 퇴학시켰다.)

1381
personalize [pə́ːrsənəlàiz]
vt. …을 개인화하다, 자기 일로 받아들이다

IN BRIEF To endow with personal or individual qualities or characteristics

+ confidential, private, individual, particular, special

> We don't want to personalize the argument.
> (우리는 논쟁을 사사로운 것으로 만들고 싶지 않다.)

1382
persuasive [pərswéisiv]
a. 설득력이 있는

IN BRIEF Tending or having the power to persuade

+ cogent, compelling, convincing, effective

> He is an eloquent and persuasive politician.
> (그는 달변에 설득력 있는 정치가이다.)

1383
pertinent [pə́ːrtənənt]
a. 적절한, 관계있는(relevant, suitable)

IN BRIEF Clearly related to a matter at hand

+ applicable, appropriate, apropos, fitting, germane, relevant

> If your question is pertinent, I will answer it.
> (당신 질문이 적절하면, 그에 대한 대답을 하겠다.)

1384
pervasive [pərvéisiv]
a. 넘치는; 만연하는, 널리 퍼진

IN BRIEF Having the quality or tendency to pervade or permeate

+ extensive, general, pervading, rampant, ubiquitous, widespread

> Her influence is all pervasive.
> (그녀의 영향이 널리 퍼져 있다.)

1385
perturb [pərtə́ːrb]
vt. 당황하게 하다, 불안하게 하다

IN BRIEF To disturb or confuse; make uneasy or anxious

+ agitate, bother, distress, disturb, fluster, upset, worry

> I was surprised but not perturbed by his sudden outburst.
> (나는 그의 갑작스런 감정 분출에 놀랐지만 불안하지는 않았다.)

1386
perverse [pərvə́ːrs]
a. 성질이 비뚤어진, 심술궂은

IN BRIEF Contrary to what is right or good; wicked or depraved

+ unmanageable, cantankerous, irascible, surly

> The perverse child did just what we told him not to do.
> (고집불통의 그 아이는 우리가 하지 말라고 한 일만 골라 했다.)

1387
pester [péstər]
vt. (사소한 일로) 괴롭히다, 성가시게 굴다

IN BRIEF To annoy persistently, as with repeated demands or questions

+ annoy, badger, bother, harass, irk, nag, torment

> Don't pester me with foolish questions.
> (어리석은 질문으로 나를 괴롭히지 마라.)

1388
petrify [pétrəfài]
v. 석화시키다, 딱딱하게 하다, 마비[경직]시키다

IN BRIEF To convert into stone or a stony substance

+ stone, harden, solidify, stiffen, frighten, deaden, numb, paralyze

> The idea of making a speech in public petrified him.
> (대중 앞에서 연설을 할 생각이 그를 돌같이 굳게 만들었다.)

1389
phase [feiz]
n. (발달·변화의) 단계, 국면

IN BRIEF A stage in development

+ facet, respect, period, stage, condition, degree development

> That is a phase all boys go through.
> (그것은 모든 소년들이 거치는 단계이다.)

1390
phenomenal [finámənl]
a. 경이적인, 비상한, 비범한

IN BRIEF Extraordinary; outstanding; remarkable

[+] great, amazing, unique, astonishing, extraordinary, marvelous, outstanding, remarkable

> The rocket travels at a phenomenal speed.
> (로켓은 굉장한 속도로 난다.)

1391
phony [fóuni]
a. 가짜의, 위조의, 사기의, 수상쩍은

IN BRIEF Not genuine or real; sham or counterfeit

[+] sham, fake, fraud, bogus, false, artificial, hypocritical, spurious

> What a phony!
> (사기꾼!)

1392
pierce [piərs]
v. …을 꿰뚫다, 관통하다; …에 꽂히다

IN BRIEF To cut or pass through with or as if with a sharp instrument; stab or penetrate

[+] puncture, spear, stab, penetrate, perforate

> The arrow pierced his shoulder.
> (그 화살은 그의 어깨를 꿰뚫었다.)

1393
placate [pléikeit]
vt. (사람)을 달래다, 진정시키다; 회유하다

IN BRIEF To allay the anger of, especially by making concessions; appease

[+] soothe, appease, assuage, pacify, mollify

> These concessions are unlikely to placate extremists.
> (이러한 양보가 극단주의자들을 회유할 수 있을 것 같지 않다.)

1394
placid [plǽsid]
a. 잔잔한, 조용한, 차분한

IN BRIEF Undisturbed by tumult or disorder; calm or quiet

[+] peaceful, sedate, serene, quiet, smooth, tranquil, undisturbed, unruffled

> She is a placid child.
> (그 애는 조용한 아이이다.)

1395
plainly [pléinli]
분명히, 똑똑히, 알기 쉽게, 있는 그대로

IN BRIEF Free from obstructions; open; clear

[+] clearly, evidently, manifestly, obviously, unambiguously

> That is plainly absurd.
> (그것은 분명 터무니없다.)

1396
plaintive [pléintiv]
a. 구슬픈, 애처로운; 하소연하는 듯한(dreary)

IN BRIEF Expressing sorrow; mournful

[+] melancholy, lamentable, mournful, pathetic, sad, sorrowful, dismal

> The music has a very plaintive air.
> (그 음악은 매우 애처로운 분위기를 가진다.)

1397
plausible [plɔ́:zəbəl]
a. 그럴싸한, 진실[정말] 같은

IN BRIEF Seemingly or apparently valid, likely, or acceptable; credible

[+] acceptable, reasonable, believable, credible, feasible, likely, possible

> The story sounds plausible.
> (그 이야기는 그럴 듯하게 들린다.)

1398
purge [pəːrdʒ]
v. 정화하다; 추방하다(evacuate, excrete)

IN BRIEF To clear (a container or space, for example) of something unclean or unwanted

[+] eliminate, eradicate, liquidate, remove, wipe out, do away with, put an end to

> Montgomery County leaders announced a costly effort to purge panhandlers from busy streets.
> (몽고메리 카운티의 지도자들은 번잡한 거리에서 걸인들을 추방하기 위한 값비싼 노력을 기울이겠다고 발표했다.)

1399
pariah [pəráiə]
n. 왕따; 부랑자; 하층민

IN BRIEF A social outcast

[+] outcast, exile, outlaw, undesirable, untouchable, leper, unperson

> After he painted his house bright orange, Paul became the neighborhood pariah. No one on the block wanted anything to do with him.
> (집을 밝은 오렌지색으로 칠한 후에, 폴은 그 동네에서 왕따가 되었다. 그 동네에 사는 어떤 사람도 그와 상관하고 싶어 하지 않았다.)

1400
put the kibosh on

~을 (방지) 막다(Restrain or check something)

IN BRIEF Prevent something that is planned from happening, To squelch someone or something; to veto someone or someone's plans

> The car industry has put the kibosh on EU CO_2 emission curbs.
> (자동차 업계에서는 이산화탄소 배출을 억제시키려는 유럽연합의 계획을 막았다.)

LESSON 29

1401
pledge [pledʒ]
n. 맹세, 약속; 공약 / v. 서약하다, 맹세하다
IN BRIEF A solemn binding promise to do, give, or refrain from doing something
- oath, plight, promise, vow, token

> The defense treaty pledges that if Korea is attacked, the U. S. will come to its aid.
> (이 방위 조약은 한국이 공격을 받을 경우 미국이 도울 것을 약속하고 있다.)

1402
plenary [plíːnəri]
a. 충분한, 완전한; 전부의; 전권의, (회의 따위가) 전원 출석의
IN BRIEF Complete in all respects; unlimited or full
- full, entire, whole

> The House speaker organized the agenda in detail to avoid afree-for-all at the plenary session.
> (하원 의장은 본회의에서 난투극을 피하도록 의제를 세심하게 조정했다.)

1403
pliant [pláiənt]
a. 휘기 쉬운, 나긋나긋한, 유연한
IN BRIEF Easily bent or flexed; pliable
- supple, impressionable, receptive, susceptible

> He is a pliant husband.
> (그는 유순한 남편이다.)

1404
plight [plait] [plaɪt]
곤경
IN BRIEF A situation, especially a bad or unfortunate one
IN BRIEF A situation, especially a bad or unfortunate one
- hardship, dilemma, predicament, crisis, difficulty, quandary

> What is the cure for the plight of the homeless?
> (노숙자들의 곤경에 대한 구제책은 무엇인가?)

1405
plunge [plʌndʒ]
v. 돌진하다; 뛰어들다
IN BRIEF To dive, jump, or throw oneself
- drive, coerce, compel, forge, lunge, rush

> The car plunged into the icy water
> (그 차는 차가운 물 속으로 뛰어들었다.)

1406
plutocracy [pluːtákrəsi]
n. 금권[재벌] 정치; 금권 정체[국가]
IN BRIEF Government of the rich, government by the affuent
- form of government, political system

> It's time we put an end to plutocracy.
> (금권 정치를 끝내야 할 때이다.)

1407
ply [plai]
v. ① (배·버스 등이) 정기적으로 왕복하다
IN BRIEF Travel regularly
- travel, go, ferry, shuttle

> We plied between Dublin and Holland.
> (우리는 더블린과 네덜란드 간을 왕복했다.)

1408
point-blank [blæŋk]
a. 표적을 똑바로 겨냥한, 단도직입의, 솔직한
IN BRIEF Aimed or fired straight at the mark esp. from close range; direct
- directly, candid, forthright, frank, free-spoken, outspoken, plainspoken

> He shot her at point-blank range.
> (그가 표적거리에서 그녀를 쐈다.)

1409
poisonous [póizənəs]
a. 독을 함유한, 유독한; 유해한
IN BRIEF Containing or being a poison
- venomous, virulent, baneful, lethal, pernicious, deleterious

> Some mushrooms are poisonous.
> (어떤 버섯은 독이 있다.)

1410
poll [poul]
n. 투표; 여론조사 / v. 투표하다, 득표하다
IN BRIEF The casting and registering of votes in an election
- opinion, sampling, survey, canvass, interview sample, vote

> The man refuted the results of the poll.
> (그 사람은 투표 결과에 반박하였다.)

1411
pompous [pámpəs]

a. 젠체하는, 거만한

IN BRIEF Characterized by excessive self-esteem or exaggerated dignity; pretentious

[+] haughty, proud, self-important, ostentatious, showy

> He's a real gentleman, if a little pompous at times.
> (비록 때때로 좀 젠체하더라도 그는 진짜 신사다.)

1412
ponder [pándə-]

v. 곰곰이 생각하다, 숙고하다

IN BRIEF To consider something deeply and thoroughly; meditate

[+] think about, consider, contemplate, meditate, muse, reflect, think

> You have pondered long enough it is time to decide.
> (당신은 충분히 숙고했다. 이제 결정할 시기다.)

1413
portal [pɔ́ːrtl]

n. (우람한) 입구, 현관, 정문

IN BRIEF A doorway, entrance, or gate, especially one that is large and imposing

[+] entrance, beginning, gate, appearance, approach, doorway, threshold

> Fifty steps lead to the cathedral's majestic portal.
> (50계단을 올라가면 대성당의 웅장한 정문에 이른다.)

1414
posterity [pɑstérəti]

n. 후손, 자손

IN BRIEF Future or succeeding generations

[+] descendants, heirs, offspring, progeny, successors

> His fame will go down to posterity.
> (그의 명성은 후손 대대로 전해질 것이다.)

1415
posthumously [pástʃuməsli]

사후에

IN BRIEF Occurring or continuing after one's death

[+] postmortem, after one's death

> His last novel was published posthumously.
> (그의 마지막 소설이 사후에 출판되었다.)

1416
postulate [pástʃəlèit]

v. (자명한 것으로) 가정하다, 추정하다

IN BRIEF To assume to be true or existent; take for granted

[+] presume, assumption, hypothesis, premise, theory

> They postulated that the collision had been caused by fog.
> (그들은 그 충돌이 안개 때문이었다고 가정했다.)

1417
potable [póutəbəl]

a. 마시기에 적합한

IN BRIEF A beverage, especially an alcoholic beverage

[+] drinkable

> This beverage is potable.
> (이 음료는 마실 수 있다.)

1418
potential [pouténʃəl]

a. 잠재적인, 가능한

IN BRIEF Possible but not yet actual

[+] eventual, latent, possible

> There may be a potential danger in the recently planned TWO project.
> (최근 계획된 TWO 사업에는 잠재적 위험이 있을 수 있다.)

1419
practically [præktikəli]

ad. 사실상(은), 실제로는, 실질적으로(는)

IN BRIEF All but; nearly; almost

[+] almost, approximately, basically, essentially, fundamentally, virtually

> He is practically dead.
> (그는 죽은 거나 마찬가지다.)

1420
pragmatically [prægmǽtikəli]

실용적으로 ; 실용주의적으로

IN BRIEF Dealing or concerned with facts or actual occurrences; practical

[+] fundamentally, practically, realistically

> We have to respond pragmatically to a crisis
> (우리는 위기에 실용적으로 대처해야 한다.)

1421
precarious [prikɛ́əriəs]

a. 불안정한, 위태로운, 위험한

IN BRIEF Dangerously lacking in security or stability

[+] dangerous, hazardous, perilous, at risk, insecure, baseless, groundless, untenable

> He was unable to get down from his precarious position on the rocks.
> (그는 바위 위의 위태로운 곳에서 내려올 수가 없었다.)

1422
precaution [prikɔ́ːʃən]
n. 조심, 예방책, 대비책

IN BRIEF An action taken to avoid a dangerous or undesirable event

[+] defense, protection, safeguard, security, anticipation, prudence

Locking doors is a precaution against thieves.
(문을 잠그는 것은 도둑을 막는 예방책이다.)

1423
precedent [présədənt]
n. 선례, 전례

IN BRIEF Law a judicial decision that serves as an authority for deciding a later case

[+] criterion, guide, example, measure, model, pattern

There is no precedent for it.
(그것에 대한 전례가 없다.)

1424
precipitate [prisípətèit]
v. 촉진 시키다, 내몰다; 재촉하다

IN BRIEF Hasten the occurrence of; to cast, plunge, or send violently; accelerate

[+] hasten, quicken, arouse, motivate, stimulate, trigger

The assassination of the president precipitated the country into war.
(대통령 암살이 그 국가를 전쟁으로 내몰았다.)

1425
precise [prisáis]
a. 명확한, 정확한

IN BRIEF Clearly expressed or delineated; definite

[+] definite, determined, distinct, explicit, accurate, correct, right, exact

What were her precise words?
(정확히 그녀가 한 말이 뭐야?)

1426
predilection [priːdəlékʃən]
n. 대단히 좋아함, 선호

IN BRIEF A predisposition, preference, or bias

[+] liking for, attraction, fondness, partiality, preference, bias, inclination, predisposition, proclivity, propensity, tendency

Ahntonio has had a predilection for Japanese food.
(안토니오는 일본 음식을 특별히 좋아해왔다.)

1427
preferment [prifə́ːrmənt]
n. 승진, 승급

IN BRIEF The act of advancing to a higher position or office; promotion

[+] promotion, rise, upgrading, dignity, advancement, elevation, exaltation

A wife was the last thing Walter Pater wanted, and he searched instead for academic preferment.
(월터 페이터(Walter Pater)는 결코 아내를 원하지 않았다. 그는 그 대신 학문적인 발전을 추구했다.)

1428
premise [prémis]
n. (…이라는) 전제, 가정

IN BRIEF To provide a basis for; base

[+] assumption, postulate, proposition, supposition

You have to start with that premise.
(당신은 그 전제에서 출발해야만 한다.)

1429
prepared [pripέərd]
a. 준비가 되어 있는

IN BRIEF Ready for something that is likely to happen done or made beforehand

[+] ready, equip, furnish

The spokesman read out a prepared statement.
(대변인이 준비된 성명서를 읽었다.)

1430
preposterous [pripástərəs]
a. 말도 안 되는, 터무니없는, 비상식적인

IN BRIEF Contrary to nature, reason, or common sense; absurd

[+] absurd, asinine, fatuous, inane, ludicrous, outrageous, ridiculous

The suggestion is preposterous.
(그 제안은 언어도단이다.)

1431
prerequisite [priːrékwəzit]
a. 필수적인, 없어서는 안 될; 미리[우선] 필요조건

[+] essential, imperative, mandatory, necessary, requirement

A degree is a prerequisite for employment at this level.
(이런 수준의 취업에는 학위가 필수조건이다.)

1432
prescribe [priskráib]
v. (약 따위를) 처방하다; 지시하다, 규정하다

IN BRIEF Appoint; to order a medicine

⊕ inquire, interrogate, solicit, beseech, entreat, implore, demand

> Ask her to prescribe something for that cough.
> (그녀에게 그 기침에 복용할 뭔가를 좀 처방해달라고 부탁해.)

1433
presently [prézəntli]
ad. 지금, 현재

IN BRIEF In a short while; soon

⊕ directly, forthwith, immediately, shortly, soon, currently, now

> The book is presently unavailable.
> (그 책은 현재 구할 수가 없습니다.)

1434
pressing [présiŋ]
a. 긴급한, 절박한, 임박한

IN BRIEF Demanding immediate attention; urgent

⊕ compelling, crucial, demanding, exigent, imperative, urgent

> He left the meeting early, saying he had a pressing engagement.
> (그는 긴급한 약속이 있다며 모임에서 일찍 떠났다.)

1435
prestigious [prestídʒiəs]
ad. 명성이 있는, 유명한

IN BRIEF Having prestige; esteemed

⊕ eminent, famed, renowned, reputable, notable, significant

> A number of prestigious persons attended the party.
> (많은 명성 있는 사람이 그 파티에 참석했다.)

1436
presume [prizú:m]
v. 추정하다, …이라고 생각하다, 여기다

IN BRIEF To take for granted as being true in the absence of proof to the contrary

⊕ assume, suppose, surmise, conclude, deduce, infer

> "Mr. Ahn, I presume?"
> ("안 선생 아니십니까?")

1437
presumptuous [prizʌ́mptʃuəs]
a. 주제넘은, 건방진

IN BRIEF Going beyond what is right or proper; excessively forward

⊕ audacious, brazen, impertinent, nervy, arrogant, disdainful, haughty, imperious, pompous

> It would be presumptuous of me to comment on the matter.
> (내가 그 문제에 논평을 하는 것은 주제 넘는 일이 될 것이다.)

1438
pretentious [priténʃəs]
a. 자만하는, 우쭐대는, 젠체하는

IN BRIEF Making claim to distinction or importance, esp undeservedly

⊕ ostentatious, pompous, affected, flaunting, insincere, snobbish

> I don't like pretentious rock groups.
> (나는 잘난 체하는 록 그룹은 좋아하지 않는다.)

1439
pretext [prí:tekst]
n. 구실, 핑계

IN BRIEF Something put forward to conceal a true purpose; an ostensible reason; excuse

⊕ excuse, pretense, defense, justification

> We'll have to find a pretext for not going to the party.
> (우리는 그 파티에 가지 않을 핑계를 찾아야 할 것이다.)

1440
prevail [privéil]
vi. (…에) 널리 퍼지다[행해지다], 보급되다, 유행하다

IN BRIEF To be greater in strength or influence; triumph

⊕ dominate, predominate, spread, prevail upon, influence

> Such ideas prevail these days.
> (이러한 생각들이 요즈음 판을 치고 있다.)

1441
prevalent [prévələnt]
a. (…에) 널리 퍼진; 보급된, 유행하고 있는

IN BRIEF Widely or commonly occurring, existing, accepted, or practiced

⊕ popular, rampant, widespread, dominant, predominant, prevailing

> This is an attitude prevalent among university students.
> (이것이 대학생들 사이에서 유행하는 태도이다.)

1442
prey [prei]
n. 먹이, 희생물

IN BRIEF An animal hunted or caught by another for food

+ target, victim, casualty, fatality, sacrifice, scapegoat

> They were prey to pickpockets and other criminal.
> (그들은 소매치기들 및 다른 범죄자들의 희생자였다.)

1443
prime [praim]
vt. (사전) 준비하다; 준비시키다 / a. 가장 중요한, 주된, 주요한, n. 전성기

IN BRIEF To make ready; prepare

+ prepare, ready, educate, instruct, teach, tutor

> The new manager was clearly well primed with information.
> (그 새 매니저는 정보가 충분히 준비되었음이 분명했다.)

1444
primarily [praim]
본래, 주로

IN BRIEF Principally; chiefly; mainly

+ essentially, fundamentally, predominately, first, initially, originally

> The purpose of the programme is primarily educational.
> (그 프로그램의 목적은 주로 교육적이다.)

1445
privatize [práivətàiz]
vt (공기업 등) 민영화하다

IN BRIEF To transfer from public or government control or ownership to private enterprise

+ personal, privy, intimate, private, individual, particular

> British Telecom was privatized in 1984.
> (British Telecom은 1984년에 민영화되었다.)

1446
poignant [pɔ́injənt]
a. 매서운, 날카로운; 통렬한

IN BRIEF Sharply distressing or painful to the feelings

+ moving, touching, affecting, upsetting, sad, bitter, intense, painful, distressing, pathetic, harrowing, heartbreaking, agonizing, heart-rending, gut-wrenching; piquant, pungent, sharp, spicy, zesty

> The opening chapters of this novel boast some of the wittiest, most poignant and sharply intelligent comic prose in the English literature.
> (이 소설 첫머리의 장들은 영국 문학에서 가장 위트 있고, 가장 신랄하면서도 번득이는 지성을 갖춘 희극 산문 가운데 일부를 뽐내고 있다.)

1447
profusion [prəfjúːʒən]
n. 대량, 풍부; 사치

IN BRIEF The state of being profuse; abundance; copiousness

+ abundance, wealth, excess, quantity, surplus, riot, multitude, bounty, plethora, exuberance, glut, extravagance, cornucopia, oversupply, plenitude, superabundance, superfluity, lavishness, luxuriance, prodigality

> Members of the academy and activist organizations mainly debate the complexity of the contemporary profusion of feminist perspectives.
> (학술 및 운동 단체들의 회원들은 현대 사회에 페미니즘의 시각이 풍부하게 존재하는 것이 갖는 복잡성에 관해 주로 토론하고 있다.)

1448
pay off
빚을 갚다, 보답하다; 성과를 내다
1. To pay the full amount on (a debt)
2. To result in profit or advantage; succeed: Your efforts will eventually pay off

> Young people have got to understand from an early age that the world pays off on results, not on effort.
> (젊은이들은 세상은 / 노력이 아니라 결과에 보답한다는 것을 어려서부터 이해해야 한다.)

1449
preferential [prèfərénʃəl]
a. 우선권[특혜]을 주는, 선택적인, 차별적인

IN BRIEF Showing or resulting from preference

+ privileged, favoured, superior, better, special, partial, partisan, advantageous

> The Los Angeles County Sheriff's Department is investigating whether Mel Gibson received preferential treatment when he was arrested.
> (로스앤젤레스카운터 경찰국은 멜 깁슨이 체포되었을 때 특별대우를 받았는지 여부를 조사하고 있다.)

1450
protrude [proutrúːd]
v. 내밀다, 밀어내다, 불쑥 나오다

IN BRIEF To extend or jut out; project

+ bag, balloon, beetle, belly, bulge, jut, overhang, pouch, project, protuberate, stand out, stick out

> Minahasa, northeasternmost portion of the longest of the four peninsulas, projects from the curiously shaped and mountai-nous island of Celebes (Sulawesi), Indonesia. The peninsula protrudes northeast between the Celebes and Molucca seas.
> (4개의 반도 중 가장 긴 반도의 최북동부 지역인 미나하사는 기이한 형태에 산이 많은 인도네시아 셀레베스 섬으로부터 불쑥 나와 있다 그 반도는 셀레베스 섬과 몰루카해 사이에 북동쪽으로 돌출해있다.)

LESSON 30

1451
probity [próubəti]

n. 정직, 성실

IN BRIEF Complete and confirmed integrity; uprightness

[+] character, decency, honesty, honor, tried integrity

> Probity is a high standard of correct moral behavior.
> (정직함이란 올바른 도덕적 행동 중에서도 상위 기준이다.)

1452
proceeds [próusi:dz]

n. 수익, 수입

IN BRIEF Commerce the profit or return derived from a commercial transaction, investment

[+] yields, gain, income, net, profits, receipts, revenue

> The proceeds were divided equally among us.
> (이익금은 우리에게 공평하게 분배되었다.)

1453
process [práses-]

n. 과정, 절차; 진행, 진전; …을 처리하다

IN BRIEF A series of actions that produce a change or development

[+] work on, procedure, rule, mechanism, operation, working

> Most of the food we buy is processed in some way.
> (우리가 사는 식품은 대부분이 어떤 식으로든 처리가 된 것이다.)

1454
procrastinate [proukræstənèit]

질질 끌다, 꾸물거리다, 지체하다

IN BRIEF To put off or defer (an action until a later time; delay)

[+] delay, defer, postpone, suspend, dawdle, hesitate, linger, loiter, tarry

> He procrastinated until it was too late to do anything at all.
> (그는 질질 끌다가 너무 늦어서 전혀 아무 것도 할 수 없게 되고 말았다.)

1455
procure [proukjúər]

v. 얻다, 획득하다, 손에 넣다

IN BRIEF To get by special effort; obtain or acquire

[+] purchase, secure, capture, grasp, seize

> She managed to procure a car.
> (그녀는 그럭저럭 차를 한 대 획득했다.)

1456
prodigious [prədídʒəs]

a. 거대한, 터무니없는, 놀랄만한

IN BRIEF Vast in size, extent, power

[+] noteworthy, wonderful, enormous, gigantic, huge, immense

> The construction was started on a prodigious scale.
> (그 공사는 엄청난 규모로 착수되었다.)

1457
profile [próufail]

n. 윤곽, (특히) 옆얼굴; 측면

IN BRIEF A side view of an object or structure, especially of the human head

[+] shape, silhouette, characterization, portrait, vignette

> She has a beautiful profile.
> (그녀는 옆얼굴이 아름답다.)

1458
progeny [prádʒəni]

n. 자식, 자손; 계승자

IN BRIEF The immediate descendant or descendants of a person, animal

[+] child, heir, offspring, descendants, posterity, seed

> His numerous progeny are scattered all over the country.
> (그의 수많은 자손들이 이 나라 방방곡곡에 흩어져 산다.)

1459
prognostication [prɑgnɑ̀stikéiʃən]

예언(예상, 예지, 예측)하기

IN BRIEF To predict according to present indications or signs; foretell

[+] forecast, outlook, prediction, prognosis, projection

> His gloomy prognostications proved to be false.
> (그의 암울한 예측은 틀린 것으로 판명되었다.)

1460
prohibit [prouhíbit]

vt. 금지하다

IN BRIEF To forbid by law or other authority

[+] ban, forbid, outlaw, impede, inhibit, obstruct, prevent

> Parking without a permit is prohibited.
> (허가 없는 주차는 금지된다.)

1461
project [prədʒékt]

n. 계획, 설계 (plan, schema, scheme) / v. 을 계획[고안]하다, …를 제출[제시]하다, 투영하다, 예측하다(conceive, design, propose, forecast, predict) / 발사하다, 불쑥 나오다, 돌출하다 (emit, protrude, shed)

IN BRIEF A proposal, scheme, or design

> The population is projected to decrease.
> (인구가 감소할 것으로 예상된다.)

1462
prolific [proulífik]

a. 다산(多産)의, 다작(多作)의(productive);비옥한

IN BRIEF Producing fruit, offspring, etc, in abundance

fruitful, fertile, abundant, teeming, bountiful, luxuriant, generative, profuse, fecund

> His prolific writings earned him the 1953 Nobel Prize in Literature.
> (자신이 쓴 풍부한 글들로 그는 1953년에 노벨문학상을 수상했다.)

1463
proliferate [prəˈlɪfəreɪt]

증식, 번식하다

IN BRIEF To grow or multiply by rapidly producing new tissue, parts, cells, or offspring

breed, generate, propagate, reproduce, rapidly, burgeon, expand, increase, multiply, spread

> At Christmastime biographies of the famous proliferate in the bookshops.
> (크리스마스 때가 되면 유명인의 전기들이 서점에 난무한다.)

1464
proliferation [prəlifəréiʃən]

확산, 급증; 증식

IN BRIEF A sudden increase, increase

rapid increase, breed, generate, propagate, burgeon, expand

> Federal policy is changing to curb the proliferation of nuclear weapons.
> (연방 정부 정책은 핵무기 확산을 억제하는 쪽으로 바뀌고 있습니다.)

1465
prologue [próulɔːg]

n. 서사, 프롤로그; 머리말

IN BRIEF An introduction or preface, especially a poem recited to introduce a play

induction, introduction, lead-in, overture, preamble, preface, prelude

> I read the prologue to the 'Canterbury Tales'.
> (나는 '캔터베리 이야기'의 머리말을 읽었다.)

1466
prolong [proulɔ́ːŋ]

vt 연장하다; 길어지게 하다; 연기하다

IN BRIEF To lengthen in duration; protract

elongate, extend, lengthen, delay, protract, retard

> They prolonged their visit by a few days.
> (그들은 방문기간을 며칠 더 연장했다.)

1467
prominent [prámənənt]

a. 저명한; 두드러진

IN BRIEF Widely known; eminent

important, manifest, obvious, pronounced, salient

> He is a prominent politician.
> (그는 저명한 정치가다.)

1468
promiscuous [prəmískjuəs]

a. 뒤섞인, 뒤죽박죽의, 난잡한, 마구잡이의

IN BRIEF Indulging in casual and indiscriminate sexual relationships

careless, haphazard, indiscriminate, uncritical, unrestricted

> She did not regard herself as promiscuous.
> (그녀는 자신을 문란하다고 여기지 않았다.)

1469
promote [prəmóut]

vt. 승진, 진급 시키다 / 장려, 진흥하다

IN BRIEF To raise to a more important or responsible job or rank

encourage, advertise, circulate, publicize

> She worked hard and was soon promoted.
> (그녀는 열심히 일해서 곧 승진되었다.)

1470
promptly [prámptli]

기민하게, 민첩하게; 즉시

IN BRIEF Carried out or performed without delay

precise, punctual, timely, immediate, instant, quickly

> She promptly accepted my offer.
> (그녀는 나의 제의를 즉시 받아들였다.)

1471
promulgate [prámǝlgèit]

vt. 공표[발표]하다; 공포하다

IN BRIEF To make known to the public; popularize or advocate

announce, circulate, officially declare, proclaim, publicize

> The American Declaration of Independence was promulgated in January 1776.
> (미국 독립 선언은 1776년 1월에 공표 되었다.)

1472
prone [proun]

a. ~경향이 있는, ~하기 쉬운

IN BRIEF Lying with the front or face downward

+ disposed, apt, liable, likely, inclined, predisposed, susceptible

> Man is prone to err.
> (인간은 잘못을 저지르기 쉽다.)

1473
propensity [prəpénsəti]

n. 경향, 버릇

IN BRIEF An innate inclination; a tendency

+ proclivity, aptitude, predisposition, tendency

> Ahntonio has a propensity to exaggerate.
> (안토니오는 과장하는 경향이 있다.)

1474
propitious [prəpíʃəs]

a. 길조의, 순조로운

IN BRIEF Favourable; auguring well

+ auspicious, fortunate, lucky, advantageous, beneficial, favorable, promising

> It was not a propitious time to start a new business.
> (그때가 새 사업을 시작하기에 좋은 때가 아니었다.)

1475
proponent [prəpóunənt]

n. 제안[제의]자, 지지자, 옹호자

IN BRIEF One who argues in support of something; an advocate

+ advocate, backer, champion, defender, patron, supporter

> She was an avid proponent of equal rights for immigrants.
> (그녀는 이민자의 동등한 권리를 열렬히 지지하는 사람이었다.)

1476
propriety [prəpráiəti]

n. 예의바름, 단정함; 적당

IN BRIEF Conformity to conventional standards of behavior or morality

+ correctness, seemliness, suitability, decorum, proprieties, amenities

> I doubt the propriety of making use of the method.
> (그 방법을 이용하는 것이 적당한지 어떤지 의문이다.)

1477
prosaic [prouzéiik]

a. 재미없는, 평범한, 단조로운, 지루한, 산문의, 산문체의

IN BRIEF Commonplace or dull; matter-of-fact; unimaginative

+ boring, common, everyday, ordinary, routine, banal, dull, trite

> He is a prosaic writer.
> (그는 산문 작가이다.)

1478
proscribe [prouskráib]

vt. …를 금지하다, 금하다, 배척하다

IN BRIEF Prohibit, censure, repudiate; to banish

+ interdict, prohibit, censure, condemn, denounce, disapprove

> Some conductors proscribe sound amplification at their concert.
> (몇몇 연출자들은 그들의 콘서트에서 음향 증폭을 금지한다.)

1479
protract [proutrǽkt]

vt. 연장하다; 오래 끌게 하다

IN BRIEF To draw out or lengthen in time; prolong

+ prolong, continue, maintain, perpetuate, sustain, lengthen

> Please don't protract the suspense tell me if I passed or not.
> (제발 불안한 상태를 끌지 말아주세요. 붙었는지 떨어졌는지 말해줘요.)

1480
provenance [právənəns]

n. 기원, 출처

IN BRIEF Place of origin; derivation

+ fount, fountainhead, origin, provenience

> I don't need to see a label to identify the provenance of a garment.
> (나는 라벨을 보지 않아도 옷의 출처를 확인할 수 있다.)

1481
provisional [prəvíʒənəl]

a. 일시적인, 잠정적인, 임시의; 조건부의

IN BRIEF Provided or serving only for the time being

+ conditional, contingent, experimental, interim, makeshift, temporary

> The booking is only provisional.
> (그 예약은 잠정적일 뿐이다.)

1482
provocation [pràvəkéiʃən]
n. 도발, 자극, 건드림

IN BRIEF The act of provoking or inciting

aggravation, cause, goad, incitement, instigation, motivation

She loses her temper at the slightest provocation.
(그녀는 사소한 자극에도 성을 낸다.)

1483
provoke [prəvóuk]
vt. 자극하다, 화나게 하다, 유발하다

IN BRIEF To incite to anger or resentment

anger, inflame, irritate, arouse, excite, goad, incite, kindle

If you provoke the dog, it will attack you.
(그 개를 자극하면 공격할 것이다.)

1484
prowess [práuis]
n. 용감함; 위대한 업적; 훌륭한 솜씨

IN BRIEF Superior skill or ability

competence, skill, talent, bravery, courage, daring, valor, vigor

We admire his prowess as a sportsman.
(우리는 그의 운동 솜씨에 감탄했다.)

1485
prowl [praul]
v. 배회하다, 기웃거리다

IN BRIEF To roam through stealthily, as in search of prey or plunder

move around, sneak, haunt

Wolves prowled the forest.
(늑대들이 숲 속을 배회했다.)

1486
proximity [praksíməti]
n. (장소·시간·관계) 가까움[to]; 근접

IN BRIEF Nearness in space or time

closeness, nearness, propinquity, environs, neighborhood, vicinity

The restaurant benefits from its proximity to several cinemas.
(그 식당은 몇 몇 영화관에 근접한 덕을 보고 있다.)

1487
prudent [prú:dənt]
a. 현명한; 신중한

IN BRIEF Discreet or cautious in managing one's activities; circumspect

politic, careful, cautious, circumspect, discreet

He is a prudent businessman.
(그는 신중한 사업가다.)

1488
prying [práiiŋ]
a. 엿보는, 흘끗흘끗 보는, 캐기 좋아하는

IN BRIEF Insistently or impertinently curious or inquisitive

interfere, inquisitive, nosy, meddle, poke, snoop

don't want you prying into my private life.
(네가 내 사생활을 엿보는 걸 원치 않는다.)

1489
pseudonym [sú:dənim]
n. (작가의) 필명, 가명

IN BRIEF A fictitious name, especially a pen name

nickname, pen name, nameless, unidentified, unknown, unsigned

She writes under a pseudonym.
(그녀는 필명으로 글을 쓴다.)

1490
psychology [saikálədʒi]
n. 심리학

IN BRIEF The science that deals with mental processes and behavior

mentality, mind, mind-set, psyche

He specialized in social psychology.
(그는 사회 심리학을 전공했다.)

1491
punctilious [pʌŋktíliəs]
a. 격식에 치우친, 세심한; 꼼꼼한

IN BRIEF Strictly attentive to minute details of form in action or conduct

careful, fastidious, meticulous, painstaking, scrupulous

Ahntonio is too punctilious in everything
(안토니오는 모든 면에서 너무 꼼꼼하다.)

1492
punctual [pʌ́ŋktʃuəl]
a. 시간[기일]을 지키는

IN BRIEF Acting or arriving exactly at the time appointed; prompt

+ on time, precise, prompt, seasonable, timely, well-timed

> He's always very punctual.
> (그는 언제나 시간을 아주 잘 지킨다.)

1493
pundit [pʌ́ndit]
n. 전문가, 박식한 사람, 학자

IN BRIEF A learned person

+ expert, savant, intellectual, philosopher, sage

> The pundits disagree on the best way of dealing with the problem.
> (그 문제를 해결하는 최선책에 대해 학자들의 의견이 다르다.)

1494
purport [pərpɔ́ːrt]
vt. 주장하다, 의도하다, 의미하다, 취지이다 / n. 요지, 취지, 뜻

IN BRIEF Meaning; significance

+ allege, aver, claim, maintain, profess, point, significance, design, intention, purpose

> I do not understand the purport of your question.
> (난 당신 질문의 요지를 모르겠다.)

1495
plethora [pléθərə]
n. 과다, 과잉(lot; extreme excess), (의학)다혈증

IN BRIEF An abundance or excess of something;

+ excess, surplus, glut, profusion, surfeit, overabundance, superabundance, superfluity

> Artists, craftsmen and entrepreneurs offer a plethora of handmade items and services.
> (예술가, 장인, 기업가들은 대단히 많은 수제품과 서비스를 제공하고 있다.)

1496
punctuate [pʌ́ŋktʃuèit]
v. 구두점을 찍다; 강조하다

IN BRIEF To provide (a text) with punctuation marks

+ emphasize, mark, stress, underline, accentuate, foreground, point up

> All such communicative events are punctuated routinely by various units of traditional material that are memorable and repeatable.
> (그러한 모든 의사소통 사건들은 기억할 만하고 반복할 만한 여러 다양한 단위의 전통적인 자료에 의해 일상적으로 강조되고 있다.)

1497
pinchbeck [píntʃbèk]
n. 가짜, 모조품(fakery)

IN BRIEF Counterfeit, imitative – not genuine; sham or counterfeit. spurious

+ copy, ersatz, imitation, simulation

> The idea that advertising was merely a method of puffing the pinchbeck has long passed.
> (광고가 단지 가짜(모조품)를 부풀려 선전하는 방법일 뿐이라는 생각은 사라진 지 오래다.)

1498
perk [pəːrk]
n. 임원직의 특전; (급료 이외의) 임시 수입(perquisite)
v. (낙담·병(病) 뒤에)생기가 나다, 건강해지다; 활기 띠다

IN BRIEF Gain or regain energy; "I picked up after a nap"

+ gain vigor, perk up, percolate, pick up, convalesce, recover, recuperate

> The perk of being a student is an inexpensive flight fee.
> (학생이 됨으로써 얻게 되는 특전은 항공요금이 싸다는 것이다.)

1499
petulance [pétʃələns]
n. 성마름, 토라짐, 안달, 무례한 태도[행동]

IN BRIEF Unreasonably irritable or ill-tempered; peevish

+ unreasonable, childish, bad temper, sulkiness, bad temper, irritability, spleen, pique, sullenness, waspishness, ill-humour, peevishness, querulousness, crabbiness, pettishness

> The child's petulance annoyed the teacher, who liked her students to be cheerful and cooperative.
> (그 아이의 무례한 태도는 선생님을 화나게 했는데, 그녀는 자신의 학생들이 쾌활하고 협동적이기를 바랐다.)

1500
pejorative [pidʒárətiv]
a. 가치를 떨어뜨리는; 퇴화적인; 경멸적인, 멸시적인(critical)

IN BRIEF Tending to demean or belittle

+ deprecative, deprecatory, depreciative, depreciatory, derogative, derogatory, detractive, disparaging, low, slighting, uncomplimentary

> The pejorative sense of the invention of tradition implies manipulation and mystification and should not be taken ascharacteristic of traditions in general.
> (전통을 창출하는 것에 들어 있는 경멸적인 의미는 조작과 속임수가 개입되었음을 암시하는 것이며, 따라서 그것을 전통이 보편적으로 가진 특징으로 간주해서는 안 된다.)

LESSON 31

1501
putative [pjúːtətiv]

a. 추정되는, 소문에 들리는

IN BRIEF Generally regarded as such; supposed

+ reputed, supposed, assumed, consider, presume, conjecture

> He's referred to in the document as the putative father.
> (그는 서류 속에서 추정상의 아버지로 언급되었다.)

1502
put-on

가장한, 거짓의, 겉으로 만의

IN BRIEF A hoax or spoof

+ phony, fraud, fraudulence, dupery, hoax, humbug

> He seems very sincere, but it's all put-on.
> (그는 아주 진실해 보이지만, 그건 모두 가장이다.)

1503
puzzling [pázliŋ]

a. 어찌할 바를 모르게 하는, 곤혹케 하는; 혼란시키는

IN BRIEF To be perplexed

+ baffle, confound, perplexing, bewilder, confuse, mystify, nonplus

> She's been puzzling over this problem for weeks.
> (그녀는 이 문제를 두고 몇 주째 어찌 할 바로 모르고 있다.)

1504
quaint [kweint]

a. 색다르고 재미있는, 진기한, 고풍스러운

IN BRIEF Attractively unusual, esp in an old-fashioned style

+ eccentric, unique, unusual, bizarre, outlandish, peculiar, old-fashioned

> What a quaint idea!
> (정말 진기한 생각이야!)

1505
qualms [kwɑːm]

n. 거리낌, 양심의 가책

IN BRIEF Uneasy feeling; pang of conscience; misgiving

+ doubt, scruple, compunction, misgiving, reservation

> He had no qualms about cheating his employer.
> (그는 고용주를 속이는 데 일말의 양심의 가책도 느끼지 않는다.)

1506
quandary [kwándəri]

n. 곤경, 궁지, 어려움

IN BRIEF A state of uncertainty or perplexity

+ dilemma, entanglement, plight, impasse, mire, bog, predicament

> North Korea's actions have created a diplomatic quandary for China.
> (북한의 행동은 중국을 외교적으로 난처하게 만들었다.)

1507
queasy [kwíːzi]

a. 구역질나게 하는, 메스꺼운

IN BRIEF Troubled; anxious; worried; nauseated; upset

+ bilious, indisposed, nauseous, qualmish, squeamish

> His stomach still felt queasy.
> (그는 아직도 속이 느글거렸다.)

1508
quintessential [kwintəsénʃəl]

본질의, 전형적인

IN BRIEF Most typically representative of a quality, state, etc; perfect

+ paradigmatic, prototypical, representative, typical

> Everybody thinks of her as the quintessential beauty.
> (모든 사람들이 그녀를 전형적인 아름다움으로 여겼다.)

1509
quiver [kwívər]

떨림, 진동

IN BRIEF To shake with a slight, rapid, tremulous movement

+ pulse, quake, quaver, shudder, tremble, vibrate

> A quiver of excitement ran through the audience.
> (청중들 사이로 흥분의 떨림이 흘렀다.)

1510
qualified [kwάləfàid]

a. 자격 있는; 제한된, 한정된

IN BRIEF Having the abilities, qualities, attributes, etc, necessary to perform a particular job or task. Satisfying certain requirements, as for selection

+ eligible, fit, fitted, suitable, worthy, limited, modified, or restricted; not absolute

A qualified number of students are allowed in Professor Martin's Classics class.
(제한된 수의 학생들만이 마틴 교수의 고전 수업을 들을 수 있다.)

1511
racism [réisizəm]

n. 인종[민족] 차별주의

IN BRIEF Discrimination or prejudice based on race

➕ discrimination, bias, bigotry, prejudice, competition

They abhor all forms of racism.
(그들은 모든 종류의 인종 차별주의를 혐오한다.)

1512
rampant [rǽmpənt]

a. 마구 퍼지는, 만연하는

IN BRIEF Extending unchecked; unrestrained

➕ prevalent, widespread, epidemic, excessive

Food was scarce and disease was rampant.
(식량은 부족했고 질병은 만연했다.)

1513
rancid [rǽnsid]

a. 악취가 나는, 썩은 냄새가 나는

IN BRIEF Having a rank, unpleasant smell or taste

➕ fetid, offensive, spoiled, reeking

There was a rancid smell in the kitchen.
(부엌에서 썩는 냄새가 났다.)

1514
random [rǽndəm]

a. 마구잡이, 무작위

IN BRIEF Lacking any definite plan or prearranged order; haphazard

➕ chance, haphazard, indiscriminate, irregular

She reads books at random.
(그녀는 닥치는 대로 책을 읽는다.)

1515
rankle [rǽŋk-əl]

v. (마음에) 사무치다; 괴롭히다

IN BRIEF To become sore or inflamed; fester

➕ fret, grate, irritate, annoy, bother, irk, pique, vex

The insult still rankled with him.
(그 모욕은 아직도 그의 마음에 사무쳤다.)

1516
rapport [ræpɔ́:r]

n. (친밀하고 조화를 이루는) 관계, 친밀감

IN BRIEF Relationship, especially one of mutual trust or emotional affinity

➕ camaraderie, compatibility, harmony understanding, relationship

He has a very good rapport with his pupils.
(그는 학생들과 훌륭한 신뢰관계를 맺고 있다.)

1517
rare [rɛə:r]

a. 드문, 유례없는

IN BRIEF Infrequently occurring; uncommon

➕ unique, unusual, exceptional, extraordinary, remarkable

It's rare to see snow in September.
(9월에 눈을 보는 것은 드문 일이다.)

1518
ratify [rǽtəfài]

vt. 인가[승인]하다; (조약)비준하다

IN BRIEF To approve and give formal sanction to; confirm

➕ approve, confirm, endorse, sanction, support, enact, validate, verify

Heads of twelve European governments will meet to ratify the treaty.
(그 조약을 비준하기 위해 유럽 12개 정부 수반들이 모일 것이다.)

1519
ration [rǽʃ-ən]

공급을 제한하다; 배급하다

IN BRIEF To supply with rations

➕ allocate, allot, apportion, dole out, mete out, proportion

The government may have to introduce petrol rationing.
(정부가 휘발유 배급제를 도입해야 할지도 모른다.)

1520
rattled [rǽtld]

놀란, 당황한, 어리둥절한

IN BRIEF Disconcerted, unnerved

➕ confused, baffle, daze, fluster, perplex, puzzle

Thunders of applause rattled the speaker.
(우레 같은 갈채에 연사는 어리둥절했다.)

1521
ravage [rǽvidʒ]
v. 파괴하다 / n. 황폐, 파괴된 자취

IN BRIEF Wreak great destruction or devastation

[+] ruin, despoil, pillage, plunder, raid, ransack, demolish, destroy, raze

> This village is a witness to the ravages of war.
> (이 마을은 전쟁의 참혹한 피해의 증거이다.)

1522
rave [reiv]
v. 열심히 이야기하다; 격찬하다; 헛소리 해대다

IN BRIEF To speak wildly, irrationally, or incoherently

[+] highly praised, roar, storm, cheer, effervesce, gush

> The play got rave reviews in the papers.
> (신문들은 그 연극을 격찬했다.)

1523
reaffirm [riːəfə́ːrm]
vt. 다시 단언하다; 다시 확인하다

IN BRIEF To affirm or assert again

[+] reiterate, repeat, restate

> She reaffirmed that she was prepared to help.
> (그녀는 도와줄 각오가 되어 있다고 재차 다짐했다.)

1524
recalcitrant [rikǽlsətr-ənt]
a. 반항[저항]하는; 고집 센

IN BRIEF Not susceptible to control or authority; refractory

[+] unmanageable, bullheaded, headstrong, inflexible, stubborn

> He is a recalcitrant child.
> (그는 반항적인 아이다.)

1525
recant [rikǽnt]
v. (진술·주장)철회하다, 취소하다; 부정하다(withdraw)

IN BRIEF Withdraw or disavow; revoke, rescind, deny

[+] disavow, disclaim, annul, cancel, repeal, revoke, rescind, retract

> He recanted his former opinions in public
> (그는 대중에 대한 자신의 이전 견해를 철회했다.)

1526
recapitulate [riːkəpítʃəlèit]
v. 요약하다, 반복하다, 요점을 되풀이 하다

IN BRIEF To repeat in concise form

[+] reiterate, rephrase, restate, reword, recount, review, summarize

> The second scene of the play recapitulates the central points of the first scene.
> (그 연극의 두 번째 장은 첫 장의 핵심 요점을 되풀이하여 말한다.)

1527
recede [risíːd]
vi. 물러나다; 멀어지다, 약해지다

IN BRIEF To move back or away from a limit, point, or mark

[+] subside, withdraw, abate, decrease, lessen

> As the tide receded from the shore we were able to look for shells.
> (해변에서 물이 빠져나가자 우리는 조개껍질을 찾을 수 있었다.)

1528
reciprocal [risíprək-əl]
a. 상호의, 서로의

IN BRIEF Done, given, felt, or owed in return

[+] mutual, shared, bilateral, common, joint

> Such treaties provide reciprocal rights and obligations.
> (그런 조약들은 상호간의 권리와 의무를 규정한다.)

1529
reckless [réklis]
a. 앞뒤를 헤아리지 않는, 무모한; 부주의한

IN BRIEF Acting or done with a lack of care or caution; careless or irresponsible

[+] irresponsible, careless, foolhardy, heedless, imprudent, thoughtless

> Ahntonio is a reckless driver.
> (안토니오는 부주의한 운전자이다.)

1530
reclaim [rikléim]
v. 되찾다; 개간하다; 재생하다

IN BRIEF To resume possession of; take back

[+] recondition, reconstruct, rehabilitate, reinstate, rejuvenate

> I went to the station to reclaim my suitcase.
> (나는 여행 가방을 되찾기 위해 역으로 갔다.)

1531
recluse [réklu:s]
n. 은둔자

IN BRIEF A person apart from the society, hermit, introvert, loner

+ secluded, solitary and shut off from society

> He's become a virtual recluse since his wife died.
> (그는 아내가 죽은 후로 그야말로 은둔자가 되었다.)

1532
recollect [rèkəlékt]
v. 기억해 내다, 생각해 내다, 회상하다

IN BRIEF To remember something

+ evoke, place, recall, remember

> I recollect that I have met her before.
> (전에 그녀를 만난 것이 기억난다.)

1533
reconcile [rékənsàil]
v. 화해시키다; 조화시키다, 감수하게 하다, 만족시키다

IN BRIEF To reestablish a close relationship between

+ make up, appease, conciliate, propitiate, reunite, adjust, harmonize

> He had to reconcile himself to his fate.
> (그는 자신의 운명에 만족해야만 했다.)

1534
rectitude [réktətjù:d]
n. 정직, 청렴 (virtuousness)

IN BRIEF Moral uprightness; righteousness

+ morality, probity, righteousness, rightness, uprightness, virtue

> He is a person of exemplary moral rectitude.
> (그는 모범적으로 도덕적 청렴함을 지닌 사람이다.)

1535
recurring [rikə́:riŋ]
a. 되풀이해서 일어나는; 〈수학〉 순환하는

IN BRIEF To happen or occur again or repeatedly

+ continue, persist, repeated, resume, return

> The recurring decimal 3. 999 … is also described as 3. 9 recurring.
> (순환소수 3. 999…는 또한 3. 9 순환으로 묘사되기도 한다.)

1536
recycle [ri:sáik-əl]
v. (폐기물) 재생 처리[가공, 이용]하다, 재활용하다

IN BRIEF To process in order to regain materials for human use

+ reprocess, reuse, salvage, reclaim, save

> The government wants everyone to recycle 25% of their household waste.
> (정부는 모든 사람이 가정 쓰레기의 25%를 재활용하기를 바란다.)

1537
redeem [ridí:m]
v. 되사다, 되찾다 / (결점 등을) 메우다, 벌충하다 / (상품권 등을) 상품권으로 바꾸다 / (약속·의무) 이행하다

IN BRIEF To recover ownership of by paying a specified sum

+ buy back, recover, regain, retrieve, reclaim, win back

> I'm going to redeem my gold watch.
> (나는 내 금시계를 다시 되찾을 것이다.)

1538
redundant [ridʌ́ndənt]
a. (문체) 장황한, 여분의, 불필요한

IN BRIEF Exceeding what is necessary or natural; superfluous

+ tautological, excessive, superfluous, unnecessary

> The report was cluttered with redundant detail.
> (그 보고서는 장황한 설명으로 뒤죽박죽이었다.)

1539
refrain [rifréin]
v. 억제[자제]하다; 삼가다, 그만두다

IN BRIEF To hold oneself back; forbear from doing something

+ stop, abstain, avoid, desist, forbear, resist

> Please refrain from smoking.
> (담배를 삼가 주십시오.)

1540
refute [rifjú:t]
vt. 반박하다, 논박하다

IN BRIEF To prove to be false or erroneous; overthrow by argument or proof

+ contradict, discredit, disprove, rebut

> He refuted all suggestions that he was planning to resign.
> (그는 자기가 사임을 계획 중이라는 모든 제안들을 반박했다.)

1541
regard [rigá:rd]

v. 간주하다, 여기다[as]

IN BRIEF To think of or consider in a particular way

+ consider, judge, think, view, admire, esteem, observe, scan

> We regard such visits as important.
> (우리는 그런 방문들을 아주 중요하게 생각한다.)

1542
regional [ríːdʒnəl]

a. 지역의, 지대의, 지방의, 지방적인

IN BRIEF Of or relating to a large geographic region

+ local, territorial, rural, rustic

> She's been shunted off to a regional office.
> (그녀는 지방 사무소로 좌천되었다.)

1543
rehabilitate [riːhəbílətèit]

vt. 복원하다, 원상태로 돌리다; 복귀시키다; 갱생시키다

IN BRIEF To restore to good health or useful life, as through therapy and education

+ restore, renovate, reeducate, reclaim, redeem, reform, transform

> The warehouses have been rehabilitated.
> (창고들이 복원되었다.)

1544
reimburse [riːimbə́ːrs]

vt. 빚을 갚다, 변상하다

IN BRIEF To repay (money spent; refund)

+ refund, remit, remunerate, repay, return

> We will reimburse the customer for any loss or damage.
> (저희는 고객 여러분께 어떤 손실이나 손상도 배상해 드립니다.)

1545
reiterate [riːítərèit]

vt. (명령·탄원 등을) 반복하다, 되풀이하다

IN BRIEF To say or do again or repeatedly

+ repeat, rephrase, restate, reword

> She reiterated her story to the police.
> (그녀는 자신의 이야기를 경찰에게 되풀이했다.)

1546
release [rilíːs]

vt. 석방하다; 풀어놓다; 개봉하다, 석방, 방출

+ disengage, distribute, present, discharge

> He has been released from prison.
> (그는 교도소에서 석방 되었다.)

1547
relentless [riléntlis]

가차 없는, 잔인한; 집요한, 끊임없는(indefatigable)

IN BRIEF Unyielding in severity or strictness; unrelenting

+ merciless, hard, fierce, harsh, cruel, grim, ruthless

> Bloodhounds are relentless trackers, but they must be kept on a leash because if a scent goes off the edge of a cliff, the bloodhound will likely follow.
> (블러드하운드는 집요한 경찰견이지만, 반드시 끈으로 묶어 두어야 한다. 왜냐하면 만약 벼랑 끝 너머에서 냄새가 나면 블러드하운드는 (그 냄새를 따라) 추적할 것이기 때문이다.)

1548
relevant [réləvənt]

a. 관련된; 적절한

IN BRIEF Having direct bearing on the matter in hand; pertinent

+ applicable, appropriate, apropos, fitting, germane, pertinent

> The evidence is relevant to the case.
> (그 증거는 이 사건과 관련이 있다.)

1549
reliant [riláiənt]

a. 의존하는, 의지하는

IN BRIEF Having or exhibiting reliance; dependent

+ concomitant, contingent, dependent, subject to

> Ahntonio is heavily reliant on bank loans.
> (안토니오는 은행 융자에 많이 의존하고 있다.)

1550
resolution

n. 결의, 결심; 해결

IN BRIEF The condition or quality of being resolute; firmness or determination

+ solution, end, settlement

> A misstep in the resolution of the dispute over tuberculosis control could have serious and unintended side effects in the entire state.
> (결핵퇴치에 대한 논쟁을 해결하는 데 있어 한 번 실수를 하면 심각하고 의도하지 않은 부작용을 국가 전체에 가져올 수도 있을 것이다.)

LESSON 32

1551
relinquish [rilíŋkwiʃ]
vt. (소유물) 포기[양도]하다; 그만두다; 버리다, 단념하다
IN BRIEF To give up or abandon
➕ give up, abdicate, forego, renounce, surrender, waive, yield

> Do you think he will relinquish his seat in the Senate?
> (당신은 그가 상원에서의 자기 지위를 포기할 거라고 생각하십니까?)

1552
reluctant [rilʌ́ktənt]
a. 주저하는, 마음이 내키지 않는
IN BRIEF Disinclined; unwilling to act
➕ disinclined, loath, opposed, unwilling, diffident, hesitant, irresolute

> She was very reluctant to admit her mistake.
> (그녀는 겨우 마지못해 자기 실수를 인정했다.)

1553
remedial [rimíːdiəl]
a. 치료[교정, 구제]하는
IN BRIEF Medicine affording a remedy; curative
➕ curative, restorative, therapeutic, correcting, healing

> He has undergone remedial therapy for a bad back
> (그는 안 좋은 허리를 위한 치료를 받고 있다.)

1554
reminisce [rèmənís]
v. 추억[회상]하다, 추억에 잠기다
IN BRIEF To think about or tell of past experiences or events
➕ remember, recollect, recall, go over in one's memory

> She often reminisced about her youth.
> (그녀는 자주 젊은 시절을 회상했다.)

1555
remiss [rimís]
a. 태만한, 부주의한
IN BRIEF Lacking in care or attention to duty; negligent
➕ careless, inattentive, lax, negligent, slack

> I have been very remiss in my duty.
> (나는 지금까지 임무에 매우 태만했다.)

1556
remedy [ˈremədi]
v. 치료하다, 고치다, 없애다 (mitigate, assuage, palliate)
IN BRIEF To counteract or rectify (a problem, mistake, or undesirable situation
➕ cure, treat, heal, help, control, ease, restore, relieve, soothe, alleviate

> In the long history of images of beauty, one staple is the male tendency to spot new flaws in women, and the female tendency to work and suffer to remedy them.
> (미적 표현의 오랜 역사에서 한 가지 주된 특징은 남성들에게는 여성들의 새로운 결함을 지적하는 경향이 있으며, 여성들에게는 그 결함을 고치기 위해 노력하며 고통을 겪는 경향이 있다는 것이다.)

1557
remnant [rɪˈzɪliənt]
n. 나머지, 잔여; 생존자; 조각, 단편; 자투리
IN BRIEF Something left over; a remainder
➕ remainder, remains, fragment, piece, relic

> The remnants of the man's clothes were found by the river.
> (그 남자의 다른 옷 조각 들은 강가에서 발견되었다.)

1558
remorse [rimɔ́ːrs]
n. 후회, 양심의 가책
IN BRIEF A sense of deep regret and guilt for some misdeed
➕ compunction, contrition, penitence, regret, repentance

> He seemed to feel no remorse at all.
> (그는 아무런 후회도 느끼지 않는 것 같았다.)

1559
remote [rimóut]
a. 멀리 떨어진(distant, far-off, faraway)
IN BRIEF Located far away; distant in space
➕ isolated, secluded, irrelevant, unrelated, aloof, detached

> My house is remote from my school.
> (내 집은 학교와 멀리 떨어져 있다.)

1560
remuneration [rimjùːnəréiʃ-ən]

n. 보답; 보수, 보상

IN BRIEF The act of remunerating

+ payment, salary, wages, damages, reparation, restitution

They demanded adequate remuneration for their work.
(그들은 자신들의 일에 대한 적합한 보수를 요구했다.)

1561
renown [rináun]

n. 명성, 유명, 명망[for] / v. 유명하게 만들다

IN BRIEF The quality of being widely known or acclaimed; fame

+ celebrity, eminence, prominence, reputation, repute

He is renowned for his paintings.
(그는 그림으로 유명하다.)

1562
repeal [ripíːl]

(정식으로) …을 취소하다, 철회하다; 무효로 하다

IN BRIEF To revoke or rescind, especially by the action of a legislature

+ annul, cancel, invalidate, recall, rescind, revoke

A repeal is the removal or reversal of a law.
(repeal이란 법을 철회하거나 제거하는 것이다.)

1563
repellent [rɪˈpelənt]

역겨운, 혐오감을 주는

IN BRIEF Inspiring aversion or distaste; repulsive

+ unpleasant, distasteful, obnoxious, offensive, repugnant, repulsive

I find his selfishness repellent.
(나는 그의 이기주의가 역겹다.)

1564
replenish [ripléniʃ]

vt. 다시 채우다; 보충[보급]하다

IN BRIEF To fill or make complete again; add a new stock or supply to

+ refill, reload, restock, furnish, provide, supply

Let me replenish your glass.
(잔을 다시 채워 줄게요.)

1565
reprehensible [rèprihénsəb-əl]

a. 비난받을 만한, 괘씸한

IN BRIEF Deserving rebuke or censure

+ heinous, despicable, disgraceful, ignoble, objectionable

Your attitude is most reprehensible.
(네 태도는 대단히 괘씸하다.)

1566
reprimand [réprəmænd]

문책하다, 질책하다

IN BRIEF A reproof or formal admonition; rebuke

+ chide, rebuke, reproach, reprove, scold

The headmaster was severely reprimanded.
(교장은 심한 견책을 받았다.)

1567
reproach [ripróutʃ]

vt. 비난하다, 질책하다

IN BRIEF To express disapproval of, criticism of, or disappointment in (someone)

+ blame, chide, condemn, criticize, rebuke, reprimand

She reproached him with aloofness.
(그 여자는 그의 냉담함을 나무랐다.)

1568
repulsive [ripʌ́lsiv]

a. 역겨운, 혐오스러운

IN BRIEF Causing repugnance or aversion; disgusting

+ repugnant, revolting, frightful, hideous, monstrous

Picking your nose is a repulsive habit.
(네 코 후비는 버릇은 역겨워.)

1569
repercussion [rìːpəːrkʌ́ʃ-ən]

n. (간접적)영향; (사건·행동 등의 오래 남는)영향

IN BRIEF An effect or result of some previous action or event

+ backlash, strong impact, outcome, repercussions, consequences

His resignation will have serious repercussions on the firm.
(그의 사직은 회사에 심각한 파장을 초래할 것이다.)

1570
requisite [rékwəzit]

a. 필요한, 필수의, 불가결한

IN BRIEF Something that circumstances make necessary

+ essential, indispensable, necessary, needful, required

The firm employs the requisite number of women.
(그 회사는 필요한 수의 여성을 고용하고 있다.)

1571
requite [rikwáit]

vt. 보답하다; 은혜 갚다, 앙갚음하다, 보복하다

IN BRIEF To make return to (a person for a kindness or injury; repay with a similar action)

➕ indemnify, pay, recompense, redress, reimburse, remunerate, repay

> I will requite like for like.
> (같은 방법으로 복수할거야.)

1572
rescind [risínd]

v. (법률·행위) 폐지하다; (계약) 무효로 하다, 취소하다(annul)

IN BRIEF Cancel. To void by legislative action

➕ declare void, recall, repeal, reverse

> The government rescinded its trade agreement after a continuous economic recession.
> (정부는 계속되는 경기침체 뒤에 그 무역협정을 폐지하였다.)

1573
resemble [rizémb-əl]

v. 닮다

IN BRIEF To exhibit similarity or likeness to

➕ favor, look like, parallel, take after

> She resembles her mother.
> (그녀는 어머니를 닮았다.)

1574
resent [rizént]

vt. 분개하다, 싫어하다, 원망하다

IN BRIEF To feel indignantly aggrieved at

➕ begrudge, take exception to, be offended by, be angry about

> He resents any allusion to his baldness.
> (그는 자기 대머리에 대해 조금만 암시해도 분개한다.)

1575
resentment [rɪˈzentmənt]

n. 분개; 원한

IN BRIEF Anger, bitterness, or ill will

➕ anger, rage, fury, irritation, grudge, wrath

> Psychologists say that people taken hostage sometimes feel not resentment toward their captors but sympathy.
> (심리학자들은 인질로 잡힌 사람들이 때때로 납치한 사람들에 대해 분노가 아니라 동정심을 느낀다고 말하고 있다.)

1576
residual [rizídʒuəl]

a. 남겨진, 나머지의, 잔류의

IN BRIEF The quantity left over at the end of a process; a remainder

➕ remaining, balance, dregs, excess, remainder, remnant

> I still felt some residual bitterness.
> (나는 여전히 괴로움의 앙금을 느꼈다.)

1577
resilient [rizíljənt, -liənt]

a. 되 튀는, 복원력 있는, 탄력 있는, 곧 기운을 회복하는 / 쾌활한, 발랄한

IN BRIEF Able to recover readily, as from misfortune

➕ elastic, flexible, rubbery, springy, stretchy

> She is very resilient to change.
> (그녀는 변화에 대한 탄력이 아주 좋다. – 즉 적응력이 좋다.)

1578
resolute [rézəlùːt]

a. 굳게 결심한

IN BRIEF Firm or determined; unwavering

➕ resolved, persevering, persistent, relentless, steady

> He is resolute to fight.
> (그는 싸울 결심을 하고 있다.)

1579
resolve [rizálv]

v. 해결하다 / 결심하다

IN BRIEF To make a firm decision about

➕ solve, conclude, decide/determine, ascertain, settle, bound

> I can't resolve this problem.
> (나는 이 문제를 해결할 수 없다.)

1580
respite [réspit]

n. (일·고통·의무 따위의) 일시적 중단[휴지], 휴식

IN BRIEF A usually short period of rest or relief

➕ relief, break, lull, recess, rest

> We worked for hours without respite.
> (우리는 중간 휴식도 없이 몇 시간 동안 일했다.)

1581
restive [réstiv]

a. 말을 잘 안 듣는, 다루기 힘든, 고집 센

IN BRIEF Restless, nervous, or uneasy

+ resolute, disobedient, recalcitrant, reluctant

Allen grew restive because his music was interrupted.
(앨런은 자신의 음악이 방해를 받자 성질이 났다.)

1582
resume [rizú:m]

v. 다시 시작하다, 재개하다

IN BRIEF To begin or take up again after interruption

+ restart, begin again, continue, proceed, recommence

The two sides have resumed fighting.
(양 팀은 싸움을 다시 시작하였다.)

1583
resurrection [rèzərékʃ-ən]

n. 부활; 소생, 그리스도의 부활

IN BRIEF The act of restoring a dead person, for example, to life

+ revival, animate, rekindle, renew, resuscitate, revitalize

The Resurrection is one of the most crucial doctrines of Christianity.
(부활은 기독교 신앙에서 가장 중요한 교리 중 하나이다.)

1584
retain [ritéin]

vt. 보유[유지]하다, 간직[기억]하다

IN BRIEF To keep possession of; continue to have

+ reserve, conserve, maintain, preserve, endure, persist

Lead retains heat.
(납은 열을 그대로 간직한다.)

1585
reticent [rétəs-ənt]

a. 과묵한, 말이 없는

IN BRIEF Unwilling to speak; reserved; taciturn, uncommunicative

+ quiet, reserved, restrained, subdued, taciturn

She is a reticent woman.
(그녀는 말이 없는 여자다.)

1586
retreat [ritrí:t]

v. 물러가다, 후퇴하다

IN BRIEF The act or process of moving back or away

+ recede, escape, evacuate, retire, withdraw

They could neither advance nor retreat.
(그들은 전진도 후퇴도 할 수 없었다.)

1587
retribution [rètrəbjú:ʃ-ən]

n. 징벌; 응보

IN BRIEF Punishment administered in return for a wrong committed

+ vengeance, penalty, punishment, reparation, requital satisfaction

Some people saw her death as divine retribution for her crimes.
(어떤 이들은 그녀의 죽음을 두고 그녀가 저지른 범죄에 대해 하늘이 내린 벌이라고 생각했다.)

1588
retrieve [ritrí:v]

v. 되찾다, 회수하다; 만회하다, 회복하다

IN BRIEF To get or fetch back again; recover

+ salvage, bring, get, reclaim, recoup, recover, redeem, regain

We taught our dog to retrieve a ball.
(우리는 개에게 공을 집어오라고 가르쳤다.)

1589
retrogress [rétrəgrès]

퇴보하다, 후퇴하다; 나빠지다, 쇠퇴하다

IN BRIEF To return to an earlier, inferior, or less complex condition

+ regress, backslide, relapse, revert, degenerate, deteriorate

There is a time in the history of many great civilizations when they begin to retrogress.
(많은 위대한 문명의 역사에는 그들이 쇠퇴하기 시작하는 시기가 있다.)

1590
revamp [ri:væmp]

vt. 수리[개조, 개선]하다

IN BRIEF To patch up or restore; renovate

+ overhaul, redo, revise, refurbish, remodel, renovate

Here is a revamped kitchen.
(여기가 개조된 부엌이다.)

1591
reverberate [rivə́ːrbərèit]

v. 반향을 일으키다, 울려 퍼지다

IN BRIEF To resound in a succession of echoes; reecho

+ echo, resound, rumble vibrate

A loud voice reverberates through the hall.
(큰 목소리가 회관 안에 울려 퍼진다.)

1592
reveal [rivíːl]

vt. 드러내다, 폭로하다, 밝히다

IN BRIEF To make known (something concealed or unknown)

+ bare, expose, show, uncover, disclose, divulge

They began to reveal their true selves.
(그들은 본성을 드러내기 시작했다.)

1593
revere [rivíər]

vt. 존경하다, 숭배하다

IN BRIEF To regard with awe, deference, and devotion

+ respect, adore, exalt, honor, reverence, venerate, worship

The students revere the professor.
(학생들은 그 교수를 존경한다.)

1594
revert [rivə́ːrt]

v. (원래의 습관·신앙·상태 따위로) 되돌아가다; 귀속하다

IN BRIEF To go back to a former condition, practice, subject, or belief

+ backslide, regress, relapse, return, reverse

The conversation kept reverting to the subject of money.
(대화는 계속해서 돈이라는 주제로 되돌아갔다.)

1595
revision [rivíʒ-ən]

n. 개정, 교정, 수정

IN BRIEF Reexamining and improving, alteration

+ amendment, change, correction, improvement, modification

That book needs a lot of revision.
(저 책은 개정할 것이 많다.)

1596
rigorous [ríg-ərəs]

a. 엄격한, 엄한, 정밀한; 정확한

IN BRIEF Thorough, demanding, harsh

+ stern, strict, tough, accurate, correct, exact, precise

The arms trade should be subject to rigorous controls.
(무기 거래는 엄격히 규제를 해야 한다.)

1597
rip-off [rip ɔːf]

도둑; 사기; 사취, 폭리, 모방, 도용; 도작 작품

IN BRIEF An act of exploitation

+ deceit, deception, trickery, ruse, sham, swindle, cheater, fake, phony, quack

$50 for a cup of coffee? What a rip-off!
(커피 한 잔에 50 달러라고요? 도둑질이 따로 없군!)

1598
riveting [rívitiŋ]

a. 매혹적인, 황홀케 하는; 재미있는

IN BRIEF Wholly absorbing or engrossing one's attention; fascinating

+ very interesting, attractive, appealing, enchanting, alluring, fascinating, seductive

Especially, the last chapter of the book was riveting.
(특히 그 책 마지막 부분이 매혹적이다.)

1599
roam [roum]

v. 배회하다, 걸어 다니다

IN BRIEF To move about without purpose or plan; wander

+ stray, wander, wander with no very clear aim, meander, stroll

He used to roam the streets for hours on end.
(그는 몇 시간 동안 계속해서 길거리를 돌아다니곤 했었다.)

1600
resilience [rizíljəns]

n. 탄성, 탄력; 회복력

IN BRIEF The ability to recover quickly from illness, change, or misfortune; buoyancy

+ bounce, buoyancy, elasticity, resiliency

An ingredient of resilience is an optimistic orientation and a focus on the positive on oneself and in human nature.
(회복력의 구성요소 가운데 하나는 낙관적인 태도, 그리고 자신과 인간본성에 존재하는 긍정적인 면에 주의를 집중하는 것이다.)

LESSON 33

1601
robust [roubʌ́st]
a. 튼튼한, 억센, 강건한
IN BRIEF Full of health and strength; vigorous
+ strong, energetic, lively, exuberant, vigorous

> You need to be robust to go rock climbing.
> (암벽 등반을 하려면 건강해야 한다.)

1602
rookie [rúki]
n. 신병; 신임 경찰관; 신출내기, 풋내기
IN BRIEF An untrained or inexperienced recruit, as in the army or police
+ first-year, apprentice, beginner, newcomer, novice, tyro

> Ah, you're the rookie.
> (아, 당신이 그 신입사원이군요.)

1603
roughly [rʌ́fli]
ad. 거칠게, 난폭하게; 투박하게, 대충, 대략
IN BRIEF Without being exact or fully authenticated; approximately
+ coarse, harsh, rugged, raging, tempestuous, tumultuous, unpolished

> It should cost roughly $100.
> (비용이 대략 100 달러는 들 것이다.)

1604
routine [ru:tíːn]
n. 일상적인 틀, 일상
IN BRIEF A customary or regular course of procedure
+ habitual, methodical, ordinary, predictable, usual

> She wants to escape from the same routine.
> (그녀는 똑같은 일상사에서 벗어나고 싶어 한다.)

1605
rowdy [ráudi]
a. 난폭한; 시끄러운; 툭 하면 싸우는
IN BRIEF Tending to create noisy disturbances; rough, loud, or disorderly
+ boisterous, disorderly, loud, unruly

> The party got a bit rowdy.
> (파티가 조금 소란스러워졌다.)

1606
rudimentary [rùːdəméntəri]
원리의, 기본의, 기초의; 초보의
IN BRIEF Basic; fundamental; not elaborated or perfected
+ basal, basic, elementary

> Her knowledge is still only rudimentary.
> (그녀의 지식은 여전히 초보적일 뿐이다.)

1607
rugged [rʌ́gid]
a. 울퉁불퉁한, 험한
IN BRIEF Rough but strong and good, uneven
+ difficult, tough, hardy, coarse, rude, uncultivated, unrefined

> This rugged road takes you to the village.
> (이 울퉁불퉁한 길을 따라가면 그 마을이 나옵니다.)

1608
ruin [rúːin]
n. 폐허, 파괴, 파멸, 황폐; 파괴하다, 파멸시키다
IN BRIEF The state of being physically destroyed, collapsed, or decayed
+ relics, remains, remnants, vestiges, demolition, destruction

> Gambling was his ruin.
> (노름 때문에 그는 파멸했다.)

1609
rummage [rʌ́midʒ]
v. 뒤지다, 샅샅이 찾다
IN BRIEF To search thoroughly by handling, turning over, or disarranging the contents of
+ search, comb, forage, ransack, pillage, raid, sack

> The doctor rummaged in his bag.
> (그 의사는 가방을 샅샅이 뒤적거렸다.)

1610
run-down [rʌn daun]
지친, 기진맥진한; 쇠약해진
IN BRIEF In poor physical condition; weak or exhausted
+ fatigued, tired-out, wearied, weariful, weary, worn-out

> He was in a run-down condition.
> (그는 기진맥진해 있었다.)

1611
run-of-the-mill
흔해 빠진, 평범한, 어디에나 있는, 보통의

IN BRIEF Not special or outstanding; average

⊕ average, banal, common, plain, prosaic, everyday, mundane, normal, regular, routine

> This book is a run-of-the-mill detective story
> (이 책은 평범한 탐정 소설이다.)

1612
rustle [rʌ́s-əl]
v. (잎·비단·종이 따위가) 바스락거리다, 사각거리다, 와삭거리다

IN BRIEF To move with soft fluttering or crackling sounds

⊕ whisper, flutter, soft sound

> I wish people wouldn't rustle their bags of popcorn during the movies.
> (나는 영화 볼 때 사람들이 팝콘 봉지를 바스락거리지 않으면 좋겠다.)

1613
ruthless [rúːθlis]
a. 무자비한, 가차 없는

IN BRIEF Having no compassion or pity; merciless

⊕ remorseless, brutal, cruel, fierce, inhuman, vicious

> He is a ruthless tyrant.
> (그는 무자비한 폭군이다.)

1614
revulsion [rɪ'vʌlʃn]
n. 반박; 혐오(odium, detestation)

IN BRIEF A sudden strong change or reaction in feeling, especially a feeling of violent disgust or loathing

⊕ disgust, loathing, distaste, aversion, recoil, abomination, repulsion, abhorrence, repugnance

> Many people in this country who admired dictatorship underwent a revulsion when they realized what their president was trying to do.
> (독재를 찬미했던 이 나라의 많은 국민들은 대통령이 시행하려고 하던 바를 이해했을 때 극도의 혐오감을 경험했다.)

1615
sacred [séikrid]
a. 신성한; (신에게) 바친

IN BRIEF Treated with great reverence, blessed, consecrated

⊕ dedicated, hallowed, sanctified, holy, pious, divine, religious

> A temple is a sacred place.
> (사원은 신성한 곳이다.)

1616
rejection [rɪ'dʒekʃn]
n. 거절; 배제, 폐기

IN BRIEF To refuse to accept, submit to, believe, or make use of

⊕ denial, veto, dismissal, exclusion, abandonment, spurning, casting off, disowning, thumbs down, renunciation, repudiation, eschewal

> Older theories are not so much abandoned as corrected. Einstein himself always insisted that his own work was a modification rather than a(n) rejection of Newton's
> (오래된 이론들은 버려지기 보다 오히려 수정된다. 아인슈타인은 자신의 연구가 뉴턴의 연구를 배제한 것이 아니라 오히려 부분적으로 수정한 것이라고 항상 주장했다.)

1617
sag [sæg]
v. (길·땅) 가라앉다, 꺼지다, (의류·바지)느슨해지다, 약해지다, 나른해지다

IN BRIEF To sink, droop, or settle from pressure or weight

⊕ droop, slouch, stoop, decline

> Your skin starts to sag as you get older.
> (나이가 들면 피부가 처지기 시작한다.)

1618
sagacious [səgéiʃəs]
a. 빈틈없는, 영리한; 현명한

IN BRIEF Having or showing keen discernment, sound judgment, and farsightedness

⊕ perceptive, perspicacious, smart, canny, clever, cunning, shrewd

> He is a sagacious person.
> (그는 현명한 사람이다.)

1619
salient [séiliənt]
a. 두드러진, 눈에 띄는, 돌출한(prominent, protruding)

IN BRIEF Prominent, conspicuous, or striking

⊕ conspicuous, noticeable, pronounced, striking

> She pointed out all the salient features of the new design.
> (그녀는 새 디자인에서 두드러지는 모든 특징들을 모두 지적하였다.)

1620
salutary [sǽljətèri]
a. 유익한, 건전한

IN BRIEF Effecting or designed to effect an improvement; remedial

⊕ useful, practical, serviceable, valuable, worthwhile

> The accident is a salutary reminder of the dangers of climbing.
> (그 사고는 등산의 위험을 상기시켜 주는 유익한 것이다.)

1621
sanction [sǽŋkʃən]

n. 인가 → 승인 → 제재하다 → 처벌하다

IN BRIEF Authoritative permission or approval that makes a course of action valid

+ approve, entitle, endorse, authorize, countenance, vouch for

The book was translated without the sanction of the author.
(그 책은 저자의 허가 없이 번역되었다.)

1622
sanctuary [sǽŋktʃuèri]

n. 신성한 장소, 성역; 피난처; 야생동물 보호구역

IN BRIEF A sacred place, such as a church, temple, or mosque

+ shrine, temple, haven, refuge, retreat, asylum, protection, shelter

This region is a wildlife sanctuary.
(이 지역은 야생생물 보호구역이다.)

1623
sanctum [sǽŋktəm]

n. (방해받지 않는) 사실, 서재

IN BRIEF A sacred or holy place

+ refuge, retreat, den, hideaway, private room, hide-out

I was allowed once into his sanctum.
(나는 그의 밀실에 한 번 들어가 본 적이 있다.)

1624
sanguine [sǽŋgwin]

a. 쾌활한, 낙천적인; (얼굴이) 혈색이 좋은

IN BRIEF Cheerfully confident; optimistic

+ buoyant, red, cheerful, hopeful, optimistic, flushed, rosy, ruddy

She remained sanguine about our chances of success.
(그녀는 우리가 성공할 가능성에 대하여 마지막까지 낙관적이었다.)

1625
sanitary [sǽnətèri]

a. 위생의, 위생적인

IN BRIEF Of or relating to health or the protection of health

+ antiseptic, clean, decontaminated, germ-free, hygienic

This building is a sanitary office.
(이 건물은 검역소이다.)

1626
sap [sæp]

v. (나무) 수액을 짜내다 → 활력을 잃게 하다 / n. 원기, 활기

IN BRIEF To deplete or weaken gradually

+ gradually weaken, deplete, reduce, rob, debilitate, enervate, exhaust

The long trek sapped our energy.
(길고 고된 여행에 우리는 진이 빠졌다.)

1627
saunter [sɔ́:ntər]

vi. 느릿느릿 걷다

IN BRIEF To walk at a leisurely pace; stroll

+ amble, mosey, promenade, stroll, wander

He sauntered by with his hands in his pockets.
(그는 손을 호주머니에 집어넣고서 어슬렁거리며 돌아 다녔다.)

1628
savvy [sǽvi]

v. 알다, 이해하다 / a. 소식에 밝은, (사정) 정통한 / n. 실제적 지식, 상식

IN BRIEF Well informed and perceptive; shrewd

+ conceive, fathom, follow, get, grasp, make out

He has a lot of savvy.
(그는 상당한 상식을 지니고 있다.)

1629
scanty [skǽnti]

a. 근소한, 모자라는; 불충분한, 부족한

IN BRIEF Small or insufficient in amount, size, or extent

+ insufficient, meager, measly, paltry, scarce, poor

The scanty rainfall is causing water shortages.
(불충분한 강우량이 물 부족을 야기하고 있다.)

1630
scathing [skéiðiŋ]

a. (비평 등이) 통렬한, 신랄한, 가차 없는

IN BRIEF Bitterly denunciatory; harshly critical

+ ruthless, biting, brutal, caustic, stinging

The report was scathing about the lack of safety precautions.
(그 보고서는 사전 안전 예방 조치가 부족하다는 것을 혹독히 비난했다.)

1631
scrap [skræp]
n. 작은 조각, 찌꺼기 / v. 쓰레기[폐물, 스크랩]로 만들다

IN BRIEF A small piece or bit; a fragment

➕ crumb, grain, fragment, particle, piece, portion, discard, junk, reject

> Lack of cash forced us to scrap plans for new house.
> (돈의 부족은 우리에게 새로운 집에 대한 계획들을 찢어버리게 했다.)

1632
screen [skri:n]
가리다; 검열하다

IN BRIEF Protect, hide, or conceal from danger or harm

➕ shield, conceal, shade, evaluate, cull, filter, sift, sort, strain

> A fifth of all applicants fail during the initial screening.
> (1차 심사에서 지원자의 5분의 1이 탈락한다.)

1633
scribe [skraib]
n. 문필가, 대서인, 서기; 달필가

IN BRIEF A writer or journalist

➕ writer, author, composer, dramatist, journalist

> In Biblical times, a scribe was a teacher of the religious law.
> (성서 시대에 문필가는 종교법을 가르치는 교사였다.)

1634
scrupulous [skrú:pjələs]
a. 세심, 꼼꼼, 정확한 → 양심적인, 성실한

IN BRIEF Conscientious and exact; painstaking

➕ careful, fastidious, meticulous, painstaking, punctilious, exact

> A scrupulous politician would not lie about his business interests.
> (양심적인 정치인이라면 자신의 사업적 이해관계에 대해 거짓말을 하지 않을 것이다.)

1635
scrutinize [skrú:t-ənàiz]
자세히 조사하다

IN BRIEF To examine or observe with great care; inspect critically

➕ examine, exam closely, inspect, observe, study, survey

> He scrutinized minutely all the documents relating to thetrial.
> (그는 그 재판에 관련된 모든 서류를 세밀히 조사했다.)

1636
scrutiny [skrú:təni]
정밀한 조사 → 응시 → 정밀조사(analysis)

IN BRIEF Examination, study

➕ check, checkup, examination, inspection

> "The media scrutiny and the reaction from government are so tremendous that it actually eclipses our ability to understand it," Assange said in an interview with Time magazine on day 3 of the data dump, which began on November 28.
> ("언론의 면밀한 관찰과 정부의 반응은 너무나 엄청나서 그것(외교문서 공개.)은 우리가 이해할 수 있는 능력을 실제로 넘어서고 있다." 라고 어샌지는 11월28일 자료공개를 시작한 지 사흘째 되는 날에 타임지와 가진 인터뷰에서 말했다.)

1637
seasoning [sí:z-əniŋ]
n. 양념(하기); 간을 맞춤; 조미료

IN BRIEF Something, such as a spice or herb, used to flavor food

➕ condiment, dressing, flavoring, spice

> Salt and pepper are the two most common seasonings in cooking.
> (소금과 후추는 요리에 가장 흔히 쓰이는 두 가지 조미료이다.)

1638
secede [sisí:d]
vi. (정당이나 모임 따위에서) 탈퇴[분리]하다

IN BRIEF To withdraw from.

➕ withdraw, pull away; split from

> He has decided to secede from the association.
> (그는 그 모임에서 탈퇴하기로 작정했다.)

1639
seclude [siklú:d]
vt. 떼어놓다(separate), 차단[격리]하다(from)

IN BRIEF To set or keep apart, as from social contact with others

➕ hide, insulate, isolate, separate, sequester

> He secluded himself from society because of shyness.
> (그는 수줍은 성격 때문에 사회로부터 은둔했다.)

1640
secular [sékjələ:r]
a. 세속의, 세속적인, 현세적인, 이 세상의

IN BRIEF Worldly rather than spiritual

➕ mundane, civil, carnal, earthly, profane, temporal, worldly

> He is concerned only with secular affairs.
> (그는 세속적인 일에만 관여한다.)

1641
sedentary [sédəntèri]
a. 앉아 있는; 잘 앉는; 앉아 일하는

IN BRIEF Characterized by or requiring much sitting

+ fixed, immobile, inactive, stationary, indolent, languid, sluggish

> I should start playing sport because my lifestyle is too sedentary.
> (내 생활 방식이 너무 앉아만 있는 것이라서 난 운동을 시작해야 한다.)

1642
segment [ségmənt]
n. 단편, 조각, 부분, 구분

IN BRIEF Any of the parts into which something can be divided

+ division, fragment, part, piece, portion, section

> Please give me a segment of an orange.
> (제발 오렌지 한쪽 좀 주세요.)

1643
sensible [sénsəbəl]
a. 분별 있는, 현명한

IN BRIEF Acting with or exhibiting good judgment; reasonable

+ intelligent, prudent, wise, cognizant, conscious, sentient

> She gave me some very sensible advice.
> (그녀는 나에게 아주 현명한 충고를 해 주었다.)

1644
sentient [sénʃənt]
a. 느끼는, 지각[감각]력이 있는

IN BRIEF Having sense perception; conscious

+ aware, cognizant, discerning, knowledgeable, deliberate, intentional

> It is hard for a sentient person to understand that.
> (지각이 있는 사람으로서는 그건 이해하기 힘들다.)

1645
shortcoming [ʃɔ́ːrtkʌ̀miŋ]
n. 결점, 단점, 불충분한 점(A deficiency; a flaw)

IN BRIEF A failing or deficiency

+ defect, deficiency, deficit, inadequacy, insufficiency, lack, paucity, drawback, imperfection, frailty, foible, weak point

> My mother was always a little troubled by my lack of beauty, and I knew it as a child senses such things. She tried very hard to bring me up well so my manners would in some way compensate for my looks, but her efforts only made me more keenly conscious of my shortcomings.
> (어머니는 항상 나의 부족한 외모에 대해 걱정했고, 나는 그런 것을 아이의 감각으로 알 수 있었다. 그녀는 내 예절이 어떤 면에서 나의 외모를 보완하도록 나를 잘 기르려고 열심히 노력했지만, 그녀의 노력은 나로 하여금 내 결점에 대해 더욱 신경 쓰이게만 했다.)

1646
setback [sétbæ̀k]
n. 걸림돌, 곤란, 문제, 패배, 좌절

IN BRIEF A check to progress; a reverse or defeat

+ frustration, hindrance, inhibition, interference, obstruction

> The defeat constitutes a major setback for the government.
> (그 패배는 정부에게 주요한 좌절이 되었다.)

1647
sullen [sʌ́lən]
a. 부루퉁한, 시무룩한, 기분이 언짢은

IN BRIEF Unwilling to talk or be sociable; sulky; morose

+ dour, gloomy, glum, moody, morose, saturnine, sour, sulky, surly

> It is not so easy to abandon the whiny toddler or the sullen teenager.
> (징징대는 어린아이나 뚱해 있는 십대아이를 그대로 내버려 두는 것은 그리 쉬운 일이 아니다.)

1648
spin controller
공보 비서관

> Spin controllers are people who try to minimize the effects of gaffes, and otherwise improve the way candidates are presented in the media generally.
> (공보 비서관은 실수로 인한 영향을 최소화하며 이외에도 일반적으로 후보자들이 언론에 노출되는 모습을 개선하기 위해 노력하는 사람들이다.)

1649
seasoned [siːznd; 시즌드]
a. 조미된; 경험 많은

IN BRIEF Rendered competent through trial and experience

+ experienced, veteran, mature, practised, old, weathered, hardened, long-serving, battle-scarred, time-served, well-versed

> Being a seasoned traveler, he was prepared for the dangers.
> (노련한 여행가였기 때문에, 그는 여러 가지 위험한 일에 대비가 돼 있었다.)

1650
sediment [sédəmənt]
n. 침전물, 앙금(dregs, deposit)

IN BRIEF Material that settles to the bottom of a liquid

+ dregs, grounds, residue, lees, deposit, precipitate, settlings

> Since 1830, suspended sediment in the river has risen continuously.
> (1830년 이후, 그 강 속의 부유 퇴적물이 계속해서 늘어났다.)

LESSON 34

1651
sever [sévər]
v. 절단하다, 끊다[from], 떼어 놓다, 가르다[from, into]
IN BRIEF To cut off (a part from a whole)
+ cleave, cut, rend, split, amputate, truncate, break off, disband

Sara hand was severed from his arm.
(Sara의 팔에서 손이 잘려나갔다.)

1652
shabby [ʃǽbi]
a. 닳아 해진, 누더기의, 초라한
IN BRIEF Howing signs of wear and tear; threadbare or worn-out
+ dilapidated, ragged, rundown, tattered, worn-out, cheap

His old suit looks shabby.
(그의 낡은 정장은 초라해 보인다.)

1653
sheen [ʃiːn]
n. 광휘, 광채; 광택; 윤; 현란한 의상; 광택 있는 천
IN BRIEF Glistening brightness; luster
+ light, luster, gloss, glow, polish, radiance, shine

Ulasteam is a shampoo to give your hair a beautiful sheen.
(윌라스팀은 당신의 머리에 아름다운 윤기를 주는 샴푸다.)

1654
sheer [ʃiər]
a. 《한정용법》 완전한, 순전한, 절대적인
IN BRIEF Not mixed with extraneous elements
+ unmixed, diaphanous, absolute, pure, unadulterated

She wore a sheer white dress.
(그녀는 얇은 하얀 색 드레스를 입었다.)

1655
shield [ʃiːld]
n. 방패, 보호물
IN BRIEF A protective covering or structure
+ armor, defence, protect, cover, guard

God is our shield.
(신은 우리의 방패이다.)

1656
shift [ʃift]
v. 이동시키다, 옮기다; (기어를) 바꾸다
IN BRIEF To exchange (one thing for another of the same class)
+ change, move, switch

We couldn't shift the heavy box.
(우리는 그 무거운 상자를 옮길 수가 없었다.)

1657
shrewd [ʃruːd]
a. 예민한, 통찰력 있는, 빈틈없는, 약삭빠른, 재빠른
IN BRIEF Having or showing a clever awareness or resourcefulness, especially in practical matters
+ calculating, crafty, astute, clever, ingenious, perceptive, wise

He is shrewd in business.
(그는 장삿속이 밝다.)

1658
shrill [ʃril]
a. 날카로운, 예리한
IN BRIEF High-pitched and piercing in tone or sound
+ penetrating, piercing, acute, keen, sharp

She scolded me in shrill tone.
(그녀는 날카로운 어조로 나를 꾸짖었다.)

1659
shrub [ʃrʌb]
n. 관목(灌木), 떨기나무
IN BRIEF A woody plant of relatively low height, having several stems arising from the base and lacking a single trunk; a bush
+ bush

This two foot tall shrub likes hot, arid climates.
(키가 2피트 되는 이 관목은 뜨겁고 건조한 기후를 좋아한다.)

1660
shudder [ʃʌ́dər]
vi. 전율하다, 진저리치다
IN BRIEF To tremble from horror, fear, or cold; quiver; shiver
+ shake with dislike, quake, quiver, shake, tremble

I shudder to think how much this meal is going to cost.
(나는 식사비용이 얼마나 나올까 생각하니 으쓱 떨린다.)

1661
shun [ʃʌn]

vt. 피하다, 비키다, 멀리하다; 꺼리다

IN BRIEF To avoid using, accepting, engaging in, or partaking of

avoid, dodge, elude, eschew, evade, ignore, reject

> She was shunned by her family.
> (그녀는 가족에게 외면당했다.)

1662
sidestep ['saɪdstep]

한 발짝 비키다; (일·책임) 회피하다

IN BRIEF To dodge an issue or a responsibility

evade, dodge, duck, evade, hedge

> He sidestepped the issue by saying it was not his responsibility.
> (그는 그것은 자기 책임이 아니라고 말함으로써 그 문제를 회피했다.)

1663
simultaneously [sàim-əltéiniəsli]

ad. 동시에, 일제히

IN BRIEF Happening, existing, or done at the same time

at the same time, coincident, concurrent, synchronous

> Two children answered the teacher's question simultaneously.
> (두 어린이가 교사의 질문에 동시에 대답했다.)

1664
sip [sip]

조금씩 마시다, 찔끔찔끔 마시다, 홀짝이다

IN BRIEF To drink in small quantities

gulp, guzzle, quaff, swallow, imbibe, drink slowly

> We were all in the bar sipping cocktails.
> (우리는 모두 바에서 칵테일을 홀짝거리고 있었다.)

1665
skeptical [sképtik-əl]

a. 회의적인, 의심하는

IN BRIEF Marked by or given to doubt; questioning

dubious, incredulous, suspicious, unbelieving

> He is skeptical about the project.
> (그는 그 프로젝트에 회의적이다.)

1666
skid [skid]

v. 미끄러지다

IN BRIEF The action of sliding or slipping over a surface, often sideways

decline, descent, down slide, downturn, slide, slump

> The car skidded across the road.
> (그 차는 도로를 가로질러 미끄러졌다.)

1667
skim [skim]

v. 대충 읽다; 스쳐 지나가다

IN BRIEF To move or pass swiftly and lightly over or near a surface; glide

look at quickly, glance, graze, ricochet, skip

> Father skims over a paper every morning.
> (아버지는 아침마다 신문을 대충 훑어보신다.)

1668
skinny [skíni]

a. 피골이 상접한, 말라빠진

IN BRIEF Having very little bodily flesh or fat, often unattractively so; very thin

bony, gaunt, lank, lean, scrawny, thin, haggard

> He is tall and skinny.
> (그는 키가 크고 바짝 말랐다.)

1669
slacken [slǽkən]

완만하게 되다, (속도) 늦어지다, 느슨해지다, 늦추다

IN BRIEF To make or become slower; slow down

slow up, abate, decrease, diminish, lessen, ease, loosen, relax

> After months of being really busy at work, things are beginning to slacken off a bit.
> (몇 달 동안 직장에서 정말 바쁘더니 일들이 조금 느슨해졌다.)

1670
sleuth [sluːθ]

n. 《구어》탐정, 형사

IN BRIEF An informal word for detective

detective, agent, investigator, scout, spy

> He is an amateur sleuth.
> (그는 아마추어 탐정이다.)

1671
slightly [sláitli]

ad. 약하게; 섬세히, 가냘프게

IN BRIEF To a small degree or extent; somewhat

a little, a bit, somewhat, moderately, marginally

> I know her slightly.
> (나는 그녀를 좀 안다.)

1672
slim [slim]

a. 가느다란, 호리호리한, 날씬한

IN BRIEF Small in girth or thickness in proportion to height or length; slender

[+] slender, thin, willowy, slight

> She has a slim waist.
> (그녀는 가느다란 허리를 가지고 있다.)

1673
sloppy [slápi]

a. (구어) 나약하고 감상적인

IN BRIEF Not neat or careful

[+] messy, unkempt, untidy → mawkish, romantic, sentimental

> Sloppy writing is difficult to read.
> (엉성한 글쓰기는 읽기 어렵다.)

1674
slovenly [slʌ́v-ənli]

a. 단정치 못한; 아무렇게나 하는

IN BRIEF Untidy, as in dress or appearance

[+] messy, shabby, careless, faulty, slapdash, sloppy

> her appearance is slightly slovenly.
> (그녀의 외모는 다소 단정치 못하다.)

1675
sluggish [slʌ́giʃ]

a. 게으른, 나태한, (반응·움직임) 둔한, 느린; (흐름) 완만한

IN BRIEF Displaying little movement or activity; slow; inactive

[+] slow to respond, drooping, languid, lethargic, listless, phlegmatic

> The flux of the traffic was sluggish.
> (교통의 흐름은 완만했다.)

1676
smack [smæk]

vi. ((구어)) 찰싹 때리다; 세게 치다

IN BRIEF To strike sharply

[+] bash, buffet, bust, punch, slap, spank, swat, whack

> I think it's wrong to smack children even when they misbehave.
> (아이들이 나쁜 짓을 하더라도 그들을 때리는 것은 잘못된 일이라 생각한다.)

1677
smudge [smʌdʒ]

더러움, 얼룩, 오점; 더럽히다, 얼룩이 지게 하다

IN BRIEF To make dirty, especially in one small area

[+] dirty, smear, soil, streak

> You've smudged my picture!
> (네가 내 그림을 더럽혀 놨어!)

1678
sneer [sniəːr]

v. 조소하다, 비웃다, 코웃음 치다[at]

IN BRIEF To show contempt by means of a derisive smile

[+] leer, smirk, deride, mock, scoff, scorn

> He's always sneering at my suggestions.
> (그는 항상 내 제안에 코웃음을 친다.)

1679
soak [souk]

v. 담그다; 잠기다; 젖다

IN BRIEF To immerse in liquid for a period of time

[+] absorb, douse, drench, saturate, penetrate, permeate

> You're soaking wet. What happened?
> (흠뻑 젖었군요. 어떻게 된 일이에요?)

1680
sober [sóubəːr]

a. 술에 취하지 않은, 진지한

IN BRIEF Not intoxicated or affected by the use of alcohol or drugs

[+] grave, serious, solemn, somber

> She is a sober and intelligent student.
> (그녀는 진지하고 지적인 학생이다.)

1681
sojourn [sóudʒəːrn]

v. 묵다, 체류하다

IN BRIEF To reside temporarily

[+] stay, visit, stop, rest, stopover

> My sojourn in the youth hostel was thankfully short.
> (내가 유스호스텔에서 머문 기간은 고맙게도 짧았다.)

1682
solace [sáləs]

n. 위안

IN BRIEF Comfort in sorrow, misfortune, or distress; consolation

+ comfort, consolation, reassurance, relief

> His work was a real solace to him at this difficult time.
> (그의 일은 이렇게 힘든 때에 그에게 정말로 위안이 되었다.)

1683
solidify [səlídəfài]

굳어지다, 단결하다

IN BRIEF To make solid, compact, or hard

+ calcify, assure, confirm, insure

> The paint had solidified in the tin.
> (페인트가 깡통 안에서 굳어 있다.)

1684
somber [sámbər]

a. 어두컴컴한, 흐린, 침울한

IN BRIEF Gloomily dark; shadowy

+ dark, desolate, dismal, dreary, gloomy, glum

> A cloudy winter day is somber.
> (구름 낀 겨울날은 어둠침침하다.)

1685
somnolent [sámnələnt]

a. 졸리는; 졸리게 하는

IN BRIEF Drowsy; sleepy

+ drowsy, groggy, nodding, sleepy, yawning

> The noise of the stream had a pleasantly somnolent effect.
> (시냇물 소리가 사근사근하게 좋은 최면 효과를 가져다주었다.)

1686
soothe [suːð]

v. 가라앉히다, 달래다, 진정시키다, 덜어주다, 편하게 하다

IN BRIEF To calm or placate

+ calm, quiet, appease, mollify, pacify, placate, console

> This medicine may soothe your cough.
> (이 약이 당신의 기침을 가라앉혀 줄 것입니다.)

1687
sophisticated [səˈfɪstɪkeɪtɪd]

정교한, 세련된, 순진성을 잃은

IN BRIEF Having refined or cultured tastes and habits

+ cosmopolitan, urbane, advanced, complex, complicated

> They are very sophisticated.
> (그들은 매우 정교합니다.)
> She loved a very sophisticated young artist.
> (그녀는 아주 세련된 한 젊은 예술가를 사랑했다.)

1688
spacious [spéiʃəs]

a. 넓은, 널찍한

IN BRIEF Having enough or abundant space or room; large in area or extent

+ big, capacious, commodious, expansive, roomy, vast

> The accommodation was spacious and comfortable.
> (숙박시설은 널찍하고 편안했다.)

1689
spawn [spɔːn]

(물고기·개구리 따위의) 알, 알을 낳다(산란), 생기게 하다

IN BRIEF To produce or deposit (spawn)

+ engender, generate, produce, multiply, proliferate, reproduce

> Frogs spawn hundreds of eggs at a time.
> (개구리는 한꺼번에 수 백 개의 알을 낳는다.)

1690
specific [spisífik]

a. 특수한, 특별한; 한정된; 분명한

IN BRIEF Explicitly set forth; definite

+ definite, precise, certain, special, unique, distinctive

> What are your specific aims?
> (당신의 분명한 목적은 무엇인가요?)

1691
specify [spésəfài]

vt. 명시하다; 일일이 열거하다, 지성하나

IN BRIEF To state explicitly or in detail

+ indicate, stipulate, define, delineate, enumerate, designate

> She did not specify reasons for resigning.
> (그녀는 사임의 이유를 구체적으로 밝히지 않았다.)

1692
specimen [spésəmən]
n. 견본, 예, 실례

IN BRIEF An individual, item, or part representative of a class or whole

➕ example, illustration, representative sample

> He's still a fine specimen of health.
> (그는 여전히 건강의 좋은 표본이다.)

1693
specious [spí:ʃəs]
외양[허울]만 좋은, 그럴듯한

IN BRIEF Having the ring of truth or plausibility but actually fallacious

➕ fallacious, misleading, deceptive, plausible, unsound, sophistic

> We have no time to discuss such specious arguments.
> (우리는 그러한 허울만 좋은 주장에 대해 논의할 시간이 없다.)

1694
spectrum [spéktrəm]
n. 범위; 스펙트럼, 분광

IN BRIEF An ordered array of the components of an emission or wave

➕ range, broad range, extent, realm, scope, distance, limit reach

> A rainbow may be regarded as a spectrum of the Sun.
> (무지개는 태양의 스펙트럼이라 볼 수도 있다.)

1695
spin-off [spin ɔːf]
파급 효과, 파생적인

IN BRIEF A product made during the manufacture of something else

➕ derivative, derived, secondary, byproduct, by-product

> The TV series was a spin-off from the movie.
> (그 TV시리즈는 영화의 부산물이었다.)

1696
suss out
의심하다, 조사하다(keep an eye on)

IN BRIEF Examine so as to determine accuracy, quality, or condition

➕ analyse, analyze, examine, study, canvass, look into

> They are approved to suss out the area to see how strong the police presence is.
> (그들은 경찰의 존재가 얼마나 강한 힘을 발휘하는지 알아보고자 그 지역을 답사할 수 있도록 허락받았다.)

1697
scintillate [síntəlèit]
v. 반짝반짝 빛나다, 불꽃이 튀다; (재치, 기지) 번득이다, 넘치다

IN BRIEF To be animated or witty; sparkle, To emit light suddenly in rays or sparks

➕ coruscate, flash, spangle, sparkle, twinkle

> There is little reason to depict the scenes with the salacious, first-person point of views they are treated with, other than to scintillate.
> (재치를 발휘하지 않고 그 장면들을 외설스럽고 1인칭적인 관점으로 다루고 묘사할 이유는 거의 없다.)

1698
stint [stint]
n. (일정 기간 동안의)일, 활동 / v. 절약하다, 아끼다

IN BRIEF A length of time spent in a particular way, especially doing a job or fulfilling a duty

➕ term, time, turn, bit, period, share, tour, shift, stretch, spell, quota, assignment

> He is returning to this country after a five-year stint in Hong Kong.
> (그는 5년간의 홍콩 근무를 마치고 귀국한다.)

1699
slip [slip]
v. 살짝 가다; (안 좋은 상황) 처하게 되다

IN BRIEF To decline from a former or standard level; fall off

> All these milder monarchies now risk slipping into the habits of the gulf's worst human-rights offenders, Bahrain and Saudi Arabia.
> (이 모든 좀 더 온건한 군주제 국가들이, 지금 걸프 지역 최악의 인권 침해국인 바레인과 사우디아라비아의 관습에, 슬그머니 젖어들려는 모험을 하고 있다.)

1700
soporific [sàpərífik]
a. 최면성의, 졸린

IN BRIEF Tending to induce sleep

➕ hypnotic, narcotic, opiate, sedative, sleepy, slumberous, somnifacient, somniferous, somnific, somnolent

> Billy finds nothing more soporific than reading classics; he's usually asleep before the end of the first chapter.
> (비리에게 고전을 읽는 것보다 더 졸린 것은 없다. 그는 대체로 첫 번째 장을 다 읽기도 전에 잠들어 버린다.)

LESSON 35

1701
splendor [spléndər]

n. 장려함, 장엄함

IN BRIEF Magnificent appearance or display; grandeur

⊕ magnificence, brightness, brilliance, luster

> Can the city recapture its former splendor?
> (그 도시가 과거의 장대함을 되찾을 수 있을까?)

1702
splice [splais]

vt. 잇다, 연결하다

IN BRIEF To join (two pieces of film, for example at the ends)

⊕ join, connect, associate, combine, consolidate, merge

> Splice things together seamlessly.
> (이음매가 안 보이게 매끈하게 이어라.)

1703
spoil [spɔil]

v. 망쳐놓다, 상하게 하다, 못쓰게 만들다

IN BRIEF To impair or destroy the quality or value of; ruin

⊕ contaminate, defile, stain, sully, despoil, pillage, disfigure, impair

> The bad news has spoilt my day.
> (그 안 좋은 소식 때문에 내 하루를 망쳤다.)

1704
spontaneous [spɑntéiniəs]

a. 자연스러운, 자발적인

IN BRIEF Occurring, produced, or performed through natural processes without external influence

⊕ voluntary, automatic, instinctive, unconscious, unprepared, unrehearsed, unplanned

> His reactions are spontaneous and instinctive rather than calculated.
> (그의 반응은 계산되었다기보다 자연스럽고 본능적인 것이다.)

1705
spooky [spúːki]

a. 유령 같은; 유령이 나올 듯한, 섬뜩한, 무시무시한

IN BRIEF Suggestive of ghosts or spirits, especially in being eerie or disturbing

⊕ eerie, ghostly, mysterious, scary weird

> We terrified the girls with spooky stories.
> (우리는 무시무시한 얘기로 여자 애들을 두려움에 떨게 했다.)

1706
sporadic [spərǽdik]

a. 때때로[산발적으로] 일어나는, 산발성의

IN BRIEF Occurring at irregular points in time; intermittent

⊕ intermittent, irregular, occasional, isolated, scattered, separate

> Sporadic gunfire continued throughout the night.
> (산발적인 발포가 밤새 계속 되었다.)

1707
spotless [spɑ́tlis]

a. 더러워지지 않은, 얼룩이 없는, 아주 깨끗한

IN BRIEF Free from stains; immaculate

⊕ immaculate, flawless, pristine, undefiled, unsullied, untainted, pure

> He keeps his room spotless.
> (그는 방을 티 하나 없이 해 놓는다.)

1708
spurious [spjúəriəs]

a. 가짜의, 위조의

IN BRIEF Lacking authenticity or validity in essence or origin; not genuine

⊕ artificial, bogus, counterfeit, fake, false, imitation, phony

> Don't spurious claims!
> (거짓 주장 하지마!)

1709
spurn [spəːrn]

v. 쫓아내다, 물리치다, 일축하다; 냉대하다

IN BRIEF To reject with disdain or contempt

⊕ defy, disdain, reject, repudiate, scorn, ignore

> She spurned his advances.
> (그녀는 그의 접근을 퇴짜 놓았다.)

1710
squalid [skwɑ́lid]

a. 더러운, 불결한, 불쌍한, 비참한

IN BRIEF Dirty or deteriorated, especially from poverty or lack of care

⊕ dirty, filthy, sordid, shabby, sleazy

> Ahntonio lives in squalid conditions.
> (안토니오는 비참한 지경에서 산다.)

1711
squander [skwάndər]

v. (돈·시간)낭비하다, 함부로 쓰다

IN BRIEF To spend wastefully or extravagantly; dissipate

⊕ consume, dissipate, fritter away, misuse, waste

> Please don't squander your youth.
> (제발 당신의 청춘을 허비하지 마세요.)

1712
squeamish [skwíːmiʃ]

a. 지나치게 예민한, 까다로운, 잘 토하는

IN BRIEF Easily nauseated or sickened

⊕ nauseated, queasy, finicky, fussy, particular, priggish, prudish

> She's really squeamish.
> (그녀는 정말 쉽게 토한다.)

1713
squeeze [skwiːz]

압착하다, 죄다, 짜내다 → (야구) 〈3루 주자〉스퀴즈로 득점

IN BRIEF To press hard on or together; compress

⊕ compress, pinch, press, bind, constrain, constrict, cramp, jam, stuff

> Squeeze me some orange juice.
> (오렌지 주스 좀 짜주세요.)

1714
stack [stæk]

n. 쌓아 올린 것, 더미 / v. 쌓아 올리다

IN BRIEF An orderly pile, especially one arranged in layers

⊕ pile, heap, hill, mound, accumulation, aggregation, collection

> The floor was stacked with books.
> (바닥에는 책이 쌓여 있었다.)

1715
stagger [stǽgər]

v. 비틀거리다, 휘청거리다(falter)

IN BRIEF To move or stand unsteadily, as if under a great weight; totter

⊕ stumble, teeter, totter, weave, lurch

> One man had managed to stagger out.
> (한 남자가 간신히 밖으로 비틀거리며 나왔다.)

1716
staggering [stǽgəriŋ]

a. 엄청나게 충격적인, 경이적인

IN BRIEF Astounding or overwhelming; shocking

⊕ amazing, astonishing, astound, shock, startle, stun

> It was staggering to total up the losses.
> (손해를 합산해 보고 망연자실했다.)

1717
staple [stéip-əl]

n. 주요 산물, 명산물; 주요 상품, 주요소, 주성분

IN BRIEF A principal raw material or commodity grown or produced in a region

⊕ important part, basic, essential, fundamental

> Bread is a staple food for them.
> (그들에겐 빵이 주식이다.)

1718
starry-eyed [stάːri aid]

a. 《구어》공상[몽상]적인, 비현실적인

IN BRIEF Having a naively enthusiastic, overoptimistic, or romantic view; unrealistic

⊕ visionary, chimerical, fanciful, idealistic, utopian

> She's got some starry-eyed notion about reforming society.
> (그녀는 사회 개혁에 대해 약간 비현실적인 생각을 갖고 있다.)

1719
starvation [stɑːrvéiʃ-ən]

n. 기아, 아사 (상태); 궁핍, 결핍

IN BRIEF The act of starving or the state of being starved

⊕ hunger, famine, voracity, craving

> The refugees are on the verge of starvation.
> (난민들은 기아선상에 놓여 있다.)

1720
state-of-the-art

(과학) 최첨단 기술, (수준) 최신식의

IN BRIEF The highest level of development, as of a device, technique, or scientific field, achieved at a particular time

⊕ up-to-date, most modern

> Cisco Systems opened a $10 million state-of-the-art child care center for all employees.
> (시스코 시스템즈는 1천만 달러를 들여 전 직원을 위한 최신식 보육원을 열었다.)

1721
stationary [stéiʃ-ənèri]

a. 움직이지 않는, 정지한, 고정된(fixed, immovable)

IN BRIEF Fixed; standing still; not movable; not changing

+ permanent, stable, inert, motionless, static, constant, steady

> A stationary object is easiest to aim at.
> (고정된 목표물은 가장 겨냥하기 쉽다.)

1722
status [stéitəs]

n. 지위, 신분; 상태

IN BRIEF Position relative to that of others; standing

+ caste, degree, position, rank, station, condition, state

> What is her status in her company?
> (그녀는 회사에서의 지위가 무엇인가?)

1723
statute [stǽtʃuːt]

n. 법령, 법규; 제정법

IN BRIEF A law enacted by the legislative branch of a government

+ act, bill, law, ordinance

> It is laid down by statute.
> (그것은 법으로 규정되어 있다.)

1724
steadily [stédili]

ad. 꾸준히, 끊임없이

IN BRIEF Firm in position or place; fixed

+ ceaselessly, continuously, incessantly, steadfastly, determinedly

> Prices are rising steadily.
> (물가가 꾸준히 오르고 있다.)

1725
stealthy [stélθi]

a. 남몰래 하는, 살그머니 하는, 남의 눈을 피하는, 은밀한

IN BRIEF Marked by or acting with quiet, caution, and secrecy intended to avoid notice

+ furtive, secret, sly, sneaky, surreptitious − overt

> The cat crept with stealthy movement toward the bird.
> (고양이는 몰래 움직여 새 쪽으로 기어갔다.)

1726
stem from [stem frʌm]

n. 기인하다, 유래하다

IN BRIEF To come, result, or develop from something else

+ arise, come, derive, result, spring, restrain

> This expression stems from an old Korean saying.
> (표현은 한국의 옛 속담에서 유래한 것이다.)

1727
sterile [stéril]

a. 메마른; 불모의, 불임의, 열매를 못 맺는

IN BRIEF Not producing or incapable of producing offspring

+ barren, fruitless, impotent, infertile, arid, desert, desolate

> Desert soil is usually sterile.
> (사막 토양은 대개 불모이다.)

1728
stifle [stáif-əl]

v. 숨 막다, 질식시키다, (감정·불평)억누르다, 억제하다

IN BRIEF To keep in or hold back; repress

+ hot, subdue, suppress, extinguish, quell, terminate, inhibit, restrain

> We were stifling in that hot room with all the windows closed.
> (창문이 모두 닫힌 그 더운 방에서 우리는 질식할 것 같았다.)

1729
stigma [stígmə]

n. 오명, 오욕, 불명예

IN BRIEF An association of disgrace or public disapproval with something, such as an action or condition

+ feeling of shame, disgrace, dishonor, blemish, stain, taint

> There is still social stigma attached to being unemployed.
> (실업에는 아직도 사회적인 오명이 따라 붙는다.)

1730
stimulate [stímjəlèit]

v. 자극[고무]하다

IN BRIEF To rouse to action or increased activity; excite

+ excite, incite, inspire, stir, encourage, spur, activate, kindle

> The lecture failed to stimulate me.
> (그 강연은 내 흥미를 자극하지 못했다.)

1731
stocky [stáki]

a. 땅딸막한, 튼튼한

IN BRIEF Solidly built; sturdy

+ short and heavy, chunky, fat, husky, stubby, thickset

> Ahntonio is a stocky little man.
> (안토니오는 땅딸막하게 작은 남자이다.)

1732
stoically [stóuikəli]

금욕적으로, 냉정하게, 태연하게

IN BRIEF Unconcerned about pleasure or pain

[+] unemotional person

> The patient bore the pain stoically, neither wincing nor whimpering when the incision was made.
> (그 환자는 절개를 했을 때 움찔하거나 흐느끼지 않고 침착하게 고통을 견뎌냈다.)

1733
strand [strænd]

좌초시키다[하다], 오도 가도 못하게 하다, 꼼짝 못하게 하다, 무일푼이 되게 하다

IN BRIEF To leave in a helpless position

[+] beach, desert, ground, shipwreck, abandon, desert, forsake

> The ship was stranded on a sandbank.
> (그 배는 모래톱에서 꼼짝 못하게 되었다.)

1734
stray [strei]

vi. 벗어나다, 빗나가다; 길을 잃다

IN BRIEF To be directed without apparent purpose

[+] rove, wander, deviate, digress, abandoned, deserted, homeless, lost

> Their home was a haven for stray animals.
> (그들의 집은 길 잃은 동물을 위한 안식처였다.)

1735
streamline [strí:mlàin]

유선형의, 유선형으로 하다, 능률적으로 하다, 합리화하다

IN BRIEF To alter so as to make more efficient or simple

[+] simplify, clarify, ease facilitate

> The new manager wants to streamline production.
> (새 매니저는 생산을 능률화하길 원한다.)

1736
strenuously [strénjuəsli]

분투하여, 맹렬하게

IN BRIEF Vigorously active; energetic or zealous

[+] arduously, exhaustingly, intensely, vigorously

> She strenuously denies all the charges.
> (그녀는 모든 혐의를 완강히 부인하고 있다.)

1737
stricken [strík-ən]

a. (무기 따위로) 상처를 받은, 괴로워하는, 고뇌하는

IN BRIEF Affected by something overwhelming, such as disease, trouble, or painful emotion

[+] blow, buffet, clout, cuff

> I tried to console the grief-stricken relatives.
> (나는 슬픔에 괴로워하는 친척들을 위로하려 애썼다.)

1738
strict [strikt]

a. 엄격한, 가혹한; 엄밀한

IN BRIEF Rigorous in the imposition of discipline

[+] stern, exacting, rigorous, stringent, uncompromising)

> His father is very strict.
> (그의 아버지는 매우 엄하시다.)

1739
strikingly [stráikiŋli]

두드러지게

IN BRIEF Arresting the attention and producing a vivid impression on the sight or the mind

[+] prominently, extraordinarily, markedly, surprisingly

> The two guys are strikingly similar.
> (그 두 남자들은 눈에 띄게 비슷하다.)

1740
stringent [stríndʒənt]

a. 엄한, 가혹한; (규칙) 엄격한, 엄중한(exacting, rigid)

IN BRIEF Posing rigorous standards of performance; severe

[+] rigorous, harsh, severe, stern, strict, forceful, persuasive

> Some of the conditions in the contract are too stringent.
> (어떤 계약 조건들은 너무 가혹하다.)

1741
strive [straiv]

vi. 노력하다; 분투하다

IN BRIEF To exert much effort or energy; endeavor

[+] make effort, attempt, endeavor, labor, struggle, try, battle, contend

> He strives hard to overcome his handicap.
> (그는 장애를 극복하기 위해 열심히 노력했다.)

1742
stroke [strouk]
쓰다듬다, 어루만지다; 달래다

IN BRIEF The act or an instance of striking, as with the hand, a weapon, or a tool; a blow or impact

+ caress, pat, rub

> She likes to stroke her dog.
> (그녀는 개를 쓰다듬기를 좋아한다.)

1743
stubby [stʌ́bi]
a. 그루터기의[와 같은]; 땅딸막한

IN BRIEF Having the nature of or suggesting a stub, as in shortness, broadness, or thickness

+ thick and short, squat, stocky, stumpy, thick

> He poked at the spider with a stubby finger.
> (그는 짤막한 손가락으로 거미를 콕콕 찔렀다.)

1744
stubborn [stʌ́bəːrn]
a. 완고한, 고집 센

IN BRIEF Hard to deal with, inflexible, intractable

+ obdurate, resolute, unyielding, mulish, obstinate, recalcitrant, persistent, relentless, tenacious

> Ahntonio is as stubborn as a mule.
> (안토니오는 똥 고집쟁이다.)

1745
stuck-up [ʃtuk ʌp]
(구어)거만한, 건방진

IN BRIEF Snobbish; conceited

+ conceited, egoistic, egotistic, vain, narcissistic, vainglorious

> She is very stuck-up. She thinks she's of a higher class than everyone else.
> (그녀는 매우 우쭐댄다. 그녀는 자기가 어떤 다른 사람보다도 상류 계층이라고 생각한다.)

1746
stumble [stʌ́mbəl]
v. 걸려 넘어지다, 비틀거리다; 실수하다, 잘못하다 (fail)

IN BRIEF To almost fall while walking or running

+ falter, lurch, reel, stagger, teeter, totter, trip

> No matter how many times the little ones stumble in their initial efforts, most keep on trying, determined to master their new skills.
> (꼬마들은 첫 시도에서 몇 번을 실수하더라도 대부분 새로운 기술을 연마하려는 결심을 하며 노력을 계속한다.)

1747
significantly [signífikəntli]
ad. 상당히, 크게

IN BRIEF In an important way or to an important degree

+ very much, greatly, hugely, vastly, notably, considerably, remarkably, enormously, immensely, tremendously, markedly

> Due to the unusually cool weather last month, the number of visitors to the state's major theme parks was significantly lower than forecast.
> (지난달 이례적으로 서늘한 날씨 때문에, 그 주의 주요 테마 파크의 방문객 수는 예상보다 상당히 더 낮았다.)

1748
scourge [skəːrdʒ]
n. 하늘의 응징, 천벌, 징벌, 재앙(chastisement)

IN BRIEF A person who harasses, punishes, or causes destruction

+ affliction, plague, curse, terror, pest, torment, misfortune, visitation, bane, infliction

> The human cost of this scourge becomes apparent to any visitor to Cambodia – the pockmarked nation has an estimated 40,000 amputees.
> (이 재앙이 가져 온 인명피해는 캄보디아를 찾아오는 누구에게나 분명하게 드러난다. 상처가 깊이 패여 있는 그 나라는 절단수술을 받은 사람이 40,000명에 이르는 것으로 추정된다.)

1749
stunt [stʌnt]
v. 성장을 방해하다, 저해하다 (hinder)

IN BRIEF Check the growth of

+ hamper, restrict, curb, slow down, hold up, interfere with, hinder, impede

> In the impetuous youth of humanity, we can make grave errors that can stunt our growth for a long time.
> (충동적인 젊은 시절에 우리 인간은 오랫동안 성장을 저해할 수 있는 중대한 실수를 저지를 수 있다.)

1750
skewed [skjuːd]
a. 왜곡된, 뒤틀린

IN BRIEF Having no balance or symmetry, turned to one side ; asymmetric (불균형의, 비대칭의)

+ inclined

> This skewed perception of risk has serious social consequences, however. We aim our resources at phantoms, while real hazards are ignored.
> (그러나 위험에 대한 이러한 왜곡된 인식은 심각한 사회적 결과를 초래한다. 우리가 실재하지 않는 환영같은 것에 우리의 자원을 쏟는 반면 실제 위험은 무시되고 있다.)

LESSON 36

1751
stupefy [stjúːpəfài]
신체기능을 둔하게 하다, (지각·감각)마비시키다
IN BRIEF To render insensitive or lethargic
➕ bedaze, bemuse, benumb, daze, stun

> I was stupefied with drink
> (나는 술을 마셔서 몽롱했다.)

1752
stupendous [stjuːpéndəs]
a. 놀랄만한, 불가사의한, 굉장한
IN BRIEF So great in scope, degree, or importance as to amaze
➕ extraordinary, incredible, marvelous, colossal, enormous, tremendous

> The opera was quite stupendous!
> (그 오페라는 정말 굉장했다!)

1753
stymie [stáimi]
n. 〈골프〉타자 공과 홀 직선상에 상대방 공이 가로놓인 상태, (비유)난처한 상태[문제], 훼방 놓다, 방해하다, 좌절시키다(block)
IN BRIEF To hinder or thwart
➕ baffle, confound, confuse, puzzle, stump, frustrate, obstruct, thwart

> Their plans to open a new shop have been stymied by lack of funds.
> (새 가게를 열려던 그들의 계획은 자금 부족으로 좌절되었다.)

1754
subjugate [sʌ́bdʒugèit]
vt. 정복하다; 복종[예속]시키다
IN BRIEF To bring under control, especially by military force; conquer
➕ conquer, defeat, vanquish, subdue, control, dominate, suppress

> She was totally subjugated to the wishes of her husband.
> (그녀는 남편의 뜻대로 움직인다.)

1755
sublime [səbláim]
a. 고상한, 숭고한, 장엄한, 기품 있는
IN BRIEF Characterized by nobility; majestic
➕ celestial, divine, glorified, marvelous, splendid, superb, wonderful

> Mountain scenery is often sublime.
> (산 경치는 이따금 장엄하다.)

1756
submerge [səbmə́ːrdʒ]
v. 물속에 가라앉히다, 빠지게 하다, 열중하게 하다
IN BRIEF To plunge, sink, or dive or cause to plunge, sink, or dive below the surface of water
➕ immerse, lower, plunge, deluge, drench, engulf

> She submerged herself in her work.
> (그녀는 일에 열중했다.)

1757
subpoena [səbpíːnə]
n. 소환장 / v. 소환하다
IN BRIEF A writ to summon witnesses or evidence before a court
➕ writ

> The court subpoenaed her as a witness.
> (법원이 그녀를 증인으로 소환했다.)

1758
subsequent [sʌ́bsikwənt]
다음의; 다음에 오는
IN BRIEF Following in time or order; succeeding
➕ next, resulting, succeeding, after, later, posterior

> Subsequent events vindicated his suspicions.
> (잇따른 사건들이 그의 결백을 입증했다.)

1759
subsequently ['sʌbsɪkwəntli]
ad. 이어서(다음에) → 그 뒤에 → 나중에(later)
IN BRIEF Following in time or order; succeeding
➕ after, afterward, afterwards, later, latterly, next, ulteriorly

> When this mixture is subsequently heated, the gluten becomes firm instead of elastic.
> (이 혼합물이 이어서 가열되면, 글루텐 성분이 말랑말랑해지지 않고 단단해진다.)

1760
subside [səbsáid]
vi. 내려앉다, 가라앉다, 진정되다
IN BRIEF To become less intense, active, or severe; abate
➕ fall, fall off, remit, slacken, slack off, wane

> The storm began to subside.
> (폭풍이 가라앉기 시작했다.)

1761
subsidy [sʌ́bsidi]

n. 보조금, 장려금, 기부금

IN BRIEF A grant paid by a government to an enterprise that benefits the public

➕ financial supports by the government, appropriation, grant, subvention

> The company was given a substantial subsidy by the government.
> (그 회사는 정부로부터 실질적인 보조금을 받았다.)

1762
substantial [səbstǽnʃəl]

실질적인, 본질적인, 상당한, 중요한 (물질개념)

IN BRIEF Considerable in importance, value, degree, amount, or extent

➕ significant, considerable, large, important, generous, worthwhile

> It made substantial changes.
> (그것 때문에 상당한 변화들이 일어났다.)
> We must all make substantial economies.
> (우리는 모두 실질적인 절약을 해야 한다.)

1763
subtle [sʌ́tl]

a. 미묘한, 포착하기 어려운; 엷은, 은은한, 희미한

IN BRIEF So slight as to be difficult to detect or describe; elusive

➕ obscure, elusive, implied, indirect, insinuated, delicate, fine

> Subtle lighting helps people relax.
> (은은한 조명은 사람들이 긴장을 푸는 데 도움이 된다.)

1764
subversive [səbvə́ːrsiv]

a. 전복시키는, 파괴적인

IN BRIEF In opposition to a civil authority or government

➕ rebellious, insurgent, seditious

> They are contaminating the minds of our young people with these subversive ideas.
> (그들은 이런 파괴적인 생각들로 우리의 젊은이들의 마음을 오염시키고 있다.)

1765
successive [səksésiv]

a. 연속하는, 잇따르는

IN BRIEF Following in uninterrupted order; consecutive

➕ consecutive, sequent, sequential, serial, subsequent, successional

> It has rained for three successive days.
> (3일 연속 비가 내렸다.)

1766
succinct [səksíŋkt]

a. (표현) 간결한, 간단명료한

IN BRIEF Marked by brevity and clarity; concise

➕ direct, pithy, terse, abbreviated, abridged, compact, condensed

> His speech was short and succinct.
> (그의 연설은 짧고 간결했다.)

1767
succulent [sʌ́kjələnt]

a. 즙[수분]이 많은

IN BRIEF Full of juice or sap; juicy

➕ juicy, luscious, palatable, savory, tasty

> These are wonderfully succulent peaches.
> (이것은 아주 즙이 많은 복숭아이다.)

1768
succumb [səkʌ́m]

vi. 굴복하다, 패하다, 지다 [to]

IN BRIEF To give way to superior force; yield

➕ capitulate, relent, surrender, yield, expire, perish

> Ahntonio succumbed to the temptation of cream coffee.
> (안토니오는 크림커피의 유혹에 지고 말았다.)

1769
suffocate [sʌ́fəkèit]

v. 숨을 막다, 질식시키다, 숨이 막히게 하다

IN BRIEF To kill or destroy by preventing access of air or oxygen

➕ asphyxiate, choke, smother, stifle, strangle

> I'm suffocating in here. can we open a window?
> (여기 있으니 질식할 것 같아. 창문 좀 열까?)

1770
suffrage [sʌ́fridʒ]

n. 투표권, 선거권, 참정권

IN BRIEF The right or privilege of voting; franchise

➕ voting right, ballot, franchise, vote

> Universal suffrage
> (보통 선거권)

1771
suit [suːt]

n. 적합하다, 맞다

IN BRIEF A legal action; a matched set of clothes; meet the requirements of

➕ accommodate, adapt, adjust, conform, satisfy

> That date will suit.
> (그 날이 적합하다.)

1772
summon [sʌ́mən]
vt. 호출하다, 소환하다; 요구하다
IN BRIEF To call together; convene
➕ call up, beckon, bid, call, rouse, command, gather, invoke, muster

> We had to summon the doctor to look at her.
> (그녀를 살펴보도록 의사를 불러와야 했다.)

1773
sumptuous [sʌ́mptʃuəs]
a. 사치스러운; 호화스러운, 화려한
IN BRIEF Of a size or splendor suggesting great expense; lavish
➕ luxurious, costly, lavish, expensive, extravagant, magnificent

> The king gave a sumptuous banquet.
> (왕은 사치스러운 연회를 열었다.)

1774
superfluous [suːpə́ːrfluəs]
a. 여분의, 남는; 불필요한
IN BRIEF Being beyond what is required or sufficient
➕ extra, dispensable, needless, useless, wasteful

> Superfluous wealth can buy superfluities only.
> (남아도는 부는 불필요한 물건만 사게 할 뿐이다.)

1775
supersede [ˌsuːpərsíːd]
v. 대신하다(replace); 경질하다, 면직시키다
IN BRIEF To take the place of; replace or supplant
➕ replace, displace, usurp, supplant

> Every few minutes, someone introduces a new antiaging cream that allegedly supersedes all the existing ones on the market.
> (몇 분마다. 시장에 나와 있는 기존의 모든 제품을 대신한다고 하는 새로운 노화방지 크림이 출시되어 나오고 있다.)

1776
superstition [sùːpərstíʃən]
n. 미신
IN BRIEF An irrational belief in or notion of the ominous significance of a particular thing, circumstance, occurrence
➕ myth, story, belief, legend

> Superstition is the religion of feeble minds.
> (미신은 연약한 사람들이 믿는 종교이다.)

1777
supervise [súːpərvàiz]
vt. 감독하다, 관리하다, 지휘하다, 지도하다
IN BRIEF To manage and direct; be in charge of
➕ control, direct, manage, oversee, administer, govern

> I'm supervising.
> (나는 감독하고 있는 중이다.)

1778
supplant [səplǽnt]
vt. 대신하다
IN BRIEF To take the place of or substitute for (another)
➕ depose, displace, replace, supersede, substitute

> Computers will never completely supplant books.
> (컴퓨터가 완전히 책을 대신하는 일은 결코 없을 것이다.)

1779
suppress [səprés]
vt. 억압하다; 진압하다
IN BRIEF To put an end to forcibly; subdue
➕ keep under, overcome, overpower, quell, subdue, repress, stifle

> He was unable to suppress a smile.
> (그는 미소를 억누를 수 없었다.)

1780
supremacy [səpréməsi]
n. 최고; 주권, 패권, 지배권(ascendance, dominance)
IN BRIEF The quality or condition of being supreme
➕ domination, paramount, predominance, preeminence, preponderancy

> Korea is challenging Japan's supremacy in the field of electronics.
> (한국은 전자 분야에서의 일본의 패권에 도전하고 있다.)

1781
surfeit [sə́ːrfit]
n. 과도, 과다; 지나치게 많은 양; 과식, 과음
IN BRIEF To feed or supply to excess, satiety, or disgust
➕ excess, intemperance, overindulgence

> A surfeit of food makes us sick.
> (과식하면 병난다.)

1782
surpass [sərpǽs]
vt. 능가하다, 넘다, 뛰어나다[in, at]

IN BRIEF To be greater than in degree, extent, etc

+ exceed, overreach, overrun, overstep, transcend

> He surpasses me in knowledge.
> (그는 지식 면에선 나보다 우월하다.)

1783
surrender [səréndər]
v. 내주다, 항복하다

IN BRIEF To give up or abandon

+ relinquish, render, renounce, resign, waive, yield

> We shall never surrender.
> (우리는 결코 항복하지 않을 것이다.)

1784
surreptitious [sə̀ːrəptíʃəs]
a. 남의 눈을 피하여 하는, 비밀의, 은밀한

IN BRIEF Obtained, done, or made by clandestine or stealthy means

+ clandestine, furtive, secretive, sly, sneaking, sneaky

> He started making surreptitious visits to the pub on his way home.
> (그는 집으로 가는 길에 은밀히 그 술집에 드나들기 시작했다.)

1785
surveillance [sərvéiləns]
n. 감시, 감독

IN BRIEF A watch kept over someone or something, esp. over a suspect, prisoner

+ observation, close observation, lookout, vigil, vigilance, watch

> The police are keeping the suspects under constant surveillance.
> (경찰이 용의자들을 계속 감시하고 있다.)

1786
susceptible [səséptəbəl]
a. 영향 받기[감염되기] 쉬운, 민감한[to]

IN BRIEF Easily influenced or affected

+ liable to, prone, sensitive, defenseless, helpless, unprotected

> Some people are more susceptible to alcohol than others.
> (어떤 사람들은 다른 사람들보다 알코올에 더 영향을 받기 쉽다.)

1787
suspend [səspénd]
v. 매달다; 연기하다

IN BRIEF To cease for a period; delay

+ interrupt, postpone, cease, discontinue, halt, hang

> Rail services are suspended indefinitely because of the strike.
> (파업 때문에 철도 운행이 무기한 중단되었다.)

1788
sustain [səstéin]
vt. (무게) 떠받치다, 지탱하다, 견디다, 지속하다

IN BRIEF To keep in existence; maintain, continue, or prolong

+ maintain, preserve, bear, bolster, support, uphold, continue

> The ice will not sustain your weight.
> (그 얼음은 네 체중을 지탱하지 못할 것이다.)

1789
sustained [sə-stān']
a. 지속된, 한결같은, 일관된(To bear up under; withstand)

IN BRIEF To keep in existence; maintain, continue, or prolong

+ continuous, constant, steady, prolonged, perpetual, unremitting, nonstop

> With so much lost ground to make up, Britain needs a sustained period of strong growth.
> (벌충해야 할 잃어버린 기반이 너무 많기 때문에, 영국은 견실한 성장을 지속적으로 할 필요가 있다.)

1790
swarm [swɔːrm]
v. 떼 지어 모이다

IN BRIEF To fill with a crowd

+ great crowd, multitude, pour, throng, troop

> Every place swarms with people on Sundays.
> (매 일요일에는 어디나 사람들로 붐빈다.)

1791
swarthy [swɔ́ːrði]
a. (피부·안색) 거무스름한, 까무잡잡한

IN BRIEF Having a dark complexion or color

+ dark, mediterranean, olive-skinned, black-a-visage, brunet, dusky

> He had a swarthy face.
> (그는 까무잡잡한 얼굴을 가지고 있다.)

1792
sway [swei]
v. 흔들리다, 흔들다, (의견·기분) 동요하다, 동요시키다

IN BRIEF To swing back and forth

[+] oscillate, swing, repetition

> She swayed her hips seductively.
> (그녀는 유혹적으로 엉덩이를 살랑살랑 흔들었다.)

1793
swell [swel]
v. 부풀다, 팽창하다, 부피가 커지다

IN BRIEF To increase in size or volume as a result of internal pressure; expand

[+] grow, distend, enlarge, expand, increase, inflate, mount

> Wood often swells when wet.
> (목재는 물에 젖으면 흔히 팽창한다.)

1794
swerve [swəːrv]
v. 빗나가다, 벗어나다, 갑자기 방향을 바꾸다[from, to]

IN BRIEF To turn or cause to turn aside, usually sharply or suddenly, from a course

[+] turn aside, deviate, digress, diverge, stray, veer

> The car swerved sharply to avoid the child.
> (아이를 피하려고 그 차는 급히 방향을 바꾸었다.)

1795
serendipitously [sèrəndípətəs-]
ad. 우연히(accidentally)

> I serendipitously found three mentors who happened to be at the vanguard of a brand-new field called positive psychology.
> (나는 세명의 스승을 우연히 발견했는데, 그들은 마침 긍정심리학이라 불리는 새로운 분야에서 선도적 지위에 있던 분들이었다.)

1796
shaggy [ʃǽgi]
a. 털투성이의; 털이 덥수룩한(thick)

IN BRIEF Having or covered with rough unkempt fur, hair, wool, etc

[+] unkempt, rough, tousled, hairy, long-haired, hirsute, unshorn

> The lion shook his shaggy mane and looked thoughtful.
> (그 사자는 덥수룩한 갈기를 흔들더니 생각에 잠기는 듯 보였다.)

1797
surmise [sərmáiz]
v. 추측하다, 짐작하다(suppose)

IN BRIEF To make a judgment about (something) without sufficient evidence; guess

[+] guess, suppose, imagine, presume, consider, suspect, conclude, fancy, speculate, infer, deduce, come to the conclusion, conjecture, opine

> He surmised that something must be wrong.
> (그는 뭔가가 틀림없이 잘못 됐다고 추측했다.)

1798
subsistence [səbsístəns]
n. 생존; 생계

IN BRIEF The means needed to support life

[+] maintenance, support, sustenance, upkeep

> The village in the remote jungle was in the condition of subsistence because it didn't have much land for cultivation.
> (정글 오지에 있던 그 마을은 재배할 경작지가 많지 않았기 때문에 겨우 생계를 유지하는 상황에 놓여 있었다.)

1799
saturnine [sǽtərnàin]
a. 성미가 까다로운; 무뚝뚝한(sullen) / n. 귀족

IN BRIEF Having a gloomy temperament; taciturn; uncommunicative

[+] gloomy, grave, sombre, dour, morose, glum, taciturn, phlegmatic, moody, sour, sulky, sullen, surly

> In the play, Huston's saturnine patrician and Jacob's plaintive everyman never faltered.
> (그 연극에서, 휴스턴(Huston)이 맡은 무뚝뚝한 귀족과 제이콥(Jacob)이 맡은 애처로운 평민의 연기는 결코 흔들리지 않았다.)

1800
sit on the fence
중립적인 태도를 취하다(take a litmusless position)

> He tends to sit on the fence at the meetings.
> (그는 회의에서 중립적인 태도를 취하는 경향이 있다.)

LESSON 37

1801
swiftly [swíftli]
재빨리, 즉각적으로
IN BRIEF Moving or capable of moving with great speed; fast
➕ quickly, breakneck, expeditious, fast, fleet, rapid, speedy

> Her hands moved swiftly over the piano keys.
> (그녀의 손이 피아노 건반 위로 날렵하게 움직였다.)

1802
swoon [swu:n]
vi. 기절하다; (좋아서) 넋이 빠지다, 정신을 빼앗기다
IN BRIEF To enter a state of hysterical rapture or ecstasy
➕ enrapture, black out, faint, keel over, pass out

> All the girls are swooning over the new history teacher.
> (모든 여학생들이 새 역사 선생님 때문에 황홀해 있다.)

1803
swoop [swu:p]
v. 덤벼들다, 홱 덮치다, 급습하다
IN BRIEF To make a rush or an attack with a sudden sweeping movement
➕ attack suddenly, dive, nosedive, plunge, header

> Police made a dawn swoop.
> (경찰이 새벽에 급습했다.)

1804
symmetrical [simétrik(əl)]
대칭적인, 균형이 잡힌
IN BRIEF Of or exhibiting symmetry
➕ well-proportioned, balanced, proportional, proportionate, regular

> The plan of the ground floor is completely symmetrical.
> (1층의 설계도는 완전히 좌우 대칭으로 되어 있다.)

1805
symptom [símptəm]
n. 증상, 징후
IN BRIEF An indication of a disorder or disease
➕ badge, indication, indicator, manifestation

> Doctors must be able to read symptoms correctly.
> (의사들은 증상을 정확히 읽을 수 있어야 한다.)

1806
synergy [sínərdʒi]
n. 공동[협동] 작용, 상승 작용; 상승효과
IN BRIEF Combined action or functioning; synergism
➕ coaction, collaboration, cooperation, teamwork

> The potential synergy between the two companies makes them ideal candidates for a merger.
> (두 회사 사이 잠재적 공동 상승이 그들은 회사 합병의 이상적인 후보가 되었다.)

1807
synonymous [sinánəməs]
a. 동의어의, 같은 뜻의
IN BRIEF Having the character of a synonym
➕ same mean, paraphrase

> The verbs 'shut' and 'close' are synonymous.
> (동사 shut과 close는 유의어이다.)

1808
synopsis [sinápsiS]
n. 개요, 개관, 요약
IN BRIEF A brief outline or general view, as of a subject or written work; an abstract or a summary
➕ abstract, outline, review, sketch, summary

> The program gives a brief synopsis of the plot.
> (그 프로그램은 그 줄거리의 간략한 개요를 보여준다.)

1809
synthetic [sinθétik]
a. 종합적인, 종합의; 합성의, 인조의
IN BRIEF Chemistry (of a substance or material) made artificially by chemical reaction
➕ artificial, imitation, plastic, pseudo, counterfeit, false, mock, phony

> The synthetic fuels project has been canceled.
> (합성 연료 개발 프로젝트는 취소되었다.)

1810
tacit [tǽsit]

a. 무언의, 말없는, 잠자코 있는

IN BRIEF Not spoken

⊕ implicit, implied, silent, unexpressed, unspoken, unstated

> The grim expression on his face was a tacit admission of failure.
> (그의 얼굴에 나타난 엄한 표정은 패배에 대한 무언의 인정이었다.)

1811
taciturn [tǽsətə̀:rn]

a. 말없는, 무언의, 입이 무거운

IN BRIEF Habitually untalkative

⊕ laconic, quiet, reserved, uncommunicative

> He was a taciturn person when I first knew him.
> (내가 그를 처음 알았을 때에 그는 말수가 적은 사람이었다.)

1812
tactful [tǽktfəl]

a. 재치 있는, 빈틈없는, 약삭빠른, (감각)세련된, (기술)적절한

IN BRIEF Possessing or exhibiting tact; considerate and discreet

⊕ delicate, diplomatic, discreet, politic, sensitive, thoughtful, careful

> Mentioning his baldness wasn't tactful.
> (그가 대머리라는 사실을 언급한 것은 재치 있는 일은 아니었다.)

1813
tamper [tǽmpə:r]

v. 참견(간섭)하다, 매수(부정수단)하다, 함부로 변경하다[with]

IN BRIEF To interfere in a harmful or disruptive manner; meddle

⊕ interfere with, intervene, intrude, meddle, fiddle

> The records of the meeting had been tampered with.
> (그 회의 기록이 함부로 고쳐져 있었다.)

1814
tangible [tǽndʒəbəl]

만져서 알 수 있는, 실체적인; 유형의(corporeal)/(사실·근거)명백한, 확실한/실재하는, 현실의

IN BRIEF Discernible by the touch; palpable

⊕ substantial, recognizable, concrete, real, palpable, tactile, touchable, detectable, discernible, actual, manifest, obvious

> A desk is a tangible object.
> (책상은 만질 수 있는 물체이다.)

1815
tantalize [tǽntəlàiz]

v. (보여서) 감질나게 [애타게] 하다

IN BRIEF To excite by exposing something desirable that remains or is made difficult or impossible to obtain

⊕ torment, tease, taunt, torture, provoke

> Movie previews are made to tantalize moviegoers.
> (영화 시사회는 영화 팬들을 감질나게 하기 위해 만들어진다.)

1816
tarnish [tá:rniʃ]

v. (명예) 더럽히다 → 흐리게 하다, 녹슬게 하다, 변색시키다

IN BRIEF To dull the luster of; discolor, especially by exposure to air or dirt

⊕ blemish, stain, corrode, discolor, oxidize, discredit, disgrace, taint

> Silver tarnishes easily and turns black if not polished regularly.
> (은은 정기적으로 닦지 않으면 쉽게 변색이 되고 검게 변한다.)

1817
tart [ta:rt]

a. (맛)시큼한(sour); 자극적인 → (대답·태도)신랄한, 톡 쏘는

IN BRIEF Having a sharp pungent taste; sour

⊕ sour, piquant, tangy, biting, caustic

> The stewed apple needs a bit more sugar —it's still a bit tart.
> (사과 스튜에 설탕을 좀 더 넣어야겠어. 아직도 좀 시큼해.)

1818
tatter [tǽtə:r]

n. 넝마, 누더기(옷); 《비유적》무용지물

IN BRIEF A torn and hanging piece of cloth; a shred

⊕ rag, tag end, shred, tag

> I really needed a new winter coat. My old one was in tatters.
> (새 겨울 코트가 하나 꼭 필요했어. 전에 입던 게 다 해어졌거든.)

1819
taunt [tɔ:nt]

vt. 조롱하다, 비아냥거리다

IN BRIEF To reproach in a mocking, insulting, or contemptuous manner

⊕ dare, derision, jeer, mockery, slur v. insult, mock, scorn, sneer

> Their taunts stung him to action.
> (그들의 조소가 그를 행동하도록 부추겼다.)

1820
tedious [tíːdiəs]

a. 지루한, 따분한, 장황한

IN BRIEF Iresome by reason of length, slowness, or dullness; boring.

boring, drab, dull, monotonous, prosaic, laborious wearisom

> His speech was long, also tedious.
> (그의 이야기는 길었고 게다가 지루했다.)

1821
temerity [təmírəti]

무모한 행위, 만용(분별없이 함부로 날뛰는 용맹), 용기

IN BRIEF The state of being foolishly bold or brash; reckless

brashness, foolhardiness, incautiousness, rashness, recklessness, temerariousness

> According to Sartre, those with the temerity to shun convention and make free choices in their search for self are "authentic."
> (사르트르에 따르면, 관습을 피하고, 자아를 찾는데 있어서 자유로운 선택을 하는 용기를 가진 사람들이 "진정한" 사람들이다.)

1822
temperamental [tèmp-ərəméntl]

성미가 까다로운; 신경질적인; 변덕스러운

IN BRIEF Easily upset or irritated; excitable; volatile

emotional, impatient, irritable, moody, sensitive, touchy, capricious, fickle, impulsive, unpredictable

> Ahntonio is very temperamental.
> (안토니오는 변덕이 심하다.)

1823
temperate [témp-ərit]

a. 절제하는, 삼가는, (기후) 온화한

IN BRIEF Moderate or self-restrained; not extreme in opinion, statement

conservative, reasonable, restrained, abstemious, abstinent, mild

> Please be more temperate in your language.
> (말을 좀 더 삼가시오.)

1824
temporary [témpərèri]

a. 일시적인, 한때의, 잠깐의, 덧없는; 임시(변통)의

IN BRIEF Lasting, used, serving, or enjoyed for a limited time

not intended to last, ephemeral, fleeting, impermanent, momentary, transient

> It is only a temporary pleasure.
> (그것은 한때의 쾌락일 뿐이다.)

1825
tenable [ténəb-əl]

a. 공격에 견딜 수 있는, (학설 따위가) 비판에 견딜 수 있는, 조리 있는

IN BRIEF Capable of being maintained in argument; rationally defensible

defensible, logical, practical, rational, viable

> The view that the earth is flat is no longer tenable.
> (지구가 평평하다는 견해는 더 이상 조리 있는 주장이 아니다.)

1826
tenacious [tənéiʃəs]

a. 단단히 잡고 [쥐고] 있는, 집요한, 끈질긴, 완강한, 고집 센

IN BRIEF Holding or grasping firmly; forceful

constant, determined, dogged, firm, persistent, stubborn

> They were confronted with a tenacious foe.
> (그들은 완강한 적과 직면했다.)

1827
tenant [ténənt]

n. 토지 차용자, 소작인; 부동산 보유자, 세입자

IN BRIEF Occupant; one who holds the right to occupy a place

inhabitant, lodger, occupant, resident

> The apartment will be completely refurbished for the new tenants.
> (그 아파트는 새 세입자를 위해 완전히 새 단장을 할 것이다.)

1828
tenement [ténəmənt]

n. 가옥, 공동 주택

IN BRIEF A building for human habitation, especially one that is rented to tenants

slum

> They live in a tenement block on the edge of the city.
> (그들은 도시 변두리의 공동 주택 지역에서 살고 있다.)

1829
tenet [ténət]

n. 주의(主義), 교의(敎義)

IN BRIEF Principle, belief, doctrine; part of a body of doctrine

canon, conviction, creed, doctrine, dogma principle

> This is one of the basic tenets of the Christian faith.
> (이것은 기독교 신앙의 기본 교의 중 한 가지이다.)

1830
tendency [téndənsi]
n. 경향, 추세, 풍조 [to, toward, to do]

IN BRIEF A characteristic likelihood

+ trend, affinity, disposition, inclination, penchant, preference

> Ahntonio has a strong tendency to exaggerate.
> (안토니오는 과장하는 경향이 강하다.)

1831
tender [téndər]
v. 제출하다, 내다; 제공하다, 제안하다

IN BRIEF To give, present, or offer

+ offer, extend, propose, submit, suggest, proffer

> Mr. Kim was reluctant to tender on apology to me.
> (김 선생은 내게 사과하는 것을 꺼려했다.)

1832
tenor [ténər]
n. 진로, 행로, 흐름; 성질, 취지[of]

IN BRIEF The general course or character of something

+ nature, character, disposition, personality, temper, temperament

> At this point the whole tenor of the meeting changed.
> (이 시점에서 그 회의의 전반적인 취지가 바뀌었다.)

1833
tentative [téntətiv]
a. 시험적인, 임시적인

IN BRIEF Not fully worked out, concluded, or agreed on; provisional

+ provisional, temporary, doubtful, hesitant, uncertain

> I have made tentative plans to take a trip to Seattle in July.
> (나는 7월에 시애틀 여행을 하기로 잠정적인 계획을 세워 놓았다.)

1834
tepid [tépid]
a. (액체가) 미지근한, 열의 없는, 활기 없는, 시들한, 김빠진

IN BRIEF Slightly warm; lukewarm

+ lukewarm, halfhearted, indifferent, unenthusiastic, uninterested − passionate

> The water was tepid.
> (물이 미지근했다.)

1835
tenuous [ténjuəs]
a. 가느다란, 얇고 가는, 가냘픈, 빈약한

IN BRIEF Weak or insubstantial; flimsy

+ rarified, airy, fine, gossamer, thin, nebulous, insubstantial

> I found an excuse to phone her, but it was rather tenuous.
> (그녀에게 전화할 구실을 찾긴 했지만 좀 빈약했다.)

1836
terminate [tə́ːrmənèit]
v. 끝나다; 끝내다; 종점이 되다

IN BRIEF To bring to an end or halt

+ end, stop, conclude, finish, complete

> The meeting terminated in disorder.
> (그 회의는 무질서하게 끝났다.)

1837
terrible [térəb-əl]
a. 형편없는; 끔찍한, 무서운

IN BRIEF Causing great fear or alarm; dreadful

+ gruesome, macabre, appalling, disturbing, horrid, shocking

> It was terrible.
> (끔찍한 일이었다.)

1838
terse [təːrs]
a. (문체·표현) 간결한, 간명한, 짧고 힘찬 → (대답)퉁명스러운

IN BRIEF Brief and to the point; effectively concise

+ brief, short, compendious, concise, laconic, lean, succinct

> Her newspaper articles are terse and to the point.
> (그녀가 쓴 신문기사는 간결하고 요령이 있다.)

1839
testify [téstəfài]
v. 증명(입증)하다, (법정)증언하다 (give evidence)

IN BRIEF To tell or give as proof, especially under oath in a court

+ swear, witness, attest, certify, vouch (for), justify, validate, verify, warrant, substantiate, affirm

> The teacher testified to the boy's honesty.
> (선생님이 그 소년의 정직을 증언했다.)

1840
thorough [θə́ːrou]
a. 완전한, 철저한

IN BRIEF Exhaustively complete

+ complete, exhaustive, careful, exact, meticulous, precise, detailed

> He is a thorough vegetarian.
> (그는 철저한 채식주의자이다.)

1841
thoroughfare [θə́ːroufɛ̀əːr]

n. 가로, 도로, 주요 도로

IN BRIEF A main road or public highway

+ street, boulevard, concourse, expressway, freeway, highway

> The Strand is one of London's busiest thoroughfares.
> (스트랜드 가는 런던의 가장 붐비는 거리 중 한 곳이다.)

1842
threshold [θréʃhould]

n. 문지방; 입구, (사물의) 시작, 발단, 출발점

IN BRIEF A piece of wood or stone placed beneath a door

+ entrance, vestibule, doorway, gate, portal

> We are at the threshold of a new era in medicine.
> (우리는 의학 분야의 새 시대로 들어가는 초입에 있다.)

1843
thrift [θrift]

n. 검약, 절약

IN BRIEF Wisdom and caution in the management of money

+ conservation, economy, frugality, prudence

> The concept of thrift is foreign to me.
> (절약이라는 개념은 내게 낯설다.)

1844
thrive [θraiv]

vi. 번영하다, 번성하다; 잘 자라다

IN BRIEF To grow vigorously; flourish

+ burgeon, flower, grow, increase, wax, flourish, prosper, succeed

> Bank business is thriving.
> (은행업은 번창하고 있다.)

1845
tidy [táidi]

a. 단정한, 정돈된, 깨끗한

IN BRIEF Orderly and clean in appearance

+ neat, orderly, meticulous, organized, systematic

> My brother always keeps his room tidy.
> (내 동생은 자기 방을 언제나 말끔히 정돈한다.)

1846
tip [tip]

v. (내용물)비우다, 버리다; (사람)내쫓다 → 끝, 첨단(point) → 팁, 사례금

IN BRIEF The end of a pointed or projecting object

+ dump, lean, slope, incline, tilt

> Tip the box up and empty it.
> (그 상자를 기울여 속에 든 것을 비워 내어라.)

1847
titter [títəːr]

vi. (신경질적으로) 킥킥 웃다, 소리를 죽여 웃다

IN BRIEF A nervous restrained laugh

+ giggle, chortle, snicker, twitter

> There was an embarrassing pause on stage and the audience began to titter.
> (무대 위에서 당황스럽게 대사가 중단되자 관객이 킥킥거리기 시작했다.)

1848
trafficking [trǽfikiŋ]

n. 밀매, 불법거래

IN BRIEF Or improper commercial activity

+ traffic in something 밀거래하다
+ to traffic in drugs 마약을 밀거래하다
+ human traffic 인신 매매

> Another human rights concern is the transnational crime of trafficking in humans.
> (또 다른 인권문제는 인간 밀매라는 초국가적 범죄이다.)

1849
tout [taut]

v. 과대 선전하다

IN BRIEF To promote or praise energetically; publicize.

+ ballyhoo, boost, build up, enhance, promote, publicize, puff, talk up

> Burma is being touted as one of the world's last virgin markets with a location between India and China that ensures access to enormous markets.
> (미얀마는 인도와 중국 사이에 위치하여 그 위치가 두 거대한 시장으로의 접근성을 확보해주는 세계에서 마지막으로 남은 미개척 시장이라고 요란하게 선전되고 있다.)

1850
toll [toul]

n. 희생, 대가

IN BRIEF An amount or extent of loss or destruction, as of life, health, or property

+ cost, expense, price, sacrifice

> Although Aesha believes that she will be able to stay in this facility until she completes her associate's degree, the ordeal of being homeless has taken a toll on her and her studies.
> (에이샤는 자신이 준학사 학위를 다 마칠 때까지는 이 시설에 머물 수 있을 거라고 믿지만, 집이 없는 시련은 그녀와 그녀의 학업에 큰 타격을 주었다.)

LESSON 38

1851
tolerate [tálərèit]

vt. 관대하게 다루다, 묵인[허용]하다, 너그럽게 봐주다; 참다, 견디다

IN BRIEF To treat with indulgence, liberality, or forbearance

⊕ Bear, put up with, stand, endure, allow, indulge, withstand, generous

> I will not tolerate your behaving in this way.
> (네가 이런 식으로 행동하는 것은 참지 않겠어.)

1852
topple [táp-əl]

v. 넘어뜨리다; (권력) 끌어내리다, 몰락시키다

IN BRIEF Fall down, as if collapsing

⊕ collapse, fall, tumble, knock down, upset, bring down

> The pile of books toppled over onto the floor.
> (책 더미가 바닥으로 와르르 무너졌다.)

1853
touchy [tʌ́tʃi]

a. (구어) 까다로운, 민감한

IN BRIEF Easily upset or irritated; oversensitive

⊕ moody, temperamental, testy, cantankerous

> He's very touchy about his baldness.
> (그는 자기의 대머리에 대해 무척 예민하다.)

1854
toxic [táksik]

a. (약품·가스 따위가) 유독한, 독성의

IN BRIEF Of, relating to, or caused by a toxin or poison; poisonous

⊕ unhealthy, venomous, virulent, deadly, fatal, lethal, mortal

> Fumes from an automobile are toxic.
> (자동차 배기가스는 유독하다.)

1855
trace [treis]

v. 자취, 흔적, 기색

IN BRIEF A visible mark, such as a footprint, made or left by the passage of a person, animal, or thing

⊕ indication, hint, touch, nuance, evidence, relic, remains, vestige, track

> We've lost all trace of him.
> (우리는 그의 흔적을 완전히 놓쳤다.)

1856
track [træk]

n. 궤도, 선로, 발자국, 흔적 ; 추적하다

IN BRIEF A mark or succession of marks left by something that has passed

⊕ trail, marks, impressions, traces, imprints, prints

> It's hard to keep track of all one's old school friends.
> (모든 옛날 학교 친구들과 계속 연락을 하기는 힘들다.)

1857
tractable ['træktəbl]

a. 다루기 쉬운, 유순한

IN BRIEF Easily handled or worked; malleable

⊕ yielding, tame, amenable, submissive, docile

> He has a highly tractable personality easily influenced by suggestions.
> (그는 제안에 쉽게 좌우되는 아주 유순한 성격을 지녔다.)

1858
traditional [trədíʃən-əl]

a. 전통적인, 관습적인

IN BRIEF Conforming to established practice or standards

⊕ typical, customary, established, habitual, historic

> She's very traditional.
> (그녀는 아주 전통적이다.)

1859
trait [treit]

n. 특성, 특징

IN BRIEF A distinguishing feature of your personal nature

⊕ feature, mark, peculiarity, property, quality, savor

> Generosity is one of her most pleasing traits.
> (관대함은 가장 호감이 가는 그녀의 특성 가운데 하나이다.)

1860
trample [trǽmp-əl]

v. 내리밟다, 짓밟다, 밟아뭉개다 → (감정·권리)유린하다, 무시하다

IN BRIEF Tread or stomp heavily or roughly

⊕ crush, pulverize, crowd, defeat, overwhelm

> Laws made by common consent must not be trampled on by individuals.
> (공동의 동의에 의해 만들어진 법은 개인에 의해 짓밟혀서는 안 된다.)

1861
tranquil [trǽŋkwil]

a. 조용한, 평온한, 잔잔한

IN BRIEF Calm, peaceful or quiet

+ calm, pacific, placid, serene, still, composed, imperturbable, sedate

> Tranquil lakes offer solitude amid the swirl of urban life.
> (고요한 호수들은 현기증 나는 도시 생활 속에 한적한 장소를 제공해 준다.)

1862
transgress [trænsgrés]

v. 위반하다, 죄를 범하다

IN BRIEF Pass beyond limits or boundaries

+ breach, break, contravene, infringe, defy, disobey, flout

> Those who transgress the laws of society can be punished.
> (사회의 법을 위반한 사람들은 처벌 받는다.)

1863
transient [trǽnʃənt]

a. 덧없는, 무상한 → 일시적인, 순간적인, 깜짝할 사이의

IN BRIEF Lasting a very short time

+ ephemeral, evanescent, fleet, fleeting, fugacious, fugitive, momentary, passing, short-lived, temporary, transitory

> How transient all happiness is in this world!
> (이 세상 행복이란 것이 모두 다 얼마나 덧없는가!)

1864
transitory [trǽnsətɔ̀:ri]

a. 오래가지 않는, 일시적인

IN BRIEF Existing or lasting only a short time; short-lived or temporary

+ brief, fleeting, momentary, passing, temporary, transient

> We hope this hot weather will be transitory.
> (우린 이 더운 날씨가 일시적인 것이기를 바란다.)

1865
transport [trænspɔ́:rt]

vt. 수송(하다); 수송 기관

IN BRIEF To move or carry (goods, for example from one place to another; convey)

+ bring, carry, convey, ferry, move

> Generally speaking, it's quicker on public transport.
> (일반적으로 말해서 대중 교통편이 더 빠르다.)

1866
traumatic [trɔ:mǽtik]

a. 잊을 수 없을 만큼, 정신적 충격이 큰

IN BRIEF Deeply shocking

+ blow, disturbance, shock, upset, breakdown, injury

> Under deep hypnosis she remembered the traumatic events of that night.
> (그녀는 깊은 최면에 빠져 그 날 밤에 일어난 충격적인 사건을 기억해 냈다.)

1867
travail [trəvéil]

v. 진통하다, 산고를 겪다 → 수고하다 → 노고, 수고 → 고통, 고뇌

IN BRIEF Work, especially when arduous or involving painful effort

+ drudgery, labor, moil, toil, work, sweat

> The travail of the British car industry are seldom out of the news.
> (영국의 자동차 산업이 겪는 진통은 뉴스에서 거의 빠지지 않는다.)

1868
traverse [trǽvə:rs]

v. 가로지르다, 넘다, 통과하다

IN BRIEF To travel or pass across, over, or through

+ cross, navigate, bridge, intersect

> The road traverses a wild and mountainous region.
> (이 도로는 험난한 산악지대를 관통한다.)

1869
travesty [trǽvəsti]

우스꽝스럽게 만듦, 희화화(풍자) → 모방작, 서툰 흉내 → 변장

IN BRIEF A composition that imitates somebody's style with humour and satire

+ burlesque, caricature, farce, mock, mockery, parody, sham

> His account of our meeting was a travesty.
> (우리 회의에 대한 그의 설명은 엉터리이다.)

1870
treachery [trétʃ-əri]

n. 배반[배신, 반역](treason); 불안정한 것, 기대할[믿을] 수 없는 것

IN BRIEF An act of deliberate betrayal

+ perfidious, treacherous, traitorous, unfaithful: disloyalty, dishonesty

> King Arthur's kingdom was destroyed by treachery.
> (아서 왕의 왕국은 배신에 의해 몰락했다.)

1871
trenchant [tréntʃənt]

(말·사람) 통렬한, 신랄한, 날카로운(sarcastic, scathing, sharp) / (사람·정책) 강력한 (방침) 효과적인, 설득력 있는 / (윤곽) 뚜렷한

IN BRIEF Forceful and clear; penetrating

➕ acute, incisive, keen, acerbic, acid, acidic, acrid, astringent, caustic corrosive, mordacious, pungent, slashing, stinging, truculent, vitriolic

> He wrote a series of trenchant articles on the state of the British theater.
> (그는 연속으로 영국 연극계의 현 상황에 대한 신랄한 기사를 썼다.)

1872
trepidation [trèpədéiʃ-ən]

n. 전율, 공포(fright), 당황 → (마음) 동요; 낭패, 혼란

IN BRIEF A feeling of alarm or dread

➕ anxiety, worry, fear, fearfulness, fright, funk, horror, panic, terror

> I waited for my exam results with some trepidation.
> (나는 약간 불안한 마음으로 시험 결과를 기다렸다.)

1873
triumph [tráiəmf]

n. 승리[감], 정복, 업적 ; 이기다, 성공하다

IN BRIEF To be victorious or successful; win

➕ achievement, victory

> Finally justice triumphed.
> (드디어 정의가 이겼다.)

1874
trivial [tríviəl]

a. 하찮은(사소한), 별것 아닌 → 진부한, 평범한 → (답)명백한

IN BRIEF Small and of little importance. Obvious and dull

➕ inconsequent, inconsequential, insignificant, little, unimportant

> She's always fussing about some trivial matter.
> (그녀는 항상 사소한 것에 대해 소란을 떤다.)

1875
trump card [trʌmp kɑːrd]

n. 으뜸 패(의 한 장), (구어) 비장의 수

IN BRIEF Something, especially something held in reserve, that gives one a decisive advantage

➕ trump

> Our rivals seem to hold all the trump cards.
> (우리의 라이벌들이 모든 으뜸 패를 다 쥐고 있는 것 같다.)

1876
truncate [trʌ́ŋkeit]

vt. (나무·원뿔)끝을 잘라내다; (문장)짧게 하다

IN BRIEF To shorten or reduce

➕ cut, abbreviate, abridge, curtail, amputate

> They published my article in truncated form.
> (그들은 내 글을 잘라서 줄인 형태로 실었다.)

1877
turbulence [tə́ːrbjələns]

n. (바람·물결) 휘몰아침, 사나움 → (사회)소란, 불온, 동란

IN BRIEF A state or condition of confusion, movement, or agitation; disorder

➕ agitation, commotion, convulsion, tumult, turmoil, uproar, wild

> The country is in a state of turbulence.
> (그 나라는 혼란 상태이다.)

1878
turmoil [tə́ːrmɔil]

n. 소란, 소동, 혼란, 동요

IN BRIEF A state of extreme confusion or agitation

➕ commotion, confusion, agitation

> The town was in turmoil.
> (그 마을은 소란에 빠졌다.)

1879
twilight [twáilàit]

n. (해뜨기 전·해진 후) 여명, 황혼, 땅거미 → 불확실한 상태(-)

IN BRIEF The period between afternoon and nighttime

➕ dusk, eve, evening, eventide, gloaming, nightfall

> The house looked peaceful in the twilight.
> (그 집은 황혼에 묻혀 평화롭게 보였다.)

1880
tyranny [tírəni]

n. 전제정치 → 포학[무도]한 행위

IN BRIEF A government in which a single ruler is vested with absolute power

➕ absolutism, autarchy, autocracy, despotism, dictatorship, monocracy, domination

> Where laws end, tyranny begins.
> (법이 끝난 곳에서 전제 정치가 시작된다.)

1881
tyro [táirou]
초보자, 초심자(novice, abecedarian)

IN BRIEF Someone new to a field or activity

➕ beginner, fledgling, freshman, greenhorn, initiate, neophyte, novice, novitiate, tenderfoot

> He is a tyro movie producer.
> (그는 초심 영화제작자 이다.)

1882
ubiquitous [juːˈbɪkwɪtəs]
a. 아주 흔한, 어디에나 있는

IN BRIEF Being or seeming to be everywhere at the same time; omnipresent

➕ ever-present, pervasive, omnipresent, all-over, everywhere, universal

> GPS has become ubiquitous in civilian and military life, with hundreds of thousands of receivers in cars and weapons system.
> (차 안과 무기시스템 안에 수십만 개의 수신기가 있는 가운데, GPS는 시민 생활과 군대 생활에 있어서 아주 흔한 것이 되었다.)

1883
ultimate [ʌ́ltəmit]
a. 궁극적인, 최후의

IN BRIEF Greatest in quantity or highest in degree that has been or can be attained

➕ fundamental, conclusive, definitive, maximum, paramount, supreme, utmost

> Peace was the ultimate goal of the meeting.
> (평화가 그 모임의 궁극적인 목표였다.)

1884
unabridged [ʌ̀nəbrídʒd]
a. 생략하지 않은, 완전한

IN BRIEF Not shortened by omissions whole

➕ not shortened, complete, unabbreviated, uncensored, uncut

> An unabridged edition(version) of 'War and Peace?'
> ('전쟁과 평화'의 무삭제판)

1885
unadulterated [ʌ̀nədʌ́ltərèitid]
a. 섞인 것이 없는, 순수한(pure)

IN BRIEF Not mixed with impurities

➕ absolute, perfect, plain, pure, sheer, simple, undiluted, unmixed

> In an attempt to experience the unadulterated, they travel up obscure places.
> (순수한 것들을 체험하기 위해, 그들은 미지의 장소를 여행한다.)

1886
unanimity [jùːnəníməti]
n. (만장) 일치, (전원)합의

IN BRIEF Showing complete agreement with no one opposed

➕ agreement, accord, consensus, concert, unity, harmony

> There was a remarkable unanimity at the meeting.
> (그 회의에서는 놀랍도록 만장일치가 이뤄졌다.)

1887
unassuming [ʌ̀nəsjúːmiŋ]
a. 주제넘지 않은; 얌전한, 겸손한

IN BRIEF Exhibiting no pretensions, boastfulness, or ostentation; modest

➕ modest, meek, unpretentious, humble, submissive

> He was shy and unassuming.
> (그는 수줍음이 많고 겸손했다.)

1888
unattended [ʌ̀nəténdid]
a. 돌보지 않는; 수행원이 없는

IN BRIEF Not being attended to, looked after, or watched

➕ unguarded, defenseless, open, unprotected, vulnerable, incautious

> Please do not leave your luggage unattended.
> (아무도 지키는 사람 없이 짐을 방치해 두지 마시오.)

1889
unbridled [ʌnbráidld]
a. 억제되지 않은, 방자한, 난폭한

IN BRIEF Being without restraint

➕ unrestrained, unbounded, unchecked, unhampered, unrestricted

> The storm had an unbridled fury as it hit the usually peaceful valley.
> (이 폭풍은 보통 평화로운 계곡을 강타하면서 억제되지 않은 맹위를 떨쳤다.)

1890
uncanny [ʌnkǽni]
a. 초자연적인, 초인적인; 불가사의한, 기괴한, 기분 나쁜

IN BRIEF Mysterious or impossible to explain, especially when causing uneasiness or astonishment

➕ odd, weird, strange, unnatural, amazing, extraordinary, incredible

> The silence was uncanny.
> (기괴할 정도로 조용했다.)

1891
uncharted [ʌntʃɑ́ːrtid]

a. 해도[지도]에 실리지 않은; 미지의

IN BRIEF Not charted or recorded on a map or plan

- unknown, unidentified, unnamed, obscure, concealed, hidden

> The party is sailing in uncharted seas.
> (그 집단은 미지의 바다를 항해 중이다.)

1892
uncomely [ʌnkʌ́mli]

a. 예쁘지 않은 → 버릇없는

IN BRIEF Not handsome or beautiful

- homely, plain, unattractive, unlovely, ugly

> uncomely person
> (버릇없는 사람)

1893
uncongenial [ʌ̀nkəndʒíːniəl]

a. 마음에 들지 않는, 싫은, 부적당한

IN BRIEF Not compatible or sympathetic, as in character

- alien, exotic, foreign, remote, strange

> It's like an uncongenial atmosphere.
> (마음에 안 드는 분위기로군.)

1894
undependable [ʌ̀ndipéndəbəl]

a. 신뢰[의지]할 수 없는

IN BRIEF Not easily relied or depended on

- irresponsible, unreliable, untrustworthy

> People who spend more than they earn are said to be undependable about money.
> (자신이 버는 것 보다 더 많은 돈을 쓰는 사람들은 돈에 관해 신뢰할 수 없다고들 한다.)

1895
undergo [ʌ̀ndərgóu]

vt. 받다, 겪다, 경험하다

IN BRIEF To be subjected to; experience

- experience, feel, go through

> The country is undergoing many changes.
> (그 나라는 많은 변화를 겪고 있다.)

1896
undermine [ʌ̀ndərmáin]

vt. 밑을 파다 → 훼손시키다 → 손상시키다

IN BRIEF To lessen or deplete the nerve, energy, or strength

- attenuate, debilitate, devitalize, enervate, enfeeble, sap, undo

> Many professors are wondering whether the lotteries' get-rich-quick appeal undermines the American work ethic.
> (많은 교수들은 복권이 가진 일확천금의 매력이 미국인의 직업 윤리의식을 약화시키는 것이 아닌지 궁금해 하고 있다.)

1897
trim [trim]

v. 다듬다, 정돈하다; (인원·예산을) 삭감하다

IN BRIEF To make neat or tidy by clipping, smoothing, or pruning

- passementerie, trimming, cut down, reduce, trim back, trim down, cut, cut back, bring down

> Despite the labor union's protest, the company decided to trim its workforce and production in response to declining demand and falling profits.
> (노동조합의 항의에도 불구하고, 그 회사는 수요 감소와 수익 저하에 대처하여 직원 수와 생산을 삭감하기로 결정했다.)

1898
tap [tæp]

v. 가볍게 두드리다; 이용하다(utilize)

IN BRIEF To strike (something) lightly and usually repeatedly

> She owes her election to having tapped deep public disillusionment with professional politicians.
> (그녀의 당선은 직업 정치인들에 대한 대중의 깊은 환멸을 이용한 덕분이다.)

1899
turpitude [tə́ːrpitjùːd]

n. 대단히 부도덕한 행위, 비열

IN BRIEF Base character or action; depravity

- wickedness, evil, corruption, criminality, depravity, immorality
- iniquity, badness, viciousness, villainy, degeneracy, sinfulness
- foulness, baseness, vileness, nefariousness

> A visitor may be denied admittance to this country if he has been convicted for a crime involving moral turpitude.
> (이 나라를 방문하는 사람이 만일 부도덕한 행위와 관련한 범죄로 유죄판결을 받을 적이 있으면 입국이 거부될 수도 있다.)

1900
table [téibəl]

v. (영국) (의안 등을) 상정하다, 토의에 부치다

IN BRIEF Up for discussion

> After long negotiations, they finally agreed to table the idea of urbanization in Parliament and the Cabinet.
> (오랜 협상 끝에, 그들은 마침내 도시화에 대한 의견을 의회와 내각에 상정하기로 합의하였다.)

LESSON 39

1901
underscore [ʌ̀ndərskɔ́ːr]

vt. 밑줄을 긋다 → 강조하다 → (영화·TV) 배경 음악

IN BRIEF To put emphasis on; stress

⊕ accent, accentuate, emphasize, feature, highlight, italicize

> The recent violence underscores the sensitivity of the issue of Jerusalem.
> (최근의 폭력사태는 예루살렘 문제가 얼마나 민감한지를 강조해 주고 있습니다.)

1902
unearth [ʌnə́ːrθ]

vt. 파내다, 발굴하다, 세상에 알리다; 폭로하다(show)

IN BRIEF To dig up. To discover or to find

⊕ excavate, exhume, disclose, discover, divulge, expose, uncover

> The dog has unearthed some bones.
> (그 개가 몇몇 뼈다귀를 파냈다.)

1903
uneasiness [ʌníːzinis]

n. 불안, 걱정 불쾌, 거북함

IN BRIEF A troubled or anxious state of mind

⊕ angst, anxiety, anxiousness, care, concern, disquiet, worry, disquietude, distress, nervousness, solicitude, unease

> The house builders listened to reports of a devastating hurricane with rising uneasiness.
> (주택 건축가들은 파괴적인 허리케인에 대한 보도를 들으며 점점 더 불안해했다.)

1904
unfold [ʌnfóuld]

v. (접은·닫힌 물건) 펼치다, 펴다, 서서히 밝히다

IN BRIEF To become clear, apparent, or known

⊕ reveal, expose, show, uncover, disclose, divulge

> The seat unfolds into a bed.
> (그 좌석을 펼치면 침대가 된다.)

1905
uninhabited [ʌ̀ninhǽbitid]

a. 사람이 없는[살지 않는]

IN BRIEF Having no residents; not inhabited

⊕ empty, unoccupied, untenanted, vacant, abandoned, deserted, forsaken

> Here is an uninhabited island.
> (여기는 무인도다.)

1906
unique [juːníːk]

a. 유일한, 독특한, 유례없는

IN BRIEF Being the only one of its kind

⊕ unusual, atypical, original, distinctive, individual, particular, peculiar

> Everyone's fingerprints are unique.
> (모든 사람의 지문은 유일무이하다.)

1907
universal [jùːnəvə́ːrsəl]

a. 우주의; 만국의; 모든 사람의, 보편적인

IN BRIEF Of, relating to, or typical of the whole of mankind or of nature

⊕ general, omnipresent, pervasive, ubiquitous, widespread, boundless

> It is a universal truth.
> (그것은 보편적인 진리다.)

1908
unkempt [ʌnkémpt]

a. 단정치 못한, 흐트러진; (정원 따위가) 손질 되지 않은

IN BRIEF Disorderly or untidy in appearance

⊕ uncombed, disheveled, messy, rumpled, slovenly, untidy

> The garden looks rather unkempt.
> (정원이 다소 너저분하게 보인다.)

1909
unnerve [ʌnnə́ːrv]

vt. 용기[자신] 잃게 하다, 무기력하게 하다

IN BRIEF To cause to lose courage or firmness of purpose

⊕ frighten, intimidate, scare, upset, worry

> His silence unnerved me.
> (그의 침묵은 내가 용기를 잃게 했다.)

1910
unpalatable [ʌnpǽlətəbəl]
a. 입에 맞지 않는, 맛이 없는; 불쾌한, 싫은

IN BRIEF Not pleasing to the taste

[+] unpleasant, disagreeable, distasteful, repulsive

> The socialism which Owen preached was unpalatable to many.
> (오웬이 주창한 사회주의는 많은 사람에게 달갑지 않게 여겨졌다.)

1911
unprecedented [ʌnprésədèntid]
a. 전례가 없는 → 전에 없던 → 새로운 → 신기한

IN BRIEF Having no previous example

[+] exceptional, original, unparalleled

> Prices have been hiked (up) to unprecedented levels.
> (물가가 유례없는 수준까지 인상되었다.)

1912
unpredictable [ʌnpridíktəbəl]
a. 예언[예보, 예측]할 수 없는

IN BRIEF Difficult to foretell or foresee

[+] indefinite, uncertain, unforeseeable, fanciful, whimsical

> She's so unpredictable.
> (그녀는 너무나도 예측 불가능하다.)

1913
unravel [ʌnrǽvəl]
v. 풀다, 해명하다, 끝까지 밝히다

IN BRIEF To undo or ravel the entangled, knitted, or woven threads of

[+] undo, unknit, unsnarl, untangle, clarify, decipher, solve

> Detectives are still trying to unravel the mystery.
> (형사들은 아직도 그 수수께끼를 풀려고 애쓰고 있다.)

1894
unrelated [ʌnriléitid]
a. 관계가 없는, 혈연이 아닌, 언급되지 않은

IN BRIEF Not of the same family or kind

[+] independent; different, irrelevant

> His doctorate is in a totally unrelated field.
> (그의 학위는 전혀 관련 없는 분야의 것이다.)

1915
unrelenting [ʌnriléntiŋ]
a. 가차 없는, 무자비한

IN BRIEF Having or exhibiting uncompromising determination; unyielding

[+] persistent, resolute, steadfast, immovable, inexorable

> Her success came through unrelenting hard work.
> (그녀의 성공은 흔들리지 않는 노력에서 왔다.)

1916
unreliable [ʌnriláiəbəl]
a. 신뢰[의지]할 수 없는, 믿을 수 없는

IN BRIEF Not reliable; untrustworthy

[+] not trustworthy, not true, undependable, untrustworthy

> She's very unreliable.
> (그녀는 정말 믿을 수가 없어.)

1917
unrestrained [ʌnristréind]
a. 억제되지 않은 → 제어되지 않은 → 거리낌 없는 → 삼가지 않는

IN BRIEF Not subject to restraint

[+] uncontrolled, uninhibited, unbridled, free, natural

> There was unrestrained joy on the faces of the people.
> (사람들의 얼굴에는 거침없는 기쁨이 감돌았다.)

1918
upbringing [ʌ́pbriŋiŋ]
n. 가정교육, 양육

IN BRIEF The rearing and training received during childhood

[+] education, guidance, instruction, schooling, training

> She had a strict religious upbringing.
> (그녀는 엄격한 종교적 양육을 받았다.)

1919
upheaval [ʌvphíːvəl]
n. (지각의) 융기; (사회의) 대변동, 격변

IN BRIEF Strong or violent change or disturbance, as in a society

[+] chaos, disruption, disturbance, tumult

> It would cause a tremendous upheaval to install a different computer system.
> (다른 컴퓨터 체계를 설치하면 엄청난 격변을 일으킬 것이다.)

1920
upright [ʌ́prait]
a. 똑바로 선 → 직립의 → 수직의(똑바른)

IN BRIEF Standing on end. Honest and trustworthy

[+] perpendicular, plumb, vertical

> The man is standing upright.
> (남자는 똑바로 서 있다.)

1921
urban [ə́ːrbən]

a. 도시의, 도시 특유의, 도시에 익숙한; 도시에 사는

IN BRIEF Having to do with cities or towns

+ city, metropolitan, municipal ↔ country, rural, suburban

> Urban planning is necessary so that people can live comfortably in cities with high populations.
> (인구가 많은 도시에서 사람들이 편하게 살 수 있도록 도시계획이 필요하다.)

1922
urge [əːrdʒ]

v. 억지로 시키다 → 강요하다 → 몰아대다 → 재촉하다

IN BRIEF To force or drive forward or onward; impel

+ exhort, press, very strong desire

> He urged me to reconsider my decision.
> (그는 내 결정을 재고하도록 촉구했다.)

1923
usher [ʌ́ʃər]

n. 안내원; 문지기 / v. 안내하다(into)

IN BRIEF An official doorkeeper, as in a courtroom

+ doorman, escort, guide, harbinger, precursor

> Ushered into a waiting car, he was driven for two hours into the Bavarian countryside.
> (그는 기다리고 있는 차로 안내되어, 차로 두 시간 동안 바이에른의 교외로 갔다.)

1924
utterly [ʌ́tərli]

ad. 전적으로, 완전히, 철저하게

IN BRIEF Completely; absolutely; entirely

+ absolutely, completely, perfectly, positively, thoroughly, totally

> Men and women are utterly different.
> (남자와 여자는 완전히 다르다.)

1925
vacant [véikənt]

a. 텅 빈, 공허한, 멍청한

IN BRIEF Containing nothing; empty

+ empty, vacuous, void, uninhabited, unoccupied, unused, blank

> There is no vacant room.
> (빈 방이 하나도 없다.)

1926
vacillate [vǽsəlèit]

vi. (사람·마음)동요하다 → 주저하다 → 망설이다

IN BRIEF To waver in one's opinions

+ go back and forth, sway, teeter, totter, waver, weave, hesitate

> She vacillated between hope and fear.
> (그녀는 마음이 희망과 두려움 사이에 갈피를 못 잡았다.)

1927
vagary [véigəri]

(날씨) 예측불허 변화[변동] → 엉뚱한 짓[생각], 언행, 변덕

IN BRIEF Unpredictable act or idea

+ caprice, conceit, freak, humor, impulse, megrim, whim

> Thanks to the vagaries of fashion, everyone is wearing tennis rackets instead of shoes this summer.
> (변덕스러운 유행 탓에, 올 여름에 사람들이 모두 신발 대신에 테니스 라켓을 신고 있다.)

1928
vague [veig]

a. (말·관념·감정) 막연한, 모호한, 애매한

IN BRIEF Not clear in meaning or expression; inexplicit

+ ambiguous, equivocal, inexplicit, obscure, indistinct, nebulous, unclear

> She was vague about her plans.
> (그녀는 자신의 계획에 대해 분명하지 않았다.)

1929
validate [vǽlədèit]

vt. 입증(확인)하다 → 인가(승인, 비준)하다 → 허가하다

IN BRIEF Ascertain the truth, authenticity of something

+ approve, authorize, certify, stamp, authenticate, verify

> This discovery seems to validate the claims of popular astrology.
> (이 발견은 대중 점성술의 주장을 입증하는 것 같다.)

1930
valiant [vǽljənt]

a. 용맹스런, 씩씩한, 장한, 영웅적인

IN BRIEF Possessing or exhibiting valor; brave

+ brave, audacious, bold, dauntless, gallant, intrepid, valorous

> Cowards die many times before their death; the valiant never taste of death but once.
> (겁쟁이들은 죽기 전에 여러 번 죽는다. 그러나 용감한 사람들은 오직 한 번 죽는다.)

1931
valor [vǽləər]
n. 대단한 용기, 용맹

IN BRIEF Courage and boldness, as in battle; bravery

+ boldness, bravery, courage, mettle, pluck

> The Medal of Honor is given for valor.
> (명예 훈장은 용맹스러움에 대해 수여되는 메달이다.)

1932
vanish [vǽniʃ]
v. (갑자기)사라지다 → 없어지다

IN BRIEF To pass out of sight, especially quickly; disappear

+ disappear, dissipate, evaporate, fade, depart, leave, withdraw

> My pen seems to have vanished without trace.
> (내 펜이 흔적도 없이 사라진 것 같다.)

1933
vanquish [vǽŋkwiʃ]
vt. 정복하다 → 이기다

IN BRIEF To defeat or conquer in battle; subjugate

+ conquer, defeat, overthrow, overwhelm, rout, overpower

> He vanquished the world.
> (그는 세계를 정복했다.)

1934
vapid [vǽpid]
a. (음식) 맛없는, 김빠진 → (말, 문장) 활기 없는, 흥미 없는(dull)

IN BRIEF Dull and uninteresting

+ Bland, innocuous, insipid, jejune, namby-pamby, washy, waterish

> The vapid food at that restaurant caused us to never eat there again.
> (그 식당의 맛없는 음식 때문에 우리는 그곳에서 다시는 먹을 수 없었다.)

1935
variation [vɛ̀əriéiʃən]
n. 변동 → 변화(change) → 변종 → 차이

IN BRIEF The act of changing. The amount of a change

+ difference, change, alternative, modification

> Variations in the color of sea water from blue to green seem to be caused by high or low concentrations of salt.
> (바닷물의 색깔이 청색에서 녹색까지 여러 가지인 것은 소금의 농도가 높거나 낮음에 기인하는 것 같다.)

1936
vast [væst]
a. 광대한; (평면적으로) 거대한

IN BRIEF Very great in size, extent, or quantity

+ huge, immense, expansive, measureless, spacious, unlimited

> His business was vast.
> (그의 사업은 방대했다.)

1937
vehement [víːəmənt]
a. 격렬한 → 맹렬한 → 열렬한 → 열정적인 (passionate, terrible)

IN BRIEF Very eager or urgent

+ passionate, opinionated, intense, desperate, fierce, furious, violent

> He has a vehement dislike of loud pop music.
> (그는 시끄러운 팝 음악을 격렬히 싫어한다.)

1938
velocity [vəlásəti]
n. 속력, 속도

IN BRIEF Rapidity or speed of motion; swiftness

+ speed, acceleration, quickness, rapidity, swiftness

> A typhoon is approaching at a velocity of 20km per hour.
> (태풍이 시속 20km의 속도로 접근하고 있다.)

1939
venal [víːnl]
a. 돈으로 좌우되는 → 매수할 수 있는 → 부패한(bribable)

IN BRIEF Open to bribery; mercenary; corruptible

+ corrupt, dishonest, buyable

> Originally there was enough money to cover all expenses but venal officials took most of it.
> (원래는 모든 비용을 충당하기에 충분한 자금이 있었는데 뇌물을 좋아하는 관리들이 대부분의 돈을 횡령했다.)

1940
verdict [vɔ́ːrdikt]
n. (배심원의) 평결; 판단, 결정

IN BRIEF Law The decision of the jury after the trial of a case

+ decision, decree, determination, judgment, resolution, adjudication

> The jury brought in a verdict of guilty.
> (배심원은 유죄평결을 내놓았다.)

1941
verge [vəːrdʒ]
n. 가장자리, 끝, 경계; ~직전에 있다; 가장자리에 있다

IN BRIEF An edge or margin; a border

➕ brink, edge, point, threshold

> She looked on the verge of tears.
> (그녀는 눈물을 터뜨리기 직전처럼 보였다.)

1942
verify [vérəfài]
vt. 확인하다; 증명하다

IN BRIEF To prove to be true or accurate

➕ authenticate, confirm, corroborate, document, support, validate

> The police verified that she had an airtight alibi.
> (경찰은 그녀에게 완벽한 알리바이가 있다는 것을 확인했다.)

1943
versatile [vɔ́ːrsətàil]
a. 다재다능한, 용도가 다양한(protean), 융통성 있는(flexible)

IN BRIEF Able to do a number of things well

➕ adjustable, all-around, many-sided, multifaceted, various, skillful, proficient, clever at various things

> Few cooking ingredients are as versatile as eggs.
> (달걀만큼 용도가 넓은 요리 재료는 거의 없다.)

1944
verbal [vɔ́ːrbəl]
a. 말[언어]의, 말[언어]에 의한, 말로서의

IN BRIEF Relating to, or associated with words

➕ speaking, oral, spoken, uttered, vocal, lexical, lingual, linguistic

> I made a verbal contract with him.
> (나는 그와 구두 계약을 맺었다.)

1945
vacuum [vǽkjuəm]
n. 진공; 공허, 공백

IN BRIEF The absence of matter

➕ emptiness, vacancy, vacuity, void

> Human actors and their actions do not exist on a(n) vacuum, but rather in a context of wider social wholes.
> (인간이라는 행위자들과 그들이 하는 행동들은 진공 상태가 아니라 더 폭넓은 사회 전체의 맥락에서 존재한다.)

1946
verbose [vəːrbóus]
a. 말이 많은, 다변의, 장황한

IN BRIEF Using or containing a great and usually an excessive number of words; wordy

➕ long-winded, wordy, garrulous, windy, diffuse, prolix, tautological, circumlocutory, periphrastic, pleonastic

> This writing is verbose; we need to edit it.
> (이 글은 장황하다. 그래서 우리는 이 글을 수정할 필요가 있다.)

1947
volitional [voulíʃənl]
a. 의지의; 의욕적인

IN BRIEF With deliberate intention

➕ free, spontaneous, uncompelled, unforced, voluntary, willful

> Genuine love is volitional rather than emotional.
> (진정한 사랑은 감정적이라기보다 의지적이다.)

1948
verbose [vɜːrˈboʊs]
a. 말이 많은, 다변의

IN BRIEF Using or containing an excessive number of words

➕ long-winded, wordy, garrulous, windy, diffuse, prolix, tautological, circumlocutory, periphrastic, pleonastic

> She found him to be unbearably verbose and would often simply turn away when he began speaking.
> (그녀는 그가 참을 수 없을 정도로 수다스러운 것을 알고 그가 말을 시작하면 종종 그저 외면했었다.)

1949
vacillating [vǽsəlèitiŋ]
우유부단한, 흔들리는, 흔들흔들하는

IN BRIEF Inclined to fluctuate; wavering → irresolute

➕ indecisive, irresolute, hesitant, uncertain, faltering, wavering, unresolved, oscillating, in two minds

> Because Marissa had always been a staunch supporter of animal rights, her audience was confounded by her vacillating stance during the debate.
> (마리사는 언제나 동물 권리의 확고한 지지자였기 때문에, 토론 내내 그녀의 우유부단한 태도에 청중들은 당황했다.)

1950
vertiginous [vərtídʒənəs]
빙글빙글(회전) 도는 → 현기증이 나는 → 변하기 쉬운 → 불안정한

IN BRIEF Turning about an axis; revolving or whirling

➕ dizzy, giddy, unstable

> The world is changing at such a vertiginous speed in this digital age. I don't think I can afford a vacation even if it is paid for.
> (이 디지털 시대에 세상은 현기증을 일으키는 속도로 변화하고 있다. 유급 휴가라 해도 나는 휴가를 가질 형편이 못된다고 생각한다.)

LESSON 40

1951
verbatim [vəːrbéitim]
축어적으로, 말대로
IN BRIEF Word for word, literally
⊕ literal, verbal, word-for-word

> He kept verbatim transcripts of discussions with his friends.
> (그는 자기 친구들과 했던 토론을 말 그대로 적어놓았다.)

1952
vestige [véstidʒ]
n. (소멸한 것의) 흔적, 자국, 유적; 잔존물
IN BRIEF A small trace, mark, or amount; hint
⊕ remaining sign, fragment, piece, relic, remains, remnant, evidence

> There was not a vestige of the castle.
> (그 성은 자취조차 없었다.)

1953
viable [váiəbəl]
a. (태아) 생존 가능한 → (계획) 실행 가능한 → (사물) 확실한
IN BRIEF Capable of occurring or being done
⊕ reasonable, practicable, feasible, possible, workable, strong

> There's no viable alternative.
> (실행 가능한 대안이 없다.)

1954
vicinity [visíniti]
가까움, 근접, 주변, 가까이 있음
IN BRIEF Nearby or surrounding area; local area
⊕ proximity, surroundings, neighborhood

> There's no hospital in the immediate vicinity.
> (가까운 인근에는 병원이 없어요.)

1955
vicious [víʃəs]
a. 나쁜(evil) → 악덕의 → 사악한 → (구어) 지독한, 심한
IN BRIEF Likely to attack or bite. Mean and cruel
⊕ wicked, malevolent, malicious, malignant, brutal, ferocious

> He's not a vicious person.
> (그는 나쁜 사람이 아니다.)

1956
vicissitude [visísitjùːd]
(사물) 변화, 변천, 교체 → (인생·운명) 영고성쇠
IN BRIEF Constant change as a natural process; unexpected change
⊕ asperity, difficulty, hardship, rigor

> We can count on the vicissitude of the seasons throughout the year.
> (우리는 1년 내내 계절의 변화를 기대할 수 있다.)

1957
vie [vai]
우열을 다투다 → 겨루다 → 경쟁하다
IN BRIEF To work to beat another
⊕ compete, contend, contest, emulate, rival

> The children tend to vie for their mother's attention.
> (그 아이들은 엄마의 관심을 얻기 위해 경쟁하는 경향이 있다.)

1958
vigilant [vídʒələnt]
a. 경계하고 있는 → 방심하지 않는 → 주의 깊게 지키는
IN BRIEF Being on the alert
⊕ watchful, careful

> Supervisors must be vigilant when it comes to safety. They must continually educate workers.
> (관리자는 안전에 대해서라면 방심해서 안 된다. 사원들을 계속 교육시켜야 한다.)

1959
vilify [víləfài]
vt. 헐뜯다 → 비방하다 → 중상하다
IN BRIEF To speak ill of; defame; slander
⊕ criticize very harshly, defame, malign, accuse

> She was vilified by the press for her unfashionable views.
> (그녀는 케케묵은 생각들 때문에 언론의 비방을 받았다.)

1960
villain [vílən]
n. 악한, 악당; 범죄자(a wicked man)
IN BRIEF An evil or wicked person in a play or novel
⊕ evil person

> He is cast as the villain.
> (그는 악역을 맡았다.)

1961
vindicate [víndəkèit]

vt. 진실임[정당함]을 입증하다 → 변호하다 → 혐의를 풀다

IN BRIEF To clear from guilt, accusation, blame, etc, as by evidence or argument

[+] prove one's innocence, absolve, exculpate, exonerate

> The evidence will vindicate the defendant.
> (그 증거가 피고의 결백을 입증해 줄 것이다.)

1962
vindictive [vindíktiv]

a. 복수심 있는 → 앙심 깊은 → 보복적인

IN BRIEF Wanting to get revenge

[+] hateful, revengeful, spiteful, vengeful, malicious

> She can be extremely vindictive.
> (그녀는 극도로 앙심을 품을 수 있는 사람이다.)

1963
virtually [və́ːrtʃuəli]

거의 → 실질적으로 → 사실상

IN BRIEF In fact or to all purposes; practically

[+] practically, almost, nearly, in effect

> In his rage, he flung virtually everything within reach at the wall.
> (그가 화가 나서 손이 닿은 곳에 있는 거의 모든 것을 벽으로 내던졌다.)

1964
virtue [və́ːrtʃuː]

n. 장점 → 미점 → 가치 → 좋은 점

IN BRIEF Moral excellence and righteousness; goodness

[+] honor, integrity, merit, advantage

> Patience is a virtue.
> (인내는 미덕이다.)

1965
vogue [voug]

n. (대)유행(fashion) → 인기 있는 물건[사람]

IN BRIEF The prevalent way or fashion. Being popular

[+] fashion; current practice, popularity

> Black is in vogue again.
> (검정색이 다시 유행이다.)

1966
volatile [válətil]

a. 휘발성의 → 변덕스러운 → 순간적인(일시적인)

IN BRIEF Changeable. Evaporating quickly

[+] explosive, changeable, unstable, whimsical, erratic, fickle

> Like many actors, he had a rather volatile temper.
> (많은 배우와 마찬가지로 그도 다소 변덕스러운 성미를 가지고 있다.)

1967
volunteer [vàləntíər]

지원(하다), 지원자, 자원봉사(하다)

IN BRIEF A person who offers to do something of one's own free will

[+] unpaid, voluntary, extend, offer, proffer

> I will volunteer to lead the hike into the nature preserve.
> (나는 자연 보호 구역으로 하이킹을 이끌기 위해 자원할 것이다.)

1968
voracious [vouʃíərəs]

a. 게걸스레 먹는(식욕 왕성한) → 몹시 집착하는(Very eager)

IN BRIEF Eating with greediness or in very large quantities

[+] very hungry, rapacious, edacious, gluttonous, greedy

> He has a voracious appetite.
> (그는 왕성한 식욕을 지녔다.)

1969
vouch [vautʃ]

v. 보증하다 → 단언하다 → 주장하다 → 증명하다

IN BRIEF To give supporting evidence. To give a guarantee

[+] give assurance, attest, certify, testify, witness, declare one's belief

> I'll vouch for him.
> (내가 그를 보증 하겠다.)

1970
vulnerability [ˌvʌlnərəˈbɪləti]

n. 약점이 있음, 취약성

IN BRIEF Susceptible to physical harm or damage

[+] exposure, liability, openness, susceptibility, susceptibleness

> Last week's icy assault on the Midwest, for all its ferocity and cost, is merely another reminder of the inescapable vulnerability of life and social well-being to the whins of the weather.
> (지난 주 미국 중서부 지방에 맹렬히 쏟아진 눈은 그 사나움과 손실에도 불구하고, 삶과 사회적 안녕이 변덕스러운 날씨에 어쩔 수 없이 취약함을 다시 한 번 상기시켜주는 것일 뿐이다.)

1971
vulnerable [vʌ́lnərəbəl]

a. 상처입기 쉬운 → 공격받기 쉬운 → 쉽게 영향을 받는

IN BRIEF That which can be hurt, destroyed or attacked. Sensitive

➕ open to attack, liable, weak, prone, subject, susceptible, precarious

> Young people are vulnerable to the influences of elevision and the internet.
> (젊은 사람들은 텔레비전과 인터넷의 영향에 민감하다.)

1972
waive [weiv]

vt. (권리·주장) 포기[철회]하다 → (요구) 보류하다, 미루다(defer)

IN BRIEF Lose or lose the right to by some error, offense, or crime

➕ give up; let go, relinquish, abandon, abdicate, cede, concede

> I will waive my rights in this matter in order to expedite our reaching a proper decision.
> (적절한 결정을 신속히 내리기 위해 나는 이 문제에 있어서 나의 권리를 포기하겠다.)

1973
wandering [wάndəriŋ]

a. (정처 없이) 돌아다니는 → 방랑하는 → 헤매는 → 종잡을 수 없는

IN BRIEF To go from place to place without a plan

➕ move about aimlessly; digress, roam, rove, stray

> The child was found wandering the streets alone.
> (그 아이는 길에서 혼자 헤매는 것이 발견되었다.)

1974
wane [wein]

vi. 작아[적어]지다 → 약해지다 → 쇠약해지다(weak, decline)

IN BRIEF A gradual decline (in size or strength or power or number

➕ diminish, lessen, flag, languish, dwindle, degenerate, deteriorate

> Life will wax and wane.
> (인생에는 성쇠가 있다.)

1975
warily [wέərəli]

신중하게 → 조심스럽게

IN BRIEF In a carefully watchful manner

➕ carefully, cautiously

> The police came up to the stranger warily.
> (경찰은 낯선 이에게 조심스럽게 다가갔다.)

1976
warrant [wɔ́(:)rənt]

v. 정당화하다 → (구어)보증하다, 단언(장담), 허가하다

IN BRIEF Formal and explicit approval right/wrong

➕ guarantee, attest, authenticate, substantiate, validate, confirm, corroborate

> Nothing warranted his behaving like that.
> (그 무엇도 그의 그 같은 행위를 정당화시키지는 못했다.)

1977
wary [wέ-əri]

a. 조심성 있는[of] → 방심하지 않는 → 세심[신중]한 (scrupulous)

IN BRIEF On guard; watchful

➕ careful, cautious, alert, heedful, vigilant, wakeful, watchful

> You must be wary of strangers bearing gifts.
> (당신은 선물을 가져오는 낯선 사람들을 조심해야 한다.)

1978
watchword [wάtʃwə̀:rd]

n. 암호(password) → 표어, 슬로건(slogan)

IN BRIEF A secret word or phrase known only to a restricted group

➕ password, word, parole, countersign

> Safety is our watchword.
> (안전이 우리의 슬로건이다.)

1979
well-being

행복 → 안녕 → 복지

IN BRIEF The state of being healthy, happy, or prosperous; welfare

➕ welfare, good, interest, health, benefit, advantage

> People are getting interested in well ageing beyond well being.
> (사람들은 웰빙을 넘어서 잘 늙어가기에 관심을 갖고 있다.)

1980
well-to-do [wel:tu:du:]

부자인 → 유복한 → 부유 계급

IN BRIEF Prosperous; affluent; well-off

➕ rich, wealthy, affluent, well-off, loaded

> To these well-to-do people, higher prices mean better quality.
> (이들 부유한 사람들에게는 높은 가격이 높은 품질을 의미한다.)

1981
whit [hwit]

(부정문)조금, 극소

IN BRIEF The least bit; an iota

+ iota, scintilla, shred, smidge

> There is not a whit of truth in the statement.
> (그 진술에는 조금도 진실성이 없다.)

1982
whitewash [hwáitwɑ̀ʃ]

눈속임하다 → 결점[과실]을 감추다 → 겉치장하다

IN BRIEF Something that glosses over faults or absolves one from blame

+ cover up the truth, palliate, extenuate, hide, erase, camouflage

> The tide of history can sweep away many things, but it can't whitewash China's collective memory of the Japanese invasion in the 1930s.
> (역사의 흐름은 많은 것들을 쓸어버릴 수 있다. 하지만 1930년대 일본의 침략에 대한중국의 집단적인 기억을 지워버릴 수는 없다.)

1983
wild [waild]

a. 길들지 않은(uncultivated) → 야생의 → 자연 그대로 자란

IN BRIEF A natural or undomesticated state

+ untamed, fierce, savage, ferocious, unbroken, feral, undomesticated

> North America has the world's best climate for wild grapes.
> (북아메리카는 야생 포도가 자라기에 세계에서 가장 적합한 기후를 가지고 있다.)

1984
winnow [wínou]

v. (좋은 부분) 골라내다 → 뽑아(선별)내다 → (낟알·겨) 키질하다

IN BRIEF To separate grain from chaff

+ separate, sift, sort, fan

> The test will winnow out the congressmen.
> (그 시험으로 국회의원들을 가려낼 것이다.)

1985
wit [wit]

n. 기지 → 재치 → 유머

IN BRIEF A message whose ingenuity or verbal skill or incongruity has the power to evoke laughter

+ humor, fun, quips, banter, puns, pleasantry

> Mark Twain, the famous American novelist, was well known for his wit.
> (유명한 미국의 소설가인 마크 트웨인은 그의 위트로 유명하다.)

1986
wither [wíðər]

v. 시들다 → 말라빠지다(shrivel) → (애정·희망)약해지다

IN BRIEF Shrink, especially from a loss of moisture; Lose freshness, vigor, or vitality

+ droop, decline, languish, benumb, numb, paralyze, petrify, stun, stupefy, wilt

> The hot sun had withered the leaves.
> (뜨거운 태양이 나뭇잎들을 시들게 했었다.)

1987
withdraw [wiðdrɔ́]

v. (예금) 인출하다 → (약속) 철회(취소)하다 → 철수(후퇴)하다

IN BRIEF To remove. To leave, retire or resign

+ take out, quit, retract, declare void, remove, abjure, recall, recant

> Our troops have withdrawn from the border area.
> (우리 군대는 국경지역에서 철수했다.)
> How much do you want to withdraw?
> (얼마나 찾으시겠습니까?)

1988
wood [wud]

n. 숲, 삼림

> Woods are very important in the conservation of nature.
> (자연 보호에 있어 숲은 대단히 중요하다.)

1989
wrap up [ræp ʌp]

(물건) 싸다; (참뜻) 숨기고 표현하다[in](cover, package, cloak, envelop, veil) / (구어) [계약]을 매듭짓다(end, finish)

> That just about wraps it up for today, gentlemen.
> (여러분, 오늘은 이만 마칩니다.)

1990
wrath [ræθ]

격노(rage), 분노

IN BRIEF Intense anger usually on an epic scale

+ extreme anger, furor, fury, irateness, ire, rage, wrathfulness

> A soft answer turns away wrath.
> (부드러운 대답은 분노를 물리친다.)

1991
wreck [rek]
(건물·차)파괴하다 → (배)난파시키다 → (계획)좌절시키다(잔해)

IN BRIEF Destroy; devastate; shatter; tear down

[+] break down, cross up, demolish, destroy, ruin, shatter, sink, smash, spoil, torpedo

> The storm caused many wrecks.
> (폭풍우로 많은 배가 조난됐다.)

1992
wretched [rétʃid]
비참(불쌍, 불행)한(miserable) → 초라한[형편없는] → 야비한

IN BRIEF Characterized by physical misery. Very unhappy, very bad

[+] terrible, abhorrent, nasty, nefarious, obnoxious, odious, repugnant

> This wretched weather gets me down.
> (이런 처량한 날씨는 나를 침울하게 한다.)

1993
yield [ji:ld]
v. 양보하다, 지다, 굴복하다[to]

IN BRIEF To give forth by a natural process, especially by cultivation

[+] give in, surrender, give way, succumb, cave in, capitulate

> She yielded to temptation and had another chocolate.
> (그녀는 유혹에 굴복하여 초콜릿을 하나 더 먹었다.)

1994
zenith [zí:niθ]
n. 천정(天頂), 정점, 절정(vertex)

IN BRIEF The highest point or state

[+] acme, apex, apogee, climax, crest, crown, culmination, height, meridian, peak, pinnacle, summit, top

> He is at the zenith of his political career.
> (그는 자기 정치 생활의 정점에 있다.)

1995
visceral [vísərəl]
a. 내장의; 노골적인; 본능적인(instinctive)

> The response was less analytical than visceral.
> (그 반응은 분석적이기 보다 본능적이었다.)

1996
vie [vai]
경쟁하다 → 겨루다 → 다투다(compete)

IN BRIEF To work to beat another

[+] compete, contend, contest, emulate, rival, conflict

> The $500 million-blockbuster "Avatar" is vying for four honors at this weekend's Oscar awards.
> (5억 달러의 막대한 돈이 든 영화 '아바타'는 이번 주말에 있을 오스카 시상식에서 4개 부문에서 상을 받으려고 경쟁하고 있다.)

1997
vital [váitl]
a. 필수적인, 매우 중요한(critical); 생명의; 생생한; 치명적인

IN BRIEF Essential to maintain life

[+] essential, important, necessary, key, basic, significant, critical, radical, crucial, fundamental, urgent,

> Gold is not vital to human existence; it has, in fact, relatively few practical uses.
> (금이 인간의 삶에 매우 중요한 것은 아니다. 그것은 사실 실용적 용도가 비교적 적은 편이다.)

1998
vociferous [vousífərəs]
a. 시끄러운 → 큰소리의 → 떠들썩한

IN BRIEF Loud and noisy in making one's feelings known

[+] loud, insistent, blatant, boisterous, clamorous, obstreperous, strident
[−] quiet, silent

> The student was extremely vociferous in declaring the winner of the match.
> (그 학생은 시합의 승자를 선언할 때 매우 큰 소리로 말했다.)

1999
volition [voulíʃən]
n. 의지(력), 결단(력)

IN BRIEF A choice or decision made by the will; discretion

[+] determination, purpose, resolve, will, agency

> She left entirely of her own volition.
> (그녀는 전적으로 자진해서 떠났다.)

2000
voluble [váljəbəl]
말이 유창한 → 입심 좋은 → 혀가 잘 돌아가는

[+] chatty, conversational, garrulous, loquacious, talkative
[−] mute, taciturn, uncommunicative

> His voluble style works well on TV.
> (그의 말 잘하는 스타일이 TV에서 효과가 좋다.)

PART 02

독논주보

(독해·논리·주제별 보카니오)

001. 줄(이)다 중요단어

- lessen 적게 하다, 줄이다
- decline 쇠퇴·하락하다, 거절하다
- diminish 줄이다, 감소시키다
- dwindle 점차 감소하다
- curtail 줄이다, 삭감하다
- retrench 단축하다, 절감·긴축하다
- slash 대폭 삭감하다, 혹평하다
- abate 감소시키다, 줄이다
- reduce 줄이다, 축소하다 중요단어
- reductionism (리덕셔니즘) 환원주의; 복잡한 데이터·현상을 단순하게 환원하려는 이론

002. 약화시키다·약화되다 중요단어

- debilitate 약화시키다
- devitalize 약화시키다
- incapacitate 무능력하게 하다
- wither 시들다, 약해지다
- enervate 약화시키다
- unnerve 무기력하게 하다
- enfeeble 약화시키다
- attenuate 가늘게·약하게 하다
- extenuate 줄여주다, 경감하다
- languish 나른해지다, 약해지다
- wane (쇠)약해지다

003. (가치를) 떨어뜨리다 중요단어

- degrade 격하·좌천·강등시키다
- depreciate 가치가 떨어지다
- devalue 가치를 떨어뜨리다
- demote 격하·강등시키다
- abase 지위·품격을 떨어뜨리다
- debase 품질·가치를 떨어뜨리다
- relegate 좌천시키다, 격하하다

004. 선언·공언하다

- pronounce 선언·단언하다
- enunciate 선언·발표하다
- proclaim 선언·선포하다
- profess 공언하다, 명백히 말하다
- predicate 단정·선언하다

005. 주장하다

- affirm 단언·확언·주장하다
- protest 단언·주장 항의하다
- declare 선언·단언하다
- allege 단언·주장하다
- assert 단언·주장하다
- persist 고집·주장하다, 지속하다
- contend 싸우다, 다투다, 주장하다

006. 강요하다

- constrain 강요하다
- enforce 시행·집행하다, 강요하다
- oblige 강제하다, 의무를 지우다
- compel 강요하다
- impel 재촉하다, 강요하다
- coerce 강제·강요하다
- intrude 강요, 침입, 참견
- obtrude 강요하다

007. 가능성 있는

- potential 가능한, 잠재하는
- latent 잠재하는
- dormant 잠자는, 휴지의, 잠재의
- plausible 그럴듯한(likely)
- feasible (실행) 가능한, 그럴듯한
- prospective 앞으로의, 가망성 있는

008. 강한·힘센·확고한

- mighty 강한, 힘센
- hardy 강한, 튼튼한
- firm 견고한, 확고한
- solid 견고한, 튼튼한
- steely 강철의, 단단한·냉혹한
- steadfast 확고한, 흔들리지 않는
- emphatic 강한, 강조된
- robust 강한, 튼튼한
- masculine 남자다운, 힘센
- muscular 근육의, 강한, 힘센
- stout 튼튼한, 견고한, 뚱뚱한
- staunch 견고한, 튼튼한
- virile 남자다운, 힘센, 강한

009. 어려운·힘드는

- demanding 힘드는, 어려운
- laborious 힘든, 어려운, 근면한
- strenuous 분투를 요하는
- arduous 어려운, 힘드는

010. 고통·고뇌·괴로움

- affliction 고통, 괴로움
- agony 고통, 고민, 고뇌
- anguish 고민, 고뇌, 고통
- angst 걱정, 고뇌
- torment 고통, 고뇌, 괴롭히다
- woe 고뇌, 괴로움, 고통

011. 신랄한·통렬한

- bitter 쓰라린, 혹독한, 신랄한
- acid 신맛의, 산성의, 신랄한
- acute 날카로운, 신랄한, 격심한, 급성의
- acrid 신랄한, 혹독한
- acrimonious 통렬한, 신랄한
- trenchant 날카로운, 통렬한
- incisive 날카로운, 신랄·통렬한
- poignant 날카로운, 신랄한
- pungent 날카로운, 신랄한

012. 역경·시련·어려움

- hardship 곤란, 어려움
- trial 시련, 고난, 시도, 재판
- adversity 역경, 시련
- ordeal 시련
- tribulation 고난, 시련
- crucible 시련

013. 곤경·궁지·여려움 [중요단어]

- cul-de-sac 막다른, 골목
- distress 고뇌, 고통, 곤궁, 곤란
- jam 곤란, 궁지
- impasse 막다른 골목, 곤경
- bind 곤경
- fix 곤경
- pinch 위기, 곤경
- plight 곤경, 궁지, 맹세, 서약
- predicament 곤경, 궁지
- quagmire 수렁, 곤경
- quandary 곤경, 난국
- difficulty 어려움, 곤경
- dilemma 궁지, 진퇴양난

014. 불안한·걱정스러운

- anxious 걱정스러운, 열망하는
- concerned 걱정스런, 관계하고 있는
- uneasy 불안한, 걱정되는
- apprehensive 걱정·염려하는

015. 칭찬하다

- applaud 박수치다, 칭찬하다
- laud 칭찬·칭송하다
- glorify 찬양·찬미하다
- commend 칭찬하다
- compliment 칭찬하다, 무료로 주다
- eulogize 칭찬·칭송하다
- exalt 높이다, 칭찬하다
- extol 칭찬·찬양하다

016. 고치다·변경하다

- remedy 고치다
- revise 교정·수정하다
- transform 변형시키다
- (a)mend 고치다, 수정하다
- vary 바꾸다, 변경하다
- alter 변경하다, 바꾸다
- modify 변경·수정하다
- rectify 개정·수정하다
- convert 전환·개조하다
- redress 바로잡다, 교정하다

017. 떼어놓다·멀어지게 하다 [중요단어]

- distance 멀어지게 하다
- dissociate 떼어놓다, 분리하다
- separate 떼어놓다, 멀어지게 하다
- sever 자르다, 떼어놓다
- detach 떼어내다, 분리하다
- estrange 떼어놓다, 멀어지게 하다
- alienate 소원케 하다, 양도하다
- insulate 격리하다, 고립시키다
- split 쪼개다 분리·이간시키다
- segregate 분리·격리하다
- seclude 차단·격리시키다
- sequester 격리하다, 은퇴시키다

018. 물러서다·후퇴하다

- recede 물러가다
- retreat 후퇴(하다)
- flee 달아나다, 도망치다
- flinch 도망치다, 꽁무니 빼다
- recoil 후퇴하다, 꽁무니 빼다
- abscond 도망치다, 자취를 감추다
- wince 주춤하다, 꽁무니 빼다

019. 관대한·너그러운

- beneficent 자선의, 관대한
- benevolent 자선의, 인자한
- generous 관대한, 풍부한
- liberal 관대한, 자유주의의, 교양의
- indulgent 관대한, 엄하지 않은
- lenient 너그러운, 관대한
- magnanimous 관대한, 도량이 큰
- lavish 아끼지 않는, 관대한, 낭비하는
- munificent 아낌없이 주는, 관대한

020. 친절한·상냥한 [중요단어]

- considerate 친절한, 신중한
- gracious 품위 있는, 정중한, 상냥한
- good-humored 상냥한, 사근한
- amiable 친근한, 상냥한
- amicable 우호적인, 친선의
- benign 친절·상냥한, 온화한, 양성의
- affable 상냥한, 사근한
- genial 친절한, 상냥한, 온화한

021. 사교적인·외향적인 [중요단어]

- sociable 사교적인
- outgoing 외향적인
- extrovert 외향적인
- gregarious 군거성의, 사교적인
- convivial 어울리기 좋아하는, 즐거운

022. 내성적인·수줍어하는 [중요단어]

- introvert 내성적인
- reserved 내향적인, 수줍은
- bashful 수줍어하는, 부끄럼타는
- timid 겁 많은, 내성적인, 수줍어하는

023. 겁 많은·소심한 [중요단어]

- coward(ly) 겁 많은, 소심한
- diffident 자신 없는, 소심한
- timid 겁 많은, 내성적인, 수줍어하는
- timorous 겁 많은, 소심한
- chickenhearted 겁 많은, 소심한
- fainthearted 소심한, 겁 많은

024. 호전적인·싸우기 좋아하는 [중요단어]

- warlike 호전적인
- militant 투쟁·전투적인
- argumentative 논쟁적인
- belligerent 호전적인
- bellicose 호전적인
- contentious 다투기 좋아하는
- pugnacious 싸움하기 좋아하는

025. 인위·인공적인

- artificial 인조의, 인공적인
- factitious 인위적인, 인공적인
- synthetic 합성의, 인조의
- manmade 인조의, 인공의

026. 능숙한·솜씨 있는 [중요단어]

- seasoned 경험이 많은; 능숙한
- skillful 숙련된, 능숙한
- handy 손재주 있는, 편리한, 가까이의
- proficient 익숙한, 능숙한
- ingenious 재간 있는, 창의적인
- adept 숙달한, 정통한
- deft 손재주 있는, 솜씨 좋은
- adroit 손재주가 있는
- dexterous 손재주 있는, 솜씨 있는
- versed 숙달한, 정통한, 조예 깊은
- knowing the ropes 능숙한

027. 솜씨 없는·서투른 [중요단어]

- inapt 서투른, 부적당한
- inept 서투른, 부적당한
- maladroit 서투른, 솜씨 없는
- clumsy 꼴사나운; 어색한, 서투른
- awkward 꼴사나운, 어색한, 서투른

028. (자세히) 설명하다

- depict 묘사·설명하다(describe)
- illuminate 해명하다, 명백히 하다
- manifest 명백히 하다
- narrate 이야기하다
- articulate 명료히 표현하다
- elucidate 해명·설명하다
- expound 상세히 설명하다
- specify 명기하다, 상술하다
- explicate 설명하다
- amplify 확대하다, 상세히 설명하다

029. 명백한·분명한 [중요단어]

- decode 해독하다 = 설명하다 = 명확
- definite 명확한
- distinct 별개의, 뚜렷한, 명확한
- evident 분명한, 명백한
- obvious 명백한, 분명한
- visible 가시의, 명백한
- manifest 명백한
- plain 평평한, 명백한, 솔직한
- transparent 투명한, 명백한
- pronounced 명백한, 뚜렷한
- lucid 빛나는, 명쾌한
- luminous 빛나는, 명쾌한
- articulate 명료한
- unequivocal 모호하지 않은, 명백한
- conspicuous 명백한, 현저·저명한
- perspicuous 명료한, 명쾌한
- explicit 명백한
- overt 명백한, 공공연한
- tangible 만져서 알 수 있는, 명백한
- palpable 매우 뚜렷한, 명백한

030. 모호한·불분명한 [중요단어]

- cloudy 흐린, 애매한
- indefinite 불분명한
- indistinct 뚜렷하지 않은
- obscure 불분명한, 모호한
- vague 막연한, 모호한
- ambiguous 모호한
- equivocal 불분명한, 모호한
- inarticulate 불명료한
- inexplicit 불명료한, 모호한
- intangible 만질 수 없는, 막연한
- impalpable 불분명한
- nebulous 성운의, 불명료한
- blurry 흐릿한

031. 순응·순종·복종·굴복하다

- obey 복종하다, 준수하다
- yield 굴복하다[to]; 산출하다
- comply 응하다, 따르다
- conform 순응하다, 따르다
- submit 복종·굴복하다[to]; 제출하다
- acquiesce 묵종하다, 따르다
- capitulate 항복하다
- succumb 굴복하다

032. 동의하다 [중요단어]

- assent 동의(하다)
- consent 동의(하다)
- accord 일치·조화하다
- concord 일치, 조화
- accede 동의하다, 응하다
- concur 동의·일치, 동시 발생
- unanimous 합의의, 만장일치의

033. 반대·불일치하다 [중요단어]

- [ ] oppose 반대하다, 이의를 제기하다
- [ ] object 반대하다
- [ ] dissent 의견을 달리하다, 불찬성하다
- [ ] discord 불일치(하다)
- [ ] diverge 의견이 갈라지다
- [ ] dissident 의견을 달리하는
- [ ] demur 반대하다, 이의를 말하다
- [ ] take exception to …에 반대하다
- [ ] take issue with 의견을 달리하다, 문제삼다

033. 저항·반항하다

- [ ] resist 저항·반항하다
- [ ] withstand 저항하다, 버티다
- [ ] rebel 모반·반역·반항하다
- [ ] defy 도전하다, 반항하다
- [ ] revolt 폭동·반란(을 일으키다)
- [ ] mutiny 폭동·반란(을 일으키다)

034. 논박·반박하다 [중요단어]

- [ ] contradict 반박하다, 모순되다
- [ ] disprove 반증·논박하다
- [ ] controvert 논쟁, 논박·부정
- [ ] refute 논박·반박하다
- [ ] confute 논박하다
- [ ] rebut 논박·반박하다
- [ ] retort 말대꾸하다, 반박하다
- [ ] gainsay 반박·부정하다
- [ ] impugn 논박하다, 비난하다

035. 부정·부인·거절하다

- [ ] decline 거절하다, 쇠퇴·하락하다
- [ ] reject 거절·부인하다(refuse)
- [ ] deny 부인·부정·거절하다
- [ ] negate 부정·부인하다
- [ ] repudiate 거절·부인하다

036. 강화·보강·지지하다 [중요단어]

- [ ] enhance 강화하다, 높이다
- [ ] fortify 강화하다
- [ ] intensify 세게 하다
- [ ] reinforce 강화·증강하다
- [ ] sustain 지탱·유지·부양·지지하다
- [ ] solidify 견고히 하다, 결속시키다
- [ ] consolidate 합병·통합 강화
- [ ] buttress 지지·보강하다
- [ ] prop 받치다, 지지·지원하다
- [ ] bolster 지지·보강하다
- [ ] bulwark 보루를 쌓다, 견고히 하다

037. 변호·옹호·지지하다 [중요단어]

- [ ] beef up 강화하다
- [ ] defend 방어·옹호·변론하다
- [ ] uphold 유지·지탱·지지하다
- [ ] advocate 변호·옹호·지지하다
- [ ] patronize 후원·후견·보호하다
- [ ] espouse 신봉하다, 지지하다
- [ ] plead 변호·변론하다, 탄원·간청하다
- [ ] prop up 지지하다

038. 창의·독창적인

- [ ] original 최초의, 독창적인
- [ ] inventive 발명의, 독창적인
- [ ] ingenious 재간 있는, 창의적인

039. 협력·협조하다 [중요단어]

- [ ] collaboration 함께 일하기, 협력
- [ ] collaborate 협력·협동·합작하다
- [ ] cahoot [kəhúːt] 공동; 공모
- [ ] cooperate 협력·협동하다
- [ ] ally 동맹·연합·제휴하다, 동맹국
- [ ] concert 협조·협정하다
- [ ] coalesce 합동·연합하다

040. 길조의·행운의

- [ ] fortunate 운이 좋은, 행운의
- [ ] favorable 호의적인, 유망한
- [ ] promising 장래성 있는, 유망한
- [ ] auspicious 길조의, 상서로운
- [ ] propitious 상서로운, 길조의

041. 불길한·나쁜 조짐의

- [ ] unfortunate 불운·불행한
- [ ] unfavorable 불리한, 불길한
- [ ] ominous 불길한, 나쁜 징조의
- [ ] sinister 불길한
- [ ] portentous 불길한, 흉조의

042. 시작·착수하다

- [ ] launch 진수시키다, 착수·시작하다
- [ ] initiate 시작·창시하다
- [ ] commence 개시·시작하다
- [ ] embark 착수·시작하다

043. 학살·살육(하다)

- [ ] holocaust 대학살
- [ ] butcher 도살·학살하다
- [ ] massacre 대량 학살(하다)
- [ ] carnage 대학살
- [ ] slaughter 도살·학살(하다)
- [ ] decimate 학살하다

044. 중재·조정하다

- [ ] coordinate 조정하다, 조화시키다
- [ ] intercede 중재·조정하다
- [ ] intervene 중재·개입하다
- [ ] interpose 중재·조정하다
- [ ] mediate 조정·중재하다

- [ ] intermediate 중재·중개하다
- [ ] arbitrate 중재·조정하다

045. 간섭·참견하다
- [ ] interfere 방해[with]; 간섭[in]
- [ ] intrude 강요, 침입, 참견
- [ ] meddle 간섭·참견하다
- [ ] butt in 간섭·참견하다
- [ ] tamper 참견하다, 간섭하다

046. 어기다·위반하다
- [ ] disobey 불복종하다, 어기다
- [ ] violate 위반·침해하다, 폭행하다
- [ ] breach 위반, 불이행
- [ ] infringe 어기다, 위반하다, 침해하다
- [ ] transgress 어기다, 위반하다, 넘다
- [ ] infract 어기다, 위반하다
- [ ] contravene 위반하다, 범하다

047. 침입·침략·침해하다
- [ ] invade 침략·침입하다
- [ ] trespass 침입·침해하다
- [ ] intrude 강요, 침입, 참견
- [ ] impinge 침범·침해하다
- [ ] encroach 침략·침입·침해하다

048. 공격·습격하다
- [ ] attack 공격하다
- [ ] raid 습격·급습·공습(하다)
- [ ] onslaught 공격, 맹습
- [ ] assail 맹공하다, 습격하다
- [ ] assault 습격·급습(하다)

049. 꾸미다·장식하다
- [ ] ornament 꾸미다, 장식하다
- [ ] adorn 꾸미다, 장식하다(decorate)
- [ ] embellish 미화·장식하다
- [ ] garnish 장식하다, 꾸미다

050. 실질적인·상당한
- [ ] considerable 상당한, 중요한
- [ ] significant 의미심장한, 상당한
- [ ] sizable 상당히 큰, 상당히, 많은
- [ ] substantial 실체의, 실질적인, 상당한
- [ ] hefty 무거운, 상당한, 많은

051. 진실한·성실한
- [ ] genuine 진짜의, 진실한
- [ ] heartfelt 진심에서 우러난(hearty)
- [ ] sincere 성실한, 진실한
- [ ] bonafide 진실한, 성실한
- [ ] cordial 진심의, 성심의
- [ ] unfeigned 거짓 없는, 진실한
- [ ] veracious 진실의, 진실한

052. 솔직한
- [ ] candid 솔직한
- [ ] plain 평평한, 명백한, 솔직한
- [ ] flat 평평한, 단조로운, 단호한
- [ ] straightforward 똑바른, 솔직한
- [ ] outright 솔직한, 노골적인
- [ ] outspoken 솔직한, 노골적인
- [ ] unreserved 기탄없는, 솔직한

053. 순진한
- [ ] innocent 죄 없는, 결백한, 순진한
- [ ] artless 꾸밈없는, 순진한
- [ ] naive 소박한, 순진한
- [ ] ingenuous 순진한, 솔직한
- [ ] credulous 속기 쉬운, 잘 믿는
- [ ] gullible 잘 속는

054. 괴롭히다 중요단어
- [ ] pick on 괴롭히다
- [ ] torture 고문하다, 괴롭히다
- [ ] annoy 화나게 하다, 괴롭히다
- [ ] distress 괴롭히다
- [ ] afflict 괴롭히다, 시달리게 하다
- [ ] agonize 괴롭히다
- [ ] crucify 몹시 괴롭히다
- [ ] excruciate 몹시 괴롭히다, 고문하다
- [ ] harass 괴롭히다
- [ ] persecute 박해하다, 괴롭히다
- [ ] pester 괴롭히다, 시달리게 하다
- [ ] plague 괴롭히다
- [ ] torment 고통, 고뇌, 괴롭히다
- [ ] molest 괴롭히다, 못살게 굴다
- [ ] tease 괴롭히다, 졸라대다

055. 회복·복구·복원시키다
- [ ] resilience 회복력
- [ ] snap back 원상태로 돌리다
- [ ] restore 복직·복위·복구시키다
- [ ] reestablish 복직·복구·회복시키다
- [ ] retrieve 되찾다, 회복하다, 구출하다
- [ ] reinstate 회복·복위·복직시키다
- [ ] restitute 복구·회복시키다
- [ ] rehabilitate 복귀·복구·복직시키다
- [ ] convalesce 건강을 회복하다

056. 덧없는·무상한·순식간의 중요단어
- [ ] momentary 순식간의, 덧없는
- [ ] evanescent 순간의, 덧없는
- [ ] transient 덧없는, 무상한
- [ ] transitory 덧없는, 무상한
- [ ] ephemeral 하루살이의, 덧없는
- [ ] fleeting 잠시의, 무상한, 덧없는
- [ ] fugitive 도망하는, 덧없는, 일시적인

057. 일시적인·임시의

- [ ] temporary 일시적인, 임시의
- [ ] tentative 시험적인, 임시의
- [ ] provisional 일시·잠정적인
- [ ] interim 당분간의, 임시의

058. 영원한·영속하는

- [ ] (ever)lasting 영원한, 영속하는
- [ ] eternal 영원한, 영구한
- [ ] durable 영속성 있는
- [ ] enduring 참을성 있는, 영구적인
- [ ] permanent 영속하는
- [ ] persistent 고집 센, 영속하는
- [ ] perennial 사철의, 영구한
- [ ] perpetual 영속하는, 영원한
- [ ] immortal 불사의, 불멸의
- [ ] immutable 불변의
- [ ] imperishable 불멸의, 불사의
- [ ] abiding 영구적인

059. 끊임없는

- [ ] consecutive 연속적인(successive)
- [ ] ceaseless 끊임없는
- [ ] unceasing 끊임없는
- [ ] incessant 끊임없는
- [ ] uninterrupted 중단되지 않은

060. 과장하다·과장된

- [ ] exaggerate 과장하다
- [ ] overrate 과대 평가하다
- [ ] overstate 과장하다, 허풍떨다
- [ ] bluff 허세부리다, 속이다
- [ ] grandiloquent 과장된
- [ ] hyperbolic 과장적인
- [ ] bombastic 과장한, 허풍떠는

061. 근접한·가까운 [중요단어]

- [ ] neighboring 이웃의, 인근의
- [ ] proximate 가까운, 근접한
- [ ] adjacent 이웃의, 인접한
- [ ] adjoining 인접한, 이웃의
- [ ] contiguous 접촉·인접하는

062. 전염의·쉽게 옮기는

- [ ] communicable 전달의, 전염성의
- [ ] contagious 전염성의, 옮기 쉬운
- [ ] infectious 전염성의, 옮기 쉬운
- [ ] catching 전염성의, 매력 있는

063. 섞다·혼합하다

- [ ] blend 섞다, 혼합하다
- [ ] compound 혼합·합성하다
- [ ] synthesize 종합·합성하다
- [ ] mingle 섞다, 혼합하다

064. 합병·통합하다 [중요단어]

- [ ] combine 결합·연합·합병하다
- [ ] incorporate 통합·합병하다
- [ ] consolidate 합병·통합·강화
- [ ] annex 부가·첨부하다, 합병하다
- [ ] merge 병합·합병하다
- [ ] fuse 융합·연합하다
- [ ] meld 혼합·융합하다
- [ ] amalgamate 합병·융합하다

065. 위조·날조하다 [중요단어]

- [ ] falsify 위조하다, 속이다
- [ ] counterfeit 위조·모조(하다)
- [ ] fake 위조·날조하다
- [ ] forge 위조·모조·날조하다
- [ ] fabricate 꾸며내다, 위조하다
- [ ] concoct 날조하다, 꾸미다
- [ ] feign 가장하다, 꾸며대다
- [ ] simulate 흉내내다, 가장하다

066. 무수한·셀 수 없는

- [ ] incalculable 헤아릴 수 없는
- [ ] immeasurable 측정불가의, 광대한
- [ ] inestimable 측정·평가할 수 없는
- [ ] interminable 끝없는, 무한한
- [ ] infinite 무한한, 무수한, 끝없는
- [ ] (in)numerous 무수한, 수많은
- [ ] innumerable 셀 수 없는, 무수한
- [ ] myriad 무수한

067. 거대한·막대한

- [ ] gargantuan 엄청난
- [ ] enormous 거대한, 막대한
- [ ] gigantic 거대한
- [ ] huge 거대한, 막대한
- [ ] vast 광대한, 막대한
- [ ] colossal 거대한, 어마어마한
- [ ] immense 거대한, 막대한, 광대한
- [ ] bulky 부피가 큰, 거대한

068. 넓은

- [ ] spacious 넓은, 광대한
- [ ] capacious 널찍한, 큼직한
- [ ] extensive 광대한, (폭)넓은
- [ ] ample 넓은, 충분한, 풍부한
- [ ] commodious 넓은, 편리한

069. 무거운

- [ ] weighty 무거운, 중요한
- [ ] massive 무거운, 육중한
- [ ] hefty 무거운, 상당한, 많은
- [ ] ponderous 무거운, 묵직한

070. 놀라게 하다
- amaze 몹시 놀라게 하다
- alarm 놀래다
- scare 깜짝 놀라게 하다, 위협하다
- stun 대경 실색케 하다
- astonish 깜짝 놀라게 하다
- astound 몹시 놀라게 하다
- startle 깜짝 놀라게 하다
- dumbfound 깜짝 놀라게 하다
- petrify 석화시키다 (깜짝 놀라게 하다)
- stupefy 마비시키다 (깜짝 놀라게 하다)
- frighten 놀라다
- be taken aback 깜짝 놀라다

071. 편리한·편의의·편안한
- convenient 편리한
- handy 손재주 있는, 편리한, 가까이의
- commodious 넓은, 편리한
- expedient 편리한, 편의의
- portable 휴대용의, 간편한
- facile 쉬운, 편리한
- cozy 포근한, 아늑한
- snug 아늑한, 안락한(comfortable)

072. 협박하다·무섭게 하다
- threaten 위협·협박하다
- frighten 위협하다
- horrify 무섭게 하다
- terrify 무섭게[겁나게] 하다
- appall 오싹·질겁하게 하다
- intimidate 협박·위협하다
- menace 위협·협박하다

073. 탓으로 돌리다 중요단어
- blame(for) ~탓으로 돌리다
- attribute(to) ~탓으로 돌리다, 속성
- accredit(with) ~의 공으로 돌리다
- impute(to) ~탓으로 돌리다
- ascribe(to) ~탓으로 돌리다

074. 도움이 되는·유용한
- serviceable 쓸모 있는, 유용한
- instrumental 수단·도움이 되는
- contributory 기여 하는, 도움이 되는
- conducive 도움이 되는, 이바지하는

075. 헛된·무익한·효과 없는
- fruitless 결과·효과 없는(unfruitful)
- vain 헛된, 무익한
- futile 효과 없는, 쓸데없는
- void 쓸모없는, 무효의, 없는, 결여된
- abortive 유산의, 실패의, 헛된

076. 다산의·다작의·비옥한 중요단어
- productive 생산적인, 다산의
- fruitful 다산의, 결실을 많이 맺는
- fructuous 다산의, 결실이 많은
- fertile 다산의, 비옥한, 기름진
- luxuriant 다산의, 기름진, 무성한
- prolific 다산·다작의, 비옥한

077. 불모의·불임의·메마른 중요단어
- infertile 메마른, 불모·불임의
- barren 불모·불임의
- sterile 불임·불모의, 살균한
- arid 건조한, 메마른, 불모의

078. 간헐적인·산발적인 중요단어
- intermittent 때때로 중단되는
- sporadic 때때로 일어나는
- irregular 불규칙한
- periodic 이따금의, 간헐적인
- occasional 가끔식, 때때로
- spasmodic 경련(성)의, 간헐적인, 산발적인

079. 소집·소환하다
- convene 소집·소환하다
- summon 소환·소집하다
- convoke 소집하다
- congregate 모이다, 집합하다
- muster 소집하다, 집합하다

080. 축적하다·쌓다
- accumulate 축적하다
- amass 쌓다, 축적하다
- pile 더미 쌓다
- stack 더미 쌓다
- heap 더미 쌓다
- garner 모으다, 저축하다 중요단어
- accrue 모으다, 축적하다(accumulate)
- agglomerate 모으다, 덩어리로 만들다
- aggregate 집합하다, 모이다
- cumulate 쌓다, 집적하다(amass)
- hive 저축하다, 모으다
- pile up 축적하다, 쌓이다
- roll up 긁어모으다
- reap 거둬들이다 중요단어

081. 모이다·모으다
- assemble (한데) 모으다, 조립하다
- compile 수집하다
- aggregate 모이다, 총계의
- congregate 모이다, 모으다
- converge 모이다, 집중·수렴하다
- flock 떼 짓다, 모이다
- cluster 떼 짓다, 밀집하다

082. 해산·해체·분해하다

- disassemble 해체·분해하다
- dismantle 분해·해체하다
- disperse 흩뜨리다, 퍼뜨리다
- disband 해산하다

083. 확산·유포·보급시키다

- scatter 흩뿌리다, 퍼뜨리다
- popularize 대중화하다
- publicize 광고·선전하다
- circulate 퍼뜨리다, 유포시키다
- diffuse 확산·보급시키다
- disperse 흩뜨리다, 퍼뜨리다
- disseminate 흩뿌리다, 퍼뜨리다
- propagate 번식시키다, 퍼뜨리다
- promulgate 공포하다, 퍼뜨리다

084. 분배·배분·할당하다

- distribute 분배·배분하다
- dispense 분배하다
- assign 할당·배당하다
- allocate 할당·배분하다
- allot 할당·배당하다
- apportion 배분·할당하다

085. 비슷한·유사(한) 중요단어

- parallel 평행의, 유사한 중요단어
- comparable 유사한, 비슷한
- akin 혈족·동족의, 유사한, 비슷한
- kindred 혈연(의); 유사한, 동종의
- analogous 유사한, 닮은
- semblance 유사, 상사, 닮음
- similitude 유사, 상사, 비슷함
- affinity 밀접·유사성, 애호, 기호

086. 같은·동등한 중요단어

- even 같은, 동일한, 대등한
- equivalent 동등한, 상당하는
- identical 동일한
- synonymous 같은 것을 의미하는
- coordinate 동등한, 대등한
- commensurate 같은 (정도의)
- tantamount 동등한, 같은

087. 다른·상이한 중요단어

- dissimilar 다른(different)
- variant 다른, 상이한
- disparate 다른, 같지 않은
- divergent 분기·발산하는, 다른

088. 동시에 일어나는

- concurrent 동시 발생의, 일치하는
- coinciding 동시 발생의, 일치하는
- accompanying 동반·수반하는
- synchronous 동시에 일어나는
- simultaneous 동시에 일어나는
- concomitant 동시에 일어나는
- contemporaneous 동시 발생의

089. 일치·조화하는 중요단어

- harmonious 조화된
- accordant 일치하여(concordant)
- corresponding 상응·일치하는
- consistent 일관된, 일치하는
- concurrent 일치하는, 동시 발생의
- coinciding 일치하는, 동시 발생의
- coherent 응집성의, 일관된
- reconcilable 일치시킬 수 있는
- compatible 양립할 수 있는
- consonant 일치·조화하여
- congenial 같은 성질의
- congruous 일치하는(congruent)
- consort ~와 어울리다·일치하다

090. 불일치 하는·모순된 중요단어

- asymmetry 비대칭, 불균형
- conflicting 모순·상충되는
- contradictory 모순된, 논박의
- inconsistent 일치하지 않는
- discordant 일치·조화하지 않는
- irreconcilable 모순되는
- incompatible 양립할 수 없는
- dissonant 조화되지 않는
- ambivalent 양면가치의, 상충되는
- incongruous 조화되지 않는
- discrepant 어긋나는, 모순된

091. 회상·회고하다

- recall 상기하다
- recollect 회상·기억하다
- retrospect 회고·회상하다
- reminisce 추억하다

092. 편협·편파적인 중요단어

- biased 치우친, 편향적인
- partial 부분적인, 편파적인
- prejudiced 선입관의
- insular 섬의, 고립된, 편협한
- tendentious 편파·편향적인
- hidebound 야윈, 편협한

093. 공정한·공평한 중요단어

- neutral 중립적인
- disinterested 공평한, 사심 없는
- impartial 공평한, 치우치지 않는 중요단어
- evenhanded 공평한, 공정한
- unprejudiced 선입관 없는, 공평한
- unbiased 편견 없는, 공평한
- equitable 공정한, 공평한

- square 정사각형의, 공명정대한
- detached 분리된, 공평한, 초연한
- above board 공명정대하게

094. 호기심이 강한
- curious 호기심이 강한
- questioning 캐묻는, 의심하는
- inquisitive 호기심이 강한
- prying 캐묻기 좋아하는
- snoopy 기웃거리는, 이것저것 캐묻는

095. 무관심한·무감각한
- insensitive 무감각한, 둔감한
- unconcerned 관심·관계가 없는
- indifferent 무관심한, 냉담한
- callous 무감각한, 냉담한
- apathetic 무감각한, 냉담한
- impassive 무감각한, 냉정한

096. 중단하다·중단시키다
- discontinue 그만두다, 중단하다
- terminate 끝내다, 종결짓다
- pause 잠시 멈추다
- cease 그치다, 그만두다
- halt 멈추다(stop)
- interrupt 가로막다, 중단시키다
- intermit 일시 멈추다, 중단시키다
- punctuate 구두점, 강조, 중단
- suspend (일시) 중지하다
- abort 유산하다, 중지시키다

097. 시끄러운·떠들썩한
- blatant 떠들썩한, 시끄러운
- obtrusive 강요하는, 주제넘은, 눈에 띄는
- obvious 명백한, 빤히 보이는
- obstreperous 소란한, 시끄러운
- strident 귀에 거슬리는
- deafening 귀청이 터질 것 같은
- clamorous 떠들썩한, 시끄러운
- vociferous 시끄러운, 떠들썩한
- boisterous 떠들썩한, 거친, 사나운
- uproarious 시끄러운, 떠들썩한

098. 조용한·침묵의
- calm 고요한, 조용한, 평온한
- pacific 평온한, 태평한
- tranquil 조용한, 고요한, 평온한
- serene 고요한, 조용한, 침착한
- placid 평온한, 조용한
- quiescent 정지한, 침묵의
- mute 무언의, 침묵의
- hushed 조용한, 고요한
- tacit 무언의, 암묵·묵시적인
- taciturn 말 없는, 과묵한(quiet, reserved)
- reticent 과묵한

099. 침착한·차분한·냉정한
- composed 침착한, 차분한
- dispassionate 냉정한, 공평한
- sober 맑은, 정신의, 냉정한
- imperturbable 침착한, 냉정한
- sedate 차분한, 침착한

100. 위험하게 하다
- endanger 위험에 빠뜨리다
- destabilize 불안정하게 하다
- jeopardize 위태롭게 하다
- imperil 위태롭게 하다

101. 위험한·불안정한 중요단어
- precarious 불확실한, 위험한
- unstable 불안정한(unsteady)
- uncertain 불확실한
- insecure 불안정한, 위태로운
- shaky 흔들리는, 불확실한
- hazardous 모험적인, 위험한
- perilous 위험한, 모험적인
- speculative 사색의, 투기의, 위험한
- wobbly 흔들거리는, 동요하는, 불안정한

102. 확실하게 하다
- ensure 확실하게 하다(assure, insure)
- secure 안전·확실하게 하다
- confirm 확실하게 하다
- certify 증명·보증하다
- ascertain 확인하다
- corroborate 확실하게 하다
- endorse 배서, 보증, 시인
- vouch 보증·보장하다(guarantee)
- warrant 정당화하다, 보증하다

103. 허락·승인하다
- approve 찬성·승인하다
- validate 유효하게 하다, 비준하다
- permit 허락·허가하다(admit)
- grant 승인·인정하다, 주다
- underwrite 서명하다, 승낙하다
- concede 양보·용인·승인·인정
- cede 양도하다, 양보하다
- sanction 재가·인가·시인하다
- ratify 승인·비준·재가하다

104. 약속·맹세·서약(하다)
- swear 맹세하다, 욕하다[at]
- vow 맹세·서약(하다)(promise)
- plight 맹세(pledge), 약혼(하다), 곤경, 궁지
- pledge 맹세(하다)
- oath 맹세, 서약
- covenant 계약, 서약(contract)

105. 정확한·틀림없는
- accurate 정확한(precise)
- unfailing 확실한, 틀림없는
- infallible 틀림없는, 확실한
- unerring 잘못이 없는, 정확한

106. 식별·분간·구별하다
- differentiate 구분 짓다, 차별하다
- distinguish 구별·식별하다
- discriminate 식별·분간하다
- discern 식별·분간하다
- demarcate 분리·구별하다

107. 잘못된·틀린·무근한 중요단어
- spurious 그럴듯한, 가짜의 중요단어
- awry 잘못된, 틀린(distorted)
- distorted 비뚤어진, 곡된
- crooked 구부러진, 굴곡된
- false 그릇된, 거짓의, 가짜의
- faulty 결점이 있는, 불완전한
- fallacious 그릇된, 오류의
- defective 결점·결함이 있는
- erroneous 잘못된, 틀린
- baseless 근거 없는
- ungrounded 근거 없는(groundless)
- unfounded 근거 없는

108. 흠 없는·죄 없는 중요단어
- faultless 결점이 없는
- spotless 오점이 없는, 흠 없는
- stainless 때 끼지 않는, 흠 없는
- flawless 흠 없는, 완벽한
- irreproachable 흠잡을 데 없는
- unblemished 흠·결점 없는
- immaculate 오점·결점 없는
- innocent 죄 없는, 결백한, 순진한
- guiltless 죄 없는, 결백한
- inculpable 죄 없는, 결백한

109. 아름다운·장관의
- pictorial 그림 같은, 아름다운
- picturesque 그림 같은, 아름다운
- gorgeous 멋진, 근사한
- scenic 경치의, 아름다운
- spectacular 구경거리의, 장관의
- splendid 화려한, 멋진
- exquisite 아주 아름다운, 절묘한

110. 장엄한·장대한
- grand 웅장한, 웅대한
- grandiose 웅장한, 웅대한
- magnificent 장엄한, 장대한
- majestic 장엄한, 장대한
- sublime 장엄한, 웅대한, 숭고한
- stately 위엄 있는, 위풍당당한
- august 위엄 있는, 존엄한

111. 고귀한·고상한
- noble 고귀한, 숭고한
- ennobled 고귀한, 고상한
- lofty 매우 높은, 고상한
- dignified 존엄 있는, 고귀한
- high-minded 고매한, 고결한
- virtuous 덕 있는, 고결한
- elevated 높은 고상한, 고결한
- exalted 높은, 고귀한

112. 불쌍한·천한·야비한
- lowly 지위가 낮은, 천한
- tragic 비극적인, 비참한
- mean 천한, 초라한, 비열한
- menial 시시한, 천한
- piteous 불쌍한, 비참한(pitiable)
- miserable 불쌍한, 비참한
- humble 겸손한, (비)천한, 초라한
- pathetic 감상적인, 불쌍한, 슬픈
- wretched 비참한, 불쌍한, 야비한
- abject 비천한, 비열한
- servile 노예(근성)의, 비굴한
- subservient 도움이 되는, 비굴한

113. 비탄·개탄하다
- sigh 한숨쉬다, 한탄하다
- deplore 비탄·개탄하다
- grieve 몹시 슬퍼하다
- wail 울부짖다, 한탄하다
- lament 비탄·한탄하다
- mourn 슬퍼하다, 한탄하다
- moan 한탄하다, 슬퍼하다

114. 슬퍼하는
- woeful 슬픈, 괴로워하는
- deplorable 통탄할
- grievous 통탄할, 슬픈
- lamentable 유감·한탄스러운
- mournful 슬픔에 잠긴
- moanful 슬퍼하는
- doleful 서글픈, 슬픈
- pathetic 감상적인, 불쌍한, 슬픈
- pensive 생각에 잠긴, 시름의, 슬픈
- disconsolate 서글픈, 비탄에 잠긴

115. 낙담한·우울한 중요단어
- melancholy 우울한(blue)
- discouraged 낙담·낙심한
- disheartened 낙담·낙심한
- depressed 의기소침한, 불경기의
- dejected 낙심한
- gloomy 어두운, 우울한 중요단어

- despondent 의기소침한, 낙담한
- morose 시무룩한, 침울한

116. 즐거운·기쁜

- joyous 기쁜, 즐거운(joyful)
- merry 명랑한, 즐거운
- agreeable 기분 좋은, 상냥한
- ecstatic 황홀한
- gay 명랑한, 즐거운
- festive 축제의, 즐거운
- jubilant 기뻐하는, 즐거워하는
- blithe 즐거운, 기쁜
- elated 의기양양한, 매우 기쁜
- rapt 넋이 나간, 황홀한 열중·몰두한
- rapturous 기뻐 날뛰는
- exultant 크게 기뻐하는, 환희의
- hilarious 유쾌한, 즐거운

117. 기뻐하다·기쁘게 하다

- delight 기쁘게 하다, 기뻐하다
- gladden 기쁘게 하다
- rejoice 기쁘게 하다, 기뻐하다
- enrapture 황홀하게[기쁘게] 하다
- exult 크게 기뻐하다
- exhilarate 기분 좋게 하다

118. 축복·은총·기쁨

- blessing 은총, 축복
- bliss 기쁨, 행복
- benediction 축복
- boon 혜택, 은총, 이익
- rapture 황홀, 환희(ecstasy)
- felicity 기쁨, 행복

119. 만족·충족시키다 = 일치 〔중요단어〕

- meet 만족·충족시키다
- suffice 만족·충족시키다
- content 만족시키다
- gratify 만족시키다, 기쁘게 하다
- satiate 만족시키다, 물리게 하다

120. 불평·불만(하다) = 불일치 〔중요단어〕

- complain 불평하다
- moan 투덜거리다, 불평하다
- grumble (about) 투덜거리다, 불평하다
- grievance 불평, 불만
- grouch 투덜대다, 토라지다
- grump 불평하다, 툴툴거리다(뿌루퉁해지다)
- whine 푸념하다, 투덜대다(우는 소리하다)

121. 축하·기념하다

- celebrate 축하하다
- commemorate 기념·축하하다
- congratulate 축하하다
- memorialize 기념하다, 기리다
- fete 경축·축하하다, 축제
- felicitate 축하하다
- solemnize (식 올려서) 축하하다

122. 감독·관리하다

- direct 지도·지시·감독하다
- supervise 감독·관리하다
- superintend 감독·관리하다
- surveil 감시·감독하다
- overlook 감독[감시]하다
- oversee 감독, 감시하다

123. 결혼의·혼인의

- marital 결혼의, 부부의
- wedded 결혼한, 부부의
- matrimonial 결혼의, 부부의
- conjugal 부부의, 혼인의
- connubial 결혼(생활)의, 부부의
- hymeneal 결혼의, 혼인의(nuptial)
- spousal 결혼의(matrimonial), 혼례의(nuptial)
- celibate 미혼(독신)남자(bachelor)
- spinster 미혼 여성

124. 경쟁하다·다투다

- compete 경쟁하다, 겨루다
- contest 다투다, 겨루다
- struggle 분투하다, 싸우다
- contend 싸우다, 다투다, 주장하다
- vie 다투다, 경쟁하다
- emulate 경쟁하다, 겨루다, 흉내내다
- rival ~와 경쟁하다, 서로 겨루다

125. 박식한·박학한

- learned 박학한, 박식한
- scholarly 학자의, 박식한
- omniscient 전지의, 박식한
- erudite 박학한, 박식한
- lettered 학문[교양, 문학적 소양]이 있는
- well-informed 박식한, 견문이 넓은

126. 무지한·무식한

- illiterate 무식한, 문맹의
  Unable to read and write. (읽을 수 없다.)
  Having little or no formal education.
  (정규 교육을 거의 혹은 전혀 받지 않은 것.)
- unlearned 배우지 않은
- nescient 무지한, 모르는
- ignorant 무식한, 무지한
- uneducated 교육을 받지 못한, 무식한
- uninstructed 무식한, 교육받지 못한
- unschooled 학교 교육[훈련]을 받지 않은, 타고난(natural)
- an unschooled talent 타고난 재능
- untaught 배우지 않은, 무지한

127. 현학적인·아는 체하는

- [ ] **bookish** 학자인 체하는, 현학적인 (pedantic)
- [ ] **pedantic** 아는 체하는, 현학적인 〔중요단어〕
- [ ] **pedagogic** 교육학의, 아는 체하는
- [ ] **academic** 학구적인, 공론(空論)의
- [ ] **donnish** 격식을 차린
- [ ] **formalistic** 형식주의의(형식에 지나치게 집착하는)
- [ ] **literary** 문학적인, 학문상의
- [ ] **scholastic** 학자티를 내는, 현학적인, 형식적인

128. 선견지명의·예지의 〔중요단어〕

- [ ] **insightful** 통찰력이 있는
- [ ] **farsighted** 원시의, 선견지명의
- [ ] **prospective** 앞으로의, 선견지명의
- [ ] **prescient** 미리 아는, 선견지명의
- [ ] **provident** 선견지명의, 절약하는

129. 아끼는·절약하다

- [ ] **economize** 절약하다(save)
- [ ] **spare** 용서하다, 아끼다, 할애하다
- [ ] **retrench** 단축하다·절감·긴축하다
- [ ] **pinch** 꼬집다, 압박하다, 절약하다
- [ ] **trim** (깎아) 다듬다 깎다, 삭감하다
- [ ] **thrifty** 검약하는, 아끼는
- [ ] **frugal** 절약하는
- [ ] **provident** 선견지명의, 절약하는
- [ ] **austere** 엄한, 금욕적인, 평이한(plain)

130. 구두쇠의·인색한

- [ ] **stingy** 인색한, 너무 아끼는, 깍쟁이의
- [ ] **miserly** 구두쇠의, 인색한
- [ ] **penny-pinching** 인색한
- [ ] **parsimonious** 인색한
- [ ] **niggardly** 인색한
- [ ] **costive** 쩨쩨한, 우유부단한
- [ ] **hard fisted** 인색한, 무자비한
- [ ] **penurious** 가난한, 궁핍한, 인색한(stingy)
- [ ] **petty** 마음이 좁은, 좀스러운, 인색한
- [ ] **pinch** 몹시 절약하다, 인색하게 굴다(on)
- [ ] **pinch and save** [scrape] 인색하게 굴어 돈을 모으다
- [ ] **pinch pennies** 지출을 극도로 줄이다
- [ ] **tightfisted** 인색한, 구두쇠의
- [ ] **mean** 인색한, 쩨쩨한, 비열한

131. 낭비하는·낭비하다 〔중요단어〕

- [ ] **luxurious** 사치스러운, 호화로운
- [ ] **wasteful** 낭비적인, 소모성의
- [ ] **lavish** 아끼지 않는, 관대한, 낭비하는
- [ ] **extravagant** 낭비하는, 지나친
- [ ] **thriftless** 낭비하는
- [ ] **prodigal** 낭비하는, 방탕한
- [ ] **squander** 낭비·탕진하다

132. 번영·번성하다 〔중요단어〕

- [ ] **flourish** 번창·융성하다(flour)
- [ ] **prosper** 번영·번창하다
- [ ] **thrive** 번영·번성하다
- [ ] **grow** 발달[발전]하다 / 재배하다(cultivate)
- [ ] **boom** 좋아지다, 폭등하다
- [ ] **score** (이익) 얻다, 올리다;〈성공을〉거두다
    The play scored a great success. (연극은 대성공이었다.)

133. 고갈·소진시키다

- [ ] **deplete** 비우다, 고갈시키다
- [ ] **exhaust** 다 써버리다, 고갈시키다
- [ ] **drain** 배수하다, 소모·고갈시키다
- [ ] **fatigue** 피곤·피로하게 하다
- [ ] **impoverish** 저하시키다(사람의 질·능력·활기)
- [ ] **enervate** 약화시키다, 기운[힘]을 빼앗다 (weaken)
- [ ] **use up** 다 써버리다, 소모시키다 (consume)
- [ ] **sap** 활력을 잃게 하다(수액을 짜내다)

134. 지치지 않는·끈기 있는

- [ ] **indefatigable** 지치지 않는
- [ ] **untiring** 지치지 않는(tireless)
- [ ] **patient** 참을성 있는 환자
- [ ] **enduring** 참을성 있는, 영구적인
- [ ] **tolerant** 참을성 있는, 관대한
- [ ] **perseverant** 참을성 있는
- [ ] **unflagging** 지칠 줄 모르는

135. 용감한·대담한 〔중요단어〕

- [ ] **brave** 용감한(courageous)
- [ ] **daring** 대담한, 용감한
- [ ] **audacious** 대담한(bold)
- [ ] **intrepid** 용맹한, 대담한
- [ ] **dauntless** 겁 없는(undaunted)
- [ ] **gallant** 용감한
- [ ] **valiant** 용맹스런, 용감한(valorous)
- [ ] **chivalrous** 용감하고, 예의바른

136. 예의바른·공손한 〔중요단어〕

- [ ] **mannerly** 예절 바른
- [ ] **respectful** 공손한, 정중한
- [ ] **courteous** 예의 바른(polite)
- [ ] **civil** 시민의, 예의 바른, 정중한
- [ ] **genteel** 가문이 좋은, 점잖은(gentle)
- [ ] **obeisant** 정중한, 공손한
- [ ] **decent** 예절 바른, 점잖은

137. 부지런한·열심인

- [ ] **industrious** 근면한(diligent)
- [ ] **laborious** 힘든, 열심인, 근면한
- [ ] **painstaking** 수고를 아끼지 않는
- [ ] **studious** 면학에 힘쓰는
- [ ] **assiduous** 부지런한, 근면한
- [ ] **sedulous** 근면한, 부지런한

138. 게으른·나태한, 느린

- faineant 게으른, 나태한
- inert 둔한, 완만한, 활발치 못한, 느린(inactive)
- idle 한가한, 나태한(lazy)
- sluggish 느린, 게으른
- slothful 나태한, 게으른
- indolent 게으른, 나태한
- tardy 더딘, 느린, 지각한
- lazy 게으른, 나태한
- sluggard 게으른, 굼뜬
- shiftless 무능한, 무기력한; 게으른

139. 노력(하다)·애쓰다

- labor 노동(하다); 노력(하다)
- struggle 분투하다, 싸우다
- strive 노력하다, 애쓰다
- toil 애쓰다, 수고하다, 노고, 수고
- endeavor 노력(하다)
- exert 쓰다, 노력하다[oneself]
- strain 힘껏 노력하다, 애쓰다

140. 연기·연장·지연하다

- extend 늘이다, 연장하다, 넓히다
- elongate 연장하다, 늘이다
- prolong 늘이다, 연장하다
- protract 길게 하다, 연장하다
- delay 늦추다, 미루다, 연기하다
- postpone 연기하다(put off)
- defer 연기하다, 미루다
- retard 늦추다, 지연시키다
- procrastinate 미루다, 지연시키다

141. 열렬한·열광적인

- passionate 열렬한, 격렬한
- enthusiastic 열렬한, 열광적인
- ardent 불타는, 열렬한
- zealous 열광적인, 열심인
- intense 강한, 격렬한, 열정적인
- fanatic(al) (열)광적인
- feverish 열이 있는, 열광적인
- fervent 뜨거운, 열렬한
- fervid 타오르는 듯한, 열렬한
- fiery 불같은, 사나운, 열렬한
- vehement 격렬한, 열렬한, 열정적인
- impetuous 맹렬, 격렬한, 성급한

142. 열망·갈망하다

- anxious 걱정하는, 열망하는
- eager 열망하는, 열성적인
- impatient 성급한, 갈망하는
- long 열망·갈망하다
- crave 열망·갈망하다
- yearn 동경하다, 열망하다
- aspire 열망하다
- covet 탐내다, 갈망하다
- lust 갈망·열망(하다)

143. 만성적인·뿌리깊은 중요단어

- habitual 습관·상습적인
- deep-seated 뿌리 깊은, 고질적인
- chronic 오래된, 만성적인, 상습적인
- inveterate 뿌리 깊은, 만성의
- ingrained 깊이 배어든, 뿌리 깊은
- embedded 깊숙이 박힌

144. 활기찬·힘찬·활발한

- energetic 정력적인, 활기찬
- vivid 활발한, 힘찬(vital)
- vivacious 활기찬, 활발한(lively)
- animate(d) 살아 있는, 활기찬
- spirited 힘찬, 생기 있는
- vigorous 정력적인, 활기 있는
- brisk 활발한, 활기 있는

145. 활기 없는·불 활발한

- inactive 활발하지 않은
- dull 무딘, 둔한, 단조로운, 활발치 못한
- inanimate 생명이 없는, 활기 없는
- weary 피곤한, 지친(fatigued)
- sluggish 느린, 활발치 못한, 게으른
- slack 늘어진, 힘없는, 활발치 못한
- lackluster 광택이 없는, 활기 없는
- languid 나른한, 활발치 못한
- languorous 나른한, 노곤한
- inert 활발치 못한
- torpid 움직이지 않는, 활발치 못한

146. 졸리는·나른한 중요단어

- dozy 졸리는
- drowsy 졸리는, 나른한, 활기가 없는
- dormant 잠자는, 휴지의, 잠재의
- hypnotic 최면(성)의
- somnolent 졸리는, 졸리게 하는
- somniferous 최면의, 졸리게 하는

147. 혼수상태의

- comatose 혼수상태의, 몹시 졸리는
- lethargic 혼수상태의, 무기력한
- stuporous 혼수의, 인사불성의
- insensible 무감각한, 무관심의
- unconscious 무의식의, 모르는
- lifeless 생명이 없는
- listless 마음이 없는, 열의 없는, 무관심한
- phlegmatic 냉담한, 느릿한,
- sluggish 게으른, 나태한

148. 평가·사정·계산하다

- estimate 평가·추정하다
- evaluate 평가·사정하다

- rate 평가하다
- value 평가하다, 존중하다
- compute 계산하다, 평가하다
- reckon 계산하다, 판단하다(calculate)
- appraise 값을 매기다, 평가하다
- assess 사정·평가하다

149. 선별·선택하다

- select 고르다(choose)
- opt 선택하다
- adopt 채용·채택하다, 입양하다
- sort 분류하다, 가려내다[out]
- assort 유형별로 분류하다(classify)
- screen 가리다, 심사·선발하다[out]
- single 골라내다, 선발하다[out]
- filtrate 거르다, 여과하다(filter)
- sift 체 치다, 선별하다, 정밀 조사하다

150. 다양한·다재다능한, 다방면의

- diverse 다양한(diversified)
- assorted 종류대로 분류된(classified)
- varied 다양한(various)
- manifold 가지각색의(multifold)
- multifarious 가지각색의, 잡다한
- multitudinous 다수의, 많은 다양한
- miscellaneous 잡다한, 갖가지의
- sundry 갖가지의, 잡다한
- versatile 다재다능한, 융통성있는
- all-around [다방면]에 걸친; 전면적인; 만능의
- many-sided 다방면의[에 걸친], 다재다능한
- multifaceted 다방면의[에 걸친], 다재다능한
- protean 다방면의, 혼자서 여러 역할을 하는
- proteus
  【그리스신화】 Proteus신의[같은]
  【그리스신화】 프로테우스
  (자유자재로 변신하고 예언의 힘을 가졌던 바다의 신)
- various 여러 가지의, 다방면의

151. 감동적인·감동시키다

- moving 움직이는, 감동적인
- touching 감동적인
- impressive 감명을 주는, 인상적인
- imprint 찍다, 감명시키다
- impassion 감동·감격시키다

152. 심사숙고하다 중요단어

- Weigh 심사숙고하다, 비교·검토하다
- deliberate 숙고하다
- meditate 명상·숙고하다
- speculate 사색하다, 투기하다
- contemplate 심사숙고하다
- weigh 무게 달다, 심사숙고하다
- ponder 숙고하다, 깊이 생각하다
- pensive 생각에 잠긴
- think about 깊이 생각하다

- muse 명상·숙고하다
- chew 깊이 생각하다, 심사숙고하다
- cogitate 생각하다, 숙고하다
- sleep on 골똘히 생각하다(dwell on)

153. 신중한·주의 깊은 중요단어

- considerate 친절한, 신중한
- alert 경계·조심하는
- cautious 조심성 있는, 신중한
- attentive 주의 깊은(prudent)
- heedful 주의 깊은, 조심하는
- circumspect 조심성 있는, 신중한
- advertent 주의 깊은
- vigilant 자지 않고 지키는, 경계하는
- conscientious 양심적인, 신중한
- scrupulous 양심적인, 신중한
- meticulous 너무 신중한, 꼼꼼한
- wary 조심성 있는, 신중한
- punctual 시간 엄수의, 꼼꼼한
- exhaustive 철저한, 소모적인 중요단어

154. 현명한·분별 있는 중요단어

- sensible 분별 있는, 현명한 중요단어
- judicious 분별 있는, 신중한
- sage 현명한, 현자, 현인
- sagacious 현명한, 영리한
- sapient 슬기로운, 지혜로운
- discreet 분별 있는, 신중한
- agile 민첩한, 예민한, 머리 회전이 빠른

155. 부주의한·경솔한 중요단어

- hasty 성급한, 경솔한
- impatient 성급한, 갈망하는
- imprudent 경솔한(thoughtless)
- inconsiderate 분별없는, 경솔한
- inattentive 부주의한, 태만한
- impulsive 충동적인, 감정에 끌린
- rash 무분별한, 경솔한
- reckless 무분별한, 무모한, 경솔한
- heedless 부주의한, 조심성 없는
- inadvertent 부주의한, 우연의
- indiscreet 지각없는, 경솔한

156. 태만의·게을리 하는

- negligent 태만한, 부주의한
- omissive 게을리 하는, 빠뜨리는
- delinquent 태만의, 비행의, 체납의
- derelict 버려진, 포기된, 직무태만의
- remiss 태만한, 게으리하는
- default 태만·불이행 (하다)

157. 예언·예측하다

- forecast 예상·예측하다(foretell)
- foresee 예견하다
- prophesy 예언하다(predict)

- anticipate 예기·예상·고대하다
- prognosticate 예지·예언하다

158. 교훈적인·교육적인
- informative 정보 제공의, 유익한
- instructive 교육적인, 교훈적인
- didactic 교훈적인, 설교적인

159. 훈계·설교·경고하다
- caution 경고하다(warn, alert)
- admonish 훈계·권고하다
- preach 설교하다
- sermonize 설교·훈계하다
- censure 비난하다, 나무라다
- chide 꾸짖다(scold), 비난하다
- reprimand 호되게 꾸짖다
- reproach 비난하다, 나무라다
- reprove 꾸짖다, 비난하다; 훈계하다

160. 주저하는·머뭇대는
- indecisive 우유부단한
- irresolute 결단력 없는
- unwilling 내키지 않는
- hesitant 주저하는, 머뭇대는
- reluctant 꺼리는, 내키지 않는
- disinclined 하고 싶지 않은
- indisposed 내키지 않는
- lingering 오래 끄는, 망설이는

161. 주저하다·망설이다
- linger 꾸물거리다, 망설이다
- hesitate 주저하다, 머뭇거리다
- scruple 주저하다, 꺼리다
- waver 흔들리다, 주저하다
- balk 방해하다, 망설이다, 머뭇대다
- vacillate 흔들리다, 망설이다

162. 무료의
- free 무료의(for nothing)
- complimentary 칭찬의, 무료의
- gratis 무료의
- gratuitous 무료의
- on the house 공짜의

163. 민감한·쉽게 영향받는 중요단어
- sensitive 민감한, 예민한
- impressionable 감수성이 강한
- susceptible 민감한·쉽게 영향받는
- vulnerable 상처·공격받기 쉬운

164. 증가하다·증가시키다
- boost 증가시키다, 후원하다
- augment 증가·증대시키다
- multiply 증가·증식·번식시키다
- proliferate 증식·번식·증가하다
- surge 급격히 오르다, 급등
- soar 급상승하다, 폭등하다
- wax 커지다, 증가하다

165. 확대하다·넓히다
- enlarge 크게 하다, 확대하다
- expand 넓히다, 확장하다(extend)
- escalate (차츰) 확대하다, 올리다
- magnify 확대하다
- aggrandize 크게 하다, 확대하다
- amplify 확대하다, 상세히 설명하다
- dilate 넓히다, 팽창시키다

166. 잉여의·과잉의
- redundant 여분의, 잉여의, 장황한
- superfluous 여분의, 남아도는
- supernumerary 여분의, 남는
- surplus 나머지의, 잔여의, 과잉의

167. 지나친·과도(한)
- far-fetched 터무니없는 중요단어
- excessive 과도한, 지나친
- undue 과도한, 부당한, 부적합한
- exorbitant 지나친, 터무니없는
- extravagant 지나친, 터무니없는
- immoderate 무절제한, 지나친
- intemperate 무절제한, 지나친
- inordinate 지나친, 과도한
- surfeit 지나침, 과도
- steep 가파른, 심한, 지나친

168. 불합리한·우스꽝스런
- unreasonable 불합리한
- inconceivable 상상할 수도 없는
- ridiculous 우스꽝스러운
- absurd 불합리한, 우스꽝스러운
- ludicrous 어이없는, 우스꽝스러운
- preposterous 앞뒤가 뒤바뀐, 불합리한
- unproven 증명할 수 없는 중요단어

169. 풍부한·가득한 중요단어
- enriched 풍요한, 풍부한
- sufficient 충분한
- plentiful 많은, 풍부한
- generous 관대한, 풍부한
- abundant 풍족한, 많은
- affluent 풍부한, 풍족한
- ample 넓은, 충분한, 풍부한
- copious 풍부한
- opulent 부유한, 풍부한
- replete 충만한, 가득한
- saturated 가득한, 충만한
- fraught 충만한
- profuse 풍부한, 넘치는

- exuberant 풍부한, 넘치는
- rife 충만한, 가득한
- teeming 풍부한, 충만한

170. 부족(한)·결핍(된) 중요단어
- deficient 부족한(insufficient)
- lacking 부족한, 모자라는
- wanting 모자라는, 결핍한
- scarce 부족한, 모자라는
- scant(y) 부족한, 모자라는
- sparse 희박한, 드문드문한
- meager 메마른, 빈약한, 결핍한
- void 쓸모없는, 무효의 없는, 결여된
- devoid 결여된, …이 없는
- destitute 결핍한, 없는, 빈곤한
- dearth 부족, 결핍
- rarity 진기, 희귀

171. 범람시키다·쇄도하다
- flood 범람시키다
- inundate 범람·침수시키다
- deluge 범람시키다
- submerge 물에 빠지게 하다

172. 유행·성행·만연하는
- current 현재의, 통용되는, 유행하는
- widespread 널리 퍼진, 만연된
- prevailing 널리 유행하는
- prevalent 유행·널리 보급된, 만연된
- pervasive 널리 퍼진, 성행하는
- epidemic 유행하는, 전염병
- rampant 유행하는, 만연하는
- universal 보편·일반적인
- ubiquitous 어디에나 있는, 편재하는
- fad (일시적) 유행, 열광
- vogue 대유행
- craze 열광, 대유행
- rage 격노, 격정, 열망, 일시적 대유행

173. 지역 고유의
- endemic 풍토성의, 그 지방 특유의
- indigenous 토착의, 지역 고유의
- local 지방의, 그 지방 특유의
- native 토착의, 원주민의
- inborn 타고난, 천부의
- inherent 본래의, 타고난; 선천적인(in)
- innate 타고난, 선천적인
- intrinsic 본질적인, 고유의(inherent)

174. 말 많은·장황한
- chatty 수다스러운(talkative, wordy)
- lengthy 긴 장황한
- redundant 여분의, 잉여의, 장황한
- loquacious 수다스러운, 말 많은
- verbose 말이 많은, 장황한
- prolix 말이 많은, 장황한
- garrulous 말이 많은, 수다스러운

175. 가난한·파산한
- penniless 무일푼의
- needy 가난한, 궁핍한
- necessitous 가난한, 필수적인
- destitute 결핍한, 없는, 빈곤한
- impoverished 가난하게 된
- impecunious 돈 없는, 가난한
- indigent 궁핍한, 빈곤한
- bust 파산한(bankrupt, broke)
- insolvent 파산한, 지불 능력이 없는
- delinquent 태만의, 비행의, 체납의
- beggarly 거지 같은, 빈털터리의
- down-and-out 무일푼의
- penurious 가난한, 궁핍한

176. 약한·깨지기 쉬운
- fragile 부서지기 쉬운, 약한
- frail 무른, 연약한, 허약한
- brittle 부서지기·깨지기 쉬운
- feeble 연약한, 허약한
- tenuous 얇은, 희박한, 빈약한
- flimsy 얇은, 연약한, 박약한

177. 의심하는·의심하다 중요단어
- distrust 의심하다(suspect, doubt)
- skeptical 의심 많은, 회의적인
- suspicious 의심 많은, 의심하는
- dubious 의심하는, 의심스러운
- incredulous 의심 많은

178. 이상한·기이한
- rare 드문, 진기한, 희박한
- extraordinary 이상한, 특이한
- abnormal 비정상적인
- anomalous 변칙적인, 예외적인
- atypical 전형적이지 않은
- eccentric 별난, 괴벽스러운
- outlandish 이국풍의, 기이한
- exotic 이국적인, 색다른, 외국산의
- odd 홀수의, 임시의, 이상한
- grotesque 괴상한, 괴기한
- bizarre 괴상한, 이상한
- weird 이상한, 기묘한
- quaint 기이한, 기묘한
- queer 기묘한, 괴상한
- aberrant 비정상적인, 이상한
- normal 정상의 중요단어

179. 독특한·고유한
- individual 개개의, 개인의, 독특한
- distinctive 특유한, 차이가 나는
- peculiar 독특·특유한, 기묘·이상한

- [ ] idiosyncratic 특유한(unique)

180. 처벌·징계하다

- [ ] discipline 훈련·단련하다, 징계하다
- [ ] chasten 처벌·징벌하다
- [ ] chastise 벌하다, 혼내다
- [ ] castigate 징계하다, 벌주다
- [ ] penalize 벌을 주다(punish)

181. 보답·보상하다

- [ ] reward 보답·보상하다
- [ ] compensate 보상·배상하다
- [ ] recompense 보답·보상하다
- [ ] reciprocate 보답하다, 보복하다
- [ ] reimburse 변제·변상·배상하다
- [ ] indemnify 보상·배상하다
- [ ] remunerate 보상·보답하다

182. 보복(하다)

- [ ] revenge 복수, 보복
- [ ] vengeance 복수, 앙갚음
- [ ] avenge 복수를 하다
- [ ] retaliate 보복하다
- [ ] reciprocate 보답하다, 보복하다
- [ ] retribution 보복, 응징

183. 암시하다·함축적인

- [ ] suggest 암시·시사하다
- [ ] imply 내포·함축하다
- [ ] implicate 연루시키다, 내포·함축하다
- [ ] implicit 함축·암시적인, 맹목적인
- [ ] allude 암시하다, 시사하다(hint)
- [ ] tacit 무언의, 암묵·묵시적인
- [ ] insinuate 암시하다, 넌지시 비치다

184. 증명·입증하다

- [ ] attest 증명·입증하다, 증언하다
- [ ] testify 증명·입증하다, 증언하다
- [ ] prove 입증·증명하다
- [ ] substantiate 구체화하다, 실증하다
- [ ] verify 증명·입증하다
- [ ] authenticate 증명하다
- [ ] vindicate (정답·결백을) 입증하다

185. 검사·조사하다

- [ ] analyze 분석하다
- [ ] examine 검사·조사하다
- [ ] investigate 조사하다
- [ ] explore 탐험·답사, 탐구·조사
- [ ] inspect 점검·검사하다
- [ ] diagnose 진단하다
- [ ] anatomize 해부하다, 분석하다
- [ ] dissect 절개·해부하다, 분석하다
- [ ] interrogate 심문하다, 질문하다
- [ ] scrutinize 세밀히 조사하다
- [ ] sift 체 치다, 선별하다, 정밀 조사하다
- [ ] probe 검사하다
- [ ] overhaul 분해·검사하다
- [ ] fathom 수심을 측정하다, 간파하다

186. 이해하다·파악하다

- [ ] comprehend 이해하다, 포함하다
- [ ] apprehend 체포, 이해, 걱정
- [ ] appreciate 인정·인식·감상·감사하다
- [ ] perceive 지각·인지하다, 이해하다
- [ ] interpret 해석하다, 이해하다
- [ ] grasp 움켜잡다, 이해하다
- [ ] construe 해석하다, 파악하다
- [ ] savvy 이해하다, 기지·재치(의)
- [ ] fathom 수심을 측정하다, 간파하다

187. 배신(의)·배반하다

- [ ] betray 배반하다
- [ ] renegade 변절·배반·배신하다
- [ ] traitorous 반역의, 배반의
- [ ] treacherous 배반·반역하는
- [ ] treason 반역, 배신
- [ ] perfidious 불성실한, 배반의

188. 감사의

- [ ] grateful 감사하는(thankful)
- [ ] appreciative 감사하는
- [ ] obliged 감사하는
- [ ] indebted 빚지고 있는, 신세를 진

189. 반복하다

- [ ] repeat 되풀이하다
- [ ] reiterate 되풀이하다
- [ ] recapitulate 반복하다, 요약하다
- [ ] recur 재발하다, 반복되다

190. 중요한·중대한

- [ ] vital 활기찬, 힘찬, 극히 중대한
- [ ] critical 비판적인, 결정적인
- [ ] crucial 결정적인, 중대한
- [ ] consequential 결과적인, 중대한
- [ ] momentous 중대한, 중요한
- [ ] principal 주요한, (단체의) 장
- [ ] grave 중대한, 무덤
- [ ] weighty 무거운, 중대한
- [ ] cardinal 주요한, 중요한, 진홍색의
- [ ] pivotal 중추적인

191. 의무·필수·강제적인

- [ ] essential 본질적인, 필수적인
- [ ] compulsive 강제적인(compulsory)
- [ ] coercive 강제적인
- [ ] mandatory 강제적인, 필수적인

- [ ] obligatory 의무적인, 필수의
- [ ] binding 구속력이 있는, 의무적인
- [ ] requisite 필요한, 필수적인
- [ ] necessitous 가난한, 필수적인
- [ ] indispensable 필수적인
- [ ] imperative 필수적인

192. 긴급한·임박한

- [ ] pressing 긴급한, 급박한
- [ ] urgent 긴급한, 다급한
- [ ] imminent 절박한, 촉박한
- [ ] impending 절박한, 박두한
- [ ] pending 임박한, 미결정된

193. 작은·미세한

- [ ] minimal 극소의(minimum)
- [ ] tiny 작은
- [ ] microscopic 현미경의, 미세한
- [ ] diminutive 소형의, 작은
- [ ] minute 작은, 미세한, 사소한, 하찮은

194. 하찮은·사소한

- [ ] subsidiary 부차적인, 자회사
- [ ] peripheral 주변의, 중요하지 않은 중요단어
- [ ] footnotes 부차적인 존재(각주) 중요단어
- [ ] subordinate 부수적인 중요단어
- [ ] minor 소수의, 중요하지 않은, 미성년
- [ ] slight 약간의 하찮은, 시시한
- [ ] negligible 무시해도 좋은, 하찮은
- [ ] petty 작은, 사소한(petit)
- [ ] trivial 하찮은, 사소한
- [ ] trifling 하찮은, 사소한
- [ ] paltry 하찮은, 보잘것없는

195. 미해결된·현안의

- [ ] unsettled 미해결의
- [ ] outstanding 눈에 띄는, 미해결된
- [ ] pending 임박한, 미결정된, 현안의
- [ ] moot 토론의, 여지가 있는, 미결정의

196. 요약·개괄하다

- [ ] summarize 요약·개괄하다
- [ ] abstract 추상적인, 요약·발췌하다
- [ ] abbreviate 생략·단축하다
- [ ] abridge 요약하다
- [ ] compress 압축하다, 요약하다
- [ ] condense 압축하다, 요약하다
- [ ] epitomize 요약하다
- [ ] recapitulate 요약하다
- [ ] synopsize 요약·개요하다

197. 간결한·간명한

- [ ] brief 짧은, 간결한(short)
- [ ] compact 꽉 들어찬, 간결한, 소형의
- [ ] concise 간결한, 간명한
- [ ] curt 간략한, 짧은, 무뚝뚝한
- [ ] terse 간결한, 간명한
- [ ] succinct 간결한, 간명한
- [ ] laconic 간결한, 간명한

198. 정복하다·복종시키다

- [ ] overthrow 뒤엎다, 정복·전복하다
- [ ] subvert 전복하다, 파괴하다
- [ ] subject 복종·종속시키다
- [ ] subordinate 종속·복종시키다
- [ ] subdue 정복하다(conquer, defeat)
- [ ] vanquish 정복하다, 패배시키다
- [ ] subjugate 정복하다, 복종시키다
- [ ] rout 패주시키다

199. 이기다·압도하다

- [ ] overpower 이기다, 압도하다
- [ ] dominate 지배하다, 위압하다
- [ ] predominate 지배하다, 우세하다
- [ ] overcome 이기다, 극복하다
- [ ] surmount 극복하다, 이겨내다
- [ ] overwhelm 압도하다, 당황하게 하다
- [ ] prevail 이기다, 극복하다, 유행하다
- [ ] daunt 위압하다, 기세를 꺾다

200. 정지한·움직이지 않는

- [ ] immobile 정지의(motionless)
- [ ] still 조용한, 정지한
- [ ] stagnant 정체된, 불경기의
- [ ] static 정적인, 정지한, 정전기의
- [ ] stationary 정지한, 주둔한
- [ ] quiescent 정지한, 침묵의

201. 면제의·면역의·특권의

- [ ] immune 면역의, 면제된
- [ ] exempt 면제하다, 면제된
- [ ] privileged 특권의
- [ ] prerogative 특권(을 가진)

202. 숨기다·감추다

- [ ] secrete 비밀로 하다, 숨기다
- [ ] conceal 숨기다, 감추다
- [ ] veil 감추다, 숨기다(hide, mask)
- [ ] camouflage 위장(하다)
- [ ] disguise 변장·위장(하다)
- [ ] cloak 뒤덮다, 은폐하다
- [ ] mantle 덮다, 가리다, 숨기다

203. 폭로하다·누설하다

- [ ] reveal 드러내다, 폭로하다
- [ ] expose 노출시키다, 폭로하다
- [ ] disclose 드러내다, 노출시키다
- [ ] unmask 폭로하다(uncover)

- [ ] unveil 베일을 벗기다, 밝히다
- [ ] unearth 발굴 밝혀내다, 폭로하다
- [ ] leak 새게 하다, 누설하다
- [ ] divulge 누설하다, 폭로하다
- [ ] uncloak 폭로하다, 밝히다

204. 복잡한·난해한·심오한

- [ ] complicated 복잡한
- [ ] abstract 추상적인, 심오한, 난해한
- [ ] intricate 얽힌, 복잡한
- [ ] perplexing 당황하게 하는, 복잡한
- [ ] profound 심오한, 난해한
- [ ] recondite 심오한, 난해한
- [ ] labyrinthine 미로[미궁]의, 복잡한
- [ ] abstruse 난해한, 심오한

205. 헤아릴 수 없는·불가해한

- [ ] incomprehensible 이해할 수 없는
- [ ] mysterious 신비한, 불가사의한
- [ ] enigmatic 수수께끼 같은
- [ ] subtle 미묘한, 이해하기 어려운
- [ ] inscrutable 헤아릴 수 없는
- [ ] unfathomable 헤아릴 수 없는
- [ ] impenetrable 헤아릴 수 없는
- [ ] occult 신비스러운, 불가해한

206. 비밀의·은밀한

- [ ] classified 분류된, 기밀의
- [ ] undercover 비밀의(secret)
- [ ] confidential 기밀의, 비밀의
- [ ] privy 비밀의, 개인적인(private)
- [ ] intimate 친밀한, 개인적인, 사적인
- [ ] covert 은밀한, 비밀의
- [ ] stealthy 몰래하는, 비밀의
- [ ] furtive 몰래하는, 비밀의
- [ ] clandestine 은밀한, 비밀의

207. 표면적인·피상적인 중요단어

- [ ] superficial 표면상의, 피상적인
- [ ] cosmetic 화장의, 표면적인
- [ ] shallow 얕은, 피상적인
- [ ] specious 외양만의, 겉만 그럴듯한
- [ ] cursory 서두르는, 피상적인
- [ ] perfunctory 형식적인, 피상적인
- [ ] coarse 조잡한, 거친(crude)
- [ ] shoddy 겉만 번지르르한, 싸구려의
- [ ] ostensible 표면상의, 허울만의

208. 명목상의·이름만의

- [ ] honorary 명예상의, 직함만의
- [ ] nominal 이름만의, 명목상의
- [ ] titular 이름만의

209. 피하다

- [ ] sidestep 회피하다
- [ ] evade (회)피하다(avoid, escape)
- [ ] elude 피하다, 회피하다
- [ ] duck 피하다, 회피하다
- [ ] dodge 확 피하다
- [ ] avert 피하다(averse, aversion)
- [ ] shun 피하다, 멀리하다
- [ ] eschew 피하다, 삼가다

210. 포기하다·단념하다

- [ ] abandon 포기·단념하다(quit)
- [ ] desert (저)버리다
- [ ] resign 사직하다, 포기하다
- [ ] despair 절망·자포자기(하다)
- [ ] discard 버리다
- [ ] forsake (저)버리다
- [ ] relinquish 그만두다, 포기하다
- [ ] renounce 포기·단념하다
- [ ] desist 그만두다, 단념하다
- [ ] disclaim 버리다, 포기하다
- [ ] surrender 포기하다
- [ ] forgo 포기하다, 삼가다

211. 삼가다·절제하다

- [ ] abstain 삼가다, 절제하다
- [ ] refrain 그만두다, 삼가다
- [ ] forbear 참다(endure, tolerate)
- [ ] persevere 인내하다, 참다
- [ ] contain 포함하다, 억누르다, 참다

212. 금지시키다

- [ ] ban 금지하다
- [ ] (de)bar 금하다
- [ ] prohibit 금지하다
- [ ] inhibit 금하다, 못하게 하다
- [ ] dissuade 단념시키다
- [ ] deter 단념시키다
- [ ] outlaw 금지하다, 무법자
- [ ] restrain 제지·금지시키다
- [ ] interdict 금지하다, 막다

213. 막다·방해하다

- [ ] obstruct 막다, 방해하다
- [ ] preclude 막다, 방해하다(prevent)
- [ ] interfere 방해하다, 간섭하다
- [ ] impede 방해하다
- [ ] hinder 방해하다
- [ ] encumber 방해하다, 막다
- [ ] hamper 방해하다, 훼방놓다
- [ ] balk 방해하다, 망설이다, 머뭇대다
- [ ] stymie 방해하다
- [ ] thwart 훼방하다, 방해하다

214. 제한·억제·속박하다

- [ ] confine 한정·제한하다

- restrict 제한·한정하다
- oppress 압박·억압하다
- suppress 억압·억제하다(repress)
- withhold 보류하다, 억제하다
- bridle 마구·구속·속박하다(curb)
- fetter 족쇄·속박·구속(하다)
- leash 속박하다, 억제하다

215. 해방하다·풀어주다
- liberate 자유롭게 하다(free)
- release 풀어놓다, 해방하다
- unbind 풀다(unchain, untie)
- emancipate 해방·석방하다
- unleash 풀다, 자유롭게 하다

216. 빼앗다·박탈하다
- dispossess 빼앗다
- seize 붙잡다, 빼앗다, 강탈하다
- deprive 빼앗다, 박탈하다
- rob 강탈하다, 빼앗다
- bereave 앗아가다
- strip 벗기다, 빼앗다, 박탈하다(rip)
- snatch 잡아채다, 강탈하다
- extort 강탈하다
- divest 빼앗다, 박탈하다
- usurp 빼앗다, 강탈하다

217. 지우다·삭제하다
- eliminate 제거·삭제하다(rid)
- delete 삭제하다, 지우다
- erase 지우다, 삭제하다
- remove 제거·삭제하다
- obliterate 지우다
- efface 지우다, 삭제하다
- expunge 지우다, 삭제하다
- censor 검열(삭제)하다

218. 파괴하다
- ruin 파멸시키다, 황폐하게 하다
- demolish 파괴하다(destroy)
- smash 때려부수다, 박살내다
- shatter 산산이 부수다, 파괴하다
- desolate 황폐시키다, 황량한, 쓸쓸한
- devastate 황폐화시키다
- raze 완전히 파괴하다
- level 평평하게 하다, 파괴하다
- wreck 난파·조난·파괴(시키다)
- havoc 파괴·황폐화(하다)
- ravage 유린하다, 파괴하다
- blot out 지우다, 파괴·섬멸하다

219. 약탈하다
- despoil 약탈하다
- depredate 약탈하다
- loot 전리·약탈품, 약탈하다
- plunder 약탈하다, 노략질하다
- ransack 샅샅이 뒤지다, 약탈하다
- pillage 약탈하다, 강탈하다
- ravage 약탈하다, 파괴하다
- sack 약탈하다

220. 근절·박멸·절멸하다
- outroot 근절시키다(uproot)
- annihilate 전멸·절멸시키다
- eradicate 박멸·근절하다
- exterminate 근절·절멸하다
- extinguish 끄다, 절멸·멸종시키다

221. 손상하다·해치다
- damage 손해·피해(를 입히다)
- injure 상처 입히다, 손상시키다
- spoil 망치다, 상하게 하다
- disfigure (외관을) 손상하다
- deface 더럽히다, 손상시키다
- undermine 손상·훼손하다
- impair 손상시키다, 해치다(harm)
- mar 흠가게 하다, 망쳐놓다
- derogate (가치를) 훼손·손상하다
- traumatize 상처 입히다, 충격을 주다

222. 흠·오점·더럽히다
- fault 결점, 흠 과실, 잘못
- defect 결점, 결함, 흠
- shortcoming 결점, 단점
- stain 얼룩, 때, 오점, 흠, 더럽히다
- spot 반점, 얼룩, 오점, 더럽히다
- blot 얼룩, 때, 오점, 흠 더럽히다
- blemish 흠, 오점, 손상하다, 더럽히다
- flaw 흠, 약점, 결함
- blunder 큰 실수(error, fiasco)

223. 완전한·완벽한
- whole 전체의, 완전한
- integral 완전한, 빠져서는 안 될
- intact 손대지 않은, 완전한
- plenary 완전한(perfect), 절대적인
- consummate 완성하다, 완전한

224. 최고의·최상의
- prime 제1의, (가장) 중요한
- premier 수상 1위의, 첫째의
- supreme 최고의, 최상의
- superb 최고의, 최상의
- superlative 최고의, 최상의
- paramount 최고의, 가장 중요한
- top-notch 일류의, 최고의
- stellar 일류의, 아주 우수한

225. 신속한·즉시의
- [ ] momentary 순식간의, 덧없는
- [ ] immediate 즉각·즉시의
- [ ] instant(aneous) 즉시·즉석의
- [ ] swift 빠른, 신속한(rapid)
- [ ] prompt 빠른, 신속한
- [ ] fleet 빠른, 신속한

226. 음모·공모하다
- [ ] conspire 공모하다
- [ ] collude 공모하다
- [ ] scheme 계획(하다); 음모(하다)
- [ ] plot 음모(하다); 계획(하다)

227. 유리한·득이 되는
- [ ] gainful 이득이 있는(beneficial)
- [ ] rewarding 할 만한 가치가 있는
- [ ] lucrative 득 되는, 수지맞는(profitable)
- [ ] paying 이득이 있는, 수지맞는

228. 건강에 좋은·위생적인
- [ ] healthful 건강에 좋은
- [ ] salutary 건강에 좋은
- [ ] wholesome 건강에 좋은, 건강한
- [ ] salubrious 건강에 좋은
- [ ] sanitary 위생의, 위생적인
- [ ] hygienic 위생적인
- [ ] sterile 무익한, 불모의, 살균한 [중요단어]

229. 인사하다·환영하다
- [ ] welcome 환영하다
- [ ] salute 인사·경례하다, 맞이하다
- [ ] acclaim 갈채·환호하다
- [ ] hail 환호해 맞이하다
- [ ] greet 인사하다, 환영하다
- [ ] hospitable 환대·후대하는

230. 미친
- [ ] lunatic 정신이상의
- [ ] demented 미친(mad, crazy)
- [ ] insane 제정신이 아닌, 미친

231. 오래된·낡은·늙은
- [ ] outmoded 구식의(outdated)
- [ ] antiquated 오래된, 낡은(antique)
- [ ] aged 늙은(old, elderly)
- [ ] senile 노쇠한, 나이 많은
- [ ] superannuated 늙은 낡은
- [ ] ragged 남루한, 초라한
- [ ] shabby 초라한, 낡아빠진

232. 젊은·새로운
- [ ] cutting-edge 최첨단, 활력소 [중요단어]
- [ ] novel 새로운
- [ ] juvenile 청소년의(youthful)
- [ ] adolescent 청년기의

233. 죽은·소멸한·없어진
- [ ] perish 죽다, 소멸하다
- [ ] obsolete 폐용이 된, 쓰이지 않는
- [ ] extinct 꺼진, 절멸된, 멸종한
- [ ] defunct 죽은, 없어져 버린
- [ ] moribund 죽어 가는(dying)

234. 일신·개편·개선하다
- [ ] innovate 혁신[쇄신]하다(reform)
- [ ] renovate 새롭게 하다, 수선하다
- [ ] realign 재편[재정렬]하다
- [ ] reshuffle 개편·재편하다
- [ ] refurbish 다시 닦다, 일신하다
- [ ] revamp 수선하다, 개조·개혁하다
- [ ] refine 정련[세련]하다
- [ ] polish 닦다, 세련되게 하다
- [ ] purify 깨끗이 하다, 정화하다(purge)
- [ ] cleanse 깨끗이 하다
- [ ] rinse 헹구다, 씻어내다
- [ ] better 개량·개선하다(improve)
- [ ] ameliorate 개량·개선하다

235. 악화시키다
- [ ] worsen 악화시키다
- [ ] aggravate 더욱 악화시키다
- [ ] deteriorate 나빠지게 하다
- [ ] deprave 나쁘게 만들다, 악화시키다
- [ ] degenerate 타락하다, 퇴보하다
- [ ] disintegrate 분해하다, 붕괴하다
- [ ] regress 되돌아가다, 퇴보하다
- [ ] retrogress 후퇴하다, 쇠퇴하다

236. 진부한·평범한
- [ ] commonplace 평범한, 진부한
- [ ] routine 일상의, 틀에 박힌
- [ ] cliched 진부한, 판에 박은
- [ ] stereotyped 판에 박은, 진부한
- [ ] stale 케케묵은, 진부한
- [ ] banal 진부한, 평범한
- [ ] mediocre 평범한, 범용한
- [ ] humdrum 평범한, 보통의, 단조로운
- [ ] trite 평범한, 케케묵은, 진부한

237. 단조로운·지루한
- [ ] monotonous 단조로운
- [ ] tedious 지루한, 지겨운(boring)
- [ ] dull 무딘, 둔한, 단조롭고, 지루한
- [ ] flat 평평한, 단조로운, 김빠진, 단호한
- [ ] dreary 쓸쓸한, 황량한, 지루한
- [ ] insipid 맛없는, 무미건조한, 재미없는
- [ ] vapid 김빠진, 활기 없는, 지루한

- prosaic 산문체의, 무미건조한
- dragging 질질 끄는, 오래 걸리는

238. 황량한·쓸쓸한

- dreary 쓸쓸한, 황량한, 지루한
- deserted 황폐한, 버림받은
- lonesome 쓸쓸한, 고독한(solitary)
- desolate 황폐시키다, 황량한, 쓸쓸한
- forlorn 버림받은, 고독한
- forsaken 버림받은, 고독한
- bleak 차가운, 황량한, 쓸쓸한
- dismal 음침[음산]한, 쓸쓸한, 황량한

239. 재미있는·우스운

- amusing 재미있는(funny)
- entertaining 재미있는
- intriguing 흥미[호기심]을 자극하는
- facetious 우스운, 익살스러운

240. 매혹하다·매료시키다

- fascinate 매혹하다(attract, charm)
- captivate 사로잡다, 매혹하다
- seduce 유혹하다, 매혹하다
- hypnotize 최면을 걸다, 매혹하다
- mesmerize 매혹하다, 매료시키다
- enamor 반하게 하다, 매혹하다
- enchant 매혹하다, 황홀하게 하다
- enrapture 황홀하게[기쁘게] 하다
- bewitch 요술을 걸다, 매혹시키다
- infatuate 얼빠지게 하다, 매료시키다

241. 부추기다·선동하다

- incendiary 선동적인, 방화의
- tempt 유혹하다, 부추기다
- entice 꾀다, 유혹하다, 부추기다
- agitate 선동하다, 동요시키다
- provoke 화나게 하다, 자극·선동하다
- stir 휘젓다, 자극·선동하다
- (al)lure (미끼로) 꾀다, 부추기다
- kindle 불붙이다, 부추기다(ignite)
- instigate 충동하다, 선동하다
- abet 부추기다, 선동하다

242. 고무·격려·자극하다

- cheer 기운을 북돋우다, 격려하다
- encourage 격려·장려·조장하다
- hearten 기운 나게 하다, 고무하다
- stimulate 자극하다, 격려하다
- foster 육성·촉진·조장하다
- motivate 동기를 부여하다
- inspire 고무하다, 격려하다 영감을 주다
- incite 자극·격려·고무하다
- prompt 자극·격려하다, 부추기다
- spur 박차를 가하다, 자극하다
- animate 생기 있게 하다, 격려하다

- energize 힘을 주다, 격려하다
- vivify 활기 띠게 하다, 격려하다
- invigorate 기운 나게 하다, 고무하다
- enliven 활기 있게 만들다

243. 진척·촉진시키다

- activate 활성화하다, 촉진하다
- hasten 재촉하다, 촉진하다
- accelerate 가속화시키다(quicken)
- promote 승진시키다, 촉진시키다
- further 조장하다, 촉진하다
- facilitate 용이케 하다, 촉진시키다
- expedite 진척·촉진시키다

244. (생각에) 사로잡힌

- enslaved 사로잡힌[by]
- preoccupied 정신이 팔린[with]
- obsessed 사로잡힌, 집착하는[by]

245. 열중한·몰두한·흡수

- mop up 빨아들이다(흡수) 중요단어
- intent 의지, 의향, 여념이 없는[on]
- keen 날카로운, 심한, 열중하여[on]
- engaged 몰두한[in]; 약혼한[to]
- absorbed 몰두한[in]; 흡수된
- immersed 열중하여[in]
- engrossed 몰두한[in]
- rapt 황홀한[with]; 열중·몰두한다[in]
- soaked 흠뻑 젖은, 몰두한[in]

246. 성향·경향

- inclination 경향, 성향
- bias 성향, 편향, 선입견(prejudice)
- (pre)disposition 성향, 경향
- propensity 경향, 성향
- proclivity 성향, 경향(tendency)
- partiality 편견, 편파 기호, 애호
- bent 경향, 좋아함

247. 기호·애호

- fondness 좋아함, 기호
- taste 맛, 기호, 취향
- appetite 식욕, 욕구, 흥미
- fancy 공상, 기호, 애호(liking)
- affinity 밀접성, 유사성, 애호, 기호
- bent 성향, 기호, 열심인[on]
- preference 더 좋아함, 우선권
- priority 우선, 우선권(precedence)

248. 자치의·자율의

- independent 독립한, 자주의
- self-governing 자치의
- self-sufficient 자급자족의
- autonomous 자치의, 자율의

- [ ] sovereign 주권의, 자주의

249. 의지하다·~에 달려있다

- [ ] lean on 기대다(rely, depend)
- [ ] count on 기대다, 의지하다
- [ ] build on 기대다, 의지하다
- [ ] turn to …에 의지하다(look to)
- [ ] recline on 기대다, 의지하다
- [ ] hinge on …에 달려있다
- [ ] contingent 조건으로 하는[on]; 우발적인
- [ ] incumbent …의 책임인[on]; 현직의

250. 고의적인·의도적인

- [ ] purposeful 의도적인, 고의의
- [ ] intentional 고의적인(intended)
- [ ] calculated 계산된; 계획된, 고의의
- [ ] systematic 조직적인, 계획적인
- [ ] deliberate 신중한, 고의적인
- [ ] designed 계획적인, 고의적인
- [ ] premeditated 계획적인
- [ ] wittingly 고의적으로, 일부러

251. 우연한·우발적인

- [ ] incidental 우연한(accidental)
- [ ] casual 우연의, 임시의, 격의 없는
- [ ] haphazard 우연한, 아무렇게나의
- [ ] inadvertent 부주의한, 우연의
- [ ] contingent 조건으로 하는[on]; 우발적인
- [ ] fortuitous 뜻밖의, 우연한
- [ ] adventitious 우연의

252. 속이다·현혹시키다

- [ ] cheat 속이다(trick)
- [ ] falsify 위조하다, 속이다
- [ ] deceive 속이다, 기만하다
- [ ] delude 속이다, 현혹하다
- [ ] defraud 속여 빼앗다, 사취하다
- [ ] swindle 속여 빼앗다, 사취하다
- [ ] entrap 함정에 빠뜨리다(ensnare)
- [ ] beguile 속이다, 현혹시키다
- [ ] dazzle 눈부시게 하다, 현혹시키다
- [ ] hoax 속이다, 골탕먹이다

253. 싫어하다·혐오(하다)

- [ ] misanthropy (사람을) 싫어함 중요단어
- [ ] hate 싫어하다(hatred)
- [ ] despise 경멸·멸시하다, 혐오하다
- [ ] abhor 몹시 싫어하다(abhorrence)
- [ ] abominate 혐오하다(abomination)
- [ ] detest 혐오하다(detestation)
- [ ] loathe 몹시 싫어하다(loathing)
- [ ] aversion 싫음, 혐오

254. 증오·적의·원한(의)

- [ ] hostile 적의의, 적대의(hostility)
- [ ] animosity 증오, 원한, 앙심
- [ ] antipathy 반감, 혐오
- [ ] enmity 적의, 증오
- [ ] antagonistic 적대하는(antagonism)
- [ ] rancorous 원한의, 증오의(rancor)
- [ ] repugnant 역겨운, 반항하는, 적의의
- [ ] spite 악의, 앙심, 원한
- [ ] grudge 원한, 악감정

255. 악의의·사악한·나쁜

- [ ] malicious 악의 있는(malice)
- [ ] malevolent 악의 있는
- [ ] malign 악의의, 악성의, 중상하다
- [ ] malignant 악의 있는, 악성의
- [ ] vicious 나쁜, 악의 있는
- [ ] evil 나쁜, 사악한, 악
- [ ] vile 몹시 나쁜, 비열한
- [ ] wicked 사악한, 부정한, 악독한
- [ ] iniquitous 부정한, 사악한
- [ ] nefarious 사악한, 극악한
- [ ] virulent 유독한, 악의 있는

256. 교활한·음흉한

- [ ] cunning 교활한, 간사한
- [ ] shrewd 빈틈없는, 약삭빠른
- [ ] crafty 교활한, 간사한(artful)
- [ ] sly 교활한, 음흉한
- [ ] insidious 교활한, 음흉한, 잠행성의
- [ ] wily 약삭빠른, 교활한

257. 무서운·끔찍한

- [ ] awful 무서운, 대단한
- [ ] formidable 무서운, 만만찮은
- [ ] horrid 무서운(horrible, horrifying)
- [ ] horrendous 무서운, 끔찍한
- [ ] ghastly 무시무시한, 소름끼치는
- [ ] spooky 으스스한, 무시무시한
- [ ] dreadful 무서운, 무시무시한
- [ ] appalling 소름끼치는, 오싹한
- [ ] hideous 끔찍한, 소름끼치는
- [ ] dire 무서운, 무시무시한
- [ ] eerie 무시무시한, 오싹한

258. 사나운·포악한·극악한

- [ ] untamed 길들이지 않은, 사나운
- [ ] notorious 악명 높은
- [ ] monstrous 괴물 같은, 극악무도한
- [ ] violent 난폭한, 폭력적인, 격렬한
- [ ] outrageous 난폭한, 포악한
- [ ] ferocious 사나운, 흉포한, 잔인한
- [ ] fierce 흉포한, 사나운, 맹렬한
- [ ] diabolic 악마의, 극악무도한
- [ ] flagrant 악명 높은, 극악한

- egregious 악명 높은, 극악한
- atrocious 극악한, 잔학한

259. 야만적인·잔인한

- brutal 짐승 같은, 잔인한(cruel)
- savage 야만적인, 미개한, 잔인한
- barbaric 야만적인, 잔인한
- barbarous 야만스런, 미개한, 잔인한

260. 냉혹한·무자비한

- pitiless 무자비한, 냉혹한
- merciless 무자비한(heartless)
- relentless 냉혹한, 가차없는
- inexorable 냉혹한, 무정한

261. 무시·멸시·경시하다

- pejorative 경멸적인 중요단어
- derision 조소, 조롱 중요단어
- belittle 얕잡아 보다
- slight 약간의, 하찮은, 경시·무시하다
- ignore 무시하다, 모르는 체하다
- neglect 태만히 하다, 무시·경시하다
- disregard 무시·경시하다
- despise 경멸·멸시하다, 혐오하다
- mock 비웃다, 무시하다, 가짜의
- contemn 경멸하다
- disdain 경멸하다
- scorn 경멸하다, 조소하다
- disparage 얕보다, 깔보다
- ridicule 비웃다, 조소하다
- deride 비웃다, 조소하다
- mock 비웃다, 무시하다, 가짜의
- satirize 풍자하다, 빈정대다
- scoff 비웃다, 조롱하다
- sneer 비웃다, 조소하다
- jeer 조롱하다, 조소하다

262. 빈정대는·비꼬는

- cynical 빈정대는, 냉소적인
- contemptuous 경멸적인
- satirical 비꼬는, 풍자적인
- sarcastic 빈정대는, 비꼬는
- sneering 비웃는, 냉소하는
- derisive 비웃는, 조롱하는 중요단어
- sardonic 냉소적인, 조롱하는

263. 비난하다·꾸짖다

- blame 비난하다, …탓으로 돌리다
- accuse 고소하다, 비난하다
- condemn 비난하다, 유죄 판결하다
- denounce 비난하다
- reproach 꾸짖다, 비난하다
- reprove 꾸짖다, 책망하다
- reprimand 꾸짖다, 질책하다
- reprehend 꾸짖다, 비난하다
- rebuke 비난하다, 꾸짖다
- censure 비난하다
- chide 꾸짖다(scold)
- decry 비난하다
- dress[strip] sb down 꾸짖다
- take to task 꾸짖다
- slash 대폭 삭감하다, 혹평하다
- impugn 논박하다, 비난하다
- scathe 혹평하다, 헐뜯다

264. 비방하다·중상하다

- curse 욕하다, 저주하다(damn)
- swear 맹세하다, 욕을 하다
- defame 중상하다
- malign 악의의, 악성의, 중상하다
- slander 중상하다
- revile 욕하다, 헐뜯다(vilify)
- libel (글로) 비방·중상하다
- calumniate 비방·중상하다
- call names 욕하다, 험담하다

265. 더럽히다·욕되게 하다

- insult 모욕하다
- dishonor 불명예스럽게 하다
- humiliate 굴욕감을 느끼게 하다
- foul 더러운, 반칙의, 더럽히다
- soil 더럽히다(stain, spot, blot, blemish)
- defile 더럽히다, 모독하다
- affront 모욕하다
- taint 더럽히다, 오염시키다
- denigrate 더럽히다, 모욕하다
- mortify 굴욕을 느끼게 하다
- stigmatize 오명을 씌우다
- profane 신성을 더럽히다
- desecrate 신성을 더럽히다

266. 불명예스런·수치스런

- disgraceful 수치스러운
- dishonorable 불명예스러운
- disreputable 불명예스러운
- inglorious 불명예스러운
- ignoble 불명예스러운, 수치스러운
- infamous 수치스러운(infamy)
- ignominious 불명예스러운
- stigmatic 불명예스러운, 오명의

267. 신성하게 하다

- consecrate 신성하게 하다
- hallow 신성하게 하다
- sanctify 신성하게 하다
- deify 신격화하다, 신성시하다

268. 신성한·성스러운
- [ ] divine 신성한(holy); 종교적인
- [ ] sainted 신성한, 거룩한
- [ ] sacred 신성한
- [ ] celestial 하늘의, 신성한, 거룩한

269. 세속적인·현세적인
- [ ] worldly 세상의, 세속적인(earthly)
- [ ] terrestrial 지구의, 지상의, 현세의
- [ ] temporal 시간의, 현세의, 속세의
- [ ] secular 세속적인, 현세적인
- [ ] carnal 육체의, 현세적인, 속세의
- [ ] vulgar 저속한, 통속적인, 세속적인
- [ ] profane 신성을 더럽히는, 세속적인
- [ ] mundane 현세의, 세속적인(worldly)

270. 존경(하다)
- [ ] admire 감탄·찬탄하다
- [ ] adore 숭배·흠모하다
- [ ] worship 숭배·경배하다
- [ ] esteem 존경·존중(하다)
- [ ] homage 경의, 존경(respect, honor)
- [ ] revere 숭배·존경하다
- [ ] venerate 존경·숭배하다
- [ ] cult 제식(rite); 숭배, 예찬

271. 소중히 하다·간직하다
- [ ] value 높이 평가하다, 소중히 하다
- [ ] cherish 소중히 하다, 간직하다
- [ ] treasure 소중히 하다
- [ ] enshrine 사당에 모시다, 간직하다

272. 내쫓다·추방하다
- [ ] dismiss 해고·면직하다(fire)
- [ ] exclude 제외·배제하다, 추방하다
- [ ] banish 추방하다, 내쫓다
- [ ] expel 내쫓다, 추방하다
- [ ] exile 추방·유배·망명시키다
- [ ] eject 쫓아내다, 축출하다
- [ ] deport 국외로 추방하다
- [ ] ostracize (도편) 추방하다
- [ ] oust 내쫓다, 축출하다

273. 구하다
- [ ] rescue 구출·구조(하다)
- [ ] save 구하다, 저축하다, 덜어주다
- [ ] salve 구조하다, 구하다
- [ ] salvage 구출·구조하다
- [ ] retrieve 되찾다, 회복하다, 구출하다
- [ ] redeem 되찾다 구조·구제·구출하다
- [ ] extricate 구해내다, 탈출시키다

274. 달래다·진정시키다 중요단어
- [ ] relieve 경감하다, 덜다, 구제하다
- [ ] soothe 달래다, 진정시키다(calm)
- [ ] lull 달래다, 어르다
- [ ] appease 달래다, 진정시키다
- [ ] pacify 진정시키다, 달래다
- [ ] console 위로·위안하다(comfort)
- [ ] solace 위안·위로하다
- [ ] placate 달래다, 진정시키다
- [ ] sedate 진정시키다, 차분한, 침착한
- [ ] tranquilize 조용·진정하게 하다
- [ ] conciliate 달래다, 회유하다
- [ ] alleviate 덜어주다, 완화하다
- [ ] mitigate 완화하다, 누그러뜨리다
- [ ] mollify 달래다, 진정시키다

275. 간청·애청·탄원하다
- [ ] implore 간청·애원하다
- [ ] petition 청원·간청하다
- [ ] plead 변호·변론하다, 탄원·간청하다
- [ ] solicit 간청하다
- [ ] supplicate 간청·애원하다
- [ ] entreat 간청·탄원하다

276. 화나게 하다
- [ ] annoy 화나게 하다, 괴롭히다
- [ ] irritate 짜증나게·화나게 하다
- [ ] offend 화나게 하다, 감정 상하게하다
- [ ] provoke 화나게 하다, 자극·선동하다
- [ ] inflame 불태우다, 격분시키다
- [ ] enrage 격노·분노하게 하다
- [ ] infuriate 격노·격분하게 하다
- [ ] resent 분개해 하다, 화를 내다
- [ ] exasperate 성나게·격분케 하다

277. 화난·성난
- [ ] furious 격노한, 격분한
- [ ] cross 기분이 언짢은, 성난
- [ ] indignant 분개한
- [ ] resentful 분개한
- [ ] irate 노한, 성난
- [ ] sullen 뾰로통한, 샐쭉한, 화난

278. 쉬 흥분하는
- [ ] irritable 화를 잘 내는, 성마른
- [ ] volatile 휘발성의, 변덕스러운, 잘 흥분하는
- [ ] inflammable 흥분하기 쉬운
- [ ] temperamental 화를 잘 내는
- [ ] irascible 성마른, 화를 잘 내는

279. 혼란·당황·좌절케 하다
- [ ] confuse 혼란시키다, 당황하게 하다
- [ ] confound 혼란시키다, 당황케 하다
- [ ] embarrass 당황하게 하다
- [ ] bewilder 당황하게 하다
- [ ] overwhelm 압도하다, 당황하게 하다
- [ ] puzzle 당황하게 하다

- perplex 당황케 하다, 혼란케 하다
- frustrate 좌절시키다
- disturb 방해하다, 어지럽히다
- perturb 혼란시키다
- baffle 당황하게 하다, 좌절시키다
- disconcert 당황하게 하다
- muddle 혼란시키다
- vex 괴롭히다, 난처하게 하다
- dismay 당황하게 하다
- nonplus 난처·당황하게 하다

280. 소란·소동·혼란(한)

- disturbance 소란, 교란, 불안
- chaotic 혼돈된, 무질서한(chaos)
- commotion 동요, 소요, 소동
- turbulent 소란스러운, 교란된
- tumult 소란, 소동, 소요
- turmoil 소란, 혼란, 소동
- uproar 소란, 소동, 법석
- bustle 야단법석, 소란(hustle)

281. 역겨운·불쾌한

- disgusting 메스꺼운, 역겨운
- sickening 구역질 나는, 메스꺼운
- disagreeable 불쾌한, 비위 거슬리는
- nasty 구역질 나는, 역겨운
- nauseating 욕지기 나는(nauseous)
- obnoxious 비위 상하는, 불쾌한
- repulsive 불쾌한, 혐오감을 주는
- repellent 불쾌한, 혐오감을 주는
- repugnant 역겨운, 반항·반대하는
- revolting 반란·모반하는, 역겨운

282. 해로운·유해한·치명적인

- injurious 해로운, 유해한(harmful)
- deleterious 해로운, 유독한
- detrimental 해로운
- nocuous 유해한
- noxious 유해한, 유독한
- pernicious 유해한, 유독한
- lethal 죽음의, 치명적인
- fatal 치명적인, 운명의

283. 유순한·순종하는 중요단어

- obedient 순종하는, 고분고분한
- subordinate 종속적인, 부하의
- tame 길들여진, 유순한, 길들이다
- flexible 유연한, 유순한, 융통성 있는
- compliant 고분고분한(compliable)
- acquiescent 묵종·순종하는
- submissive 복종·순종하는
- tractable 순종하는, 유순한
- docile 온순한, 유순한
- supple 유연한, 유순한
- ductile 유연한, 유순한, 고분고분한

284. 순종하지 않는·반항하는 중요단어

- disobedient 순종하지 않는
- rebellious 반란·모반·반항하는
- insubordinate 순종하지 않는
- defiant 도전하는, 반항하는
- repugnant 역겨운, 반항·반대하는
- revolting 반란·모반하는, 역겨운
- insurgent 반란·모반하는

285. 고집, 완고, 완강 중요단어

- inflexible 굽히지 않는, 완고한
- opinionated 완고한
- persistent 고집 센, 영속하는
- diehard 완강한, 완고한
- wayward 말 안 듣는, 고집 센
- obstinate 완고한, 고집 센
- obdurate 완고한(unyielding)
- tenacious 고집하는, 집요한, 완강한
- stubborn 완고한, 고집 센
- intractable 완고한, 고집 센
- bull-headed 완고한, 고집 센
- dogged 완고한, 끈덕진
- bigoted 완고한, 고집불통의
- headstrong 완고한, 고집 센
- mulish 노새 같은, 고집 센
- pertinacious 집요, 완고, 끈기 있는
- perverse 외고집의, 심술궂은
- pig-headed 고집이 센
- stiff-necked 목이 뻣뻣해진, 완고한, 고집 센
- indocile 순종하지 않는, 말을 잘 듣지 않는

286. 정복·극복할 수 없는

- unconquerable 정복할 수 없는
- insuperable 이기기 어려운
- insurmountable 이겨내기 어려운
- invincible 정복할 수 없는
- indomitable 굴복하지 않는, 불굴의
- impregnable 난공불락의

287. 변덕스러운

- variable 변하기 쉬운(inconstant)
- mutable 변하기 쉬운
- moody 변덕스러운, 우울한
- capricious 변덕스러운
- arbitrary 변덕스러운, 독단적인
- volatile 휘발성의, 변덕스런, 쉬 흥분하는
- fickle 변하기 쉬운
- whimsical 변덕스러운
- erratic 산만한, 변덕스러운
- desultory 산만한, 변덕스러운
- vagrant 방랑하는, 변하기 쉬운

288. 엄한·엄격한

- rigid 엄격한, 엄밀한
- rigorous 엄한, 엄격한

- [ ] severe 엄격한, 심한, 혹독한
- [ ] harsh 거친, 가혹한, 엄한
- [ ] stern 엄격한, 단호한
- [ ] strict 엄격한, 엄밀한
- [ ] stringent 엄중한
- [ ] grim 엄한, 엄격한, 잔인한, 냉혹한

289. 절제하는·금욕적인

- [ ] puritanical 청교도적인, 금욕적인
- [ ] stoic 극기의, 금욕의
- [ ] abstinent 절제하는, 금욕적인
- [ ] continent 절제하는, 자제하는
- [ ] temperate 절제하는, 적당한, 알맞은
- [ ] moderate 절제하는, 알맞은, 적당한

290. 욕심 많은·탐욕스러운

- [ ] greedy 욕심 많은, 탐욕스러운 〔중요단어〕
- [ ] insatiable 탐욕스러운
- [ ] acquisitive 탐내는, 욕심 많은
- [ ] voracious 게걸스레 먹는, 탐욕적인
- [ ] covetous 몹시 탐내는, 탐욕스러운
- [ ] avaricious 욕심 많은, 탐욕스러운
- [ ] avid 욕심 많은, 탐욕스러운, 열렬한

291. 현저한·유명한

- [ ] distinguished 두드러진, 저명한
- [ ] marked 현저한, 저명한(noted)
- [ ] renowned 유명한, 명성 있는
- [ ] outstanding 눈에 띄는, 미해결된
- [ ] remarkable 주목할 만한
- [ ] striking 현저한, 두드러진
- [ ] conspicuous 명백한, 현저·저명한
- [ ] illustrious 빛나는, 저명한, 유명한
- [ ] eminent 저명한, 두드러진
- [ ] prominent 두드러진, 현저한
- [ ] preeminent 뛰어난, 현저한
- [ ] salient 현저한, 두드러진

292. 취소하다·폐지하다

- [ ] invalidate 무효로 하다
- [ ] withdraw 철회·취소하다
- [ ] void 무효의·없는, 결여된·무효로하다
- [ ] annul 무효로 하다, 취소하다(nullify)
- [ ] repeal 무효로 하다, 폐지하다
- [ ] retract 취소·철회하다
- [ ] revoke 취소하다, 무효로 하다(cancel)
- [ ] scrap 폐기·파기하다
- [ ] abolish 폐지하다
- [ ] countermand 취소·철회하다
- [ ] abrogate 폐기·폐지하다

293. 돌이킬 수 없는

- [ ] incurable 불치의
- [ ] irreparable 회복할 수 없는
- [ ] irreversible 되돌릴 수 없는
- [ ] unalterable 바꿀 수 없는
- [ ] irremediable 불치의, 회복불능의
- [ ] irrevocable 취소할 수 없는

294. 후회하는·뉘우치는

- [ ] regretful 뉘우치는, 후회하는
- [ ] apologetic 사과하는, 변명의
- [ ] repentant 후회하는, 뉘우치는
- [ ] penitent 회개하는, 참회하는
- [ ] remorseful 후회하는, 가책되는
- [ ] contrite 깊이 뉘우치는, 회오의

295. 겸손한

- [ ] humble 겸손한, (비)천한, 초라한
- [ ] modest 겸손한, 적당한, 알맞은
- [ ] unpretending 체하지 않는, 겸손한
- [ ] condescending 겸손한
- [ ] unassuming 주제넘지 않은, 겸손한

296. 거만한·오만한·건방진

- [ ] arrogant 거만한
- [ ] conceited 자만하는, 젠체하는
- [ ] domineering 거만한, 횡포한
- [ ] haughty 오만한, 거만한(arrogant)
- [ ] imperious 거만한, 오만한, 전제적인
- [ ] impudent 뻔뻔스러운, 건방진
- [ ] pompous 거만한, 젠체하는
- [ ] insolent 건방진, 오만한
- [ ] overbearing 거만한, 횡포한
- [ ] assuming 주제넘은, 건방진
- [ ] impertinent 건방진, 부적절한
- [ ] presumptuous 주제넘은, 건방진

297. 대신하다·대체하다

- [ ] substitute 대신·대리하다(replace)
- [ ] supplant 대신·대체하다
- [ ] supersede 대신·대리하다
- [ ] surrogate 대리·대신하다, 대리의

298. 대신의·대리의

- [ ] substitutional 대리·대용의
- [ ] surrogate 대리·대용의
- [ ] vicarious 대리의

299. 예고·전조·조짐

- [ ] forerunner 선구자, 선조, 전조, 예고
- [ ] foreboding 육감, 예고, 전조
- [ ] omen 예언, 전조, 조짐
- [ ] precursor 선구자, 선임, 전조
- [ ] premonition 예고, 전조
- [ ] presage 전조, 조짐, 예감
- [ ] portent 조짐, 전조

300. 끌어내다·유래하다
- originate 비롯하다, 생기다[from]
- derive 끌어내다, 유래하다[from]
- stem 유래하다, 생기다[from]
- extract 뽑아내다, 끌어내다
- elicit 도출하다, 이끌어내다
- deduce 연역·추론하다(infer)

301. 관련된·적절한
- appropriate 적당한, 적절한
- apposite 적당한, 적절한
- apropos 적당한, 적절한
- relevant 관련된, 적절한
- germane 밀접한, 적절한
- proper 적당한, 적절한(fit, suitable)
- apt 적절한, 적당한, ~하기 쉬운
- pertinent 적절한, 관계있는

302. 짐작하다·추측하다
- presume 가정·추정하다(assume)
- conjecture 추측하다, 짐작하다
- surmise 짐작하다, 추측하다

303. 잊혀지지 않는
- memorable 기억할 만한
- haunting 잊혀지지 않는
- indelible 지울 수 없는, 잊혀지지 않는
- oblivious 잘 잊어버리는(forgetful)

304. 휴식·휴회(하다)
- recess 휴식, 휴회(rest)
- repose 휴식(하다)
- unwind 긴장을 풀다, 편히 하다
- adjourn 휴회·휴정하다, 연기하다

305. 타고난·선천적인
- innate 타고난, 선천적인(inborn)
- inherent 고유한, 타고난
- intrinsic 고유한, 본질적인
- immanent 내재하는, 내재적인
- gifted 타고난, 재능이 있는
- endowed (재능을) 타고난
- congenital 타고난, 선천적인

306. 초래하다·야기하다
- generate 낳다, 일으키다
- engender 발생시키다(produce)
- effect 결과, 효과 초래하다
- spark 불꽃, …의 발단이 되다
- breed 낳다, 기르다, 일으키다
- induce 야기하다, 일으키다, 귀납하다
- trigger 방아쇠, 촉발시키다
- incur 초래하다
- entail (결과로서) 수반하다
- beget 낳다, 생기게 하다
- spawn (알) 낳다, 산란하다, 발생시키다

307. 용서하다·묵인하다
- overlook 묵과·간과·대충 보다
- acquit 무죄로 하다, 방면하다
- condone 용서·묵과하다(pardon)
- wink 못 본 체하다[at]

308. 사기·속임·부정(의)
- deceitful 기만적인, 사기의
- fraudulent 사기의, 부정의(fraud)
- crooked 구부러진, 부정직한
- manipulative 속임수의, 부정의
- feint 가장, 시늉, 속임수
- swindle 사취·사기(하다)
- imposture 사기, 협잡(trickery)
- sham 속임수(의), 허위(의), 가짜(의)
- pseudo 가짜의, 사이비의

309. 부과하다·짐 지우다
- impose 부과하다, 강요하다
- levy 부과하다, 징수하다(charge)

310. 명령·규정·요구하다
- necessitate 필요로·요구로 하다
- prescribe 규정하다, 처방하다
- dictate 명령하다, 요구하다
- enjoin 명령하다, 요구하다(demand)
- exact 요구로 하다(demand)
- stipulate 규정하다, (조건으로) 요구하다

311. 독재적인·전제적인
- authoritarian 권위주의적인
- oppressive 압제적인
- dictatorial 독재적인
- tyrannical 전제적인, 압제적인
- imperious 거만한, 오만한, 전제적인
- despotic 독재적인, 전제적인

312. 살찐·비만한
- fat 뚱뚱한
- fleshy 살의, 살찐
- obese 비만의(overweight)
- plump 포동포동한, 토실토실한
- stout 튼튼한, 견고한, 뚱뚱한
- corpulent 뚱뚱한, 비만한
- portly 비만한, 비대한
- rotund [routʌ́nd] 토실토실 살찐

313. 시작·초기·발단의
- cut their teeth on 중요단어 최초의 경험을 쌓다
- initial 처음의, 시초의
- come into being 탄생하다

- nascent 발생하려고 하는, 초기의
- incipient 시작의, 발단의(inceptive)
- budding 싹트기 시작한, 신진의
- embryonic 배·태아의, 미발달된
- fledgling [fléd3liŋ] 깃털이 갓난
- rudimentary 기본의, 초보의(elementary)

314. 능가하다·~보다 낫다; 더 크다

- exceed 초과하다, 능가하다(excel)
- surpass …보다 낫다, 능가하다
- transcend 초월하다, 능가하다
- outstrip …보다 낫다, 능가하다(outdo)
- outweigh 더 크다 중요단어

315. 방랑하는·헤매는

- wandering 방랑하는
- migratory 이주하는, 이주성의
- vagrant 방랑하는, 변하기 쉬운
- vagabond 방랑·유랑하는
- stray 길 잃은, 헤매는(astray)
- nomadic 유목(민)의, 방랑의

316. 즉흥적인·임시변통의

- stopgap 임시변통(의), 미봉책(의)
- impromptu 즉석에서의, 즉흥적인
- improvised 즉석에서의, 즉흥의
- makeshift 임시변통(의), 일시적인
- instant(aneous) 즉시·즉석의
- extemporaneous 준비 없는, 즉흥적인, 즉석의
- spontaneous 자발적인(voluntary)
- unrehearsed 연습[리허설]을 하지 않은

317. 재난·재앙(의)

- disastrous 재난의, 재앙의
- catastrophic 대이변·참사·재앙의
- apocalyptic 종말적인
- calamitous 재난의, 참화의
- cataclysmic 격변의, 대 변동의
- upheaval 대 변동, 대 격변

318. 방탕한·방종한

- prodigal 낭비하는, 방탕한
- fast 빠른, 방탕한, 단식(하다)
- licentious 방탕한, 방종한
- promiscuous 난잡한, 무차별한

319. 사라지다

- vanish 사라지다(disappear)
- fade 사라지다, 희미해지다
- evaporate 증발하다, 사라지다

320. 즐기다·좋아하다

- fancy 공상하다, 좋아하다
- relish 맛 맛보다, 즐기다
- savor 맛, 맛보다, 감상하다
- revel 한껏 즐기다

321. 선조·조상

- forebear 조상, 선조
- forefather 조상, 선조(ancestor)
- predecessor 전임자, 조상
- forerunner 선구자, 전조, 예고
- precursor 선구자, 선임 전조
- progenitor 선조

322. 후손·자손

- descendant 자손, 후손
- offspring 자손, 결과
- posterity 자손, 후손
- progeny 자손

323. 초조한·긴장된

- nervous 긴장되는, 초조한
- tense 팽팽한, 긴장한(strained)
- edgy 날카로운, 초조한(on edge)
- uptight 초조해하는, 긴장한
- jittery 신경과민의(have the jitters)

324. 횡령·유용·사용하다

- appropriate 사용·착복하다
- embezzle 횡령·착복하다
- divert 유용·전용하다
- peculate 유용·횡령하다

325. 음란한·음탕한

- obscene 외설적인, 음란한
- filthy 더러운, 음탕한
- lewd 음란한, 외설적인
- salacious 음란한, 음탕한
- indecent 버릇없는, 음란한
- lewd 추잡한, 음란한
- smutty 더러워진, 음란한
- vulgar 저속한, 속된
- disgusting 구역질 나는
- loathsome 불쾌한, 역겨운
- offensive 불쾌, 무례, 음란한

326. 미온적인

- lukewarm 미지근한, 미온적인
- tepid 미지근한, 미온적인

327. 지속할 수 있는

- tenable 유지·지속할 수 있는
- viable 생존 가능한, 지속 가능한

328. 사실상·실질적으로

- substantially 실질적으로, 상당히

- [ ] effectively 실질적으로, 사실상
- [ ] virtually 사실상, 실질적으로

329. 주다

- [ ] confer 협의하다(consult), 주다
- [ ] render 주다, …하게 하다
- [ ] impart (나누어) 주다
- [ ] bestow 주다, 수여하다
- [ ] grant 주다, 수여하다

330. 다음의·잇따르는

- [ ] succeeding 계속되는, 다음의
- [ ] subsequent 다음의, 잇따르는
- [ ] ensuing 다음의, 뒤이은

331. 합법적인·정당한

- [ ] legitimate 합법적인, 정당한
- [ ] authentic 인증된, 믿을만한
- [ ] valid 유효한, 확실한
- [ ] legal 합법적인, 정당한

332. 거물, 실력자

- [ ] magnate 거물, 큰 손
- [ ] mogul 거물, 실력자
- [ ] potentate 강한 지배자, 통치자
- [ ] tycoon 거물

PART 03

숙토니오

A

- artisanal foods 명품음식
- about-face (주의, 태도) 180도 전환 → 태도 변화
  (change one's mind and assume the opposite viewpoint)
- act of God 불가항력 → 천재지변
  (a sudden action of natural forces that could not have been prevented, as an earthquake or hurricane → calamity, catastrophe, tragedy, disaster, cataclysm)
- act with great aplomb 아주 침착하게 행동하다.
- a square peg in a round hole 부적격자, 부적임자
- a feather in one's cap 자랑거리, 훌륭한 업적
- as thick as thieves 아주 친한(very friendly)
- a drug on the market 팔리지 않는 물건 → 공급과잉상태인 상품
- a bundle 많은 비용 (a lot of expense, a bunch)
- a can of worms 골치 아픈 문제(complicated problem)
- a mixed blessing
  1) 좋은 일이 있으면 나쁜 일도 있다(새옹지마)
  2) (구어) 좋기도 하고 나쁘기도 한 것
  3) something good, pleasant, fortunate, etc. which also has disadvantages
- a couch potato 나태한 사람(감자 칩 먹으면서 소파에 앉아 TV나 보는)
- a couple of 두 셋의
- at sixes and sevens about
  1) 당황한 → 혼란스러운 → 일치하지 않는
  2) In a state of confusion or disorder → in confusion; completely disorganized
- pull someone up short ~를 당혹하게 하다
- a slap in the face 모욕, 거절 (insult, contempt)
- a sticking point 걸림돌, 장애가 되는 것(obstacle, barrier)
- a chip off the old block 아버지를 꼭 닮은 아들 → 부전자전
- a track record 업적, 실적 (a record of actual performance)
- a variety of 다양한
- abide by 따르다, 이행하다 (follow, comply with)
- above all (thing) 무엇보다도, 특히 (first of all, especially)
- above board 정직한 → 솔직한 → 공정한
  (in the open; without dishonesty, concealment, or fraud)
- above oneself 분수를 모르는, 자만하는
- according to ~에 따르면
- account for 설명하다, 비율을 차지하다, 원인이 되다, 유발하다
  (explain, prove)
- across the board 전면적으로, 포괄적인(uniformly, all-out, blanket)
- act up 상태가 나쁘다, 이상이 있다 (not work properly)
- add fuel to the fire(flame) 불난데 부채질하다, 악화시키다
- add insult to injury 사태를 더욱 악화시키다 (worsen the situation)
- after all 결국
- again and again 자꾸자꾸 반복적으로(recurrently)
- against the clock 시간을 다투어, 시간에 맞추려고 (to be on time)
- all alone 혼자서, 혼자 힘으로
- all along 줄곧, 죽, 내내(from the beginning to the end)
- all at once 갑자기
- all but impossible 거의 불가능한(almost impossible)
- all of a sudden 갑자기 (suddenly, abruptly)
- all one's life 한평생 (for a whole life)
- all set 준비된 (ready and prepared)
- all the way 내내, 멀리서(from start to finish, from the distance)
- all thumbs 손재주가 없는, 서투른(clumsy, awkward, inept)
- allow for ~를 참작하다, 고려하다(consider, take into account)
- alongside of ~곁에, 나란히 (side by side, together with)
- an all-time record 전대미문의 기록, 유례없는 기록 (the highest record)
- an arm and a leg 엄청난 금액, 터무니없는 비용(an exorbitantly high price)
- an old flame 옛 애인(old girlfriend/boyfriend)
- apart from ~는 별개로 하고, ~는 제쳐놓고(aside from)
- apply for ~에 신청하다, 지원하다(ask for)
- apple-pie order 잘 정리된 것 → 자로 잰 듯 반듯함
- around the corner 바로 다가와서, 임박해서 (near at hand, close at hand)
- around the clock 24시간 계속하여, 주야로 (day and night, for 24 hours a day)
- as a rule 대체로, 일반적으로 (in general, at large)
- as a matter of fact 사실은
- as a result 그 결과로
- as a whole 전체로서, 대체로, 총괄하여 (on the whole, at large, all together)
- as far as ~에 관한 한, ~까지 (as regards, until)
- as for ~에 대하여 말하면, ~에 관해서는 (concerning, in regard to)
- as is often the case 흔히 있는 일이지만 (as often happens)
- as it happens 마침, 공교롭게도 (by coincidence, by chance)
- as likely as not 아마 (perhaps, maybe)
- as luck would have it 운 좋게도, 운 나쁘게도 (luckily or unluckily)
- as of ~일부로
- as often as not 종종, 대체로 (often, usually)
- as the crow flies 일직선으로
- as the case may be 상황에 따라서 (as circumstances are applicable)
- ascribe A to B : A에 대해 B 탓으로 돌리다(attribute A to B)
- ask out 데이트 신청하다(영화를 보러 가자는 등) (invite out)
- at a loss 어쩔 줄을 몰라서, 당황하여(embarrassed)
- at a loss for words 말이 막힌 (so amazed or shocked by something)
- at a sail's pace 아주 느리게(very slowly)
- at all costs 어떤 대가를 치르더라도(at all events, by all means)
- at all times 언제나, 항상
- at ease 편하게 (easily, in comfort)
- at face value 액면대로 (as what is said or acted)
- at logger-heads with 심한 의견 차이를 보이다 → 마찰을 빚다
- at first sight 첫눈에, ~를 보고 (after a first quick look)
- at issue 문제가 되는, 논쟁 중인 (in dispute, at debate)
- at it (일) 힘을 쏟아 → (싸움에) 열중하여(very active, bent on)
- at large 일반적으로, 자세히 붙잡히지 않고(in general, in detail, free)
- at odds over(with) ~와 불화하여, 사이가 좋지 않아(in disagreement, in conflict)
- at one's own discretion 재량으로, 임의로(not according to some rule)
- at one's own expense 자기 희생하여(paying for something oneself)

- at present 현재는
- at short notice 즉시, 급히, 예고 없이(immediately, quickly)
- at stake 위험한, 내기에 걸려있는(dangerous)
- at the age of ~의 나이에
- at the drop of a hat 즉시, 지체 없이(immediately, without hesitation)
- at the eleventh hour 마지막 순간에 (at the last possible moment)
- at the expense of ~를 희생해서, ~의 비용으로 (at the cost of)
- at the last minute 마지막 순간에(at the final moment)
- at the latest 늦어도
- at the moment 지금, 지금으로서는 (for now, now)
- at(on)the tip of one's tongue 생각날 듯 말 듯 하다 (trying to remember)
- at (the) best 잘해야, 기껏해야
- at one's best 가장 좋은 상태에 → 전성기에
- at the most 기껏해야, 아무리 많아도
- at times 때때로, 가끔 (sometimes, now and then)
- at work 일하는 → 직장에서 → 작업 중인 → 활동하는
- attribute A to B : A를 B 탓으로 돌리다(ascribe / impute A to B)
- a basket case 사지를 절단한 환자 → 노이로제에 걸린 사람 → 완전 무능력자
  (One that is in a completely hopeless or useless condition)
- a bird in the hand 확실한 소유물
- a bone of contention 분쟁의 원인(a subject of quarrel)
- a chip off the old block (기질) 부모를 꼭 닮은 자식
- a couple of 두 개의, 두셋의
- a pretty kettle of fish 난처한 일(골치 아픈 일)
- a drop in the bucket 아주 적은 양(a very small amount)
- a good mixer 교제술(사교술)이 좋은 사람
- a handful of 소수의
- a flash in the pan 반짝[일시적인]성공 → 용두사미(한때 반짝 뜨고 말다)
  (sudden success that is not repeated)
- a hard(tough) nut to crack 어려운 문제(사람), 다루기 어려운 것(사람)
- a moving spirit 주동자, 주창자(a person who causes it to start)
- a pain in the neck 두통거리, 골칫거리
- a piece of cake 매우 쉬운 일(very easy)
- a rule of thumb 손대중, 주먹구구
- a slip of one' tongue 실언 (an unintentional verbal mistake)
- A stitch in time saves nine 호미로 막을 것을 가래로 막지 마라
- a trump card 으뜸패 (비장의 수단)
- a world of 아주 많은(a large number (amount) of)
- a slap (모욕, 비난, 찰싹) on the wrist(리스트:손목의 힘) 경고[가벼운 꾸지람]
- a slap in the face (고의적인) 모욕[면박]
- abandon oneself to ~에 탐닉하다(빠지다) (indulge oneself in)
- above one' head 너무 어려워서 이해할 수 없는(above the head of)
- account for 설명하다(explain, expound upon)
- accuse A of B : A를 B의 혐의로 기소하다
- across the board 전면적인, 종합적인(overall)
- add to ~에 더하다
- add up 이해가 되다(make sense)
- after dark 어두워진 후에
- again and again 반복적으로(recurrently)
- against the grain of 성질에 맞지 않게, 비위에 거슬리는 (contradicted)
- agree on ~에 동의하다, 의견을 같이 하다
- ahead of ~보다 앞서
- all at once 갑자기
- all of a sudden (on a sudden) 갑자기
- all but 거의
- all in all (보통 문두) 대체로, 대강 말하면 (to make a longstory short)
- all over 도처에, 모든 점에서(in every respect)
- all the rage 매우 유행한(very fashionable)
- all the same 아주 같은, 아무래도 상관없는, 그래도 역시
- all the time 항상(always, invariably, ever, continuously)
- all thumbs 손재주가 없는(very poor, clumsy, awkward)
- amount to 총계 ~가 되다(add up to, come up to)
- an apple of the eye 매우 소중한 것
- the apple of discord 분쟁의 씨
- answer for 책임을 지다(be responsible for, account for, be accountable for, be responsible for, be charged for)
- be in charge for, take charge of → pass the buck 책임을 전가하다
- answer to 일치(합치)하다(be as described)
- approve of 승인하다, 찬성하다
- as a last resort 최후의 수단으로서
- as a matter of fact 실제에 있어서, 사실은(really, in fact)
- as a result of ~의 결과로(because of, in the wake of : ~직후에)
- as a rule 일반적으로(generally, in general)
- as deaf as a post 귀가 전혀 안 들려서
- as far as it goes 그 일에 관한 한, 어떤 범위 내에서는
- as fit as a fiddle 매우 건강한, 원기 왕성한
- as good as one' word 약속을 이행하는, 언행이 일치하는, 약속을 지키다
- as like as two peas 흡사한, 꼭 닮은
- as luck would have it 다행히도, 운 나쁘게(fortunately, unfortunately)
- as sick as a dog 몹시 아픈, 메스껍고 토하는(Very ill, especially stomach malady)
- as per ~에 관하여
- aside from ~은 차치하고, ~을 제외하고
- ask for a lady' hand 여자에게 청혼하다(ask for marriage, court)
- at a loss 당황하여(perplexed, embarrassed, at one's wit's end)
- at a low ebb 쇠퇴기인(in a bad or inactive state)
- at a person' disposal 마음대로 할 수 있는
- at an additional cost 추가 비용으로
- at eleventh hour 아슬아슬한 때에(sooner or later)
- at every turn 아주 자주, 늘, 예외 없이(very often, always, without exception)
- at large 마음대로, 자유로이, 전체로서, 널리
- at length 마침내, 드디어, 자세히(at last)
- at odds (with) 의견이 일치하지 않는(in disagreement)
- at once ~ and~ : ~하기도 하고~하기도 하다(both~and ~)
- at one' discretion ~의 재량으로, ~의 판단으로
- at one' expense 자기를 희생시켜 → 자비로, ~의 비용으로
- have a lot to do with ~와 많은 관련이 있다
- at one' finger' ends ~에 정통한(adept at, be conversant with,

249

be versed in, be well grounded in, be well read in)
- **at random** 무작위로, 함부로, 닥치는 대로(aimlessly, without plan)
- **at reasonable rate** 적당한 가격으로
- **at sixes and sevens** 혼란하여(in great confusion, in a mess)
- **at stake** 위기에 처한, 위태로워(at risk, at bay, in the lurch, in the soup)
- **at the eleventh hour** 마지막 순간에(at the very last moment)
- **at the end of** ~의 끝 무렵에
- **at the expense of** ~을 희생하면서(at the cost of)
- **at the latest** 늦어도
- **at the mercy of** ~에 좌우되는(under(at) the control of)
- **at the rate(cost) of** ~의 비용으로
- **at the risk of** 위험을 무릅쓰고
- **at the same time** 동시에(simultaneously)
- **at the speed of** ~의 속도로
- **at will** 뜻대로, 임의로(at one's pleasure)
- **avail oneself of** ~을 이용하다(utilize, make use of, take advantage of)(capitalize on → cash in on)
- **a baker's dozen** 빵집의 한 다스(13개) → 옛날에 빵집에서 하나씩 더 얹어준 것에서 비롯되었다.
- **a sight for sore eyes** 정말 보기 좋은 것[보기만 해도 즐거운 것] (a person or thing that one is pleased or relieved to see) 만나서 정말 반갑다(You are a sight for sore eyes)
- **a bad apple** 불량한 사람
- **a babe in arms** 젖먹이; 풋내기, 세상 물정 모르는 사람
- **a beggar for work** (구어) 일하기 좋아하는 사람
- **a bit of fat** (구어) 뜻밖의 행운[기회] → 벌이가 좋은 일
- It was a bit of fat that I won the lottery. (내가 복권에 당첨된 것은 뜻밖의 행운이었다.)
- I'm a chip off the old block. 나는 (아빠나 혹은 엄마) 꼭 빼닮았어요.
- I'm a pretty likable guy. 난 꽤나 호감형인 남자죠.
- Why the long face? 왜 그렇게 우울한 얼굴이니?
- **at one's wits end** 난처하여, 어찌할 바를 몰라
- **deep end** 수심이 깊은 쪽, 어려운 상황
- **make ends meet** 수입과 지출의 균형을 맞추다, 수입에 알맞은 생활을 하다
- **have something in view** (목표, 계획) 마음(염두)에 두고 있다
- **take a poor view of** 비관적으로 보다
- **a bird's eye view** 조감도, 전경, (사물의) 개관
- **put one's foot down** 단호한 태도를 취하다, 반대하다(refuse very firmly to do or accept something)
- **set foot on** 발을 들여놓다, 방문하다, 상륙하다(land)
- **put one's feet up** 누워서 쉬다, 긴장을 풀다, 안심하다(relax)
- **get off on the wrong foot** 첫발을 잘못 떼다, 첫 단추를 잘못 끼우다
- **fire and brimstone** (지옥을 연상케 하는) 불과 유황

B

- **bring halt to** 중단하다(discontinue)
- **Be on cloud nine**
  1) 기분이 매우 좋다, 매우 행복하다 → 9층 구름 위에 있다 → 기분이 뿡 가도록 좋다
  2) feel extreme happiness or elation → euphoria(유포리아) → elysium(엘리시움)

- **in seventh heaven** (over the moon)
  1) 너무나도 행복한
  2) I'm in seventh heaven! (기분이 끝내줘요! 야호!! 기분이 끝내줘요!!!)
  3) "I'm on cloud nine(I'm in seventh heaven)"
- **bend the law** 법을 악용하다(do something illegal)
- **bail out** 곤경에서 구하다(help out)
- **bailout** (정부의 자금 지원에 의한) 기업 구제(조직)
- **bustle about** 분주히 돌아다니다(walked energetically)
- **be in the way** 방해하다, 간섭하다(intrude)
- **be loaded with** ~로 가득 차다(teem with, awash in, fraught with, abound with(in))
- **bonanza** 대성공 → 행운 → 노다지 → 운수 대통 → (농장) 대풍년
- **be traced to** ~에서 유래하다, ~에서 찾다(found to originate from)
- **brace oneself** 대비하다, 준비하다(prepare)
- **be on ~ terms** : ~사이이다
- **branch out** 확장하다, 영역을 넓히다(expand)
- **break with** 단절하다, 절연하다(abandon)
- **break a leg** 행운을 빌다(good luck, keep one's fingers crossed)
- **break down** 고장나다, 분류하다, 부셔버리다(crash, classify)
- **break one's neck** 몹시 노력하다 → 전력을 다하다
- **break even** 손실과 이득이 없이 되다(no gain and no loss)
- **break ground** 시작하다 → 착공하다, 땅을 파다(begin a construction)
- **break out** 발발하다, 일어나다(begin, occur, take place, erupt)
- **break the ice** 서먹한 분위기를 깨다 → 실마리를 찾다(find the clue)
- **break up** 헤어지다, 해산하다, 박살 나다(divorce, disperse, break into pieces)
- **bring home to** 절실히 느끼게 하다(make someone realize)
- **bring to an end/a close/a stop** 끝내다, 종결시키다(put an end)
- **bring to light** 밝히다, 폭로하다(reveal)
- **be off to** ~로 떠나다
- **be one's cup of tea** 바로 ~ 가 좋아하는 것(taste, hobby)
- **be in need of** ~가 필요하다
- **be liable to** ~하기 쉽다(be prone to)(open, likely, prone, subject, susceptible, vulnerable)
- **be made of** ~로 만들어져 있다
- **be on easy street** 유복하게 지내다
- **be satisfied with** ~에 만족하다
- **be supposed to** ~하기로 되어 있다
- **be through with** ~를 끝마치다
- **be born from** ~에서 태어나다
- **be used to –ing** ~에 익숙해져 있다
- **be worth –ing** ~할 만한 가치가 있다
- **bear in mind** 명심하다
- **bear on/upon** 영향 미치다, 관계있다(influence on, have a relationship with)
- **beat around/about the bush** 변죽을 울리다, 요점을 말하지 않다 (drop a hint → say indirectly)
- **beat one's time** 남의 애인을 가로채다, 경쟁자에게 이기다
- **beat/jump the gun** 서두르다 (start before the starting signal)
- **beef up** 강화하다, 보강하다(strengthen, tighten up)

- beggars can't be choosers 찬밥 더운밥 가릴 때가 아니다
- behind schedule 일정보다 늦은
- behind the closed doors 비밀히, 비공개로(not open to the public)
- behind time 지각하여, 늦은
- believe it or not 믿거나 말거나 (it may sound odd but it is true)
- below par/under par/not up to 표준 이하로, 건강이 좋지 않은
- bend over backwards 최선을 다하다, 열심히 노력하다 (make great effort)
- beneath notice[contempt] 주의[경멸]할 가치도 없는
- beneath one's dignity ~의 위신과 관계된
- bent on ~에 열중하여, ~를 결심한 (determined)
- between ourselves 우리끼리만의 얘기인데 (between you and me)
- beyond description 말로 이루 다 표현할 수 없는 (indescribable)
- bite off more than one can chew 분에 넘치는 일을 하다
- bite one's nails 불안해하거나 긴장하다 (get nervous)
- bite the bullet 악전고투하다 (bear it patiently)
- bite one's tongue 혀(입술)를 깨물다 → 꾹 참다(struggled not to say)
- black out (일시적으로) 의식을 잃다 (lose consciousness)
- black sheep (한집안의) 말썽꾼 ☆ a white crow (진귀한 것) (a person who is regarded as a disgrace or failure by his family or peer group)
- blast off 발사되다 (lift off)
- block off 폐쇄하다, 막다(block up)
- blow one's own trumpet 자화자찬하다 (blow one's own horn)
- blow the whistle 밀고하다, 폭로하다 (divulge)
- blow one's cool 흥분하다
- boast of 자랑하다 (brag about)
- bottle up (감정을) 억누르다 → 묻어두다(suppress)
- bog down to 수렁에 빠지다, 막다른 골목에 이르다(come to a dilemma)
- boil down to 결국~이다(become something in the end)
- beef up 강화하다 (보강하다) → beef about 불평하다
- bolster up 기운을 북돋우다, 강화하다(make someone feel more confident)
- botch up 실수하여 망쳐버리다(ruin something by mistake)
- bother to R : 일부러~하다
- bottom out 바닥에 이르다(be in the worst situation)
- bow out 사직하다, 물러나다(leave, resign)
- bring up 제기하다, 키우다(mention, raise)
- broken English 엉터리 영어 (imperfect English)
- brush off 무시하다 → 털어 버리다, 거절하다 퇴짜를 놓다 (brush aside, reject)
- brush up on ~를 다시 연마하다, 복습하다(begin study again, improve)
- buckle down to 전념하다, 집중하다 (work/study hard)
- burn the candle at both ends 기진맥진하다 → 녹초가 되다(to work very hard and stay up very late at night)
- bump into 우연히 만나다(run into, come across)
- burn one's fingers 손을 데다 → (참견했다가)혼나다 → (투기로) 손해보다
- burn out 녹초가 된, 지친(exhausted)
- burn the midnight oil 밤늦게까지 일하다(공부) (work or study till late at night)
- bury the hatchet 화해하다 → 싸움을 그만두다(make peace, stop fighting) (mend the fence, come to terms with, make up with)
- butt in 간섭하다, 참견하다(cut in, intervene)
- by and large 전반적으로, 대체로(generally)
- by chance 우연히, 뜻밖에(by accident)
- by choice 스스로 택하여(voluntarily)
- by dint of ~에 의해서, ~의 힘으로(by the strength of)
- by the skin of one's teeth 아슬아슬하게, 간신히(narrowly)
- by the time ~할 무렵에는
- by virtue of ~의 힘으로, ~에 의하여 (by dint of)
- by word of mouth 구두로, 입소문으로(verbally)
- back down 손을 떼다, 취소하다, 양보하다(cancel, give in)
- back off ~에서 손을 떼다, 취소하다, 양보하다 (cancel, withdraw)
- back to/at square one 원점으로 돌아가서 (back to the beginning)
- back to the wall 막다른 골목에 이르러, 궁지에 빠져 (in a trap, in trouble)
- back up 후원하다, 지지하다, 후진하다 (support, reverse direction)
- balk at 주저하다, 망설이다 (not want to do)
- bank on 의지하다, 믿다, 기대하다(trust, rely on)
- bark up the wrong tree 잘못 짚다, 허방 짚다(have a wrong address)
- be a must 꼭 필요한 것이다 (requirement)
- be about to 막~하려고 하다
- be booked up 예매가 매진되다(be sold out)
- be bound for ~행의
- bury one's head in the sand
  1) 현실을 회피하다 → 골치 아픈 현실을 외면하다
  2) 타조가 위험에 처했을 때 몸은 밖에 둔 채 머리만 모래 속에 파묻는다는 데에서 나온 말
- by rule of thumb 대충, 주먹구구식으로
- back-seat driver 참견 잘하는 사람
- bark up the wrong tree 헛물켜다, 잘못 짚다
- be absent from ~에 결석하다
- be absorbed in ~에 몰두하다, 전념하다
- be accustomed to ~에 익숙해지다
- be acquainted with ~을 잘 알다
- be addicted to ~에 중독되다
- be appreciative of ~에 감사하고 있다
- be apt to R ~하기 쉽다
- be assigned to 할당되다(designate, set aside, allocate, earmark)
- be at home in ~에 정통해있다, ~에 익숙하다(be familiar with)
- be authorized by 권한을 부여받다
- be aware of 알고 있다, 의식하고 있다
- be based on ~에 근거를 두다
- be bent on ~에 열중하고 있다, ~하려고 결심하다 (be absorbed in, be determined to)
- be bound to R ~하지 않을 수 없다
- be capable of ~할 능력이 있다
- be charged with (일, 임무를) 맡다
- be checked for ~을 확인받다
- be comparable to ~에 필적하다
- be concerned about ~에 대해 걱정하다
- be concerned with ~에 관심을 갖다(be interested in)
- be condensed into ~으로 압축되다, 요약되다

- be conscious of ~을 의식하고 있다
- be consistent with 일관성이 있다, ~와 일치하다
- be contingent upon ~을 조건으로 하다, 좌우되다
  (be dependent upon)
- be crazy about ~에 열중하다(hang in around)
- be credited to ~덕분(덕택)이다, ~의 공으로 돌려지다
  (be ascribed to)
- be dead set against 완전히 반대하다(completely oppose)
- be dissatisfied with ~에 불만족스러워하다
- be divided into ~로 분류되다, 나뉘어지다
- be dressed to kill 멋지게 옷을 입다(be dressed to attract attention)
- be eligible for/to R ~할 자격이 있다, 적격이다
- be engaged in ~에 종사하다
- be engrossed in ~에 열중하다(be absorbed in, be lost in)
- be entitled to ~의 자격이 있다, 권리가 있다(have a right to)
- be equal to ~와 같다, 감당할 수 있다, ~에 합당하다
- be exposed to ~에 노출되다
- be faced with ~에 직면하다
- be familiar to ~에게 잘 알려져 있다
- be fed up with ~에 질리다 → 싫증나다(sick and tired of → Enough is enough → have enough of)
- be geared to ~에 놓여지다, 맞추어지다
- be good at ~에 능숙하다(do well, be clever or skillful)(have a knack for, have a way with, have at one's finger tips)(feel at home with, know the ropes about)
- be hard on ~에 모질게 대하다(bother, be not gentle)
- be hard up for (돈 따위에) 쪼들리다, 궁색하다(be in great need of (money)
- be implicated in ~에 연루되다(be involved in)
- be in charge of 책임지다
- be in the red 적자를 내다, 빚을 지고 있다
- be inclined to R ~하는 경향이 있다
- be inconsistent with ~와 반대이다(contradict)
- be indifferent to ~에 무관심하다
  (be not interested in, do not care about)
- be indulged in ~에 빠지다, ~에 탐닉하다(allow oneself to)
- be interested in ~에 관심이 있다
- be involved in ~에 연루되다, 관여하다
- be known by ~으로 알 수 있다
- be least likely to win ~이길 것 같지 않다
- be likely to R ~하기 쉽다, ~할 것 같다
- be noted for ~로 유명하다
- be obligated to R ~하지 않을 수 없다
- be one' age ~와 동갑이다
- be opened to ~ 받기 쉽다. 면할 수 없다
- be played out 기진맥진하다, 녹초가 되다
  (be exhausted, be worn out)
- be poor at ~에 서투르다(be not good at)
- be proud of ~을 자랑으로 여기다, 뽐내다
- be rapt in ~에 열중해있다
- be responsible for ~에 책임을 지다 → 원인이 있다
- be robbed of ~ 을 빼앗기다, 강탈당하다
- be saddled with (책임, 부담) 지다(be burdened with)
- be set against ~에 반대하다(be opposed to)
- be snowed under 눈에 묻히다, 수량으로 압도당하다
  (being overwhelmed)
- be subject to ~을 받기 쉽다, ~에 걸리기 쉽다
- be subordinate to ~에 종속하다, 부속하다
- be survived by ~보다 먼저 죽다
- be susceptible to ~에 영향 받기 쉽다, ~에 걸리기 쉽다
- be suspicious of 의심하다
- be taken by surprise 기습공격을 받다
- be tied up 바쁘다(be busy, have one's hands full)
- be true of 적용되다(apply to, hold true of)
- be up to ~에게 있다, 달려 있다(rest with)
- be up to one' ear 깊이 빠져 있다, 몰두하다(be busy)
- be well-grounded in 기초가 탄탄하다(know thoroughly)
- be willing to R 기꺼이 ~하다
- bear a grudge 원한(나쁜 감정)을 품다(continue ill feeling toward)(have a bone to pick with → have a score to settle with → have it in for)
- bear (something) in mind ~을 기억하다, ~을 명심하다
- beat about 이리저리 찾다 (seek anxiously)
- beat around the bush 빙빙 둘러서 말하다(take around the point)
- become of ~이 (어떻게) 되다
- beef up 강화하다(reinforce, strengthen, fortify)
- before long 머지않아
- before you can say Jack Robinson 눈 깜짝할 사이에[아주 빨리] (very quickly or suddenly)
- behind (the) bars 옥중에서(in prison)
- behind the times 시대에 뒤진
- below normal 정상치보다 낮은
- beside the beach 해변에
- better off 부유한(richer than now)
- beware of ~을 주의하다, 조심하다
- beyond repair 수리의 가망이 없는
- beyond the control of 통제수준을 넘어서
- beyond the pale 일반적으로 용인될 수 없는
  (socially unacceptable)
- Birds of a feather flock together 유유상종
- bite off more than one can chew 힘에 겨운 일을 계획하다
- bite the bullet 이를 꽉 물다, 어려움을 감내하다
- black eye (얻어맞아 생긴) 눈언저리의 검은 멍 → 수치 → 불명예(shame, dishonor, infamy)
- black out 잠시 의식을 잃다, 등화관제하다; 등화관제, 잠시 의식을 잃음
- black sheep 악한, 망나니, (한집안의) 말썽꾼 (villain)
- blow one' own horn 자랑하다 → 떠벌리고 다니다
  (brag → show off)
- blow one' own trumpet 자화자찬하다(boast of one's work)
- put on airs 거만하게 굴다
- ride the high horse 뽐내다 → 거만하게 행동하다(옛날 영국에서 신분이 높을수록 높은 말(큰 말)을 탈 수 있었던 관행에서 비롯된 말이다)
- come down off one's high horse 콧대를 낮추다
- boil down to 결국 ~이 되다, 결국~로 (집약)되다(end up, come down to)
- bone up (on) 열심히 공부하다, 벼락공부하다
  (study hard, study quickly, cram for)
- box up(in) 가두다(confine, detain, enclose in a small space)
- break down 파괴하다, 고장나다; 실패하다; 건강이 쇠약해지다; 분류하다

- break even 손실과 이득이 없이 되다, 비기다
- break ground for 착공하다, 새 사업을 시작하다(start in on)
- break in 길들이다; 침입하다, 끼어들다, 말참견하다 (tame invade, cut in, interfere with)
- break in on 방해하다 (interrupt)
- break off 중단하다, 멈추다(stop, halt, come to an end)
- break out (전쟁, 화재가) 발생하다(begin)
- break the ice 말을 시작하다; 어색한 분위기를 깨뜨리다(start to speak)
- break the news to 중요한 소식(대개 나쁜 소식)을 전하다
- break up 해산시키다(disband, dismiss, scatter)
- bring out (성질을) 나타내다, 발휘하다(reveal)
- bring something to light ~을 밝히다, ~을 폭로하다
- bring to an end 끝내다
- bring to light 알리다, 세상에 내놓다, 세상에 알리다, 폭로하다
- bring up 양육하다, ~에 대해 언급하다(raise, nurse, rear, mention)
- brush up on 재검토하다, 자세히 검사하다, 복습하다, 몸단장하다
- burn the midnight oil 밤늦게까지 일(공부)하다(work(study) late at night)
- button up 단추를 꼭 채우다
- by the same token 마찬가지 이유로, 게다가(for the same reasons)
- by all means 꼭
- by and large 대체로, 일반적으로, 대개(on the whole)
- Buy a pig in a poke(bag) 물건을 보지도 않고 사다 → 충동 구매하다
  물건을 살 때는 당연히 이모저모를 살피고 마음을 결정한다. '자루 속에 있는 돼지를 그대로 사다'라는 식으로 된 'buy a pig in a poke'라는 표현이 있다. 뼈만 앙상하게 남은 비루먹은 녀석인지 통통한 놈인지조차 살피지 않고 선뜻 사버리는 것처럼 '물건을 살피지 않고 사다'라는 뜻을 가진다.
- by dint of ~에 의해서(by means of)
- by halves 불완전하게(imperfectly, incompletely)
- by hook or by crook 무슨 짓을 해서라도, 어떻게 해서라도
- by leaps and bounds 일사천리, 급속하게(very rapidly)
- by means of ~에 의하여
- by no means 결코 아니다, 결코~하지 못하다(anything but; far from being)
- by telephone 전화로
- by the book 규칙대로 → 정확하게(flawlessly) → 원칙대로 → 정식으로
- by the skin of one' teeth 가까스로, 간신히(with the narrowest margin)
- be loaded with ~로 가득 차다 (A abound with B : A에 B가 풍부하다)
- bounceback-ability (바운스배커빌리티) (신조어)
  1) (스포츠팀, 선수가) 완패나 부정적 언론 보도 이후 복귀할 수 있는 능력(역전능력)(the ability to recover after a setback, esp in sport)
  2) 경기에서 열세를 극복하고 승리를 이끌어낼 수 있는 능력을 뜻한다.
- bounce back (병·곤경에서) 다시 회복되다
- bring up the rear 맨 뒤에 오다 → (경주에서) 꼴찌가 되다
  A teacher told him to bring up the rear. (선생님께서는 그에게 맨 뒤에 오라고 말씀하셨다.)

- besides (전치사) ~외에도 → (부사) 게다가, 뿐만 아니라
- back number 시대에 뒤진 사람[방법, 물건]; (명성·인기를 잃은) 과거의 사람
- back scratcher 등긁이(scratchback) → 아첨꾼 → 서로의 이익을 위해 한 패가 된 사람
- back to back 연속적인 → back to back home run (연속홈런)
- bad blood 악감정, 증오
- banana head 바보 → 멍텅구리(blubber head, bone-head)
- band wagon 인기 있는 그룹 → 시류 → 유행
- blabber-mouth 수다쟁이 → 비밀을 경솔하게 지껄이는 사람
- boob (구어)실수, 실패 → 얼간이 → (속)breast
- boob tube 바보상자(텔레비전)
- boondoggle 쓸데없는[무익한] 일(시간과 돈을 낭비하는 일)
- buck passer (구어) 사사건건 책임을 전가하는 사람
- pass the buck 책임을 전가하다
- bummer 기대에 어긋나는 경험 → 실패, 실망(시키는 것)
- brass tacks (사물의)핵심 → 진실 → 요점 → 중대한 사항
- Can I bum a cigarette? → 담배를 빌리다(담배 한 대 빌려 줄래요?)
- I'm between Jobs at the moment. → 구직 중인, 실직상태인(나는 현재 구직 중에 있습니다.)
- break even 본전치기하다
- butt in 끼어들다 → 참견하다
- I'd like to put my two cents in if it's okay with you. 당신이 괜찮다면 제가 조언 한마디 드리고 싶네요 → 조언(의견)을 말하다
- I wasn't born yesterday. 나는 세상 물정 모르는 바보가 아니다 → 세상 물정 모르는 바보다

C

- chastise a man for his fault 과실에 대해서 벌주다
- cater to 부응하다, 만족을 주다 → (저속한 욕구) 영합하다 (pander)
- call names 욕하다
  (Verbally abuse someone, use offensive epithets)
- come under fire 집중포화를 받다 → 비난받다
  (received criticism)
- clear the way (사전) 준비를 하다; 모든 장애물을 제거하다
- cultural myth 문화 통념, 문화적 신화
- colour-blind 색맹의 → 인종 차별을 하지 않는
- cut the Gordian knot
  1) 어려운 일을 단번에 해결하다
  2) 어려운 문제를 단순하고 과감하며 극단적인 방식으로 쉽게 해결한다 → 알렉산더 대왕이 도저히 풀 수 없는 매듭을 잘라버린 데서 유래
  3) cut the Gordian knot (고르디우스의 매듭을 끊다)
  4) the Gordian knot (복잡 미묘한 문제)
  5) He is a marvelous man. He cut the Gordian knot in difficulty situation. (그는 정말 대단한 사람이다. 어려운 상황에서도 일을 단번에 해결했다.)
- cut no ice with ~에 영향을 끼치지 않다(do not influence)
- chicken-and-egg 닭이 먼저냐 달걀이 먼저냐의
- chew the cheese 토하다, 게우다
- chew the cud 새김질하다, 곰곰이 생각하다, 심사숙고하다[of]
- chew the fat 수다를 떨다, 담소를 나누다
- chew the rag 불평을 늘어놓다, 나무라다(구어)
- chew the scenery 과잉 연기를 하다

- chew the cud 심사숙고하다, 깊이 생각하다, (소) 되새김질하다 (ruminate)
- chew the fat 수다를 떨다 → 담소를 나누다(shoot the breeze, shoot the bull)
  1) fat는 지방 덩어리 → 수다를 떨고 있는 모습이 질긴 지방 덩어리를 씹고 있는 것에 비유한 구어 표현
  2) 친한 사람들과 오랜 시간 동안 별로 중요하지 않은 내용의 수다를 떠는 것
- call a spade a spade 사실 그대로 말하다(speak frankly)
- call at (건물을) 방문하다(visit)
- call down 꾸짖다(scold, admonish, rebuke, reprimand, reproach)
- call it a day 일을 마치다, 하루를 마치다(finish work of the day)
- call it quits 끝내다, 사임하다, 물러나다(finish, resign, retire)
- call it square 결말을 짓다
- call off 취소하다, 중지하다(cancel, stop)
- call on (사람을) 방문하다(visit)
- call one's shots 솔직하게 말하다
- call the shots 지배하다, 감독하다(dominate, supervise)
- can't hold a candle to someone 비교도 안되다 → 발밑에도 못 따라가다(not [to be] equal to someone; unable to measure up to someone)
- can't make heads or tails of 이해할 수 없다; ~를 알 수 없다(It beats me, you search me, It's all Greek to)
- cannot see the wood for the tress 나무만 보고 숲을 보지 못하다
- capitalize on 이용하다, 편승하다(cash in on, make the best of, make the most of, make use of, take advantage of, avail oneself of, draw on)
- carrot and stick 당근과 채찍, 회유와 위협 (reward and punishment)
- carry out 수행하다, 성취하다 (perform, accomplish → implement)
- carry the ball 책임을 지다, 선수를 치다, 주도권을 잡다(be responsible for)
- case by case 한 건씩, 개별적으로
- case in point 적절한 예(good example)
- Catch you later 나중에 봐요
- cash in on 이용하다, ~에서 이익을 내다(take advantage of)
- catch as catch can 한사코 붙잡다, 기를 쓰고 달려들다
- catch cold 감기에 걸리다(get a cold)
- catch fire 불이 붙다(burn)
- catch on 인기를 얻다, 유행하다(become popular)
- catch on (to something) (~을) 이해하다 → 터득하다, 적응하다 (adapt)
- catch up with 따라잡다, 만회하다(overtake, keep up with)
- chances are (that) ~할 가능성이 높다, 아마~일 것이다
- chase a rainbow 불가능한 것을 추구하다
- cede to 양도하다 → 할양하다(abandon, abdicate, demit, forswear, hand over, quitclaim, relinquish, render, renounce, resign, surrender, waive, yield)
- chill the/one's spine 등골을 오싹하게 하다(cause feelings of fear and horror)
- chip in 기부하다, 끼어들다(pitch in)
- chip on one's shoulder 시비조, 걸핏하면 싸우려 드는 성질 (aggressive attitude)
- churn out 대량 생산하다(crank out)
- claim check 보관증, 예탁 증서(claim tag)

- clean bill of health 건강 증명서, 적격증명서 (a medical certificate)
- cliffhanger 가슴 조이게 하는 것(a very suspenseful race/game)
- close at hand 가까이에(nearby)
- close call/shave 위기일발, 아슬아슬한 위기(a narrow escape from danger)
- close down 폐쇄하다, 중지하다, 휴업하다(stop operations)
- close out 다 팔아치우다, 헐값으로 팔다(sell off goods at low prices)
- close round 포위하다
- coast is clear 지금이 적기다, 지금이 호기다(no one is around)
- cold feet 겁내는 모양, 도망칠 자세(a loss of courage or nerve)
- cold snap 한파(cold wave)
- come to pass 사건이 일어나다 → 생기다(occur)
- comb through 샅샅이 뒤지다(sift through)
- come to grief 실패하다, 재난을 당하다(end in total failure)
- come clean 실토하다, 자백하다(admit, confess)
- come down with 병에 걸리다(become sick with)
- come in handy 도움이 되다, 유용하다(be useful)
- compose oneself 진정시키다, 마음을 가라앉히다(control his feelings)(To make (oneself) calm or tranquil) (Compose yourself and deal with the problems logically)
- come to think of it 다시 생각해 보니까(As I think again, on second thought)
- come true 실현되다(really happen, be realized)
- coming right up 곧 나옵니다(패스트푸드점에서 주문을 하면 들을 수 있는 대답)
- come up 나타나다(turn up, show up)
- come out of nowhere 아무 데도 없는 곳에서 나오다 → 유명해지다 → 갑자기 뜨다(appearing suddenly, without warning)
- come up with 생각해내다, ~를 따라잡다(find out, catch up)
- come up in the world 출세하다
- common ground 공통 기반, 견해의 일치점 (shared beliefs/interests)
- comply with 따르다 → 응하다 → 준수하다(follow, obey)
- conform to 따르다, 일치시키다(abide by)
- congratulate on ~를 축하하다
- consist of ~로 이루어져 있다(comprise, be made up of)
- cook up 날조하다, 조작하다(fabricate, concoct)
- (as) cool as cucumber 아주 침착한(composed, calm)
- cope with 대처하다, 극복하다(deal effectively)
- copycat 모방하는 사람(imitator, mimic)
- count for much 중요하다(be important)
- count in 계산에 넣다(figure in)
- count on 의지하다, 기대하다, 믿다 (fall back on, rely on, depend on)
- count out 제외하다(exclude, leave out)
- cover up 감추다, 숨기다(hide, conceal)
- crack down on 단속하다, 단호한 조치를 취하다 (clamp down on)
- cream of the crop 가장 좋은 것(the best, top choice)
- cross a bridge before one comes to it 일어나지도 않을 일을 걱정하다
- cross one's mind 생각이 떠오르다(hit upon an idea)
- cross the line 선을 넘다(go too far)
- cry over spilled milk 저질러진 일을 후회하다
- cut back 삭감하다, 줄이다(reduce)

- cut corners 돈을 절약하다, 지름길로 가다(economize)
- cut down 줄이다, 베어 넘기다(reduce)
- cut in 방해하다, 끼어들다(interfere, interrupt)
- cut out for ~에 적격인, ~에 적합한(be suited for)
- cut short 단축하다, 갑자기 끝내다(shorten, stop abruptly)
- calibrate (캘리브레이트)
  1) 정확하게 조정하다 → 보정하다 → to correct or adjust(the scale or instrument)
  2) 테스터기를 작동시키기 전이나 이상이 있을 경우, 처음의 영점 조정을 검사하거나 수정하는 것을 이른다.
- call collect 수신자부담 전화를 하다(the receiver pays for the call)
- call for 불러오다, 요구하다, 요청하다, 필요로 하다(require, demand)
- call it a day 하루 일을 마치다, 오늘은 그만두다; 단념하다
- call long distance 장거리 전화를 하다(make a long distance call)
- call one' names 비난하다(abuse, curse each other)
- call the roll 출석을 부르다(read the list aloud to see if everyone is there)
- Can I drop you off? 함께 편승할까요?
- cannot ~ too 아무리 ~해도 지나치지 않다
- care for ~을 좋아하다, 돌보다
- carry ~ to excess 지나치게 ~ 하다
- carry away 흥분시키다, 가져가 버리다(excite)
- carry on 계속 진행하다(continue, run on)
- carve out a career for oneself 자력으로 길을 개척해나가다
- cast a doubt 의심하다(be doubtful, be suspicious)
- catch a glimpse of it ~을 흘끗 보다
- catch someone red handed 현행범으로 잡다
- catch up with 따라 잡다
- chain smoker 줄담배를 피우는 사람
- check up 조사하다
- clear away 치우다, 제거하다(remove, eliminate, get rid of)
- clear one' throat (말을 시작하기 전에) 헛기침을 하다
- close call 위기일발, 아슬아슬한 순간(narrow escape, narrow squeak)
- coincide with ~와 동시에 일어나다(occurred at the same time as)
- collect 수신자가 부담하는(paid for by the receiver)
- come across 우연히 만나다, 마주치다(encounter)
- come between 사이를 가르다, 이간질하다
- come in 관여하다
  That's where the paralegal come in. (그 업무에는 변호사 보조원이 관여한다.)
- come by 곁을 지나가다, 들르다; 손에 넣다, 얻다(buy, get, obtain)
- come close to 거의 ~하게 되다, 자칫 ~할 뻔하다
- come down with 질병에 걸리다 (contract, catch an infectious illness)
- come home to 가슴에 사무치다, 큰 감동을 주다 (deeply impress)
- come down to 귀결되다, 요약되다(is reduced to)
- come in third 3등으로 들어오다
- come into (재산을) 물려받다; ~에 들어가다, ~에 가입하다 (inherit; enter)
- come into being 생기다, 태어나다
- come into effect 효력을 나타내다, 실시되다, 발효하다
- come into one' own 자기 역량을 충분히 발휘하다(show one's ability)
- come into one' thought 생각이 떠오르다(cross one's mine)
- come natural to ~에게는 쉽다
- come off 이루어지다, 행해지다, 실현되다, 성공하다(succeed)
- come to 정신이 들다, 의식을 회복하다, 결국 ~가 되다(regain)
- come to an end 멈추다, 끝나다
- come to blows 주먹질이나 말로 싸우다(hit each other)
- come to life 의식을 되찾다(recover oneself)
- come to nothing 소용없다, 무위로 끝나다, 수포로 돌아가다
- come to pass 일어나다, 생기다(occur)
- come to a halt 멈추다, 정지하다
- come to terms with 타협하다 → (사태 등을) 감수하다
- come to the fore 두드러지다, 표면화되다, 세상의 이목을 끌다 (prominent)
- come to the point 요점을 말하다
- come under fire 집중포화를 받다, 비난받다(receive criticisim)
- come up against ~에 대항하다, (곤란, 반대) 직면하다(face, confront)
- come up to ~에 부응하다, ~쪽으로 오다, 필적하다
- come up with 제안하다, 아이디어를 생각해 내다 (suggest, propose)
- come upon 우연히 발견하다(find expectedly)
- compensate for 보상하다 (To offset; counterbalance: redeem) (indemnify, recompense, redress, reimburse, remunerate, repay, requite)
- comply with 따르다, 순응하다, 동의하다 (conform to, obey, conform to)
- conceive of 생각하다(think of)
- conjure up (상상으로)만들어내다, 출현시키다
- concentrate on ~에 집중하다(focus on)
- confer with ~와 협의하다
- consist of ~으로 구성되다
- conflict-of-interest 이익충돌(두 가지 동시에 동등하고 공정하게 양립하기 어려운 상황)(A conflict between a person's private interests and public obligations)
- contingent upon ~좌우되는 → ~을 조건으로 하는(determined by conditions or circumstances that follow)
- contrary to ~에 반하여
- contribute to ~에 공헌하다, ~에 기여하다
- cook one' goose 실패하게 되다, 망쳐놓다(ruin one's chances)
- cool (kick) one' heels 오랫동안 기다리다(wait long)
- cope with 대처하다(deal with, treat; get over, overcome)
- correspond to 일치하다, 상응하다(be equivalent to)
- correspond with ~에 부합하다
- cost an arm and a leg 엄청난 비용이 들다
- cost a fortune (톡톡히) 비싼 값을 치루다
- cost a pretty penny 많은 돈이 들다, 많은 돈을 치르다(cost a lot of money)
- count on 의지하다, 믿다(rely on, depend on, count on)
- crack a joke 농담하다(tell a humorous story, tell a joke)
- crack down 단속하다, 엄하게 다스리다, 엄한 조치를 취하다(on) (enforce law; take strong and severe action to deal with something bad)
- cross one' mind 생각이 떠오르다; (생각이) 마음에 떠오르다 (occur to, come into one's thoughts, occur to someone, strike

- someone)
- **cut a fine (brilliant, conspicuous) figure** 두각을 나타내다
- **cut back on** (비용을) 절감하다, 줄이다
- **cut corners** 지름길로 가다; (돈, 시간, 노력을) 절약하다 (take a shorter way; reduce(money, time or labor required)
- **cut down** 줄이다(reduce, lower, lessen, cut back)
- **cut ice** 효과가 있다(have effect)
- **cut no ice with** 아무런 효과가 없다(have no effect)
- **cut off** 중단하다, 끊다, (통화) 가로막다, 베어내다, 삭제하다 (stop, delete, erase)
- **cut from whole cloth** 완전한 거짓말이다 (sharing a lot of similarities)
- **cut someone dead** 보고도 보지 못한 체하다 (refuse to: recognize someone you know in order to be rude)
- **cut someone to the quick** 감정을 몹시 상하게 하다
- **cut-and-dried** 미리 준비된, 미리 결정된; 신선함이 없는, 틀에 박힌, 진부한 (already settled and unlikely to be changed; banal, clich, stereotyped)
- **cover one's back**
  1) 미리 핑계거리를 만들어 놓다 → 미리 구실을 하다
  2) 문제가 생길 경우를 대비하다
  3) 전투에서 동료를 위해 뒤에서 엄호사격을 하는 것에서 유래한 것
- **Cold call** (상품 판매 권유를 위해) 영업전화를 하다
- **Cut the crap** 헛소리 집어치워
- **congruent-incongruent effect** 일치-불일치 효과 (Corresponding; congruous → compatible)
- **customized production** 주문 제작방식
- **customize** [컴퓨터] 커스터마이즈하다 ((자기 취향에 맞도록 설정을 바꾸다)) 이용자가 사용 방법과 기호에 맞추어서 하드웨어나 소프트웨어를 설정하거나 기능을 변경하는 것

D

- **desensitize** [디센서타이즈] 둔감하게 만들다 → 냉담[무관심]하게 하다(to)(insensitive or less sensitive → cause not to be sensitive)
- **dispersity** 분산도(a characteristic of particle dimensions in disperse systems)
- **disperse** 흩어지다, 해산하다; 해산시키다, 흩어지다
- **dispersed** 흩어진, 분산된
- **Dibs on the cold pizza!** 식은 피자는 내가 찜! → ~은 내가 찜!
- **Get with the times!** 시대에 발좀 맞춰!
- **You're stylin!** 간지 나는데 (굉장히 스타일 좋을 때) 스타일린
- **I know he's not much to look at.** 그게 볼품없게 생겼다는 거 나도 알아.
- **Is she a Hottie?** 그 여자애 섹시녀냐?
- **He's quite a catch, isn't he?** 그는 꽤나 킹카죠, 그렇지 않아요?
- **You knockout** 넌 끝내주게 매력적인 여자야
- **doctor accounts** 계산을 속이다(manipulated)(to make different in order to deceive, tamper with, falsify, or adulterate)
- **deracinate** [디래시네이트] 뿌리 뽑다 → 근절시키다 (root out, extirpate, uproot)
- **drown out** 떠내려 보내다 → 몰아내다
- **dumb down** 지나치게 단순화하다(suppressed) (to make or become less intellectually demanding or sophisticated)
- **dead-head** 무료 입장재[승객] → 빈 차 → 승객 없이 달리다 (travel empty)
- **drive up** (값을) 올리다
- **date back to** ~로 거슬러 올라가다(go back to the past)
- **dawn on** (생각이) 떠오르다 (come across one's mind)
- **day in and day out** 날이면 날마다, 매일(everyday)
- **dance on a rope** 교수형에 처해지다
- **days are numbered** 수명이 다되다(not many days are left)
- **dead heat** 대접전, 거의 동시에 골인하는 것(close race/game)
- **deal in** 취급하다(trade in)
- **deal with** 다루다, 처리하다(treat, handle)
- **decide on** ~하기로 결정하다(agree on)
- **deep down** 내심은
- **deep water** 곤경, 궁지, 어려움 (hot water, trouble: grid lock, dead lock)
- **delve into** 탐구하다(search thoroughly for facts)
- **depend on** ~에 의존하다(rely on → contingent upon) (bank on, count on, rely on, rest on, fall back on, lean on) (resort to, have recourse to, rest with, be up to, hinge on)
- **die away** 차차 약해지다, 수그러들다 (gradually become weaker)
- **dig in one's heels/toes** 자신의 입장을 고수하다 (stick one's heels in)
- **dime a dozen** 흔해 빠진, 싸구려의(easy to get, common)
- **do favor** 호의를 베풀다(help somebody)
- **do away with** ~를 없애다, 폐지하다(get rid of, abolish)
- **do good** 이롭게 하다(be helpful)
- **do harm** 해를 끼치다(damage)
- **do the dishes** 설거지하다
- **down in the dumps** 우울한 → 낙심된 (down in the mouth, long face, be in the blues)
- **down in the mouth** 우울한 → 낙담한(depressed)
- **catch 40 winks** 잠깐 자다
- **doze off** 꾸벅꾸벅 졸다(drowse)
- **hit the hay** 잠자다(hit the sack)
- **sleep like a log** 깊이 자다(sleep like a top)
- **drag on** 질질 오래 끌다(prolong)
- **drag one's feet/heels** 일부러 꾸물거리다, 늑장 부리다(act slowly on purpose)
- **draw the line** 한계를 정하다(set the limit)
- **draw up** 작성하다
- **drink like a fish** 술을 과하게 마시다(drink like a horse)
- **drink to** 건배하다, 축배를 들다(toast)
- **drive away** 몰아내다, 없애다
- **drive home to** 납득시키다, 통감하게 하다(make clear) (convey a message forcefully)
- **drop/send a line** 몇 줄 써 보내다(send a short letter)
- **drop by** 잠깐 들르다(stop off at, stop by)
- **drop in the bucket** 새발의 피(a drop in the ocean)
- **drop off** 내려놓다
- **drop the ball** 일을 망치다 → 중대한 실수를 하다 (commit a faux pas or a fault or make a serious mistake)
- **drop out** 그만두다, 중퇴하다(quit, stop, leave)
- **drum up** 북을 쳐서 모으다, 선전하다
- **dry as dust** 무미건조한
- **dry behind the ears** 경험 있는(experienced)

- due to ~로 인해
- dwell on 곰곰이 생각하다(excogitate, ruminate)
  (mull over, muse about, think about:contemplate)
- day in and day out 언제나(continually)
- deal with 다루다, 처리하다
- delve into 탐구하다, 깊이 파고들다
- depend on 의존하다
- devil's advocate 반대입장을 취하는 사람(dissident) → 트집을 잡는 사람
- depend upon it 틀림없다(to be sure)
- deprive A of B : A로부터 B를 빼앗다
- dine out 외식하다(eat out)
- discrepancy 차이(differnce)
- dispense with ~없이 지내다(do without, go without → forgo ~ 없이 때우다
- dispose of 처분하다; 제거하다(sell; get rid of)
  (disposition 배열, 배치 → 처리, 처분 → 경향, 소질, 기질)
- do a favor for a person ~에게 은혜를 베풀다
- do away with 없애다, 폐지하다(discard, abolish, eliminate)
- do one's best 최선을 다하다
- do one's favor ~의 부탁을 들어주다
- doubting thomas 의심이 많은 사람
- do one's utmost 최선을 다하다, 온 힘을 기울이다
- do someone or something in 파멸시키다, 못쓰게 만들다(ruin)
- do the cleaning 청소하다, 세탁하다
- do up 수리하다, 고치다(repair, mend)
- do with (어떻게) 때를 보내다; 처치하다, 처분하다
- do without ~없이 지내다
- dog in the manger 심술쟁이(be cross or ill-natured)
- double-cross 배반(배신)하다(cheat especially someone with whom one has already agreed to do something dishonest)
- down and out 가난한(destitute, impoverished, indigent, needy)
- down in the mouth 낙담하여, 풀이 죽어
  (in low spirits, depressed)
- down-to-earth 현실적인, 실제적인(practical)
- drag on 질질 끌다
- drape the table 식탁을 덮다
- draw a blank 허탕짚다 → 실패하다 → 아무런 결과를 얻지 못하다
  (not succeed in finding or getting something)
- draw forth 이끌어내다(elicit)
- draw up 문서를 작성하다
- dress down 꾸짖다, 매질하다
  (chide, rebuke, reprimand, reproach, reprove)
- dress up 잘 차려입다, 쫙 빼입다, 정장하다
  (put on nice clothes, put on one's clothes, put on formal clothes)
- drive someone up a wall 누구를 화나게 하다(enrage, drive someone mad)
- drive something home (못 등을) 단단히 박다, 납득시키다
  (make something unmistakably clear)
- drivie ~ crazy 미치게 하다, 화나게 하다
- drop off 데려다 주다
- drop one's line 편지쓰다
- drop out 참석이나 참가하는 것을 그만두다
- drop a dime [다임] (경찰에) 밀고하다
- sheer drudgery 아주 고된 일
  (hard monotonous routine work)

E

- It's kind of a Catch-22 일종의 진퇴양난인 상황이죠
- I'm on a roll. 나 잘 나가고 있어(직장, 일, 이성 관계)
- You've crossed the line. 넌 도가 지나쳤어.
- I hit rock bottom. 전 바닥까지 내려가다. → (인생)밑바닥까지 내려가다.
- Let's just keep our fingers crossed. 우리 그냥 행운을 빕시다
- Everything's gonna turn out fine. 모든 일이 잘 풀리다 → 잘 풀리다
- You're on thin ice. 너 위태위태 하구나. → 위태위태한
- With all due respect. 외람된 말씀입니다만 (상대방의 의견 → 정중하게 반대할 때)
- Over my dead body. 눈에 흙이 들어가지 전에는 안된다(강력한 반대)
- I weigh the pros and cons. 장점과 단점을 저울질하죠. (이해득실)
- I'm just playing the devil's advocate. 전 그냥 반대하는 입장에서 말해보는 겁니다.
- You're way off base on this 이 부분은 네가 헛다리 짚은 거야
- When will he give us the green light? 그가 언제 우리에게 승낙을 주실까요?
- I can't argue with you. 토를 달수가 없네. (동감해)
- Do we see eye to eye? 우리 서로 의견이 일치하는 건가요?
- we're on the same page. 같은 생각이다
- They're all tone-deaf 그들은 모두 음치예요
- Every. Let's take five. 여러분 잠깐 휴식을 취합시다
- embark on 시작하다, 착수하다(start out on)
- earn one's living 생계를 꾸리다(make a living)
- easier said than done 말보다 실천이 어렵다
  (to do is more difficult than to say)
- end up 결국 ~가 되다(end in)
- enjoy oneself 즐기다(have fun, have a good time)
- enroll in 등록하다, 입학[입회]시키다(register)
- entitled to ~를 받을 자격이 있는(having a right)
- every cloud has a silver lining 하늘이 무너져도 솟아날 구멍이 있다
- an eye for an eye 눈에는 눈(a tooth for a tooth)
- except for ~를 제외하고
- earn a good wage 상당한 급료를 받다
- eat crow 굴욕을 참다 → 마지 못해 자기의 실패[패배, 잘못]를 인정하다(To be forced to accept a humiliating defeat)
- eat one's words 앞서 한 말을 취소하다
  (withdraw one's statement)
- egg on 선동하다(instigate, abet, incite, urge on)
- enter by forces 완력으로 밀고 들어가다
- enter into 공감하다; 시작하다, 관여하다(sympathize, commence)
- elephant in the room 금기시되는 주제(서로 말하기 꺼리는)
  (an obvious truth that is being ignored or goes unaddressed)
  1) 좁은 방안에 들어와 있는 코끼리처럼, 못 본 척 하거나 무시할 수 없는 데도 외면하고 있는 진실 → 모든 사람이 문제라는 것은 알고 있지만 쉽사리 꺼내지 못하는 이슈
  2) The term refers to a question, problem, solution, or controversial issue that is obvious, but which is ignored by a group of people, generally because it causes embarrassment or is taboo
- every inch 완전히(completely, thoroughly)
- Every cloud has a silver lining.

257

(괴로움의 반면에는 기쁨이 있다, 쥐구멍에도 볕들 날 있다)
- eat one's heart out 비탄(큰 슬픔)에 빠지다

F

- bridge and tunnel 촌뜨기
- She's a trainwreck. 그녀는 사고만 치고 다니지.
- My life's fucked up! 내 인생은 *됐어
- You can't go cold turkey. (마약, 담배, 술) 완전히 끊다.
- It's all Greek to me. 무슨 말인지 전혀 모르다
- That's news to me. 그건 금시초문이네요. (새로운 소식)
- That figures! (예상하고 있던 상황에 대해) 그럴 줄 알았어!
- First things first. 중요한 일부터 하자.
- fly by the seat of one's pants
  1) (계기에 의존하지 않고) 직감으로 [손으로 더듬어] 조종하다
  2) It was a dangerous moment. Pilots had to fly by the seat of their pants.
  (위험한 순간이었다. 조종사들은 계기에 의존하지 않고 직감으로 조종해야 했다.)
- face off 대결하다(fight, take on)
- face the music 책임을 지다 → (자신의 행동에 대해) 비난[벌]을 받다
- face-to-face 얼굴을 마주 보고(facing each other)
- factor in 계산에 넣다(include a particular thing) → 고려하다[감안하다]
- fall asleep 잠들다
- fall back on 의지하다(rely on, depend on)
- fall behind 뒤떨어지다, 기일에 늦다(can't keep pace)
- fall for (이성에) 반하다, 매혹되다(fall in love with)
- fall short 부족하다, 모자라다(be lacking, be insufficient)
- fall out with 사이가 틀어지다 → 다투다
  (Disagree, quarrel, contend with)
- fall through 그르치다, 수포로 돌아가다(fail)
- fed up 물린, 싫증이 난(getting sick of)
- feel free to 자유롭게~하다
- fight off 격퇴하다, 퇴치하다(defeat)
- figure out 이해하다, 풀다, 해결하다, 계산하다(understand, settle)
  (come across, get across, put across, catch on, get the picture, make sense of)
- fill in 자세히 알려주다, 빈칸을 채우다, 구멍을 메우다(inform in details)
- fill out 빈 곳을 채우다, 작성하다, 기입하다, 완성시키다(complete)
- fill up (기름, 가스) 채우다(make a container full)
- fish in troubled water 어부지리를 얻다 → 혼란을 틈타 한몫 보다
- fit like a glove 꼭 맞다[끼다](fit perfectly)
- flare up 확 타오르다(fly into rage)
- fly in the ointment 옥에 티(tiny flaw in a gem) → 연고 속에 빠져 있는 날 파리(A detrimental circumstance or detail; a drawback)
- fly the coop 떠나다, 도망가다, 달아나다[날다] (Escape, run away)
- follow suit 선례를 따르다 → 남이 하는 대로 하다(do as others do)
- follow up on 끝까지 추적하다(add further on)
- for a rainy day 만일을 위하여(against a rainy day)
- for all I know 아마~일 것이다

- for good 영원히(forever, permanently)
- for one's part ~로서는(as for)
- for one thing 첫째로
- for sale 팔려고 내놓은(available for purchase)
- for short 줄여서, 생략해서
  (by way of abbreviation or contraction)
- for sure 확실히(certainly, surely)
- for the most part 대부분은, 대개는(mostly, chiefly)
- for the record 공식적으로(officially, formally)↔(off the record)
- for the sake of ~를 위하여(to one's advantage, in the favor of)
- for the time being 당분간(for now, for the present)
- for this reason 이런 이유로
- frame up 조작하다, 날조하다(manipulate)
- free-for-all 누구나 참가할 수 있는, 무료의(open to everyone)
- from somebody's point of view ~의 입장에서 보면
  (from somebody's viewpoint)
- from scratch 무에서, 처음부터, 맨 처음부터
  (from the beginning)
  (fledgling, embryonic, rudimentary, incipient, fetal)
- from the beginning 처음부터(from the start)
- from the bottom of one's heart 진심으로
  (most sincerely, with all one's heart)
- from the horse's mouth 확실한 소식통으로부터(from the reliable sources)
- from time to time 때때로, 가끔(sometimes, occasionally)
- by hook or by crook 수단과 방법을 안 가리고[어떻게 해서든지]
- fight tooth and nail
  싸우다(모든 수단을 다해) → 싸우다(이로 물고 손톱으로 할퀴면서)
  (to use a lot of effort to oppose someone or achieve something)
- face the music 벌을 받다, 잘못을 인정하다
  (accept the consequences, accept punishment)
- fall back on ~에 의지하다(have recourse to)
  (bank on, count on, rely on, rest on, lean on, resort to, be up to)
- fall into servitude 노예화되다(be(become) enslaved)
- fall out with 다투다, 싸우다(quarrel, brawl, bicker, altercate)
- fall to (어떤 것을 하기) 시작하다
- farrago[파라고]
  이리저리 긁어모은 것, 뒤섞은 물건, 뒤범벅(medley, confused mixture → hotchpotch)
- fall upon 불행 등이 닥치다, ~에 착수하다
- familiarize A with B : A가 B에 익숙하게 하다
- far and away 훨씬, 단연; 틀림없이, 분명히
  (very much, by far; without exception)
- far from ~ ing : ~하기는커녕(not at all)
- fasten one's seatbelts 안전 벨트를 매다
- follow one's nose 직감에 의존하다 → 곧장 앞으로 나아가다
- feed on ~을 먹이(주식)로 하다(live on)
- feel at home 마음 편하다
- feel blue 우울하다(be depressed, be low-spirited)
  (be) a feather in one's cap
  1) 명예 → 자랑거리(an honor; a reward for something)
  2) 과거 전쟁 중 적의 병사를 죽였을 때 죽인 수만큼 모자에 깃털을 달아주고 이를 자랑스러워 한것에서 유래
- feel for 동정하다; 더듬어 찾다(sympathize with; grope for)
- feel like ~ ing : ~하고 싶은 마음이다
- fend for 돌보다, 부양하다, 보살피다(look after)
- figure out 이해하다, 계산하다(understand)

- [ ] file a lawsuit 소송을 제기하다
- [ ] fill in for 대리 역할을 하다, 대신하다(substitute, replace)
- [ ] fill it up ~을 가득 채우다
- [ ] fill out 빈 곳을 채우다, 써넣다, 작성하다(complete)
- [ ] find (someone or something) out 찾아내다, 알아내다
- [ ] fix up 완전히 고치다, 수리(수선)하다(repair, mend)
- [ ] flare up 확 타오르다, 불끈 성내다
- [ ] flat broke 무일푼의
- [ ] fly in the face of (공공연히) 반대하다(go against)
- [ ] follow in someone's footsteps ~의 선례(전철)를 따르다
  (do the same things as someone do earlier)
- [ ] follow suit 선례를 따르다(do the same)
- [ ] follow up on (약속 등을) 잘 이행하다, 적절한 처리를 하다
- [ ] for a limited time 제한된 시간 동안
- [ ] for a more extensive description 보다 더 종합적인 설명을 위해서
- [ ] for all ~에도 불구하고
- [ ] for all ~에도 불구하고
- [ ] for good 영원히(forever, permanently)
- [ ] for next to nothing 거의 공짜로
- [ ] for nothing 공짜로
- [ ] for one thing 무엇보다도(above all, first of all, more than anything else)
- [ ] for the life of one 도저히, 아무리~해도 (않다)
- [ ] for the long pull 긴급상황에 대한(for emergency)
- [ ] for the time being 당분간
- [ ] fret over ~에 대해 우려하다, 걱정하다(worry about)
- [ ] fringe benefit 부가급부(연금, 유급휴가, 보험급여 등)
  (an added favor or service given with a job, besides wages, such as the use of car, free of cheap meals, or free insurance)
- [ ] from hand to mouth 그날 벌어 그날 먹는, 겨우 생계를 유지하는
  (with only just enough money to live on and nothing for the future)
- [ ] from now on 지금부터, 금후
- [ ] from scratch 날것으로부터, 처음부터(using fresh foods)
- [ ] fall on deaf ears 무시되다 → 귀 기울여지지 않다(Be ignored or disregarded)

G

- [ ] Drop the gun! (총 등의 무기) 버리다 → Freeze 꼼짝마! 움직이지마!
- [ ] Copycat 모방범죄(자) → 표절쟁이
- [ ] No one's getting hustled. 어떤 누구도 속임을 당하지 않을거야 → 속이다
- [ ] Am I being followed? 저 미행 당하고 있는 건가요? → 미행 당하다
- [ ] Do I need to Laywer up? 제가 변호사를 선임해야 할까요? → 변호사를 선임하다
- [ ] We just solved the case. 저희가 방금 사건을 해결했어요.
- [ ] We have a warrant for your arrest. → 영장을 가져오다
  저희는 당신을 체포하기 위한 영장을 가져왔습니다.
- [ ] I got busted in Boston with some dope. → 체포되다
  난 마약을 가지고 있다가 보스턴에서 체포 당했어요.
- [ ] You're on suspension. 넌 정직처분 되었어.
  수사드라마를 보면 실수를 한 형사가 얼마간의 기간동안 경찰배지(badge)을 뺏기고 활동을 못하게 되는 경우 → 정직처분

- [ ] He maxed out the limit. 한도를 초과하다(신용카드, 체크카드)
- [ ] gnomic[노믹] 격언의, 격언적인 (aphoristic, sententious)
- [ ] gift of gab 능변, 말재주
- [ ] get over 극복하다(overcome)
- [ ] glance through 짧은 시간에 훑어보다
- [ ] get a new lease of life 활기를 되찾다
- [ ] give vent to 표출하다, 발산하다(express → give off → give out)
- [ ] gain/get access to ~에 접근할 수 있다 (reach)
- [ ] get a head start 다른 사람보다 일찍 시작하다
  (start earlier than someone else)
- [ ] get a kick out of ~에서 즐거움을 얻다 (find great pleasure in)
- [ ] get around to ~할 시간이 생기다(have time to)
- [ ] get away from it all (일 등을 잊고) 완전히 푹 쉬다(rest up)
- [ ] get away with murder 죄를 짓고 처벌을 받지 않다(get away with)
- [ ] get cold get 겁을 먹다, 낙담하다 (be frightened, be scared)
- [ ] get hold of 연락을 취하다, 손에 넣다(reach)
- [ ] get in touch with 통신하다, 접촉하다(communicate with, contact)
- [ ] get it straight from horse's mouth 본인에게서 직접 듣다
  (hear directly from somebody)
- [ ] get lost 길을 잃다(lose one's way)
- [ ] get nowhere 성공하지 못하다, 효과 없다, 아무 소용없다(not succeed)
- [ ] get off the ground 이륙하다(take off, launch)
- [ ] get off the hook 곤경에서 벗어나다(get free)
- [ ] get off to a good start 출발이 좋다(begin well)
- [ ] get one's money's worth 본전 뽑다, 최대한 이용하다(make the most of)
- [ ] get out of hand 통제가 안 되다(get out of control)
- [ ] get rid of 제거하다, 없애다(eliminate, remove)
- [ ] get the ax 해고되다, 제적 당하다(get the bag/boot)
- [ ] get the boot 해고되다, 제명되다(be fired, be kicked out)
- [ ] get the green light 허가를 얻다(get the go-ahead)
- [ ] get the better of 이기다, 능가하다(defeat)
- [ ] get the hang of ~의 요령을 터득하다 (get the knack of)
- [ ] get the short end of the stick 불리한 입장에 서다 → 운이 나쁘다
- [ ] get the picture 상황을 파악하다(understand the whole situation)
- [ ] get the word/message 이해하다, 해결하다(understand)
- [ ] get together 모이다, 단결하다(gather)
- [ ] get wind of ~에 대한 소식을 듣다(hear about)
- [ ] get worked up 신경이 곤두 서있다, 흥분하다(get nervous, upset)
- [ ] give a big hand 열심히 칭찬하다, 찬사를 보내다(praise)
- [ ] get promoted 승진하다
- [ ] give a break 기회를 주다, 한번 봐주다(give an opportunity)
- [ ] give a call 전화하다(give a ring/buzz)
- [ ] give a hard time 괴롭히다(bother)
- [ ] give a party 파티를 열어주다
- [ ] give away 남에게 무료로 주다(give for free)
- [ ] give birth to 낳다(bear, deliver)
- [ ] give credit for 인정하다(believe that somebody possesses something)
- [ ] give it a try 한번 해보다(try, attempt)
- [ ] give off (빛, 열, 향기) 방출하다, 발하다(emit, release)
- [ ] give one's word 약속을 하다, 언질을 주다(promise)
- [ ] give rise to 야기시키다 (cause, lead to)

- give someone a lift ~를 태워주다
- give someone the boot 쫓아내다, 해고하다(kick out, fire)
- give something one's best shot 어떤 일에 최선을 다하다(do one's best)
- give the ax 갑자기 관계를 끊다, 해고하다, 제명하다(give the boot/bag)
- give the benefit of the doubt 확실하지 않을 때는 무죄라고 판단하다
- give way 양보하다, 무너지다(surrender, collapse)
- gloss over 그럴듯하게 얼버무리다(try to make what is wrong seem right)
- go aground 좌초하다, 좌절되다(run aground)
- go by the book 규칙을 그대로 따르다(follow the rules)
- go down in history 역사에 남다[기록되다](be remembered for good)
- go downhill 악화하다, 쇠퇴하다(worsen decline)
- give the shirt off one's back 아낌없이 주다, 남에게 무엇이든 주다
- go up and down 오르락내리락하다(fluctuated)
- go Dutch 각자 부담하다(split the bill, go fifty-fifty)
- go halfway 타협하다(compromise)
- go into a huddle with 밀담을 나누다
- go into effect 효력을 발생하다(take effect)
- go out of business 망하다 (fail in business, go bankrupt)
- go out of one's way 특별히 노력하다(make an extra effort)
- go to great lengths 많은 애를 쓰다
  (to try very hard to achieve something)
- go steady 이성과 교제하다(go on dates)
- go under the knife 수술을 받다 (undergo an operation)
- good at ~에 능숙한(proficient)
- goof off 게으름피우다, 빈둥거리다(goof around)
- grow up 자라서 ~이 되다
- grumble at/about/over 불평하다(complain about)
- go broke 파산하다(go bankrupt)
- go into bankruptcy 파산되다(run out of money)
- gain ground 지지를 얻다, 확고한 기반을 쌓다, 우세해지다, 유행하다(become more accepted)
- gear up 준비를 갖추다(prepare for)
- get a fix on 이해하다(understand)
- get a grip on 이해하다(understand, figure, make out, comprehend)
- get a head start 먼저 출발하다(start earlier)
- get a point 논지를 파악하다, 요점을 이해하다
- get across 설명하다, 이해시키다
  (make clear, explain, make the meaning clear, put across)
- get along 살아가다(get on)
- get along with ~와 잘 지내다, 사이좋게 지내다
- get around (법) 빠져나갈 구멍을 찾다(avoid), 잘피하다
- get at ~에 도착하다; ~을 파악하다; ~에 착수하다
  (get to, arrive at, reach; discover; start to work on)
- get away with 처벌을 모면하다(not be punished for)
  (go unpunished for, do something without being caught)
- get back 돌아오다
- get carried away 무아지경이 되다; 넋을 잃다, 정신이 나가다
  (become too excited; get fascinated, get enchanted)
- get cold feet 겁먹다; 낙담하다(become timid; get discouraged)
  (chiken out, cop out 꽁무니를 빼다)
- get even (with) 복수, 보복하다(retaliate, revengeful)
  (repay, retaliate, take revenge on, revenge, get back at, pay back)
- get in someone's hair 괴롭히다(bother)
- get in the way of 방해하다(prevent)
- get in touch with ~와 연락하다, 접촉하다
- get married 결혼하다
- get off the ground 행동으로 옮겨지다, 진척되다, (일을) 진행시키다; 이륙하다
  (make progress; take off → started to be successful)
- get on one's nerves 신경을 건드리다, 짜증나게 하다
  (irritate, make one irritable)
- get on with 의좋게 지내다, 진척시키다
- get out of hand 통제를 벗어나다
  (jump the track, get out of control, become uncontrollable)
- get over 극복하다, 회복하다(overcome)
- get someone wrong 오해하다(misunderstand someone)
- get somewhere 성공하다(succeed, make good, come off)
- get starry-eyed 몽환의, 몽상에 찬 눈빛의
- ditch (곤경에 있는 동료를) 버리다
- lay off 해고하다
- get the ax 자루가 짧은 손도끼, 참수, 해고
- get the sack 해고하다
- get the pink slip 해고당하다
- get the boot 부츠, 장화, 신병, 차기 : kick, 해고
- get the bullet 탄알, 해고, 콩
- get the bucket 죽다(양동이, 궁둥이)
- get the air 버림받다, 해고하다
- get the better of ~에 이기다
- get the edge on 조금 우세하다(have a slight advantage over)
- get the hang of 요령을 터득하다 (get used to:knack)
- get the picture 상황을 이해하다
- get hooked on ~열중하다, ~에 빠지다, 중독되다
- get through with ~을 끝내다(finish, complete)
- get to ~에 도착하다(come to, reach, arrive at(in)
- get to first base (부정문, 의문문) 다소 진전하다
  (have any success whatsoever)
- get (have) wind of ~을 풍문으로 듣다
  (hear or know about (something secret or private) especially accidentally or unofficially)
- get [put, set] one's back up 화나게 하다, 성나게 하다(became enraged)
- girl Friday 여사무원, 여비서, 여자 조수
  (a female secretary or general helper in an office)
- give ~ a hand 도와주다, 박수치다
- give a ride 차를 태워주다 (give a lift)
- give a ring 전화하다 (give a buzz, call up)
- give a wide berth 멀리하다 → 피하다 → 일정 거리를 두다
  (keep an adequate distance from, avoid coming into contact with)
- give directions 길을 가르쳐주다 (tell the way, show the way)
- give evidence 증언하다 (testify)
- give in 제출하다, 건네다
- give in to ~에 굴복하다, 양보하다 (yield to)
- give ~ a lift : ~을 차로 태워주다
- give one's right arm 큰 희생을 치르다 (sacrifice a lot)
- give out 배포하다, 나눠주다 (distribute, hand out)
- give rise to 일으키다

- give someone to understand that ~에게 ~라고 넌지시 말하다, 알리다 (advise)
- give standing ovation 기립박수를 쳐주다
- give the cold shoulder to a person ~에게 쌀쌀하게 대하다
- give the devil one's due 공평하게 대하다
- give up 포기하다 → 철회하다 (abandon, relinquish, yield, waive)(throw in the towel → throw up one's hands)
- give vent to 표현하다 (express)
- give way to 항복(굴복)하다, ~에 의해 대체되다, ~에 양보하다 (yield, surrender)
- gloat over (남의 불행을) 고소한 듯이 바라보다 (gaze with great satisfaction)
- go a long(great) way 크게 도움이 되다 (be very useful, be of great use)
- go back on one's word
  (약속) 어기다, 취소하다, 속이다, 배반하다(break, cheat, betray)
- go by ~에 따라 행동하다, 의지하다 (follow)
- go down with 병에 걸리다
- go over like a lead balloon 완전한 실패로 끝나다(come a cropper)
- go Dutch (비용을) 각자 부담하다 (pay expense individually)
- go for ~에 들어맞다, ~에 적용할 수 있다, ~하러 가다 (be applicable to)
- go from rags to riches 벼락 부자되다 (get rich very quickly)
- grease(tickle, gild) one's palm 뇌물을 주다
- go home 정곡을 찌르다 (hit the target)
- go in for 참가하다, 열중하다, 종사하다, 시험을 치르다 (take part in)
- go into bankruptcy 파산하다 (go bankrupt)
- go off 음식이 상하다, 나빠지다, 자명종이 울리다 (become worse, become rotten)
- go off the deep end 자제력을 잃다; 위험을 무릅쓰다 (lose one's self-restraint; run a risk)
- go on a spending spree 돈을 흥청망청 써대다 (spend a lot of money)
- go on strike 파업하다
- go out of business 폐업하다, 파산하다 (go bankrupt)
- go out of fashion 유행이 지나다
- go over the top 한도를 넘어서다 → 할당액[목표]을 초과하다 (overspend)
  1) We didn't go over the top. We didn't get half of what we planned to collect.
     (우리는 목표를 달성할 수 없었다. 당초 예상한 액수에 반에도 도달하지 못했다.)
  2) over the top 과장된[지나친]
- His performance is completely over the top.
  (그의 연기는 완전히 과장된 것이다.)
- go over 검토하다, 복습하다, (설명을) 되풀이하다 (examine carefully(closely), review)
- go round (around) ~에게 모두 돌아가다 (be enough for all)
- go through (고난, 경험 등을) 거치다, 경험하다, 관통하다
- go through the motions 마지못해 시늉만 해 보이다 (play without effort)
- go through the roof (가격, 판매가) 최고에 달하다, 벌컥 화를 내다
- go through with ~을 해내다 (complete)
- go to great lengths 무슨 짓이든지 하다 (endeavor)
- go under 밑으로 가다, 실패하다

- go up (값 등이) 오르다 (be raised)
- go with ~와 어울리다 (match)
- get a life 인생 똑바로 살다
- go without ~없이 지내다
- gild the lily
  1) 백합에 금을 입히다
  2) 망치다 (이미 좋은[아름다운] 것을 지나치게 꾸미려다)
- go to the wall (자금 부족으로) 실패하다
- get the hooked on (무언가에) 빠지다 → 중독되다
- She Grew on me 그녀가 점점 마음에 들게 됐어요. → Grow on
- When do you Get off work? → 퇴근하다
  (언제 퇴근하시나요?)
- She's really Gullible. 그녀는 정말 귀가 얇아요. (귀가 얇은, 잘 속는)
- We do have chemistry. 우리는 통하는 것이 있다(공감대가 있다)
- give a person the slip 남을 속이고 달아나다(get away from)

H

- hang in the balance 미해결 상태에 있다 → 위기에 처해있다 (jeopardy → on the line)
- Hit a sore spot. 아픈 곳을 건드리다.
- I'm your groupie. 전 당신의 열성팬입니다.
- I'm a happy has-been. 전 행복한 왕년 스타입니다.
- have a bee in one's bonnet/head
  1) 머리가 좀 이상해져 있다
  2) (머리가 이상해질 정도로) 어떤 생각에 골몰해 있다
  3) 망상에 사로잡히다
  4) When he came back to his hometown, he seemed to have a bee in his bonnet.
     (그가 고향에 돌아왔을 때 그는 미쳐있는 것 같았다.)
- have nothing to do with ~과 아무 관련 없다; ~와 교제를 안하다
- hang over 연기되다, 미결인 채로 남다; 다가오다
- haggle with 논쟁하다(argue with:contentious) → 끈질기게 깎다
- had better ~하는 것이 좋겠다
- haggle over 옥신각신하다, 승강이를 벌이다 (try to settle the price)
- hammer and tongs 맹렬히
- hammer away 열심히 일하다, 여러 번 강조하다
- hammer out 고심하여 생각해내다 (come up with)
- hand and foot 수족이 되어, 정성껏
- hand over fist (많은 양) 빨리빨리, 척척
- hand and/in glove 단짝인, 절친한 (very close)
- hand in 제출하다 (turn in, submit)
- hand in hand 손에 손을 잡고 (holding hands)
- hand out 나누어주다 (distribute)
- hands down 힘들이지 않고, 수월하게 (easily, in comfort)
- hang back 주춤하다, 머뭇거리다
- hang in (there) 버티다, 곤란을 견디다 (persist, not give up)
- hang in the balance 몹시 불안정한 상태에 있다 (be uncertain)
- hang up 전화를 끊다
- happen to 우연히~하다, 마침~하다(do something by chance)
- have a ball 재미있게 보내다, 멋진 시간을 보내다 (have a blast)
- have a bearing on ~와 관계가 있다 (be relates to)
- have a bone with ~와 따질 것이 있다 (have something to argue about)

261

- **have a card up one's sleeve** 숨겨둔 비책이 있다(keep a hidden card)
- **have a chip on one's shoulder** 시비를 걸다, 시비조로 말하다 (say rudely)
- **have/get a crush on** ~에게 홀딱 반하다, 푹 빠지다 (dig someone)
- **have/take a look at** ~를 언뜻 보다, ~를 훑어보다 (look at)
- **have a fit** 화가 나다, 갑자기 병이 들다 (get angry, get sick suddenly)
- **have an ax to grind** 딴 속셈이 있다
- **have a good command of** ~를 잘 구사하다 (do something very well)
- **have a hand in** ~에 관여하다, 일부 책임이 있다 (partly responsible for)
- **have the world by the tail** 잘 나가다, 남부러울 것이 없다
- **have a say** 발언권이 있다 (have a voice)
- **have a thing about/for** ~를 몹시 좋아[싫어]하다 (like somebody romantically)
- **have a word with** ~와 잠시 대화를 나누다 (speak with somebody briefly)
- **have one's foot on the ground** 현실적이다, 분별력이 있다
- **have access to** ~에 접근[사용]할 수 있다 (be able to reach)
- **have one's heart in one's mouth**
   1) 몹시 놀라다 → 혼비백산[기절초풍]하다 → 안절부절 못하다 (to be extremely frightened or anxious)
   2) 만화영화 같은 데에서는 너무나 놀란 모습을 묘사할 때 턱이 털썩 내려앉는 모습으로 그려내기도 한다. 기절초풍하도록 놀란 이는 입을 다물지 못한 채 얼이 빠져 버리기 때문일 것이다. '심장이 입에까지 나와 있다.'라는 식의 'have one's heart in one's mouth'라는 표현은 '기절초풍하다'라는 의미를 가진다.
- **have at one's fingertips** ~를 잘 알고 있다 (know well)
- **have/get cold feet** 겁을 먹다, 겁이 나다 (be scared)
- **have enough** (of) ~를 충분히 갖고 있다 (have had it)
- **have ~in common** 공통점을 가지고 있다 (have some common points)
- **have misgivings about** ~에 불안을 느끼다 (be anxious about)
- **have mixed feelings** 생각이 착잡하다, 희비가 엇갈리다(think in two opposite ways)
- **have no objection to/against** ~에 이의가 없다 (make no objection on)
- **have no inkling of** 조금도 알아채지 못하다 → 전혀 모르다 (didn't know)
- **have nothing to do with** ~와 아무런 관계가 없다
- **have one's hands/plate full** 매우 바쁘다, 꼼짝 못하다 (be very busy)
- **have one's nose to the grindstone** 쉴새없이 일하다 (work without rest)
- **have the nerves to** ~할 용기가 있다, 뻔뻔스럽게 ~하다
- **have his heart set on** 열망(갈망)하다 → ~하기로 마음을 정하다(long for)
- **have what it takes** ~할 능력, 소질 (have the ability)
- **have a soft spot for** ~무척 좋아하다
- **head for** ~로 향하다, 떠나다 (head to)
- **head off** 떠나다, 막다, 저지하다(left, forestall)
- **hear through the grapevine** 소문으로 듣다 (hear by way of rumor)
- **help oneself to** ~를 마음대로 먹다 (serve oneself)
- **help out** 도움을 주다 (be helpful)
- **hinge on** 의존하다, ~에 따라 결정되다(depend on)
- **hit a snag** 뜻하지 않은 장애에 부딪히다 (face an obstacle)
- **hit it off** 사이좋게 지내다 (become friends)
- **hit off** 즉석에서 짓다, 흉내내다
- **hit on** 유혹하다, 발견하다, 생각해내다 (proposition, discover)
- **hit the books** 열심히 공부하다 (study hard)
- **hit the bottle** 술을 많이 마시다 (hit the booze)
- **hit the ceiling** 몹시 화를 내다 (hit the roof)
- **hit the hay/the sack** 잠자리에 들다 (go to bed)
- **hit the headline** 대서특필되다 (make the headlines)
- **hit the jackpot** 대성공하다, 땡잡다 (make a great success)
- **hit the nail on the head**
   핵심을 찌르다 → 요점을 찌르다(hit the bull's eyes, to the point)
- **drive(bring) home the point** → hammer home the point
- **say a mouthful** (단 몇 마디 단어로)중요한 말을 하다
   (pertinent, apposite, apropos, appropriate)
   변죽을 울리다 (beat around the bush)
   빗나가다 → 벗어나다
   (beside the mark, wide of the mark, off the base, off the beam, off the track)
- **hit the road** 여행을 떠나다 (go on a trip)
- **hit the spot** 더할 나위 없다 (satisfy one)
- **Hobson's choice**
   1) (제의를 받아들이는 것 외에) 달리 선택의 여지가 없는 상황
   2) 주는 대로 받아야 하는 상태
   Hobson's choice(주어진 것을 갖느냐 안 갖느냐의 선택, 골라잡을 수 없는 선택)는 영국의 마차업자이자 말 대여업자인 토머스 홉슨(Thomas Hobson, 1544~1631)의 말 대여 규칙에서 비롯된 표현이다. 그는 케임브리지대 근처에서 말을 빌려주는 사업을 했는데, 손님들이 좋은 말만 선호하는데다 젊은이들이 말을 거칠게 타는 바람에 그 말들이 혹사당하는 것을 염려해 새로운 영업 방침을 내세웠다. 모든 말을 순서대로 타야 한다는 것. 즉, 손님에겐 말의 선택권이 없고 홉슨이 정한 순서에 따라 주어진 말을 타느냐? 안 타느냐? 하는 선택만 하라는 것이었다.
- **hold good** 유효하다, 지속하다 (remain valid)
- **hold one's horses** 기다려라, 참아라, 진정해라 (wait, be patient)
- **hold one's tongue** 잠자코 있다, 입을 다물고 있다 (keep silent)
- **hold out for** ~를 강경하게 요구하다
- **hold over** 연기하다 (postpone, put off)
- **I'm Hanging in there** 버티다 → 견디다 → 그럭저럭 버티며 살다
- **hold true/good** 진리이다, 유효하다 (be effective)
- **hold water** 물이 새지 않다, 이치에 맞다 (not leak)
- **hole up** 숨어 있다 (hide out)
- **hook up** 접속하다, 중계하다 (connect)
- **hot and strong** 호되게, 맹렬히
- **hot potato** 곤란한 문제 (difficult to settle)
- **hot under the collar** 화를 내어, 흥분하여 (angry)
- **hot water** 어려움, 곤경 (deep water)
- **huddle together** 한 데 모이다 (move close together)
- **hunker down** 쭈그리고 앉다 (squat)
- **hunt down** 추적하다 (track down)
- **hand down** (후세에) 전하다, (판결을) 선고하다
- **hand in** 제출하다 (submit)
- **hand out** 나누어주다 (distribute)
- **hand over fist**(hand) 성큼성큼 (very quickly and in large

amounts)
- **hang around** 기다리다, 어슬렁거리다, 배회하다 (remain)
- **hang by a thread** 매우 위태롭다 (be in a very uncertain state)
- **hang on** (전화를 끊지 않고) 기다리다 (hold on, wait)
- **hang out with** 어울려 다니다, 친하게 지내다
- **hang up** 전화를 끊다 (end a phone call and put back the receiver)
- **hard and fast** 엄격한, 단단히 고정된
- **have a bee in one's bonnet** 뭔가를 골똘히 생각하다, 머리가 좀 이상해지다
  (have a fixed idea about something)
- **have a big mouth** 말이 많다, 허풍을 떨다 (talk big)
- **have a fat chance of** 가망이 전혀 없다 (Very little or no chance)
- **have a chip on one's shoulder** 시비조이다, 싸우려 들다
  (try to pick a quarrel)
- **have a finger in the pie** 관여하다, 참견하다
  (participate in, share with, be involved)
- **have a go at** ~을 해보다; 상연하다
- **have a lot of nerve** 아주 뻔뻔스럽다, 정말 철면피다
- **have a person in** ~를 초대하다, 맞아들이다
- **have a profound influence on** ~에 깊은 영향을 미치다
- **have a reluctance to** ~하기를 꺼려하다
- **have a way with** 잘 다루다 (have the ability to deal with)
- **have a word with** ~와 말다툼하다, ~에게 할 말이 있다
- **have an alibi for** ~에 대한 알리바이가 있다
- **have an ax to grind** 딴 속셈이 있다 (have hidden intention)
- **have an eye for** 안목이 있다, 기호나 취향을 가지다
- **have butterflies in one's stomach**
  (걱정으로) 두근두근거리다 → 조마조마하다
  (feel very nervous before doing something)
- **have difficulty ~ing** ~하는데 고생하다
- **have in mind** 염두에 두고 있다, 계획하고 있다
- **have it both ways** 양다리 걸치다
  (gain advantage from opposing opinions or actions)
- **have it in for** 꾸짖거나 벌할 계획을 하다, 벼르고 있다
- **have it out** (have things out) 거리낌 없이 토론하다, 토론으로 결말을 내다 (settle(a difficulty) by talking freely and openly, sometimes angrily)
- **have mixed feelings** 착잡한 느낌을 가지다
  (like something in some ways but not in others)
- **have no idea** ~을 알지 못하다
- **have one's cake and eat it too**
  동시에 가질 수 없는 두 가지를 가지게 하다, 임도 보고 뽕도 따다
- **have one's hair done** 머리를 하다
- **have one's hands full** 몹시 바쁘다 (extremely busy)
- **have one's head in the cloud**
  1) 공상에 잠기다 → 비현실적이다 → 몽상에 잠겨있다
     (be daydreaming)
     (pipe dream → castle in the air → pie in the sky → cloud-cuckoo land)
- **have one's heart in one's mouth** 몹시 걱정하다, 안절부절 못하다
  (feel anxious, full of fear for a short time, be very nervous, be on edge)
- **have the guts** 용기가 있다 (have the heart (courage))
- **have the say** 발언권(결정권)이 있다 (have the power of acting or deciding)

- **have yet to** 아직 ~하지 못하다
- **in the doghouse**
  1) (구어) 난처한 입장에 처하다 → I am in the doghouse
  2) (구어) 면목이 없다 → I'm always in the doghouse because I don't help my wife clean the house.
     (집안 청소 안 도와줘서 늘 아내에게 면목이 없어요)
  3) 이 표현은 미국에서 흔히 애완견이 잘못했을 때 집 안에 들이지 않고 벌주기 위해 집 밖에서 있도록 하는 데서 생겨난 것으로 볼 수 있습니다.
- **have someone over a barrel** (구어) 꼼짝 못하다 → 궁지에 몰리다~좌지우지하다
- **behind the eight-ball** 궁지에 빠진 → 불리한 입장인
  (in trouble, stymied or thwarted, in an awkward position or out of luck)
- **head off** 가로막다, 저지하다 (block (off), forestall)
- **help out** 돕다 (assist, give help, aid)
- **high and low** 도처에, 모든 곳에 (everywhere)
- **hinge on** ~에 달려있다 (depend on, rely on)
- **hit below the belt** 반칙행위를 하다, 비겁한 짓을 하다
  (attack unfairly, act in dishonorable way)
- **hit it off** (with) 성미가 잘 맞다, 친구가 되다, ~와 잘해 나가다, ~와 타협하다
- **hit the ball** 척척 진행하다 (go well)
- **hit the book** 열심히 공부하다 (study hard, bone up on)
- **hit the booze** 술을 마시다 (hit the bottle)
- **hit the ceiling** 화를 내다, 몹시 성나다 (become angry)
- **hit the jackpot** 대성공하다 (come off, have a big success)
- **hit the nail on the head** 핵심을 찌르다, 바로 알아 맞히다
  (say exactly the right thing, arrive at the correct answer)
- **hold back** 억제하다 (control, restrain)
- **hold good** 유효하다 (remain, valid)
- **hold over** 연기하다 (postpone, defer, delay, put off)
- **hold up** 강도질하다, 지탱하다, 버티다, 위로쳐들다, 올리다
  (stop forcibly and rob → mug)
- **hold water** 이치에 맞다 (be logical, add up, make sense)
- **hook up** 접속하다, 부품 등을 짜 맞추다 (connect)
- **hot air** 과장 (exaggerated talk, big talk → Empty, exaggerated talk)
- **How come?** 왜인가(그런가)?
- **have the last word** (토론) 마지막 말을 하다 → 최종결정을 내리다
  (to say the last statement in a discussion or argument)
  (to make the final decision about something)

I

- **I'm in the zone** 난 컨디션이 최상이야!
- **incontrovertible**
  논쟁[논박]의 여지가 없는 → 부정할 수 없는 → 의심할 수 없는 → 명백한
- **absolute and incontrovertible truth** 명백한 절대적 진리
  같이 꼭 외워버리자!
- **ample[clear, conclusive, concrete, convincing, definite, incontestable, incontrovertible, indisputable, irrefutable, living, positive, tangible, undeniable, unquestionable] proof**
  명백한 [결정적인, 확실한, 반박의 여지가 없는] → 증거, 확증
- **in the wake of** ~의 바로 뒤에, ~의 결과로서 (come after,

- follow)
- indulge oneself in 탐닉하다, ~에 빠지다
- impoverishing our civil discourse 시민토론의 질을 저하시키다
- in the face of ~에 맞서서; ~에도 불구하고
- in ~ terms : ~측면에서
- idle about/around 시간을 헛되이 보내다 (spend one's time idly)
- if in were not for 만약 ~가 없다면 (but for, without)
- if the shoe fits, wear it 그 말이 타당하면 순순히 받아들여라
- in one's Sunday best/clothes 나들이 옷을 입고
- ill at ease 불안한, 안절부절못하는 (feel uncomfortable)
- in a flash 순식간에 (very suddenly)
- in a fog 당황하여, 어찌할 바를 몰라, 오리무중인 (in a haze)
- in a nutshell 간단히 말해서, 한 마디로 (in a few words)
- in one's birthday suit 발가벗고, 알몸으로
- in a sense 어떤 의미에서 (in some way but not in all)
- in/as a token of ~의 표시로써 (in sign of)
- in a way 어떤 점에서는
- be in a double bind 딜레마에 빠져 있다
- in a bind 곤경에 처한, 속박되어(in distress)
  (In a difficult, threatening, or embarrassing position; also, unable to solve a dilemma)
- in addition to ~이외에
- in advance 미리, 앞당겨 (beforehand)
- in any case (사정이) 어떻든 간에 (no matter what happens)
- in arrears 미납된, 체불된 (behind in payment)
- in case (that) ~하는 경우에는, ~의 경우에 대비하여 (if it should happen)
- in charge of ~를 담당하고 있는 (take charge of)
- in comparison with ~에 비하면
- in deep water 곤경에 처한 (in hot water)
- in detail 상세히 (at length, at large)
- inconsistent with 일치하지 않다, 모순되다(contradicted)
- in dispute 논쟁 중인 (being argued)
- in effect 실제적으로, 사실상 (in fact)
- in (the) event if ~의 경우에는 (in case of)
- in every respect 모든 면에서 (in every aspect)
- in favor of ~에 찬성하여 (in support of)
- in fear of ~를 두려워하여
- in for ~를 당하게 되어 (unable to avoid)
- in force 대거, 전원 합세하여 (in a large group)
- in full swing 한창인, 절정인 (actively going on)
- in general 일반적으로, 대개 (generally)
- in harmony with ~와 조화되어 (well-matched with)
- in honor if ~에 경의를 표하여, 기념으로 (for showing respect)
- in hopes 바라면서 (hoping)
- in hot water 곤경에 처한 (in deep water)
- in less than ~도 못되어
- in life 인생에서
- in nothing flat 눈 깜짝할 사이에 → 순식간에
- in line with ~와 일직선상에, 일치하여, ~에 순응하여 (in harmony with)
- in luck 운이 좋은 (lucky)
- in many respects 여러 가지 점에서 (in many aspects)
- in one piece 상처 없이 → 무사히 → 안전히[하나도 상한데 없이] (intact)
- in one's prime 전성기에 한창 때에 (in one's best days)

- in one's shoes ~의 처지가 되어, ~의 입장이 되어 (in someone's position)
- in one's spare time 한가한 때에 (at one's leisure)
- in order to ~하기 위해
- in other words 다시 말해서 (that is to say)
- in person 몸소, 직접 (personally)
- in place 적소에, 그 자리에 (in the right place)
- in place of ~대신에
- in private 비밀히, 조용히 (secretly)
- in public 공공연히, 사람들 앞에서 (publicly)
- in reply to ~에 답하여
- in return 답례로써 (in order to give back something)
- in search of ~를 찾아, ~를 구하려고
- in secret 비밀리에 (secretly)
- in short order 재빨리, 즉시
- in seventh heaven 아주 행복한 (on cloud nine)
- in shape 좋은 상태인, 건강한 (healthy)
- in short 한 마디로 말해서, 요컨대 (in a word)
- in sight 보이는 곳에, 보이는 거리에 (able to be seen)
- in some respects 어떤 점에서는 (in some ways)
- in spite of ~에도 불구하고 (despite, with all)
- in store 일어나려 하여, 비축하여 (ready to happen)
- in style 유행인 (in fashion)
- in terms of ~의 관점에서 (on the subject of)
- in that ~라는 점에서
- in the bag 보장된, 확실한 (certain)
- in the black 흑자인(profitable)
- in/on the cards 있을 수 있는 (likely to happen)
- in the case of ~에 관해서는 (as regards)
- in the center of ~의 한복판에
- in the dark 알지 못하고, 비밀로 하고 (not knowing)
- in the doghouse 찬밥 신세인
- in the doldrums 침울한, 불황인
  (down in the mouth, long face, be in the blues)
- in the end 마침내, 결국 (finally, at last)
- in the face of ~에 직면하여, ~에도 불구하고 (in spite of, despite)
- in large measure 대부분, 상당히(mostly)
- in the first place 맨 먼저, 우선 (first of all)
- in the interest of ~를 위하여 (for the sake of)
- in the light of ~에 비추어, ~의 관점에서 (judging from the point of view)
- in the limelight/spotlight 각광을 받고 (at the center of attention)
- in the long run 장기적인 안목으로, 결국에는 (eventually)
- in the red 적자인 (lose money)
- in the same boat 같은 처지에, 같은 운명에 (in the same situation)
- in the short rum 단기적으로 (for the immediate future)
- in the wake of ~의 결과로써, ~의 바로 뒤에 (following)
- in the works 진행[준비] 중인 (being worked on)
- in turn 차례로 (each following another)
- in this respect 이 점에 있어서
- in vain 헛되이, 보람 없이 (without getting the desired result)
- include of ~를 빼다, 제외하다
- infringe on 침해하다 (encroach on)
- instead of ~대신에, ~하지 않고
- into something ~에 열중하여 (indulged in)

- iron out 원활하게 하다, 이견을 해소하다 (find a solution for)
- It is no use –ing ~해봐도 소용없다 (There is no use in –ing)
- (It is) no wonder that~ ~하는 것은 당연하다 (take for granted)
- itch for ~하고 싶어 좀이 쑤시다
  (want very much to do something)
- ill at ease 거북한
- I'm completely broke 가진 돈이 없다 (I have no money)
- I'm in line with you 너의 생각에 동의한다
- impose on ~에 편승하다 (take advantage of)
- impose upon ~을 이용하다 (take advantage of, exploit)
- immune from 면역이 된 (exempt from)
- in a bind 속박되어, 딱하게 되어, 곤경에 처하여 (in distress)
- in a jam 곤경에 처한
- in a muddle 어리둥절하여
- in a nutshell 아주 간결하게
  (very clearly and briefly, in a few words, shortly)
- in a row 연속하여
- in a timely manner 시기적절하게
- in accordance with ~에 따라서
- in addition to ~에 더하여
- in advance 미리 (beforehand)
- in all senses 모든 점에서 (in all respects)
- in an effort to R ~하는 노력으로
- in behalf of ~의 이익을 위해, ~을 대신해서 (in the interest of)
- in case ~에 대비하여, ~한 경우에
- in charge of ~을 맡고있는, 담당의 (responsible for)
- in comparison with 비교하여
- in conjunction with ~와 함께, ~와 관련하여(together with)
- in comparison with ~와 비교하여
- in compliance with ~에 따르는, 순응하는
- in conclusion 결론적으로
- in deep water 곤경에 처한 (in trouble)
- in despair 절망하여
- in detail 상세히
- in duplicate 두 통씩
- in earnest 본격적으로; 진지하게, 진심으로 (to a great extent, seriously)
- in favor of ~에 찬성하여, ~에 유리하도록
- in full accord 만장일치의 (unanimous)
- in good state 점잖은, 격조 높은, 멋있는 (polite)
- in high relief 아주 돋보이게, 눈에 띄게 (with designs that stick out a lot)
- in honor of ~에게 경의를 표하여, ~을 기념하여
- in no time 곧, 바로, 즉시 (soon, at once, immediately)
- in observance of ~을 준수하여, 기념하여
- in person 본인이, 자기 스스로
- in person 직접
- in proportion to ~에 비례하여 (in comparison with)
- in reference to ~에 관하여
- in response to ~에 응해, ~에 대한 답변으로
- in retrospect 회고해 볼 때 (looking back)
- in return for ~에 대한 답례로
- in round numbers 어림으로, 대략 (roughly, approximately)
- in someone else's shoes 다른 사람의 입장이 되어
- in spite of ~에도 불구하고
- in spite of oneself 자신도 모르게, 무의식적으로
  (taking no notice of, unconsciously)
- in store (운명 등이) 기다리고 있는 (waiting, about to happen)
- in terms of ~의 견지에서, ~의 점에서 보아
- in that ~하기 때문에
- in two shakes 순식간에 → 눈 깜짝할 사이에
- in the absence of ~가 없는 가운데
- in the balance 결정되지 않은 상태에서 (in jeopardy)
- in the bargain 게다가, 덤으로(as well)
- in the black (재정이) 흑자로
- in the distance 먼 곳에, 저 멀리
- in the end 결국, 마침내 (finally, ultimately, at last)
- in the event of (that S+V) ~할 경우를 대비하여
- in the face of ~에도 불구하고 (despite, with all, for all, notwithstanding)
- in the foreseeable future 가까운 장래에, 머지않아(soon)
- in the last analysis 결국, 마침내 (eventually, finally, ultimately, at last)
- in the nick of time 때마침, 마침 제때에 (just in time)
- in the red (재정이) 적자로
- in the same boat 같은 입장인, 같은 처지에 놓여 있는
- in the strongest possible terms 가능한 한 강한 말로
- in the suburbs 교외에
- in time 때맞추어
- in token of ~의 표시로
- in transit 통과 중, 수송 중, 이송 중
- in(into) the bargain 게다가 (besides, in addition, furthermore)
- inch along 조금씩 움직이다 (move barely)
- inflict A on B : A를 B에게 가하다
- ins and outs 세부사항 (the details of a difficult situation, problem etc.)
- instead of ~ 대신에
- interfere with 방해하다
- irrespective of ~에 관계없이 (regardless of, without regard to)
- It doesn't make any difference to me 전 아무 데나 좋습니다
- It is needless to say ~을 말할 필요도 없다
- It's a bit a lark. 즐겁다, 유쾌하다
- It's all Greek to me. 금시초문이다, 전혀 이해할 수 없다
  (It's incomprehensible to me.)
- It's all set. 모두 다 준비되어 있습니다
- It's no big deal. 별것 아니다
- It's water under the bridge. 한번 엎지른 물은 다시 주워 담지 못한다
  (What's done is done. There is no use crying over spilt milk.)
- inchoate ideas 이제 시작 단계인 아이디어들[막 떠오른 발상들]
  (In an initial or early stage; incipient → Imperfectly formed or developed)

J

- Jump to conclusion 속단하다
- You're so full of it. 너 정말 허풍쟁이구나 → 허풍쟁이인
- Don't go around advertising. 여기저기 떠벌리고 다니다
- They are not bluffing. 그들은 허풍을 치고 있는 게 아니에요
- John Doe
  1) 존 도우 (특히 법정에서, 남자의 이름을 모르거나 비밀로 할 경우에 쓰는 가명)
  2) 미드제목 → 익명인 : 정체불명의 사나이 (John Doe)
  3) 미국에서는 수사 당시에 신원이 밝혀지지 않는 사람을 '존 도

(John Doe)'라고 부른다.
여성의 경우에는 '제인(Jane) 도', 아이에게는 '베이비(Baby) 도'라고 한다.
한국식으로 표현하자면 아무개, 홍길동 등이 이에 해당한다 → 가명

- John Doe and Richard Roe [리처드 로] 원고와 피고(법률재판)
- juice up 가속하다; 기운 나게 하다
- jack up 인상하다, 들어 올리다 (raise, lift, elevate)
- judging from ~로 판단해보면 (if we judge from)
- jack-in-the-box
  도깨비 상자 → 깜짝 장난감 상자(뚜껑을 열면 용수철에 달린 인형 등이 튀어나오게 되어 있음)
- jump off 공격을 개시하다, 나서다, 시작하다
- jump out of one's skin (기뻐서, 놀라서) 펄쩍 뛰다
- jump the gun 서두르다 (be too hasty)
- jump down someone's throat 심하게 야단치다 → 심하게 화내다
  throat은 목구멍인데, "Jump down someone's throat"은 "내 목구멍으로 뛰어들지 말아라."라는 의미다. 즉, "나를 숨 막히게 하지 말라."
  "나를 화나게 하지 말라."라는 뜻이다.
- jump the track 탈선하다 (go off rails)
- jack of all trades
  (a person who can do many different kinds of work, but perhaps does not do them very well)
  1) 팔방미인 (이것저것 잘하는 사람) → 긍정의미
  2) 특별히 잘하는 것은 없는 사람 → 부정의미
- jump/rush to the conclusion 속단하다 (decide too quickly)
- just like that 그렇게 단순한 방법으로, 손쉽게 (with ease)
- Jóhn Háncock[존 핸콕] (구어) 자필 서명(signature)
  1) (John Hancock이 미국 독립 선언서의 서명자)
  2) The contract is ready. Just put your John Hancock on it.
  (계약서가 준비되었습니다. 여기에 당신의 자필 서명을 하기만 하면 됩니다)
- Judas Kiss [성서] 유다의 키스 → (친절을 가장한) 배신행위
- jones for (주로 음식, 담배, 커피) 간절히 당기다 → 땡기다
- Jane is stubborn as a mule 제인은 고집불통이다
- jack up 밀어 올리다, 들어올리다 (elevate, lift up)
- jot down 적어두다, 메모하다 (write down, record)
- jump the track (rails) (차량이) 탈선하다 (derail, get out of control)
- jump (get, hop, climb) on the bandwagon
  시류에 편승하다, 우세한 쪽에 붙다
  (join a popular cause or movement → follow the majority)
- just around the corner 임박하여 (very near)
- jump the shark 한물가다 → 한창때가 지나다

K

- keep one's shirt on 진정하다 → 흥분하지 않다
- keen to ~하는 데 열성적이다, ~하고 싶어 하다
- of that message 메시지의 핵심(core)
- the long and short of it 핵심, 요점
- keep a low profile 저자세를 취하다, 눈에 띄지 않다 (maintain a low profile)
- keep a straight face 진지한 표정을 짓다 (hold oneself back from smiling)
- keep an/one's eye on ~에서 눈을 떼지 않다 (keep watch)
- keep at bay 접근시키지 않다 (let somebody not approach)
- keep somebody at arm's length 멀리하다, 쌀쌀하게 대하다
- keep bad/late hours 밤늦게까지 자지 않다
- keep ~in the dark 고의로 알리지 않다 (deliberately not inform)
- keep in touch with ~와 접촉[연락]을 유지하다 (keep in contact with)
- keep one's fingers crossed 성공이나 행운을 빌다(wish somebody luck)
- keep one's head above water 빚을 지지 않고 버텨 나가다 (keep out of debt, make both ends meet)
- keep one's promise 약속을 지키다 (abide by one's promise)
- keep one's shirt on 냉정을 유지하다, 침착하다 (keep one's temper)
- keep one's word 약속을 지키다
- keep out of 가담하지 않다, ~에 관계하지 않다 (stay out of, keep away from)
- keep someone company ~와 사귀다, 동석하다, 동행하다 (make friends. Keep company with)
- keep someone from –ing ~에게 ~를 못하게 하다
- keep someone posted ~에게 가장 최근의 뉴스를 알리다 (keep someone informed)
- keep something dark ~를 알리지 않다 (hide out)
- keep something under one's hat 비밀로 하다 (keep secret)
- keep the ball rolling 끊이지 않도록 계속하다 (get the ball rolling)
- keep one's head above water 빚지지 않고 살아가다, 간신이 먹고살다
- keep the lid on ~를 통제하다, 단속하다 (keep under control)
- keep track of ~를 놓치지 않다
- keep body and soul together 간신히 연명하다
  (to manage to keep existing, especially when one has very little money)
- keep up with 뒤떨어지지 않다 (keep abreast of, catch up with)
- kick off 시작하다, 출발하다 (start, begin)
- kick out 쫓아내다, 해고하다 (fire, boot)
- kill time 시간을 때우다, 소일하다(spend time by doing something)
- kill two birds with one stone 일석이조, 일거양득
  (get two results from one effort)
- know better than ~할 만큼 바보는 아니다(be wise enough not to) know by heart 암기하고 있다 (learn by heart)
- touch wood (←knock on wood)
  부정(不淨) 타지 않기를[행운을] 빌다
- know one's stuff 능란하다, 수완이 있다 (know everything)
- know the ropes 요령을 알다 (have the knack)
- know the score 사실[사정]을 알고 있다 (know what's happening)
- knuckle under 굴복하다 (surrender)
- Kudos(쿠다스) to you 너 대단하구나!
  (상대방의 행동이나 성과에 대해 칭찬하고자 할 때)
- keen on ~하는데 열성적인 (interested in)
- keep ~ company ~와 동행하다
- keep a straight face 웃지 않다, 정색하다
  (refrain from smiling, remain serious)
- keep abreast ~와 보조를 맞추다
- keep an eye on ~을 감시하다, ~에 유의하다 (take care of)

- keep ~ at arm's length 멀리 하다, 쌀쌀하게 대하다
- keep away 피하다, 거리를 두다 (avoid, shun, eschew, evade)
- keep body and soul together 겨우 살아 나가다
  (have enough money, food, etc to live on)
- keep close tabs on ~에서 눈을 떼지 않다, ~에 주의(감시)하다
  (watch closely)
- keep cool 냉정을 유지하다
- keep down 억누르다, 줄이다, 억제하다
- keep good time 시간이 잘 맞다
- keep in mind 기억하다, 명심하다 (remember)
- keep in touch 계속 연락하다
- keep an ear to the ground 새로운 정보에 귀를 기울이다
  (To be on the watch for new trends or information)
- keep one's eye on the ball 방심하지 않다 (be watchful and ready)
- keep one's fingers crossed 행운을 빌다 (hope for good luck)
- keep one's head over water 빚지지 않고 있다
  (be only just able to live on one's income)
- keep one's post 알려주다
- keep one's temper 화를 참다
- keep someone posted 소식을 알려주다
  (keep someone informed, let someone know the news)
- keep track of 추적하다
- Keep up the good work! 수고하세요!
- keep up 계속하다, 지탱하다, 유지하다 (continue, keep on, maintain, preserve)
- keep up with 따라가다, 뒤지지 않다
- keep up with the joneses (존씨즈)
  (재산·사회적 성취 등에 있어서) 남에게 뒤지지 않으려 애쓰다 → 허세 부리다
- keep (have) one's nose to the grindstone
  죽으라고 일만하다 (work hard all the time)
- kick the bucket 죽다 (die)
- Kill two birds with one stone. 일거양득이다
- kiss off 거절하다, 없어진 것으로 생각하다, 단념하다(give up, abandon, dismiss)
- knock up (급히) 만들다 (finish up, prepare quickly)
- know by heart 암기하여 외우다
- know the ropes 요령을 잘 알다 (be experienced, know knack)
- put one's shoulder to the wheel 열심히 일하다(공부하다)
- keep one's nose to the grindstone
  1) 열심히 일하다 → 뼈 빠지게 일하다(to work hard and constantly)
  2) (멧돌에 코박고) 죽어라 일만하다
  3) 쉬지 않고 죽어라 하고 일하다(work long and hard)

L

- we're tight 우리 친해요
- lay an egg 알을 낳다, 기초를 만들다, 창시하다 → (흥행, 농담) 완전히 실패하다
- look beyond 건너편을 보다, ~너머를 보다
- late bloomers 대기만성형, 늦게 꽃이 피는 사람
- lame duck 무능자 → 재선거에 낙선하고 남은 임기를 채우고 있는 지사[대통령]
- landslide victory/win 대승, 압승 (overwhelming victory)
- last but not least 마지막으로 말하지만 결코 무시하지 못할
- last ditch 끝, 마지막 (last minute)

- lay aside 저축하다, 간직하다, 따로 두다(set aside → earmark → designate)
- lay off 일시 해고하다(temporarily dismiss → fire → discharge → ditch)
- lay/put one's finger on 정확하게 지적하다
  (say exactly what something is)
- lay/put the blame on ~에게 책임을 지우다 (blame someone for)
- lead to ~에 이르게 하다, 초래하다 (cause, trigger)
- leaf through ~를 훑어보다
- learn by heart 암기하다 (memorize)
- leave in the air 불안하게 두다
- leave no stone unturned 가능한 모든 수단을 동원하다
  (try all the possible means)
- leave nothing to be desired 더할 나위 없이 좋다 (very satisfied)
- leave out in the cold 무시하다, 냉대하다 (ignore)
  (look down on, brush off)
- Long time no see 오랜만이다
- Hello, stranger. 아니 이게 누구신가
- Look who's here! 이게 누구야!(우연히 예상치도 못했던 곳에서)
- leave something holding the bag 책임을 떠맡기다
  (let someone be responsible)
- lend/give a hand 도움을 주다 (help)
- let/leave alone ~는 말할 것도 없고 (to say nothing of)
- let down 실망시키다, 낙담시키다
  (disappoint, cast down, break one's heart)
  (down in the dumps, down in the mouth, in the doldrums)
- let on 비밀을 알리다, 폭로하다 (reveal)
- let the cat out of the bag 비밀을 누설하다, 무심코 말하다
  (spill the beans)
- let up 수그러들다, 그치다, 가라앉다 (become weaker, lessen)
- lie through the nose 의도적으로 거짓말을 하다
- lie in ~에 있다 (consist in)
- like a bolt out of the blue 갑자기, 청천벽력으로 (suddenly)
- like a flash 곧, 순식간에 (quickly)
- like father, like son 부전자전 (like mother, like daughter)
- live it up 편하게 놀고 지내다 (enjoy the life)
- live off ~의 신세를 지다, ~에 의존하다 (get money for one's support)
- live up to 기대에 부응하다, ~에 따라 행동하다
  (meet one's expectation)
- look after ~를 돌보다
- look up to ~를 우러러보다, 존경하다 (respect)
- lose face 체면을 잃다, 낯이 깍이다 (suffer humiliation)
- lose one's mind 미치다 (go insane, demented, nutty)
- lose one's temper 화를 내다 (get angry, get sick suddenly)
- lose out 지다, 실패하다 (fail to win)
- lose sleep 걱정하다, ~에 신경쓰다 (worry about)
- lose track of ~를 놓치다, 잊어버리다 (miss)
- lag behind 뒤지다
- laugh (smile) in (up) one's sleeve 뒤에(숨어)서 웃다 (giggle)
- lay bare 밝히다, 드러내다 (expose, reveal)
- lay by 저축하다 (lay aside, save, set aside)
- lay down 규정하다 (prescribe)
- lay down the law 꾸짖다, 야단치다

(reprimand, scold, call down, dress down)
- [ ] **lay off** (일시) 해고하다 (fire temporarily, dismiss, discharge, get sacked)
- [ ] **lay out** 배열하다 (arrange or plan)
- [ ] **lay up** (병으로) 몸져눕다
- [ ] **lead off with** 시작하다 (start, begin, launch)
- [ ] **leave ~ out of account** ~을 고려에 넣지 않다
- [ ] **leave a word with** 위탁하다
- [ ] **leave for the day** 퇴근하다 (leave office)
- [ ] **Leave it to me.** 나에게 맡겨 (I'll take care of it)
- [ ] **leave no stones unturned**
  백방으로 노력하다, 온갖 수단을 강구하다 (use every means possible)
- [ ] **leave nothing to be desired** 더할 나위없이 좋다, 완벽하다(be perfect)
- [ ] **leave out** ~을 내놓은 채로 내버려두다, 빠뜨리다, 생략하다, 제외하다 (omit, exclude, rule out)
- [ ] **leave someone in the lurch**
  곤경에 빠진 사람을 내버려두다, 돕지 않고 내버려두다
  (desert, leave someone alone and without help in a place or time of difficulty, desert someone)
- [ ] **let ~ go** 풀어주다, 놓아주다
- [ ] **let alone** ~은 물론이고 (not to a mention)
- [ ] **let bygones be bygones** 과거는 과거일뿐 (let the past be forgotten)
- [ ] **let down** 실망하게 하다 (disappoint)
- [ ] **let go of** 가도록 허락하다, 해고시키다
- [ ] **let out** 입 밖에 내다, 누설하다
- [ ] **let on** 밀고하다, 드러내다 (reveal, disclose, divulge)
- [ ] **let the cat out of the bag** (무심결에) 비밀을 누설하다
- [ ] **let up** (비나 눈이) 멈추다, 잠잠해지다, 늦추다 (stop, lessen)
- [ ] **Let's call it a day.** 오늘 하루일을 그만 마치자 (Let's stop now)
- [ ] **like a fish out of water** 불편한 (uncomfortable)
- [ ] **like anything** 열심히
- [ ] **like clockwise** 규칙적으로 (regularly)
- [ ] **live on ~** : ~에 의지하여 살다
- [ ] **living up to** 기대에 부응하다, 실천하다(fulfilling)
- [ ] **look after** 돌보다
- [ ] **look around** 둘러보다, ~을 찾아 돌아 다니다
- [ ] **look a gift horse in the mouth** 흠을잡다 → 트집잡다
  (To be critical or suspicious of something one has received without expense)
  (선물로 받은 말의 입 속을 들여다보다)
- [ ] **Never look a gift horse in the mouth.**
  (선물에 대해 흠을 잡지 말라)
- [ ] **look down on** 깔보다, 경멸스럽게 여기다 (despise)
- [ ] **look for** 찾다
- [ ] **look forward to ~ing** ~을 기대하다 (expect)
- [ ] **look in on** 방문하다, 잠깐 들르다
- [ ] **look into** 조사하다
- [ ] **look on the bright side of things**
  사물의 밝은 면을 보다, 낙관적으로 생각하다
  (be cheerful and hopeful in spite of difficulties; be optimistic)
- [ ] **look out** 주의하다, 경계하다
- [ ] **look out for** ~을 조심하다 (be on guard against)
- [ ] **look over** 조사하다; 눈감아주다 (examine, look into)
- [ ] **look to** ~에 유의하다, ~의 도움을 받으러 가다, 의존하다

- [ ] **look up to** 존경하다 (respect, admire, esteem, venerate, revere)
- [ ] **lose face** 창피를 당하다 (be humiliated in front of others)
- [ ] **lose one's heart** 용기를 잃다, 낙담하다
  (break one's heart, cast down, let down, down in the dumps)
  (down in the mouth, in low spirits, in the doldrums)
- [ ] **under the black dog** 우울하다(depression or melancholy)
  (영국 수상 처칠 → '나는 평생 검은 개 한 마리와 살아왔다'에서 유래)
- [ ] **She didn't anything under the black dog.**
  (그녀는 우울하여 아무것도 할 수 없었다)
- [ ] **lose one's marbles** 머리가 이상해지다 → 발광하다
- [ ] **lose one's temper** 화를 내다 (become angry, hit the ceiling)
- [ ] **lose track of** 상황을 도중에 모르게 되다, ~을 잊어버리다
  (forgot, miscalculate)
- [ ] **level with** ~에게 털어놓다
- [ ] **in the chips** 부유한, 부자인(wealthy; having lots of money)
- [ ] **live like fighting cocks**
  1) 사치스럽게 살다(싸움닭처럼 맛있는 것만 먹고)
  2) Paris Hilton lives like fighting cocks. (패리스 힐튼은 사치스럽게 산다)
- [ ] **born with a silver spoon in one's mouth** 부잣집에 태어난
- [ ] **born in the purple** 왕족의 집안에서 태어난
- [ ] **I Laze around all day.** 빈둥거리다.
- [ ] **I'm a loner.** 전 왕따예요.
- [ ] **She was withdrawn.** 그녀는 내성적이었어요.

M

- [ ] **My ears are burning.** 귀가 근질근질하다
- [ ] **I'm totally neurotic.** 난 완전 신경이 예민해요.
- [ ] **I easily get nervous.** 난 쉽게 신경질적이 돼.
- [ ] **I've been a little jumpy.** 내가 조금 신경이 예민했어.
- [ ] **Picky** 변덕스러운(extremely fussy or finicky, usu. over trifles)
- [ ] **mood swings** 변덕 → (정신의학) (조울증 등에서 볼 수 있는) 기분의 두드러진 변화
- [ ] **muster up** 소집하다, 모으다(gather)
- [ ] **meddling with** 간섭하다, 참견하다(interring in)
- [ ] **make oneself understood in** 의사소통하다
- [ ] **McDonald's its burgers**
  (맥도날드는 동시에 자신의 햄버거를 선전한다 → broadcast)
- [ ] **make a fuss** 소란을 피우다
- [ ] **make a clean breast of** 다 털어놓다, 자백하다 (confess)
- [ ] **make a comeback** 재기하다, 인기를 만회하다 (return to prominence)
- [ ] **make a difference** 차이가 나타나다, 차이를 두다
  (change the nature of something)
- [ ] **make a duplicate of** ~의 사본을 만들다
- [ ] **make/pull a face** 얼굴을 찌푸리다, 인상쓰다 (express dislike)
- [ ] **make a fool of** 놀리다[웃음거리로 만들다] → 조롱하다
  (to make (someone) appear ridiculous or stupid)
  (make an ass of, make fun of, make sport of, play a joke on, play a trick on)
- [ ] **make a long story short** 짧게 말하다 (summarize)
- [ ] **make a mountain (out) of a molehill** 뻥치다, 과장하여 말하다
- [ ] **make a pass at** ~를 유혹하다, ~를 시도하다 (seduce)
- [ ] **make a point of** ~를 주장[강조]하다 (stress)

- make a scene 한바탕 소란을 피우다 → 야단법석을 떨다
- make a speech 연설하다
- make a splash 인기를 끌다, 센세이션을 일으키다 (become popular)
- make advances 접근하다 (make passes at)
- make capital (out) of ~를 이용하다 (make advantage of)
- make haste 서두르다
- make no difference 차이가 없다, 중요하지 않다 (not important)
- make one's mark 성공하다, 유명해지다 (succeed, become famous)
- make or break 흥하거나 망하거나 (sink or swim)
- make sense 이치에 맞다 (be understandable)
- make the grade 만족스럽다, 성공하다, 잘 해내다 (be satisfactory, succeed)
- make up for 보상하다, 벌충하다 (compensate for, off-set)
- make up of ~로 만들다, 구성하다 (compose of)
- make waves 소동을 일으키다, 평지풍파를 일으키다 (create a disturbance)
- manage to 가까스로 ~하다
- map out ~를 계획하다 (plan)
- mark my word(s) 내 말 명심해 (remember what I'm telling you)
- meet halfway 타협하다 (compromise with)
- meet the requirements 요건을 충족시키다 (meet the demand)
- mince (one's) words 삼가서 말하다, 완곡하게 말하다 (speak euphemistically)
- miss the point 핵심을 놓치다 (miss the crucial part)
- most likely 아마, 십중팔구 (probably)
- most of all 가장
- mull over 심사숙고하다 (dwell on)
- make a song and dance about
  1) 호들갑 떨다 → 야단법석을 떨다
  (worry or be excited about something which is not very important)
- made for 꼭 닮은, 꼭 알맞은
- maintain (keep) the status quo 현상을 유지하다 (keep things)
- major in ~을 전공하다
  (study as the chief subject(s) when doing a university degree)
- make a bet 내기하다
- make a blunder 실수하다 (mistake)
- make a decision 결정하다
- make a difference 중요하다 (count, matter, be significant)
- make a face 얼굴을 찌푸리다
  (grimace, show an expression of disgust, pull faces)
- make a scene 소란을 피우다, 다투다 (have a violent argument)
- make a beeline for 직선으로 나아가다(직선, 최단코스)
- make a speech 연설하다
- make no bones about something 솔직히 털어놓다 → 솔직히 인정하다
  (be frank about something → To be forthright and candid about → acknowledge freely)
- make allowances for 참작하다
  (take into account(consideration))
- make believe ~인 체하다 (pretend, feign, put on)
- make both ends meet 빚지지 않고 살다
- make do with 임시변통하다 (manage with)
- make for ~로 향하다; ~에 이바지(공헌)하다
  (go forward, go in the direction of; be conducive to)

- make good 성공하다 (succeed, come off)
- make good on 약속을 이행하다, 빚을 갚다
- make good time 빠른 속력으로 나아가다
- Make hay while the sun shines. 해가 날때 건초를 말려라.
- make head or tail of (부정문)이해하다, 분간하다 (understand, comprehend)
- make it 해내다, 성공하다; (장소에) 닿다, 도착하다
- make most of ~을 최대한 이용하다
- make no difference 차이가 없다
- make no provision for ~을 위한 준비를 하지 않다
- make off 급히 떠나다, 도망치다 (depart suddenly)
- make one's way 나아가다, 출세하다; 성공하다 (progress, advance; come up in the world; succeed, come off, make good)
- make oneself at home 마음을 편하게 먹다
- make oneself understood 남에게 자기의 생각을 이해시키다
- make out 이해하다 (understand)
- make room for ~을 위하여 자리를 마련하다 (arrange space for)
- make sense 이해하다, 뜻을 이루다 (add up)
- make short work of 재빨리 해치우다 (finish rapidly)
- make something of oneself 성공하다, 출세하다 (get on in the world)
- make sure ~을 확실히 하다
- Make that two. 나도 같은 걸로 주세요.
- make the best of ~을 최대한 이용하다
- make the most of ~을 잘 이용하다 (capitalize on)
- make the rounds 순시하다; 소문이 퍼지다
- make up 보충, 꾸며, 날조, 구성, 화해, 해결, 화장하다
- make up for 보상하다, 보충하다, 메우다 (compensate for)
- map out (토지, 통로 등을 지도에) 정밀하게 표시하다, 계획을 세밀히 세우다 (plan in detail in advance)
- mark one's words ~의 말에 주의(주목)하다
  (pay close attention to what one says)
- measure up to ~에 들어맞다, 부합하다, 일치하다 (emulate)
- meet a person halfway 타협하다 (compromise)
- meet the mark 목표에 도달하다(achieve the goal)
- meet the needs 욕구를 충족시키다
- minister to 도움이 되다, 공헌하다 (serve)
- move heaven and earth ~하기 위해 전력을 다하다
- mull over 숙고하다, 머리를 짜내다 (consider)
- muse about ~을 깊이 생각하다(pensive)
- My lips are sealed. 비밀을 지키다.
- make it up 화해하다 → 변상하다
- more often than not 자주, 대개(frequently)
- He moonlights → 부업을 하다
  (그는 부업을 뛰죠)

N

- I'm a real People person. 전 정말로 사교성이 좋아요.
- I started getting bummed out, so I came here. (기분이 꿀꿀한, 슬픈)나 기분이 꿀꿀해 지기 시작해서 여기에 온거야.
- I'm not macho. 난 남자답지 않아.
- You've been kind of grumpy all day. (투덜대는, 짜증 부리는) 너 거의 하루 종일 투덜거렸어.

- I'm completely stumped. 전 완전히 난처합니다(난감한, 난처한)
- nail down 최종적인 것으로 하다 (make sure)
- narrow down 좁히다, 제한하다 (limit)
- near/close at hand 바로 가까이에, 곁에 (nearby)
- neck and neck 막상막하의, 용호상박의 (close)
- next to ~와 나란히, 곁에, 거의 (close to, almost)
- next/second to none 최고인, 어느 누구에게도 뒤지지 않는 (the best)
- nine cases out of ten 십중팔구 (most likely)
- nip something in the bud 미연에 방지하다 (prevent)
- no matter what happens 어떤 일이 있어도 (by all means)
- no picnic 쉬운 일이 아닌 (difficult to settle)
- no way 절대로 안 된다, 말도 안 돼 (no possibility)
- not able to see the forest for the trees 나무를 보느라 숲을 보지 못하는
- not always 반드시 ~한 것은 아니다
- not hold (any) water 이치에 닿지 않다
- not on your life 결코~아닌 (be illogical)
- not one's cup of tea 좋아하지 않는 것 (never ever)
- not sleep a wink 한잠도 못 자다 (not something one likes)
- not to mention ~는 말할 것도 없고 (to say nothing of)
- nothing/little short of 아주 ~한, 거의 ~나 다름없는(almost same as)
- (every) no and then 때때로, 이따금 (occasionally, from time to time)
- nuts and bolts 기본 사항 (basics)
- nail down 확실하게 하다, 해결하다 (make certain, settle)
- narrow down to 선택범위를 ~로 좁히다
- next to 거의 (almost, nearly, all but)
- no more than 단지, 오로지 (only, merely)
- No sweat. 걱정마라, 힘든 일은 아니야.
- nobody's fool 영리한 사람, 속이기 힘든 사람 (a sensible and wise person who is not easily deceived)
- none of your business 네가 관여할 일이 아니다
- nose into ~에 간섭하다 (meddle in, cut in, put in a word)
- not a bit 결코~하지 않는 (never, anything but, not ~at all, on no account)
- Nothing ventured, nothing gained. 호랑이를 잡으려면 호랑이 굴에 들어가야 한다.
- nuts and bolts (기계의) 작동부, (사물의) 요점 (basic practical detail)
- neck and neck (경주·시합에서) 막상막하로[대등하게] (So close that the lead between competitors is virtually indeterminable)

O

- out of the wood 위기를 벗어난(stabilized)
- Over the moon 아주 행복하여 → 몹시 흥분하여(overjoyed)
- Objection! 이의 있습니다!
- Booze talking. 술을 마시고 지껄이는 말(술김에 한 소리)
- Passed out. 필름이 끊긴 것 같아요. (술을 더 많이 마셔서)
- Another round over here. 여기 한잔 더요.
- Beer on tap. 생맥주
- on the wagon. 술을 끊다
- One's number goes[is] up 죽어가다, 임종이 가깝다, 운이 다하다, 곤경에 빠지다 (one's time to die—or to suffer some other unpleasantness—has come)
- on the fly 자동적으로, 비행 중인, 날고 있는, 서둘러, 바삐, 작동 중인
- on no account 결코 ~(하지) 않다(=never)
- one-size-fits-all 만능의, 일률적인, 범용의
- one-way operation 일방통행(도로상의 교통을 한 방향으로만 통과시키는 것)
- only to 결국 ~하고 말다
- object to 반대하다, 이의를 말하다 (be opposed to)
- odds and ends 잡동사니, 나머지, 시시한 것 (bits and pieces)
- off the top of one's head 즉석에서, 깊이 생각하지 않고
- off and on 불규칙하게, 단속적으로 (on and off) (↔on and on)
- off the cuff 즉흥적인, 즉석의(impromptu, extemporaneous)
- off-the-record 비공개의, 비밀의 (secret, confidential)
- on a par 똑같은, 동등한 (equal, normal condition)
- on a waiting list 대기자 명단에 올라 (waiting for an opportunity)
- on account of ~ 때문에 (because of)
- on an/the average 평균하여 (usually)
- on behalf of ~를 대신하여, ~를 대표하여 (as the representative of)
- on board 탑승[승선, 승차]한
- on cloud nine 아주 행복한 (in the 7th heaven)
- on duty 근무 중인
- on edge 흥분하여, 안절부절못하여 (so tense or nervous)
- on guard 경계하고
- on hand 가까이, 출석하여, 동석하여 (near, taking part in)
- on hold 보류 중인 (temporarily halted)
- on one's feet 독립하여, 회복하여 (independently)
- on one's own 혼자의 힘으로
- on one's way to ~로 가는 길에
- on pins and needles 불안하여, 걱정되어, 흥분되어 (tense)
- on sale 팔려고 내놓은, 특가로 (available for purchase)
- on second thought 다시 생각해보니까 (after much thought)
- on strike 파업 중인
- on tap 언제든지 따를[쓸] 수 있도록 준비되어 (readily available)
- on the back burner 뒷전으로 밀려, 뒤로 미루어져 (delayed)
- on the ball 빈틈없이, 잘 알고 있는, 유능한 (intelligent)
- on the blink 고장이 난, 못 쓰게 되어 (break down, crash)
- on the button 정각에, 적중하여 (on the nose)
- on the contrary 반하여, 도리어 (contrarily)
- on the dot 정각에, 정시에 (exactly on time)
- On the double 황급히 → 신속히(Immediately → In double time) On the double은 원래 군대 용어로 '뛰어', '구보로'라는 말이다. 이것이 일상회화에서 "빨리 빨리해"의 뜻으로 쓰이게 되었다
- on the ground that/of ~의 이유로, ~를 구실로 (by reason)
- on the heels of ~직후, ~에 잇따라 (in the wake of)
- on/in the hot seat 곤경에 처한 (in a difficult situation)
- on the house 공짜로, 무료의 (paid for by the owner)
- on the map 중요한, 세상에 알려진 (important, well-known)
- on the market 팔려고 내놓은, 특가로 (for sale)
- on the nose 정확하게, 정각에 (on the button)
- on the one hand~, on the other hand 한편으로는, 또 한편으로는
- on the part of ~의 편에서는 (on one's part)
- on the rocks 파경에 이르러, 파산하여, 물을 타지 않고 얼음을

- 넣은 (ruined)
- on the shelf (팔리지 않아) 선반에 얹힌 채, 보류되어 (inactive)
- on the side 요점에서 벗어난, 부업으로
- on the spot 현장에서, 그 자리에서, 곤경에 처하여(then and there, right away)
- on the strength of ~의 도움으로, ~에 힘입어 (relying on)
- on the verge of 직면하여, 바야흐로 ~하려고 하여 (on the brink of)
- on the whole 전체로 보아서, 대체로 (generally)
- jump (get, hop, climb) on the bandwagon
  시류에 편승하다 → 우세한 쪽에 붙다
  (join a popular cause or movement → follow the majority)
- on the wagon 금주하는(teetotal : 절대 금주하다)
- fall off the wagon 다시 술을 마시기 시작하다 → 절제를 잃다
- on top of ~위에, 게다가, 더하여 (in addition to)
- on one's toes 빈틈없는 → 활발한, 원기있는
- once and again 몇 번이고 반복해서
- once and for all 끝으로 딱 한 번만 더, 단호히 (one time and never again)
- once in a lifetime chance 평생에 단 한 번 있는 기회
- once in a while 이따금, 드물게 (sometimes)
- one of a kind 독특한(unique)
- one and only 유일무이한 (only one)
- one for the books 주목할 만한 일, 굉장한 일 (very unusual)
- one way or another 어떻게 해서든 (somehow)
- one's bread and better 생활 수단, 밥줄 (one's means of making a living)
- one's own –ing 자신이 직접~한
- open and shut 명쾌한, 명백한
- open secret 공공연한 비밀
- open the door to ~에게 문호를 개방하다 (give an opportunity)
- opt for ~하는 쪽을 고르다, 선택하다 (choose)
- or so 약, 대략
- out in the cold 혼자서, 무시되어 (alone)
- out of a clear/blue sky 뜻밖에, 청천벽력으로 (suddenly)
- out of business 파산[폐업]하여 (go bankrupt)
- out of commission 퇴역하여, 사용 불능인 (not in use)
- out of date 시대에 뒤진, 구식의 (outdated, obsolete)
- out of it 관계가 없는, 고립된
- out of luck 운이 나쁜 (unlucky)
- out of one's mind 미친 (crazy)
- out of order 고장난, 순서가 잘못되어 (on the blink)
- out of sorts 기분이 안 좋은, 의기소침한 (unwell, in a bad mood)
- out of the blue 느닷없이, 뜻밖에 (suddenly, unexpectedly)
- out of the question 문제가 되지 않는, 전혀 불가능한
  (not to be discussed at all)
- out of the woods 위기를 모면하여 → 곤란을 벗어난 (out of danger)
  (off the hook, over the hump [험프])
- out of town 도시를 떠나, 시골에 (in the countryside)
- out on a limb 위태로운 처지에 → 곤경에 처한 (in danger)
  (at bay, at stake, in deep water, in hot water, in the lurch [럴취], in the soup)
  (on the line, on the rocks, up a tree, on the spot, at the end of one's rope)
- over all 전체적으로, 전반적으로
- over and above ~에 더하여, ~외에 (besides, more than)

- over one's dead body 죽었다 깨나도, 하늘이 무너져도(That will be the day)
- over the hill 한물간, 고비를 지나서 (past one's prime)
- over the long haul (비교적) 장기적으로
  (for a relatively long period of time)
- owe A to B : A는 B의 덕분이다
- own up to ~의 죄를 인정하다, 고백하다 (confess)
- on the level 합법적인, 정직한(fair)
- on the whole 대체로
- odds and ends 나머지, 잡동사니 (miscellaneous)
- of itself 저절로
- of moment 중요한 (important, momentous, significant)
- of one's own accord 자발적으로 (voluntarily, willingly)
- off hand 즉시 (at once, immediately, without time to think or prepare)
- off the record 비공식적으로, 비공식적인, 발표해서는 안 될
  (not known to the public, not intented for publication)
- off the wagon 술을 다시 마시는 (starting to drink alcohol again)
- off the beam 항로를 벗어난 → 틀린 → 잘못된
- on the beam 정상항로를 가는 → 올바른 → 정확한
- old hand 경험이 많은 사람
- on the straight and narrow 정직하게 사는
- on a clear day 맑은 날에
- on a par with ~과 동등한 (similar to , equivalent to)
- on a roll 잘 나가는
  (at a high point, having great success which seems likely to continue)
- on account of ~때문에
- on and on 계속해서 (continuously)
- on behalf of ~을 대신하여
- on closer examination 보다 더 면밀한 조사를 하자마자
- on cloud nine 매우 행복한, 날아갈 듯이 기쁜 (very happy, cheerful)
- on edge 안절부절못하여 (nervous)
- on good (friendly) terms with ~와 친한
- on hand 이용 가능한; 가까이 있는 (available; near)
- on leave 휴가 중인 (away from work)
- on par with 똑같은, 동등한 (equivalent to)
- on pins and needles 조심하는, 불안한 (nervous)
- on pain of ~라는 조건으로, 위반하면(at the risk of paying)
- on purpose 고의적으로 (intentionally, deliberately, purposely)
- on the alert 경계하는 (watchful, open-eyed, vigilant, wakeful, wide-awake)
- on the blink 고장이 나서; 몸 상태가 좋지 않은
  (not working properly; under the weather)
- on the booze 몹시 취하여 (very drunk)
- on the ball
  빈틈없는 → 유능한 → 빈틈없다, 똑똑하다(alert; competent and knowledgeable)
- on the brink of ~의 직전에
- on the contrary 반대로 (opposite)
- on the fence 관망하고 있는, 결정되지 않은 (undecided)
- on the go 쉴새 없이 활동하는, 바쁜 (busy)
- on the ground that ~라는 이유로
- on the heels of ~의 직후에, ~바로 뒤를 따라서 (directly after)
- on the horns of a dilemma 진퇴양난인 (in a quandary, in a dilemma)

- on the house 공짜로, 술집에서 서비스로 주는 (with no payment)
- on an even keel 안정된, 평온한 (steady)
- on the point of ~ing 바야흐로 ~하려고 하다 (be about to)
- on the quiet 비밀로, 은밀히 (secretly)
- on the recommendation of ~의 추천으로, ~의 권고로
- on the rise 증가추세에 있는
- on the run 달리는, 도주하는 (in flight, trying to escape or hide)
- on the spur 전속력으로, 매우 급히
- on the square 정직한, 믿을만한 (honest, on the level, trustworthy)
- on the tip of one's tongue 혀끝에서 맴도는, 생각이 안 나는
- on the wagon (선거 등에서) 인기가 있는, 우세한; 술을 끊고 (no longer willing to drink alcohol)
- on the waiting list 대기자 명단에
- on the wane 줄어가는, 하락하는 동 (dwindling, on the decline, on the decrease)
- on the wax 증가하는 (on the increase, increasing)
- on the whole 전반적으로, 대체로 (generally)
- on the button 정확하게, 정각에 (on the nose)
- once and for all 최종적으로 (for the last time)
- once in a while 가끔씩 (occasionally, from time to time, now and then)
- One's eyes were bigger than one's stomach. 먹을 수 있는 음식보다 더 많이 챙기다.
- out of bounds 출입금지 지역의 (not allowed to go there)
- out of date 구식의, 시대에 뒤떨어진 (outdated, oldfashioned)
- out of humor 불쾌해서, 화가 나서 (in a bad temper, moody)
- out of one's wits 제정신을 잃고
- out of order 고장 난 (not working properly)
- out of place 장소에 어울리지 않는, 불편한 (uncomfortable)
- out of print 절판된
- out of question 틀림없이, 물론 (undoubtedly, surely)
- out of stock 품절 되어, 재고가 바닥난 (unavailable)
- out of the blue 뜻밖에, 불시에 (unexpectedly, suddenly, without any advance notice)
- out of the question 불가능한 (impossible)
- owe A to B : A는 B 덕분이다
- owe ~ to ~ : ~의 은혜를 입다
- on no account 결코 ~(하지) 않다 (never)
- on a lark 즉흥적으로, 장난삼아 (spontaneously)
- out of the way 별난, 엉뚱한, 진기한, 기이한 (eccentric)

P

- Is he is a ladies' man? 바람둥인가요?
- You can google it. 검색해봐
- Are You online? 인터넷 접속 중이다
- Pig out 과식하다 (to eat too much or a lot of food)
- Your business went under 당신 사업은 실패했습니다
- I make a good living 전 돈을 많이 벌어요
- pinch-pennies 한푼이라도 아끼다
- perk it 뽐내다, 젠체하다, 주제넘게 나서다
- perk up 기운을 차리다 (gain or regain energy) → 증가하다 → perk : 특전
- plead no contest to ~에 대해 유죄를 인정하다 (plead guilty to)
- pull[take, get]one's finger out (다시 한번) 열심히 일하기 시작하다
- pull oneself together 냉정을 되찾다, 침착해지다 (caim) (level-headed → calm down → cool off → composure)
- phase out 단계적으로 제거하다 (remove over time) (root out, stamp out, wipe out, weed out)
- push the envelope (분야) 인간 위업의 한계를 넓히다 (go beyond the limits of what is allowed)
- put down (이름·생각) 적어두다 → (폭동·운동) 진압하다
- pick on 괴롭히다, 못살게 굴다, 비난하다
- palm off 가짜를 속여 팔다 (foist off → fob off, foist, pass off, put off)
- pain in the neck 골칫거리, 싫은 사람(일) (pain in the ass)
- paint the town red 술 마시고 흥청대다 (celebrate wildly)
- pare away/down/off 깎아서 다듬다 (trim down)
- part company 교제를 끊다 (sever the relationship)
- pass over 무시하다, 못 본 체하다, 넘겨주다, 양도하다 (disregard)
- pass away 돌아가시다 (die)
- pass out 의식을 잃다 (lose consciousness)
- pass the buck to 책임을 전가하다 (put blame on somebody or something else)
- The buck stops here 모든 책임은 내가 진다
- pat~on the back : ~의 등을 두드려 격려하다 (encourage, praise)
- pave the way to/for ~를 용이하게 하다 (prepare the way for)
- pat a tribute to ~에게 찬사[경의]를 보내다 (express one's admiration)
- pay a visit 방문하다, 문병하다 (make a visit)
- pay/give attention to ~에 주의하다, 주목하다 (listen to carefully)
- pay lip service 입에 발린 소리를 하다
- pay off 성과를 거두다, 효과를 보다, 빚을 다 갚다 (work, pay up)
- pay on the nail 즉석에서 지불하다
- pay through the nose 터무니없는 돈을 치르다 (pay an arm and a leg)
- phase out 단계적으로 폐지[제거]하다 (gradually stop using something)
- play second fiddle to 들러리를 서다, ~보다 못한 취급을 받다
- pick fight 싸움을 시작하다 (begin a fight)
- pick on 괴롭히다, 고르다 (bully, harass, single out)
- pick out 고르다, 선택하다 (choose, select)
- pick up 정돈하다, 치우다, 익히다, 터득하다, 데려다주다, 체포하다, 회복되다
- pick up the tab 계산하다 → 셈을 치르다 (pick up the bill)
- pie in the sky 그림의 떡 → 천국 → 이상향
- cloud-cuckoo land 현실성 없는 계획
- pipe dream 허황된생각 → 몽상 → 환상 (impossible) (bubble, castle in the air, chimera, illusion, delusion)
- piece of cake 누워서 떡 먹기, 쉬운 일 (a very easy thing to do)
- pile up 쌓다, 쌓아 올리다 (stack up)
- pin one's faith on ~를 굳게 믿다 (believe firmly)
- pit against 경쟁시키다 (match against)
- pitch in 협력하다 (help each other)
- play a part 역할을 하다 (play a role)
- play fast and loose
  1) 되는대로(무책임하게) 행동하다 → 다루다
     (to behave cavalierly toward → deal irresponsibly with)
- play hooky 농땡이 치다 (ditch the class)

- [ ] **play it by ear** 임기응변으로 일을 하다(improvise: act as the situation demands)
- [ ] **play up** 강조하다, 중시하다 (emphasize)
- [ ] **plenty of** 많은
- [ ] **plow into** 열심히 일하다, 세게 부딪다 (work vigorously)
- [ ] **point the finger at** ~를 비난하다, 손가락질하다 (blame someone for)
- [ ] **point out** 지적하다
- [ ] **pressed for time/money** 시간/돈이 없는, 쪼들리는 (lacking of time/money)
- [ ] **prick up one's ears** 귀를 쫑긋 세우다, 주의해서 듣다 (begin to listen carefully)
- [ ] **pull/make/wear/put on a long face** 침울한 얼굴을 하다 (look depressed)
- [ ] **pull off** 성공하다, 잘 해내다, 달성하다 (succeed, do well)
- [ ] **pull one's leg** ~를 놀리다, 속이다 (deceive, kid fool)
  1) beguile, betray, bluff, cozen, delude, double-cross, dupe, finagle fool, hoodwink, humbug, mislead, take in, trick. bamboozle, hoax
  2) pull the wool over someone's eyes
  3) double-cross → pull a fast one on (slang)
- [ ] **pull up stakes** 이사하다, 전직하다 (move, transfer)
- [ ] **push for** ~를 밀어붙이다, 강력히 요구하다 (strongly demand)
- [ ] **push someone's buttons** 화나게 하다(아픈 곳을 건드려)
- [ ] **put an ad in** ~에 광고를 내다
- [ ] **put an end to** 종식시키다 (stop, finish)
- [ ] **put in a good word for** 추천하다 (recommend, praise)
- [ ] **put/bring in/into practice** ~를 실행하다 (execute, perform)
- [ ] **put/set one's house in order** (신변을) 정리하다, 행실을 바로잡다
- [ ] **put one's foot in one's mouth** 실언하다★ (자기의 입에 자기의 발을 넣다 → 부주의로 말을 실수하다★ 하지 말아야 할 말을 했다는 뜻이다)
- [ ] **put off** 연기하다, 미루다 (postpone)
- [ ] **put one's money where one's mouth is** 자신이 말한 것에 대하여 실제 행동으로 증명하다
- [ ] **put one's two cents in** 의견을 첨가하다 (add one's comments)
- [ ] **put oneself in someone else's place/shoes** 다른 사람의 입장에서 보다
- [ ] **put/lay/place the blame on** ~를 비난하다, 탓하다 (blame someone for)
- [ ] **put together** 조립하다, 짜 맞추다 (assemble)
- [ ] **put up with** ~를 참다, 견디다 (stand, endure, bear)
- [ ] **progressive disorder** 진행성 질환(parkinson)
- [ ] **part and parcel** 중요 부분, 요점 (integral part)
- [ ] **participate in** 참가하다
- [ ] **pass away** 죽다 (die)
- [ ] **pass for** ~로 통하다 (be (mistakenly) accepted or considered as)
- [ ] **pass out** 기절하다; 나누어주다 (accept the consequences; distribute)
- [ ] **pass out of existence** 사라지다 (disappear, vanish, fade)
- [ ] **pass over** 무시하다, 빼놓다, 넘겨주다 (disregard)
- [ ] **Pyrrhic victory**
  1) 보람 없는 승리 → 막대한 희생을 치른 승리
  2) 너무 많은 희생[대가]을 치르고 얻은 승리
  3) 기원전 279년에 에피루스(Epirus)의 왕 피루스(Pyrrhus)가 로마군과 싸워 이겼으나 많은 전사자를 낸 것에서 나온 표현.
- [ ] **pass the buck** 책임을 전가하다
- [ ] **pass up** 거절하다 (reject, turn down, decline)
- [ ] **patch up** 일시적으로 수습(해결)하다 (settle a quarrel or disagreement)
- [ ] **pave the way for** ~의 길을 열다, ~을 가능하게 하다(prepare for, make possible)
- [ ] **pay attention to** ~에 주의를 기울이다
- [ ] **pay back** 상환하다 (return)
- [ ] **pay off** 성과를 거두다, 좋은 결과를 낳다 (be worth while)
- [ ] **pay through the nose** 엄청난 돈을 쓰다, 바가지를 쓰다 (pay far too much)
- [ ] **pay tribute to** 경의를 표하다 (honor, pay homage to)
- [ ] **peeping Tom** 엿보기 좋아하는 호색가 (a person who secretly looks at others who don't know they are being watched, especially when they are undressing)
- [ ] **pick on** 괴롭히다, 흠을 찾아내다, 혹평하다(annoy, find fault, criticize severely)
- [ ] **pick one's pocket** 소매치기하다 (commit pocket-picking)
- [ ] **pick up** (도망자 등을) 붙잡다, 검거하다 (seen and arrested)
- [ ] **pick up** (자동차를) 태워주다 (arrange to go and get)
- [ ] **pick up the tap** 셈을 치르다 (pay for)
- [ ] **picture to oneself** 상상하다 (imagine, envision, visualize, fancy)
- [ ] **pinch pennies** 절약하다, 인색하게 굴다 (economize, save, be stingy)
- [ ] **place (set, put) much value on** ~을 높이 평가하다 (value highly)
- [ ] **play a key role in** 중요한 역할을 하다
- [ ] **play ducks and drakes with money** 돈을 물쓰듯 쓰다 → 낭비하다
- [ ] **cut it fine** (시간, 돈)바싹 줄이다 → 절약하다(to allow little margin of time, space)
- [ ] **cut corners** 절약하다 → 지름길로 가다 → 안이한 방법을 취하다
- [ ] **play fast and loose** 무책임하게 행동하다 (act in an irresponsible manner)
- [ ] **play it by ear** 임기응변으로 ~하다, 즉흥 연주하다 (improvise)
- [ ] **play by the rules** 원칙대로 하다
- [ ] **play on** ~을 이용하다, 자극하다 (exploit, take advantage of, impose on)
- [ ] **play hooky** 땡땡이 치다
- [ ] **play trick on** ~에게 장난을 치다
- [ ] **play possum** 죽은체하다, 위장전술을 펴다
- [ ] **play up** 과장하다; 장난치다 (exaggerate, overstate, hyperbolize)
- [ ] **point up** 강조하다 (show clearly, underline, emphasize)
- [ ] **pore over** 심사숙고하다 (contemplate, ponder, think over, mull over)
- [ ] **prevail on** 설득하다 (persuade, sway)
- [ ] **pride oneself on** 자랑하다 (be proud of, take pride in)
- [ ] **prior to** ~보다 앞선, 이전에(before)
- [ ] **probe into** ~을 조사하다 (look into, examine)
- [ ] **prop up** 떠받치다, 버티다, 지지하다, 보장하다 (support)
- [ ] **provide A with B** : A에게 B를 제공하다
- [ ] **pull a long face** 우울한 얼굴을 하다, 우울한 표정을 짓다 (wear a gloomy expression, look sad)
- [ ] **pull one's weight** 자신의 임무(역할)을 다하다 (do one's full share of work or part)
- [ ] **pull over** 정차하다
- [ ] **pull (draw) the wool over one's eyes**

남의 눈을 속이다(trick someone by hiding the facts)
(pull a fast one on, do a snow job, take in)
- **speak through one's teeth** 새빨간 거짓말을 하다
- **put ~ on** 입다, 쓰다, 신다, 놀리다, 속이다
- **put ~ on a pedestal** 존경하다, ~를 연장자로 모시다
- **put oneself in a person's shoes** 누구의 입장이 되어 생각하다
- **put a question to someone** ~에게 질문하다 (ask someone a question)
- **put a stock in** ~을 신용하다
- **put across** 명료하게 설명하다, 훌륭히 해내다, 성공시키다 (explain)
- **put by** 모아두다, 비축해두다
- **put on a garb of** ~의 옷을 입다, (모습, 특징) 띠다(assumed)
- **put down** 적어 넣다 (write)
- **put in for a transfer** 전근을 요청하다
- **put off** 연기하다 (postpone)
- **put on** 입다, 쓰다, 신다, 지니다 (assume)
- **put on the dog** 부자인(고상한, 잘난)체하다 → 거드름을 피우다
(To make an ostentatious display of elegance, wealth, or culture)
- **put on an act** ~인 체하다 (make believe, feign, put on, pretend)
- **put on weight** 살이 찌다
- **pop the question** 청혼하다(ask (someone) to marry you)
- **put on (stand in) a white sheet** 참회하다, 회개하다 (repent)
- **put one's foot in it** (부주의로 말미암아) 실수하다
- **put one's foot in (into) it (one's mouth)**
실수하다, 부주의로 곤경에 빠지다
(do a wrong thing, make a blunder, be in hot water by carelessness)
- **put one's heart and soul into** ~에 열중, 몰두하다
- **put one's life on the line** 목숨을 걸다 (risk one's life)
- **put one's nose into** ~에 간섭하다 (interfere in, meddle in, intervene in)
- **put out** (불을) 끄다, 출판하다, 내쫓다, 번거롭게 하다
- **put someone through** ~을 연결시키다 (connect)
- **put something on the back burner** 어떤 것을 뒷전으로 미루다
(leave something behind)
- **put ~ on the back corner** 유보하다, 뒤로 미루다
- **put through** 성취하다, (전화를) 연결시키다 (complete)
- **put up a tent** 천막을 치다 (set a tent)
- **put up at** ~에 투숙하다 (stay at)
- **put up with** 참다, 견디다 (bear, stand, endure, tolerate)
- **put ~ in one's place** 입장을 바꾸어 보다
- **push the envelope** (어떤 분야에서) 인간 위업의 한계를 넓히다
(go beyond the limits of what is)
- **put down** (이름·생각 등을) 적어두다; (폭동·운동 등을) 진압하다
- **put the cart before the horse**
1) 수레를 말 앞에 놓는다는 뜻 → 앞뒤가 바뀐 상황
2) 본말을 전도하다 → 일의 순서가 뒤바뀌다
- **proximity of blood** 근친(近親) → 친족 관계
- **propinquity**[프러핑쿼티] (장소, 관계, 시간) 가까움 → 근접 → 유사
- **My Pet Peeve is rude people.** 혐오하는 것 → 발끈하게 하는 것
(내가 혐오하는 건 무례한 사람들이에요)
- **penny-wise and pound-foolish** 소탐대실하다
- **He is Loaded** 그는 갑부이다
- **premature diagnosis** 섣부른 진단
1) diagnosis 진단법 → (문제, 상황) 원인실태 분석

(문제의 원인이나 성질의) 판단 분석 → (문제의)해답, 해결
IN BRIEF A conclusion reached after a study of the symptoms conclusion, determination, identification, analysis, examination, investigation
- **give a diagnosis of pneumonia** (폐렴 진단을 내리다)
- **make a diagnosis** (진단하다)
의사가 환자가 지니고 있는 이상 상태를 정확하게 파악하고 이에 따라서 적절한 처치를 내리기 위한 근거를 얻는 것을 말한다. 진단의 목표는 단순히 질환명을 결정하는 것뿐만이 아니라 환자가 나타내는 이상 상태를 정확하게 파악하는 것이다.
2) prognosis (의학)예후(豫後) → 예상, 예측
IN BRIEF Forecast, The prospect of recovery from a disease forecast, outlook, prediction, prognostication, projection. See foresight
병세의 진행, 회복에 관한 예측을 의미하는 의학용어
- **prolix** 지루한 → 장황한
IN BRIEF Too wordy(diffuse, long-winded, periphrastic, pleonastic, redundant, verbose, wordy)
- **prolixity** 장황함 → 지루함(boring verbosity)
(excessive wordiness in speech or writing; longwindedness)
- **avoid prolixity** 장황함을 피하다
- **public scrutiny** 공개 심사, 감시, 감독

Q

- **quite a bit** (구어) 꽤, 상당히
- **quite a few** 꽤 많은
- **quite right** 좋아; 고장 없다, 무사하다(all right)
- **quote unquote** 《구어》 말하자면, 다시 말해서
- **quite a few** 많은 (many, a lot of, a great number of)
- **quake in one's boots** 겁내다; 무서워하다
Mel Gibson alone can quake in their boots.
멜 깁슨 혼자서도 그들을 떨게 할 수 있다
- **qualify oneself for** ~에 대한 자격을 갖추다
I think I qualify myself for the job.
내 생각엔 내가 그 자리에 대한 자격을 갖추었다.
- **Queen Anne is dead.** (구어) 그것은 낡아빠진 이야기다
- **queer a person's pitch= queer the pitch for a person**
(구어) 남의 계획을 망치다
You have queered my pitch today.
오늘 넌 내 계획을 망쳤다.
- **queer in the head** 머리가 이상한[어떻게 된]
I think he is queer in the head.
내 생각엔 그의 머리가 좀 이상한 것 같다.
- **quick on the draw** 기민하게 반응하다; 이해가 빠르다
She's really quick on the draw.
그녀는 정말 반응이 빠릅니다.

R

- **red flannel** 《구어》 혀(tongue)
Watch out your red flannel.
혀를 함부로 놀리지 마라.
- **read between the lines** (글의) 행간을 읽다, 숨은 뜻을 알아채다
- **raise sand** 《미국·구어》 큰 소동을 일으키다

- The tanks raised sand in the town.
  탱크들이 마을에서 큰 소동을 일으켰다.
- raise hob with 《구어》 ~을 어지럽히다[망가뜨리다]
  Do not raise hob with this thing.
  이건 망가뜨리지마.
- raise[lift] a blockade 봉쇄를 풀다
  They decided to raise a blockade and let her in.
  그들은 봉쇄를 풀고 그녀를 들여보내기로 결정했다.
- reinvent[invent] the wheel 《구어》 일부러 처음부터 다시 하다
- raise cain 《구어》 (큰) 소동을 일으키다; 화내어 날뛰다
- raise a question 문제를 제기하다, 문제 삼다
- raise (up) the ante 《구어》 (1) 분담금[자금]을 인상하다 (2) (합의하기 위하여) 양보하다, (양보하여) 의견의 일치를 보다
- rake it in 《구어》 한밑천 잡다[벌다] → 돈을 잔뜩 벌다
  The salesperson raked it in here for two months and then left.
  이곳에서 판매원이 두 달간 한밑천을 잡은 후 떠났다.
- rake off [뇌물 따위를] 챙기다[먹다]
  The corrupt official raked off bribes.
  부패한 관리가 뇌물을 챙겼다.
- rare old 《구어》 매우 좋은[나쁜], 대단한
  This is a rare old vintage.
  이것은 최고급 포도주입니다.
- rat on (약속을) 취소하다, 이행하지 않다; (빚을) 떼어먹다; 배신하다
  If you ever rat on, I will never see you again.
  만약 날 바람맞힌다면, 다신 널 보지 않을 거야.
- rat race 생존 경쟁; 출세 경쟁; 과당 경쟁; 성공을 위한 치열한 투쟁;
  Bob is tired of the rat race. He's retired and lives in the country.
  밥은 치열한 출세 경쟁에 진저리가 났다. 그는 은퇴하여 시골에 살고 있다.
- read a dream 해몽하다
  Fortunetellers can read your dreams.
  점성술사들은 당신의 꿈을 해몽해줄 수 있다.
- receive[take] with a grain of salt 에누리하여[가감하여] 듣다
- reckon for ① ~의 책임을 지다 ② ~의 준비를 하다
  You must reckon for your behavior.
  너의 행동에는 책임을 져야 한다.
- reckon on ~을 의지하다; ~에 기대를 걸다
  Rosa reckons on her parents.
  Rosa는 부모님께 의지한다.
- red tape 관료주의; 형식주의; (특히 정부나 관공서의 부서가) 규칙이나 규정된 말씨 등 지나치게 까다로운 관료적인 것(영국 관공서에서 공문서를 묶는 데 쓴 빨간 끈에서)
- rain cats and dogs 《구어》 비가 억수같이 퍼붓다
- He had a quick temper. 그는 성질이 급해.
- I'm such a klutz. 난 정말 덤벙대는구나. (덩벙덤벙)
- rub salt into the wound 사태를 더 골치 아프게 만들다
  (make something worse, add insult to injury, fan the flames, aggravate matters, magnify a problem)
- red-herrings(레드헤링) (주의나 관심) 딴 데로 돌리는 것 (irrelevant comments), 속이다, 현혹시키다
- rack up 성취하다, 달성하다, 해내다(gain)
- running down 헐뜯다 → 비방하다(criticizing)
- round off(up) 마무리하다(finish)

- rack one's brain(s) 머리를 짜내다(try to solve something)
- raise an objection to/against 이의를 제기하다
  (take issue with → express dissent → question → doubt)
- raise eyebrows 사람들을 놀라게 하다 (surprise)
- remain on the right side of
  ① ~와 사이가 좋다 ② [사람]을 괴롭히지 않다
  Bob remains on the right side of Peter.
  밥은 피터와 사이가 좋다.
- render down [문제·생각 따위를] 단순화하다, 정리하다
  Render it down, so we can talk about it more easily.
  좀 정리하면 더 쉽게 얘기해 볼 수 있을 거야.
- renounce friendship[one's friend] 친구와 절교하다
  I had to renounce friendship because everything was not the same.
  모든 것이 전과 달라졌기에 나는 친구와 절교해야 했다.
- ride off on a side issue 지엽적인 문제로 요점을 회피하다
  Don't ride off on a side issue but talk about the main point.
  지엽적인 문제로 요점을 회피하지 말고 내게 요점을 말하오.
- right in the head 《구어》 분별이 있는
- raise Cain
  1) 소동을 일으키다[with] → (큰 소리로)화내다 → 불평하다 → 호통치다
  2) 카인은 최초의 인류인 아담(Adam)의 첫째 아들로 그에게는 아벨(Abel)이라는 동생이 있었다. 그는 아벨이 신에게 인정을 받자 시기심과 질투심으로 인하여 아벨을 들로 데리고 나가서 돌로 쳐 죽이고 만다. 이후로 카인은 불순종과 시기심의 대명사처럼 쓰이게 되었다.
- raise the roof 화내다 → 호통치다, 불평하다
  (blow a fuse, blow one's lid, blow one's top, blow off one's steam)
  (fly off the handle, hit the ceiling the roof, be hot under the collar)
  (jump down one's throat, see red)
- rally around 집결하다, 단결하다 (gather, support)
- ramble on 장황하게 이야기하다, 횡설수설하다
- remind A of B : A에게 B를 생각나게 하다
- rank and file 대중, 평민, 평사원, 평회원 (ordinary people)
- read between the lines 말 속에 담긴 속뜻을 파악하다
- read through 독파하다, 통독하다 (read to the last page)
- reckon with 처리[청산]하다, ~를 고려하다 (settle accounts with)
- reflect on 곰곰이 생각하다, 반성하다 (ponder on)
- renege on 약속을 어기다 (break one's promise)
- resort to (수단)호소하다(appeal to → make use of)
- rest up 충분히 쉬다 (relax)
- result in ~로 끝나다 (end as a consequence)
- ride again 원기를 회복하다
- ride out (폭풍, 곤란 따위)이겨내다 (endure successfully)
- right away 즉시, 당장에 (immediately)
- right up/down somebody's alley 적성에 맞는, 적격인(one's cup of tea)
- ring/hit a bell 생각나게 하다 (make one remember something)
- ring down the curtain 끝마치다, 폐막의 신호를 하다
  (bring down the curtain)
- rip off 속이다, 사취하다, 바가지 씌우다 (fleece)
- rob Peter to pay Paul 빚을 내어 빚을 갚다
- rob the cradle 요람을 훔치다 →
  훨씬 나이 어린 상대와 결혼하다 [고르다, 사랑하다]

- [ ] rock bottom 최저 (the lowest possible point)
- [ ] rock the boat 문제[풍파]를 일으키다 (cause the problem)
- [ ] roll out 펴다, 처음으로 공개하다 (introduce)
- [ ] roll out the red carpet 정중히 맞이하다 (give a hearty welcome)
- [ ] root for 응원하다 (cheer, support)
- [ ] rob Peter to pay Paul 빚으로 빚을 갚다(베드로+바울) (take money from one area and spend it in another)
- [ ] root out 뿌리째 뽑다, 근절하다 (eradicate)
- [ ] round up 체포하다 → 일망타진하다
- [ ] rub elbows with 유명인사와 사귀다 (rub shoulders with)
- [ ] tub somebody the wring way 신경을 건드리다, 화나게 하다 (annoy)
- [ ] rule out 배제하다, 제거하다(exclude)
- [ ] run a risk 위험을 무릅쓰다 (take a risk)
- [ ] run a temperature 열이 있다 (have a fever)
- [ ] run across 우연히 만나다 (come across)
- [ ] run up against (곤란) 부딪치다, 마주치다(to experience a difficulty or a problem)
- [ ] run errands 심부름 가다 (go on errands)
- [ ] run for 입후보하다 (become a candidate)
- [ ] run in the blood/family 혈통을 물려받다
- [ ] run into 우연히 만나다 (bump into)
- [ ] run out of ~를 다 써버리다, 바닥이 나다 (deplete)
- [ ] run up (빚 등을) 갑자기 늘리다 (add to the amount of)
- [ ] run-of-the-mill 평범한, 보통인 (common, average in quality)
- [ ] rack one's brains 머리를 짜내다 (think very hard)
- [ ] rain cats and dogs 비가 억수같이 내리다 (rain heavily)
- [ ] rain or shine 날씨에 상관없이
- [ ] raise an objection 이의를 제기하다 (take exception)
- [ ] raise one's hand 손을 들다
- [ ] read between the lines 행간(숨은 의미)을 알아내다(read hidden meanings)
- [ ] record time 최단시간 (the shortest time)
- [ ] red tape 관료적 형식주의 (silly detailed unnecessary official rules that delay action)
- [ ] redound to 이익 등이 돌아가다 (increase)
- [ ] refer to ~대해 언급하다
- [ ] refrain from ~ing 삼가다
- [ ] regardless of ~에 상관없이
- [ ] rely on ~에 의지하다, 신뢰하다
- [ ] remain stable 안정세를 유지하다
- [ ] remain unoccupied 입주가 안 된 상태로 있다
- [ ] remind A of B : A에게 B를 상기시키다
- [ ] resign oneself to 체념하다 (accept without complaint)
- [ ] ride out (폭풍, 곤란)이겨내다, 극복하다
- [ ] rid ~ of 제거하다, 해방하다
- [ ] rife with ~로 가득찬 (full of)
- [ ] ring a bell 연상하게 하다 (sound familiar)
- [ ] rip off 바가지를 쒸우다
- [ ] rip-off 바가지요금, 터무니없이 비싼 가격 (act of charging too much)
- [ ] rise to fame 명성을 얻다 (come to fame)
- [ ] root out 뿌리 뽑다, 근절하다 (eradicate, get rid of)
- [ ] round off 마무리하다 → 끝내다(finish) (get through with, go through with, have done with, wind up, wrap up) (Let's call it a day, Let's call it quits, so much today)

- [ ] round out 완성하다, 마무리하다 (complete, finish)
- [ ] round the clock 24시간 내내 (day and night, 24 hours a day)
- [ ] round up 체포하다, 모으다 (arrest, apprehend)
- [ ] rub the wrong way ~를 화나게 하다 (irritate, annoy someone)
- [ ] rule out 배제하다, 제외하다 (exclude, be lost in)
- [ ] run a risk of ~의 위험을 무릅쓰다
- [ ] run across 우연히 만나다 (come across, run into, meet by chance, encounter, bump into)
- [ ] run away 달아나다, 도망치다 (escape)
- [ ] run for ~에 출마하다
- [ ] run into 충돌하다, 우연히 만나다
- [ ] run out of ~이 바닥나다, 떨어지다, 고갈되다, 다 써버리다 (become used up, be exhausted, use up, exhaust)
- [ ] run out of gas 기름이 떨어지다
- [ ] run over (차가) 사람을 치다 (hit, knock down and pass over the top of)
- [ ] run short 모자라다, 불충분하다
- [ ] run-of-the-mill 보통의, 일반적인, 평범한 (ordinary, average, mediocre)
- [ ] rough up 학대하다, 괴롭히다
- [ ] ring a bell 생각나다 → 떠오르다

S

- [ ] single-handedly 혼자 힘으로 → 한 손으로 → 단독으로
- [ ] Don't be wishy washy. 우유부단하게 굴지마. (우유부단한, 줏대가 없는:indecisive)
- [ ] Kathy has a mind of her own. 케이씨는 주관이 뚜렷했어요.(주관이 뚜렷한)
- [ ] Thank you for being so Open-minded. 정말 편견 없이(개방적인) 대해주셔서 감사해요.
- [ ] She seems so good-natured. 그녀는 정말 마음씨가 좋아 보여요.
- [ ] I used to have morning sickness. 전 입덧을 하곤 했었어요.
- [ ] we were like newly-weds. 우리는 마치 신혼부부 같았어요.
- [ ] Tie the knot. 결혼하다.
- [ ] We were engaged. 우리는 약혼했어요.
- [ ] pop the question 청혼하다.
- [ ] I'm sorry, but I'm already spoken for. 죄송해요. 전 이미 임자가 있어요.
- [ ] It's a great pick-up line. 훌륭한 작업용 멘트네요.
- [ ] I'm trying to play hard-to-get. 밀고 당기기를 하다 → 비싸게 굴다
- [ ] She's into you. 그녀는 너한테 반했어.
- [ ] saturate with ~으로 가득차 있다 → 흠뻑 적시다, 담그다
- [ ] shoot off one's mouth(face) 입방아 찧다, 과장해서말하다, 경솔하게 지껄이다
- [ ] be scared stiff 깜짝 놀라다 → 몹시놀라게하다(petrified, take aback)
- [ ] stuck-up 건방진, 거만한
- [ ] sneak a smoke 몰래 담배를 피우다
- [ ] stick with 끝까지 충실하다; 떨어지지 않다; 지키다 → 바꾸지 않다(not give up on it)
- [ ] skin deep 거죽 한 꺼풀 깊이의 → 피상적인
- [ ] succumb to 굴복하다
- [ ] safe and sound 무사히 (safe and sure)

- salt of the earth 세상의 소금, 세상에서 중요한 사람 (a very good person)
- save one's face 체면을 세우다 (keep one's dignity)
- save one's skin 목숨을 건지다
- saved by the bell 공이 살려준 (saved from trouble by unexpected situation)
- scale down 줄이다 (reduce → slash)
- score of 많은 수의, 많은 (a great many)
- set the thames /river on fire 대단한 일을 하다, 세상을 깜짝 놀라게 하다
- scramble for ~를 차지하려고 다투다 (struggle to get)
- scrape through 간신히 통과하다 (barely pass)
- scratch the surface 수박 겉핥기만 하다 (deal with only a small part of)
- screen out 가려내다 (select)
- screw up 혼란시키다, 뒤죽박죽 만들다 (make a mess)
- seamy side of life 인생의 좋지 않은 면 (dark side of life)
- see eye to eye (with) (전적으로) 의견이 일치하다 (agree completely → concur)
- see little of ~를 잘 만나주지 않다
- see off 배웅하다, 전송하다 (go to say goodbye)
- see red 노발대발하다, 격노하다 (be angry)
- see to it that ~하도록 조처하다 (make sure something is done)
- sell like hot cakes 날개 돋친 듯이 팔리다 (sell very fast)
- sell out 다 팔아치우다, 배신하다 (be all out, betray)
- serve right 거참 고소하다, 꼴 좋다
- set a precedent 전례를 만들다 (establish a pattern)
- set aside 따로 챙겨두다 (put aside)
- set fire to ~를 불태우다 (set on fire)
- set the pace 모범을 보이다, 보조를 맞추다 (make the pace)
- set the table 식탁준비를 하다 (lay the table)
- set up 준비하다, 시작하다, 설립하다, 조작하다 (make preparations, start, establish, frame up)
- settle down 정주하다, 정착하다, 가라앉다
- settle for 불만스럽지만 받아들이다, ~로 만족하다
- settle on 정하다, 동의하다 (decide on)
- settle up 해결하다, 청산하다
- shake a leg 서두르다 (hurry)
- shame on you 창피한 줄 알아라 (what a disgrace!)
- shed light on 밝히다, 해명하다 (elucidate, clarify)
- shoot the breeze 잡담하다, 수다떨다 (chat)
- shoot up 치솟다, 빨리 자라다 (soar)
- short of ~가 부족한 (lacking of time/money)
- shortcut 지름길 (fastest way)
- shot in the arm 활력소 (something encouraging)
- show around 여기저기 안내하다
- show up 나타나다 (turn up, appear)
- shut down 휴업하다 (close down)
- sick and tired of 넌더리가 난, 지긋지긋한 (disgusted)
- side with 편을 들다, 지지하다 (support)
- sift through 철저히 조사하다, 샅샅이 뒤지다 (come through, scrutinize) (over-haul → look into → vet)
- sign up for ~에 등록하다, 신청하다 (apply for)
- single out 고르다, 선발하다 (choose)
- sink or swim 성공하느냐 실패하느냐, 흥하든 망하든 (make or break)
- sit in 수강하다, 참석하다 (attend, take part in)
- sit in for somebody ~를 대신하다, 대리하다 (substitute for)
- sit it on ~를 방청[참관, 청강]하다 (attend, be present at)
- sit through 끝까지 앉아 있다, 끝까지 보다[듣다]
- sit up (밤늦게까지) 자지 않고 있다 (not sleep till late at night)
- size up 평가하다, 판단하다 (assess)
- skim through 대충 훑어보다 (read quickly through)
- slack off 느슨하게 하다, 늦추다 (relax)
- sleep in 늦잠 자다 (oversleep)
- sleep off 잠을 자서 낫게 하다, 잠으로 씻어 버리다
- sleep on ~를 하룻밤 자면서 생각하다 (dwell on)
- slip one's mind 깜박 잊다 (forget)
- slip up 잘못하다, 실수하다 (make an error)
- slow down 속력을 늦추다 (slacken)
- snarl up 얽히게 하다, 혼란시키다 (complicate)
- sneak up 살짝[몰래]다가가다 (come near to quietly)
- so to speak 말하자면
- so-called 소위 (what is called)
- sooner or later 조만간 (in the near future)
- sort out 가려내다, 골라내다 (classify)
- sound fishy 수상쩍게 들리다
- sound out 타진하다 (try to find out)
- spaced out 멍한, 정신이 나가있는
- speak ill of ~를 나쁘게 말하다 (slander)
- speak of the devil (and he will appear) 호랑이도 제 말하면 온다 (talk of the devil)
- speak up 큰 소리로 말하다 (speak loudly)
- speak well of ~를 좋게 말하다 (speak highly of)
- speaking of ~에 관해서라면, ~의 이야기라면
- speed up 빠르게 하다 (make it faster)
- spell out 자세히 설명하다, 또박또박 말하다 (shed light on)
- spick-and-span 깨끗한, 말쑥한 (clean)
- spill the beans 비밀을 폭로하다, 비밀을 누설하다 (reveal)
- split hairs 사소한 일을 꼬치꼬치 따지다
- split the difference 타협하다, 절충하다 (make a compromise)
- spruce up 단정하게 하다 (tidy up)
- square away 갖추다, 준비하다, 처리하다 (put in order)
- stack up 쌓아 올리다 (pile up)
- stamp out 근절시키다, 박멸하다 (eradicate)
- stand a chance 가능성이 있다, 승산이 있다 (have a chance of winning)
- stand by ~의 편을 들다, 찬성하다, 기다리다 (support, approve of)
- stand fo ~를 뜻하다, 나타내다, 의미하다 (mean, show, represent)
- stand out 두드러지다 (be noticeable)
- stand up for 옹호하다 → 지지하다 → 변호하다 (defend, back up)
- stand up to ~에 용감히 맞서다 (confront bravely)
- stare at ~를 빤히 쳐다보다, 노려보다
- start from scratch 처음부터 다시 시작하다 (start from the beginning keep the ball rolling)
- start/get/set the ball rolling 일을 개시하다 (keep the ball rolling)
- stave off 간신히 모면하다, 피하다 (ward off)
- stay away from 결석하다, 부재중이다 (be absent, be away)
- stay up 밤을 새우다 (sit up all night)
- steep in 깊이 빠지다 → 몰두하다
- steal the show (조연이 주연의) 인기를 가로채다

- steer clear of 회피하다 → 피하다 (avoid → stay away from) (To stay away from; avoid)
- stem from ~에서 유래되다 → ~에서 시작되다 (originate from → to result from something)
- step by step 한 걸음 한 걸음, 착실하게 (little by little)
- step down ~하여 하다, 은퇴하다 (leave office)
- smell a rat (이상하다는)낌새를 채다 → 의심이 들다 (to suspect that something is wrong)
- step on the gas 서두르다, 속력을 내다 (press on the accelerator)
- stick around 곁에서 기다리다, 부근에서 어슬렁거리다 (stay near)
- stick one's nose in something 다른 사람 일에 관여하다 (poke one's nose in something)
- stick to 고수하다 (not give in)
- stick to one's guns 고집하다, 주장하다 (stand firm, dig in one's heels)
- stop by 잠시 들르다 (drop by)
- stop off at 잠깐 들르다 (drop by)
- stop short ~까지는 이르지 않다(not go too far)
- stumbling block 걸림돌, 장애물 (obstacle)
- substitute A for B : B대신에 A를 사용하다, 바꾸다(use in place of another)
- suited for 어울리는, 적합한 (fit, suitable)
- sum up 요약하다 (summarize)
- swear in 선서하고 취임하다
- sweep the board 싹쓸이하다 (take all the prizes)
- sell someone short (구어)얕잡아 보다 → 능력을 과소평가하다
- save one's face 체면을 지키다, 체면을 세우다
- second to none 누구에게도 뒤지지 않는, 어느 것에도 뒤지지 않는, 최고의 (better than all others, better than at least, the best)
- second-rate 2류의, 열등한, 평범한
- see A as B A를 B로 간주하다
- see eye to eye 견해가 일치하다 (agree)
- see red 격노하다 (become angry, get infuriated)
- see to 주의하다, 배려하다 (take care, pay attention to)
- see to it that 꼭~하도록 보내다, ~을 확실히 하다 (make sure that ~)
- sell like cakes 날개 돋친듯이 팔리다
- separate A from B : A를 B로부터 분리하다
- serve one's turn 목적에 적합하다 (suit one's purpose)
- set about 시작하다
- set at naught 무시하다, 경멸하다(make light of → down-play) (ignore, neglect, not to care about or not fear: make little of)
- set back 방해하다 (hinder)
- set forth 보이다, 진열하다, 시작하다 (present)
- set free 석방하다 (release, liberate)
- set off 일으키다, 유발(촉발)하다, 출발하다, 시작하다 (start, make begin, begin a usually long or difficult course of action with a clear purpose, trigger)
- set oneself apart 고립시키다 (isolate, insulate, cut off)
- set out 출발하다, 말하다, 착수하다, 시작하다, 떠나다, 꺼내 놓다 (start journey, leave, start)
- set store by ~을 중요시하다 (make much of, think highly of)
- set one's teeth on edge 역겹게 하다, 불쾌하게 만들다
- set the seal on ~을 마무리하다 (bring to an end in a suitable way; formally end) (round off, round out, round up, put through)
- set up 세우다, 짜 맞추다, 설립하다, 새로이 만들다
- set up for ~을 준비하다 (prepare for)
- shed crocodile tears 거짓 눈물을 흘리다 (pretend grief)
- shed light on 설명하다 (explain, account for, spell out)
- show off 자랑하다, 과시하다(hot air : 허풍 → full of bunk → bluffs)
- show respect for another opinion 다른 의견을 존중하다
- show up 나타나다, 참석하다
- side by side with ~와 결탁하여
- sign up for ~에 등록하다
- sit in on ~에 참석하다, 구경하다 (participate in)
- sit on ~의 일원이다 (be a member of)
- sit on the fence 형세를 관망하다, 중립을 지키다 (remain neutral)
- slack off 늦추다, 줄어들다 (become slow moving)
- slip one's mind 깜빡하다, 잊다 (forget something)
- smoking gun 확실한 증거 (concrete evidence)
- snow job 감언이설
- snow someone under 압도하다(was overcome with)
- so much for ~에 대해서는 이만하면 충분한 (enough has been said about)
- soap opera 연속 멜로드라마 (a television or radio program about the continuing daily life and troubles of characters in it)
- Speak of the devil 호랑이도 제 말하면 온다더니
- speak excitedly 흥분하여 말하다
- speak ill of ~ : ~를 나쁘게 말하다
- speak one's mind 솔직하게 이야기하다 (speak frankly)
- speak to A about B : A에게 B라고 말하다
- speculate on 추측하다 (divine, forecast, forestall, prophesy)
- spill the beans 비밀을 누설하다
  '콩을 엎지르다'라는 식으로 된 이 표현은 '비밀을 누설시키다'라는 뜻(divulge confidential information or secrets)
- split hairs 쓸데없이 따지다 → 지나치게 구분하다 (argue about small and unimportant differences)
- sprain one's ankle 발목을 삐다
- spread oneself too thin 일을 너무 많이 벌이다 (to do so many things at one time that you can do none of them well)
- stand (someone) up 데이트에서 바람맞히다 (ail to meet (someone, especially of the opposite sex) as arranged)
- stand by 지지하다
- stand for 상징하다, 나타내다, 대표하다; 지지하다 (symbolize, represent)
- stand in 대역을 하다; 가담하다
- stand (put on) in a white sheet 유감으로 여기다, 죄를 뉘우치다 (repent)
- stand to reason 이치에 맞다 (be logical, add up, make sense)
- stand up for 옹호하다, 지지하다 (support, defend, back up → back stop)
- stand ~ in good stead ~에게 큰 도움이 되다
- stare at ~을 응시하다, 노려보다
- status quo 현상 (the state of things as they are)
- steal away 몰래 떠나다 (leave furtively)
- stem from ~에서 기원하다 (originate in)
- step on ~을 밟다

- step on the gas 속력을 내다, 서두르다 (speed up, accelerate, hurry)
- step out (특히) 장소를 잠깐 떠나다
- stick to one's guns 주장을 고수하다 (hold fast to one's own opinion)
- stop at nothing 무엇이든 다 하려 들다 (be ready to take any risk)
- stop by ~에 잠시 들르다, 잠깐 들르다 (drop in, drop by, make a stop by)
- stop from ~ ing ~하지 못하게 하다
- straight from the horse's mouth 믿을 만한 소식통으로부터, 본인의 입으로부터
- straight from the shoulder 솔직하게, 직접, 정면에서 (frankly)
- strike out 고안해내다, 발명하다, 삭제하다
  (invent, contrive; remove from a record)
- strike tent 천막을 철수하다
- strike up (대화를) 시작하다
  (invent, contrive; begin, start, commence)
- stuck-up 거만한, 건방진, 거드름피우는 (conceited)
- subscribe for 잡지 예약하다, 구독하다(take in) → (to) 동의하다
- subscribe for(to) (신문, 잡지) 구독하다
- substitute A to B : A대신 B로 대처하다
- such as it is 있는 그대로, 변변치 못한
- suit oneself 마음대로 하다
- support a load 짐을 지탱하다
- surf the Internet 인터넷을 검색하다
- weigh one's words 말조심하다
- swallow(eat) one's words 한 말을 취소하다
  (eat one's words, recant one's words)
- swarm with 충만하다 (be rife with, be full of, teem with)
- sweet talk 감언((cajolery), 아첨쟁이 → sweet-talk a woman (여자를 후리다)
- square the circle
  1) 불가능한 일을 시도하다(the task was proven to be impossible)
  2) 원과 면적이 같은 정사각형을 만들다
  3) 원과 같은 면적의 정사각형을 만드는 것처럼 불가능하거나 매우 어려운 상황을 묘사
- square with ~와 직각이 되다, ~와 일치하다
- squeaky(스퀴키)-bum time 긴장감이 최고조에 달하는 시간
  2003년 퍼거슨이 경기가 끝나기를 바라며 초조하게 시계를 바라보던 장면이 방송에 포착됐는데, 이를 퍼거슨 본인은 "긴장감이 최고조에 달하는 시간"이란 의미로 '스퀴키 붐 타임'(squeaky bum time)이란 말을 처음 사용
- squeaky(스퀴키) wheel gets the grease
  1) 우는 아이에게 떡 하나 더 준다((aggressive attitude)
  2) 삐걱거리는 바퀴는 기름을 쳐야 한다
  3) 우는소리 한다고 다 되는 것이 아니라 핵심을 알고 요구해야 한다는 표현이다. 그래서 나온 말이 'The squeak gets the grease'이다. '삐걱 소리가 나면 기름을 친다'는 이 말은 어떤 잡음을 내느냐가 중요하고, 문제의 핵심을 정확히 표현해야 한다는 의미다.
  4) 원하는 것은 쟁취하되 남에게 반감을 사지 않는 스타일을 약간 적극적인(passive-aggressive) 스타일이라고 말한다. 조용히 대처하고(Silent treatment) 슬며시 앞서가는(get ahead) 편이다. 개성파(assertive)는 솔직담백하며 자존심을 지키고 자중자애하는 스타일이다.
- shoot from the hip
  1) 성급하게 반응하다 → 성급하게 행동하다 → 즉흥적으로 행동하다, 성급하게 말하다 (react quickly without thinking carefully first)
  2) 깊이 생각하지 않고 바로 반응하여 이야기하는 사람에게 하는 말입니다.
  서부의 총잡이를 보면 엉덩이에서 총을 꺼내어 빠른 반응으로 상대에게 총을 겨누는 것
- Shape up or ship out! (구어) 열심히 하지 않으려면 나가라!
- security blanket
  1) 담요(어린애가 안도감을 얻기 위해 안거나 어루만지는)
    (A blanket carried by a child to reduce anxiety)
  2) 안도감을 주는 것[사람](Something that dispels anxiety)
- substantive nation 독립 국가
- substantive duration 독립적 존재
- say a mouthful (구어) 중요한[적절한] 말을 하다 → 핵심을 찌르다
- shake on it (구어) 동의하여 악수하다
  The leaders shook on it eventually (결국 지도자들은 동의하여 악수했다)
- see with ~와 의견이 일치하다 → 동의하다
  I see with your dad. (난 네 아빠에 동의해)
- say ditto to (구어) 의견에 전적으로 동의하다
- say amen to (구어) 동의[찬성]하다
  He said amen to the bill. (그는 법안에 동의했다)
- say nix on 반대하다 불허하다
  We all say nix on the bill. (우리는 모두 그 법안에 반대한다)
- set one's teeth against 단호히 반대하다
  We set out teeth against the plan.
  (그 계획을 우리는 단호히 반대한다)
- say away[on] (구어) 거침없이 말하다
  She said away that it was her own fault.
  (그녀는 그것이 자신만의 잘못이라고 거침없이 말했다.)
- say for oneself 변명하다 → 해명하다
- say nice things 아양 떨다 → 입에 발린 말을 하다
  Don't say nice things because it will not change the decision.
  (어차피 결정에 영향을 주지 않을테니 아양은 그만 떨어라)
- score a bull's eye [a bull] 핵심을 찌르다
  Her question scored a bull's eye.
  (그녀의 질문은 핵심을 찔렀다.)
- score a success 성공하다
- scot free (구어) 완전히 자유롭게 → 형벌 받지 않고 → (다친 데 없이) 무사히
- screw up one's courage 용기를 내다; 용기를 쌓다
- scrub along (구어) 가까스로 생계를 유지하다
  Poor Charlie scrubs along(가난한 찰리는 가까스로 생계를 유지했다)
- scrub round (구어) 피하다, 무시하다
- search one's heart (구어) 반성하다 → 자기 비판을 하다
  She searched her heart because of the mistake she did.
  (그녀는 실수했던 것 때문에 반성했다)
- second off (구어) 두 번째로
  She was not the best, but the second off best.
  (그녀는 최고는 아니었지만 두 번째로 최고였다)
- see light[daylight] (구어) (문제 해결의)실마리를 찾다 → 돌파구가 보이다
- see sense 도리를 알다, 분별력을 갖다

A man who sees sense (분별력 있는 남자)
- see the sun 출생하다 → 태어나다 → 살아 있다
- see through 꿰뚫어 보다 → 간파하다
- sell a person a packet (구어) 남에게 거짓말을 하다
  Don't sell me a packet. (내게 거짓말 마라)
- sell a person a pup (구어)속이다 → 바가지 씌우다
- sell a person down the river (구어) 남을 속이다, 배신하다
- sell smoke 속이다, 협잡하다 → We were sold smoke (우리는 속았다)
- sell someone a bill of goods 속이다 → 남에게 사기치다
- sell like hot cakes 불티나게 팔리다
  This CD sells like hot cakes. (이 씨디는 불티나게 팔린다)
- sell one's birthright for a mess of pottage
  팥죽 한 그릇에 장자의 권리를 팔다 →
  (눈앞의 이익을 위해)영구적인 이익을 팔다(←창세기(Gen.))
  The stupid man sold his birthright for a mess of pottage. (어리석은 남자는 눈앞의 이익을 위해 영구적 이익을 팔았다.)
- send a person about his business (구어) 즉석에서 해고하다 → 쫓아 버리다
  The boss sent Tom about his business. (상사는 톰을 즉석에서 해고했다.)
- send a person packing (즉석에서) 남을 해고하다
  I was sent packing. (난 해고당했다)
- set a thing at naught[nothing] 무시하다
  She set my ideas at naught. (그녀는 내 의견을 무시했다.)
- set the world on fire 눈부신 성공을 거두다 → 크게 출세하다
- shaggy-dog story (듣는 사람에게 따분한) 장광설
- shake the money tree (구어) (큰) 이익을 낳다, 크게 벌다
  The businessman shook the money tree. (기업인은 큰돈을 벌었다.)
- shift one's ground
  (토론·상황 따위에서) 주장[입장, 의견, 의도]을 바꾸다, 변절하다
  They shifted their ground suddenly. (갑자기 그들은 입장을 바꾸었다.)
- shoot from the hip (구어) 충동적인 언동을 하다 → 생각 없이 행동하다
  John tends to shoot from the hip, but he speaks the truth. (존은 앞뒤 생각 없이 함부로 말해 버리는 경향은 있으나, 사실대로는 말한다.)
- shoot one's grandmother (구어) 낙담하다 → 실망하다
  The class shot its grandmother. (학급은 실망했다.)
- simmer down 식어 가다; 조용해지다, 흥분이 가라앉다
- sing dumb 침묵하다 → 침묵하고 있다
  He just sang dumb. (그는 단지 침묵했다.)
- sing for air (구어) 숨차다 → 헐떡이다
  The runner sang for air. (그 달리기 선수는 숨이 찼다.)
- sink into oblivion 망각되다
  The fact sank into oblivion. (그 사실은 망각되었다.)
- sink into obscurity 세상에서 잊혀지다 → 초야에 묻히다
- sink into one's boots (구어) (기분·정신 등이) 가라앉다
  I sank into my boots. (난 기분이 가라앉았다.)
- sit in the catbird seat (구어) 유리한[우세한] 입장에 있다
  Mr. Smith sat in the catbird seat. (스미스씨는 유리한 입장이었다.)
- small-time 하찮은; 시시한; 3류의; 작은; 소규모의
- He is solving this case Single-handedly → 혼자 힘으로, 단독으로

(그는 이 사건을 혼자 힘으로 해결하는 중이에요.)
- I'm Swamped right now. → 정신없이 바쁜(늪에 빠진 것처럼) (전 지금 정신없이 바빠요.)
- Scout's honor (구어) 맹세하다 (내가 한 말이 사실임을)
- sell someone down the river 배신하다
- succession of the Olympic Games 계속되는 올림픽대회
  연속 → 연속물 → 상속 → 계승(a following of one thing after another in time)
- in succession 계속하여 → 연속하여 → 연달아
  → one after the other, running, successively,
  → consecutively, on the trot (informal), one behind the other
- sugar daddy 《구어》 (선물 따위로) 젊은 여자를 후리는 돈 많은 중년 남자
- sugarcoat 먹기 좋게 하다 → 겉을 잘 꾸미다 *표면을 덮다, 입히다
  (To cause to seem more appealing or pleasant)
  "더 이상의 사탕발림(sugarcoat)은 의미 없다. 충격적이다." 2일 (미국 동부시간) 미국의 제조업 경기 급락에 대해 금융 전문 매체인 마켓워치는 이와 같이 진단했다
- sack in[out] 《구어》 잠자리에 들다
- sail with every (shift of) wind
  세상 물결을 잘 타다, (정세 변화를 이용하여) 처세를 잘하다
  If you want to be a politician, you must sail with every wind. 정치가가 되고 싶다면 처세를 잘 해야 한다.
- salt of the earth 인격이 뛰어난 사람; 가장 고결한 인물
- Same[The same] here (구어)
  ① (남이 한 말을 받아서) 나도 마찬가지다
  ② (음식점에서 주문할 때) 나도 같은 것을 주시오
  Same here, coffee, please. 저도 똑같이 커피 주세요.
- saunter through life 빈둥거리며 일생을 보내다
  The beggar sauntered through life.
  그 거지는 빈둥거리며 일생을 보냈다.
- save something for a rainy day 만일에 대비하다; 장래에 대비하다
- save the day 《구어》 가까스로 승리[성공, 해결]하다 → 궁지를 벗어나다
  We saved the day last day.
  우리는 어제 경기에서 가까스로 이겼다.
- say a mouthful 《구어》 중요한[적절한] 말을 하다

T

- take a detached view 객관적인[공정한] 견해를 가지다
  He take a detached view.
  그는 객관적 견해를 가지고 있다.
- take a disgust at 넌더리를 내다, 정나미가 떨어지다
  I took disgust at his behavior.
  나는 그의 행동에 정나미가 떨어졌다.
- take a dim[dark, gloomy, poor] view of ~찬성하지 않다, 회의적으로 보다, 비관하다
  We must take a dim view of the facts.
  우리는 그 사실에 대해 비판적이어야 한다.
- Top-dollar 최고가의 → 최고의 수입을 벌어들이는(the highest paid)
- The cat's out of the dog. 비밀이 탄로나다.
- That's a tough call. 그거 결정하기 힘든 일이네요.
- We just clicked. 우리는 마음이 맞다. → 마음이 통하다.

- I'll be your wingman. 내가 네 지원군이 되어줄게.
- I really gotta buckle down. 나는 집중해서 열심히 공부해야 해
- You suck at math. 너 수학 더럽게 못하는구나 → 형편 없이 못하다
- runner-up 2등
- Well done! Top notch! 잘했어! 최고야!
- Throw a party. 파티를 열다.
- They are neck and neck. 그들은 막상막하다.
- turn the trick 일이 잘되다, 목적을 이루다
- take a nose dive 급하강하다 → 대폭락하다(plummet)
- take in (one's) stride 수월하게[냉철하게] 해내다(not be upset by)
- take blood sample 혈액 채취하다
- take the lead 선두에 서다 → 솔선수범하다
- throw up 음식을 토하다
- take no stock in 신용하지 않다(distrust)
- the cat has got his tongue 그는 말이 없다(he was speechless)
- turn a cold shoulder to 냉대하다 → 무시하다
- tack on 첨가하다, 추가하다 (add on)
- tag along ~를 따라가다, 붙어 다니다 (stalk)
- take a back seat to 낮은 지위를 감수하다 (accept a lower position)
- take the rap (자기 일이 아닌 일에) 비난(벌)을 받다
- take a break 잠깐 쉬다 (take a short rest)
- take a dim view of ~를 비관적으로 보다 (have doubts about)
- take A for B : A를 B로 착각하다 (confuse)
- take a rain check 다음으로 미루다 (postpone)
- take a turn for the better 호전되다 (begin to improve)
- take a turn for the worse 악화되다 (become worse)
- take advantage of ~를 이용하다 (make use of)
- take in 가서 보다, 기장을 줄이다, 속이다 (go and see)
- take into account 고려하다, 감안하다 (take account of)
- take it easy 쉬엄쉬엄해라 (relax)
- take it for granted that ~를 당연시하다 (take something as a matter of course)
- take it or leave it 하려고 하고 말려면 마, 싫으면 그만둬라 (decide yes or no)
- take oath 선서하다 (make oath)
- take off 급히 가다 → 이륙하다 → 벗다(get going, get off the ground) 상승하기 시작하다 → 일이 순조롭게 잘 시작되다 (=succeed)
- take off (from work) 휴가로 일을 쉬다 (not go to work)
- take office 취임[취직]하다 (take up one's post)
- take on 싸우다, 다투다, 떠맡다, 대전하다 (fight, undertake, confront)
- take one's breath away ~를 움찔 놀라게 하다
- take one's time 천천히 하다, 서두르지 않다 (act slowly)
- take part in 참가[참여]하다 (participate in)
- take place 일어나다, 생기다 (happen, occur)
- take a shine to 홀딱 반하다
- take root 뿌리박다, 정착하다
- take something with a grain of salt (남의 얘기를)에누리하여 듣다
- take steps 조치를 취하다 (take actions)
- take the bull by the horns 의연하게 난국에 맞서다, 대처하다
- take the cake 상을 타다, 빼어나다 (win the prize, excel)
- take the heat 비난을 받다 → 비난을 감수하다
- take the Fifth 묵비권을 행사하다 → 답변을 거부하다 (refuse to answer)
- take the floor 발언대에 서다
- take the initiative 솔선하다, 주도하다 (take the lead)
- take the law into one's own hands 본인이 알아서 처리하다
- take the plunge 과감하게 하다 (do something risky)
- take the stand 증언대에 서다, 증인석에 앉다
- take the words out of someone's mouth ~가 말하려는 것을 앞질러 말하다
- take up someone's time ~의 시간을 뺏다 (waste one's time)
- take aback 깜짝 놀라다 (surprise)
- talk big/tall 허풍치다 (exaggerate)
- tall order 어려운 주문 → 무리한 요구(목표)
- talk someone into something 설득해서 ~하게 하다 (persuade)
- tamper with 함부로 변경해버리다, 손대다 → 뇌물을 주다, 매수하다
- taper off 차츰 소멸되다, 차츰 줄어들다 (become weaker gradually)
- teem with ~로 가득차다, 많이 있다 (be filled with)
- tell apart 분간하다, 구별하다 (distinguish one from another)
- thanks to 덕분에
- That will be the day 절대로 그런 일은 발생하지 않을 것이다 (not on your life)
- the rest of ~의 나머지
- The shoe is on the other foot 입장(사정)이 뒤바뀌다
- these days 요즈음
- think out loud 혼자 말로 지껄이다
- think twice 재고하다, 다시 생각하다 (think over again)
- thrash out 철저히 토의하다 (discuss completely)
- throw a dust in one's eyes 속이다
- throw/give/have a party 파티를 열다 (hold a party)
- throw a (monkey) wrench 방해하다, 망치다, 실패시키다
- throw in the towel 패배를 인정하다, 항복하다 (give up, surrender)
- throw the book at ~를 엄벌에 처하다, 최대 형량을 언도하다 (punish severely)
- throw up 토하다(vomit) (To eject the contents of the stomach through the mouth)
- tie the knot 결혼하다(marry → walk down the aisle) 청혼하다(ask for one's hand → pop the question) 헤어지다, 이별하다 (be through with → break up with → split up with)
- tighten one's belt 허리띠를 조르다, 절약하다 (spend less money)
- time and again 여러 번 반복하여 (repeatedly)
- twiddle one's thumbs (지루해서) 손가락을 비비다 → 빈들빈들하고 있다(to do nothing; be idle)
- time is up 시간이 다 됐다 (time has run out)
- tip off 밀고하다, (농구 경기가) 시작되다 (tell secret facts to)
- to tone in with 어울리다, 조화되다(to harmonize with)
- to begin with 우선, 첫째로 (to start with)
- to blame 책임이 있는 (be responsible for)
- to make a long story short 간단히 말해서, 한 마디로 (in short)
- to make matters worse 설상가상으로 (what is worse)
- to one's disappointment 유감스럽게도 (to one's regret)
- to one's surprise 놀랍게도 (to one's astonishment)
- to say nothing of ~는 말할 것도 없고, ~는 제쳐놓고 (not to

mention)
- **to some extent** 어느 정도(까지는) (to a certain extent)
- **to (the best of) somebody's knowledge** ~가 아는 바로 (as far as one knows)
- **to sum up** 요약하면
- **to tell the truth** 실은, 사실대로 말하자면 (to speak the truth)
- **to the best of one's ability** 힘닿는 데까지 (to the utmost of one's power)
- **to the bone** 철두철미하게 (to the core)
- **to the core** 철저하게 (completely)
- **to the effect that** ~라는 취지로 (with the purport)
- **to the letter** 정확하게, 엄밀히, 문자 그대로 (precisely, literally)
- **to the tune of** 거금, 무려 ~에 이르는
- **toe the line** 규칙[명령]대로 따르다 (toe the mark)
- **tone down** 감정을 누그러뜨리다 (lessen the intensity)
- **tongue in cheek** 농담조로 (jokingly)
- **too close for comfort** 절박한, 아슬아슬한 (be dangerously close)
- **touch off** ~를 유발하다(lead, induce)
  (bring about, bring on, cause, effect, effectuate, generate, ingenerate)
  (lead to, make, occasion, result in, set off, stir1(up), touch off, trigger)
- **touch on** ~에 대해 간단히 언급하다 (speak about briefly)
- **tout for** 열심히 홍보(크게 선전)하다 → 몹시 칭찬하다
- **track down** 추적하여 잡다 (hunt down)
- **touch and go** 아슬아슬한 → 불안한
- **trial and error** 시행착오
- **trim down** 삭감하다 (cut down)
- **try on** 입어보다, 신어보다 (put on something to test)
- **tune in** 주파수를 맞추다
- **turn down** 거절하다, (소리, 온도) 줄이다 (reject, decline, refuse)
- **turn in** 제출하다 (hand in, submit)
- **turn one's stomach** 역겹게 하다, 불쾌하게 하다 (feel disgusted)
- **turn out** ~라는 것이 판명되다, 모이다, 생산하다 (prove to be)
- **turn over a new leaf** 마음을 고치다, 새 생활을 시작하다
- **turn the corner** 비를 넘기다, 모퉁이를 돌다 (begin to improve)
- **turn thumbs down** 거절하다, 찬성하지 않다 (turn down, disapprove)
- **turn to** ~에 의지하다, 호소하다 (resort to, appeal to)
- **turn up** 모습을 나타내다, 발견하다, 소리를 높이다 (appear, discover)
- **twist someone's arm** ~에게 강요하다 (pressure someone into doing)
- **tar and feather** 호되게 벌하다
  tar and feather a person
  (사형(私刑)·모욕으로써) 남의 온몸에 타르를 칠하고 그 위에 깃털을 씌우다
- **tar and feather a black slave** 흑인 노예를 사형하다
  (타르를 온몸에 칠하고 그 위에 새의 깃털을 꽂거나 하여)
- **table** (의안) 상정하다
  They have tabled a motion for debate at the next Party Conference.
  (그들은 차기 당대회에서 토의될 발의안을 상정해 놓고 있다.)
- **on the table** 상정되어 있는
  Management have put several new proposals on the table.
  (경영진에서 몇 가지 새로운 제안들을 상정해 놓고 있다.)
- **take out** 꺼내다; 데리고 나가다
- **take a dim view of** ~을 못마땅하게 생각하다(비판적, 불찬성) (have a little confidence, have a negative opinion of, disapprove of)
- **take a hit** 타격을 입다(→ take toil on → hard hit)
- **take A for B** : A를 B로 잘못 알다 (mistake A for B)
- **take a bath** 돈을 잃다 → 손해를 보다(To experience serious financial loss)
- **take A into consideration** : A를 고려하다
- **take A into custody** : A를 구금시키다
- **take a person to task** ~을 꾸짖다, 책망하다 (scold)
- **take a pinch [grain] of salt** ~을 에누리해서 듣다
- **take a rain-check** (약속, 초대를) 뒤로 미루다 (delay, invitation)
- **take a sip** 조금씩 맛보다
  (drink, taking only a little at a time into the front of the mouth)
  take advantage of 이용하다(cash in on → avail oneself of)
  (utilize, impose, capitalize on, play on, exploit) take after ~을 닮다(resemble, bear a resemblance to, be the very image of)
- **take against** 반항하다, 반감을 갖다(be allergic to → dislike)
- **take back** 도로 찾다, 취소하다
- **take care of** ~을 돌보다
- **take down** 적어두다, 받아 적다 (record)
- **take in** 속이다; 이해하다; 체포하다; 마시다; 숙박시키다
  (double cross, deceive, delude, cheat; comprehend; arrest, round up)
- **take in account** 셈에 넣다, 계산에 넣다
- **take in one's stride**
  냉철하게 대처하다; 수월하게 어려움을 극복하다; (장애물을) 쉽게 뛰어넘다 (deal calmly with, meet without much surprise)
- **take into account** 고려하다
  (consider, allow for, make allowances for)
- **take a dim[dark, gloomy, poor] view of**
  ~에 찬성하지 않다 → ~을 회의적으로 보다 → 비관하다
  We must take a dim view of the facts.
  (우리는 그 사실에 대해 비판적이어야 한다)
- **take issue with** 이의를 제기하다 → 논쟁하다 (argue, debate)
- **take exception**
  1) 이의를 제기하다[against, to, at] → 성내다, 화를 내다[to, at]
- **show a bold front** 단호히 반대의 태도를 보이다
  I showed a bold front. (난 단호히 반대했다.)
- **sit down (hard) on[upon]** 강경하게 반대하다
  My parents will sit down on my plan.
  (부모님이 내 계획에 강경히 반대할 것이다)
- **take a detached view** 객관적인[공정한] 견해를 가지다
- **sit on the fence** 형세를 관망하다 → 중립을 지키다
- **Take it easy** 조심해서 가라, 안녕, 걱정하지 마라, 서두르지 마라
- **take it for granted** ~을 당연히 여기다
- **take it out of** ~을 지치게 하다, ~을 못살게 굴다, ~에게 앙갚음 (보복)을 하다 (exhaust, annoy, pick on, get even, revenge, retaliate, repay)
- **take it out of someone** 괴롭히다, 지치게 하다
- **take lion's share** 최대의 몫을 갖다
- **take no stock in** ~을 믿지 않다, 신용하지 않다 (do not believe in)
- **take notice of** 알아차리다, 주의하다
- **take off** 이륙하다; (옷 등을) 벗다 (depart; undress, take off)
- **take one's time** 서두르지 않다 (don't hurry)
- **take over** 인수하다, 떠맡다
- **take part in** ~에 참석하다 (participate in, go in for)

- take place 일어나다, 발생하다 (occur, happen)
- take place of ~를 대신(대체)하다(replace)
- take precaution 경계하다, 조심하다
- take pride in ~을 자랑하다 (be proud of, pride oneself on)
- take sides 편들다 (support, side with)
- take something to heart ~에 대해 노심초사하다 (consider seriously)
- take something with a grain(pinch) of salt
  ~을 에누리해서 듣다, 액면 그대로 믿지 않다
  (not necessarily believe all of, remain doubtful about something)
- take the bull by the horns 과감하게 행동하다, 난국에 맞서다
- take the lead 앞장을 서다, 주도권을 잡다
- take to the cleaners 빈털터리가 되다 → 돈을 모두 잃다
  (to get a lot of money from someone, usually by cheating)
- take to 정들다, 좋아하다
- take to one's heels 도망가다 (run away, flee, take flight)
- take turn 교대로 하다
- take someone by storm 매혹하다 → 마음을 사로잡다
  (to captivate completely; to fascinate → riveting)
- take up 착수하다, 시작하다 (begin, commence, launch, start)
- take your time 천천히 하세요
- take (catch) 40 winks 잠깐 눈을 붙이다 (take a nap)
- tale down 적어두다 (write down, jot down)
- talk turkey 사실대로(솔직하게, 까놓고)말하다(To speak frankly)
- talk down to 무시하는 투로 말하다 (speak in an impolite manner)
- talk shop 전문적인 (일, 전문분야) 이야기를 하다 (talk about things in one's work or trade)
- tamper with 개조하다, 고치다, 변조하다, 참견하다, 간섭하다
  (alter, meddle in, cut in, interfere with)
- taste good 좋은 맛이 나다
- team up with ~와 협력하다(cooperate, collaborate)
- tease out (정보를) 빼내다 (uncover)
- tell A about B : A에게 B에 대해 말하다
- tell on 영향을 미치다, 비밀을 누설하다
  (have an effect on, let on, reveal, disclose → work on)
- ten to one 십중팔구, 아마도 (probably, nine out of ten)
- That's no big deal at all. 문제없어. (There's no problem)
- the nuts and bolts 기본[기초]적인 사항들
  (너트와 볼트는 기계의 가장 기본적인 부분이잖아요? 그래서 기본이란 뜻)
- the Midas touch 돈 버는 재주 (the ability to make money)
- the name of the game 본질, 가장 중요한 것
- the cream of the crop
  최고 중에 최고 → 가장 좋은 것(the best of a particular group)
  cream이란 우유에서 가장 질 좋은 부분을 뜻하므로 비유적으로는 「최고, 최상의 것」(the best)이란 의미로 쓰인다.
- The proof of the pudding is in the eating. 백문이 불여일견
- Cat got your tongue? (왜 말이 없지?) speechless
- the salt of the earth 세상의 소금, 건전한 사회지도층
- the upper hand 장점 (advantage, merit, virtue, edge)
- Think nothing of it 별말씀을
- This is on me. (음식값은) 이번 것은 내가 낼게.
- throw a fit 노발대발하다 (become upset) → 화내다
  (blow a fuse, blow one's lid, blow one's top, blow off one's steam
  fly off the handle, hit the ceiling, hot under the collar, jump down one's throat, see red, walk up the wall

- throw in the sponge 패배를 인정하다, 항복하다 (admit defeat, surrender)
- throw in the towel 패배를 인정하다, 항복하다 (admit, defeat, surrender)
- throw (have) a fit 노발대발하다 (become upset, be very angry)
- throw in its lot with 운명을 같이하다, 지지하다(supports)
- tick off 확인하다, 점검하다 (show with marking)
- tie up 중단시키다 → 구속하다 → 꼼짝 못하게 하다 → (hinder) → 바쁘게 만들다(busy)
- to a fault 지나치게, 극단으로 (too much, excessively)
- to a wall 궁지에 빠져 (into a trap, into the corner → stalemate, mire, quagmire
- to date 지금까지(until now)
- to look quickly through 책을 처음부터 빨리 읽다(skim)
- to the contrary 그와 반대로, 그와는 달리
- to the effect that ~라는 뜻(취지)으로 (with the purport that ~)
- to the fullest extent 완전한 정도까지
- to the letter 충실히 (faithfully, exactly, to the fullest degree)
- to the point 적절한 (pertinent, suitable, relevant, germane)
- to the quick 절실히, 뼈에 사무치게 (deeply, home)
- to what extent 어느 정도까지
- tone in with 조화하다 (harmonize)
- too wide of the mark 터무니없는 (too irrelevant)
- tool around 마차나 차로 돌아다니다 (take a ride in or on a vehicle)
- tooth and nail 전력을 다하여, 필사적으로
- trains of thought 끊임없이 이어지는 생각의 흐름
- truck farm 시장판매용 채소재배 농원 (market garden)
- turn a blind eye 못 본척하다 (ignore)
- turn a deaf ear to 듣고도 못 들은척하다, ~에 조금도 귀 기울이지 않다
- turn aside 빗나가다, 벗어나다, 굴절되다 (deflect, avert, divert)
- turn away 들어오지 못하게 하다, 내쫓다
- turn down 거절하다 (reject)
- turn in 물건을 돌려주다, 제출하다 (submit)
- turn into ~로 변하다, (어떤 것이) 되다(become)
- turn one's head (성공이) 우쭐하게 만들다, (마음을) 뒤집히게 하다 (make one proud of oneself)
- turn one's nose up at ~을 경멸하다 (ridicule)
- turn out to be 결국 ~이 되다, 판명되다 (prove)
- turn over 뒤집어엎다; 양도하다 (capsize, turn upside down, transfer)
- turn over a new leaf 새로운 삶을 시작하다 (begin a new life)
- turn the table 역습을 가하다, 전세를 뒤집다
- turn to ~에 의지하다
- turn up 나타나다, 도착하다, (악기를) 조율하다 (appear, arrive, reach)
- toe the line
  (1) (경주에서) 발끝을 출발선에 나란히 하다.
  (2) 규칙[통제, 명령, 규칙] 따르다.
  (3) 책임을 지다; 의무를 다하다.
- the name of the game
  1) 가장 중요한 점[자질] → 승패를 판가름하는 관건
  2) Persistence is the name of the game.
    (끈기야 말로 중요한 것입니다.)
- tug of war 줄다리기(경쟁) → 주도권 쟁탈(세력다툼) → A struggle for supremacy
- Tom, Dick, and Harry

(anyone or everyone indiscriminately → Anybody at all; a member of the public at large)
보통 사람들 → 극히 평범한 사람들 → 너나할 것 없이 모두 → 어중이떠중이 → 개나소나

- [ ] **every Tom, Dick, and Harry**
  1) (너나 할 것 없이)모두 → 아무나 → 차별없이 모든사람 → 보통 사람들 → 개나 소나
  2) Mary's sending out very few invitations.
  She doesn't want every Tom, Dick, and Harry turning up.
  (메리는 겨우 몇 장밖에 초대장을 보내지 않았다.)
  (그녀는 누구나 참석하기를 원치 않은 것이다.)

- [ ] **take a dive** (다이브)
  1) (~에) 몰두하다[into]
  2) (주식 따위가) 폭락하다 → (기온이) 급강하다
  The stock is taking a dive (그 주식은 폭락하고 있다)
  3) (구어) 실패한 척하다 → (복싱) 승부 담합 시합에서 패배하다

- [ ] **tail off**
  1) 차츰 감소하다[시키다] → (목소리가) 가늘어지다[지게 하다]
  2) (구어)달아나다; 퇴거하다

- [ ] **tag and rag** 하층민, 사회의 쓰레기
- [ ] **take a (firm) hold on oneself** 자제하다 → 냉정하게 행동하다
- [ ] **take coolly** 태연자약하다
- [ ] **take a front seat** (구어) 중요한 지위를 차지하다
- [ ] **take a person down a notch**(or two) (구어) 남의 콧대를 꺾다
- [ ] **take a tumble to** (구어) ~을 깨닫다, 알아차리다
- [ ] **take forever** (구어) 엄청난[오랜] 시간이 걸리다
- [ ] **take it** (구어) 벌을 받다 → 참다, 견디다
- [ ] **take no notice of** ~을 무시하다
- [ ] **share the blame for** ~에 대해 공동 책임을 지다
  The teachers will share the blame for his behavior.
  (교사들이 그의 행동에 공동 책임질 것이다.)
- [ ] **take[assume] the responsibility of[for]** ~의 책임을 지다
- [ ] **take on the mantle of** ~의 책임을 떠맡다
  He took on the mantle of the project.
  (그는 그 계획의 책임을 맡았다.)
- [ ] **shift off** [의무·토론 따위] 피하다 [책임]을 전가하다
  Don't try to shift off your duty.
  (네 의무를 피하려 하지마.)
- [ ] **shift the blame[responsibility] (on) to another** 책임을 남에게 전가하다
- [ ] **disclaimer** 디스클레이머(금융기관이 투자에 대한 책임을 지지 않음을 첨부하는 공지)
  (제품에 표시하는) 주의[경고](문) → 단서(상품의 사용상 주의 사항이나 영화·TV·언론 따위의「미성년자 관람 불가」「실존 인물[실재 사실]과 무관함」따위 → 책임 경감용
- [ ] **skirt around[round]** [문제]를 회피하다
  Do not skirt around this matter. (이 문제를 회피하지 마라.)
- [ ] **take one's own life** 자살하다
- [ ] **take the (gas) pipe** 자살하다
- [ ] **shoot oneself** 자살하다
- [ ] **take (the) pet** 뚱하다 → 토라지다 → 부루퉁하다
  She took the pet (그녀는 토라졌다)
- [ ] **take the sweet with the sour** 인생의 고락을 감수하다 → 낙천적으로 받아들이다
  His good ting is to take the sweet with the sour.
  (그의 장점은 인생을 낙천적으로 받아들이는 것이다.)
- [ ] **the back of one's hand** (구어) 비난 → 거절

- [ ] **the best of the bunch** (구어) 엄선한 것 → 가장 뛰어난 것

U

- [ ] **under a cloud** 의심을 받는(suspected)
- [ ] **Never underestimate your opponent.**
  1) 절대 상대를 과소평가하지 말아라.
  2) 낮게[적게] 어림하다 → 과소평가하다 → 얕잡아 보다 → 경시하다
  ➕ undervalue, understate, underrate, diminish, play down, minimize, downgrade, miscalculate, trivialize
  ➖ exaggerate, overstate, overestimate, overrate, inflate
- [ ] **upend** 거꾸로하다 → 뒤집다 → 파괴시키다(destroy, or change completely; overthrow)
- [ ] **My car's on the fritz.** 내 차가 고장나다
- [ ] **My battery is dead.** 배터리가 다 달다 (run out)
- [ ] **Key is stuck in the lock.** 열쇠가 자물쇠 안에 꽉 박혀버렸어 → 꽉 껴서 박히다
- [ ] **My toilet's Clogged.** 저희 변기가 막혔어요.
- [ ] **Would you like to say grace?** 당신이 식사 기도를 하실래요?
- [ ] **The room is a pigsty.** 이방은 돼지우리구나. → A dirty or very untidy place.
- [ ] **Maybe he was in the john.** 그는 아마도 화장실에 있을거에요.
- [ ] **under age** 미성년의 → 규정에 미달인
- [ ] **under an alias** 가명으로
- [ ] **under duress** 협박당하여, 강압하에
- [ ] **under the radar** 눈에 띄지 않는(두드러지지 않는) (inconspicuous)
- [ ] **under the guise of** ~를 가장하여(in pretense of)
- [ ] **under a cloud** 의심을 받아 (under suspicion)
- [ ] **under construction** 건설 중인
- [ ] **under fire** 공격[비난]을 받아 (under attack)
- [ ] **under the aegis of** ~의 비호하에, ~을 방패삼아
- [ ] **under close questioning** 철저한 심문을 받고
- [ ] **under[below] one's breath** 소곤소곤, 낮은 목소리로
- [ ] **under the circumstances** 그러한 상황 하에서는, 현 상황에서
- [ ] **under the influence of** ~의 영향으로, ~의 힘으로 (affected by the influence of)
- [ ] **under the table** 비밀히, 뇌물로 (covertly)
- [ ] **under the weather** 기분이 언짢아, 몸 상태가 좋지 않아 (not feeling well)
- [ ] **under way** 진행 중인 (in progress)
- [ ] **under wraps** 비밀로 되어 있는 (in secrecy)
- [ ] **under one's hat** (구어) 비밀리에, 남몰래
- [ ] **under the counter** (거래 따위를) 비밀리에, 암거래로; 몰래, 슬그머니
- [ ] **to the hammer** (구어) 더할 나위 없이 훌륭한 → 일류의
- [ ] **up to snuff** (구어) (건강·품질 따위가) 양호하여, 만족할 만한
- [ ] **up to scratch** (구어) 좋은 상태로 → 표준에 달하여
- [ ] **unheard of** 알려지지 않은, 들어본 적이 없는 (unknown)
- [ ] **up the mark** (구어) 수준[목표]을 높이다
- [ ] **up against** 부닥쳐서, 직면하여 (faced with)
- [ ] **up the wall** (구어) 몹시 화가 나서
- [ ] **up in the air** (구어) 들떠서; 당황하여 → 성나서, 흥분하여
- [ ] **up in the fly** (연극) 성공적인
- [ ] **up and around/about** (환자가) 침대에서 일어나서, (일어나서)

- 돌아다니게 되어
- **up for grabs** 마음만 먹으면 쉽게 얻을 수 있는 (easily available)
- **up in the air** 미정의 (undecided)
- **up one's sleeve** 몰래 준비하여, 숨겨서 (hidden)
- **upon the place** 즉석에서
- **up one's alley** ~의 능력(취미, 적성)에 맞는 (suitable)
- **up shit[shit's] creek** (without a paddle) 궁지에 몰려
- **up to one's ears** 열중한, 몰두한, 빠져 있는 (up to one's eyes/neck)
- **up to one's[the] elbows** 몰두하여, 매우 분주하여[in]
- **up to one's pits in work** 일에 몰두[전념]하여
- **up to par** 표준에 달하여 (up to the standard)
- **up to here** 여기까지 → (구어) 일이 너무 많아 → (구어) 감당 못하게 되어
- **up to something** ~를 꾸며, 계획하여 (planning/ plotting)
- **up to the minute** 최신의(up-to-date → cutting-edge 최첨단 → state of the art)
- **ups and downs** 영고성쇠, 오르막과 내리막(rise and fall → wax and wane)
- **upside down** 뒤집혀서, 전복되어 (reverse)
- **up-to-date** 현대적인, 최신의 (modern, sophisticated, up to the minute)
- **use language** 욕을 퍼붓다(abuse → revile at → slander) (call name → speak ill of → chew out → find fault with → point a finger at)
- **use one's head** 머리를 쓰다, 생각하다 (use one's brain)
- **use up** 다 써버리다(depleted, exhaust)
- **used to** ~하곤 했다
- **usher in** ~의 도래를 알리다
- **Uncle Sam**
  1) 미국 정부(a personification of the United States government)
  2) 미국 정부(때때로 흰 수염에 높은 중절모를 쓴 키 큰 남자로 묘사됨)
- **under consideration** 고려 중인
- **under construction** 건설 중
- **under no circumstances** 결코~이 아닌 (never, anything but, far from)
- **under one's breath** 작은 목소리로, 소곤소곤 (quietly)
- **under the management of** ~의 관리(경영)하에 있는
- **under the seat** 좌석 밑에
- **under the counter** 비밀리에, 불법적으로
- **over the counter** (약) 처방전 없이 살 수 있는
- **under the weather** 아픈, 기분이 좋지 않은 (sick, feeling unwell)
- **under way** 진행 중인 (going on)
- **unequal to** 능력을 넘어선
- **until further notice** 더 이상의 통보가 있을 때까지
- **up in the air** 계획이 미정으로, 막연하여, 미결정의 (uncertain, unsettled)
- **up for grabs** 이용 가능한
- **up to** ~에 달려있는 (depend on)
- **upon request** 요청하자마자
- **ups and downs** 기복
- **up-to-the-minute** 최근의 (latest, abreast, up-to-date, read-hot, contemporary)
- **use up** 다 써버리다, 고갈시키다, 소모하다 (exhaust, deplete, consume)
- **usher in** 알리다, 예고하다 (herald)

- **ugly enough to tree a wolf** 지독히도 못생긴(늑대도 무서워서 나무 위로 도망칠 만큼) She was disappointed his face that ugly enough to tree a wolf. (그녀는 지독히도 못생긴 그의 얼굴에 실망했다.)
- **um and aah** (구어) 주저하다 → 말이 막혀 우물거리다 The foreigner asked him the way to station, but he couldn't answer um and aah. (외국인이 그에게 역까지 가는 길을 물어보았으나 그는 말이 막혀 대답하지 못했다.)
- **under-the-table practices** 불법적인 관행 (Not straightforward; secret or underhand → behind-the-scenes, sub-rosa)
- **questionable business practices** (미심쩍은 기업 관행) 의심스러운 (행동) ; 수상한; 문젯거리의
- **up to scratch** 만족스러운 → 훌륭한 상태에 있는 (as good as the standard; satisfactory)

V

- **vacate[resign] one's seat** 의원직을 그만두다 Please don't vacate your seat. We need you. 제발 의원직을 그만두지 마십시오. 우리는 당신이 필요합니다.
- **Variety is the spice of life.** 다양성은 인생의 양념이다; 이질성과 변화가 인생을 재미있게 한다는 것을 뜻하는 속담
- **Vanity of vanities;all is vanity.** 헛되고 헛되니 모든 것이 헛되도다. 《전도서 1:2》
- **vent one's spleen** 화풀이하다; 울분을 풀다 Jack vented his spleen at not getting the job by shouting at his wife. (잭은 아내에게 고함을 질러 일자리를 얻을 수 없었던 화풀이를 했다.)
- **veer and haul** 풍향이 시시각각 바뀌다 Because it veers and hauls, we must be careful. 풍향이 시시각각 바뀌기 때문에 우리는 조심해야 한다.
- **verdant lawns** 파릇파릇한 잔디밭 → 초록의(green) → 미숙한 (inexperienced)
- **I'm running late.** 나 늦어요 → 지각이다
- **I totally lost track of time.** 난 정말 시간 가는 줄 몰랐다
- **veer off** 갑자기 방향을 바꾸다(suddenly change the direction)
- **vent one's spleen on** 화풀이하다 (give vent to one's anger)
- **vent oneself** 감정을 속 시원히 털어놓다[폭발시키다] I only can vent myself to my mom. (나는 엄마에게만 감정을 속 시원히 털어놓을 수 있다)
- **vex oneself** 안달하다, 화내다(vex)
- **vibe on** 공감하다 → 뜻이 통하다 Most people in this room vibed on his opinion. (이 방 사람 대부분은 그의 의견에 공감하였다)
- **villain of the piece** 장본인; 문제의 원흉; 나쁜 일이나 잘못된 일에 책임이 있는 사람이나 물건
- **vie with** 다루다, 경쟁하다 (fight with)
- **vote against** ~에 반대투표를 하다 (ballot against)
- **vote down** 부결시키다 (reject, decline)
- **vote for** 찬성 투표하다 (ballot for)
- **vote on** 표결하다 (take a vote)
- **vouch for** 보증하다
- **value oneself for** ~을 뽐내다 → 자만하다

- **va piano** 계속 약하게
  My computer makes a noise va piano.
  (내 컴퓨터는 계속 약하게 소리를 낸다.)
- **vacate[resign] one's seat** 의원직을 그만두다
  Please don't vacate your seat. We need you.
  (제발 의원직을 그만두지 마십시오. 우리는 당신이 필요 합니다.)
- **vindicate oneself** 변명[소명(疏明)]하다 → 자기의 주장[권리]을 옹호하다
  They vindicated themselves.
  (그들은 자기의 주장을 옹호했다.)

W

- **what it takes** 《미국·구어》 (성공 따위를 얻는 데 필요한) 조건(아름다움·매력·재능·재력 따위)
  People ask me what it takes to be a leader.
  사람들은 제게 리더가 되기 위해 갖춰야 할 자질이 무엇인지 묻습니다.
- **wild goose chase.** 헛수고 → 부질 없는 짓
- **I'm going to get forty winks.** 나 잠깐 눈 좀 붙일거야.
- **Have it your way.** 좋을 대로 하세요. 마음대로 하세요
- **waltz a person around** 남을 따돌리다, 속이다
  They waltz me around, and leave me entirely out of their conversation.
  그들은 나를 따돌리고 말 상대를 하지 않는다.
- **waltz around** 논의가 (요점을 피해) 겉돌다
  I don't know why his speech waltz around.
  나는 왜 그의 연설이 겉도는지 모르겠다.
- **waltz around with** ~을 마음대로 조종하다
  His mom waltzed around with him.
  그의 어머니는 그를 마음대로 조종하였다.
- **waltz into** 공격[비난]하다, 야단치다
  He waltzed into a long diatribe against the government's policies.
  그는 정부 정책에 대해 길고 통렬한 비난을 하였다.
- **war of nerves** 신경전
- **war of words** 설전(舌戰), 논쟁
- **warm a person's ear** (구어) 남에게 (세상 이야기 따위를) 장황하게 들려주다
  My grandfather loves to warm a person's ear about his life.
  할아버지는 남에게 자신의 삶에 대한 얘기를 장황하게 들려주는 것을 좋아한다.
- **warp out** 《구어》 신속히 이동하다, 재빨리 가버리다
  He wrapped out to the door at the sight of the policeman.
  그는 경찰관을 보자마자 문으로 재빨리 가버렸다.
- **warts and all** 《구어》 (결점도 빼지 않고) 있는 그대로, 모조리
  Jim has many faults, but Jean loves him, warts and all.
  짐은 결점이 많으나 진은 그 결점이 있는 그대로의 그를 사랑하고 있습니다.
- **Was my face red!** 《구어》 창피해서 홍당무가 되었다!
- **wash one's dirty linen in public**
  집안의 수치를 남 앞에 드러내다; 자신의 개인적인 문제를 남의 앞에서 논의하다
  I wish he wouldn't wash his dirty linen in public.
  집안의 수치를 밖에 노출시키는 짓은 하지 않았으면 좋겠어.
- **wash one's hands**
  ① 《완곡적》 화장실에 가다 ② 손을 끊다, 관계를 끊다, 손을 떼다 [of] (←마태 복음(Matt 27:24))
- **wash one's hands in invisible soap** (아첨·당황의 표현으로) 손을 비비다
  In front of her boss, she washed her hands in invisible soap.
  그녀는 상사 앞에서 손을 비볐다.
- **Waste not, want not.** 《속담》 낭비가 없으면 부족도 없다.
- **waste one's breath[words]** 쓸데없는 말을 하다; 말해봐야 소용 없다
  It's waste your breath to tell him what to do.
  그에게 무엇을 하라고 시키는 것은 말해봐야 소용없는 것이다.
- **watch one's mouth[tongue]** 말[입]조심하다
  Please watch your mouth in front of my mom.
  엄마 앞에서 제발 말조심하세요.
- **watch out** 《미국·구어》 조심하다, 주의하다; 경계[감시] 하다 [for]
  You'd better watch out for the computer virus.
  컴퓨터 바이러스를 조심하는 게 좋겠군요.
- **water under the bridge= water over the dam**
  (구어) 지나간 일, 끝난 일, 어쩔 수 없는 일
  I can't change the past. It's water under the bridge.
  나는 과거를 바꿀 수는 없다. 지난 일은 어쩔 수가 없는 것이다.
- **wax and wane** (달이) 찼다 이울었다 하다; 성쇠하다 → 증감하다
  Life will wax and wane.
  인생에는 성쇠가 있다.
- **We was[wuz] robbed!** (부당한 판정[불운]으로) 승리를 빼앗겼다, 속았다, 협잡이다
  A man rushed to the stairs and said 'We was robbed!'.
  그는 급히 계단을 뛰어 올라가면서 '속았다!'라고 말하였다.
- **weak in the head** 《구어》 머리가 나쁜, 바보인
  People think she is a madwoman who is weak in the head.
  사람들은 그녀가 머리가 나쁜 미치광이라고 생각한다.
- **wear on[upon]** [남의 신경]을 거스르다; [남]을 안달나게 하다
  His word and behavior wore on me.
  그의 언행과 태도는 나의 신경을 거슬렀다.
- **wear one's heart on[upon] one's sleeve**
  감정을 감추지 않고 드러내다, 생각하는 바를 숨김없이 말하다 (sleeve)
- **wear the breeches**
  (구어) 남편을 깔고 뭉개다, 내주장하다 → (가정 내에서) 아내가 주도권을 잡다
  The woman who lives next door often wears the breeches.
  옆집에 사는 여자는 종종 남편을 깔고 뭉갠다.
- **wear the willow**
  ① 실연하다 ② (애인이나 신부의 죽음을 슬퍼하여) 상복을 입다 《옛날에 버들잎 화환을 가슴에 달고 그 뜻을 표시하였음》
  After she wore the willow, she has pined away.
  그녀는 실연한 뒤에 초췌해졌다.
- **weather through** [곤란 따위]를 뚫고 나아가다
  Don't worry. I can weather through the difficulties.
  걱정마. 난 어려움을 뚫고 나아갈 수 있어.
- **weave all pieces on the same loom** 모두 같은 방법으로 다루다
  It leaves much to be desired as she weaves all pieces on the same loom.
  그녀가 모두 같은 방법으로 다루기 때문에 불만스러운 점이 많아.
- **(Well,) did you ever!** 《구어》 어어!, 놀랐어!, 뜻밖이군!
  You really worked as a model? Well, did you ever!

당신이 모델로 활동했다고? 그것 놀랄 일인데!
- [ ] **Well done!** 《구어》 잘 했어!, 훌륭했어!
  Well done! You are so great!
  잘했어! 너 참 멋져!
- [ ] **well-off** 유복한; 부유한
- [ ] **well up in** ~에 정통한(well-informed on)
  Ellen is well up in pop music.
  엘렌은 대중음악에 정통하다.
- [ ] **wet behind the ears**
  《구어》 미숙한, 젊고 경험이 없는(immature)
  He may be wet behind the ears, but he's well trained and totally competent.
  그는 경험이 적을지 모르지만 잘 단련되어 있고, 아주 유능합니다.
- [ ] **What a liberty!** 《구어》 참 제멋대로군! (무례한 행동을 하는 사람에게 쓰는 말)
  What a liberty! I have never seen someone like you before.
  참 제멋대로군! 너 같은 사람은 본 적이 없어.
- [ ] **What can I say?** 《구어》 무어라 말할지 설명할 도리가 없다
  What can I say? I am so sorry.
  무어라 말할지 설명할 도리가 없어. 정말 미안해.
- [ ] **What goes around comes around**
  일어날 일은 어차피 일어나기 마련이다; 살다 보면 좋은 일도 생기는 법이다; 자업자득(自業自得), 인과응보(因果應報), 역사[유행]는 되풀이된다
  You are right. What goes around comes around!
  맞아. 남에게 잘못한 만큼 자신에게 돌아오는 법이지!
- [ ] **What is it?** 《구어》 무슨 일이야?, 뭐야?
  What is it? Did you get hurt?
  무슨 일이야? 어디 다쳤어?
- [ ] **You got a booger.** 너 코딱지 보여
- [ ] **I've seen you burp.** 트림하다
- [ ] **She got her period.** 그녀는 생리기간이다.
- [ ] **You just cut in line.** 당신 방금 새치기 했죠.
- [ ] **wise up** ~에게 알리다; 알다
- [ ] **writ** (법률) 영장
- [ ] **wrongful dismissal**(termination) (법률) 부당해고
- [ ] **write down** 지위[가치·가격]를 떨어뜨리다
- [ ] **wipe out** 닦다, 지우다; 전멸하다(destroy)
- [ ] **with no strings attached** 아무런 조건 없이
- [ ] **wager on** ~에 돈을 걸다 (bet on)
- [ ] **wait and see** 관망하다 (watch)
- [ ] **walk away with** 쉽게 이기다, 낙승하다 (win easily)
- [ ] **walk on air** 황홀해하다 (be ecstatic)
- [ ] **walk on eggs** 조심스럽게 행동하다 (act carefully)
- [ ] **walk out** 퇴장하다, 파업하다 (stop working in protest)
- [ ] **walk (all) over** 독주하다, ~에 낙승하다
- [ ] **walk tall** 뻐기며 걷다
- [ ] **walk the chalk/line** 명령[규정]에 따르다 (walk the chalk mark)
- [ ] **wash one's hands of** ~에서 손을 떼다, ~와 관계를 끊다 (withdraw from)
- [ ] **watch and ward** 엄중한 경계, 끊임없는 감시
- [ ] **watch out** 조심[주의]하다 (be careful)
- [ ] **watch one's step** 신중하게 행동하다 (act carefully)
- [ ] **water down** 희석시키다, 약하게 하다 (weaken)
- [ ] **wean off** ~를 떼어놓다
- [ ] **wear the pants** 좌지우지하다

- [ ] **wear the trousers** 여자가 입김이 더 세다, 남편을 깔아뭉개다 (wear the pants)
- [ ] **wear two hats** 두 가지 직책을 가지다 (have two jobs)
- [ ] **week in, week out** 매주 (every week)
- [ ] **weigh one's words** 신중하게 말하다 (speak carefully)
- [ ] **welcome someone with open arms** ~를 환대하다, 따뜻하게 맞이하다 (welcome warmly)
- [ ] **well off** 유복한, 잘 사는 (rich, affluent)
- [ ] **wet behind the ears** 미숙한, 풋내기의 (inexperienced)
- [ ] **what's up?** 별일 없지? → Nothing much 잘, 지내,
- [ ] **what do you say to** ~하는 거 어때? (how about something)
- [ ] **what the doctor ordered** 원했던 거, 바람직한 것 (a desirable thing)
- [ ] **what's the big deal?** 뭐가 문제야? 그게 무슨 상관이야 (what's the problem)
- [ ] **what's the good of something?** ~가 무슨 소용이냐? (what's the use of something?)
- [ ] **when it comes to** ~에 대해서라면 (in regard to)
- [ ] **when the chips are down** 위급할 때, 돈이 떨어졌을 때 (at stake, in crisis)
- [ ] **wide of the mark** 과녁을 빗나간(away from the target)
- [ ] **wide-awake** 완전히 잠이 깬, 정신을 바싹 차린 (completely awake)
- [ ] **wind up** ~를 끝내다, 태엽을 감다 (finish)
- [ ] **wishful thinking** 소망 사항
- [ ] **with a view to** ~할 목적으로 (for the purpose of)
- [ ] **with all one's heart** 진심으로, 충심으로 (sincerely)
- [ ] **with no strings attached** 아무 조건 없이 (without any strings attached)
- [ ] **with one's tail between one's legs** 기가 죽어, 위축되어 (cowed)
- [ ] **with respect to** ~에 관해서는 (with reference to)
- [ ] **with surprise** 놀라서
- [ ] **with the exception of** ~를 제외하고, ~외에는 (except)
- [ ] **within a stone's throw of/from** 매우 가까운 곳에 (not far from)
- [ ] **without fail** 틀림없이, 꼭 (surely)
- [ ] **wipe out** 파괴하다, 없애버리다(destroy)
- [ ] **without reserve** 거리낌 없이 (without hesitation)
- [ ] **wipe away** 제거하다, 없애버리다(efface)
- [ ] **worth one's salt** 제 몫을 하는
- [ ] **word of mouth** 소문, 가십 (rumor)
- [ ] **work one's fingers to the bone** 뼈 빠지게 일하다 (work like a horse)
- [ ] **work out** 잘 해결하다, 마련하다 (find an answer)
- [ ] **wrap up** 끝내다, 마무리하다 (finish, finalize)
- [ ] **wreak havoc on** 황폐하게 하다 (make havoc of)
- [ ] **write down** 써두다, 기록하다 (put down)
- [ ] **write off** 장부에서 지우다, 가치가 없다고 간주하다
- [ ] **ait on** 시중들다 (serve, attend on)
- [ ] **walk on air** 매우 행복하다
- [ ] **walk out on** 버리다, 떠나다 (desert, leave)
- [ ] **walks of life** 신분, 지위, 직업
- [ ] **ward off** 쫓아버리다(repel → fend off → head-off → stave off)
- [ ] **wary of** 조심하는 (cautious of wash one's dirty linen in public)
- [ ] **waste~on** : ~하느라 ~을 허비하다
- [ ] **watch over** 감독하다 (supervise, oversee)
- [ ] **Way to go!** 그거다, 힘내라!
- [ ] **wear one's heart on one's sleeve**

감정을 노골적으로 나타내다 (show one's emotions)
- wear out 낡게 하다 (be no longer useable)
- weed out 제거하다(eliminate → get rid of → do away with → put an end to → wipe out)
- well-to-do 유복한
- wet behind the ears 미숙한, 풋내기의
  (very young and without experience)
- wet blanket 흥을 깨뜨리는 사람
  (a person who discourages others or prevents them from enjoying themselves)
- What time is it now? 지금 몇 시입니까? (Do you have the time?)
- When in Rome, do as the Romans do.
  로마에서는 로마법이 하듯이 하라
- white elephant 성가신(처치 곤란한) 물건
  (something that is useless and unwanted, especially something that is big and(or) costs a lot of money)
- wide of the mark 적절치 못한, 요점에서 벗어난 (irrelevant)
- wind up 끝내다 (finish, stop, bring to an end gradually)
- windfall profit 초과이윤, 우발이익, 불로소득
  (an unexpected lucky gift or gain)
- with all ~에도 불구하고
  (despite, in spite, of, for all, notwithstanding)
- with (all) one's heart and soul 온 정성을 다하여
  (with all one's attention and strength)
- with caution 주의 깊게
- with a vengeance 완전히, 철저하게, 심하게(in the fullest sense)
- with equanimity 침착하게 (calmly)
- with flying colors 당당하게 (in triumph, triumphantly)
- with little concern for public opinion
  여론에 대한 관심을 거의 가지지 않고
- with regard to ~에 관하여
- with the aim of ~을 목적으로
- with the exception of ~을 제외하고
- with tongue in cheek 놀림조로, 본심과는 반대로 (insincerely)
- within 24 hours 24시간 내에
- within the guideline 지침 안에서
- without limits 제한 없이, 무한한(boundless)
- without regard to ~을 고려하지 않고
- work from home 재택 근무를 하다
- work out 연습하다, 훈련하다, 운동하다; (애써서) 성취하다, (문제를) 해결하다 (resolve, solve, settle)
- work (do) wonders (miracles, magic) 기적이 일어나다
  (bring unexpectedly good results)
- worth one's salt 급료 값을 하는 (worthy of respect or of being so called)
- wreck havoc on ~을 파괴하다 (ruin, destroy, raze)
- wrestle with 악전고투하다 (have difficulty making a decision about)
- write off (감가상각으로) 값을 줄이다
  (reduce the estimated value of, remove (especially a debt) from the records of accounts)
- Where is the john? 남자 화장실이 어디입니까?
- with the wisdom[benefit] of hindsight
  1) 뒤늦게 깨달은 것이지만 → 소 잃고 외양간 고치는 격이지만
  2) 사정을 다 알게 됨(일이 다 벌어진 뒤에) → 뒤늦은 깨달음

- hindsight bias
  1) 사후 과잉확신 → 사후 해석 편파
  2) 이렇게 될 줄 미리 알았다!
  3) 사후예측 혹은 사후확증 편향(hindsight bias)이라는 말이 심리학에 종종 등장한다. 이는 어떤 일이 벌어진 이후에 그 일이 결국에는 벌어질 수밖에 없었다고 이전부터 알고 있었던 척하는 말이나 행동을 일컫는 현상이다.
  사실 그 일이 일어날지를 전혀 모르고 있었음에도 말이다. 예를 들어 주가가 며칠 사이에 폭락하게 되면 많은 TV나 라디오에서 관련 전문가들이 출연해 이런 일이 일어날 줄 이미 오래 전부터 알고 있었다는 듯한 말투로 폭락에 다다를 수밖에 없는 연결고리들을 하나씩 설명해 주곤 한다.
- waifs and strays 부랑아들; 잡동사니
- wage the peace 평화를 유지하다
  To wage the peace, they had a fight with bad people.
  (평화를 유지하기 위해 그들은 나쁜 사람들과 싸움을 했다.)
- wade in
  (1) 여울[얕은 물]에 들어가다
  (2) (구어) 싸움[논쟁]에 참가하다; 간섭하다
  (3) (구어) (어려운 일 등에) 결연히 착수하다
- walk in the woods 두 사람만의 비공식 회담
- Everybody's Working late. → 야근하다(work late)
  (모두들 야근을 하고 있습니다.)
- wait-and-see attitude → to be patient until a later time
  사태를 관망하는 태도; 회의적인 태도; 사람의 반응을 기다려 그 추세를 보려고 하는 분명치 않은 태도
- wait in the wings 《구어》 대기하다
- walk a fine line 줄타기를 하다; 위험한 일을 하다
  I hate you when you walk a fine line.
  나는 당신이 위험한 일을 하는 것이 싫어요.
- walk down the aisle 결혼하다 → (신랑, 신부가 식후에) 정면 통로로 나오다
- walk on eggs 신중히 처리하다; 아주 주의하다
  The manager is very hard to deal with. You really have to walk on eggs.
  그 지배인은 상대하기가 몹시 힘들다. 정말 신중히 처신하지 않으면 안 된다.
- walk out on 《구어》 버리다(desert); 포기하다:
- walk out on one's wife 처를 버리다
- walk the talk 말한 것을 실행[실천]하다
  He always walks the talk. 그는 항상 말한 것을 실행한다.
- walk through → to act or recite (a part) in a perfunctory manner, as at a first rehearsal
  ① (연극) (연기를 중심으로) 분장 없이 연습하다[시키다] 대본을 대충 읽어보다 → (리허설 따위에서)[배역]을 임시변통으로 연기하다
  ② [일·시험 따위]를 대충 해치우다
- walk turkey 《구어》 ① 거드름을 피우며 걷다 ② (배가) 상하 좌우로 흔들리다
  Since he was promoted, he walked turkey.
  그는 승진한 후, 거드름을 피우며 걸었다.
- walk with God 고결하게 살다, 바르게 살다
  They can live happily with their family if they walk with God.
  그들은 바르게 살면 가족과 함께 행복하게 살 수 있을 것이다.

Y

- cook up a story[report] 이야기[보고]를 날조하다(조작하다 → 속이다)
  (to invent a story, an excuse or a plan, especially a very clever or dishonest one)
- You have the right to remain silent. 너는 묵비권을 행사할 수 있는 권리가 있어.
- year in, year out 해마다 (every year)
- you bet 물론, 틀림없이, 두말하면 잔소리지 (surely, absolutely)
- You can say that again 내 말이 그 말이야 (You said it)
- Your guess is as good as mine 나도 모르겠는데요 (I don't know either)
- Your head is full of stump water. (구어) 너는 골 빈 녀석이다.
- Your trumpeter's dead. 《구어》곧이 들리지 않는데. 《남이 허풍 떨 때 대꾸하는 말》
- yearn for 동경하다, 갈망하다
- You said it 내 말이 그 말이야, 바로 그거야 (I quite agree with you)
- You are telling me. 맞았어, 바로 그거야 (I quite agree with you)
- You can lead a horse to water, but you can't make him drink. 평양감사도 자기 싫으면 그만
- You cannot make an omelet without breaking egg. 희생 없이 목적을 달성할 수 없다.
- You've got to be kidding! 농담하지마!, 믿을 수 없어 (Your attitude is unbelievable)
- yell one's head off[guts out] (구어) 1) 큰 소리로 외치다 2) 불만을 토하다 → 큰 소리로 불평을 하다
- yea, yea, nay, nay 찬성이면 찬성, 반대면 반대라고 솔직히
- yea and nay 우유부단(한) → 수시로 바뀌는 (일) → 주저, 망설임
- yank a person's crank 남을 놀리다[조롱하다]
- yank a person's chain (구어) 남을 속이다, 곤란하게 하다

Z

- zero in on 집중하다 → 겨냥하다 → 정조준하다 (aim at → focus on)
- zebra crossing 흑백 사선이 칠해진 횡단 보도
  (black and white stripes on the road where people may cross)
- Zip (up) your lips! (구어) 입을 다물다 → 말하지 않다
- zoom in on (구어) (이야기) 집중되다, (사람) 노력을 집중하다
- I pulled a few strings. 내가 인맥을 이용하다 → 연줄을 사용하다
- zip across the horizon (구어) 갑자기 유명해지다
- zing up 원기[활기]를 북돋우다
  Zing up! You have plenty of time to do it again.
  힘을 내! 다시 해 볼 시간은 충분히 있어.
- zip across the horizon (구어) 갑자기 유명해지다